THE INSIDERS' ® GUIDE
TO
Virginia's Blue Ridge

THE INSIDERS'®
GUIDE
TO
VIRGINIA'S Blue Ridge

by
Lin Chaff
and
Margaret Camlin Ritsch

THE INSIDERS'®
GUIDE

The Insiders' Guides, Inc.

Co-published and marketed by:
Richmond Newspapers, Inc.
333 East Grace Street
Richmond, VA 23219
(804) 775-8079

Co-published and distributed by:
The Insiders' Guides, Inc.
P.O. Box 2057 • Highway 64
Manteo, NC 27954
(919) 473-6100

•

THIRD EDITION
1st printing

•

Copyright ©1994
by Richmond Times Dispatch

•

Printed in the United States
of America

•

•

ISBN 0-912367-57-1

Richmond Newspapers, Inc.
Supplementary Publications

Director, Marketing Development
Bob Bowerman

Manager
Ernie Chenault

Account Executives
**Heidi Crandall, Adair Frayser-
Roper, John Wade**

Project Coordination
Bonnie Widener

Artists
**Susan Reilly, Ronnie Johnson,
Sean Contreras, Chris Novelli,
Ben Schulte**

The Insiders' Guides, Inc.

Publisher/Managing Editor
Beth P. Storie

President/General Manager
Michael McOwen

Creative Services Director
Michael Lay

Project Designer
David Haynes

Partnership Services Director
Giles Bissonnette

Editorial Staff
**Theresa Shea, Eileen Myers —
Project Editor**

Distribution Manager
Julie Ross

Fulfillment Coordination
Gina Twiford

Controller
Claudette Forney

Preface

Welcome to our favorite place. Many Americans still long for a simpler way of life in smaller towns. This is where they find it, trading in business suits for blue jeans. It's a privilege to live in the Blue Ridge of Virginia, pure and simple. Every day is a feast for the senses. And at night, you can drift off to sleep knowing that if your environment can impact upon your sense of well-being, you are one of the luckiest — and happiest — people around.

This is the nostalgic land of Earl Hamner's John-Boy and the Walton family. You can still find lots of general stores like Uncle Ike's. You can still find clucking, blue-haired ladies preparing banana pudding and fried chicken for Sunday School picnics in the country and small congregations worshipping in white, clapboard chapels. You can still find the strong family values that compel generations of extended families to all live down the same country lane. You'll find neighbors who mind their own business but are ever willing to lend a helping hand.

Welcome to a place where people still wave to strangers on back country roads, and our children and the family dog still swim with patched innertubes in pristine creeks under covered bridges. Welcome to life in the slow lane, with the same benefits but few of the hassles as life in the fast lane.

For sheer beauty and tranquility, nothing equals the Blue Ridge of Virginia's mountains, flora, fauna, rivers and lakes. We're a rhapsody of riotous yellow fuchsia and redbuds in the spring. We're a sonnet of sunny meadows with hovering hummingbirds and singing songbirds in the summer. We're a painter's palette of colors in the autumn. We're an aria to the simple setting of the first Christmas as we celebrate with handwrought wreaths and the tree we just cut out back on the snow-covered mountain.

We revere our environment, realizing a covenant with the land. We pull our cars off our highways to watch the sun go down and are filled with a sense of awe that a pinpoint of light bursting through a cloud can make a mountain appear to be wrapped in red velvet.

Ours is a land of great dynamics. We are inventors, like Cyrus McCormick, whose Shenandoah Valley mechanical reaper revolutionized the world. We are the land of Thomas Jefferson, the quintessential Renaissance man, who invented not only the concept of democracy in America, but also the dumb waiter, the original mimeograph and the brave art of eating the "love tomatoe." We are the land of robots and fiber optics in Roanoke, smart road technology in the New River Valley and solar-powered SIRUS Earthship homes in Floyd County.

We are a land of great leaders. On our Natural Bridge, George Washington left his initials and then stayed to later bail Washington & Lee University out of impending bankruptcy. Our's is a land where Robert E. Lee led our troops to great valor and honor during a four-year Civil War that was supposed to last just a few weeks. Our Shenandoah Valley is where Stonewall Jackson exasperated his students at the Virginia Military Institute with his toughness and humorlessness then went on to create a legend in military strategy that is still taught by U.S. military leaders today.

We are a land that reveres its history and honors its dead. We preserve our crumbling cemeteries and battlefields as hallowed ground. We build museums in the tiniest of communities as we welcome at least half a million people a year to Monticello and Montpelier in Charlottesville. We build monuments to every Civil War battle ever fought and museums to honor our fallen soldiers.

We are a land of great scholarship and creativity, where the slave Booker T. Washington grew up in Franklin County to become one of the great African-American thinkers and leaders of all time. Here, the great Harlem Renaissance poet, Anne Spencer, entertained Martin Luther King, Congressman Adam Clayton Powell, Justice Thurgood Marshall and singers Paul Robeson and Marion Anderson at her Lynchburg garden home.

This is also a land of enormous, diverse culture. We flatfoot on Friday nights in the Alleghany Highlands. We go to drive-in movies and eat buttered popcorn in Rockbridge County while celebrities fly in from around the world to see our American Film Festival in nearby Charlottesville. In Amherst County, near Lynchburg, we provide one of the largest residential colonies in the world for international artists and writers to stir their creative juices. At our colleges and cities, we display works of art and crafts equal to that of any metropolitan area in the country.

We're a big playground where you can camp, hike, bike, canoe, golf, boat, swim, horseback ride, hunt, fish, hang glide and soar until you drop!

We're a land of festivity looking for excuses to celebrate. We stage festivals to honor everything from apples, strawberries, garlic, dogwoods, ramps, wine and maple sugar to folklife and railroads.

This is also a land of superlatives. No matter which region of the Blue Ridge you visit, you'll find "the biggest," "the oldest," "the most important," or "nationally known," and "internationally acclaimed." Every region is a gem of multifaceted culture, like precious stones on a necklace, the common thread being the beauty of the Blue Ridge and our vast quality of life.

We are Charlottesville, land of Jeffersonian mystique and international chic. We are Staunton, heart of the Blue Ridge with our famous July Fourth picnics in Gypsy Hill, where your hosts, the world-famous

Statler Brothers, come home to celebrate with their friends. We are Harrisonburg, with fields of golden, waving grain and hills white with turkeys, and Roanoke, "Capital of the Blue Ridge," the largest metropolitan area off the Blue Ridge Parkway, voted by travel writers as the most beautiful road in the world. We are the intellectually stimulating New River Valley, home to gigantic Virginia Tech, as well as a tie-dyed counterculture that came to Floyd County and never left the '60s. We're the staid German Baptists at Smith Mountain Lake, the playground of western Virginia, and we still hunt for the cryptic, elusive Beale Treasure in nearby Bedford County. We're Jerry Falwell and the Moral Majority in Lynchburg, the home of one of the largest churches in America. We're the residents of the pastoral Alleghany Highlands, where the sheep outnumber the human population, and life is as slow and sweet as the maple sugar that trickles down the trees in the spring.

Welcome to our favorite place. Everywhere you travel, you'll find beauty that stops you in your tracks, people who are courteous, trusting and kind, and the opportunity to be transformed by the goodness of your environment.

Visit with us awhile. Rock on our wide front porches and sit a spell. Join us in our favorite pastime of watching the sun set over the Blue Ridge of Virginia. Have some peach cobbler and Virginia-made wine to settle you for the night. And when the stars blanket the Blue Ridge of Virginia, pack away your worries and tough times and mount a carousel horse (you can buy one in Newbern!) to ride through your dreams. Now, say good night to John-Boy Walton and the rest of the family. Dream of waking up to the warmth and promise of Blue Ridge sunshine and the goodness it will bring.

Good night, John-Boy.

Good night.

Acknowledgements

Lin acknowledges the Smith Mountain Lake Partnership; Andy Dawson, Shenandoah Valley Travel Association; Martha Doss, Lexington Visitors Center; Sergei Troubetzkoy, City of Staunton Department of Economic Development and Tourism; Stevie Dovel, Lynchburg Convention & Visitors Bureau; Nita Echols, the *Vinton Messenger;* Kitty Ward Grady, Town of Wytheville; Larry Hincker, Virginia Tech University Relations; Helen Looney, Craig County Historical Society; Martha Mackey, Catherine Fox and the entire staff, Roanoke Valley Convention and Visitors Bureau; Ned McElwaine and Donna Johnson, Botetourt County; Russ Merritt, Franklin County Chamber of Commerce; Franklyn Moreno, New River Valley Economic Development Alliance; Anne Piedmont, Roanoke Valley of Virginia Economic Development Partnership; Barbara Ring, Bedford County Chamber of Commerce; Christine Roberts and Heather Cormany, Lin Chaff Public Relations and Advertising; Prof. James Robertson, Virginia Tech; John Strutner and Martha Steger, Department of Economic Development, State of Virginia; Gary G. Walker, Civil War expert of Southwestern Virginia; Michelle Wright, Alleghany Highlands Chamber of Commerce; the New River Valley Hosts; the directors of the 14 Southwestern Virginia counties' Chambers and Economic Development groups; and a host of others who firmly believe the Blue Ridge of Virginia is the most beautiful, special place on earth.

Steve thanks his wife, Stacy, for spending the better part of her married life helping him navigate the slow, winding mountain roads of the Virginia Blue Ridge. Also, contributing either insight, inspiration, the occasional iced-down cooler or other general acts of mountain kindness and wisdom were Brian T. Cook, Joshua Rubin, Craig Leisher, John Marks, Willis Smith, Don and Robin Martin, Mariella and Vito Corrachano, Kathy and Roy Dawson, Paul and Margo McGinn, Matt and Deanna Soltis, Gordon and Betty Beasley, Dewey and Hall — along with just about anyone else he's ever had the pleasure of venturing into the Blue Ridge with. Steve dedicates his efforts to the Piedmont Environmental Council, the Nature Conservancy, the National Park Service and the myriad other groups and individuals working to preserve a green and open Virginia.

About the Authors

Lin **D. Chaff** arrived in Blacksburg fresh out of West Virginia University in 1972, as the editor of the *Blacksburg Sun*. While there, she fell in love with the Blue Ridge of Virginia and ever since has made it her life's mission to live and work there, taking time out to earn a graduate journalism degree at Northwestern University.

Before moving back in 1978 to become a reporter for the New River Valley Bureau of the *Roanoke Times*, she worked for Gannett newspapers and Associated Press and on Capitol Hill and received a string of journalism awards.

After the birth of her first daughter, she became manager of publicity for Dominion Bankshares Corp. (now First Union) in Roanoke. After the birth of her second daughter, she started her own public relations, marketing and advertising firm, in part to promote tourism in western Virginia. The firm's work has been honored by Virginia's premier Public Relations Society of America competition and the American Advertising Federation.

Chaff belongs to numerous tourism marketing groups, including the Blue Ridge Commission's Marketing Committee, and is accredited by PRSA. She thanks her husband, John Wade, and her daughters, Elizabeth and Priscilla, for their patience, support and shared enthusiasm for this labor of love.

Margaret **Camlin Ritsch**, a native of South Carolina, came to the Blue Ridge in early 1988 to work for *The Winchester Star* after earning a master's degree in journalism from the University of Wisconsin at Madison.

The next year, she married and became an education writer for the *Roanoke Times & World-News* New River Valley Bureau. Ritsch received her undergraduate degree in English from the College of William & Mary in 1980. She won a first-place award from the Virginia Press Association for in-depth and investigative reporting in 1989 while at *The Winchester Star*.

Her articles have appeared in *Mid-Atlantic Country, Virginia, Blue Ridge Country, Episcopal Life, Iris-A Journal About Women* and numerous newspapers.

Ritsch recently relocated to Wilmington, Delaware, with her husband, Fritz, and her daughter, Sara Caitlin. She is a member of the Public Relations Society of America and the Delaware Press Women and is director of communications for The Placers Inc., a staffing firm with offices in Delaware, Pennsylvania and New Jersey.

Stephen **Soltis** is a contributing writer for this edition. A former senior writer and editor for *Washington Flyer Magazine*, Soltis also co-authored the *Insiders' Guide to Metropolitan Washington, D.C.*

Photo: Wintergreen Resort

A breathtaking Blue Ridge vista.

Table of Contents

Overviews 9
The Civil War 83
The Blue Ridge Parkway 99
and Skyline Drive 99
Recreation 111
Skiing 141
Wineries 149
Other Attractions 161
Annual Events 175
Arts and Culture 199
Shopping 259
Resorts 299
Bed and Breakfast Inns and Country Inns 315
Other Accommodations 379
Restaurants 399
Nightlife 453
Real Estate and Retirement 461
Airports and Bus Lines 479
Education 487
Southwestern Virginia 501
Index of Advertisers 536
Index 538

Directory of Maps

Overview 3
Shenandoah Valley 4
East of the Blue Ridge 5
New River Valley 6
Alleghany Highlands 7
Southwestern Virginia 503

Photo: Wintergreen Resort

The Blue Ridge Mountains offer the ideal getaway for families.

How to Use This Book

When we decided to produce an Insiders' Guide® to the Blue Ridge, the most time-consuming discussions went into figuring out just how to present the material on such a large geographic area in a sensible and accessible way. It wasn't easy! If you are already familiar with this region, you'll sympathize with us . . . from, roughly, Winchester down through the New River Valley then over to the Alleghany Highlands and Southwestern Virginia, a lot of ground is covered, with so much to do and see in between that we hardly knew where to start recommending! But we think we've produced a guide that is organized so you can easily find what you're looking for.

In this book, each chapter is presented geographically, in regional segments, from north to south and east to west. We've defined four regions: the Shenandoah Valley, East of the Blue Ridge (also sometimes referred to as "the foothills"), the New River Valley and the Alleghany Highlands. So, each chapter starts with a regional header to orient you, followed by information about towns and cities in that region, with the overall geographic "traffic pattern" flowing south from the top of the Blue Ridge area, zigzagging back and forth from east to west.

We begin the book by introduc-ing, in a general way, the four main regions of the Blue Ridge, as noted earlier, and their cities and towns. Then, sections on such topics as Civil War sites, restaurants and accommodations follow, using the same geographical framework. In other words, if you're interested in visiting a winery that's located in the Shenandoah Valley, look under that region's heading in the Wineries chapter. The same rule applies with nightspots, shopping, bed and breakfast inns and most all the other topics we cover. The Recreation chapter is organized by type of activity and Annual Events by months, but the geographic flow continues under those headings.

One exception to this organization is the chapter on Skyline Drive and the Blue Ridge Parkway. Here, we let you know where you can eat and spend the night without departing from the two connecting mountaintop highways.

Some special chapters, such as Restaurants or Arts and Culture, will describe all the best restaurants or museums, galleries and dance groups in a given city in alphabetical order. In other chapters, such as Shopping, we let you know about our favorite stores in a given neighborhood or shopping center in every major city or town. But you still need to look first for the major region, for example, the

Shenandoah Valley. Then, under the Shenandoah Valley headline, you look under Lexington for a description of all the neat little boutiques and shops in its historic downtown district.

At the end of the book, we provide you with a comprehensive look at the area known as Southwestern Virginia. This huge region, falling to the south and west of the New River Valley and including towns such as Marion, Wytheville and the vast Jefferson National Forest, is made up of 14 counties, all distinct and interesting in their own right.

We've included maps to help you, and it's a good idea, especially if you aren't familiar with this area, to spend some time studying them before you dive into the book. They will help you understand visually how the regions are divided and what towns and cities belong in each one.

This is not meant to be the kind of guide that you must read from beginning to end to reap the benefit of buying it. But we do recommend that you start out by reading our introductions to each region; these will give you a flavor for what the areas have to offer — what makes our cities, towns and little hamlets unique and worth visiting.

One important note to keep in mind as you use this guide: On July 15, 1995, the 703 Area Code that precedes many of the phone numbers in the Blue Ridge will change to 540.

We hope you have a good time exploring both this guide and the beautiful Blue Ridge area. Let us know what you think of the book, its organization and helpfulness. We really want your input. Write us at:

The Insiders' Guides® Inc.
P. O. Box 2057
Manteo, North Carolina 27954

Virginia's Blue Ridge

(Showing Counties)

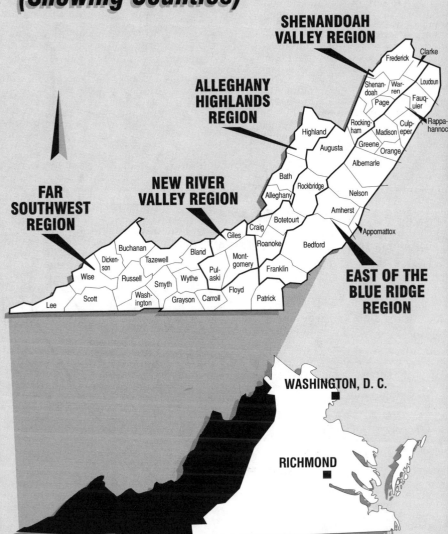

SHENANDOAH VALLEY REGION

ALLEGHANY HIGHLANDS REGION

NEW RIVER VALLEY REGION

FAR SOUTHWEST REGION

EAST OF THE BLUE RIDGE REGION

Frederick
Clarke
Shenan-doah
Warren
Loudoun
Page
Fauquier
Rocking-ham
Madison
Culpeper
Rappahannock
Highland
Greene
Orange
Augusta
Albemarle
Bath
Rockbridge
Nelson
Alleghany
Amherst
Botetourt
Appomattox
Giles
Craig
Roanoke
Bedford
Buchanan
Bland
Dickenson
Tazewell
Montgomery
Wise
Russell
Pulaski
Franklin
Smyth
Wythe
Lee
Scott
Washington
Grayson
Carroll
Floyd
Patrick

WASHINGTON, D. C.

RICHMOND

New River Valley Region

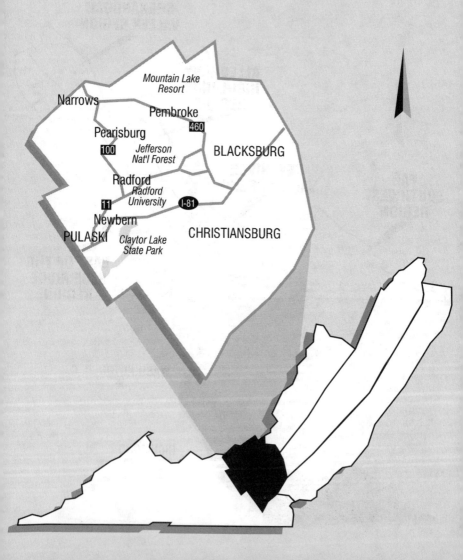

Mountain Lake Resort

Narrows

Pembroke

Pearisburg

460

100

Jefferson Nat'l Forest

BLACKSBURG

Radford
Radford University

11

I-81

Newbern

PULASKI

Claytor Lake State Park

CHRISTIANSBURG

Alleghany Highlands Region

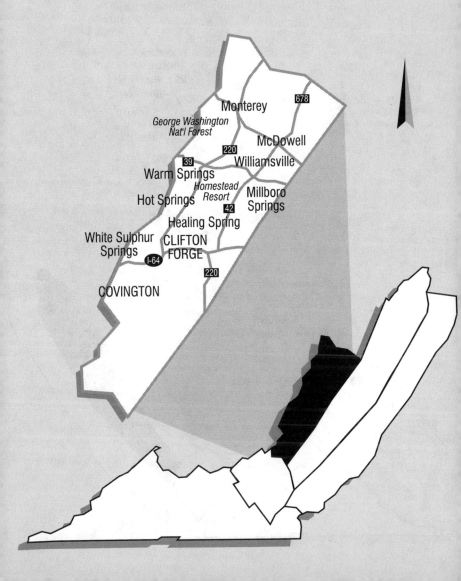

George Washington Nat'l Forest

Monterey

678

McDowell

220

Williamsville

39

Warm Springs

Homestead Resort

Millboro Springs

Hot Springs

42

Healing Spring

White Sulphur Springs

CLIFTON FORGE

I-64

220

COVINGTON

Shenandoah Valley Region

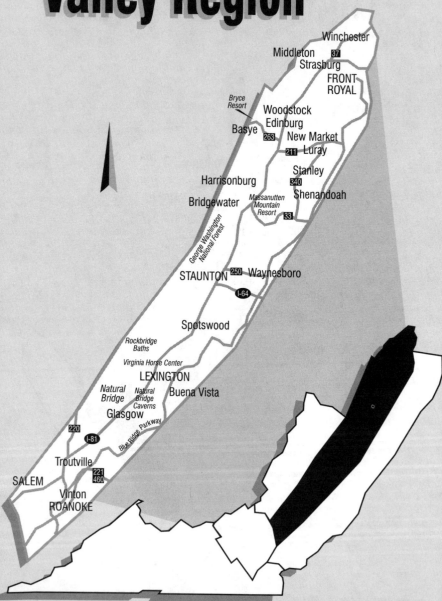

Winchester
Middleton
37
Strasburg
FRONT ROYAL

Bryce Resort
Woodstock
Edinburg
Basye
263
New Market
211
Luray
Stanley
340
Harrisonburg
Shenandoah
Bridgewater
Massanutten Mountain Resort
33

George Washington National Forest

STAUNTON
250
Waynesboro
I-64

Spotswood

Rockbridge Baths

Virginia Horse Center
LEXINGTON
Natural Bridge
Natural Bridge Caverns
Buena Vista
Glasgow
Blue Ridge Parkway
220
I-81
Troutville
SALEM
221
460
Vinton
ROANOKE

East Of The Blue Ridge Region

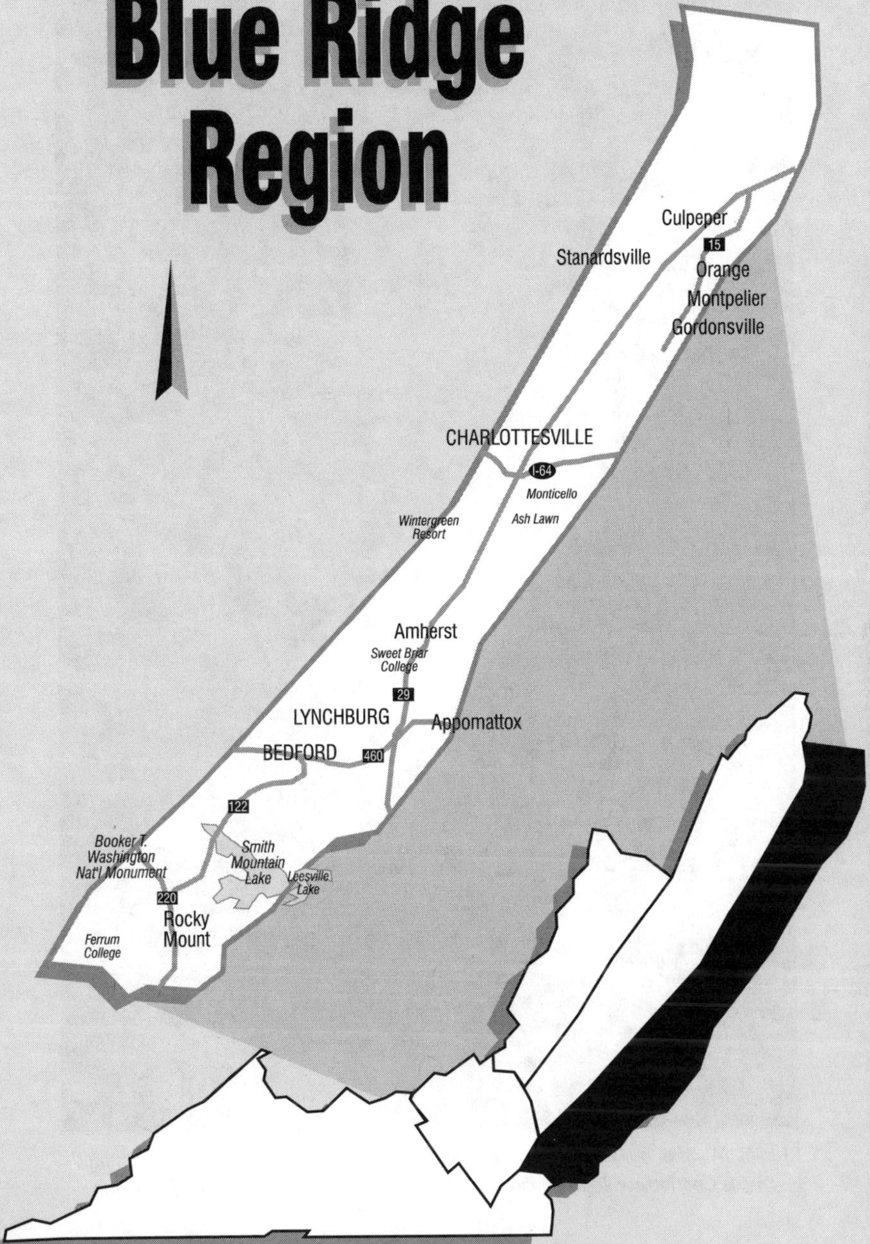

Culpeper

Stanardsville

15

Orange

Montpelier

Gordonsville

CHARLOTTESVILLE

I-64

Monticello

Wintergreen
Resort

Ash Lawn

Amherst

Sweet Briar
College

29

LYNCHBURG

Appomattox

BEDFORD

460

122

Booker T.
Washington
Nat'l Monument

Smith
Mountain
Lake

Leesville
Lake

220

Ferrum
College

Rocky
Mount

Source: Richmond Times Dispatch

James Monroe, our nation's fifth president, made his home at Ash Lawn-Highland near Charlottesville to be closer to his friend and mentor, Thomas Jefferson.

City, Town and County
Overviews

Shenandoah Valley Region

Shenandoah — the name conjures up images of rolling green farmland, beautiful old barns and the legendary Shenandoah River that winds its way to Harpers Ferry, West Virginia.

Shenandoah means "Daughter of the Stars," a name Native Americans gave this 200-mile-long valley stretching from Frederick and Clarke counties in the north to nearly Roanoke in the south. White explorers traveled through the valley as early as the mid-1600s, but it wasn't until the early 1700s that the first German and Scotch-Irish families began to put down roots here. They had migrated south in most part from Maryland and Pennsylvania, seeking rich, cheap land and greater freedom for themselves and their children.

The German families settled mainly along the land extending from Winchester to Staunton; the Scotch-Irish, on the other hand, chose Staunton and the valley south for their homesites. This is only a general pattern of settlement; to some extent both groups were interspersed along the entire length of the valley.

Original barns and homesteads dot the landscape up and down the valley, and many museums along Interstate 81 give visitors a closer look of the daily lives of these rugged pioneers.

From the Woodstock Museum in Shenandoah County and the lovely Virginia State Arboretum in Clarke County, to the Cyrus McCormick Farm near Steele's Tavern and the Museum of American Frontier Culture in Staunton, all offer a glimpse into the Shenandoah's past. You can see early American farm equipment, pottery, furniture, Native American artifacts and Civil War exhibits and watch costumed interpreters perform such pioneer chores as churning butter and shearing sheep.

The fertile, wheat-producing Shenandoah Valley was known as the "Breadbasket of the Confederacy" — that is until Union Gen. Philip Sheridan began torching nearly all the barns and mills in the valley. Crops were destroyed, and livestock and horses confiscated to the extent that "a crow flying across the Valley would have to pack its lunch."

Some of the heaviest fighting during the Civil War took place in the valley, and many of the war's hardiest soldiers hailed from here. According to Lt. Col. C.F.R. Henderson, author of the two-volume *Stonewall Jackson and the Civil War*, " . . . no better material for soldiers ever existed than the men of the valley. . . . All classes mingle in the ranks, and all ages. . . . They were a mountain people, nurtured in a wholesome climate bred to manly sports, and hardened by the free life of the field and forest. To social distinctions they gave little heed. They were united for a common purpose . . . and their patriotism was proved by the sacrifice of all personal consideration and individual interest."

The valley is the burial place of many heroes of that terrible war. Both Robert E. Lee's and Stonewall Jackson's resting places are in Lexington; Lee was president of the city's Washington College (now Washington and Lee) after the war, and Jackson had taught natural philosophy at the Virginia Military Institute for years. Jackson's horse, Little Sorrel, remains close to his master in Lexington. Still standing in the VMI Museum, the preserved horse is a little mangy — but you would be too if you had to keep standing more than 100 years after you died. (Actually, it is the real hide, stretched over a plastic form!)

Jackson is memorialized in a rollicking musical called *Stonewall Country*, performed under the stars every summer at Lexington's Lime Kiln Theater.

The Shenandoah Valley was also home to other great leaders of our nation; Woodrow Wilson was born in Staunton, and a fascinating museum next to his birth place tells all about his life and his vision for world peace. Also in Lexington is a museum honoring George C. Marshall, a VMI graduate who went on to lead the U.S. Army during World War II and later devise a plan to rebuild Europe after the war.

Visitors to the valley need not have a strong interest in history to enjoy themselves. There are great caverns offering cool tours among rooms filled with ancient and colorful calcite formations. There's the magnificence of Natural Bridge, once owned by Thomas Jefferson. There are rivers running through the valley where you can take a quiet, lazy canoe trip or an action-packed whitewater run.

Antique lovers will be wowed by the shops in charming small towns and out in the "middle of nowhere." And if you time your visit right, you can catch some of the East's finest fairs and festivals: Virginia's number one Agricultural Fair at Harrisonburg, the Maple Festival in Highland County and the wildly popular Apple Blossom Festival in Winchester.

There are downtown districts that are great to explore on foot in the valley, offering a concentration of beautiful architecture, fine restaurants, boutiques and galleries. You can spend hours exploring Roanoke's city market area, or historic downtown Lexington or Staunton.

All kinds of modern accommo-

Photo: Winchester-Frederick Co. Chamber of Commerce

Abram's Delight Museum is the oldest house in Winchester, built in 1754.

dations can be found throughout the valley, and there are also dozens of inns and bed and breakfasts in beautifully restored old homes. The Virginia Division of Tourism will recommend bed and breakfasts and make reservations, (804) 786-4484. There are also other reservation services (see our Bed and Breakfasts Inns and Country Inns chapter).

The Shenandoah Valley has many more villages and towns worth exploring than we were able to highlight in this book because of its large scope.

But we hope the following introductions will give you a taste of what each area has to offer. For more detailed information on restaurants, museums, accommodations, antiquing and more, read on!

Winchester

Once called Frederick Town after Frederick, father of King George III, Winchester is full of reminders of our nation's early history. The city and surrounding area was first settled by Pennsylvania Quakers in 1732; soon after, Germans, Scotch, Irish, English, Welsh and French Huguenots also followed the Great Wagon Road from Pennsylvania and put down roots here. Winchester was a thriving center of commerce during the settlement of our nation; pioneers obtained their wagons and provisions here for trips farther west and south.

The city saw much action during the Civil War. Five battles and many skirmishes were fought within or near Winchester, which changed hands more than 70 times. Stonewall Jackson used a home on Braddock Street for his headquarters during the war, and today his office remains much the way it was during his stay. The new Kurtz Cultural Center downtown opened a permanent exhibit last year called "Shenandoah — Crossroads of the Civil War." All kinds of displays provide details on the major battles here.

The father of our country started his career in Winchester when he was 16, as a surveyor for Lord Thomas Fairfax (owner of a 5-million-acre royal grant) who lived in nearby White Post. George Washington later held great responsibility for protecting Virginia's frontier as a colonel. He oversaw the construction of Fort Loudoun, today a museum in Winchester. He also was elected to his first political office — as a member of the House of Burgesses — in Winchester.

Country music fans know Winchester as the birthplace of Patsy Cline, that spunky, honey-voiced singer made famous by her renditions of "I Fall to Pieces, "After Midnight," and "Sweet Dreams" in the early '60s. In 1963 Cline was killed in an airplane crash when she was 30; she was buried at the Shenandoah Memorial Cemetery on Highway 522 S., also known as the Patsy Cline Memorial Highway. The singer's mother and sister still live in town.

On a literary note, the Winchester area was also the birthplace of another pioneering woman — the novelist Willa Cather. Cather's family moved from Frederick County to Nebraska when she was 10.

Winchester is probably best known for its annual Shenandoah Apple Blossom Festival. Every spring, Winchester plays host for four days to more than 250,000 visitors who converge to enjoy the Grand Feature Parade, the Queen's coronation, arts and crafts festivals, races, dances and a circus.

For more information about attractions, events and tours of the Winchester area, contact the Chamber of Commerce and Visitor Center, 1360 S. Pleasant Valley Road, Winchester, Virginia 22601, (703) 662-4135.

Middletown

This quaint little town in southern Frederick County lies along U.S. Highway 11, once the Great Wagon Road, the most important frontier highway in ColonialAmerica.

It has always been a favorite stopping place for valley travelers. A tavern was built in 1797 that later became a stagecoach relay station and an inn. It is still in operation today as the Wayside Inn and Restaurant, a beautifully restored watering hole in the center of town. The inn is a paradise for antique lovers. You'll find Colonial furnishings, rare antiques and historic paintings throughout the place, which is also famous for its hearty regional American cuisine.

Middletown is also home to Belle

Grove plantation, a large stone mansion built between 1794 and 1797 by Isaac Hite, who married James Madison's sister. The mansion served as Union Gen. Philip Sheridan's headquarters during the decisive 1864 Battle of Cedar Creek, which occurred two miles south of town.

Every October, the plantation grounds attract huge crowds for a major Civil War re-enactment, hosted by the Cedar Creek Battlefield Foundation Inc. The foundation is raising money to secure complete ownership of the 158-acre Cedar Battlefield that lies adjacent to the plantation.

Wayside Theatre in downtown Middletown is the second oldest theater in the state, performing dramas, comedies and mysteries from May through December. Some famous faces got their start here, including Susan Sarandon, Jill Eikenberry of "L.A. Law," and Peter Boyle.

For more information about Middletown attractions, contact the Winchester-Frederick County Chamber of Commerce at 1360 S. Pleasant Valley Road, Winchester, Virginia 22601, (703) 662-4135.

Front Royal

This northern Blue Ridge town was once known as "Helltown" for all the shootings, brawls and hard drinking that went on here in the mid-1700s.

Today Front Royal and the surrounding Warren County are fast becoming a bedroom community of Washington, D.C., whose beltway is only 57 miles away. But Front Royal is also the gateway to the wilderness of the Shenandoah National Park. The north and south forks of the majestic Shenandoah River come together here, and campgrounds and canoe outfitters abound.

Front Royal has a revitalized downtown district, full of interesting boutiques and antique shops. An old fashioned town clock sits in the Village Common, where a gazebo and picnic tables welcome tourists and downtown workers to sit for a spell.

The town has a Confederate Museum that documents how this important rail and river junction witnessed numerous clashes during the Civil War. Belle Boyd, the beautiful aristocratic Confederate spy, stayed for a while in Front Royal during

The tiny hamlet of Washington, Virginia, is actually older than its bigger "little brother" to the east. In fact, the Rappahannock County community is the oldest of the 28 cities in the United States named after our first president. We'll go so far as to say that it's also the prettiest.

Insiders' Tips

the war and one night was upstairs in the same home where a Union general and his officers stopped to make plans for further maneuvers.

Belle watched and listened through a small hole in the closet floor and heard every word of their plans. She wrote down in cipher each plan, stole down the back steps and rode horseback for 15 miles in the middle of the night to carry the message to Confederate troops.

Abundant attractions in the Front Royal area include Skyline Caverns, the Skyline Drive and two wineries offering tours and tastings: Oasis Vineyard and Linden Vineyards and Orchards, both about eight miles south of town.

Front Royal pulls out the stops every May for the Virginia Mushroom Festival. Virginia shiitake mushrooms, which are cultivated in the Warren County area, are featured, along with wine tastings, arts and crafts exhibits and cooking demonstrations.

For more information, contact the Chamber of Commerce of Front Royal and Warren County, 414 E. Main Street, Front Royal, Virginia 22630, (703) 635-3185.

Strasburg

Staufferstadt was the original name of Strasburg, a busy little town just south of Middletown. German Mennonites and Dunkards, who had migrated from York County, Pennsylvania, settled the village, and Peter Stover petitioned for a charter for the town in 1761. He then changed the name to Strasburg, in honor of its home city in Germany.

Later, the town was nicknamed "Pottown" for the high quality pottery produced here during the antebellum period. The first potter came in 1761, and since then at least 17 potters have produced earthen and stoneware in Strasburg.

You can see some of this pottery in the Strasburg Museum and Gift Shop, which was originally a steam pottery built in 1891. Also in the museum are Civil War relics, Native American artifacts, blacksmith collections and displays from Colonial farms and businesses.

Antique lovers will have a heyday in Strasburg. Nearly 100 dealers of high quality antiques are housed under one roof in the downtown Strasburg Emporium. You'll find not just furniture representing every American era, but also carriages, chandeliers, rugs, quilts, lace, old carousel horses and pottery.

The place to stay overnight in town is the Hotel Strasburg, a renovated Victorian hotel whose rooms are decorated with antiques that are also for sale. The hotel's restaurant has a popular following among folks from nearby valley towns and is by far the best place to dine for miles around. For more information on Strasburg, Woodstock, New Market and other Shenandoah County towns, such as Edinburg, Mt. Jackson, Basye and Orkney Springs, call the Shenandoah County Travel Council, Woodstock, at (703) 459-5522.

Woodstock

This charming valley town was originally called Muellerstadt after its founder Jacob Mueller, who arrived from Germany in 1749. In 1761, the frontier settlement was chartered by an act of the Virginia Assembly, sponsored by George Washington, a representative from Frederick County. Its name was then changed to Woodstock. Artifacts recalling the valley's early settlement can be seen at the Woodstock Museum on W. Court Street. These include Native American tools, maps, ledgers, portraits, furniture, quilts, a moonshine still and Civil War memorabilia.

The museum sponsors a walking tour through town, where you can see examples of Federal, Greek Revival and Classic Revival architecture. The courthouse, whose original section was built in 1795, is the oldest courthouse west of the Blue Ridge in continuous use as a court building.

Nearby Orkney Springs hosts the Shenandoah Valley Music Festival every spring and summer. Concerts are held in a covered, open-air pavilion and on the grounds of the historic Orkney Springs Hotel, a 19th century mineral springs spa and resort.

New Market

Here you will find caverns, museums, golf, a battlefield historical park and an excellent tourist information center for the whole Shenandoah Valley.

New Market was a little later in becoming settled than other valley towns. English settlers from the north and east settled here and named their village after a horse-racing town in England named New Market. In the early days, there was a racetrack near New Market about a mile long.

New Market is famous for the 1864 battle that drew in 247 eager cadets fresh from the classrooms of the Virginia Military Institute. A stirring account of the battle can be seen on film at the Hall of Valor Museum at the New Market Battlefield Historical Park. The museum also presents a nonpartisan view of major Civil War events with its artifacts, murals and life-size models. Also on the 220-acre battlefield is the restored farm of Jacob and Sarah Bushong, whose home became one of the hospitals and whose orchards became the killing fields of war. Equipped wheelwright and blacksmith shops, loom house and a summer kitchen have the workings of a typical 19th-century valley farm.

New Market is a center of caverns in the valley: Shenandoah Caverns are to the north and Endless Caverns to the south, and within a short drive you can also reach Luray and Grand Caverns.

Many historic buildings continue to stand in the downtown and can be seen along a walking tour. While it may sound like a sleeper of an attraction, you shouldn't miss the Bedrooms of America Museum on Congress Street (U.S. Highway 11). There are 11 different rooms of authentic furniture showing every period of America's bedrooms, from William and Mary (c. 1650) through Art Deco (c. 1930). The museum is housed in the same 18th century building used by Gen. Jubal Early as his headquarters during the Civil War.

For shopping, don't miss Paper Treasures, also on the main drag of Congress Street . The store has an extraordinary collection of old books, maps and magazines, such as *Ebony, Collier's Weekly* and the *Saturday Evening Post.* The store also sells framed, hand-tinted illustrations from some of these old magazines.

The River Farm is a working sheep farm near town that offers weekend workshops in spinning, weaving and dying, as well as lodging for students. A shop sells fleece, fibers, spinning wheels and looms.

You can also see a marvelous old covered bridge north of town, about two miles south of Mount Jackson. Meem's Bottom Bridge stretches 191 feet across the north fork of the Shenandoah River. Built in 1892, it is the longest covered bridge of the nine remaining in Virginia and the last crossing the Shenandoah.

Luray

There is no agreement as to how this town got its name. Some insist that the Huguenots who escaped from France and migrated to the valley named the new settlement Lorraine and that Luray is a corruption of the former name.

Luray is a central gateway to the 105-mile-long Skyline Drive. The Shenandoah National Park borders Page County on the east and the George Washington National Forest on the west.

As the county seat of Page, Luray is the home of the internationally famed Luray Caverns, which are open every day of the year. The magical underground world of stalactites, stalagmites and crystal-clear pools can be explored in an hourlong guided tour. Housed in the same complex is the Historic Car and Carriage Caravan, an exhibit of antique cars, carriages, coaches and costumes dating back to 1625. Rudolph Valentino's 1925 Rolls Royce is here!

Shenandoah River Outfitters in Luray and the Down River Canoe Company in nearby Bentonville both offer canoe trips on the south fork of the Shenandoah River, which travels the entire length of Page County. Guilford Ridge Vineyard is just a few miles out of town and offers tours and tastings of its wines by appointment. And would you believe one of the state's largest reptile collections is in Luray? The Luray Reptile Center and Dinosaur Park on Route 211 will keep your kids squealing for hours. Its petting zoo has tame deer and llamas.

A good time to visit the area is on Columbus Day weekend in October, when Page County throws its annual Heritage Festival. First held in 1969, it is one of the oldest arts and crafts shows in Virginia. Craft demonstrations range from quilt making, woodworking, wheel spinning and soap making to apple butter boiling and apple cider pressings. The festival offers an antique tractor steam and gas engine show, mule train rides, country bands and clogging demonstrations.

For more information about attractions and events in Page County contact the Chamber of Commerce, 46 E. Main Street, Luray, Virginia 22835, (703) 743-3915.

Harrisonburg

Harrisonburg is a thriving city and the seat of one of the nation's leading agricultural counties. In fact, so valuable is poultry to Rockingham County's economy that a proud statue of a turkey stands alongside U.S. Highway 11 south of town. And every May Harrisonburg hosts the week-long Poultry Festival, which includes a "Friends of Feathers" banquet.

There are more than 2,000 farms in the county, and nearly half the land is classified as agricultural. The county is the state's leading producer of dairy, poultry and beef products. The city also is home to 20 major industries and serves as the major financial and retail center for eight counties, including three in neighboring West Virginia.

Opportunities for higher education abound in the area. Bridgewater College, Eastern Mennonite College and Seminary and James Madison University are all here, so students and professors comprise a large part of the population.

In 1778, Virginia Governor Patrick Henry named Rockingham County for the Marquis of Rockingham, one of the few friends Virginia had at the Court of London. The following year, a prominent farmer named Thomas Harrison donated two and one-half acres for a courthouse, and the city of Harrisonburg was born.

During the Civil War, productive farms in the area helped feed the Confederate army. Stonewall Jackson used Harrisonburg as one of his headquarters, and today his military strategies that so confounded Union officers are described by way of an electric, wall-sized map at the Shenandoah Valley Heritage Museum in nearby Dayton.

Testimony to other battles can also be seen at Dayton's Daniel Harrison House, also known as Fort Harrison. This beautiful stone house was built in the mid 1750s, when bands of Native Americans frequently roamed the area threatening the settlers. The house served as a fort and had a stockade and underground passage to a nearby spring.

Dayton is also home to a wonderful indoor Farmer's Market, where you will find fresh cheeses, baked goods, antiques, bulk grains and spices and a fantastic country restaurant run by a former Mennonite missionary.

It's not unusual to see a black carriage or two with horses parked out front; about 1,000 Old Order Mennonites live in the greater area and are easily identified by their simple style of dress, including white hats for women. Their horse-drawn buggies and immaculate farms are a common sight in the southwestern region of the county.

More than 139,000 acres of George Washington National Forest lie in western Rockingham County. On the east, the county is bordered by the Shenandoah National Park. The Massanutten Mountain range is just east of town and is home to Massanutten Resort, a year-round residential community known for its ski slopes, golf courses and impressive indoor sports complex. Here, visitors can also fish swim, hike and ride horses.

Another recreational attraction near Harrisonburg (but in Augusta County) is Natural Chimneys, a place where huge rocks tower to heights of 120 feet. From one perspective, these rocks resemble a foreboding medieval castle with turrets and towers, and this may have inspired the creation of the Natural Chimneys Jousting Tournament more than 150 years ago. The tournament is the oldest continuously held sporting event in America, having begun in 1821. Modern-day knights still match their skills in the ancient art of jousting here on the third Saturday in August every year.

The Natural Chimneys Regional Park has 120 campsites, a swimming pool, picnic area, camp store, nature and bike trails and more.

For more information about attractions in the Harrisonburg and Rockingham County area, contact the Chamber of Commerce at 191 S. Main Street, Harrisonburg, Virginia 22801, (703) 434-3862.

Staunton

Staunton is a great city to explore on foot — full of Victorian era architecture and unique shops, one-of-a-kind eateries and important historical sites. The city is the birthplace of President Woodrow Wilson, who was born in 1856 to a Presbyterian minister and his wife in a Greek Revival manse on Coalter Street. Today the manse is open for tours and sits next door to a fascinating museum where you can learn all about Wilson's life, his political views and his vision for world peace. The new Woodrow Wilson Museum also houses the president's 1919 Pierce Arrow limousine.

Another major attraction in Staunton is the Museum of American Frontier Culture, an indoor-outdoor living museum that features four authentic working farms from Germany, England, Northern Ireland and early America. Children love this place, where lambs, chickens, cats and all kinds of farm critters animate the landscape. In 1993, it received the Phoenix Award of excellence from the National Association of Travel writers.

Staunton is an appropriate place for a museum that documents life in frontier America. It is the seat of Augusta County, which once stretched all the way to Mississippi. Most early settlers in the area were Scotch-Irish, including John Lewis, the first white man to build a homestead here in 1732. In 1749, Lewis' son Thomas laid out lots and streets for the new town of Staunton, named in honor of Lady Rebecca Staunton, Gov. William Gooch's wife.

Staunton became Virginia's capital for 17 days in June, 1781, as Gov. Thomas Jefferson and the General Assembly fled advancing British troops led by Tarleton. Those redcoats had already captured seven Virginia delegates in nearby downtown Charlottesville, including Daniel Boone.

Nineteenth century Staunton grew by leaps and bounds following incorporation as a town in 1801. Education became a priority, with the establishment of the Virginia Institute for the Deaf and the Blind in 1839, Augusta Female Seminary in 1842 (now Mary Baldwin College), Virginia Female Institute in 1844 (now Stuart Hall School) and Staunton Military Academy in 1884.

The railroad came to Staunton in 1854, and this stimulated the city's growth as a center of commerce for the region. Today Amtrak continues to serve the city, and the old C&O train station is a showcase of meticulous restoration work.

There, you'll find an authentic 1880s Victorian Ice Cream Parlor serving dense, Italian style ice cream in a room with antique parlor and drug store furnishings from ceiling to floor. Next door, the Depot Grille boasts a gorgeous, hand-carved antique walnut bar, and in the same building, Depot Antiques sells fine collectibles, Victorian and country furniture.

The wharf area is undergoing much restoration work; the old mill buildings and warehouses already house antique shops, a pottery workshop and studio and a marvelous antique car dealership, and you can expect much more in the future. The Historic Staunton Foundation has produced a detailed brochure to guide visitors on a walking tour of the city, as well as a new guide to antique shops.

Other attractions in Staunton include the beautiful Gypsy Hill Park, which has tennis courts, softball fields, a lake and a duck pond. Right across the street is the Statler Brothers museum and office complex. Yes, these famous, down-home country music stars actually live and work in Staunton and their children go to school here. For 25 years the Statler Brothers have thrown a huge "Happy Birthday U.S.A." celebration in Gypsy Hill Park, complete with concerts, firework displays, free tours of their museum and patriotic speeches.

For additional information about Staunton, contact the Augusta-Staunton-Waynesboro Visitors Bureau at (800) 342-7982.

Waynesboro, Stuarts Draft and Fishersville

Named in honor of Revolutionary War hero Gen. Anthony Wayne, Waynesboro thrived as an industrial community during the late 1800s and the trend continues today. Thanks in part to its convenient location just eight miles east of the intersection of I-81 and I-64, DuPont, Genicom and Hershey are a few of the plants located here.

Waynesboro is also known for being a friendly town and a wonderful place to raise children. Nearby Stuarts Draft and Fishersville are also attractive communities for families.

Waynesboro extends to Afton Mountain, from which you can see clear to Charlottesville and farther east. The Shenandoah National Park's southern tip ends on that mountain, and the Blue Ridge Parkway begins its southern trek there. One note of caution: It's not a fun mountain to cross during foggy weather; many fatal accidents have occurred here due to fog so thick you can barely see car lights in front of you. So, park yourself in pleasant Waynesboro if such conditions exist.

In Waynesboro, the P. Buckley Moss Museum, named for "The People's Artist," is located in a tall brick house surrounded by trees — a scene reminiscent of one of her watercolors. Since the early 1960s, the world-renowned, multimillionaire artist and philanthropist has found her inspiration and much of her subject matter in valley scenery and in the Amish and Mennonite people of the area. The museum is within easy walking distance of the Waynesboro Outlet Village, a fantastic place to find bargains in designer clothing, leather goods, imported china and much more.

While in Waynesboro, you can also watch age-old techniques of brass molding at the Virginia Metalcrafters factory showroom. The Shenandoah Valley Art Center in downtown Waynesboro offers residents and visitors a place to enjoy the arts through exhibits, workshops, classes and performances.

Mennonites who live in the area have established some businesses that provide a refreshing alternative to standard grocery stores. Kinsinger's Kountry Kitchen, on Route 651 off Route 608, sells yummy homemade pies, cinnamon rolls, cakes, cookies and jams — all made from scratch by Mennonites. The Cheese Shop up the road on Route 608 sells fresh cheeses at great prices, along with bulk nuts and seeds, dried fruits and baking ingredients. Milmont Greenhouses on Route 340 started as a Mennonite housewife's hobby nearly 20 years ago and today offers a large selection of house plants, perennials, annuals and vegetables, depending on the season.

Speaking of green things, one of the leading perennial nurseries in the nation is based in Fishersville and is definitely worth visiting. Andre Viette Farm and Nursery has beautiful gardens that feature more than 1,000 varieties of day lilies,

HEART OF
THE VALLEY

STAUNTON-
WAYNESBORO AND
AUGUSTA COUNTY

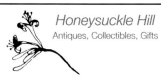

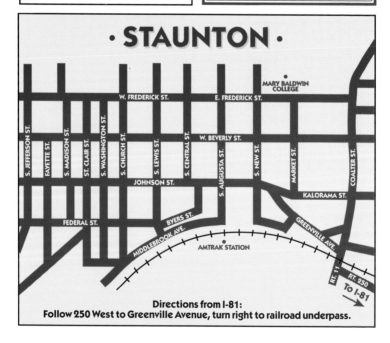

· STAUNTON ·

MARY BALDWIN COLLEGE

W. FREDERICK ST.   E. FREDERICK ST.

W. BEVERLY ST.

S. JEFFERSON ST.
FAYETTE ST.
S. MADISON ST.
ST. CLAIR ST.
S. WASHINGTON ST.
S. CHURCH ST.
S. LEWIS ST.
S. CENTRAL ST.
S. AUGUSTA ST.
S. NEW ST.
MARKET ST.
COALTER ST.

JOHNSON ST.

KALORAMA ST.

FEDERAL ST.

BYERS ST.

MIDDLEBROOK AVE.

AMTRAK STATION

GREENVILLE AVE.

RT. 11   RT. 250
To I-81

Directions from I-81:
Follow 250 West to Greenville Avenue, turn right to railroad underpass.

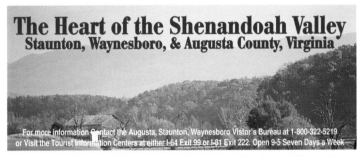

The Heart of the Shenandoah Valley
Staunton, Waynesboro, & Augusta County, Virginia

For more information contact the Augusta, Staunton, Waynesboro Vistor's Bureau at 1-800-322-5219 or Visit the Tourist Information Centers at either I-64 Exit 99 or I-81 Exit 222. Open 9-5 Seven Days a Week

Augusta County, Staunton and Waynesboro

Nestled in the heart of the Shenandoah Valley lies some of Virginia's richest treasures: the

communities of Staunton, Waynesboro and Augusta County. This unique area also offers excellent museums, fine restaurants, lovely bed & breakfasts, hospitable inns and motels, quaint shops, and various preforming arts.

Staunton

Situated just off of two of the countries busiest and important interstates, Staunton is a great city to explore ...on foot.
The city is the birthplace of President Woodrow Wilson, who was born in 1856 to a Presbyterian minister and his wife.
Another major attraction in Staunton is the Museum of American Frontier Culture, an indoor-outdoor living museum that features four authentic working farms from Germany, England, Northern Ireland and Early American. In 1993, it received the Phoenix Award of excellence from the National Association of Travel writers.
Staunton became Virginia's capital for 17 days in June, 1781, as Gov. Thomas Jefferson and the General

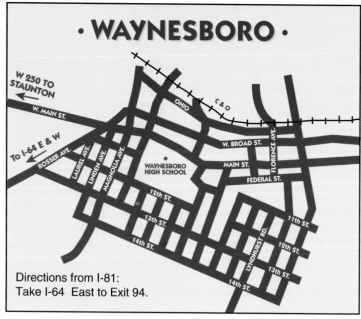

Directions from I-81:
Take I-64 East to Exit 94.

Assembly fled advancing British troops led by Tarleton. Those redcoats has already captured seven Virginia delegates in nearby downtown Charlottesville, including Daniel Boone.

The railroad came to Staunton in 1854, and this stimulated the city's growth as a center of commerce for the region. Today, Amtrak continues to serve the city, and the old C&O train station is a showcase of meticulous restoration work.

Other attractions in Staunton include the beautiful Gypsy Hill Park, which has tennis courts, softball fields, a lake and a duck pond. Right across the street is the Statler Brothers museum and office complex.

For additional information about Staunton, Contact the Office of Tourism, P.O. Box 58, Staunton, VA 24401, (703) 885-2839.

Waynesboro

Waynesboro is known for being a friendly town and a wonderful place to raise children. But it's also a great place for visitors to stop and spend some time. The city actually extends to Afton Mountain, from which you can see clear to Charlottesville and further east. The Shenandoah National Park's southern tip ends on that mountain, and the Blue Ridge Parkway begins its southern trek there.

The P. Buckley Moss Museum, named for "The People's Artist," is located in a tall brick house surrounded by trees-a scene reminiscent of one of her watercolors. The museum is within easy walking distance to the Waynesboro Outlet Village, a fantastic place to find bargains in designer clothing, leather goods, imported china and much more.

While in Waynesboro, you can also watch age-old techniques of brass molding at the Virginia Metalcrafters factory showroom.

The Shenandoah Valley Art Center in downtown Waynesboro offers residents and visitors a place to enjoy the arts through exhibits, workshops, classes and performances.

Recreational opportunities abound in the area. The Sherando Lake State Park is just outside Waynesboro, and Shenandoah Acres Resort is a Stuarts Draft.

For more information about attractions in the Waynesboro-East Augusta County area, contact the Chamber of Commerce, 301 W. Main St., Waynesboro, VA 22980-0339, (703) 949-8203.

VIRGINIA'S ANTIQUES AND COLLECTIBLES

Afton House Antiques
P.O. Box 46
Afton, VA 22920
(703) 456-6759

Depot Antiques
40 Middlebrook Ave.
Staunton, VA 24401
10:00 am-5:00 pm
Mon.-Sat.
1:00-5:00 pm Sunday
(703) 885-8326

Jolly Roger Haggle Shop
27 Middlebrook Ave.,
Staunton, VA 24401
9:00 am-5:00 pm
Mon.-Sat.
1:00-5:00 p.m.
(703) 886-9527

Dusty's Antique Market
On Rt. #11, two miles
south of Exit 235 off I-81
Mount Sidney, VA 24467
9:00 am-5:00 pm
Mon.-Sun.
(703) 248-2018

Pat's Antique Mall
Route #11
North of Verona, VA
9:00 am-5:00 pm
Mon.-Sun.
(703) 248-7287

Rocky's Gold and Silver Antique Mall
Toure #11
Weyers Cave, VA
9:00 am-5:00 pm
Mon.-Sat.
(703) 234-9900

Whitehouse Antiques
Rt. 2 Box 271
Afton, VA 22920
(703) 942-1194 (Day)
(703) 361-9137 (Night)

Tuckahoe Antique Mall
Rt. 151
Nellysford, VA 22958
10:00 am-5:00 pm
Thurs.-Sun.
(804) 361-2121

hosta, Oriental poppies, peonies and irises — as well as many rare species of other flowers and plants. Garden tours, lectures and free garden design assistance are all offered here. The nursery is on Route 608, 2.5 miles north of Route 250 in Fishersville.

Recreational opportunities abound in the area. The Sherando Lake State Park is just outside Waynesboro, and Shenandoah Acres Resort is in Stuarts Draft. At the latter, you can swim, ride horses, play badminton, mini-golf, croquet and volley ball and camp or stay in cottages that are available year round.

For more information about attractions in the Waynesboro-East Augusta County area, contact the Augusta-Staunton-Waynesboro Visitors Bureau at (800) 342-7982.

Lexington

Perhaps more than any other place in the valley, downtown Lexington has retained the graceful beauty and genteel character of its prosperous past.

And no other city or town in the Blue Ridge has a history that is so well preserved and honored by its citizens. It is a town whose heritage includes four of America's greatest generals.

It seems that everywhere you go, you are walking on historic, hallowed ground.

Filmmakers agree. In 1992, tons of dirt were dumped on downtown streets along an unusual number of 19th Century buildings for scenes in the Civil War-era movie, *Sommersby*, starring Richard Gere and Jodie Foster.

Throughout Lexington's history, the presence of its great military leaders has inspired its preservation efforts. They are George Washington, the father of our country; the great Confederate generals Robert E. Lee and Thomas J. "Stonewall" Jackson; and World War II hero Gen. George C. Marshall, the Nobel Peace Prize-winning creator of the Marshall Plan that rebuilt war-torn Europe.

Lexington is the historic and cultural heart of Rockbridge County (population 32,000), whose most prosperous residents enjoy a genteel country-estate way of life. Many are early retirees from New York, New Jersey, Connecticut and elsewhere, who devote their considerable knowledge and energy to the community as volunteers and activists. Others are college professors at nearby Virginia Military Institute and Washington and Lee University.

The county boasts the breathtaking three-mile-long Goshen Pass, a journey along the Maury River through rhododendron, laurel, ferns, mosses, magnificent pines, hemlocks, maples, dogwood and mountain ash.

Goshen Pass, a popular place for swimming, tubing, canoeing and picnicking, is so beautiful that one prominent Lexington citizen, Matthew Fontaine Maury, asked that his body be carried through the pass when the rhododendron was in bloom after he died. Complying with his request in 1873, Virginia

Military Institute cadets formed an honor guard and gave their professor his last wish.

The roles that Lexington's world-famous universities, VMI and Washington & Lee University, have played in the area's historic culture cannot be underestimated. In 1796, George Washington saved W&L from bankruptcy with a gift of $50,000 that still receives dividends. VMI cadets are immortalized forever both on campus, with the statue of "Virginia Mourning Her Dead," and at the New Market Battlefield Museum and Hall of Valor (an hour north of the city), for their role in the Civil War.

The Civil War Battle of New Market in 1864 was the first and only time in American history that an entire student body was recruited to fight a war. When the smoke cleared, 10 cadets lay dead, including Cadet Thomas G. Jefferson, 17, progeny of our nation's third president.

As a city that has had more than its share of encounters with famous presidents, it has had one rather unlikely encounter. Visitors can see the National Historic Landmark cadet barracks where actor Ronald Reagan's movie *Brother Rat* was filmed. The movie's premiere was held at Lexington's State Theatre.

VMI is now facing one of its toughest battles ever, answering the question why the college, supported by public tax dollars, should not become coed. Rounds one and two were awarded to VMI by a sympathetic judge, who ruled that a similar program at Mary Baldwin College evens up the inequity. But the fight is expected to reach the highest court of the land. In the meantime, you can still see the all-male cadet corps and marvel at its precision during one of the formal dress parades.

Many of Lexington's attractions focus on its famous former citizens. There's the Stonewall Jackson House, where the tough general lived while teaching natural philosophy at VMI, and the Stonewall Jackson Cemetery, his final resting place after he was mistakenly killed by his own soldiers. You can see his bullet-pierced raincoat at the VMI Museum, along with the curious taxidermy display of his favorite war horse, Little Sorrel. Jackson's birthday is celebrated in Lexington every January 21 with a ceremony, cake and a free tour of the only home he ever owned.

Lee Chapel, still in use by W&L

The largest county in all of Virginia is located in the Blue Ridge. Augusta County stretches from the Blue Ridge Parkway in the east clear across the Shenandoah Valley to nearly the summit of West Virginia's Shenandoah Mountain in the west. Still, less than 55,000 people call this gorgeous stretch of land "home."

Insiders' Tips

students, is another famous site. The famous striking white statue of the recumbent Lee by sculptor Edward Valentine is alone worth a visit to Lexington. The chapel also is the site of the famous Peale portrait of George Washington. You can see Lee's office as he left it in 1870 after assuming the presidency of W&L following his Civil War defeat. Lee's favorite mount, Traveller, also is buried on campus.

The third famous military landmark to see is the George C. Marshall Museum, where Marshall, VMI Class of 1901, began a remarkable military career that led to U.S. Army Chief of Staff and later the Nobel Prize in 1953. An electric map detailing the military march of World War II shows you the breadth of what this military genius accomplished and why the United States earned a reputation world wide as a country with a heart in the aftermath of the war.

Lexington's historic sites are well documented by its history-loving populace. You can even see the troughs where its famous equestrian residents, Little Sorrel and Traveller, refreshed themselves. A complete map and guide called "One Hundred Historic Sites and Structures in Rockbridge County" will keep you exploring enough bridges and locks, churches, cemeteries, houses, mills, baths and springs to quench even the most avid history buff's thirst for knowledge. It is available at the Visitors Center at 102 East Washington Street or by calling (703) 463-3777.

The Center, run by an extremely able director and an enthusiastic staff and volunteers, can tell you everything you want to know about the historic downtown and its surrounding area, from a walking map of historic sites to historic homes. They'll also let you know there's much more than history to keep you busy here and ply you with pamphlets on shopping, restaurants, bed and breakfasts, hotels and Lexington's many other attractions, including a nearby museum dedicated to Cyrus McCormick (inventor of the mechanized reaper).

Every day, the Lexington Carriage Company leaves its hitching post at the Visitors Center and carries passengers from 9:30 AM to 5:30 PM. You can ride the same streets as Jackson and Lee did on their famous horses.

Since the memory of two famous horses are awarded such places of honor in Lexington, it stands to reason that the Commonwealth of Virginia saw fit to award Lexington its $12 million Horse Center, situated on 400 rolling acres. It is one of the top equine facilities in the United States with 4,000 spectator seats, 610 permanent stalls and a gigantic show arena. Its schedule of events includes everything from the Bonnie Blue Nationals to the Northeast Peruvian Horse Club Show. Recently it hosted the return of the Rockbridge Regional Fair after 50 years' absence following World War II. This year the fair will be held again July 25 through 30 and is expected to be a regular event.

Also bringing fame and visitors to the area is Lime Kiln Theatre, named by *Theatre Journal* magazine as "the most unusual theater set-

Historic Lexington

★★★ FOR MORE INFORMATION, CALL OR STOP BY ★★★
Historic Lexington Visitor Center   102 E. Washington Street • (703) 463-3777

ting in the United States" because of its location in an abandoned kiln beside a craggy hillside overgrown with wildflowers. Lime Kiln puts on an array of plays and musicals every summer that highlights the history and culture of the Southern mountains. The theater also offers a Sunday night concert series with an eclectic slate of musicians from across the country and around the world. Every year, Robin and Linda Williams of National Public Radio's "Prairie Home Companion" fame also perform at one of the concerts. They make their home in nearby Staunton.

Going out into the countryside, there's the beautiful Chessie Nature Trail along the Maury River and numerous hiking paths in nearby mountains — among them the Appalachian Trail. If you'd like to see 100 years of nostalgia, stop by Maury River Mercantile on the way to Goshen Pass, in Rockbridge Baths. If you're into horseback riding, Virginia Mountain Outfitters will put together half-day or overnight trips that will take you along forest trails and trout-filled rivers to the tops of mountains. The phone number is (703) 261-1910.

If canoeing is your passion, the James River Basin Canoe Livery will outfit you with boats, supplies, maps and a shuttle service for a trip along with the mighty James River and the rushing Maury, (703) 261-7334.

The great outdoors should also include a visit to Hull's Drive-In, one of the premier mom-and-pop operations anywhere and one of the few surviving drive-in theaters in Virginia. It's open weekends mid-March through November.

In Buena Vista, six miles east of Lexington and the only other city in the county, you will find much of the county's manufacturing industry. You'll also find The General Store, a trip back in time for an unusual shopping experience. Every Labor Day, Buena Vista attracts huge crowds and state political leaders to a popular festival in Glen Maury Park.

Do not leave Rockbridge County without visiting Natural Bridge, one of the seven wonders of the natural world. The awesome limestone bridge is 23 stories high and 90 feet long. A beautiful walking trail allows you to hike along a wide stream until you are directly beneath the bridge (and beyond). You may strain your neck when you look up and try to take in the entire view of the awesome structure. It is easy to see why the Monocan Indians considered it such a sacred place.

One of the most spiritually moving Easter Sunrise Services in the world is conducted there annually to a hushed crowd of several thousand. The Natural Bridge Wax Museum and gift shop are also loads of fun, especially for children, who will love to fool their friends with candy that looks like real rocks.

Whether visiting the Lexington area for its history, beauty or attractions, you'll be impressed with its sense of historical importance, its gracious old homes and its vibrant downtown district with fine restaurants and one-of-a-kind shops.

Roanoke Valley Region

God lives here. You can tell from the scenery. So does Elvis, at least in miniature, at Miniature Graceland in Roanoke. The Roanoke Valley of Virginia, including the bedroom communities of Botetourt and Craig counties, is home to about a quarter million people who work and play in a cultured, historical place of incredible beauty.

Even the interstate (I-81) that connects the Roanoke Valley is beautiful. One of the first things visitors usually say is that they can't get over the absence of potholes and rough pavement. Then they marvel at all the wildflowers, redbud, yellow forsythia and flowering orchards along western Virginia's main thoroughfare.

People usually don't set out to move to the Roanoke Valley. Instead, they are converted into relocating here. When you talk to people about how they came to live here, so many times the story starts out, "We were driving down the (fill in the blank with either A. Interstate or B. Blue Ridge Parkway), when we were so smitten that we moved here without even having jobs." Or else they discovered the Roanoke Valley while hiking on the Appalachian Trail, taking the Bikecentennial path coast to coast or vacationing at nearby Smith Mountain Lake. Inevitably, the conversation ends with, "...and we'd never go back home. We'll never leave this place."

Consider this: The Roanoke Valley of Virginia was the first in the state to have curbside recycling, mandatory comprehensive recycling and a downtown recycling program that also was a first on the North American continent. This should tell you something about Valley citizens' overwhelming sensitivity to their environment.

Parenting magazine calls the

Roanoke Valley one of the 10 best places to raise a family in the United States. The U.S. Department of Education has recognized Roanoke Valley schools for being among the nation's best. *Inc.* magazine named the Roanoke Valley one of the country's top 100 hot spots for business development. The region is blessed with many community-minded businesses and industries, such at Cox Cable of Roanoke, a dynamic civic booster, and Signet Bank, which sponsors a number of benefit events in the area.

Whether they live in Historic Botetourt County, the lush, forested Catawba Valley of Craig County, the energetic cities of Roanoke or Salem, suburban Roanoke County or the quaint town of Vinton, Roanoke Valley residents are always glad to come home . . . and most of them never leave.

Botetourt County

If Virginia can be referred to as the "Mother of States," then Botetourt could be called the "Mother of Counties." With a population of 25,000, the county is home to an independent, history-loving people who are smug in the fact that their county, a land grant to Lord Botetourt, once stretched the whole way to the Mississippi River. Historic Fincastle has been the county seat since 1770. This vast tract of land once included the entirety of the present state of Kentucky and much of what is now West Virginia, Ohio, Indiana and Illinois.

George Washington, Patrick Henry and Thomas Jefferson either appeared in Fincastle or sent their agents to lay claim to tracts of wilderness lands. Jefferson designed a county courthouse. After the Lewis and Clark expedition west, William Clark returned to Fincastle to marry resident Judith Hancock.

Thousands of English, German and Scotch-Irish pioneers passed through on their way down the great Valley Road that traversed the famed Shenandoah Valley to settle the western frontier country.

Combining the talents of German craftsmen and Scotch-Irish merchants and lawyers, Fincastle built a town of well proportioned houses and public buildings, a substantial number of which still survive. These include the Old Jail Building, the Court House Complex, the Presbyterian Church, the Botetourt Museum Building and the Botetourt County Courthouse. Newer buildings, such as the historic Bank of Fincastle, a major force in the community, are centrally located to carefully blend into the historic environment. Guided tours, by appointment, are happily arranged by Historic Fincastle Inc. Write them at P.O. Box 19, Fincastle, Virginia 24090.

On your tour you will see beautiful wrought iron fences, balconies and gates, flagstone walks from the early 19th century, horse mounting stones in front of the Presbyterian Church and early gravestones in church cemeteries, with the oldest dating to 1795. Steeples contain bells, the focal point of a much publicized and honored tradition

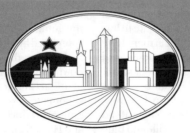

of ringing out the old and ringing in the New Year.

It stands to reason that Botetourt County residents love antiques. The Chamber of Commerce will send you a brochure listing 25 different shops, most of them clustered in Troutville and Fincastle. The Troutville Antique Mart has a plethora of these shops. Located across the street is Goodwill Tinker Mountain Industries, a sheltered workshop for Roanoke Valley's handicapped where you can donate secondhand items to its retail stores in Hollins and Salem, named the nation's best Goodwill retail store in 1993.

People love to come to Botetourt County in the spring. For a breathtaking view of orchards in bloom, take Laymantown Road left past Troutville Baptist, a cut-through road to U.S. Route 220. The mounds of blooming apple trees in the setting sun are indeed a sight to behold. In the fall, the fruit of the harvest is available for the picking at seven different orchards, most of them huge operations that also offer seasonal items, such as acres of pumpkins for Halloween. Agriculture is still a big industry, but farmland is at a premium. There are bounties on Botetourt County real estate, with people desperate to buy the scenic farmland. Farmers have lived there for generations, and people with an independent streak are attracted to the county.

There is even a farm for emus and ostriches off Blue Ridge Road (T-652) between Troutville and Blue Ridge. Residents on the road love to exchange stories about the time

an ostrich got loose, blocked the road and caused drivers to think they were losing their minds. It took a rodeo cowboy with a lasso to catch the errant fowl, truss it up and carry it home in a flatbed truck.

Two scenic landmarks tourists especially enjoy are the unusual, huge, jutting Eagle Rock boulders off U.S. Route 220; they appear as if they'll fall off any moment into the gorge below. Beyond on Route 220 is Eagle Rock's Roaring Run Furnace, part of the Jefferson National Forest and typical of the scores of iron furnaces that were scattered throughout the hills and mountains of western Virginia. The single-stack, hot-blast charcoal furnace, built of large, squared stones, was constructed in 1832, rebuilt in 1845 and rebuilt again early in the Civil War. Most of the pig iron produced was shipped to Richmond for the war effort.

A third landmark on the National Register of Historic Places is Wilson Warehouse, built in 1839 and now Buchanan's Community House. Located at Washington and Lowe streets, it is a relic of western Virginia antebellum prosperity.

It stands to reason that Botetourt County's largest and most popular festival is Historic Fincastle Days in the autumn. Attending the festival, sponsored by Historic Fincastle Inc. and held in the charming, historic downtown, is serendipity to lovers of fine art and crafts, since Fincastle is home to several well-known Virginia artists including Mark Woodie and Harold Little. The show is hung in the historic town square.

Recreational opportunities

abound, including hiking the Appalachian and Bikecentennial trails that pass by Blue Ridge Road (T-652) in Troutville. Other major activities are canoeing or floating the James River and Craig's Creek and hunting, camping and fishing.

Although Botetourt County is a county with a past, it is definitely one with a bright future while it tries to hang on to its pastoral environment. A major grassroots organization is working hard to keep a hazardous waste-burning operation from starting up there. For more information, contact the Botetourt County Chamber of Commerce at P.O. Box 92, Fincastle, Virginia 24090, (703) 473-8280.

Craig County

Just as Botetourt residents are trying to protect their pristine environment, the rural residents of pastoral Craig (population 4,500) fiercely guard their stake in God's

Country. Tourism is a major industry in this county, which is more than half covered by the Jefferson National Forest.

The county got its name from Robert Craig, delegate to the General Assembly from Roanoke County who was instrumental in legislation that formed Craig County in 1851. New Castle was designated the county seat, and the historic courthouse was erected the same year by slave labor. Its bell was cast at the same foundry as the Liberty Bell.

Early settlers probably first traveled up Craig's Creek, the county's major waterway, in the 1730s. By the end of the Indian Wars of 1756-1762, 45 families lived along the creek. George Washington reportedly passed through the junction of Craig's Creek and Meadow Creek, the site of New Castle.

The county seat contains several charming old buildings that have been designated historical landmarks, including the courthouse (which was miraculously spared during the Civil War), a jail, Central Hotel and Star Saloon (now official headquarters of the Craig County Historical Society), First National Bank and the G.W. Layman office building. You'll see several lovely old homes in the area, including the Layman house (c. 1901), on the corner of routes 311 and 42, and the big, brick "castle" — the Todd house — at the top of the hill going out of town on Route 42.

Also worth a visit is Tingler's Mill at Paint Bank. While this particular mill was built in 1873, grinding had been going on at the site since 1783. Henry Tingler was excused from military service for the Confederate Army because grinding meal was a higher war need. After 182 years of daily operation, the mill closed in 1965 but is now being restored.

One interesting, little-known fact that would stump any game show contestant is that, because of Civil War geographical boundary changes, the mill has been in two different states and five different counties without ever having been moved! In 1783, the land was part of Botetourt County, remaining so until 1792, when Monroe County, Virginia, was created. In 1851, Craig County was carved from parts of Botetourt, Monroe, Roanoke and Giles counties. In 1863, that portion of the county joined Monroe County when West Virginia was formed during the Civil War, but was returned to Craig County after the war.

The route of Gen. David Hunter's retreat in the summer of 1864 still has natives talking. The soldiers burned marriage records and Deed Book 1 and spilled ink on all the others. Then they chopped up parts of the courthouse for kindling. However, an order to burn the courthouse was somehow overlooked.

This gentle beauty of a county, rich in history, is noted as one of the most popular playgrounds in western Virginia. The scenery is spectacular! If you want to see the epitome of a quaint country road, travel Route 42 from New Castle to Giles County. This delightful road, which crosses the eastern Continental Divide, passes old farms with rail fences, graveyards of Civil War veterans and late 19th-century houses.

Route 658 in the John's Creek area takes you to the sites of two now defunct summer resorts where people would come to "take the cure" of the orange sulphur mineral waters. The 1987 movie, *In a Shallow Grave*, used the site of Blue Healing Springs resort's crumbling dance hall.

Another site to see is Hebron Church, built in 1830, complete with its own slave balcony. Locked during the week, arrangements may be made to visit through the Craig County Historical Society (see the Arts and Culture chapter).

The Appalachian Trail is one of the county's major attractions with 30 miles of the Maine-to-Georgia footpath available, with several shelters and camping facilities along the way. The Trout Branch to Dragon's Tooth section is seven rugged miles, but the views are spectacular. There's a parking lot off Route 311 in Roanoke County.

For mountain bike enthusiasts, hikers and horseback riders, Craig County is full of trails that range from the easy to challenging and all with scenic value. Some local favorites include Route 179, the road over Bald Mountain, and Route 177 over Potts Mountain. Route 188, the road across the top of Brush Mountain, will take you past the monument where World War II hero Audie Murphy's plane crashed.

Camping enthusiasts will enjoy Craig Creek Recreation area, Steel Bridge and the Pines. Some of the best information on Craig County can be obtained from the New Castle Ranger Office by calling (703) 868-5196 weekdays. It is located on Route 615, three miles east of New Castle.

If you're looking for adventure, wildlife and blessed isolation and meditation, Craig County is the place to live or visit. For more information, contact the County of Craig, Corner of Court and Main streets, New Castle, Virginia 24127, (703) 864-5010.

Roanoke

Capital of the Blue Ridge, Roanoke (population 96,400) has it all — history, culture, close-knit neighborhoods and a heady sense of environment. Its downtown was the first in North America to offer recycling, thanks to Downtown Roanoke Inc.

These happy environmental facts are due to a cutting-edge grassroots environmental group, Clean Valley Council, gutsy government officials willing to take a stand and Cycle Systems, a 75-year-old, fourth-generation recycling firm that has led Virginia in the recycling effort. Just like at Disneyland, you can count the moments before a piece of dropped litter is whisked out of sight . . . that is, if anybody has the gall to drop a piece in this earth-conscious area.

And also like at brightly lighted Disneyland, you'll probably do a double take the first time you see Roanoke's landmark Mill Mountain Star, seen nightly glowing for a radius of 60 miles. The 43-year-old, 100-foot-high star is a popular landmark for airplane pilots who frequently feel compelled to explain to passengers that what they think they're seeing below really is a gigantic, man-made star. The star has lured many people, including Elvis Presley, who donned a disguise to see it following a concert after his curiosity got the best of him. Beside the star, there are scores of happy, well-illuminated animals at Mill Mountain Zoological Park.

And, just in case you think that Roanokers are the only ones who brag about their community, let's talk about awards. A University of Kentucky study calls Roanoke one of the nation's top 20 cities for quality of life. Zero Population Growth says Roanoke is one of the 10 least stressful cities for quality of life. Downtown Roanoke's revitalization has been touted as one of America's 10 best by the National Trust for Historic Preservation. And twice in the past decade Roanoke has received the "All-America City" designation.

A crossroads for commerce, Roanoke's history began in the early 17th century. Indian resistance to settlers was fierce. The city, formerly called Big Lick (for its salt marshes), was later named Roanoke. "Rawrenock," meaning white beads — shells with holes, worn on strings around the neck and arms and passed as currency among Native Americans — was described early on by Captain John White, who attempted to settle Roanoke Island in North Carolina.

Little towns first formed what is now the city of Roanoke. New Antwerp appeared in 1802 followed by Gainesborough in 1825 and Old Lick in 1834. In 1874, the town of Big Lick, population 500, was chartered. It became a railroad crossroads, eventually home to the Norfolk and Western Railroad in 1882. This marked the start of Roanoke's rapid growth. Its historic city market, also begun in the early years, still functions and is the anchor of the revitalized City Market square downtown.

Today, Roanoke is the largest metropolitan city in Virginia west of Richmond and off the widely traveled Blue Ridge Parkway. It is the major center for transportation, ranging from the Norfolk Southern Railway to its Valley Metro bus system, which energetically and conveniently serves city residents. The city sports a new $25 million

Photo: Roanoke Convention and Vistors Bureau

Center in the Square in Roanoke.

airport terminal and is also the medical center of western Virginia, with more than 2,400 hospital beds and a gigantic medical center, Roanoke Memorial Hospitals.

The Roanoke Valley has a culture all its own. The Roanoke Symphony and its darling of the media, conductor Victoria Bond, have been featured on the "Today Show" and in the *New York Times* and *Wall Street Journal*. There's Opera Roanoke, a popular cultural complement, and Center in the Square, a unique, multicultural institution that is home to five resident organizations of art, history, theater and science.

A new national exhibition, "To the Rescue," puts Roanoke on the map as the birthplace of the volunteer rescue squad movement. The

Explore Project, open but a work in progress, is a re-creation of an 18th-century pioneer village on nearly 1,500 acres.

Perhaps the most curious of Roanoke's attractions is Miniature Graceland, a private collection of miniature buildings built by Kim Epperly, the editor of the international Elvis newsletter and the Ultimate Elvis Fan. Elvis lovers are invited to stroll through the Miniature Graceland grounds beside Epperly's house on Riverland Boulevard and hear an Elvis song anytime of the day or night as a revolving Elvis doll sings to an audience of adoring Barbies. A "world first" exhibition of Epperly's private Elvis memorabilia was displayed at the history museum at Center in the Square last January.

An innovative Roanoke landmark was recently added. Cycle Systems, a leading East Coast recycling firm, presented a 75th anniversary gift to the City of Roanoke. It is a lighted fountain of recycled metal that can be seen off I-581 beside the Cycle Systems scrap yard.

There's family entertainment a-plenty in Roanoke. Striving to live up to its name as "Festival City of Virginia," Roanoke hosts the blockbuster, two-weekend-long Festival in the Park each May. Festival is a massive celebration of art, music and the human spirit and nearly 400,000 people who agree show up to enjoy it. It's Roanoke's signal that summer is ready to begin!

There are other festivals ranging from a celebration of African-American culture on Henry Street in the fall to the Chili Cook-off and Community School Strawberry Festival, held on the first May weekend, when palates burning from flaming chili can get cooling ice cream and berries just down the block.

Roanoke is a great center for jumping off to other trips nearby. The number of attractions within an hour's radius is unbelievable, and you'd need a good week's stay at a great place, such as the Roanoke Marriott or the historic Radisson Patrick Henry Hotel downtown, just to have time to see and do even half of what's available. Be sure to stop by the Roanoke Valley Convention & Visitors Bureau on the City Market. An enthusiastic staff and a dynamic director will guide you to the many local attractions. You can contact them at (800) 635-5535.

Roanoke County

Roanoke County (population 80,000) is the mostly affluent suburban area surrounding the city of Roanoke. It includes the placid, comfortable town of Vinton as well. The county is noted for its superior school system, network of top-notch recreational centers and willingness to pay to support a superior quality of life.

Roanoke County celebrated its 150th birthday in 1988. In 1838, it was carved out of the huge county of Botetourt. The mountainous county has many areas named for its peaks. One of the most unique may be Twelve O'Clock Knob, so named because slaves west of Salem could look at the mountain and tell it was time for lunch when the sun was at a point just over the 2,707-foot peak.

Another of its natural resources, underground springs, sparked names for many areas, such as Virginia Etna Springs, site of a former water bottling plant, and Big Cook Spring in Bonsack, an area heavily touched by the Civil War due to several blanket factories located there. Legend has it that one was burned to the ground by the Yankees but the other was spared because its owner, with fingers crossed, promised not to sell blankets to the Confederate merchants down the road in Roanoke City. Another spring, Botetourt Springs, became the site of Hollins College, one of the most prestigious undergraduate women's colleges in America. Graduate programs are coeducational.

Bonsack, east of Vinton, also was the home of Jim Bonsack, who quit Roanoke College to work on a competition for the first cigarette-rolling machine. Young Bonsack won the $75,000 competition, patented it in 1880 at the age of 22, made a fortune and spawned a national industry.

Roanoke County's pioneering spirit has extended to modern times. The county was the Roanoke Valley's pioneer in curbside recycling and has led the rest of the Valley in environmental concerns and issues. It also has been nationally recognized for governmental cooperation in a joint industrial park and library built with Botetourt County. In 1987, community leaders began the Blue Ridge Region economic marketing group, a legislative group targeting General Assembly action to improve the area's quality of life. In 1989, Roanoke County was named an All-America City for its governmental cooperation, quality of life and support of the Explore Project.

Explore, a unique recreational and educational experience, is the county's tourism focus. It opened to the public in July. Many events are being held there now including astronomy field trips, bird watching, Sierra Club hikes and Scout projects. The restored Hofauger Farmhouse, the focus of the park, is complete and available for use with advance reservations.

Explore's three main parts include a frontier settlement, a North American wilderness zoological park and an environmental education center. The park will be completed in various phases, with a major emphasis on environmental preservation.

Recreation and historical preservation have been a focus for Roanoke Countians. Green Hill Equestrian Park is the site of the annual autumn polo match benefiting the Roanoke Symphony. This year, again, the Park hosts a Civil War battle recreation, Gen. David Hunter's Retreat. It is one of 44 parks and recreational facilities.

Roanoke County is known for its family-oriented neighborhoods with a wide range of styles and prices. Available are urban townhouses, bucolic farmhouses and suburban subdivisions. The average price of a Roanoke County home is $85,000.

Many move to the county for its superior school system. Both remedial education as well as classes for the gifted are available.

Roanoke County also is a popular industrial site. Major employers include ITT, manufacturer of night vision goggles, Ingersoll Rand and Allstate Insurance.

For shopping, Tanglewood Mall is a popular place visited regionally by many looking for a wide variety of speciality shops. In the same area are numerous family restaurants that serve as a magnet for the whole valley.

Most of all, however, Roanoke County is known as a desirable place to live because of the high quality and variety of suburban services it offers residents. For more information, contact the Roanoke County-Salem Chamber of Commerce at 7 S. College Avenue, Salem, Virginia 24153, (703) 387-0267.

Salem

There's an old story in the *Roanoke Times* newspaper office about a young cub reporter who had just moved to Salem. Feeling a sense of isolation, she asked a Salem native reporter, ready to retire, about just how long it would take to get "accepted" by her neighbors.

"Oh, about three," the Salem native replied.

"Three years?" responded the incredulous cub.

"No, three generations, my dear!" was the reply.

To say that the City of Salem (population 25,000) has a sense of its own history and self-sufficiency is an understatement. Salem, its name derived from "shalom," meaning peace, is the oldest and southernmost community in the Roanoke Valley. That historical fact pervades Salem's quaint, charming culture. Many of its historic downtown Victorian homes with stained glass windows, tin roofs and pointed towers are on the National Historic Register.

Gen. Andrew Lewis started the settlement in 1768 when he acquired his estate named "Richfield." In 1806, a charter to James Simpson created the town of Salem out of the Lewis estate, bounded by Union Street, Church Alley, Clay and Calhoun streets. Salem was chartered as a city in 1968. The local historical society recently opened a museum downtown.

Salem also has an excellent sense of community, especially when it comes to sports. The Salem Civic Center is the site of the fabulous Salem Fair and Exposition, an event that is a real coup for Salem and the largest of its kind in Virginia. You can do everything there from bungee jump to watch pigs race. The Civic Center seats 7,500 and offers a wide and varied program of community events. For example, it's home to the Roanoke Valley Horse Show, one of the 10 largest in the country. Salemites' love for athletics borders on the fanatic and considerable emphasis is placed on recreation, with more opportunities available than in most other areas of similar size. Facilities recently were expanded to include an

8,000-seat football stadium for the beloved Salem High Spartans.

Salem also provides exciting Class A professional baseball through the Salem Buccaneers, a Pittsburgh Pirate farm team that plays at Salem Municipal Field. There are also three golf courses in Salem. In 1994, Salem will once again be the site of the national Alonzo Stagg Bowl.

Salemites also have a heart that never stops beating for their own. When high school football star Chance Crawford was paralyzed by a spinal injury during a football game in the early '80s, the townspeople rallied to pay his medical expenses. Beyond that, an annual ball tournament was arranged to assure the Crawfords would have no financial worries. As a final tribute, Crawford was overwhelmingly elected to public office.

Festivals are especially popular. Old Salem Days in September features one of the largest antique car shows on the East Coast, as well as fine Salem art. One of the Roanoke Valley's best-known artists, Walter Biggs, lived here, and his legacy is carried on by Salem artists, such as Harriet Stokes.

Salem is also a town full of strong, large industries, such as General Electric, and the regional Veterans Administration Hospital. It is home to Roanoke College, a Lutheran-affiliated private liberal arts school that lends enormous culture to the area's charm. Salem's shopping district downtown is full of antique stores and mom-and-pop operations and Roanoke College students enjoy the local hangouts, Mac & Bob's and Macados.

Many of Salem's citizens work, live and play within its boundaries and never feel the need to leave their beloved city, regardless of how long it really takes to become an insider. For more information, contact the Roanoke County-Salem Chamber of Commerce at 7 S. College Avenue, Salem, Virginia 24153, (703) 387-0267.

Vinton

Vinton, a small, unpretentious town (population 7,665) east of Roanoke, must be doing something right. Over the past several decades, in the midst of its homespun lifestyle, it has spawned and nurtured some of Virginia's most important modern leaders.

On any given day, Virginia House Majority Leader C. Richard Cranwell, called "the most powerful man in the Blue Ridge of Virginia," can be found having lunch downtown with his constituency, who call him "Dicky" and tell him how to run Virginia's Legislature. Fortune 500 Norfolk and Southern CEO David Goode still visits his wise dad, Ott, founder of Vinton's famous Dogwood Festival, at Ott's 50-year-old downtown real estate business to get advice.

Vinton also is an important leader in its own right. In 1990 it put other Virginia municipalities on notice when its forward-looking town council began the first mandatory comprehensive recycling program in the state, effectively reducing landfilled solid waste by 25 percent. Vinton is also proud of a school system ranked among the state's top 10, and its populace comes out in droves for the William Byrd High Terriors. Its school system has the highest average achievement scores in the Valley, and teachers' salaries rank ninth in the state.

From what beginnings did such an important town spring? Gish's Mill, built prior to 1838, provided a start for the town. David Gish sold his mill to Isaac White Vineyard in 1867, and by this time enough people had settled around the mill to form the basis of the town of Vinton. Although the mill burned, some of the brick walls still are standing. The town was chartered in 1884 and relied on the railroad for employment. Moving into the future, the N&W Railway continued to be Vinton's most important industry. Today, Precision Weaving is Vinton's largest employer.

Vinton residents play as hard as they work. The town is strategically located beside the Blue Ridge Parkway, providing easy recreational access. Vinton's Folklife Festival and Farmer's Market are annual excuses to have a good time. And the oldest festival in the Roanoke Valley, the Dogwood Festival is held in Vinton and has hosted a number of celebrities during the past 38 years. It is always a pageantry of queens, bands, floats and politicians. The first-class, All-American parade always ends at the Vinton War Memorial, Vinton's landmark building and cultural center.

An incredibly moving parade followed the Persian Gulf War, when the slain former William Byrd High School star athlete and straight-A student VMI cadet Terry Plunk was honored with a dogwood tree planted at the War Memorial by the Kuwaiti ambassador. Vinton also received national recognition for its downtown Persian Gulf War information and support center, in the true spirit of Small Town, USA.

Vinton serves its citizens well with wonderful recreational and spectator sports activities. Its municipal pool is beautiful and its recreation department program and special events are second to none.

Vinton's untapped tourism potential is enormous. It is the center of the politically designated Blue Ridge Region of Virginia. In addition to its proximity to the well-traveled Parkway (9 million annual visitors through the Virginia section), Vinton is the last commercial center before Smith Mountain Lake, the state's largest lake. It also is the gateway to the Explore Project.

In the meantime, it's the epitome of the best of small town living. The best is yet to come. For more information, contact the town of Vinton at 311 S. Pollard Street, Vinton, Virginia 24179, (703) 983-0613.

East of the Blue Ridge Region

This gorgeous stretch of land begins in Loudoun County, with its famous Hunt Country and landed gentry, and sweeps southward along the mountains all the way through Charlottesville and Lynchburg to Franklin County south of Roanoke.

For the most part, we are talking about rural territory with few glaring billboards, convenience stores and shopping malls. It's an area rich in history that has little in common with the Shenandoah Valley across the mountains.

Whereas the valley was settled primarily by Scotch-Irish and Germans who migrated south from Pennsylvania and Maryland, the foothills east of the Blue Ridge — especially Charlottesville and to the north — became home to families moving west from Richmond and the Tidewater.

No superhighway cuts through the region, as does Interstate 81 in the Valley. Route 29 is the major artery from Culpeper to Lynchburg, where you will find wineries, splendid antique shops and quaint country stores right off the road. The secondary roads winding through the region will also carry you to gorgeous country inns and bed and breakfasts, vineyards, pick-your-own apple orchards and historic mansions open for tours.

It takes a little more effort to tour this region and do it right. But it is well worth it.

In the north, Loudoun, Fauquier and Culpeper counties claim some of the most productive bluegrass pastures in America — places where thoroughbreds run supreme and the economy is still largely driven by a multi-million-dollar equine industry. Indeed, this is a land straight out of a Grandma Moses painting. The postcard-perfect villages of Waterford, Hillsboro and Middleburg in Loudoun County, Paris and Upperville in Fauquier County and Jeffersonton in Culpeper County afford some of the most scenic and historic real estate in the Old Dominion. Rappahannock County, just to the south, is home to one of the most charming, even utopic, towns in America — "Little" Washington. It is the oldest of the 28 towns in the United States named for the Father of Our Country, who surveyed and laid out the town around 1749. Washington has its own internationally known five-star restaurant and inn, a performing arts center, an artists' cooperative and several classy galleries, boutiques and antique shops.

Rappahannock's county seat, historic Sperryville, sits below the entrance to Skyline Drive. It's a great little town to explore on foot, with antique stores, galleries, arts and crafts studios and a shop where you can buy Native American weavings, jewelry, quilts and crafts.

In the northern foothills region are two entry ways into Shenandoah National Park: Thornton Gap at Route 211 near Sperryville and Swift Run Gap at Route 33 through Greene County.

There is no road into the park from Madison County — a source of long-standing frustration among many residents. Madison County lost more land to the national park than any other county and was reportedly promised an entryway. But for some reason, national leaders reneged. This history explains in large part the level of outrage local residents felt when park officials proposed expanding the national park's boundaries into the county.

The officials eventually dropped the idea, realizing how ugly a battle it would have become.

Madison County's earliest settlers were German iron workers. When they had completed the terms of their indentured servitude at Lord Spotswood's Germanna mines in Orange County, the Germans set out to build new lives for themselves as craftsmen and farmers. That tradition continues in Madison County. Many craftspeople — furniture makers, potters, wood carvers, quilters and jewelry artisans — make this area their home.

The same can be said for Greene County, where you can drop by the Blue Ridge Pottery on Route 33 to Skyline Drive and chat with local potter Alan Ward as he works at his wheel. The store is kind of a headquarters for arts and crafts made especially in Greene County. Situated in the former Golden Horseshoe Inn built in 1827, Blue Ridge Pottery sells beautiful religious pewter jewelry made in nearby Stanardsville, pottery, weavings, Virginia wine and much more.

To the east, the rolling hills of Orange County hold many historical attractions, foremost being Montpelier, a 2,700-acre estate that was the lifelong home of James Madison and his equally famous and more popular wife, Dolley.

Orange County is also home to the prestigious Barboursville Vineyards, situated on the bucolic grounds of what was once an imposing brick mansion designed by Thomas Jefferson. The ruins and surrounding towering boxwoods form the backdrop for summer Shakespeare productions by the Four County Players of Barboursville.

This Italian-owned winery is one of many in the foothills region, which is truly the heart of Virginia wine country. Within a couple of miles is the family-owned Burnley Vineyards. Linden, Oasis and Farfelu vineyards lie in the northern foothills near Front Royal. Farther south in Madison County, Rose River Vineyards hugs the mountains near Syria. The award-winning Misty Mountain Vineyards lies farther south in Madison, and Virginia's largest and most successful winery, Prince Michel Vineyards, is located off Virginia Highway 29 near Culpeper.

Charlottesville and Albemarle County boast six wineries, including one located on the same property where Thomas Jefferson hired an Italian viticulturalist to grow grapes more than two centuries ago.

Nelson County, southeast of Charlottesville, is home to three wineries, eight bed and breakfast inns and the spectacular four-season Wintergreen Resort. It is also where Earl Hamner — a.k.a. "John-Boy" Walton, spent his youth. A museum dedicated to the heartwarming television series, "The Waltons," opened in 1992 in the same school where John-Boy and his siblings learned their ABCs.

Another budding attraction in Nelson County is Oak Ridge, a fabulous, early 19th-century estate situated on 4,800 acres. Oak Ridge once belonged to Thomas Fortune Ryan, a local boy who became one of nation's 10 wealthiest men at the turn of the century. The mansion, Italian gardens and grounds are being restored and are open to the public (please refer to our Arts and Culture chapter for more details about the Walton's Mountain Museum and Oak Ridge).

Major urban centers in the foothills region are Charlottesville and Lynchburg, both thriving university cities that are rich in history, culture and natural beauty. We'll tell you more about these cities in separate introductions farther ahead.

When Thomas Jefferson needed to escape the pressures of domestic life in Monticello he would head south to Poplar Forest, his retreat in Bedford County near Lynchburg. There, Jefferson designed what became the first octagonal home built in America. The beautiful residence still stands and today houses the Poplar Forest Foundation.

Most of Smith Mountain Lake lies in Bedford and Franklin counties. This is Virginia's largest lake, with 500 miles of shoreline. It is truly a recreation paradise, offering endless opportunities for swimming, sailing, water-skiing and camping, as well as sophisticated restaurants, inns and bed and breakfasts.

The southernmost county that we consider part of the foothills — or east of the Blue Ridge region — is Franklin (neighboring Floyd County is part of the New River Valley). The ethnic diversity of Franklin County makes it unusual for Southwest Virginia. There's a sizeable German Baptist population, a people whose habits and beliefs are somewhat similar to the Amish. They operate some of the county's most impeccable farms and bake the most delicious sticky buns you'll find this side of heaven. Boone's Country Store in Burnt Chimney, run entirely by German Baptists, is one place to buy these treats.

Booker T. Washington was born in Franklin County, and a strong and vibrant African-American community resides there. The county's Ferrum College is home to the National Blue Ridge Folk Life Institute, which preserves and documents the culture of the region and every October throws a huge folk life festival.

The following introductions will give you more of an in-depth look at the major cities and some of the counties in the area east of the Blue Ridge.

Orange County

Northeast of Charlottesville lies Orange County, a beautiful, hilly land with a fascinating history. Lt. Gov. Alexander Spotswood used Germanna in Orange County as a base for exploring the Shenandoah Valley in the early 1700s. He and his fellow English explorers scaled what is now called Swift Run Gap to see the fertile valley for the first time, and many suffered fevers and chills and no doubt a few hangovers on the trip (one of the explorers wrote about drinking to the Royal family's health in brandy, shrub, rum, champagne, canary, burgundy and many more spirits). In jest, the group decided to call themselves the "Knights of the Golden Horseshoe."

Historians relate that when Spotswood returned to Williamsburg he promptly wrote a letter to His Majesty King George and told him of the wonderful country beyond the Blue Ridge. He also asked for a grant for the Order of the Knights of the Golden Horseshoe.

In time, a proclamation arrived from England creating the Order, and included were 50 tiny golden horseshoes inscribed in Latin. King George must have had quite a sense of humor, because along with granting Spotswood the title of Knight, he sent him a bill for the golden horseshoes. Reportedly, Spotswood paid for them out of his own pocket without a complaint.

Today, visitors can see the Enchanted Castle at the Germanna Archeological Site, where Spotswood built an elegant brick mansion in the early 1720s. The house burned around 1750, and the site is undergoing extensive archeological research. It's under shelter and open to visitors, and an exhibit tells the story of Germanna and the life and contributions of Gov. Spotswood.

Orange County later became home to James Madison, the fourth U.S. president and the "Father of the Constitution." Madison's own grandparents first settled Montpelier, a 2,700-acre estate that is now owned by the National Trust for Historic Preservation and open for tours. This is a fascinating place to watch the restoration process un-fold, as staff archeologists and architectural historians work on site to discover more about the vast property during Madison's time there.

The James Madison Museum is located in nearby downtown Orange, where you can also visit the only surviving example of Thomas Jefferson's design for church architecture, St. Thomas Episcopal Church.

Also located in Orange County are reminders of the terrible war that nearly split our country in two. The Wilderness Battlefields in the eastern end of the county were the scene of the first clash between Robert E. Lee and Ulysses S. Grant in May, 1864. The battle resulted in 26,000 casualties. The battlefields are open for self-guided tours.

Nearby Gordonsville is home to the Exchange Hotel, a restored railroad hotel that served as a military hospital during the war. It now houses an excellent Civil War museum.

Closer to Charlottesville are the Barboursville Ruins — what's left of a mansion designed by Jefferson for James Barbour, Governor of Virginia, U.S. Senator, Secretary of War and Minister to England.

Orange County boasts the most acres of grape production of any county in the Commonwealth. Along with the Barboursville Winery, which has been praised by *Wine Spectator* magazine, the county is home to the smaller Burnley Vineyards, one of the oldest vineyards in the region.

The Montpelier estate hosts a wine festival every May, featuring live music, crafts, food and local wines. Montpelier is also the scene of steeplechase and flat track races on the first Saturday every November. This is a hallowed tradition in its 51st year that draws huge crowds of horse-lovers.

For more information about these and other attractions and fine bed and breakfasts in Orange County, contact the Visitors Bureau, P.O. Box 133, Orange, Virginia 22960, (703) 672-1653. A Visitor's Center is also located in the James Madison Museum at 129 Caroline Street in Orange, (703) 672-1776.

Nelson County

Roughly a quarter of this rural, agricultural county lies in the George Washington National Forest. Wintergreen Resort, a four-season vacation paradise with a year-round residential community, hugs the mountains in the western part of the county. Crabtree Falls, a spectacular series of cascades, is one of the highlights of the forest along Route 56, the scenic road that crosses the mountains and enters the Shenandoah Valley at Vesuvius.

But, it's probably fair to say that local leaders want the county to remain clean, beautiful and rural. Apples are the chief crop of the area's agricultural economy, and beef cattle is the second leading industry.

Earl Hamner Jr., a.k.a. "John-Boy" Walton, grew up in the tiny town of Schuyler, a mecca for fans of the popular, heartwarming television series of the '70s. For years, fans have flocked to Schuyler to track down the old home place and other reminders of "The Waltons." Now they can go to the fascinating Walton's Mountain Museum. The museum opened in October of 1992 in the same school attended by Hamner and his siblings. This year, the University of Richmond is donating 62 boxes of Hamner memorabilia, including scrapbooks, fan mail and photographs, to the museum. Don't miss the regularly shown video documentary with interviews with Hamner and the actors and screenwriters.

Visitors will not want to miss the intriguing Swannanoa Marble Palace and Sculpture Garden, with its romantic history and gorgeous grounds. This Afton Mountain wonder is also the site of the University of Science and Philosophy, a fascinating storehouse of New Age school of transcendental thinking. (Read more about it in our Arts and Culture chapter.)

Another attraction under development in Nelson County is Oak Ridge, a fabulous 4,800-acre estate that belonged to Thomas Fortune Ryan, a leading financier at the turn of the century. The mansion, formal Italian gardens, greenhouse and other buildings are being renovated by its new owners, a Tidewater couple who are building a horse racing track on the estate. They host all kinds of community and cultural events and festivals on the magnificent grounds.

Nelson County has three vineyards offering tours and wine tasting — enjoyable outings any time of year, but especially in the autumn.

Accommodations in the county include luxury condominiums and suites at Wintergreen Resort and eight bed and breakfast inns.

One of the best places to eat — and eat hearty — is Rodes Farm Inn on Route 613 near Nellysford. Owned by Wintergreen Resort, Rodes Farm Inn is an unpretentious country-style restaurant (housed in a 200-year-old farmhouse) that serves home-cooked Southern fare.

For more information about Nelson County, contact the Nelson County Department of Tourism at (800) 282-8223.

Charlottesville

Charlottesville is a crown jewel of a city, with so much beauty, history, culture and lively commerce that it's no wonder it is growing by leaps and bounds.

If he were alive, Thomas Jefferson, native of the territory, would probably roll his eyes and sigh at the traffic congestion that now clogs such major arteries as routes 250 and 29 at times. Such is the cost of the city's allure.

Fortunately, Albemarle County, which surrounds Charlottesville on all sides, remains largely rural, with rolling pastures, elegant horse farms and lush forests that lead up to the wilderness of the Shenandoah National Park. And the city itself contains many enclaves of natural beauty — from the lovely gardens along the colonnade at the University of Virginia to the fine old homes surrounded by mounds of azaleas, rhododendrons and camellias.

Reminders of the nation's early history abound in the Charlottesville area. The city took its name from the popular Queen Charlotte, wife of King George III. Albemarle County dates back to 1744, when it was named in honor of William Ann Keppel, second Earl of Albemarle, who was governor general of the colony of Virginia. The Earl never laid foot in the county, but two U.S. presidents, Jefferson and James Monroe, made it their home.

Monticello, the architectural wonder that Jefferson designed and never stopped tinkering with, remains the area's leading attraction. The mountaintop estate opens its doors to visitors seven days a week, inviting all to glimpse Jefferson's genius through his architecture, gardens and innovations. Another fascinating exhibit about Jefferson's domestic life at Monticello lies down the hill and next to I-64 at the Thomas Jefferson Visitors Center.

Thanks to Jefferson's architectural abilities, the campus of the University of Virginia is considered one of the most beautiful in the nation. Jefferson designed the Rotunda of his "academic village" after the Roman Pantheon. The graceful Rotunda, the pavilions and their gardens and the whitewashed colonnade comprise the original University buildings. The American Institute of Architects voted the original campus as the most outstanding achievement in American architecture in 1976.

Not far from Monticello on another mountain slope is Ash Lawn-Highland, home of James Monroe, Jefferson's friend and America's fifth president. Strutting, showy peacocks grace the lawn at Ash Lawn-Highland, where visitors can witness Monroe's cultured lifestyle and learn about a working farm of the 19th century. The boxwood-covered grounds at Ash Lawn come to life in the summer, when light opera performances entertain guests under the stars.

There are reminders of history also in the streets of downtown Charlottesville, especially around Court Square, where Jefferson and Monroe spent much of their leisure time. Here every building bears a plaque dating it to the early days of the city, making it easy to imagine what the city must have looked like when Jefferson practiced law here.

The Albemarle County Courthouse, built in 1762, served as the meeting place of the Virginia Legislature as they fled Cornwallis's approaching army in 1781. State Legislator Daniel Boone was one of the seven men captured in a surprise raid on Charlottesville led by British Cavalry Gen. Banastre Tarleton during that campaign. Tarleton failed at capturing then Gov. Jefferson, but nabbed Boone at the corner of Jefferson and Park streets.

History buffs are not the only ones interested in the downtown historic district. Folks of all ages enjoy strolling along the pedestrian-only downtown mall, lined on both sides with specialty boutiques, antique stores, outdoor cafes, ice-cream shops and great book stores.

Also within easy walking distance are galleries, including McGuffey Art Center, a transformed elementary school where you can observe artists at work in their studios, buy fine handcrafts, pottery, paintings, photos and prints and visit the Second Street Gallery inside. Adjacent to the McGuffey Art Center and across the street is Vinegar Hill Theater, a place to see foreign films, documentaries and movies not usually shown in standard theaters. Within walking distance are also museums, libraries and more than 25 restaurants to choose from.

Speaking of food, the culinary scene in Charlottesville has become rather lively and diverse. If you want hot and spicy Southern barbecue or country ham and biscuits, you'll find it here. But you may also be tempted by the Indian, Vietnamese, French, German, Italian, Brazilian and American nouvelle cuisine in the area.

At the risk of sounding trite, we must not forget the famous figures of the film world who make Charlottesville their home. Charlottesvilleans are reportedly known for their ability to fake nonchalance at the sight of such figures as Sam Shepard, Jessica Lange and Sissy Spacek. It is considered gauche to gawk or ask for an autograph, and this must be one reason why these famous folks and their families seem to have found such a comfortable life here.

Of course, Charlottesville's association with the rich and famous is nothing new. The area was the setting for part of *Giant*, the western starring Elizabeth Taylor, Rock

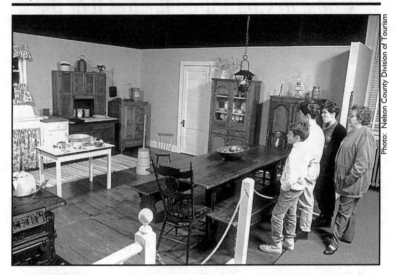

Photo: Nelson County Division of Tourism

Walton Mountain Museum in Nelson County, the birthplace of the popular TV series "The Waltons."

Hudson and James Dean. Randolph Scott, a leading star in *Ride the High Country,* one of the greatest westerns ever made, lived at Montpelier for a couple of years when he was married to Marion Dupont.

Land has become very expensive in the Charlottesville, so that it is nearly impossible for people of moderate means to purchase their own place. The gulf between the "haves" and "have-nots" in Charlottesville is widening so much that even the local association of Realtors is disturbed, making the issue of affordable housing their highest priority this year.

For instance, several new developments are selling homes on lots no larger than three acres for between $300,000 and $800,000; homes that cost around $130,000 are considered low end.

One new development east of town called Keswick is being sponsored by Sir Bernard Ashley of the Laura Ashley group. The club will cost $25,000 per person to join, and the golf course is being designed by Arnold Palmer himself. An overnight stay at the posh hotel at Keswick costs between $200 and $600 a night — expensive even by Charlottesville's standards.

The new affluence of Charlottesville has its positive side: the backing of such cultural resources as the Virginia Festival of American Film. Patricia Kluge, ex-wife of the richest man in America, provided the primary means to establish the festival, which is held at UVA every fall. Illustrious special guests have included Jimmy Stewart, Gregory Peck, Ann Margret, Charlton Heston and a host of screenwriters, critics and academics.

More than 2,000 accommodations are available in the Charlottesville area, ranging from economy motels to some of the most elegant inns and bed and breakfasts imaginable.

A trip to Charlottesville isn't complete without at least one stop at a local winery for a sample, a bottle, or a tour to learn how wine is made. There are ten wineries within easy driving distance of Charlottesville, the wine capital of Virginia. Jefferson would be proud to know this; he often dreamed of producing fine Virginia wines and experimented with grape growing for more than 30 years.

One of the region's finest wineries, Simeon Vineyards, is situated on the same property near Monticello that Thomas Jefferson donated to an Italian winegrower in 1773. The Italian, Philip Mazzei, had early success at making wine, but his efforts were interrupted by the Revolutionary War and his grapes were trampled to death by the horses of a Hessian general who had rented the property.

For more information about wineries, accommodations, restaurants, night life, shopping, real estate, retirement and cultural life in the Charlottesville area, please refer to the specific chapters farther on in this guide. The complimentary *Charlottesville Guide*, which can be found in hotels and all over the city, also tells visitors what to do, where to go and how to get there. The Guide also provides information about Orange and Madison counties, Waynesboro and Staunton.

In addition, much helpful information can be obtained by writing or calling the Charlottesville/ Albemarle Convention & Visitors Bureau, P.O. Box 161, Route 20 S., Charlottesville, Virginia 22902, (804) 977-1783.

Lynchburg

"I consider it one of the most interesting spots in the state. . . ." — Thomas Jefferson.

Democracy's founding father, who scandalized Lynchburg society by eating a "love apple" (tomatoes were thought to be poisonous), summed up best how Lynchburg's citizens feel about their city and its vast array of cultural, educational and recreational opportunities.

For the past decade, the national spotlight has shone on Lynchburg's politically active pastor of the internationally known Thomas Roads Baptist Church here, the Rev. Jerry Falwell. Known as the "City of Churches," Lynchburg (population 70,000) has 129 other houses of worship in addition to the church that launched the Moral Majority. Although the Quakers were the first religious group to settle here and strongly influenced Lynchburg's history, their opposition to slavery caused them to migrate to Ohio and Indiana.

Long before Falwell built his national church from a small Lynchburg congregation, Lynchburg's central location and role in transporting goods by river and railroad had already made it famous.

Lynchburg was named for its founder, John Lynch, the son of Charles Lynch. A 15-year-old Irish runaway, Charles Lynch decided to learn a trade and apprenticed himself to a wealthy Quaker tobacco planter. The relationship worked out so well that the Roman Catholic Lynch married the planter's daughter. Also an enterprising young man, their son John Lynch, reared as a Quaker, started a ferry service when he was 17 across the James River in 1757. In 1786, the Virginia General Assembly granted him a charter for a town, 45 acres of his own land. Lynchburg was incorporated as a town in 1805 and a city in 1852. Lynch also built the city's first bridge, replacing his ferry in 1812.

Historically known as the "Hill City," Lynchburg attracted industrial magnates who dealt in tobacco and iron, the chief products of early Lynchburg. Their ornate, luxurious homes, bordered by enormous decorative wrought iron fences, are alone worth a visit. Three of them have been made into sumptuous bed and breakfasts, Madison House, The Mansion and Langhorne Manor. All of their proprietors will make every effort to pamper you just like the original inhabitants. They are located in Lynchburg's seven original neighborhoods, its "hills." By name, they are College Hill, Daniel's Hill, Diamond Hill, Federal Hill, Franklin Hill, Garland Hill and White Rock Hill. Walking tour maps of the area are available from Lynchburg's dynamic tourism marketing team at its Convention & Visitors Bureau. You can call them at (804) 847-1732 for a rundown on so many attractions that it will take you a good week to see them all. There are many fine restaurants and great shopping here as well.

In the decade before the Civil War, Lynchburg was one of the two wealthiest cities per capita in the

United States. As you would expect, its moneyed citizenry spawned a rich culture. Sarah Bernhardt and Anna Pavlova appeared at the Academy of Music, which opened in 1905. The old music hall has been purchased by Liberty University, which plans to restore it. Jones Memorial Library was completed in 1908 and is one of America's foremost genealogical research libraries. Lynchburg's Fine Arts Center, the city's cultural nucleus, houses two art galleries, a theatre, two dance studios and the oldest continuous theatre group in the country. Each year, 100,000 people (more than the city's population) take classes, hear concerts and see plays, ballet and art exhibits at the center.

Scores of famous authors sprang from Lynchburg's culture. Two of its most famous, curiously enough, gained their fame for their books on the opposite sides of democratic and racial issues.

The great historian Dr. Douglas Southall Freeman, born in Lynchburg in 1886, received 24 honorary degrees and two Pulitzer Prizes. One was in 1936 for his four-volume work, *The Life of Robert E. Lee*, the great Confederate general. (The other, in 1948, was for a series on George Washington.)

Anne Spencer, an African-American poet born in 1882, is the only Virginian whose works are included in the *Norton Anthology of Modern American and British Poetry*. She helped establish Lynchburg's first lending library for African-Americans and started Lynchburg's first NAACP chapter.

Frequent visitors to Spencer's restored home, garden and studio, "Edankraal," (open by appointment to visitors at 1313 Pierce Street), included Dr. Martin Luther King, Dr. George Washington Carver, Jackie Robinson and Marion Anderson, the African-American singing star who was denied entrance to perform in Washington's Daughters of the American Revolution concert hall because of her race. Interestingly enough, one of the founders of the DAR, Ellet Cabell, was born at Point of Honor, a beautifully restored Lynchburg mansion, now a museum, in the same area as Spencer's house.

Point of Honor, so named for the gun duels fought there, was built by Dr. George Cabell Sr., whose most famous patient was Patrick Henry. East of Lynchburg, at Brookneal, is Red Hill Shrine, the last home and burial place of Henry, the great patriot and orator. Point of Honor is part of Lynchburg's city museum system — one which other cities would do well to emulate.

Any discussion of Lynchburg's history must also include the influence of Carter Glass, born in Lynchburg in 1858 and Secretary of the Treasury under President Woodrow Wilson. Glass served as Virginia State Senator from 1899 to 1902, in the U.S. House of Representatives from 1902 to 1918 and represented Virginia in the U.S. Senate from 1920 to 1946. He was the first living person to appear alone on a regular U.S. coin. Glass contributed greatly to Lynchburg's civic life.

Lynchburg's quality of life is also

greatly enhanced by its bustling community market at Bateau Landing, where shoppers can choose fresh produce and homemade goods. The annual Festival on the James and The Bateau Festival held in June celebrate the historic James River's contributions with entertainment, historic crafts exhibits and the start of the bateau race to Richmond. Kaleidoscope is an annual fall festival celebrating life in Central Virginia with an arts festival, bands, Riverfront Jamboree, craft show, pops picnic (dining on the lawn to some great music) and the Lynchburg Symphony.

Lynchburg has long been a leading industrial city. It has the highest per capita manufacturing employment in Virginia. Today it is also home to 3,000 businesses and led the way in developing one of the state's first small business incubators.

It is extraordinary how many early industries are still in business. The second-oldest funeral home in America, Diuguid's, has been comforting the bereaved since 1817. Lynchburg Gas Co., founded in 1851, was one of the first in the country to shed light on operating a gas utility. Wiley & Wilcox Engineering, started in 1901, is one of the oldest engineering firms in the United States. In 1901, John Craddock tried the first shoe company in the South on for size in Lynchburg, founding Craddock-Terry. It was a perfect fit. Today, Craddock-Terry's downtown outlet store offers a dazzling array of 300,000 pairs of shoes, including many odd sizes.

In 1889, the young pharmacist Charles Brown began selling his Chap-Stick lip balm. Since, his C. B. Fleet Company's product line has expanded to other national lines, including the first disposable enema and Summer's Eve douche. Babcock & Wilcox Co. and General Electric are other major employers.

As an important manufacturing center, Lynchburg played an important role in the Civil War. Perhaps none was more important than the advance of medicine for Civil War soldiers brought to the "Pest House" by Dr. John Jay Terrell. Located in the historic Lynchburg Confederate Cemetery, within the City Cemetery, the Pest House is open to visitors with displays of Dr. Terrell's pace-setting work in establishing sanitary standards, including his 19th-century medical kit.

As a major educational center, Lynchburg is home to nine diverse colleges. Randolph-Macon Woman's College was the first woman's college in the South to be accredited and the first to receive a Phi Beta Kappa chapter. The Maier Museum, an outstanding collection of American art, is also at the college. Sweet Briar is another famous woman's college and is affiliated with the Virginia Center for the Creative Arts, an internationally recognized working retreat for writers, artists and composers in Amherst County. Other colleges are Jerry Falwell's Liberty University, Lynchburg College, a liberal arts school, and a community college, seminary and two business colleges.

Lynchburg's public schools also are outstanding. Both of its high schools and one of its middle schools have been designated model schools by the Commonwealth of Virginia. The city also has 10 private schools. The most famous is The Virginia School of the Arts, a private boarding school for students grades 7 through 12. Talented young people from around the nation compete to enter the school, which encourages them to achieve the highest standards for performance in dance, drama, music or the visual arts.

High school sports also are popular. Lynchburg is home to the Virginia High School Coaches Association All-Star Games, bringing the best in high school sports to the area. Colleges offer spectator sports, and when springtime comes fans head for the diamond to see the area's only Double A professional sports team, the Lynchburg Red Sox.

Golf, tennis and swimming are popular pastimes. The city operates 10 parks, 24 playgrounds, 34 tennis courts, 26 baseball diamonds and eight community centers. Miller Park is home to an Olympic size pool. In the heart of Lynchburg is Blackwater Creek Natural Area with the Ruskin Freer Preserve, a 155-acre animal sanctuary.

A major medical center, Lynchburg's two hospitals, Virginia Baptist and Lynchburg General, have gained national attention by sharing staff and services to avoid duplication and keep down expenses.

Lynchburg is served by a new $8 million airport terminal. A hub for daytrips, tourists can go north to Schuyler, (pronounced Sky-ler), the restored home of Earl "John-Boy" Hamner, author of the book on which "The Waltons" TV series was based. Just west of the city is Poplar Forest, Jefferson's summer retreat under restoration and open to the public. Twenty miles east is Appomattox, the site where our nation reunited after the Civil War. Monument Terrace, in the center of Lynchburg's downtown, honors the heroes of all wars.

Whatever you decide to see and do while in Lynchburg, you'll probably echo the words of Thomas Jefferson in deciding that it is one of the most interesting spots in the state. For more information, contact the Greater Lynchburg Chamber of Commerce at P.O. Box 2027, 2015 Memorial Avenue, Lynchburg, Virginia 24501, (804) 845-5966.

Amherst County

North of Lynchburg is Amherst County (population 29,000). The Monocan Indians were the first humans to populate the area. It is named for Sir Jeffrey Amherst, the British commander of all forces in America from 1758 to 1763. Amherst led the British armies that successfully drove France from Canada and was the British hero of the Revolutionary War battle of Ticonderoga against the upstart Americans.

In 1761 Amherst County was created from a section of Albemarle County. In 1807, Amherst was divided and the northern part became Nelson County. Tobacco was an early cash crop, as were apples.

Three-fourths of the county's rolling terrain is forests. The Blue Ridge Parkway offers dramatic views while providing the perfect spot for an afternoon picnic. It is a popular recreational area with magnificent mountain views, clean air and thousands of acres of unspoiled forests, rivers and lakes. Numerous leisure and recreational activities can be found in the George Washington National Forest. The Appalachian Trail bisects Amherst County and affords the serious hiker the ultimate challenge.

Winton Country Club, the 18th-century manor that was the former home of Patrick Henry's sister, opens its 18-hole championship golf course to the public here.

Twenty industries also are tucked away in the hills, including a German cuckoo clock-maker, Hermle-Black Forest Clocks.

Sweet Briar College, a private woman's college built on the grounds of an old plantation near the town of Amherst, contributes to the arts experience and educational quality of life. Recently it has hosted anthropologist Jane Goodall, the Glenn Miller Orchestra and Isaac B. Singer, winner of the Nobel Prize in Literature.

The most famous Sweet Briar affiliation is The Virginia Center for the Creative Arts, an artists-in-residency program that brings in the world's most talented writers, visual artists and composers and gives them a place of peace and quiet to help foster creativity.

Visitors will enjoy the Amherst County Historical Museum, located in the German Revival-style Kearfott-Wood House, built in 1907 by Dr. Kearfott. When renovations are completed, the museum will house four exhibit rooms and a gift shop. The upstairs is used for storing the museum's collection and office space. A reference library located there is available to the public.

Amherst County serves as a springboard into many other daytrips. It is close to Charlottesville and Wintergreen Resort.

Smith Mountain Lake

How do you spell relief?

L-A-K-E. Smith Mountain, that is, western Virginia's biggest playground and Virginia's largest lake. Smith Mountain Lake is 20,000 acres of placid waters, 40 miles long and surrounded by 500 miles of shoreline.

It touches Franklin, Bedford and Pittsylvania counties (combined population 142,000). The lake is a colorful place where people love to go and hate to leave. The sunsets are streaked with purple. The water is a stunning blue. Wildlife, like glossy green-headed mallard ducks and chubby, gray-striped bass, add to the local color.

Until recently, Smith Mountain Lake was a place for people who owned their own vacation home or knew somebody who owned a boat. Thanks to the state's finally opening a public beach at Smith Mountain Lake State Park, the lake is now for everyone to enjoy.

Photo: Lynchburg Chamber of Commerce

Poplar Forest, Thomas Jefferson's retreat in Bedford County.

As lakes go, Smith Mountain is relatively new. Like its older sister to the south, Claytor Lake in Pulaski, the lake was formed to dam a river and generate electrical power for Appalachian Power Company. It took six years and a crew of 200 to move 300,000 cubic yards of earth to make way for the 175,000 cubic feet of concrete used to build the Smith Mountain Dam, where full pond is 613 feet above sea level. The Roanoke River started filling Smith Mountain Lake on September 24, 1963, and reached capacity on March 7, 1966.

Archeologists examining the excavation necessary to build the dam determined that the Algonquins fished and hunted here long before anybody else did.

While Smith Mountain was a popular spot from day one, a real breakthrough for the lake was when developer Dave Wilson started Bernard's Landing Resort in the early '80s. Wilson, who later ran into financial problems, is widely credited with being the moving force behind opening the lake to everyone and making it a major western Virginia tourism attraction.

Since, Bernard's Landing Resort and its gourmet restaurant have become the most important tourist attractions at the lake, bringing in people from around the country as condominium owners, many of whom offer public rentals. For people who enjoy bed and breakfasts, the historic Manor at Taylor's Store on Route 122 was recently featured in *Southern Living* magazine.

A second important addition to the lake's culture was the building of Bridgewater Plaza at Hales Ford Bridge on Route 122. The center of Smith Mountain's social and night life, it offers restaurants, a marina, small shops and Harbortown Miniature Golf Course, which is built out over the water. The Bluewater Cruise Company's *Virginia Dare*, a 19th-century side wheeler that offers lunch and dinner cruises, calls the Plaza home port. Bands play here weekends during the summer. It's a really fun place to take the kids to ride the carousel or just pick up an ice-cream cone while listening to the band.

The year-round lake community itself is comprised of about 5,000 residents. Some of them you will never have the opportunity to associate with. Throughout the area, its significant staid German Baptist population rarely mingles socially with outsiders. They dress similarly to Mennnonites and can be identified by the women's mesh bonnets and the men's long beards. Widely known for their agricultural prowess, they live on some of the most beautiful farms you've ever seen and make or grow virtually everything they need.

The anchor of community events is the Smith Mountain Lake Chamber of Commerce/Partnership, whose members support the lake's goals and run a Welcome Center staffed entirely by volunteers. Many of them are retirees from the North. At the Partnership, (703) 721-1203, you can pick up lots of brochures and material about marinas, jet ski and boat rentals, lake homes for rent, campgrounds, fishing guides and anything else you need to have a good time during your stay.

Annual events include the Partnership's Fall Festival, the Wine Festival held at Bernard's Landing, various golf tournaments and dances and the Smith Mountain Tour of Homes to benefit the National Multiple Sclerosis Society. Last year's event was one of the most successful fundraisers in the nation as people from all over came to see lake living at its best. The 1994 event will be held in October.

There are plenty of things to do at the lake weekdays and weekends. The major attraction is Booker T. Washington National Monument, the former home of the famous African-American statesman. It is six miles south of Hales Ford Bridge on Route 122. Also stop by APCO's Visitor Center at the Dam off Virginia Route 40 on Route 908. It's full of hands-on exhibits for the kids and interesting audiovisuals about how the lake was formed. Smith Mountain Lake State Park has a full calendar of summertime activities including swimming, fishing and canoeing. Call them at (703) 297-6066. The park is open from 8 AM until dusk and is located off Virginia Route 626 near Huddleston. You'll find a snack bar, pavilion and information center.

Golf is a major attraction for residents. However, unless you're a member of the Waterfront or Water's Edge residential communities, your game will be at Chestnut Creek, 18 holes of beauty. Chestnut Creek's restaurant is also open to the public. As with the other planned communities, it sells villa homesites for those who want to live and play by a golf course.

Other pastimes are balloon flights offered by Blue Ridge Balloons of Vinton, (703) 890-3029;

parasailing at Bridgewater Marina, (703) 721-1203; and jet-skiing. There are plenty of places that rent the controversial water motorcycles (jet skis). Just call the Partnership for a list. The same goes for a host of boat rental locations.

For the serious boater, of which there are many, there is the Smith Mountain Yacht Club and at least several dozen marinas offering services ranging from restaurants to dry-dock. Again, the Partnership will give you a complete list. A word of caution: If you are interested in a quiet day on the water, Saturday probably is not the day to be out and about. That seems to be when weekenders, intent on an extra good time and sometimes bolstered by too much drink, take to the water. Sundays and weekdays, however, are relatively calm.

Now, let's talk about fishing, the original reason many people came to the lake. Smith Mountain has a well-deserved reputation as an angler's paradise, especially for striped bass. Some coves literally churn with stripers, especially in the autumn. Getting them to bite your bait is another matter.

The state's largest striper, 44 pounds 14 ounces, was caught here in 1992. At the rate these whoppers are growing, that record will probably soon be surpassed. If you're serious about getting one of the big ones, a professional guide is a great idea. Some good ones are R. M. King, (703) 721-4444; Dave Sines, (703) 721-5007; or Spike Franceschini, (703) 297-5611. They'll try to ensure you don't go home with only tales about the one that got away.

Now that you've hooked your fish and are also hooked on the lake, let's turn our attention to buying your own vacation home here. Many a millionaire was made from lake real estate. People all over western Virginia are kicking themselves that they didn't buy when land was cheap. There are many tales of people recouping their original investment 10 times over within a decade. Those days, however, are long gone. A prime waterfront lot can easily sell at a starting point of $100,000. Still, lake property remains inexpensive to Northerners used to New Jersey-type real estate prices.

Real estate costs range from the older neighborhoods, like Isle of Pines in Bedford County, in the $165,000 beginning range, to a $300,000 average at Mountain View Shores, also in Bedford County. Many people buy condos or mobile homes for their weekend retreats. A condo at Bernard's starts at $80,000, for example, still a bargain if you're from Manhattan.

Regardless of whether you're just visiting or planning to buy real estate and stay, Smith Mountain will win your heart while you're here. There's nothing more spectacular than a Smith Mountain sunset or more beautiful than the early morning mist that blankets the lake. You'll return many times to enjoy the view and have some fun. That's no fish tale!

Bedford City and County

It's here that Thomas Jefferson came to get away from it all at his summer home in Poplar Forest. That alone should tell you something about the quality of life in Bedford County. And some things never change. Even if nobody ever finds the famous Beale Treasure here, you can easily make a case that Bedford County and its charming county seat are a real "find" in themselves. More about the tantalizing treasure later . . . let's talk history.

The fastest-growing county outside Virginia's Urban Crescent of Northern Virginia, Bedford County (population 45,349) borders Smith Mountain Lake and is home to Smith Mountain Lake State Park. Bedford also is off the Blue Ridge Parkway, close to one of the Parkway's main attractions, the Peaks of Otter Lodge and Restaurant at Milepost 86, located on a spectacularly beautiful twin-peaked mountain that can be seen for miles.

Bedford city is a Main Street Downtown Revitalization City with organizations devoted to its historic past. A wonderful museum is located downtown, as is the Bedford County Public Library.

Bedford County was named for John Russell, fourth Duke of Bedford, who, as Secretary of State for the Southern Department of Great Britain, had supervision of Colonial affairs. It was formed in 1754 from Lunenburg County and part of Albemarle County. The city of Bedford was chartered in 1968 and in the early '80s renovated its historic downtown area.

Today you will see many interesting downtown shops and restaurants. There are two quaint bed and breakfasts, Bedford House and Otters Den. If you're into natural organic food, however, try the Gunstock Creek Cooperative, a quaint 19th-century store on Route 640 in Wheats Valley at the foot of the Blue Ridge.

Recreation abounds in Bedford County, with the Jefferson National Forest on the north offering the many diversions of the Blue Ridge, including hunting, fishing, camping, picnicking and trails for both horseback riding and biking. Part of the Appalachian Trail passes through the area, with this section especially full of wildflowers and wildlife. The James River flows through in the northeast. City residents enjoy 59-acre Liberty Lake Park, the heart of recreation. Bedford Lake and Park, 35 acres with a white sand beach off Route 639, offers swimming, boating, fishing and camping.

The county is largely rural, with half of its land devoted to farming, dairy and beef cattle and orchards. One of the oldest trees on record, definitely the oldest in Virginia, stands at Poplar Park in Bedford County.

Bedford also is a manufacturing base of many different industries that make everything from pottery, clocks and golf carts to food flavoring and stew.

Bedford citizens have a rich small-town culture. There's The Little Town Players, a community theatre organization. The county's Sedalia Center offers classes in everything from classical music to "back to the land" survival skills and is a tremendous asset to the community.

Every Christmas, an estimated 100,000 visitors come to see the lighting display erected by the 200 retired Benevolent and Protective Order of Elks at that fraternal organization's national home.

Poplar Forest, just outside of Lynchburg, is one of the area's most popular destinations as history-lovers flock to see the ongoing excavation and renovation of Thomas Jefferson's beloved octagonal vacation home.

The devout Christian with an imagination will enjoy seeing Holy Land USA, a 400-acre nature sanctuary whose aim is to be a replica of the Holy Land in Israel. Its owners invite study groups and individuals for a free walking tour. Primitive camping is allowed.

Since you're still reading this, you probably want to know more about Bedford's world-famous hidden treasure. We've put it last in the Bedford section just to make sure you read the rest and make the super people at the Bedford Chamber of Commerce happy. OK, are you ready? Thousands of others with shovels and backhoes over the past century have been ready, too, and have come up empty-handed, but that's not to say YOU will! But beware . . .100 members of the Beale Cypher Association, comprised of the country's most renowned computer experts, are still

trying to crack the last two treasure codes.

This is how the story goes: The legend of the Beale Treasure began in 1885 with the publication of the Beale Papers in Lynchburg. The author told how the Beale Papers came into his possession through Robert Morris, a respected Lynchburg hotel owner. It seems that on several occasions Morris gave room and board to Thomas Beale. On his last visit in 1822 he entrusted Morris with a metal box and asked him to keep it for him.

A few months later Beale wrote a letter explaining that if he did not return within 10 years, the important papers inside should be read. He explained, however, that without a "key" that a St. Louis friend would be mailing the three papers would be unintelligible.

Beale never returned and no key ever arrived. After 23 years, Morris finally opened the box and tried to read its incomprehensible contents. One letter he could read, however, stated that Beale and his party of 29 friends had come to Bedford County several times to bury a treasure they found out west. It would be worth $23 million today. The other two documents, written in cryptic ciphers, told where it was.

After 20 years of trying, Morris was only able to break the ciphers (what cryptanalysts call multiple substitution ciphers) on one document that outlined the content of the treasure — 2,981 pounds of gold and 5,092 pounds of silver, plus jewels. This key was based on the Declaration of Independence.

Since 1885, all attempts to break the two remaining ciphers have been unsuccessful. Over the years, many treasure hunters have by-passed the ciphers and just started digging. Both the town's librarian and postmistress say they regularly receive correspondence and inquiries from around the world regarding the treasure. Recently, one woman, her dog and the man whose backhoe she hired were arrested for digging up a corpse in a cemetery. The two humans were jailed and fined, and poor Fido was incarcerated in the county pound.

The most recent hunter was Mel Fisher, the famous searcher who has recovered millions of dollars from wrecked Spanish galleons. After the local newspaper offered a blow-by-blow account of his daily diggings he abandoned his search in 1989 but vowed to return. So the question remains — is there really a Beale Treasure, or is the whole incredible story just a ruse?

Nobody knows for sure. But most people figure that if Thomas Jefferson himself kept returning to Bedford County there must be treasure enough that is much easier to find. For more information, contact the Bedford area Chamber of Commerce at 305 East Main Street, Bedford, Virginia 24523, (703) 586-9401.

Franklin County

Franklin County calls itself the "Land Between the Lakes," Smith Mountain and Philpott. More miles of shoreline touch Franklin County than either of the other two counties, Bedford or Pittsylvania. Without part-time residents who own lake vacation homes, Franklin County's population is 39,549.

For such a small, rural area, Franklin County has several important national claims to fame. It has one of the proudest African-American cultures of any place in the Blue Ridge. That's because of the Booker T. Washington National Monument, home of the famous slave who became one of America's most important scholars and educators. The park, on Route 122 six miles south of Hales Ford Bridge, is operated as a working farm. Visitors may view a slide presentation on the life of Booker T. then tour the historic area and the reconstructions of the cabins and structures of the Burroughs Tobacco Plantation in the post-Civil War era. Summers offer continuing education programs, such as "Black Women — Achievement Against the Odds" and "The Black Experience in Virginia."

Franklin County's other national claim to fame is a Blue Ridge researcher's dream, the acclaimed Blue Ridge Institute at Ferrum College, whose Folklife Festival each October is a tribute to the treasured, yet nearly forgotten, skills of its Blue Ridge culture.

The Blue Ridge Institute is a great national treasure whose outreach in promoting its culture greatly transcends what many Franklin Countians take for granted as everyday life. The Institute offers a museum, archives and records division and a re-created 1800s German-American farmstead to preserve the best of Blue Ridge culture. One of is finest creations, produced for Franklin County's Bicentennial in 1986, is a pictorial record of Franklin County life and culture.

Visitors to the farmstead will see the architecture, gardens, livestock, furnishings, tools and housewares of the farm. The tours are led by costumed interpreters who work at appropriate chores, such as baking, cooking and gardening. The farm museum also offers a Day on the Farm with hands-on experiences incorporating the tastes, smells and activities of the era. Other activities may include spinning, broom making and livestock care.

The Blue Ridge Institute's Fall Festival brings many skilled, working craftspeople in for the delight of visitors. You will see demonstrations of spinning, quilt making, shingle chopping and other homespun crafts. The Festival also offers unique spectator sports, such as Coon Dog Trials. For more information on the Institute and the Festival, see our Arts and Culture chapter.

Another popular festival is the Boones Mill Apple Festival held each fall. Boones Mill is a great place for antiquing on the Route

220 corridor connecting with Roanoke. One word of caution, however, when driving through — slow down! The speed limit changes abruptly when you enter the town, and Boones Mill's town officer has had national write-ups for his official police car, a white Camero, that sits on the curb and catches lots of out-of-state speeders. It might be an important source of revenue to the town, but you'll probably want to make your donations to the county in another manner!

Ferrum College greatly enriches the quality of life for Franklin Countians. Its Fine Arts Program supports the Jack Tale Players, whose song and drama touring company brings to life the legends of the Upland South. Its Poetic Arts Company demonstrates through performance how poetry plays a vital role in everyday life. Both students and residents enjoy participating in the Blue Ridge Summer Dinner Theatre.

The county is also known for something most Franklin County residents would prefer to put behind them — a long history of "moonshining," the illegal manufacture of whiskey. The reason they can't put it behind them is that it still goes on in the mountainous,

When considering trips to the Blue Ridge, think about a "hub and spoke" concept: Stay in a metropolitan area and take side trips to smaller towns and attractions. After your first day, you'll get a feel for how long it takes to get places and allow you to pace yourself.

Insiders' Tips

rural county. There's rarely a month that goes by without a story in the local newspaper about someone being arrested for moonshining, often for the second or third time.

Some people admit to subscribing to the *Franklin County Post* just to read the excuses given by those who get caught with their hands on the still. At one recent hearing, one moonshiner solemnly pleaded "Not Guilty." When the judge asked him just what he had intended to do with the trainload full of sugar on the track by his backyard, he replied that his wife "is fond of putting up preserves."

Some residents hold in awe the folklore of independent, enterprising mountain men doing what it took to survive, while others pretend moonshining never existed and still doesn't. Although the county's underground industry has been to some the source of amusement and the butt of jokes, a new breed of moonshiner — one selling illegal drugs, as well — is causing fewer people to be amused.

The culture of the lake is vastly different, from the early settlers in the county seat of Rocky Mount to the transplanted Northerners at Smith Mountain Lake. There is yet a third culture, the German Baptist population, that mostly keeps to itself. One exception is Boone's Country Store in Burnt Chimney. The best sticky buns on earth and other tempting edibles are prepared daily at this German Baptist store. They are truly addictive and people who live an hour's drive away admit to negotiating the winding road up Windy Gap Mountain just to stock their freezer with their "fix" of the sweet pastry.

Franklin County's history is as rich and varied as its people. Its first residents were German, French, English and Scotch-Irish settlers who moved from Pennsylvania in 1750. The county was formed in 1786 by the General Assembly. Munitions for Revolutionary War patriots were made from locally mined iron ore at an iron works on Furnace Creek, which is the county's oldest landmark.

One of the Civil War's most respected Confederate leaders, Lt. Gen. Jubal Early, second in command only to Gen. Stonewall Jackson, was born here. Rocky Mount is full of many interesting historical buildings. One, the Claiborne House bed and breakfast, is open to the public. The Chamber of Commerce, in the courthouse downtown, can give you other pamphlets on historical tours and antique shopping opportunities.

Franklin County is also an outdoor paradise for hunting and fishing. Both Smith Mountain and Philpott lakes offer wonderful fishing if you have the patience and the right bait. Philpott, a 3,000-acre lake built by the U.S. Army Corps of Engineers, is more rustic than Smith Mountain and also offers boating, a beach and camping. Smith Mountain Lake has been called the best bass fishing lake in the country. For hunting, wild turkey proves to be the most popular game in the area.

The county's recreation department also offers a host of leisure-time sports and a county recreation program including the largest volleyball league in the state. Ferrum College also gives you a chance to root for championship teams in both men's and women's sports.

Another popular site in Franklin County is Whitey Taylor's Franklin County Speedway, with one of the best payoffs for a short track 75-lap race in the country, a $5,000 fund. Lots of race car fans travel to the Speedway to "go racin'."

Of all the counties surrounding the lake, Franklin's housing costs and taxes are generally the lowest, excluding its lakefront property. Farm land, scarce in so many areas of the Blue Ridge, is plentiful here. You're within easy commuting distance of either the Roanoke Valley or Martinsville, a furniture and knitting mill area with great furniture outlets (Stanleytown and Bassett) and the Tultex (sweatsuit) outlet stores. Franklin County's low taxes attract a lot of manufacturing industry. Cabinet makers, such as the 50-year-old MW Company and Cooper Wood Products, call the county home.

When you're between stops visit the land between the lakes. Whether you play, shop or visit one of its national attractions, you'll find plenty to fill up your time. For more information, contact the Franklin County Chamber of Commerce at 124 E. Court Street, P.O. Box 158, Rocky Mount, Virginia 24151, (703) 483-9542.

New River Valley Region

The academically stimulating, scenic and mountainous New River Valley of Virginia is one of the most steadily growing areas of the Blue Ridge. It includes Montgomery County and the towns of Blacksburg and Christiansburg, the city of Radford, and Floyd, Giles and Pulaski counties. Although all are situated in the same area, you couldn't find a more diverse cultural group. The common thread, again, is the sheer beauty of their environment.

From the '70s decade to 1990, the New River Valley's population grew by nearly a fourth, to 152,720. People just keep on coming, and few ever leave. That's due to the presence of Virginia Tech, Virginia's largest university with 22,000 students, as well as Radford University's 8,000 students. Every year, scores of mountain-struck students are smitten by the New River Valley Flu, a curious mental illness that causes them to turn down lucrative jobs in the big city and vow to flip hamburgers, or do whatever they have to, in order to stay.

Blacksburg, named by Rand McNally as one of the top 20 places to live in the United States. A publication for mature adults names it as one of the best retirement spots in the country. The reasons why are diverse but mostly involve the winning combination of a scenic mountain vacation land and extraordinary cultural enrichment from its multinational university population.

An interesting historical fact is that the New River is actually old — really old! Legend has it that it's the second oldest river in the world;

only Egypt's historic Nile is older. The 300 million-year-old river is an anomaly because first, it flows from south to north and, next, cuts through the Alleghenies from east to west. The New River is 320 miles long from its headwaters near Blowing Rock, North Carolina, to the point in West Virginia where it tumultuously joins the Gauley River to form some of the best whitewater rafting in the East. Outfitters at the Gauley River Gorge regularly host celebrities and nearby Washington politicians, such as Ted Kennedy, who are looking for a refreshing crash of water instead of a staggering crush of paper.

Unlike the populous Nile River area, the New River Valley was a vast, empty land with no permanent inhabitants when the first white explorers saw the area in 1654. Drapers Meadow near Blacksburg is regarded as the first New River settlement. Germans in Prices Fork and Dunkards in Radford established themselves about the same time. Native Americans ventured in only to hunt.

For the first settlers, the natives were a threat greater than cold or starvation. Bands of Shawnees periodically would sweep in to kill settlers and destroy their homes. One such episode — a 1755 massacre of many Drapers Meadow residents — became the inspiration for a play. In the attack, Mary Draper Ingles and Betty Robinson Draper were taken hostage; Mary escaped and found her way home by following the New River. Her riveting saga, *The Long Way Home,* is recreated each summer on an outdoor stage in Radford. It is acted out at the homestead where Ingles and her husband eventually lived. Until her death in 1988 Ingles' great, great, great granddaughter, Mary Louise Jeffries, who lived on the homestead, played the part of Ingles' mother, Elenor Draper.

Although the New River Valley has an exciting textbook history, its research and development history has been equally exciting. Virginia Tech's IBM 3090 supercomputer was the first in the nation to be fully integrated with a university's computing network and made generally available to faculty and students. It's a fact that there are more computers than telephones on campus!

Virginia Tech's Corporate Research Center has 500 employees looking into everything from why illnesses can affect the immune system, very important to AIDS virus research, to robotics and fiber optics, all on the same 120-acre site. All total, $100 million is spent each year by Virginia Tech researchers, many of whom enjoy a national reputation. Business and industry are the largest users of the Center and often bring their problems for analysis by some of the nation's greatest minds.

Here is a brief overview of the New River Valley's communities, with a short history and current attractions, many of which can be found outlined in detail in other chapters.

Blacksburg

The largest town in Virginia,

Blacksburg (population 35,000) sits majestically on a mountain plateau between two of nature's masterpieces, the Blue Ridge Mountains of Virginia and the great Alleghenies.

The growing town has a national recognition as an ideal community, charming, but with a constant flow of professors and students who lend to it most of its culture. Rand McNally has rated Blacksburg in the top 20 places for both quality of life and retirement. Newcomers, students and others are easily and quickly assimilated into the town's uniquely wonderful, abundant social life.

Touring Broadway shows, well-known speakers and popular musicians appear regularly on campus. Several university performing arts groups, the Audubon Quartet and Theatre Arts Program, are recognized nationally. Tech's NCAA Division I basketball and football teams often appear in postgame contests, and tailgating is THE event every autumn. You've never seen anything until you see the enthusiasm (and the traffic!) when the Tech Hokies meet the University of Virginia Cavaliers!

These glowing quality of life reports can be attributed to the sprawling presence of Virginia Tech, its students and 5,000 employees and its innumerable cultural offerings, many of which are free to the Blacksburg community. It would be difficult to find another community in Virginia with as many professionals of every type, from educators to seafood industry experts. One of its most famous, Prof. James Robertson (see the Civil War chapter) was named "the foremost Civil War historian in America" by the United Daughters of the Confederacy.

Tech's outreach into the community through its Extension Service and other programs affects the quality of life across Virginia. While businesses are sending their problems to researchers, local veterinarians, for example, routinely send their toughest cases to Tech's Veterinary School.

However, Tech wasn't always the town's main focal point. Blacksburg's name comes from the William Black family, which contributed acreage after Blacksburg was granted a town charter in 1798. For 75 years, it was known as a quiet and pleasant place to live. Then, in 1872, Dr. Henry Black petitioned the General Assembly to establish a land-grant university in his town. The university opened with one building and 43 students.

Since, the town-gown relationship has made for an ideal community that combines a small-town atmosphere with big-city sophistication. Shopping malls and Blacksburg's active downtown offer many things you usually see only in places like Washington, D.C. Its restaurants are the same, from student hangouts like Buddy's, to age-old traditions like the Greeks, to the Marriott.

The pace of life is relaxed. You won't see any smog to speak of, smell many fumes or be bothered by excessive noise. Blacksburg takes its quality of life very seriously. Its town council is mostly made up,

Shenandoah Valley Profile:
Rupert Cutler

Dr. Rupert Cutler may very well be the most interesting man in the Shenandoah Valley. He is definitely its most notable raconteur. If you've never before met a man who can talk to anybody, anywhere, about anything — meet Rupert Cutler.

Mostly, he talks about Virginia's Explore Park. Explore, many say, was the inspiration behind the controversial Disney's America project that may or may not get built in Haymarket, Virginia, by 1998.

Dr. Rupert Cutler

First, Explore was going to be a zoo. Then it was going to be the Colonial Williamsburg of the Western frontier, with advice from an all-star cast of historians. The Explore Park that opened on July 2, 1994, bears little resemblance to any of the much-hyped and much-changed plans touted by its founders nine years and $30 million dollars ago.

The fact that Virginia's Explore Park, western Virginia's newest attraction, opened at all is a tribute to Cutler, a tall, physically fit 61-year-old whose low-key personality belies his determination and power of persuasion.

After being drafted into the job of park director, Cutler seized the vision of the impossible task before him and shot every arrow from his political quiver to change the political boondoggle that was Explore into a viable attraction the public could identify with and buy into.

How Cutler, with a long pedigree of heading environmental causes, ended up in that position, as well as executive director of the Virginia Recreational Facilities Authority, was something even Cutler himself didn't expect.

After being told of the project in the early '90s by its brilliant but controversial founder, Bern Ewert, Cutler asked to come aboard and offered to raise his own salary. Ewert was happy to oblige.

Cutler had something Ewert lacked — a diplomatic personality and experience raising funds for environmental causes within Washington, D.C.'s, inner sanctum. His most visible position was assistant secretary for Conservation, Research and Education under the Carter Administration.

From 1988 to 1990, Cutler was CEO of the 80,000-member Defenders of Wildlife. From 1984 to 1988, he was executive director of Population-Environment Balance, educating the public about the effects of population changes on the quality of life. Prior to that, he was senior vice president for programs and chapter relations for the National Audubon Society. The rest of his biography reads like a "Who's Who" of environmental causes.

Apart from his political finesse, Cutler's greatest gift is probably his ability to impart passion for Explore to everyone he meets, from the hunter in the woods to the wealthy matrons of Hunt Country. Cutler can talk the talk and walk the walk.

He talks about Explore in an educational image. So far, it consists of a reassembled 1830s farmstead with interpreters, garbed in native dress, acting out lives from that period of time.

Cutler calls it "a living-history museum in a wilderness-like setting."

It seems that everybody thought of a million different reasons why Explore would never open. That was before they met Rupert Cutler and he told them a million different reasons why it should. Every chance he got.

He's expecting 100,000 visitors a year.

traditionally, of Tech educators who put their theories into practice.

Amidst all this heady academia, there's a universal love for recreation. Virtually any can be found within minutes. Floating down the New River with an innertube and cooler is a popular pastime. There's swimming in Blacksburg's municipal pool, which sits on a ledge overlooking the spectacular mountain range, hiking in the Jefferson National Forest and sight-seeing along the Blue Ridge Parkway.

Transportation is efficient, with a terrific bicycle path reminiscent of big-city parks. Its municipal bus system has been recognized as the best in the nation for its size, according to the National Association of Public Transit authorities. The heavily used Virginia Tech Airport sees many corporate jets.

As one of the fastest-growing, progressive communities in Virginia, many more people come to Blacksburg than leave. And, with all the area has to offer, that's liable to remain the trend for a long, long time. For more information contact the Blacksburg Chamber of Commerce at 141 Jackson Street, Blacksburg, Virginia 24060, (703) 552-4061.

Christiansburg

Montgomery County's seat, Christiansburg, the fourth largest town in Virginia, is a charming, historic town anchoring a county population of 73,913. The county's rural villages of Shawsville and Riner are equally quaint. Route 8 West connects the county to the 469-mile-long Blue Ridge Parkway.

A quiet river that flows under Main Street (the old Wilderness Trail) marks the continental divide. That's where flowing groundwater changes its course toward the Ohio-Mississippi river system.

The last legal gun duel in this country, the Lewis-McHenry, was fought in Christiansburg's renovated Cambria historic district. Depot Street, location of the Christiansburg Depot Museum, was the site of the depot burned in 1864 by the Union Army. The Cambria Emporium, built in 1908, is now the site of a fabulous antique mall with its own antique General Store.

The town's skyline is dotted with history including the steeples of Old Methodist Church, built sometime in the early 19th century, Christiansburg Presbyterian, c. 1853, and Schaeffer Memorial Baptist, erected in 1884.

Christiansburg's founder was Col. William Christian, an Irish Colonial settler. It served as an outpost on the Wilderness Trail, opened by Daniel Boone as the gateway to the west for settlers, such as Davy Crockett.

In 1866, the legendary Booker T. Washington of nearby Franklin County supervised the Christiansburg Industrial School for black children.

The northern portion of Montgomery County contains nearly 20,000 acres of the Jefferson National Forest. The Bikecentennial and Appalachian trails pass through the county. Between Blacksburg and Christiansburg, on U.S. Highway 460, is the 90-acre Montgomery County Park, one of the area's many recreational facilities, which includes a swimming pool, bathhouse, fitness trail and picnic area. In all, the county contains four 18-hole golf courses, 68 outdoor and five indoor tennis courts, 18 swimming pools, 37 ballfields and numerous playgrounds.

An added plus for the area is that real estate, both land and houses, is significantly less costly than in Blacksburg. For the same money you can get so much more, with a fantastic quality of life as well.

Floyd County

Follow Route 8 south from Christiansburg and you'll find yourself in Floyd County (population 12,005). Just as movie stars are attracted to Charlottesville, '60s-era holdouts have been migrating to Floyd for the past 30 years. Their tie-dyed counterculture communes nestle quietly along with small farms in a county whose promotional material lists an employer of six (Chateau Morrisette Winery) as one of its major industries. Many residents live quietly off the land.

Another employer makes gaso-

Visit

FLOYD

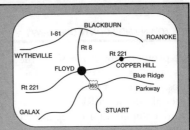

Located 6 miles off
Blue Ridge Parkway,
mile marker 165.

SCHOOLHOUSE FABRICS
"A Sewing Paradise"

An old 3-story schoolhouse
filled with all types of fabric.

Rt. 8 Floyd, Va. 24091
Mon. - Sat. 9:00 - 5:30
703 - 745-4561

BLUE RIDGE

RESTAURANT, INC.
HOMESTYLE COOKING
LOCATED IN DOWNTOWN
FLOYD VIRGINIA

DAILY SPECIALS
DELIS-BURGERS
REAL MASHED POTATOES
HOMEMADE DESSERTS
BREAKFAST
LUNCH-DINNER

PHONE#745-2147

DISCOVER THE BEAUTY OF FLOYD COUNTY

Wintergreen Farm Sheepskin Shoppe
(703) 745-4420

Highway 221 just 2 miles south
of Floyd in the beautiful Blue
Ridge Mountains of Virginia

AMERICAN HANDCRAFTS
SHEEPSKIN PRODUCTS
UNIQUE WALKING STICKS
ANTIQUES

TURN OF THE CENTURY
FARMSTEAD MUSEUM

WOODWRIGHT/BLACKSMITH
SHOPS

hol, promoted by some since the '70s gas crisis as the only way to fuel autos. Other promotional county material outlines SIRUS (Solar Innovative Republic for Independent United Survival) in Earthships, a planned counterculture community in Riner with restricted living. SIRUS accepts you only after you've been interviewed and analyzed according to what you can offer the community and humanity. Call them at (703) 763-2651 for a video showing the property and discussing the concept, which is based on homes with 3½-foot thick rammed earth walls and inspiration. The latter is furnished by author Mike Reynolds' books *Earthship, Vol. I and II*, and *A Coming of Wizards*.

Just don't go to Floyd actively looking for the counterculture. They have ingratiated themselves to the local farmers with their true sense of community spirit and are safely tucked away, bothering no one and expecting the same treatment, in the hills of Floyd.

They are most visible elsewhere, actually, at regional arts and crafts shows, where they sell their wares ranging from twisted grapevine baskets to tie-dyed and batik clothing and pottery. However, you don't have to leave Floyd to buy their wares.

One of the most prolific and amazing arts and crafts stores in the Blue Ridge, New Mountain Mercantile, six miles off the Blue Ridge Parkway on Locust Street, is the central location for area craftspeople to display and sell. You can spend hours investigating the

building, art gallery and upstairs Byrd's Walden Pond Products, which offer self-help tapes and herbal body care, among other back-to-the-earth products.

Locals also can be found hanging out at the Blue Ridge Restaurant, located in an early-1900 bank building, and Pine Tavern Restaurant and Lodge, a comfortable country inn where fine food includes vegetarian fare.

The most famous regional landmark for both locals and tourists is the inimitable Cockram's General Store, where every Friday is a hoedown! During the day, the store sells the likes of corn cob jelly and local crafts. There's no admission for the Friday Night Jamboree with pure mountain music and dancing and a fun, friendly family atmosphere. Next door is the largest distributor of bluegrass and old-time music in the world. Browsers are welcome to look through more than 5,000 tapes, records, books and videos. If you like sewing, there's Schoolhouse Fabrics, housed in what was once an 1846 school, with rooms of bargain fabric and quilts. Brookfield Christmas Tree Plantation, a national shipper of holiday trees, and Chateau Morrisette Winery and Le Chien Noir Restaurant in Meadows of Dan are other places that endear Floyd County to shoppers seeking the wild and wonderful. (See Shopping and Arts and Culture chapters for the whole scoop.)

The most famous national landmark is the picturesque Mabry Mill Blue Ridge Parkway visitors center, campground and recreation area.

Visit

FLOYD

Located 6 miles off
Blue Ridge Parkway,
mile marker 165.

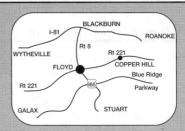

The restaurant here is quite good. The real feast, however, is one for the senses at the old-time, water-powered grist mill and interpretive historical buildings. This is usually the first place western Virginians take internationals for a true taste of American history and beauty.

The history of Floyd is actually rather sketchy, according to its Chamber of Commerce. Early land surveys showed an attempt to settle the area in 1740. The county was officially formed from Montgomery County in 1831. Floyd's original name was Jacksonville, named for Andrew Jackson, our nation's seventh president. Incorporated in 1858, the town changed its name to Floyd in 1896, although there's no official reason why.

When you visit the New River Valley, take a day to check out Floyd County, mingle with the locals, see some terrific arts and crafts and listen to some of the best bluegrass and gospel you'll ever hear. Floyd County truly is a sightseer's delight and photographer's paradise with the Blue Ridge Parkway's misty mountain views and miles of split-log fences. A map is smart when traveling Floyd's miles of rural, obscure back roads. You can receive this map and other information at the Floyd County Chamber of Commerce, P.O. Box 510, Floyd, Virginia 24091, (703) 745-4407.

Giles County

If you love dramatic mountain scenery, don't miss Giles County, especially the autumn vista from U.S. Highway 460 traveling south from Blacksburg. Giles County (population 16,366) is a mountain haven of forests, cliffs, cascading waterfalls, fast-flowing creeks and streams and, of course, the scenic New River. Its county seat of Pearisburg is one of only two towns located on the Maine-to-Georgia Appalachian Trail. Of the four covered bridges left in the Blue Ridge, two are in Giles County at Sinking Creek (see the Other Attractions chapter).

Giles County is a paradise for the lover of the outdoors. Whether your preference is for golfing a challenging emerald-green course, fly casting in an ice-cold mountain stream for trout, canoeing the New River's white water or hiking, Giles has it all.

Giles' most scenic attraction, one of the most-photographed in the Blue Ridge, is the Cascades waterfall that follows a rigorous, three-mile hiking trail in Pembroke (see our Recreation chapter); it is not recommended for small children. After your uphill pull, which seems to last forever, your excellent reward for this adventure is bathing at the foot of the tumbling, 60-foot-high waterfall.

A tamer destination, just as much fun for kids, is Castle Rock Recreation Area, which offers an 18-hole golf course, tennis and swimming. Canoe and kayak rentals are available in Pembroke at the New River Canoe Livery, (703) 626-7189.

Giles County's most famous attraction is the fabulous Mountain Lake Hotel and Resort, set atop the second highest mountain in Virginia and overlooking the town of Blacksburg, miles away. There's more information about this spot in our Resorts and Restaurants chapters. For years, it has been known for the beauty of its stone lodge and its gourmet cuisine. Of late, it is best known for the movie *Dirty Dancing*, filmed here as the epitome of early '60s-era great resorts. Mountain Lake is ageless and timeless and is not to be missed while in Giles County.

Another popular scenic destination is the attractive village of Newport, with its country store and steepled church. The quaint hamlet nestles at the foot of Gap Mountain at Sinking Creek.

Formed in 1806, the county was named for Gov. William Giles. In addition to tourism, Giles County's biggest employer is the Hoechst-Celanese Plant in Narrows. A bedroom community to many professionals, Giles' school system has one of the lowest student to teacher ratios in the state, 16 to 1, emphasizing a personal approach to instruction.

In addition to far-flung outdoor recreation Giles also offers the culture of its historic Andrew Johnston House, Giles Little Theatre and great antique shopping. Lots of Virginia Tech educators and professionals have discovered Giles, so you may have trouble finding available farmland. However, there are many gorgeous, mountaintop chalets and homes on the market at any given time. Contact the New River Board of Realtors. For more information on Giles County, contact the Chamber of Commerce at P.O. Box 666, Pearisburg, Virginia 24134, (703) 921-5000.

Radford

For quality of life, Radford City (population 15,940) has the whole country beat — that is, if you want to stake it on longevity. The late Margaret Skeete, who recently died there at the age of 114, was considered the oldest person in the United States and was listed in *The Guinness Book of Records*. Maybe living beside one of the oldest rivers in the world, the New River, had something to do with Skeete's remarkably long life. The river, which flows through this university city, adds something truly special to its quality of life.

Radford, the region's only independent city, was incorporated in 1892 and grew to be an important rail division point. It also became the home of Radford University, enrollment 8,000, and is the site of Virginia's only outdoor historical drama, *The Long Way Home*, depicting the famous story of Mary Draper Ingles' escape from the Shawnees.

Another of Radford's major attractions is 58-acre Bisset Park, with a walking trail beside nearly a mile of the tree-lined New River. This perfect park is capped off with a gazebo, swimming pool, several playgrounds and a tennis court. Colorful hot-air balloons also take off from the park. If you were to design the most charming, perfect recreational area of your dreams, this would probably be it!

Radford's energetic downtown is a Main Street community and has seen numerous unique small businesses start up, many serving the student population. To encourage small business development, Radford even publishes its own "New Business Start-up Guide."

The impact of Radford University on the city is comparable to that of neighboring Virginia Tech on the town of Blacksburg. The Dedmon Center, a $13 million athletic facility, is an unbelievable community gem featuring an air-supported fabric roof atop a gymnasium and natorium. The adjacent grounds have several softball, soccer, field hockey and flag football fields. Radford is also fanatic about its high school Bobcats' sports teams.

Other noted Radford facilities include 2,000-square-foot Flossie Martin Art Gallery, one of the Blue Ridge region's finest. A guest professor program has brought in entertainer Steve Allen, civil rights activist Jesse Jackson, Nobel Prize winner Elie Wiesel, Egypt's widowed Jihan Sadat (who displayed her own personal Egyptian art collection) and columnist Jack Anderson.

The city also has an outstanding academic tradition with its primary and secondary schools. Its school system, heavily influenced by college educated parents, has been nominated by the Commonwealth of Virginia as one of the nation's best. The highest passing percentage on national standardized tests in Virginia — 90.4 — recently was achieved by Radford's sixth-graders.

So, if you're looking for a casual but academically stimulating small city, look no farther than Radford. Its environment beside the sometimes placid, sometimes raging New River is symbolic of Radford's placid yet dynamic quality of life. For more information, contact the Radford Chamber of Commerce at 1126 Norwood Street, Radford, Virginia 24141, (703) 639-2202.

Pulaski

The town of Pulaski and Pulaski County (population 34,496), named for Count Pulaski of Poland, a Revolutionary War hero, is a special place with attractions ranging from the historic to vast water recreation and sports including a speedway and farm baseball team. No matter what your taste, you'll find entertainment here.

Most special is the town of Old Newbern, Pulaski's first county seat and the only town in Virginia that is totally an historic district, recognized by both the National Historic Register and the Virginia Landmarks Commission.

Here, you can tour the Wilderness Road Museum, treat yourself to ice cream at the old-timey soda fountain at PJ's Carousel gift shop and village and then stop by the local historic restaurant, Valley Pike Inn, for a family meal. This family tour can be easily taken in two hours, unless someone in the crowd is an avid shopper. In that case, avoid PJ's, one of a trio of shops that manufactures and sells hand-carved, full-size and miniature wooden carousel horses and other gift items. Be sure to let the kids ride the 1923 Carousel from the Cincinnati Zoo, one of 3,000 that once flourished at the peak of America's fascination with the art form!

Pulaski's newly renovated historic Main Street is also a fun stroll, featuring 20 charming shops and quaint restaurants, arts and crafts and examples of Victorian architecture. Pulaski's downtown also is blessed with the New River Valley's cultural gem, its Fine Arts Center. Located in an 1898 Victorian commercial building, the Pulaski Fine Arts Center has a full agenda and is well utilized by the local population. There are performances, exhibits, classes, the Art Mart Gift Shop, a school outreach program and art library.

Outdoor enthusiasts will adore Claytor Lake. Like its younger counterpart, Smith Mountain, it was formed by Appalachian Power Company in 1939 for the generation of electricity. Since, it has become a haven for boaters, anglers, campers and swimmers. Its white sand beach will make you think you're at the ocean. Nearby is a spectacular condominium development, Mallard Point.

Claytor Lake State Park's 472 acres offer four campgrounds, 12 housekeeping cabins, tent spots and horseback riding. The park's visitor center is located in the 1879 Howe House and has educational displays.

Another nice park is Gatewood Reservoir Park, off Route 99. You can camp on 42 sites or park your RV along the shores of Gatewood Reservoir and fish or boat surrounded by the Jefferson National Forest.

Sports fans will appreciate the Pulaski County Speedway, located on Route 11. Open early April through late September, it is a NASCAR-Winston racing series track that seats 10,000.

Pulaski County also is home to the highly respected New River Community College in Dublin. The New River Valley Fair also is held in Dublin each summer and offers such charming events as a children's pet show.

Pulaski County workers also have an impressive mix of job opportunities. The Volvo White Truck Corp. is one of the largest employers, as well as Burlington Industries, Western Electric and the Pulaski Furniture Company.

Whether you're a nature, water, fine arts or history lover, you'll find plenty to do in Pulaski County. For more information, contact the Pulaski County Chamber of Commerce at P.O. Box 169, Pulaski, Virginia 24301-0169, (703) 480-1991.

Alleghany Highlands Region

Alleghany County

Alleghany County, (population 27,820) situated on the Allegheny mountain range, is the western gateway to Virginia. Half of the county is within the George Washington

National Forest. The county is a mountain playground for a multitude of fabulous vacations in gorgeous scenery. It's also next door to wild, wonderful West Virginia's Greenbrier County, home of the world-famous Greenbrier Resort.

Outdoor lovers, sportspeople, antique aficionados, railroad buffs, history lovers and gourmets all will find something to get really excited about here.

Before the formation of Alleghany County, property records were provided from Fincastle in Botetourt County, a two-day trip. So, in 1822, the County of Alleghany was formed, named after the mountains in which they lie, although the mountains are spelled differently than the county.

Its county seat, Covington, was named in honor of Gen. Leonard Covington, hero of the War of 1812 and confidante to James Madison and Thomas Jefferson. Clifton Forge, the county's other populous area, was named for its iron production and contributed cannons and cannonballs to the Civil War effort. During the Civil War, Alleghany County furnished more soldiers to the Confederacy than it had voters. The county suffered greatly in the war, since it was located next to West Virginia, which joined the Union. It took years to recover from the losses sustained.

After the war, Clifton Forge was selected by the Chesapeake and Ohio Railway as the site of its new depot. The coming of the railroad signaled important growth and in 1906, Clifton Forge received its city charter.

Hemp, used in rope production, was another important early product. Natural resources have always been Alleghany County's main industry. The biggest boost to industrial progress in the area was the decision in 1899 by the West Virginia Pulp and Paper Co. to locate a mill at Covington. The coming of the pulp mill stimulated the development of growth of other industrial and commercial interests.

Both the railroad and Westvaco Paper Mill continue to play important roles in the county's culture and economy. As expected, many of its attractions are tied to its history.

In the charming historical city of Clifton Forge, the C&O Historical Society Archives preserves artifacts and equipment of the C&O Railroad. It is one of the largest railroad historical societies in the United States. Also worth a visit is the Alleghany Highlands Arts and Crafts Center, displaying fine regional arts and crafts. (See our Arts and Culture chapter.)

Lucy Selina Furnace stacks, more than 100 feet tall, are reminders of the area's 19th century iron industry. A stunning Victorian mansion built by the owner of the rich iron mines has been turned into the charming Firmstone Manor Bed & Breakfast. Local lore says a staff of eight was required just to maintain its gardens! Nearby is the Longdale Recreation Area, which features miles of mountain trails, camping and sand beach swimming. All are located off Interstate 64's Exit 10 on Route 269 in Longdale.

Roaring Run Recreation Area,

the site of the ruins of an 1838 iron furnace, is another wonderful place to hike and picnic. It's located off Route 220 S. Follow the signs to Route 615 and then Route 621.

Other historic points of interest are Fort Young, a reconstruction of the original French and Indian War fort on I-64, Exit 4, near Covington. Lovers of architecture will enjoy seeing Oakland Grove Presbyterian Church, which served as a hospital during the Civil War. It can be seen in Selma off I-64, Exit 7.

Water has also played a large role in the history and life of the county. The unassuming, unmarked site of the source of Quibell Water, rivaling Perrier nationally, is located by a cattle grate crossing close to Sweet Chalybeate Springs, where trucks transport it daily for bottling in Roanoke.

Sweet Chalybeate (pronounced Ka-lee-bee) Pools and gazebo off Route 311 near the West Virginia border dates back 150 years as a great pre-Civil War resort. Recently renovated after lying in waste following the demise of the Civil War aristocracy, the pools now offer bathers the most highly carbonated mineral water in the world. Locals swear by the water's healing powers and many either take a dip or drink its water daily. For more information, write them at Route 3, Sweet Chalybeate, Covington, Virginia 24426.

Twelve miles of water bring in visitors to Lake Moomaw, a relatively new lake formed for power generation 19 miles from Covington. Signs point the way. Residents and visitors have taken advantage of water skiing, boating, fishing and swimming.

Douthat State Park's 50-acre lake also offers a beach, bathhouse, boating and excellent trout fishing. Other facilities include a Visitor's Center, restaurant and lodge as well as cabins, campgrounds and miles of hiking trails.

The world's largest pump storage facility in the world, Virginia Power's Back Creek Pump Storage Station, is also worth seeing. It's located on a 325-acre recreation area with a visitor's center on Route 600. Call (703) 279-2389.

For obvious reasons, anglers find Paint Bank State Trout Hatchery on Route 311 an interesting place to visit. It is open daily from 7:30 AM until 4 PM. Rock lovers will want to visit Rainbow Gap or Iron Gate Gorge, which create a geologist's paradise a mile south of Clifton Forge on Route 220. For 12 million years, the Jackson River has been working on this masterpiece.

Across the border in West Virginia, the attractions also are overwhelming. The big one, of course, is the world-famous Greenbrier Resort. Take a look around its magnificent grounds while you're in the area. The resort welcomes visitors, even if you don't spend the night. Several nice restaurants are open. If you're just in the area for the day, you and the kids may enjoy just having dessert in the ice cream parlor with its pink and green striped awnings and pink crystal glasses. It's a really special experience that even those on a tight budget can afford.

Also close to the West Virginia

border, but still in Virginia, is a great dining experience in a place called Crows. If you blink your eyes, you'll miss it, so keep a look out for the rustic sign with the Eagle, indicating Eagle's Nest Restaurant. Built beside a rolling waterfall, the gourmet food is so good that corporate officials flying into the area from around the world are some of its most loyal customers.

Several other West Virginia attractions within an hour's drive are north up Route 92. Blue Bend swimming hole in Alvon, one of the best in the Blue Ridge, is one of them. Lake Sherwood, farther up Route 92, is nice, too, and rents paddleboats. The Cass Scenic Railroad is close to Marlinton, as is Snowshoe Ski Resort. The town of Lewisburg, cultured and sophisticated, is also worth a visit for its charming downtown shops and Carnegie Hall, built by the same industrialist tycoon as its more famous counterpart.

Another aspect that makes Alleghany County so popular with visitors is that the locals really want you to visit and stay awhile! The people are country, friendly and downright glad to see you. Brochures of all the area's attractions can be picked up at the Jerry's Run Virginia Visitor's Center at I-64's Exit 1. Better yet, contact the Alleghany Highlands Chamber of Commerce at 403 E. Ridgeway Street, Clifton Forge, Virginia 24422, (703) 962-2178.

Bath County

Nestled between Alleghany and Highland counties and bordering West Virginia, Bath County (population 4,799) doesn't even have a stop light. Nearly 90 percent of Bath County is forest. What it does have is pleasures of every kind for its visitors, whether they're on a budget or staying at the world-famous Homestead resort.

The bubbly mineral springs, or "baths," whence the county got its name, are a source of pleasure for visitors. Bath County was founded in 1745 by pioneers of mostly Scotch-Irish descent, most notably John Lewis, who settled at Fort Lewis. One son, Charles, died in the historic Battle of Point Pleasant in 1774. The other son, John, built the first hotel on the site of the present Homestead resort in 1766. His structure was destroyed by fire in 1901. In the meantime, M. E. Ingalls, president of the Chesapeake and Ohio Railroad, bought the site and the modern era of the resort was launched.

Some historic sites in the county are the Warwickton Mansion Bed and Breakfast at Hidden Valley, site of the movie *Sommersby;* the Anderson Cottage in Warm Springs; and Windy Cove Presbyterian Church at Millboro.

The real history of the county, however, lies in its springs, which have been drawing people for more than 200 years. Wrote one visitor in 1750, "The spring water is very clear and warmer than new milk." Thermal springs are found at Warm Springs, Hot Springs and Bolar Springs, at temperatures ranging from 77 degrees F to 106 degrees F. They flow at rates ranging from

2,500 to 5,000 gallons a minute. The water has a soft fizz of tickling bubbles, and taking of the baths is like lowering yourself into a warm vat of Perrier (or Quibell, whose source springs are in Alleghany County).

Public pools have been open at Warm Springs since 1761 and look today much as they did then. The covered pools were the cultural center of the rich and famous. Thomas Jefferson "took the waters" here for his health, as did the frail Mrs. Robert E. Lee (she had crippling arthritis), whose chair, used to lower her into the pool, is still on display at the ladies' pool.

Thus, the stage was set for the aristocracy to visit this scenic land. That's how the internationally known Homestead resort, detailed in our Resorts chapter, came into being. As Bath County celebrated its Bicentennial in 1991, the Ingalls family celebrated its 100th year of running the famous Homestead resort. The resort was purchased in 1993 by Resorts International of Dallas, Texas. At The Homestead you will see a place of style and grandeur equalled only by its neighbor, The Greenbrier resort, in nearby White Sulphur Springs, West Virginia.

The Homestead offers the superlative of everything — recreation, shopping and gourmet restaurants. Its sporting activities attract enthusiasts from around the world. You can ski, ride horseback on hundreds of miles of trails, play tennis on 21 professional courts, fly fish at an Orvis Fishing School, shoot skeet and golf on three championship courses including the nationally known Cascades.

The same crowd that goes to The Homestead are regulars at an absolutely serendipitous place, Garth Newel Music Center. The sound of critically acclaimed chamber music wafts through the mountains throughout the year with summer picnics and holiday events. Garth Newel attracts cultured people from around the world, and you never know who you'll see there taking in a concert while staying at The Homestead or with friends at a country estate. Many celebrities have been spotted, according to locals . . . who leave them alone.

You don't need to be rich, however, to really enjoy your stay in Bath County. There are many nice bed and breakfasts and several really outstanding ones, Meadow Lane Lodge and Fort Lewis Lodge. At Fort Lewis, hunting is the autumn and winter mainstay, and spring and summer offer lazy tubing down the placid Cowpasture River, hiking and camping and Caryn Cowden's wonderful cooking. It's a wholesome, airy retreat the whole family will enjoy.

There are very nice places to eat downtown as well. The Inn at Gristmill Square, restored by the Hirsh family, is the center of Warm Springs with its dining and interesting shops. Lodging also is available there.

Quaint shopping offers interesting opportunities, especially at the Bacova Outlet in Warm Springs. Its silk-screened gifts and household goods are made at the Bacova Guild Factory, located in an old

1920s lumber mill town restored in 1965 by the Hirsh family.

There are many outdoor adventures waiting for you in Bath County. Burnsville's large caverns and sunken caves are open for the pleasure of spelunkers.

You can hike, hunt, fish or ride on some of the most beautiful forests and mountains you'll find. The George Washington National Forest, Gathright Game Management Area and Douthat State Park are in the county. The Homestead also offers any type of arranged sporting event imaginable.

Although The Homestead is Bath County's crowning jewel, there are countless other gems in this pastoral, genteel land of sophistication. The Bath County Chamber of Commerce has a wonderful visitors guide that will tell you everything you need to know. Contact them at P.O. Box 718, Hot Springs, Virginia 24445, (800) 628-8092, for the entire story of the county known for pleasure and relaxation. Then, go and take advantage of it!

Highland County

Nicknamed the "Switzerland of Virginia," scenic Highland County (population 2,800) has more sheep than people, on land with a higher mean elevation than any county east of the Mississippi River.

Environment is everything to county residents who live in the rarefied air. Even Highland County's official brochure invites businesses to locate, providing their "environment won't be endangered." Few places have preserved their surroundings and privacy so well. One of the most influential conservation groups in America, the Ruffled Grouse Society, was founded here in 1961. Highland County was established in 1847 from the counties of Bath and Pendleton, in what is now West Virginia. Its county seat, Monterey, sits 3,000 feet above sea level, while its western border in the Allegheny Mountains reaches elevations of 4,500.

Once the hunting grounds for the Shawnees, Highland's borders were first crossed by European settlers in the 1700s, when it was still a part of Augusta County, which it remained until 1787.

In the Indian War of 1754, which lasted 10 years, the county was on the frontier. Highland men also made up the company that fought the Battle of Point Pleasant under the command of Col. Andrew Lewis.

An interesting note: Highland was visited by German Gen. Erwin Rommel, the "Desert Fox," prior to World War I so he could study Stonewall Jackson's military tactics at McDowell. Talk about biting the hand that feeds you! Later, Rommel used the same tactics against the United States and its allies.

To the visitor, Highland County is both beautiful and spectacular as well as stark and severe. The natural setting is augmented by pleasant activities and facilities. Every March, this small population rallies to put on an event ranked among the top 20 festivals in America, the Highland County Maple Festival, which draws 70,000 over a two-weekend span. The festival takes you back to the time when "tree sugar" and "tree lasses" were found on every table, when "opening" the trees and "boiling down the sugar water" were highland spring rituals. The tours and exhibits are both educational and enjoyable. The pancake (with maple syrup, of course) and trout suppers centered around the county seat of Monterey are unforgettable.

A Sugar Tour winds through some of the loveliest spots in Virginia, routes 637 and 640. Maple sugar camps throughout the county welcome visitors to view the actual process of syrup-making, from tapping the trees to collecting the colorless, almost tasteless sugar water. Gathered in plastic buckets or by plastic tubing, the water is then boiled in kettles, pans or evaporators, until a barrel is finally reduced to a gallon of pure maple syrup. The camp sites are Rexrode's Sugar Orchard, Puffenbarger's Sugar Orchard, Sugar Tree Country Store & Sugar House and Eagle's Sugar Camp. Tour maps are provided at the festival.

One of the best things about the festival is tasting and shopping for all the pure maple syrup goodies, available at a cost vastly below retail. There's sugar candy, donuts glazed with maple syrup and funnel cakes. Highland's downtown antique stores also open for the occasion. Most are clustered around the classic Victorian Highland Inn. This downtown landmark, c. 1904, has been restored and is now on the National Register of Historic Places. Its 20 rooms are furnished with antiques.

Be sure and see the Maple Museum on U.S. Highway 220, one mile south of Monterey. This replica of an old-time sugar house features exhibits showing the making of maple syrup and sugar from the earliest known methods used by Native Americans to modern techniques. Tools and equipment are on display. Admission is free and the museum is always open.

Summers are as cool here as any in the East. One word of warning — if you're driving in from another part of the Blue Ridge, expect to find snow on the ground as late as April, since Highland County gets about 65 inches of the white stuff a year. Bring a jacket for the kids, since the temperature will probably be at least 10 degrees colder than where you came from.

Outside of the maple culture, there are other interesting places to visit. If you want to see where many of those mouth-watering trout come from — and part of the reason behind this area's distinction as "Trout Capital of the Eastern United States" — visit the Virginia Trout Company, on Route 220 north of Monterey. In business for 30 years, the Virginia Trout Company hatches rainbow trout from eggs and raises them to adulthood. You can fish for your own, buy them frozen or just watch them swim in the cold mountain water. The hatchery is open seven days a week, weekdays from 8 AM to 4 PM and weekends from 9 AM to 4 PM.

While you're in Highland County, you also can see the Confederate Breastworks (breast-high trenches) built in 1862 by 4,000

AREA CODE CHANGE
ON JULY 15, 1995, THE
703 AREA CODE THAT PRECEDES
MANY OF THE PHONE NUMBERS IN
THE BLUE RIDGE WILL CHANGE TO 540. KEEP
THIS IN MIND AS YOU USE THIS GUIDE.

Confederate troops as a defense against Union soldiers. They are located at the top of Shenandoah Mountain on U.S. Highway 250 at the Highland-Augusta county line.

Also on U.S. Highway 250 east of McDowell is the McDowell Battlefield, where 4,500 Confederate troops under Gen. Stonewall Jackson defeated 2,268 Union soldiers in a bloody conflict in 1862. This engagement was the first victory in Jackson's famous Valley Campaign. Nearby McDowell Presbyterian Church was used as a hospital and soldiers are buried there. The battlefield recently was purchased by the Association for the Preservation of Civil War sites.

Highland County is one of the few places where time seems to stand still. People enjoy Highland as much for what is missing — traffic, pollution, nose and crowds — as for what is there. The pace is slow and the scenery is beautiful. It's considered the best place in Virginia to bird watch, and fans say species that have flown the coop from other parts of the state can still be found here.

If you feel like flying the coop yourself, come to Highland and slow down like the maple sugar in January. Contact the Highland County Chamber of Commerce at P.O. Box 250, Monterey, Virginia 24465, (703) 468-2550.

Inside
The Civil War

It was, as the poet Walt Whitman described, "A strange, sad war." More Americans lost their lives in the Civil War (1861 to 1865) than in both world wars combined. No other state has suffered the trauma that Virginia endured in the Civil War, say some historians. Beginning with the war's first major battle at Bull Run (First Manassas) and ending with the surrender in the tiny, peaceful village of Appomattox Court House, 60 percent of the Civil War's battles were fought in Virginia.

Interest in the Civil War has never been keener. So many inquiries have been made that the Insiders Guides® Inc. and *Richmond Times Dispatch* have published a separate book, *The Insiders' Guide to the Civil War in the Eastern Theater*, available for $12.95 in most book stores.

The Old Dominion was one of the last states to leave the Union, but because it was the most exposed geographically of the seceding states, Virginia became the major battleground of the Civil War. One borderline Shenandoah Valley city, Winchester, changed hands from Confederate to Yankee no fewer than 72 times. Thousands of men, out of a strong sense of duty and honor, heeded the call to arms and never returned. Is it any wonder

that, nearly 130 years later, the War Between the States is not forgotten? Certainly, it is not forgotten in the Blue Ridge, where generations of family farms and history were laid waste, sometimes out of spite rather than necessity.

It is not unusual to find senior citizens who fondly remember former slaves called "Auntie and Uncle," revered as family and given plots of land on the family farm after they refused to leave their masters when they were freed. On the flip side, you can see some of the earliest tintype photos ever taken showing slaves whose backs were ribbons of scars from the beatings they endured at the hands of their taskmasters. Who was in the right, and just what was the Civil War all about? Slavery alone?

The answer to those questions can be found in the Blue Ridge, the site not only of some of the bloodiest battles in the Civil War, but also home to one of the country's most noted Civil War scholar and author.

History Professor James I. Robertson of Virginia Tech is past executive director of the U.S. Civil War Centennial Commission. His most recent book, *Civil War! America Becomes One Nation*, an illustrated history for young readers, probably best answers those questions in a way that young and old can clearly understand. Robertson, whose books have been nominated for the Pulitzer Prize, teaches a Civil War class that is one of the hottest tickets on campus. His enthusiasm for Civil War history comes as no surprise, since his great-grandfather was the great Confederate General Robert E. Lee's cook.

Robertson's latest book takes into account the political and socio-economic mood of the 1860s and the events that set off a movement that the South anticipated would be over within weeks, but which, in fact, lasted four years and destroyed a way of life.

The fact that the Confederacy even survived for the duration of the war was the result, in large measure, of the excellent military leadership furnished by the Blue Ridge of Virginia's generals, Robert E. Lee and Thomas J. "Stonewall" Jackson. Jackson's nickname came, so the story goes, out of the battle of First Manassas. Gen. Barnard Bee of South Carolina pointed to Jackson's troops and shouted, "There stands Jackson like a stone wall." In addition to his legendary nickname, Jackson's Rebel yell became his battle signature. To this day, the U.S. Army regularly conducts "staff rides" into the Shenandoah Valley for its officers, following the course of Jackson's famed Foot Cavalry.

Tragically, according to Robertson, Northerners and Southerners were both fighting for the same thing: America, as each side interpreted what America should be.

On the other hand, within time, the Civil War contributed to a stronger union of the United States of America, allowing it to withstand foreign leaders bent on conquering the world just 50 years later during World War I, followed by World War II. If the South had won the war, would the history of the 20th century have been drastically rewritten? Would we be speaking German today instead of English?

When discussing the role the Blue Ridge played in the Civil War, Robertson emphasizes the Shenandoah Valley's geographical position as a spear pointing into the North and as the "Breadbasket of the Confederacy." The number of major battles in the region attests to the constant wrenching for control of the Valley, which prompted Jackson, the "pious blue-eyed killer," to push his men so hard in the spring of 1862 that their shoes fell apart in the fields.

And who can ever forget the heartbreaking Battle of New Market, when the fateful day, May 15, 1864, is retraced and its startling events reenacted? On that rainy Sunday afternoon, 247 Virginia Military Institute cadets advanced side by side with veteran Civil War infantrymen into a hellish cannon and rifle fire. The soldiers forged onward with parade ground precision, using each step to free the other from the furrows of mud caused by the heavy rainstorm.

The Confederate commander of Western Virginia, Major Gen. John C. Breckinridge, had enlisted the

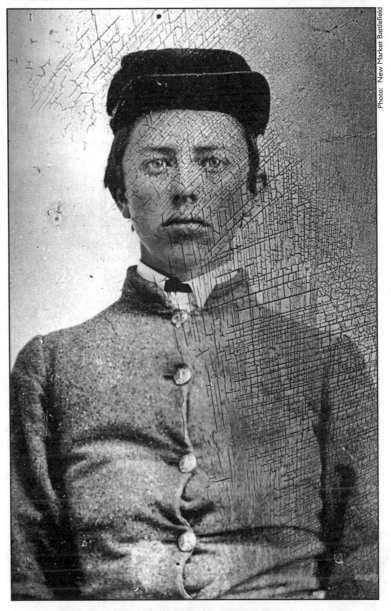

A young soldier in the Civil War, Thomas Garland Jefferson, was mortally wounded in the Battle of New Market at age 17. He was a descendant of President Thomas Jefferson.

cadets to join his ragtag force of 4,500. The cadets marched forward, their muzzle-loading muskets slung over shoulders that were destined to bear a far heavier load, their VMI flag leading the way. Looming ahead was a battle that would go down in American history as one of the most valorous and one of the last Confederate victories in the Shenandoah Valley. As the smoke of the battle cleared, 10 cadets lay dead, including Cadet Thomas G. Jefferson, 17, descendant of our nation's third president. Another 47 cadets were wounded.

Visitors can relive this segment in American history by touring the New Market Battlefield Park and its museum, the Hall of Valor. Together, they honor these 247 brave, young cadets. In the Hall of Valor are displays of Civil War muskets, uniforms, tintype photos, day-to-day accessories and a replica of the type cannon captured by the cadets. It is one of the most stirring of all the Blue Ridge Civil War sites. Young and old alike are fascinated by its sense of history and urgency.

Beyond the Shenandoah Valley, Southwestern Virginia was also a region of vital importance to the Confederacy, points out Robertson. Through it ran the Virginia and Tennessee Railroad, the only lifeline between Richmond and the West. The lead mines at Austinville, the salt works at Saltville and the coal mines throughout the region provided the embattled South with essential natural resources. The May, 1864, Battle of Cloyd's Mountain near Dublin in Pulaski County remains the largest engagement ever fought in Southwestern Virginia. A future president, Col. Rutherford B. Hayes, was a hero of the battle. Today, only a marker commemorates the site.

Roanoker Gary C. Walker, author of *The War in Southwest Virginia* and *Hunter's Fiery Raid Through Virginia's Valleys*, outlines in great detail the way the war was fought in this region of Virginia. He captures the mood of the area, geographically a third of Virginia, which broke away to join the Yankees and form its own state, West Virginia.

Walker's book on Maj. Gen. David Hunter, known for his unquenchable hatred of slavery, shows how Hunter wreaked his vengeance upon Southwestern Virginia before its secession. States Walker, "Civilian property became an official military target. Both men and women were arrested without charge. Routinely, Southern ladies

Insiders' Tips

Because of growing interest in the Civil War, some Blue Ridge colleges and universities sponsor special seminars on campus. Many of them are adjacent to important battlefields. A popular one is the Civil War Institute at Shenandoah University in Winchester.

and their crying babies were forced from their homes with nothing but the clothes on their bodies. Their manor houses were plundered and burned before their horrified eyes." In Hunter's books, one can almost smell the smoke, feel the perspiration drip from the brow and hear the heart pound as the lines clashed and the men fell with hideous and gaping wounds.

Walker also is a consultant to the growing number of hobbyists of Civil War battle re-enactments, held throughout the East Coast. The most recent Blue Ridge addition is Roanoke County's re-enactment of Hunter's Raid at Green Hill Park, held on July 29 and 30, 1994. Also during 1994, Civil War buffs can see a re-enactment at Cedar Creek October 15 and 16 in Middletown.

The Battle of Cedar Creek, 1864, marked the end of Confederate dominion over the Shenandoah Valley and its essential food supplies. It also marked the end of famed Gen. Jubal Early's career and of the war-weariness that had plagued the North. This battle also put to rest any hopes the Confederacy may have had for a negotiated peace with the Union. The victory freed Gen. Philip Sheridan and his men, including Gen. George Custer (who had the misfortune of tangling with Chief Sitting Bull at the Battle of Little Big Horn) to play crucial roles in the final battles of the Civil War the following spring.

The Cedar Creek Battlefield Foundation is fighting to save the battlefield's 158 acres from development. So far, $125,000 of the $450,000 needed has been raised. If the rest is not forthcoming, the land will be developed. In the meantime, the history preservationists are hoping their museum, relic shop and annual battle re-enactments will help stave off the bulldozers. Their October event includes open camps, drills, dress parades and demonstrations of military and civilian life. For more information call (703) 869-2064 or write: P. O. Box 229, Middletown, Virginia 22645.

For schedules of battle re-enactments throughout the country, write the Camp Chase Gazette, P. O. Box 707, Marietta, Ohio 45750. If you've never seen one of these events, you're in for a real experience. The men who do this take it very seriously, as does Vinton attorney Bruce Mayer. Since taking up his hobby seven years ago, Mayer has appeared in the movies, *Glory* and *Lincoln*, in a National Geographic TV special and in the TV film, *North South*. His 15-man unit performed at a birthday party for actor and Civil War buff Richard Dreyfuss at Smith Mountain Lake during the filming of *What About Bob?* He also is in *Killer Angels*, based on the Battle of Gettysburg.

Mayer says authenticity is a "must." Sack cloth, shell jacket and frock coat are required of all participants on the field. Eyeglasses must be of period construction. Only period footwear is allowed, preferably mule hide with square toes and wooden pegs. Uniforms must be woolen. Many of the soldiers carry their own original binoculars, pistols and bayonet rifles. No, they don't use real bullets, but they do use real gunpowder.

Regardless of whose side, if any, you believe was right in the War Between the States, there are hundreds of monuments, museums and battle re-enactments awaiting you in the Blue Ridge of Virginia. There are also more than 250 historic markers that are on-the-spot history lessons. In the pages that follow, we list only actual sites where you can see or do something. For a complete list of Virginia Civil War battlefields and markers, write the state of Virginia at 1021 East Cary Street, Richmond, Virginia 23219 or call (804) 786-2051. A great guide is Robertson's book, *Civil War Sites in Virginia, a Tour Guide*, published by the University Press of Virginia. And, our sister publication, *The Insiders' Guide to the Civil War in the Eastern Theater*, provides 15 tours that anyone interested in the Civil War — including kids — will enjoy.

Unless otherwise noted, admission is free of charge.

Shenandoah Valley Region

Winchester

GEN. STONEWALL JACKSON'S HEADQUARTERS

515 N. Braddock St.   (703) 667-3242
Open 9 AM-5 PM daily April-Oct.
Weekends in Nov. and Dec.
Adults $3.50, Children $1.75

From this brick house, Jackson commanded his forces in defense of the strategic Shenandoah Valley.

The French-style house contains artifacts of Jackson, Gen. Turner Ashby, Jackson's calvary chief, and others.

STONEWALL AND NATIONAL CEMETERIES

Several blocks east of business district

Buried in these two cemeteries are 3,000 Confederate and 4,500 Union soldiers killed in nearby battles. National is one of the largest national cemeteries in Virginia.

Middletown

BELLE GROVE PLANTATION

Cedar Creek Battlefield   (703) 869-2028
Open daily March-Nov. 10 AM-4 PM
Mon.-Sat., 1-5 PM Sun.
Adults $3.50, Ages 6 to 12 $2

Spared during the Civil War even though it served as Gen. Philip Sheridan's headquarters during the decisive 1864 Battle of Cedar Creek, Belle Grove was built between 1794 and 1797 with the design assistance of Thomas Jefferson. James and Dolley Madison honeymooned there. Today, the house and grounds exemplify the home and working farm of a wealthy Federalist planter.

CEDAR CREEK BATTLEFIELD FOUNDATION RE-ENACTMENT

Cedar Creek Battlefield   (703) 869-2064
Adults $5, Children younger than 6 free

On October 15 and 16, 1994, the Cedar Creek Battlefield Foundation, which is striving to save the 154-acre historic battlefield from development, will stage a Civil War Living History Weekend. Re-enactments of the battle will take place at

New Market Battlefield Historical Park

- ► *Civil War Museum*
- ► *19th Century Farm*
- ► *Scenic Overlook*
- ► *280 Acre Park*
- ► *Picnic Facilities*

Exit 264, I-81

Hall of Valor Civil War Museum   703-740-3101

4 PM Saturday and 2 PM Sunday. Various drills, dress parades and military and civilian demonstrations will be presented throughout the weekend. Sutlers (vendors) Row, presented by the Frederick Ladies Relief Society, will be a living history in Belle Grove. All proceeds go to the preservation of the battlefield.

CEDAR CREEK RELIC SHOP
7841 Main St.   (703) 869-5207
Open Fri.-Mon. 10 AM-6:30 PM

Cedar Creek Relics has the largest collection of authentic Civil War relics for sale in the Shenandoah Valley. This includes swords, bayonets, carbines, muskets, buttons, plates, artillery shells, tintypes, documents and other relics. The store also sells tapes and books. Civil War and antique weapons are bought and sold.

Strasburg

HUPP'S HILL BATTLEFIELD PARK & STUDY CENTER
Rt. 11 S.   (703) 465-5884
Open 10 AM-4 PM Mon., Wed., Thur., Fri.; 11 AM-5 PM Sat. and Sun.
Adults $3.50, Ages 7 to 16 $2.50

A living history learning experience, Hupp's Hill features the third-largest collection of Confederate currency in the world, a 100-foot, hand-painted mural depicting the history of the Civil War and the world's largest map on the Battle of Cedar Creek. The museum is dedicated to teaching visitors, especially children. They can try on costumes and uniforms, among other hands-on experiences.

STRASBURG MUSEUM
East King St.   (703) 465-3175
Open 10 AM-4 PM, May-Oct.
Adults $2, Children $1

There are many quality Civil War and railroad relics to see here. You'll

Photo: Alleghany Highlands Chamber of Commerce

Period dress by re-enactors at the Confederate Soldier Monument in Covington.

enjoy the blacksmith, cooper and potter's shop collections.

Front Royal

BELLE BOYD COTTAGE
101 Chester St.   *(703) 636-1446*
Open 10 AM-4 PM Mon.-Fri., Nov.-April;
10 AM-4 PM Mon.-Sat. and noon-4 PM
Sun., May-Oct.
Adults $1, Ages 12-16 50¢

This cottage museum, dedicated to the famed Confederate spy, teen-ager Belle Boyd, depicts life in Warren County and Front Royal during the Civil War. Belle was famous for the information she gathered that helped Jackson win the Battle of Front Royal on May 23, 1862.

WARREN RIFLES
CONFEDERATE MUSEUM
95 Chester St.   *(703) 636-6982*
Open 9 AM-5 PM weekdays,
noon-5 PM weekends, April 15-Nov. 1

Included in this museum is memorabilia from generals Lee, Jackson, Early, Ashby and Boyd. Other artifacts of the war in the Shenandoah are abundant.

PROSPECT HILL CEMETERY

Within the cemetery, you will find a memorial, Soldier's Circle Monument, over the graves of 276 Confederate dead. Also there is Mosby Monument, flanked by two Parrott rifled cannon. The marker is a memorial to seven members of a Confederate group named Mosby's Rangers, illegally executed as spies in 1864.

Edinburg

EDINBURG MILL
Rt. 11

In 1864, Union soldiers began a systematic destruction of the Shenandoah, known as "The Burning." Recently re-opened as a restaurant and noted for its child ghost, "Frankie," Edinburg Mill was miraculously spared when two young women tearfully begged Gen. Sheridan to spare it, since it was Edinburg's only livelihood. Sheridan ordered his soldiers to extinguish the flames. There are several stories about just who the child ghost is, but the most noted is that Frankie was a slave who was caught in the mill wheel. Waitresses over the years have claimed he plaintively appears and reappears at unusual times.

New Market

NEW MARKET
BATTLEFIELD HISTORICAL PARK
I-81, Exit 264   *(703) 740-3101*
Open daily 9 AM-5 PM except holidays
Adults $5, Ages 7 to 15 $2

New Market Battlefield Historical Park, owned and operated by Virginia Military Institute, offers a family adventure into one of America's most dramatic eras and is one of the finest Civil War museums in Virginia. Children can climb on cannons where, in 1864, 6,000 Federals clashed with 4,500 Confederates, including the famous VMI cadets desperately recruited from college to help the South's cause. It was the first and only time

Photo: R. J. Reber

The Exchange Hotel, a restored railroad hotel that served as a Civil War hospital, is now an excellent Civil War museum.

in American history that an entire student body was recruited to fight a war.

The Hall of Valor, focal point of the 260-acre battlefield park, presents a concise, graphic survey of the entire war. Exhibits highlight the war chronologically. There are two films, including a stirring account of the cadets' baptism by fire and one about Stonewall Jackson, a former VMI professor. You will see a life-size artillery unit, a model railroad, exquisitely sculptured soldiers and four battle scenes among the three-dimensional exhibits in the Virginia Room.

The c. 1825 Bushong farmhouse, around which part of the battle swirled, still stands, with its reconstructed blacksmith shop, meat and loom house, wheelwright shop, oven, hen house and other artifacts of life in the 1860s. It served as a

hospital after the battle. Scenic pathways lead to the "Field of Lost Shoes," where the mud was so thick that soldiers' mulehide shoes were often irretrievable. The celebrated Shenandoah River flows nearby.

NEW MARKET
BATTLEFIELD MILITARY MUSEUM

Collins Dr.   *(703) 740-8065*
Open 9 AM-5 PM daily, March 15-Dec.
and by appointment
Adults $5, Ages 7 to 14 $2.50

Modeled after Gen. Robert E. Lee's Arlington House, the museum stands where the battle of New Market began in the spring of 1864. The museum houses a fine collection of more than 2,500 artifacts focusing on the Civil War and other American wars from 1775 to the present. A film shown regularly gives patrons an overview of the Civil War in the museum's 54-seat theater.

Harrisonburg

WARREN-SIPE MUSEUM
Harrisonburg-Rockingham
Historical Society
301 S. Main St.   (703) 434-4762
Open 10 AM-4 PM, April-Oct. Call ahead since
hours fluctuate due to volunteers.

The highlight of this museum is its huge electrified relief map with accompanying audio cassette outlining Stonewall Jackson's Valley Campaign of 1862 for control of the Shenandoah Valley. There are many interesting artifacts, photos and paintings that help illustrate what happened in Rockingham County. Don't miss it for a blow-by-blow scenario of the great Jackson.

FORT HARRISON
Off Rt. 42 S., Dayton   (703) 879-2280
Open 1 PM-5 PM weekends May 31-Oct. 31

Guided tours are available for the home of Daniel Harrison, brother of Harrisonburg founder Thomas Harrison. The stone house was a natural fort used by local citizens when tribes of Native Americans terrorized the area during the 18th century and later, during the Civil War.

Lexington

STONEWALL JACKSON CEMETERY
300 Block, S. Main St.

Marked by Edward Valentine's bronze statue of the general, which faces South, Stonewall Jackson Memorial Cemetery contains the remains of the 39-year-old leader of battle, who died May 10, 1863, from wounds received at the Battle of Chancellorsville. The statue is prob-

ably the only time Jackson ever turned his back on his enemy. Some 400 other Confederate soldiers also are buried there. John Mercer Brooke, the inventor of the ironclad ship, the *Merrimac*, is at final rest here. So is William Washington (1834 to 1870), well-known artist of the Civil War period. He is especially known for his painting of the Battle of Lantane.

STONEWALL JACKSON HOUSE
8 E. Washington St.   (703) 463-2552
Open Mon.-Sat., 9 AM-5 PM, Sun. 1-5 PM;
until 6 PM June, July and Aug.
Closed holidays.
Adults $4, Ages 6 to 12 $2

Built in 1801, the only home Jackson ever owned is furnished with his personal possessions. A brief slide show and guided tours interpret Jackson's life as a citizen, soldier, VMI professor of natural philosophy, church leader and family man. Guided tours of the home and restored garden are given every half hour. You may also visit the museum shop, which specializes in books, prints and Victoriana.

WASHINGTON AND LEE UNIVERSITY
Main St.   (703) 463-8400

W&L's beautiful front campus includes Lee Chapel, the focal point of the campus. Robert E. Lee served as the school's president in the five years after the Civil War. The remains of Lee and most of his family are entombed here. Edward Valentine, who also did the statue of Stonewall Jackson in the cemetery, sculpted the famous pose of the recumbent Lee. In the basement is a museum emphasizing Lee. His office is preserved as he left it.

VIRGINIA MILITARY INSTITUTE AND MUSEUM

VMI Parade Grounds
N. Main St. (703) 464-7000
Open 9 AM-5 PM Mon.-Sat., 2-5 PM Sun.
Closed holidays.

Since its establishment in 1839, VMI has been known for the officers and men it contributed to the Confederacy. In the center of campus is a statue of Jackson standing in the wind. Nearby are cannons from the Rockbridge Artillery. The famous statue, "Virginia Mourning Her Dead," a monument to the VMI cadets who fell at New Market, stands on the Parade Ground. In Jackson Memorial Hall is a mural of the historic cadet charge during the battle. The VMI Museum includes Jackson's beloved war horse, Little Sorrel (yes, the real hide, stretched over a plastic form . . . considered state-of-the-art taxidermy in those times), among many other Civil War exhibits.

East of the Blue Ridge Region

Charlottesville

JACKSON STATUE

Fourth St.
Charles Keck created a bareheaded Jackson galloping forward on his favorite mount, Little Sorrel.

LEE STATUE

Park between First and Second Sts.
The work of sculptors H.M.

Shrady and Leo Lentelli, this is an equestrian statue of Lee.

UNIVERSITY CEMETERY

Alderman and McCormick Rds.
North of UVA Football Stadium

Even during the Civil War, Charlottesville, was known for its health-care facilities. The remains of 1,200 Confederate soldiers lie in University Cemetery, most the victims of disease. A bronze statue of a bareheaded Confederate soldier is at the center.

Lynchburg

APPOMATTOX COURT HOUSE NATIONAL HISTORICAL PARK

Appomattox, located 20 minutes east
of Lynchburg (804) 352-2621

This site is not to be missed! If you're going to Lynchburg to see Civil War history, just 20 minutes farther will put you at Appomattox, where our nation reunited on April 9, 1865. Living history exhibits are held during the summer, and the park is open daily except holidays November through February. In the park, you will find a totally restored village as it was during the day when generals Grant and Lee ended the war on a handshake. There are Meeks Store, Woodson Law Office, Clover Hill Tavern and Surrender Triangle, to name a few. You will find the Appomattox County Museum located in Court House Square. Every autumn, Appomattox is the site of its famous Railroad Festival.

DANIEL MONUMENT

*Intersection of Park Ave., Ninth
and Floyd Sts.*

John Warwick Daniel was a member of Gen. Jubal Early's staff who went on to become a distinguished orator and U.S. senator. This monument to the "Lame Lion of Lynchburg," so named for Daniel's wound at the Battle of the Wilderness, was created by Sir Moses Ezekiel, a famous postwar sculptor.

LYNCHBURG MUSEUM
AT OLD COURT HOUSE

*Fifth St.   (804) 847-1459
Open daily 1-4 PM. Closed holidays
Adults $1, Students 50¢*

The tragedy of the Civil War is one of many facts gleaned from the exhibits seen in this historical representation of Lynchburg's history. The city was at the center of Confederate supply lines, making it a frequent target. Housed in Lynchburg's Old Court House, built in 1855, it is one of Virginia's outstanding Greek Revival civil buildings.

PEST HOUSE MEDICAL MUSEUM
AND CONFEDERATE CEMETERY

*Old City Cemetery
Fourth and Taylor Sts.   (804) 847-1811
Open sunrise to sunset, self-guided tours
or by appointment*

Founded in 1806, Old City Cemetery contains graves of 2,701 Confederate soldiers from 14 states. The Pest House Medical Museum is a restored white frame building that was built in the 1840s and served as the medical office of Dr. John Jay Terrell. By 1861, Lynchburg was a major Civil War hospital center, and the Pest House was used as the quarantine hospital for Confederate soldiers. The dead were buried a few yards away. Dr. Terrell discovered the wretched conditions of the Pest House and assumed responsibility for the soldiers. The reforms enacted by Dr. Terrell reduced the Pest House mortality rate from 50 percent to 5 percent. On display are medical instruments from the 1860s, including a surgical amputation kit used on many soldiers. Dr. Terrell died at age 93, leaving a heroic medical legacy to Lynchburg.

SPRING HILL CEMETERY

Fort Ave.

Buried here is Gen. Jubal Early, who saved the city of Lynchburg from destruction during 1864 when he ran empty railroad cars up and down the tracks to convince the Yankees that Confederate reinforcements were arriving for a major battle. The Union forces retreated, and Lynchburg was saved from the destruction of Gen. David Hunter.

SOUTHERN SOLDIER STATUE

Monument Terrace, Center of Downtown

Honoring heroes of all wars, a statue of a Southern infantryman stands at the top of Monument Terrace. It was designed by James O. Scott and erected in 1898.

RIVERSIDE PARK

2240 Rivermont Ave.

Here you will find a fragment of the hull of the canalboat *Marshall*, which transported the body of Jackson from Lynchburg to Lexington for burial in 1863.

Bedford

BEDFORD CITY/COUNTY MUSEUM
201 E. Main St.   *(703) 586-4520*
Open 10 AM-5 PM Tues.-Sat.
Adults $1, Children 50¢

This interesting local collection includes a number of artifacts from the Civil War, including weapons, flags, photos and personal effects.

LONGWOOD CEMETERY
Bridge St.

A Civil War monument of valor marks the final resting place of soldiers who died at one of five Confederate hospitals located in and around Bedford. A tall obelisk stands over the single grave of 192 soldiers and a nurse.

New River Valley Region

Pulaski County

THE WILDERNESS ROAD MUSEUM
Newbern   *(703) 674-4835*
Open 10:30 AM-4:30 PM weekdays and Sat.; 1:30-4:30 PM Sun.

Operated by the New River Historical Society, there are three historic structures on this six-acre tract.

There are various Civil War displays, including a drum, since the area is close to Cloyd's Mountain, the major Civil War battle (May 9, 1864) site for Southwestern Virginia.

Alleghany Highlands Region

Bath County

WARM SPRINGS SPA
Warm Springs

In the Ladies Bath House of the spa is a chair made especially for the arthritically crippled Mrs. Robert E. Lee, who came often while her husband undertook his duties as a professor at Washington and Lee University after the Civil War.

Highland County

McDOWELL PRESBYTERIAN CHURCH
U.S. Hwy. 250 W.

McDowell is the site of the second major battle of Jackson's valley campaign; a roadside marker commemorates the event. Inside the village is McDowell Presbyterian Church, used as a hospital during and after the fighting.

Photo: Richmond Newspapers

Drivers on the Skyline Drive will frequently see deer along the roadside.

Inside
The Blue Ridge Parkway and Skyline Drive

It seems almost a miracle that in the late 20th century you can drive from practically one end of an East Coast state to another and see no fast-food restaurants, trucks or glaring billboards.

This miracle in Virginia is a scenic stretch of highway that begins in Front Royal as Skyline Drive, running the entire length of Shenandoah National Park and becoming the Blue Ridge Parkway at Waynesboro. From Waynesboro, the Blue Ridge Parkway meanders 469 miles all the way to the Great Smoky Mountains in North Carolina, offering magnificent views of valleys, forests and mountain ranges.

In 1931, construction of Skyline Drive began, spurred on by President Herbert Hoover who spent many a weekend at his fishing camp in the area. Reportedly, Hoover was riding his horse along the crest of the Blue Ridge Mountains one day in 1930 when he turned to a companion and said: "These mountains are made for a road, and everybody ought to have a chance to get the views from here. I think they're the greatest in the world, and I've been nearly everywhere in the world."

A year later, construction began. Mountaineer farmers provided the labor with help from the Civilian Conservation Corps, and finished the 105-mile-long Skyline Drive on August 29, 1939, during the administration of Franklin D. Roosevelt.

Today it costs $5 per vehicle to enter Skyline Drive at any point. That fee and the 35 mile-per-hour speed limit help keep the road free of commuters and speedsters.

Most visitors traveling Skyline Drive expect to see clear, sublime views of the Shenandoah Valley and distant mountain ranges. Unfortunately, this is not always possible. Visibility in Shenandoah National Park has dropped 50 percent over the past 40 years and is at its worst during summer months. In fact, visibility has declined by 80 percent during the summer over the past four decades.

At least 75 percent of the haze seen on hot summer days is pollution — much of it caused by coal-burning power plants in the Ohio Valley and from as far away as northern Indiana. And unless the trend is reversed, the problem is likely to worsen.

In 1993, a fifth of the days from May to October were classified by the National Park Service as having visibility of zero to 10 miles. Only 40 percent of the days had good visibility, and July had very few good days at all.

In the last six years, the Virginia Air Pollution Control Board has approved permits to build at least 23 coal-fired power plants in the state. Two other coal-fired power plants are planned for Pennsylvania and Maryland; these would be close enough to affect visibility.

Park officials say the Virginia Air Pollution Control Board has never denied a permit to a power plant. The proposed plants would emit many more tons of sulfur dioxide, further reducing visibility in the park and the Shenandoah Valley. If this makes you mad, then write to your congressional representative or the White House, Park officials suggest.

Meanwhile, if you're planning a trip to Shenandoah National Park and want to know what the visibility is like, you can call the dispatch office at (703) 999-3644 or (703) 999-2243. Everyday, park officials do a visibility check at 1 PM and post the results at 2 PM around the park.

Now, on to information about the beauty of Skyline Drive and the Parkway — of which there is still much to say. This chapter will tell you all about where you can eat and stay overnight without departing from either Skyline Drive or the Blue Ridge Parkway, because once you enter these pristine mountains you may not want to leave. A new tourist assistance group, Virginia Parkway Hosts, has opened a visitor's center at Milepost 195.5 at

Orchard Gap to help you find places to go that you'd need years to discover on your own. The center, covering the Rocky Mount District of the Blue Ridge Parkway, has brochures, maps and information. It also contains a display of 120 items from artwork and crafts to food and wine, the bounty of nearby shops. The area it covers is about 50 miles of road, ranging north from Floyd down to Fisher's Peak in the south. The center is open from 10 AM to 4 PM Sunday through Thursday and 10 AM to 6 PM Friday and Saturday. For information, call (703) 398-3311 or write Virginia Parkway Hosts at Route 2, Box 84, Fancy Gap, Virginia 24328.

Along the road you'll find lodges, cabins and campsites where you can spot deer and raccoons from your doorstep. You'll find plenty of way-stations with souvenirs, fudge and ice cream and restaurants offering Southern specialties like Virginia ham, blackberry cobbler and buckwheat pancakes.

Of course, there are hundreds of restaurants, motels, hotels and bed and breakfast inns a short drive from Skyline Drive and the Blue Ridge Parkway. But this chapter includes only places situated along the scenic highways. The facilities in Shenandoah National Park are operated by concessionaires for the National Park Service. By contrast, some of the restaurants and accommodations along the Blue Ridge Parkway are privately owned and operated. This is because the parkway's boundaries are quite narrow in places, bordering private

East of the Blue Ridge Profile:
Governor George F. Allen

He dips Copenhagen, drives a pickup truck, listens to bluegrass music and owns a log cabin in the Blue Ridge Mountains of Albemarle County.

Sounds like your basic Blue Ridge Everyman, right?

Well, not exactly. He is George F. Allen, the young, iconoclastic governor of Virginia.

To put it mildly, he's not your typical governor. And Virginia — a state synonymous with time-honored traditions — hasn't seen the likes of such a chief executive for a long, long time.

Governor George Allen

That's no knock against Allen. His meteoric rise through Old Dominion politics, capped by an unbelievable come-from-behind gubernatorial victory in 1993, has earned the 42-year-old Republican a healthy dose of respect. From the white-collar power corridors of Richmond and Northern Virginia to the mist-shrouded hollows of Cumberland Gap, the mere mention of the governor's name can launch an hour's worth of policy discussions. But no matter where they side, all Virginians agree that Allen's successful bid for the Governor's Mansion represents a sweeping mandate for political change.

Allen's professional accomplishments, which have also included terms in the Virginia House of Delegates and the U.S. House of Representatives, seem even more extraordinary when you consider his past. Allen grew up in Southern California, the son of the famous football coach of the Los Angeles Rams. When George Allen Sr. took over the helm of the Washington Redskins in 1971, George junior also came east, enrolling at the University of Virginia, where he went on to play football and earn bachelor's and law degrees. Of course, during this time, Coach Allen's winning ways in Washington made him as popular a figure in Virginia as any modern-day governor.

The younger Allen, however, soon forged his own strong identity as a Charlottesville lawyer, part-time farmer and avid outdoors enthusiast. Like many of his Blue Ridge brethren, Allen is affable but fiercely independent. For relaxation, when he's not with his wife Susan and children Tyler and Forrest, the governor is more than likely hunting deer or hiking in the thick woods surrounding his western Albemarle County log home.

While a transplant, a California transplant at that, Allen has put down deep roots in Virginia and the Blue Ridge Mountains. He says moving to these hills — and staying — "was one of the best decisions I've made in life."

property where people live or make a living.

Accommodations, restaurants and snack bars described below are organized from north to south. Along Skyline Drive and the Blue Ridge Parkway you will see num-

Photo: Roanoke Convention and Visitors Bureau.

Bikers ride through an underpass of the Blue Ridge Parkway near Roanoke.

bered mileposts, starting at 0.6 at the Front Royal Entrance Station. The listings in this chapter indicate the milepost where the facility is located. To make matters somewhat confusing, however, the numbering system starts again at zero when Skyline Drive becomes the Blue Ridge Parkway at Rockfish Gap. But, so long as you know to look out for it, it's not too confusing. By the way, you'll find a Howard Johnson's restaurant and a Holiday Inn where the two highways come together at Rockfish Gap.

For more information about accommodations, restaurants and attractions along and near to Skyline Drive and the Blue Ridge Parkway, write to: The Blue Ridge Parkway Association, P. O. Box 453, Asheville, North Carolina 28802.

The Parkway Association will send you a complete directory and a four-foot strip map of the parkway that you can't find at many of the information centers that are privately operated.

Accommodations Along Skyline Drive in the Shenandoah National Park

SKYLAND LODGE
Mile 41.7(800) 999-4714, (703) 999-2211
This is the first lodging facility you come to when driving south on Skyline Drive, after entering at Front Royal. Once a private resort, the lodge was built in 1894 by

George Freeman Pollock, one of the people instrumental in establishing the Shenandoah National Park.

It occupies the highest elevation along Skyline Drive, and most of its 186 guest rooms overlook the Shenandoah Valley. The facilities include the lodge, some quaint rustic cabins, a glass-walled dining room, tap room and entertainment most weekend nights in the summer. There are no phones in the guest rooms, but most have televisions. Service shelters have pay phones, ice and soda machines.

Skyland is a lively place for a family vacation. There are guided horseback trips for adults and pony rides for children. There's a playground with swings, bars, seesaws and plenty of grass and dirt. An amphitheater serves as an outdoor classroom where the National Park Service conducts educational programs. Naturalists lead hikes along numerous trails near the lodge in spring and summer and offer evening programs on such topics as bird watching, wildflowers and acid rain. You can also gaze through a telescope at the brilliant stars. Skyland also has a shop stocked with beautiful mountain crafts, photo supplies and a newsstand with daily papers and magazines.

Rates range from $70 per night for a single unit on weekdays to $130 per night for a suite with living room on weekends. Rustic cabins cost anywhere from $41 to $70 per night on weekdays and from $43 to $72 per night on weekends. The lodge is usually open from late March to the end of November.

The most popular month is October, that magical time of brilliant color in the Blue Ridge. Room rates are slightly higher this month. Reservations are often made a year in advance for these autumn nights. It's not a bad idea to make reservations well in advance for summer nights, too.

Skyland Lodge also has meeting rooms and audiovisual equipment to accommodate conferences.

BIG MEADOWS LODGE

Mile 51.3   (800) 999-4714,
                     (703) 999-2221

Nine miles south of Skyland Lodge you come to a clearing, the only large treeless area in the Shenandoah National Park. Big Meadows was probably created by fire, either accidentally by lightning or on purpose by Native Americans to encourage the growth of wild berries. The Park Service keeps the area clear to this day, and it's an excellent place for visitors to see a diversity of wildlife, including berries and wildflowers.

The best time to view the extraordinary vistas of Skyline Drive and the Blue Ridge Parkway is during the winter months, when the haze has receded and the crowds have thinned.

Insiders' Tips

The resort is situated on the meadow and includes a big lodge built in 1939 by mountaineers. The mountaineer builders used native chestnut for the lodge's paneling; this wood is nearly extinct today due to the chestnut blight in the early 1930s. The resort includes several rustic cabins and some smaller, more modern lodges with suites. The main lodge's 21 rooms offer spectacular views of the valley, while the cabins with fireplaces sit among the trees. The most modern units feature king-sized beds, a fireplace and sitting area with TV.

The main lodge has an outdoor deck where guests can lounge by day and star gaze by night. For a quarter you can look more closely at the stars through a telescope.

The main lodge's lofty central room is a relaxing, casual place to hang out day or night. Several board games are available, and there are lots of comfortable old sofas and chairs and two fireplaces. The lodge also has a dining room with huge windows and a tap room open from 4 to 11 PM. Big Meadows Lodge offers naturalist activities and a children's playground.

One plus of staying at Big Meadows is the Byrd Visitor Center within walking distance. Here you will find fascinating exhibits about the park's history and the folkways of its former inhabitants. There is also an exhibit about the growing threat of air pollution and decreasing visibility in and near the park. Dozens of books for children and adults are for sale, from wildflower coloring books to histories of the region.

The resort is open from early May through October. Rates range from $60 per night in the main lodge on weekdays to $102 per night for a suite with a living room on weekends. Rates are slightly higher in October.

LEWIS MOUNTAIN CABINS
Mile 57.5   (800) 999-4714,
                           (703) 999-2255

For an even more tranquil experience, you can spend the night in one of the cabins on Lewis Mountain. There are no room phones or televisions to disturb your peace and quiet. The cabins have furnished bedrooms and private baths, heat, towels and linens. Cooking is done in the connecting outdoor area where there is a fireplace, grill and picnic table.

The cabins are open from mid-May through October. Rates range from $50 per night on weekdays for a single room cabin to $77 per night on the weekends for a two-room cabin. Rates are slightly higher in October.

CABINS IN
SHENANDOAH NATIONAL PARK

The Potomac Appalachian Trail Club also operates six cabins in the back country of the Shenandoah National Park.

This can be a gritty or sublime experience, depending upon your perspective. You've got to hike in, chop your own firewood and draw your own water from a nearby spring. Each cabin has a table and fireplace, bunks for up to 12 people and a pit toilet. There's no electricity, so you must also bring your own source of light.

Photo: ARA Virginia Skyline Co.

White Oak Canyon waterfalls in Shenandoah National Park.

But at just a few dollars a night per person, it's no wonder these cabins are so popular. Friday and Saturday nights are usually taken by Trail Club members. Nonmembers may reserve a cabin no more than three weeks in advance.

The cabins are Range View, Corbin, Rock Spring, Pocosin, Doyles River and Jones Mountain (accessible from Criglersville but not from Skyline Drive).

The cabins are locked, so a key must be obtained from the PATC, by mail, prior to your visit. For reservations, call (202) 638-5306 or write PATC, 1718 N Street, N.W., Washington, D.C. 20036.

CAMPGROUNDS IN
SHENANDOAH NATIONAL PARK

Most years, Shenandoah National Park operates three campgrounds on a first-come, first-served basis: at Mathews Arm (Mile 22), Lewis Mountain (Mile 57.5) and Loft Mountain (Mile 80). However, because of budgetary constraints on the Park Service Mathews Arm was closed last year. At Big Meadows Campground, reservations are recommended from late May through October and can be made by calling (800) 365-2267 no more than eight weeks in advance.

All campgrounds have a 14-day limit, allow pets and do not accept credit cards. The campgrounds accommodate tent campers, recreational vehicles and tent trailers. Water and electric hookups are not available for RVs, however.

For further information, call Park Headquarters at (703) 999-2229 or refer to the Recreation chapter of this book.

PRIVATE CAMPGROUNDS

WALNUT HILLS CAMPGROUND
391 Walnut Hills Rd.
Staunton   (703) 337-3920

Steve and Karyn Albrecht are hosts at this multifaceted camping facility, located just minutes off of the Blue Ridge Parkway and Skyline Drive. This is a great central location for travellers with McCormick's Farm, American Museum of Frontier Culture, historic Staunton and the Statler Brothers Museum all within a 10-mile radius! Walnut Hills can accommodate travel trailers, motor homes and tents. There are large level RV sites with water, electric and sewer hook-ups. Free showers are available and there is a grocery store for campers' convenience. You can take your meals at your campsite or at the group picnic area. A private four-acre stocked lake and its meandering creek is great for fishing. Other amenities include a large swimming pool, children's playground, game room, volleyball area and horseshoe pit, making this the perfect place for families. Music and dancing every Saturday night in the pavillion and hay wagon rides across the grounds round out the fun. Afterwards, relax by the campfire or drift off to sleep under the stars.

Places to Eat Along Skyline Drive

ELKWALLOW WAYSIDE

Mile 24.1 (800) 999-4714

From May to late October, this stop along the drive offers groceries, camping supplies, wood, ice and gasoline. Sandwiches, burgers, fries and ice cream are sold for carry-out.

PANORAMA RESTAURANT

Mile 31.5 at U.S. Hwy. 211 (800) 999-4714

This restaurant is situated in a complex with two interesting gift shops and an information station for the Shenandoah National Park.

The restaurant serves breakfast, lunch and dinner seven days a week from April to mid-November. You'll find soups, salads, fried catfish, lasagna and Virginia ham for lunch or dinner. Breakfasts are also hearty.

SKYLAND LODGE

Mile 41.7 (800) 999-4714

The glass-walled dining room here serves breakfast, lunch and dinner every day from late March through November. For breakfast you can have Virginia-style eggs Benedict, biscuits and gravy or plainer offerings. Dinner selections include prime rib, trout with pecan butter and barbecued ribs. A tap room serves beer, wine and spirits from 3 to 11 PM daily.

BIG MEADOWS

Mile 51.2 (800) 999-4714

The menus at this restaurant sound equally yummy: for breakfast there's the Skyline Egg Bake — an open-faced omelet with ham, scallions, potatoes and apples and topped with herbed cream cheese. For lunch there are sandwiches, soups, quiche, steak and more. The dinner menu includes pizza, Shepherd's pie, catfish and fried chicken. The restaurant serves three meals a day May through October. There's also a pub open from 4 to 11 PM. The Big Meadows Wayside, which is closer to Milepost 51, has a coffee shop and counter service.

Accommodations Along the Blue Ridge Parkway

PEAKS OF OTTER LODGE

Mile 86 (703) 586-1081
In Virginia (800) 542-5927

Unlike the lodges in Shenandoah National Park, Peaks of Otter is open year round. The lodge is nestled in a valley in Bedford County, surrounded by gentle mountains and facing a beautiful

Thanks to the Skyline Drive-Blue Ridge Parkway wilderness corridor, you can drive from Front Royal, Virginia, to the Great Smoky Mountains National Park without ever hitting a stop light or spotting a McDonalds.

Insiders' Tips

lake. Each room has two double beds, a private bath and a private balcony or terrace that overlooks the lake. There are no televisions or telephones in the guest rooms.

The lodge's restaurant serves hearty Southern fare and has an unusually large salad bar. A gift shop features very fine Virginia crafts, stationery, books, jellies and more.

Camping is also available at Peaks of Otter. Park rangers give talks on nature topics during peak season, and hikers can enjoy miles of well-marked trails near the lodge.

Rates are available by calling the lodge.

ROCKY KNOB CABINS
Mile 174   *(703) 593-3503*

These cabins were built in the 1930s for the Civilian Conservation Corps workers who constructed much of the Blue Ridge Parkway. They have no fireplaces and no other source of heat, so it's understandable that they are only open from late May through Labor Day. The cabins have completely furnished electric kitchens but no bathrooms. However, within 50 feet of each cabin are private shower stalls and a washer and dryer. Rates are $41 for two and $5 for each extra person. Children 12 and younger stay for free.

DOE RUN LODGE RESORT AND CONFERENCE CENTER
Mile 189   *(703) 398-2212*

This family-oriented resort sits on beautiful Groundhog Mountain and offers tennis, swimming, saunas and golf. There are pool-side chalets, townhouse villas, tennis center chalets and single-family residences. Natural stone, wooden beams and floor-to-ceiling windows make this resort a tribute to the environment. All of the accommodations are large suites that have a fireplace, two bedrooms, two full baths and a living/dining area. Many have complete kitchens. The High Country restaurant offers seafood, steak and Southern specialties. Doe Run also offers a honeymoon package at its "Millpond Hideaway" and a range of golf packages.

Families can especially benefit from the good deals here. The $89 weekday rate can accommodate two parents and up to four children; remember, we're talking about two bedrooms, two baths and a living room. Weekend rates range from $109 per night for a chalet to $119 per night for a two-story villa. But for parties of more than 12 people, there is a $15 charge for each additional person. These rates are true May 1 to November 1. During the winter season rates are lower. The resort is open year round.

Places to Eat Along the Blue Ridge Parkway

WHETSTONE RIDGE
Mile .29   *(703) 377-6397*

Located near Montebello, this casual dining spot serves hearty fare from early May through October. It offers such breakfast specialties as buckwheat pancakes, and sandwiches and burgers are popular lunch items. The simple dinner menu lists fried chicken, hamburger steak, flounder or country ham. Don't miss the warm apple dumpling for dessert.

OTTER CREEK RESTAURANT
Mile 60.8   *(804) 299-5862*

Family favorites make up the menu, which is the same as Whetstone Ridge, listed above. The restaurant is located next to a year-round campground and small gift shop and is open mid-April through mid-November.

PEAKS OF OTTER LODGE
Mile 86   *(800) 542-5927*

Friendly service and hefty portions make this a popular dining spot among locals and visitors alike. Both the lodge and restaurant are open year round. Breakfasts are hearty, and lunches include big salads, burgers and ham steak with buttered apples. The dinner menu offers Southern dishes like barbecued ribs and salty country ham, as well as prime rib and tenderloin steak. The coffee shop sells picnic lunches to guests wanting to eat outdoors.

HIGH COUNTRY RESTAURANT
AT DOE RUN LODGE
Mile 189   *(703) 398-2212*

Open year round, this restaurant serves breakfast, lunch and dinner seven days a week. The menu is seasonal and offers such gourmet selections as she-crab soup, venison, fresh rainbow trout from Doe Run's stocked pond, lamb, duck, steaks, country ham and more. The restaurant also offers picnic lunches "to go."

MABRY MILL COFFEE SHOP
Mile 176   *(800) 542-5927*

Located at Mabry Mill, a famous pioneer attraction along the parkway, the coffee shop offers a single menu all day. Country ham, barbecue, and corn and buckwheat cakes are specialties. Mabry Mill is open from late April through October. Hours are 8 AM to 7 PM during summer months and from 8 AM to 6 PM during May, September and October.

ORCHARD GAP DELI
Between Mileposts 193 and 194
       (800) 542-5927

This private establishment about 50 yards off the parkway in Fancy Gap serves big deli sandwiches, homemade sourdough and raisin bread, Moravian sugar cake and imported and domestic beer and wine. It's open seven days a week. The deli also offers a full line of groceries, fresh produce and gasoline.

Photo: Wintergreen Resort

Anglers enjoy fly fishing in a multitude of streams in the Blue Ridge.

Inside
Recreation

Recreation: It's a concept we learn from our kindergarten days that never leaves us. The whole world loves to play. That's the major reason why visitors come to the Blue Ridge Mountains. Historically, visitors flocked to this region to partake of its pristine waters and gaze on its lofty mountains as a tonic for both body and soul. That's still true today.

The name "Blue Ridge" is synonymous with recreation to many visitors and residents. There are so many leisure activities here that the wise visitor will plan an itinerary well in advance. However, getting sidetracked is a regional pastime in the Blue Ridge, hazardous only to a tight vacation schedule, certainly not to the spirit or health.

People come to play, and many of them stay or return. There is a common bond among residents of the Blue Ridge. A smug feeling that only they have the privilege of living every day in a lush area that has brought Virginia international recognition in the realm of outdoor recreation. It's a reverence that they, as residents of the Blue Ridge, can live each day in an area that others travel hundreds, even thousands, of miles to visit.

The big draw, of course, is the scenery. Mother Nature blessed Virginia's Blue Ridge with lush greenery, bands of misty purple haze surrounding jutting mountain peaks and cool, rocky streams. She blessed us with waving grain in golden fields and meadows populated by languid dairy cattle meandering at dusk through wildflowers to quaint country barns.

The Blue Ridge's recreational wonders vary widely. One, Natural Bridge, has been called one of the seven wonders of the natural world. And the good news is that the offerings are plentiful, whether you're on a shoestring budget or have saved all year to play golf and stay at the Homestead or the Greenbrier, two of our nation's Mobil Four- and Five-Star resorts.

Many believe that the Blue Ridge's greatest strengths are its camping opportunities and national forest recreation. Two national parks, legends for their wilderness recreational opportunities, have been preserved here — the Jefferson and George Washington. The Shenandoah National Park, Virginia's mountain playground, is here. State parks, including Claytor, Douthat, Sky Meadows and Smith Mountain Lake, offer recreational opportunities galore, from horseback riding trails to cross-country skiing.

Two outdoor mega-attractions are here also. The fabled Bikecentennial Trail that stretches from Williamsburg, Virginia, to the West Coast, and the Appalachian Trail, stretching from Maine to Georgia. Natives in towns such as Troutville take for granted a continuing stream of blaze orange-clad backpackers and bikers enjoying country byways.

The forest preserves naturally offer some of the finest fishing and hunting in the Southeast. Hunters and anglers appreciate both primitive sporting opportunities as well as those that are well-planned, with guides who will do their best to ensure a trophy goes home with each participant. Licenses can be obtained at a variety of stores.

Visitors with picnic gear wishing to look, instead of stalk, will appreciate outdoor sports with a wide variety of wildlife that includes black bear, deer, wild turkeys and a great mixture of song birds.

A bounty of fresh mountain streams and rivers and the largest lake in Virginia, Smith Mountain, bordering Franklin, Bedford and Pittsylvania counties, are here. They offer the popular sports of boating, canoeing, swimming and tubing — a pastime especially enjoyed by college students who like to carry a drink and snack-stocked cooler on an extra inner tube as they float through the water on a hot, lazy afternoon.

A subterranean underground noted for its commercial caverns also offers plenty of action for spe-lunkers and rock climbing enthusiasts.

Or, if you prefer that your most rugged outing be on a sandtrap, there is a nationally known offering of public, semiprivate and resort courses. Many family attractions are within minutes of the 18th hole almost anywhere in the Blue Ridge.

As you're probably beginning to suspect, looking for recreation in the Blue Ridge Mountains is like trying to select a buffet meal from a mile-long Virginia groaning board. With so much to do and so many of our offerings in primitive wilderness areas, information in advance is a must.

There are far too many recreational opportunities to list completely in these pages. We highly recommend that you send for brochures and guides offered by the Commonwealth of Virginia and tourism and recreational associations. This is especially important to avoid disappointment for many camping reservations. Look for information contacts listed within the various recreation categories in the following pages. Then, go out there and have fun! You'll be in good company.

Hiking

It almost goes without saying that Virginia is a hiker's nirvana. There are so many hundreds of trails over such diverse terrain, from rhododendron-covered meadows to mountain peaks and rushing cascades, that it is not possible to describe them all in a book of this scope. Many good reference books have already been written on the subject of hiking in Virginia's mountains. Among them, we recommend: *Hiking the Old Dominion* by Allen de Hart (a Sierra Club Totebook), *Walking the Blue Ridge* by Leonard M. Adkins and *Backpacker Magazine's Guide to the Appalachian Trail* by Jim Chase.

But before you go rushing to your local library, let us introduce you to the major areas for hiking in the Blue Ridge region.

Hiking the Appalachian Trail

First you have the famous **Appalachian Trail**, which zigzags along the crest of the Appalachian Mountains from Georgia to Maine. More than 500 miles of the AT — about a quarter of its total distance — wind through Virginia. The portion of the trail that runs through the Shenandoah National Park, starting in Front Royal and ending at Rockfish Gap at I-64, is considered one of the most beautiful parts of the Appalachian Trail by veteran hikers.

The trail continues south through the George Washington and Jefferson national forests then winds through the Mount Rogers National Recreation Area, a spectacular stretch of land in Southwestern Virginia that includes the state's two highest peaks.

Hiking in the Shenandoah National Park Region

Let's move back to the Shenandoah National Park. Its 194,327 acres contain not just the AT but also 421 miles of other hiking paths. These range from rugged climbs up steep, rocky terrain to lazy nature trails with interpretive guideposts. Some of the best day hikes on the AT in the park include:

• **White Oak Run.** A cascade hike along this trail offers you a view to six falls ranging in height from 35 to 86 feet over a distance of about a mile. This trail can be reached from Skyland Lodge (Mile 41.7 on Skyline Drive) on the White Oak Canyon Trail.

• **The Ridge Trail.** This trail leads to Old Rag Mountain, the park's most celebrated peak. On this route, the AT travels through narrow rock-walled corridors that are the remains of the dikes through which lava flowed 700 million years ago. This is a challenging hike. But the rewards are great when you reach the top, catch your breath and stretch out on a boulder to gaze at the view over the vast, rolling mountains.

• **Big Meadows Trail.** Big Meadows, the only large treeless area in the park, is great for hiking. Depending upon the season, you'll find wildflowers, strawberries and blueberries along the path. This is also an excellent place to see a diversity of wildlife, since many animals depend on this grassy area for sustenance. Big Meadows is at the lodge that goes by the same name at Mile 51.3 on Skyline Drive.

Excellent hiking maps and trail guides to the Shenandoah National Park are available at both visitor centers, entrance stations and by mail from the Shenandoah Natural History Association, Route 4, Box 348, Luray, Virginia 22835. Or call (703) 999-3581.

The Shenandoah National Park and Skyline Drive end at Rockfish Gap just east of Waynesboro. Here is the gateway to the Blue Ridge Parkway, the 469-mile-long scenic route that travels all the way past the Cherokee Indian Reservation in North Carolina.

Hiking Along the Blue Ridge Parkway

Along the parkway are dozens of trails that are managed by the National Park Service. These are highly accessible, even for the laziest of walkers. But if you've got the energy, you can hike through tunnels of rhododendron that lead you to rushing waterfalls or out to soaring peaks covered with mountain laurel and spruce.

Hiking in these mountains also provides a glimpse of what life was like for its early settlers. It's not uncommon to stumble upon the crumbling rock foundation of a cabin no longer in existence or a stone wall that used to keep in the livestock. The ridges and valleys were inhabited when the Park Service began to obtain land for the Parkway decades ago.

Many trails lead to farms and communities that have been reconstructed by the Park Service. For instance, at the Mountain Farm Trail near Humpback Rocks (close to Charlottesville) you might see a

ranger posing as a grandma churning butter on the front porch of an old cabin and brother John plucking on a handmade dulcimer nearby.

Many interpretive programs are offered by the Park Service along the Blue Ridge Parkway trails. Rangers conduct guided walks during the heaviest tourist months, talking about everything from endangered plants to old-time farming methods.

Most Blue Ridge Parkway trails are so short and well-marked that you don't need a map to walk them. But it would be helpful to have a national forest map or two when driving along the Parkway, because they can lead you to additional trails, campsites and campgrounds. Also, if you are going to hike any of the other trails in either the George Washington or Jefferson national forest, you ought to have a map, since these trails are used less than the Parkway trails and are not maintained as well.

For a map of the George Washington National Forest (which covers the Blue Ridge Parkway from Mile 0 to 63.7) write to: Forest Supervisor, G.W. National Forest, P.O. Box 233, Harrisonburg, Virginia 22801. For a map of the Jefferson National Forest, Glenwood Ranger District Map (which covers the Parkway from Mile 63.9 to 104.3) write to: U.S. Forest Service, Jefferson National Forest, 3517 Brandon Avenue, Roanoke, Virginia 24108.

Some of the best day hikes along the Blue Ridge Parkway include:

• **Mountain Farm Trail.** This quarter-mile trail at Mile 5.9 along the Parkway is an easy, self-guiding route that begins at the Humpback Rocks Visitor Center, not too far from Charlottesville. It travels along beside log cabins, chicken houses and a mountaineer's garden and presents a good introduction to the everyday life of the Blue Ridge's former inhabitants.

• **Humpback Rocks Trail.** This is a steep and rocky section of the Appalachian Trail that you can easily hike to from the Mountain Farm trail described above. Then it is a strenuous hike for nearly four miles to the summit of Humpback Mountain, from which you can see Rockfish Gap and the Shenandoah National Park to the north, the Shenandoah Valley to the west and the Rockfish River Valley to the east. In late spring, mountain laurel and azaleas are blooming all along the path and make for a colorful, fragrant hike.

• **Crabtree Falls Trail.** This three-mile hike in Nelson County passes along what are the highest cascading falls in Virginia. Its trailhead is a parking lot on Virginia Route 56, a few miles east of Montebello. Five major cascades tumble down the mountain, and beautiful, well-worn trails make is possible to enjoy it all without getting dangerously close to the falls. Hikers are advised to stay on the trails and off the slippery rocks — too many careless individuals have met their maker or, at least, suffered injuries from a fall.

• **Rock Castle Gorge Trail.** This 10-mile, round-trip hike in northern Patrick County is one you shouldn't miss. You'll see high open meadows, panoramic views, tumbling cascades and historical sites on the way to the summit of Rocky Knob, at 3,572 feet. Until the 1920s, a mountain community thrived in this rugged area, where the rushing waters of Rock Castle Creek fueled sawmills and grist mills. You'll see many reminders of these days along the trails. This hike is merely one of hundreds in the 4,500-acre Rocky Knob Recreation Area, which has a Park Service visitor center, campground, rustic cabins for rent and picnic grounds.

• **Mount Rogers National Recreation Area.** Farther west of the Blue Ridge Parkway lies this enormous stretch of land 55 miles long and nearly 10 miles wide. This spectacular area, part of the Jefferson National Forest, is often said to resemble the Swiss Alps because of its high plateau and wide, open Alpine-like meadows.

The area has 300 miles of trails, many of which climb to the crest zone — where three mountains reach to nearly 6,000 feet. At Mount Rogers, you will find dazzling displays of purple rhododendron, dense red spruce and Fraser fir, wild horses and vast, panoramic views. For more information, contact the area's headquarters at Route 1, Box 303, Marion, Virginia 24354, (703) 783-5196.

• **The Virginia Creeper Trail.** This is the former railroad grade between Damascus at the southern-most tip of the Mount Rogers area and Abingdon. The entire trail is 34 miles long, but there are many starting and stopping points. This is a wonderful, easy trail — great for enjoying fall foliage without working up too much of a sweat.

• **Little Stoney Creek Trail.** In Giles County, west of Blacksburg, there are wonderful hikes along the Appalachian Trail and other recreation areas. One excellent two-mile day hike is alongside Little Stoney Creek, which takes you to the 60-foot Cascades waterfall. The Civilian Conservation Corps constructed this beautiful trail in the 1930s. It is well-maintained, with benches along the creek and pretty wooden bridges. In the summer, the pathway is lush and heavily shaded — the perfect place to cool off. You can also take a dip in the clear mountain pool at the base of the falls. To get there, go to Pembroke then take the road marked Cascades Recreation Area just east of the Dairy Queen on Route 460.

Hiking in the Blue Ridge Region's State Parks and Recreation Areas

There are also countless possibilities for hiking in the Blue Ridge region's state parks and in its city and county recreation areas. Some of our favorites include the following:

• **Sky Meadows Trails.** Just outside of Paris, in Fauquier County, rolls Sky Meadows State Park, (703) 592-3556, the public's access to Hunt Country living. Once a working Piedmont plantation, Sky Meadows' 1,100 acres along the eastern slope of the Blue Ridge entice weekend warriors with its maze of hiking trails, including a stretch of the Appalachian Trail.

• **Wildlife Management Area Trails.** Between Lexington and Staunton, the state operates a 34,000-acre wildlife management area. Here, alluring trails offer solitude and scenic views of the Maury River, the gorge at Goshen Pass and all manner of flora and fauna.

• **Laurel Run Trail.** This is a moderately easy trail in this area. It starts near the wayside picnic area at Goshen Pass on Virginia Route 39 and travels two miles uphill along a tumbling creek that pours into the Maury River. Rosebay rhododendron, oaks, maples and hemlock abound.

• **Old Chessie Trail.** Nearby, this seven-mile trail links historic Lexington with Buena Vista. This is an easy, flat pathway that provides glimpses of the Maury River and its gorgeous rocky banks. Wildflowers

Photo: Nathan Beck

Riders with Mountain Outfitters of Buena Vista cross their horses over Irish Creek in the Blue Ridge Mountains.

are abundant in the spring. It follows the old railroad grade of the Chesapeake and Ohio and is owned and maintained by the Virginia Military Institute Foundation. In Lexington, you can get to the trail from North Main Street at VMI by taking a side street down to Woods Creek and a parking area on VMI Island. Follow trail signs, cross a pedestrian bridge over the Maury River, and pass under the U.S. Highway 11 bridge.

• **Buck Lick Trail.** Don't miss this easy hike in Douthat State Park, which spans Bath and Alleghany counties with 4,493 acres of scenic high ridges and more miles of hiking trails than almost any other state park. Buck Lick Trail was constructed by the Civilian Conservation Corps in the '30s and has 17 interpretive signs about geological features, trees, wild animals, lichens,

forest succession and more. The park's trails are color-coded and generally in good condition. A hiking map from the visitor center is recommended for long hikes.

• **Sounding Knob Trail.** In Highland County, best known for its annual Maple Festival, there are also endless possibilities for hiking in a 13,978-acre wilderness area operated by the state. One option is a strenuous five-mile hike up an old fire road to Sounding Knob, at 4,400-feet, the best-known landmark in the county. The mountain top includes a grazed open area, and the views are splendid. The trail begins at the junction of Route 615 and the Fire Trail Road, established by the Civilian Conservation Corps.

• **Ivy Creek Natural Area.** There are also nature trails in municipal parks throughout the region. In

Charlottesville, for instance, the 215-acre Ivy Creek Natural Area is an unspoiled stretch of forest, streams and fields traversed only by footpaths. A network of six miles of trails includes self-guided ones. This area is on Hydraulic Road, two miles north of the city.

• **Ash Lawn Historical Trail.** Several miles away at Ash Lawn, a 535-acre estate that was once home to President James Monroe, a historical trail leads you through pastures and woods to the top of Carter's Mountain. Ecology markers are posted along the three-mile-long trail, which begins at the museum shop. Ash Lawn is just off I-64, 2½ miles beyond Thomas Jefferson's Monticello (see the Arts and Culture chapter for more information about Ash Lawn and other historical sites).

Boating

Canoe Outfitters

You can find many reputable canoe outfitters in the Blue Ridge region. Several are located along the South Fork of the Shenandoah River, which meanders between the Massanutten and Blue Ridge mountain ranges. These outfitters also rent rubber rafts and inner tubes, if you prefer the kind of trip that allows you to turn off your brain and relax.

Other outfitters are located near the James River, the longest and largest river in Virginia. Only Lexington's James River Basin Ca-

noe Livery leads canoe trips down both the Maury and the James rivers.

Farther southwest, in Giles County, the New River Canoe Livery in Pembroke runs trips down the magnificent New River, which many claim is the second oldest river on earth.

Most canoe outfitters will only allow you to travel down familiar waters, unless you're an expert and willing to assume the risks (financial and otherwise) of canoeing a less-traveled tributary. Generally speaking, a single fee includes the canoe rental, paddles, life jackets, maps, shuttle service and an orientation. The shortest trips cost anywhere from $22 to $28 per canoe, while longer all-day trips run anywhere from $40 to $50. Tubing costs much less.

Here are some good places to rent boats and equipment in the Blue Ridge region, from north to south:

FRONT ROYAL CANOE CO.
Front Royal   (703) 635-5440
March 15-Nov. 15

Located three miles south of the entrance to Skyline Drive, this outfit rents canoes, tubes and flatbottom boats. It offers trips on the Shenandoah River that range from leisure fishing to whitewater adventures. Multiple-day canoe trips can also be arranged. Reservations are recommended. This company will also provide a shuttle service for people with private canoes.

DOWNRIVER CANOE COMPANY

Bentonville   *(703) 635-5526*
April 1-Oct. 31

This company leads canoe trips along the South Fork of the Shenandoah River for novices and moderately experienced canoeists. Detailed maps describing the river course and the best way to negotiate it are provided. The maps also point out the best camping areas, picnic sites, swimming holes and fishing spots.

Multiple-day trips can also be arranged. Reservations are recommended, but last-minute canoe trips are often possible. This company also offers a shuttle service for people with their own canoes.

RIVER RENTAL & CAMPSTORE

Bentonville   *(703) 635-5050*
March 15-Nov. 1; Also open weekends in Nov. by reservation

"Bring us your weekend . . . and we'll do the rest!" is this business's motto. It offers canoe and tube trips down the Shenandoah River, and organizes fishing, camping, hiking and biking trips. The outfit will custom-design a weekend vacation for the entire family and offers packages with the nearby Skyline Bend Farm, Warren County's oldest licensed bed and breakfast inn.

Reservations are strongly recommended for weekends and holidays.

The business also rents kayaks, 10-speed bicycles, fishing equipment and camping gear and sells fishing tackle and all kinds of supplies.

SHENANDOAH RIVER OUTFITTERS INC.

Luray   *(703) 743-4159*
Open all year

This outfit offers canoe and tube rentals and canoe sales, and it organizes overnight trips complete with tents, sleeping bags and even music. It is situated on the Shenandoah River between the Massanutten Mountain Trails and the Appalachian Trail in the George Washington National Forest. All-you-can-eat steak dinners can even be arranged in advance. Reservations are recommended.

JAMES RIVER RUNNERS INC.

Scottsville   *(804) 286-2338*
Open March-Oct.

This business 35 minutes south of Charlottesville offers canoe and rafting trips down the James River. Families are its specialty. Owners Christie and Jeff Schmick will arrange a variety of outings suitable for families (children older than six), as well as challenging whitewater runs.

They also arrange day and overnight trips for larger groups — even conventions. A special two-day package features canoeing for nine miles the first day, camping overnight by the river and tubing the next day.

Tubing trips for up to 600 people can be arranged, and groups of 25 or more get a discount. Reservations are recommended for small parties and obviously necessary for small groups.

James River Reeling and Rafting

Scottsville   *(804) 286-4FUN*
March 1-Oct. 31

This business offers canoe, rafting and tubing trips for people at all levels of experience. It specializes in customizing overnight trips to suit the customer's fancy. "Describe what you want and let us design a trip for you," reads its brochure. Trips can be organized for convention groups, which get a 10 percent discount when five or more boats are rented. The company also rents fishing equipment.

It is located at the corner of Main and Ferry streets in downtown Scottsville at the James River Trading Post. Here you will find fishing and camping supplies and anything else you may have left behind.

James River Basin Canoe Livery Ltd.

Lexington   *(703) 261-7334*
Open year round, depending upon river conditions

This outfit arranges day and overnight trips down both the Maury and James rivers. You can take an adventurous run down Balcony Falls, the mighty rapids where the James breaks through the Blue Ridge Mountains. Or you can spend a couple of hours paddling down a slow stretch of the breathtakingly beautiful Maury.

Owner Glenn Rose gives a solid orientation with instructions on safety and basic canoeing strokes. A video program also familiarizes canoeists with the stretch of river about to be boated.

New River Canoe Livery

Pembroke   *(703) 626-7189*
April-Oct.

Owner Dave Vicenzi rents canoes and tubes for trips along the vast New River in Giles County. Vicenzi takes a laid-back approach to orienting his customers to the river: "They give me five minutes to tell 'em what to do." The easiest trip is a seven-mile run from Eggleston to Pembroke. The most popular trip is an 11-mile run from Pembroke to Pearisburg, with a number of Class II (intermediate) whitewater drops.

In the spring when the water is high Vicenzi allows customers to canoe down Walker and Wolf creeks, both tributaries of the New River. Multiple-day trips can also be arranged, but customers must supply their own camping gear.

Other Boating Possibilities in the Blue Ridge

Let's not forget boating on Virginia's beautiful lakes. There are three state parks in the heart of the mountains where boats can be rented.

At Douthat State Park near Clifton Forge, you can rent rowboats and paddleboats on a 50-acre lake. You can also rent rowboats and paddle boats on a 108-acre lake at Hungry Mother State Park, in the far reaches of Southwestern Virginia, near Marion. In Pulaski County, about an hour south of Roanoke, the 4,500-acre Claytor Lake in Pulaski County also rents rowboats.

Generally, boats are available on weekends beginning in mid-May and daily from Memorial Day through Labor Day weekend. Smith Mountain Lake's 500 miles of winding shoreline and 20,600 acres of sparkling waters also offer countless possibilities for boating. There are about a dozen places where various types of boats can be rented, from yachts and pontoons to motor boats, sailboats and house boats. For information and brochures, contact the Smith Mountain Lake Welcome Center at (703) 721-1203.

Swimming

Swimmers who enjoy the outdoors can count on the Blue Ridge of Virginia's cool mountain streams, lakes and even waterfalls for the most refreshing dip they'll ever take.

Municipal pools, such as the Town of Blacksburg's, perched atop a mountain vista, or the City of Radford's, beside the ancient New River, are a panacea to the eye and spirit by virtue of their environmentally beautiful settings.

Some of the best swimming can be found in the area's state parks and national forests. Picture yourself swimming at the bottom of a sparkling waterfall after a two-mile hike at the Cascades in Pembroke in Giles County. Or how about lying on Claytor Lake's white sand beach in Pulaski County while horseback riders amble by! For the strong in spirit, there's icy cold Cave Mountain Lake near Glasgow. All have sparse, but clean and accommodating, changing and shower facilities.

Primitive swimming fans will find the 10-mile venture across the West Virginia border near Covington worthwhile to delight in the coldest water in the Blue Ridge at Blue Bend.

Families with small children will be interested in an abundance of private campgrounds with lovely swimming areas overseen by lifeguards. One of the best-known is Shenandoah Acres Resort at Stuart's Draft, near the Waynesboro intersection of Skyline Drive and the Blue Ridge Parkway.

Following is an Insiders' list of swimming lovers' sites definitely worth the drive from anywhere.

Municipal Pools

CITY OF WAYNESBORO
(703) 949-7665

War Memorial Pool is located in the center of lovely Ridgeview Park. Surrounded by a playground, tennis courts, a baseball diamond and an open field, the managers of this Olympic-size pool pride themselves

---

If you love to photograph white-tailed deer in their natural habitat, you don't have to stray too far off the beaten path. Loudoun County, in suburban Washington, D.C., has the highest density of deer in the state.

Insiders' Tips

on its cleanliness and pleasing view. Open from Memorial Day to Labor Day, the pool's general admission hours are from noon to 6 PM Monday through Saturday and 1 to 6 PM on Sunday. Family Swim, when parents only must pay, is offered from 10 AM to noon Monday through Saturday. Fees are $1 for ages 15 and younger and $2 for ages 16 and older.

CITY OF STAUNTON
(703) 886-7946

Gypsy Hill Park Pool is a fairly new L-shaped pool, having opened several years ago. The pool is Olympic-size and has a wading pool. The facility opens for the season around Memorial Day and closes Labor Day. Open from 11 AM to 6 PM Monday through Saturday and from 1 to 6 PM on Sunday. The fee is $3 for all day, all ages.

CITY OF CHARLOTTESVILLE

Washington Park Pool, 14th St. and
Preston Ave.   *(804) 977-2607*
Onesty Pool, Meade Ave.
                            (804) 295-7532
Crow Pool, Rosehill Dr.
                            (804) 977-1362
Smith Pool, Cherry Ave.
                            (804) 977-1960
McIntire Pool, 250 Bypass
                            (804) 295-9072
Forest Hills Pool,
Forest Hills Ave.   *(804) 296-1444*

The city of Charlottesville boasts six municipal pools: two outdoor — Washington Park Pool and Onesty Pool; two indoor — Crow and Smith pools; and two wading pools — McIntire and Forest Hills. The outdoor and indoor pools are all 75 feet long and the facilities feature showers, hair dryers and lockers. The indoor pools are heated. The wading pools are small and shallow, designed for children 12 and younger. The outdoor and wading pools are open from Memorial Day to Labor Day. The hours for the outdoor pools are noon to 6 PM Monday through Friday and noon to 5 PM Saturday and Sunday. The wading pools are open 10:30 AM to 4:30 PM Monday through Friday and noon to 5 PM Saturday and Sunday. The indoor pools are open year round, but hours are widely varied, so call ahead of time. Admission for nonresidents for the outdoor and indoor facilities is $1.25 for children and $2.75 for adults. There is no charge for the wading pools.

CITY OF LYNCHBURG
(804) 528-9794

Two play areas and a place for picnics surround this pool, located in Miller Park. The Olympic-size pool features a high dive and a kiddie area. Lessons are offered each morning. Miller Park Pool is open from Memorial Day through Labor Day. On Monday, Wednesday, Friday and Saturday, the hours are noon to 6 PM; Tuesday and Thursday, noon to 5:30 PM and 6:30 to 9 PM; Sunday from 1 to 7 PM. Admission is $1.50 for ages 2 and older. The charge for the evening swims is $1. Pass books of 10 tickets can be purchased for $10. These can be used for afternoon or evening swim sessions.

TOWN OF BLACKSBURG
(703) 961-1103

Mountain scenery lovers will gasp at the view from this mountain-top panorama. You'll bathe in mountain beauty as you swim.

The facility is open June through August 15, 1 to 5:30 PM, seven days a week. The fee is 75¢ for ages 3 to 14 and $1 for ages 15 and up. The pool is located on Graves Avenue, off South Main Street, past Blacksburg Middle School. And better still, Blacksburg's new 25-yard indoor swimming facility sports six lanes, sauna, spa and diving area. It is located on Patrick Henry Drive across from Blacksburg High.

CITY OF RADFORD
(703) 731-3633

Radford's city pool is an Olympic-size swimming pool located in Bisset Park, just off Norwood Street in Radford, bordering nearly a mile of the scenic New River. Its setting in a 58-acre municipal park makes this pool unique. It is surrounded by six lighted tennis courts, lighted picnic shelters, playgrounds, a gazebo and fitness station. The facility is open May 23 through Labor Day. Hours are Monday through Thursday 1 to 5 PM and 7 to 8:30 PM; Friday, 1 to 5 PM; and weekends 1 to 8:30 PM. Admission is 50¢ for ages 7 to 15 and 75¢ for ages 16 and older. Children younger than 6 are admitted free with a paying adult.

Photo: Abingdon Convention and Visitors Bureau

The Virginia Creeper Trail, which begins in Abingdon, has been praised as one of the most beautiful trails in the East.

State Parks

CASCADES
(703) 921-5000
Directions: From Pembroke in Giles County, return to U.S. Hwy. 460, head north and west about a mile, then turn right onto Va. Rt. 623 to Cascades State Park.

Cascades State Park features a three-mile hike to a 60-foot waterfall. Picture yourself hiking and then jumping into a cool, placid pool of water right under a thundering waterfall. This is one of the most photogenic sites in the New River Valley. Warning: Don't try jumping into the water from the cliffs of the waterfall. There have been at least three deaths in recent memory from careless youths who did! This swimming area is not recommended for small children. Call the Giles County Chamber of Commerce for more information (above) or write: P.O. Box 666, Pearisburg, Virginia 24134.

CLAYTOR LAKE
Off I-81 at Exit 33 *(703) 674-5492*
This beautiful park area is located near Dublin in Pulaski County. You'll think you're on an ocean beach, with the ample white sand surrounded by a full-service boat marina beside the sparkling water. Camping, horseback riding rentals and sports fishing are also popular at this 4,500-acre lake. Its historic Howe House (c. 1879) features exhibits about the life of early settlers in the region. June kicks off with a family fishing tournament and Labor Day weekend brings the annual Appalachian Arts and Crafts Festival.

SMITH MOUNTAIN LAKE
(703) 297-4062
Directions: From U.S. Hwy. 460, take Va. Rt. 43 to Rt. 626 S.

This lakefront beach nestled in the tall blue mountains of Bedford County offers a never-ending show of gliding sailboats in the distance. It's a paradise for water enthusiasts and has a visitor center with especially good nature programs for the whole family during the summer. Special events include the Ruritans Bass Fishing Tournament in March, an Arts in the Park in June and Ruritan Supper and Festival in September.

National Forests

GEORGE WASHINGTON NATIONAL FOREST
Sherando Lake *(703) 433-2491*
Off I-64, near Waynesboro, Sherando Lake offers a pristine beach within a natural paradise of camping, boating and fishing. Daily swimming fee is $4 per vehicle or $1 per person.

JEFFERSON NATIONAL FOREST
Cave Mountain Lake *(703) 291-2189*
Directions: Off of I-81, take Natural Bridge Exit 49 or 50 and turn onto Va. Rt. 130 at Natural Bridge. Follow this road 3.2 miles, then turn onto paved Va. Rt. 759, which you'll follow for 3.2 miles and then turn right onto paved Va. Rt. 781. Drive 1.6 miles to the recreation area's paved entrance road.

The long trip to isolation is worth it. Cave Mountain Lake Campground is nearby with its unusual picnic tables and sites often surrounded by stone, set amidst large pines and hardwoods. There is a large open field with plenty of sunshine and the lake is cool and re-freshing. It's a real getaway.

MONONGAHELA NATIONAL FOREST (WEST VIRGINIA)

Blue Bend Recreation Area
(304) 536-1440
Directions: From I-64, take the White Sulphur Springs, W.Va., Exit to Rt. 92; go north 10 miles to Alvon. Turn left at the Blue Bend sign and proceed several miles to the Blue Bend Recreation Area.

A true "swimming hole," Blue Bend is known for its chilling mountain stream waters surrounded by huge, flat rocks for sunbathers. Built by the CCC camp workers during the Great Depression, the rock craftsmanship makes this place unusual. There is no other more invigorating feeling in the world than baptism by Blue Bend's waters. Swimming is within view of an authentic swinging foot bridge. Primitive camping and picnic tables are nearby in this deeply wooded, out-of-the way area populated mostly by locals. Don't miss this place, but be prepared for a chilly experience. Blue Bend is said to earn its name from the color of the swimmers' lips when they emerge!

Private Swimming Areas

SHENANDOAH ACRES RESORT
(703) 337-1911
Directions: From Skyline Drive and Blue Ridge Parkway, follow the signs from the Waynesboro Exit.

Often called "America's Finest Inland Beach," this site is reminiscent of the 1930s, with its board-walk-enclosed pavilion. Swimming is superb with a sand-bottomed lake of pure, soft, water — 500,000 gallons a day.

Children are giggly and ecstatic playing with the bubbling water as it emerges from pipes. There are slides, merry-go-rounds, a drop cable and even water volleyball. Life guards are on duty at all times, May through September. The recreational area includes camping, cottages, picnic tables and fireplaces. This is a wonderful family retreat. For more information, write: Shenandoah Acres Resort, P.O. Box 300, Stuarts Draft, Virginia 24477.

Fishing

Naturalist Henry David Thoreau of Walden Pond fame once commented, "In the night, I dream of trout-fishing." In Virginia's Blue Ridge, anglers see their dreams become reality in clear, cold mountain streams, rivers and lakes. Visitors can rest easy at night knowing that, at any given moment, millions of fish are surging upstream or lying tantalizingly in wait in stone river recesses.

An aggressive conservation effort by the state is part of the fishing charm of the Blue Ridge. For example, the mountain streams found in Shenandoah National Park are one of the last completely protected strongholds of the native Eastern brook trout. Savvy Virginia tourism experts report that since Robert Redford's naturalistic film on fly fishing, based on the book, *A River Runs Through It*, hit the screens, the numbers of fly fishing anglers in Virginia were thicker than the black flies they're trying to imitate. But don't worry. The out-of-the-way waters far outnumber those that aren't.

Outstanding waters by species include: brown trout — Lake Moomaw, Mossy Creek and Smith River; large-mouth bass — James River; small-mouth bass — James River, Smith Mountain Lake, Claytor Lake and Lake Philpott; striped bass — Claytor Lake and Smith Mountain Lake; and walleye — Smith Mountain Lake, Philpott Lake, Claytor Lake, Carvins Cove and the Roanoke River.

And now for bragging rights! To name a few records: small-mouth bass — 7 lbs., 7 oz, New River; Roanoke bass — 2 lbs., 6 oz., Smith Mountain Lake; striped bass — 44 lbs., 14 oz., Smith Mountain Lake; walleye — 12 lbs., 15 oz., south fork of Holston River; and northern pike — 27 lbs., 12 oz., Hungry Mother State Park. By the time you read this, some of these probably already will be broken.

Figures for fish citations are equally impressive. For 1993, the James River set the record with 584 citations of 17 species, followed by Smith Mountain Lake with 259 citations of 12 species; the New River with 93 of 10; Lake Moomaw with 108 of 11; Claytor Lake with 97 of 14; and Philpott Reservoir with 27 of 6 species.

The primary objective of this chapter is to give directions to some of the Blue Ridge's classic streams, rivers and lakes — the ones where anglers aren't falling over each other. After you get to your spot, you may want to rough it on your own. Or, you can hire your own guide.

Otherwise, there are literally hundreds of fishing places recommended by the Virginia Department of Game and Inland Fisheries. You can find out about real gem daytrips. An especially fun one for lovers of both fishing and horseback riding is the package offered by Virginia Mountain Outfitters in Buena Vista, near Lexington. Trips range from one day to five and include a clinic. Call Deborah Sensabaugh at (703) 261-1910 at Outfitters to find out more.

Farther north, at the charming tin-roofed town of Edinburg, Murray's Fly Shop is the place to find out where you can fish in the Shenandoah Valley for the really big ones. Harry Murray is the author of several books, including *Trout Fishing in the Shenandoah National Park*, and promises to help you catch Valley fish. Murray offers numerous clinics and can be reached at (703) 984-4212 for a complete list.

Wintergreen Resort in Wintergreen offers Fly Fisher's Symposiums. Call Chuck Furimsky at (800) 325-2200 for more information on fishing and lodging at a first-class resort that also offers great golfing and skiing. Also for fly fishing supreme, go westward in Bath County to Meadow Lane Lodge, site of a former Orvis Fishing School on the Jackson River. Call (703) 839-5959.

For details and the widest array of locations, the Department of Game and Inland Fisheries' *Virginia Fishing Guide* is a must. Traditionally, topographic maps published by the U.S. Geological Survey have been the most useful sources of information for anglers. These maps can tell you whether streams flow through open or forested land, how steep the land is and where tributaries enter. Directions on how to get both guides are listed at the end of this fishing section.

So, now you're excited about all the fishing possibilities, we hope. But, don't forget your license. It can be obtained from county circuit court clerks, city corporation court clerks and authorized agents (usually small retail stores in fishing country). License requirements and fees for both residents and nonresidents follow.

RESIDENT

County or city resident to fish in county or city of residence — $5.50

State resident to fish only — $12.50

Resident to fish statewide for five consecutive days in private waters or public waters not stocked with trout — $5.50

State and county resident to trout fish in designated waters stocked with trout, in addition to regular fishing license — $6.50

Age 65 and older state resident license to fish — $1.50

Virginia resident special lifetime to fish — $250

NONRESIDENT

To fish only — $30.50

To fish for five consecutive days statewide in private waters or public waters not stocked with trout — $6.50

To fish in designated waters stocked with trout in addition to regular fishing license — $30.50

Virginia nonresident special lifetime to fish — $500

Licenses can be obtained from some county circuit court clerks, city corporation court clerks and a variety of other authorized agents. The first Saturday and Sunday in June have been designated as Free Fishing Days in Virginia. No fishing license of any kind will be required for rod and reel fishing ex-

Photo: Wintergreen Resort

An afternoon ride through the mountains.

cept in designated stocked trout waters. A detailed booklet describing licensing requirements, game fish size and catch limits, special regulations (specific to certain areas) and other regulations can be obtained from the Virginia Department of Game and Inland Fisheries (see address at the end of this section).

Regardless of whether you're testing the waters of the Blue Ridge as an experienced angler or a novice, it doesn't hurt to remember safety at all times, especially cold weather hazards. Although getting away from it all is most of the fun, don't forget to let somebody know where you are. Despite the best of precautions, you'll probably fall in at some point. In hot weather, it's an inconvenience. In cold weather, which is most of the year, it can be fatal. Many anglers do not realize that hypothermia can strike when the temperature is in the 40s. Prevention is always best, including wearing waders with rough soles in our streams and life preservers in our rivers and lakes. And don't forget snakes (timber rattlers and copperheads are the two poisonous species) and ticks, the latter of which are "fishing" for you!

Listed below are some favorite fishing areas of the Blue Ridge. Source material for complete listings is at the end of this fishing section.

RIVIANNA RESERVOIR

Located just outside Charlottesville, this is often called the best bet for fishing in the area surrounding this historic city. It supports good populations of bass, crappie, bream and channel cats, with occasional walleye and muskie. There is a public boat ramp near the filtration plant of the Charlottesville water supply reservoir, which may be reached from U.S. Highway 29 north of Charlottesville by taking routes 631 (Rio Road) or 743 to routes 659 or 676. The ramp is at the end of Route 659.

LAKE MOOMAW
(703) 962 -2214

This flood control reservoir was completed in 1981 with the closing of the Gathright Dam on the Jackson River. Ever since, its 43-mile shoreline has proven to be a popular playground for residents of Alleghany, Bath and Highland counties. Much of the shoreline is adjacent to the Gathright Wildlife Management Area. Crappie fishing is outstanding, with 1.5-pounders common. There is an equal complement of large- and small-mouth bass. Thirty-seven citation rainbows have also been pulled from the lake. For more information, call the James River Ranger District in Covington at the number above.

SMITH MOUNTAIN LAKE
(703) 297-4062

The striper population is the most noticed at Smith Mountain, bordering Bedford, Pittsylvania and Franklin counties. It's been the source of numerous citation fish. More anglers appear to be converting to fishing live bait over artificials. A real pro, who has been fishing the lake since its beginnings with Appalachian Power Company in the '60s, says the secret for big stripers is live shad, which can be caught at dockside in casting nets. For a great fishing guide, call Bob King at (703) 721-4444. The lake provides lots of camping and recreational opportunities, including a swimming beach, through Smith Mountain Lake State Park.

CLAYTOR LAKE
(703) 961-1103

This lake, also impounded by Appalachian Power, on the New River near Dublin, is known as a fantastic white bass fishery, producing many citations annually. Claytor has traditionally been a good flathead catfish lake, too, with fish going up to 25 pounds or more. Crappie also have shown good growth rates. Claytor Lake State Park provides fine marinas, camping, cottages and a swimming beach.

HUNGRY MOTHER LAKE
(703) 783-3422

Located in the rustic highlands of its namesake state park near Marion, this lake provides good fishing for large-mouth bass, bluegill and crappie (up to 13 inches). Camping is available and boats can be rented.

REFERENCES FOR THE TOTAL SCOOP ON FISHING

The following titles are available from the Virginia Department of Games and Inland Fisheries, 4010 Broad Street, P.O. Box 11104, Richmond, Virginia 23230-1104, (804) 367-1000.

Sportsman Calendar
Virginia Fishing Regulations
Virginia Fishing Guide
Fishing with Nets
National Forest Maps
Virginia Freshwater Fish Identification Booklet
Fishing the Water James
Trout Fishing Guide
References for Fresh Water Fishing Guides

INDIVIDUAL U.S. GEOLOGICAL SURVEY MAPS

Distribution Branch, U.S. Geological Survey, Box 25286, Federal Center, Denver, Colorado 80225

AN OUTSTANDING COLLECTION OF VIRGINIA TOPOGRAPHIC MAPS

Virginia Atlas & Gazetteer, the DeLorme Mapping Company, P.O. Box 298, Freeport, Maine 04032

LAKE AND RIVER MAPS

Alexandria Drafting Company, 6440 General Green Way, Alexandria, Virginia 22312

Planning to go camping in the Blue Ridge? Be sure to book early — some of the choicest facilities have waiting lists from year to year. Call ahead so you won't be disappointed.

Insiders' Tips

GREAT TROUT STREAM BOOKS

Virginia Trout Streams by Harry Slone, published by Backcountry Publications

A Fly Fisherman's Blue Ridge, by Christopher Camuto, published by Henry Holt & Company

Golf

The Blue Ridge of Virginia is for golf lovers. Many golfers and their families keep coming back year after year, since the Blue Ridge offers golfers an entertaining and challenging mix of courses. The quality of golf in the foothills of the Blue Ridge Mountains, like its quality of life, has always been nothing short of outstanding.

An area rich in history, golfers will find the nation's oldest first tee still in use at the Homestead, a Four-Star Mobil Award, Gold Medal Golf Resort in Hot Springs, near golf legend Sam Snead's estate. Its top-rated course, Cascades, has been the site of numerous USGA championships and the 1988 U.S. Amateur. Special treats await golfers there. One example is just behind the Cascades' 13th green, where a clear mountain stream tumbles into the gorge — an idyllic picnic site! Just 30 scenic miles away is yet another ultimate in golfing at another Five-Star Mobil resort, the Greenbrier, at nearby White Sulphur Springs, West Virginia.

An example of a great place to golf in Southwestern Virginia is Olde Mill Golf Resort in Laurel Fork, 14 miles east of Hillsville in Carroll County. The Ellis Maples-designed course is both challenging and beautiful. The middle handicapper will enjoy play from the white tees, while more advanced golfers will find play from the blues quite demanding. The course's yardage/rating/slope statistics are: championship tees, 6,833/73.5/121; regular tees, 6,185/69.5/113; and women's tees, 5,293/66.0/106. A drive from an elevated tee to an hourglass-shaped fairway bordered by water on both sides makes up the par four signature 10th hole. Fees for 18 holes are $23 Monday through Thursday and $28 Friday through Sunday. Carts are $12 per person. A special twilight rate (including cart) goes into effect every day after 2 PM. Olde Mill also has condominiums off the 13th fairway available for over night stays. Groups of up to 52 can be accommodated, and two-night packages are available. Just take U.S. Highway 58 to Route 645.

The Shenandoah Valley sports multirecreational playgrounds at Wintergreen and Massanutten resorts, where you can actually play golf and ski on the same day. Nearby, Shenvalee's 18-hole PGA course has been entertaining New Market visitors for years. Chestnut Creek at Bernard's Landing, at Smith Mountain Lake, is one of the area's newest and has been winning fast and true fans since the day it opened.

Other challenging courses, such as the Roanoke Valley's Hanging Rock in Salem, are adding to Virginia's growing reputation as a top-notch golfing state with more than 135 public, semiprivate and resort courses available. The best are here in the Blue Ridge.

Photo: Lance Hill

Whitewater Katayaking on the Russell Fork River in Dickenson County.

With far too many courses to list, we at *The Insiders' Guides*® recommend three sources for a complete listing of public, semiprivate and military courses. They include the number of holes, par length, description, location and phone number of each course.

Virginia Golf Association, (804) 378-2300

Tee Time Magazine and *Mid-Atlantic Golf Magazine*, 12407 New Point Drive, Richmond, Virginia 23233, (804) 360-3336 or (301) 913-0061

Virginia Division of Tourism, 1021 East Cary Street, Richmond, Virginia 23219, (800) 93-BACK 9

Camping

From primitive campsites to modern RV campgrounds with all the amenities, camping in the Blue Ridge Mountains is a four-season activity.

Forests cover two-thirds of Virginia's total acreage, with most of it in Virginia's Blue Ridge Mountains and national forest regions. Camping here is a huge, inexpensive, family-oriented recreational pastime, whether you like KOA Kamping Kabins with all the comforts of home or just a rustic plot of beautiful land. At Blue Ridge of Virginia campgrounds, you'll usually find swimming in cool mountain streams or lakes and the hiking experience of a lifetime. Some even have boat rental and horseback riding.

NATIONAL FOREST CAMPGROUNDS

National forest areas accept no reservations. Family campgrounds are on a first-come, first-served basis. The only exception is group camping, which requires reservations, which can be made up to 120 days in advance and must be made 10 days in advance. No rental cabins or other lodging facilities are available in the national forest campgrounds. But, if you want to bring along your pets for protection or company, that's just fine.

VIRGINIA STATE PARK CAMPGROUNDS

Virginia state parks do accept and highly recommend reservations up to 364 days in advance. The maximum camping period is 14 days, and, again, pets are permitted.

DEVELOPED CAMPSITES

Developed campsites can accommodate one piece of camping equipment and/or one motor vehicle and a maximum of six people. Expect a grill, picnic table and access to bathhouses.

ELECTRICAL AND WATER HOOKUP

Electrical/water hookup sites are generally larger and can accommodate recreational vehicles and campers. They are available at Claytor Lake and Fairy Stone parks.

CABINS

Cabins are located in Claytor, Douthat and Fairy Stone state parks and are available from the end of

May through Labor Day. There is a $4.50 fee for advance registration. Reservation periods begin on Monday at 3 PM and end the following Monday at 10 AM. Any cabins not reserved become available on a first-come, first-served basis for a minimum of two nights.

GROUP CAMPING

Group camping is available, with a minimum of three sites.

Camping Fees (Nightly Rates):
Primitive sites, $6
Developed sites, $8.50
Group sites, $8.50
Electricity & water, $12
Pet fee, $1
Advance reservation, $4.50 per site
Cancellation fee, $5 per ticket
Off-season primitive, $4 to $6

Cabin Fees (Nightly):
One Room, $168
One Bedroom, $198
Two Bedroom, $282
Lodge (Douthat Only), $550
Extra Bed, $21
Pet fee, $3

FOR CAMPING AND VISITOR INFORMATION AND MAPS, CONTACT:

Virginia Campground Association (private campgrounds), 9415 Hull Street Road, Suite B, Richmond, Virginia 23236, (804) 276-8614

George Washington National Forest, Harrison Plaza, 101 North Main Street, Harrisonburg, Virginia 22801, (703)433-2491

Jefferson National Forest, 210 Franklin Road S.W., Caller Service

2900, Roanoke, Virginia 24001, (703) 982-6270

Shenandoah National Park, Route 4, Box 348, Luray, Virginia 22835, (703) 999-2243

Virginia State Parks, Department of Conservation & Recreation, Division of State Parks, 203 Governor Street, Suite 306, Richmond, Virginia 23219, (804) 786-1712

• General Information: (804) 490-3939

• Reservations by Phone: (804) 371-9502 (TDD number)

• State Forest Superintendent: Route 1, Box 250, Cumberland, Virginia 23040-9515, (804) 492-4121

• Blue Ridge Parkway Camping: 200 BB&T Building, One Pack Square, Asheville, North Carolina 28801

• U.S. Army Corps of Engineers (Philpott Lake, Bassett only): Wilmington District, Philpott Lake, Route 6, Box 140, Bassett, Virginia 24055

Virginia Division of Tourism: Telephone requests only at (804) 786-4484. Mail requests only at Bell Tower on Capitol Square, Richmond, Virginia 23219

Shenandoah Valley Travel Association, P.O. Box 1040, Department TG92, New Market, Virginia 22844, (703) 740-3132

To get information on private campgrounds, call or write the Virginia Campgrounds Association.

Horseback Riding

Virginia's Blue Ridge should not be explored just by automobile or on foot. There is a wealth of horse-

The Wonderful World of Miniature Horses
Theme Park

U.S 29 P.O. Box 440
Madison, Virginia 22727 (703)948-4000

back riding outfitters up and down the Shenandoah Valley, offering one-hour trips for beginners, half- or full-day explorations for those with tougher hides, and all kinds of overnight trips.

You can rough it and camp beside a trout stream with Deborah Sensabaugh's Virginia Mountain Outfitters, grilling fresh trout over a campfire and listening to the whippoorwills at sunset. Or you can sit back and be served dinner by candlelight with Overnight Wilderness Camping, which offers the thrill of the wild without the sweat. You'll find country inns that specialize in guided trail riding, and horse outfitters that offer packages with nearby bed and breakfast inns so that you can soak in a hot tub after a long day's ride.

If you yearn to travel the mountains in October to see the brilliant foliage, consider going by horseback. "It's the best way to see the leaves, rather than bumper-to-bumper on the parkway," says Tom Seay of Overnight Wilderness Camping.

In this section, we only list places that rent horses to the public and lead guided trips. In Virginia's Blue Ridge there are also many private liveries, horse clubs and an endless number of trails, both public and private.

MOUNTAIN SPRINGS STABLES
Sperryville   (703) 987-9545

Owners and operators Heather Marsh and Daphne Lowrie offer private trail rides seven days a week that give visitors an up-close look at the Blue Ridge foothills. They lead journeys through open fields and forests and along streams and rivers, with unspoiled views of rolling mountains. They offer catered picnics and romantic moonlit rides and can arrange either English or Western riding styles. Marsh, also an experienced professional photographer, takes her camera along so clients can take the view and their memories back home with them. The facilities also include indoor and outdoor riding arenas, private riding lessons and videod instructions. Please call for reservations, but don't hesitate to contact her on short notice in case there's an opening.

OVERNIGHT WILDERNESS CAMPING
Locust Grove   (703) 786-7329

This sophisticated operation leads cushy, overnight trail rides in the Shenandoah National Park, serving up everything from a candlelight dinner on china to well-cushioned sleeping bags and spare

toothbrushes. "We just wait on 'em hand and foot," says Tom Seay, a former producer of TV outdoor sporting shows. "The only rule we have is, 'Take your watch off when you show up.'"

Seay and his partners will meet riders in Washington, Richmond or on Skyline Drive — wherever clients want to be picked up — then head for the hills with their horses.

Amazingly, it only costs $99 a day per person, and that includes the use of a horse, a minimum of three guides, meals, a sleeping bag, tent and other equipment you might need, including fishing or hunting gear. Trips are offered year round, depending upon the weather. Small children — even toddlers — are welcome.

SHENANDOAH NATIONAL PARK
Luray   (703) 999-2210

Guided trail rides leave from the National Park's Skyland Lodge several times daily. The horses follow a trail called the White Oak Canyon, with several waterfalls along the way. Rides cost $16 per person per hour and must be booked one day in advance. There's also a more advanced, 2½-hour ride leaving early in the morning on weekdays in the summer.

MARRIOTT RANCH
Hume   (703) 364-2627

This 4,200-acre beef cattle ranch, owned and operated by Marriott Corporation, is home to one of the largest Western trail ride operations in the northern Virginia piedmont. Rides are usually 1½ hours long and are available every day of the week except Mondays. On weekdays, rides go out at 10 AM and noon, Saturdays at 10 AM, noon, 2 and 4 PM and Sundays at 10 AM, noon and 2 PM. Rates are $22.50 per person on weekdays and $27.50 on weekends; group rates are available. The minimum riding age is 10. The trails run through winding streams, open valleys and wooded hills on the ranch. Horse-drawn buggy, stage coach and haywagon rides are also offered. Reservations are required for all types of rides.

Marriott Ranch also specializes in corporate Western special events like barbecues and country and western dances, as well as formal affairs such as wedding receptions and garden parties.

Saturday nights in September and October are lively ones at the ranch. They have parties called "Steak Bake and Boot Scoot" that include haywagon rides, Western-style steak cookouts, country and western dance instructions and Western comedy entertainment. The price is $55 per person and reservations are required.

JORDAN HOLLOW FARM INN
Stanley   *(703) 778-2285*

This is a wonderful vacation spot for horse lovers. The 145-acre farm is nestled in a secluded hollow between the Massanutten and Blue Ridge mountain ranges, six miles south of Luray.

You can spend the night at the 200-year-old restored country inn or one of the two lodges, dine on "country cosmopolitan" cuisine and ride horses through lovely meadows or woods. The facilities also include a pub, recreation room with a pool table and fully equipped meeting rooms.

The inn offers three beginner trail rides a day, Western style, for $20 per person per hour. A more advanced, two-hour ride is also offered daily, on either English or Western saddle. Pony rides are available for children younger than 8.

All-day rides for experienced riders must be arranged in advance; they cost $10 per person for a minimum of six hours, with a minimum of two riders in the party. There's also a flat fee of $80 for the guide and horse transportation, to be divided among the participants. The all-day riders travel exciting trails in the Blue Ridge and Massanutten mountains.

Jordan Hollow Farm also claims to be the only country inn in Virginia with a full program for carriage driving.

WOODSTONE MEADOWS STABLE
McGaheysville   *(703) 289-6152*

Located in the Shenandoah Valley across from Massanutten Resort, this outfit offers leisurely trail rides in the rugged Massanutten Mountains. They match horse and rider according to the rider's ability and give everyone instructions before taking off. Trail rides cost $18 per person if you pay at least an hour in advance. Otherwise, they cost $20. The rides last an hour.

MOUNTAINTOP RANCH
Elkton   *(703) 298-9542*

The folks at this mountain-top ranch, located between Shenandoah and Elkton, lead trail rides throughout its 3,000 acres. It is surrounded on three sides by the Shenandoah National Park. Rides last anywhere from one hour to two days and cost $20 per person for the shortest trip. Fees are $55 for ½-day and $80 for full-day rides, which includes lunch. Two days and one night cost $200 per person. Groups of 10 or more receive a discount. The wilderness trails pass through meadows and forests and along waterfalls and babbling brooks.

The ranch also has a fully furnished cabin that sleeps eight. It can be rented for $80 a night on weekdays and $100 on Friday or Saturday nights.

OAK MANOR FARMS

Rt. II   *(703) 234-8101*
Located halfway between Harrisonburg and Staunton, this company leads guided trail rides up and down a small, beautiful mountain in the Blue Ridge. The thoroughbred horses are reportedly very gentle. Trips last about an hour and cost $20 per person. Appointments are necessary.

MONTFAIR STABLES

Crozet   *(804) 823-6961*
Fifteen miles west of Charlottesville, this ranch offers half-hour, one-hour, half-day and all-day rides for the beginner or expert, on Western or English saddle. The stables are located at the foot of Pasture Fence Mountain in the Blue Ridge and are open year round, weather permitting.

Owners Julie and Sam Strong also lead overnight trail rides once a month from May through September. On the overnighter, an afternoon ride up Pasture Fence Mountain is followed by dinner around the campfire. Riders sleep outdoors in a tent and have breakfast the next morning before heading back down the mountain. These overnight trips are for experienced riders and cost $125 per person. Reservations fill up quickly!

General fees range from $12 for a half-hour ride to $60 for a half-day ride. Discounts are offered for groups of eight or more. Rides are scheduled by reservation.

WINTERGREEN RESORT — RODES FARM STABLES

Wintergreen   *(804) 325-2200, Ext. 819*
Guided trail rides in the mountains and Rockfish Valley are offered daily (except Wednesdays) mid-March through December. The activities include pony rides for kids, sunset trail rides through Rockfish Valley, riding lessons, horsemanship classes and private rides for advanced riders.

Trail rides (all on English saddle) last one hour and 15 minutes. The cost is $25 for resort guests and $30 for the public during the week. On the weekend, rides cost an additional $3. Pony rides are $10 for guests and $12 for other children. Reservations are required. (For more information on Wintergreen, see our Resorts chapter.)

RIVER RIDGE RANCH

Millboro   *(703) 996-4148*
This 377-acre ranch, located about 10 miles from The Homestead in Bath County, has about 15 horses for guided trail rides through

unspoiled forests and fields. There are breathtaking mountain-top views of the Cowpasture River Valley and an abundance of wildlife that roams the vast ranch. Riders can use English or Western tack. Fees are $25 for an hour's ride or $70 for a half-day ride, plus $5 for lunch. A 10 percent discount is offered to groups of four or more for half-day rides.

Highly popular are the Saturday night haywagon rides and cookouts at the top of River Ridge Mountain. We're not talking hotdogs on a clothes hanger, but New York strip, barbecued chicken or fresh mountain trout grilled over a campfire.

River Ridge Ranch has a honeymoon cabin, lodge and another family unit for overnight accommodations. The ranch, which also offers fishing, swimming in the Cowpasture River and hiking, can accommodate 12 guests; a full country breakfast is always provided. The ranch is open year round.

THE HOMESTEAD
Hot Springs   (703) 839-5500

Guided trail rides are among the multitude of activities offered at this five-star resort in Bath County. There are more than 100 miles of trails, and you can ride either Western or Hunter (English) style. The escorted trail rides are private — in other words, you need not bear the company of strangers while getting to know your horse and the terrain. Reservations should be made as far in advance as possible. The rides last between 45 minutes and one hour and cost $42 per person. Chil-

dren who are at least four feet tall are welcome.

VIRGINIA MOUNTAIN OUTFITTERS
Buena Vista   (703) 261-1910

Deborah Sensabaugh runs a year-round horseback outfitter service, offering a variety of trips in both the Blue Ridge and Alleghany mountains. Half-day trail rides from Buena Vista up to the Parkway and back last about four hours and provide majestic views of the Shenandoah Valley. Half-day rides cost $45 per person, and a hearty picnic lunch is included.

Full-day rides travel along the Pedlar River, through farms and foothill country and into the mountains. The price is $80 per person, and the trip lasts nearly seven hours. You can fish for trout on the return trip if you like — there's no hurry.

Sensabaugh also organizes overnight rides and furnishes her riders everything except sleeping bags and personal items. Riders usually camp beside a mountain river or stream and cook dinner over a campfire. This costs $150 per person, which also includes all meals, from lunch on the arrival day to lunch and an afternoon snack the following day.

She also offers three- to five-night pack trips for die-hard riders. "You'll ride in all kinds of weather, all kinds of terrain, with a generous dose of history and trail lore along the way," Sensabaugh says. Camping is primitive. The trips cost $80 per person per day — a price that includes all meals, tents and camping gear other than sleeping bags.

Sensabaugh's most popular package, called "Horse Lovers Holiday," combines two all-day horseback trips with overnight stays at a nearby bed and breakfast inn, Lavender Hill Farm. You can work up quite an appetite riding in these mountains, a hunger that Lavender Hill's hearty European cuisine will more than satisfy. The cost is $225 per person, which includes two nights at Lavender Hill, all meals and the horseback trips and equipment.

An even more deluxe bed and breakfast package is offered with Irish Gap Inns, which is located high in the mountains and just off the Blue Ridge Parkway. Innkeeper Dillard Saunders charges between $98 and $118 night for a stay at her luxurious inn, and Sensabaugh leads horseback trips from the inns.

DUN ROAMING STABLES
Smith Mountain Lake
Moneta   (703) 297-6844

Danny Wagner came up with this unusual name for his stables after reflecting on his years of roaming as a horseman. "I'm 30, so I reckon it's time to settle down," Danny explained when we first talked with hime several years ago. He and his wife, Cindy, lead guided horse rides along Smith Mountain Lake, through woods, along creeks and through fields. Fees are $15 per hour per person. Dinner rides cost $36 and include a campfire-cooked dinner and a two- to three-hour trip. Overnight trips cost $48 per person a night, including dinner and breakfast. You must bring your own camping equipment. Reservations are required for all trail rides.

Southwestern Virginia has two state parks with horse rentals and guided trail rides.

HUNGRY MOTHER STATE PARK
Marion   (703) 783-3422

A few miles north of Marion is a state park known for its beautiful woodlands and placid 108-acre lake in the heart of the mountains. It's also home to a Hemlock Haven, an attractive conference center.

At Hungry Mother, guided trail rides lasting a half hour cost $6 per person. If you have small children, just sit 'em right behind you on the park's gentle horses.

Hunting

A fellow once commented that he hunted to feed his body and his soul. In the Blue Ridge of Virginia, no hunter goes hungry.

As expected, wildlife is concentrated around farmland or other areas where there is food. With much of the Blue Ridge lying in the 1.5 million acres of the George Washington and Jefferson national forests and state lands, food for wildlife is abundant. An annual $3 stamp is required to hunt in the national forest and can be purchased at most outlets that sell hunting licenses. Maps of the forests are available for purchase through their regional offices listed at the end of this chapter. Also ask about hunting regulations, license outlets and seasons and bag limits for the particular county you plan to visit.

Hunting is allowed in designated areas of five Virginia state parks, including Fairy Stone in nearby

Patrick County, Cumberland State Forest and Grayson Highlands State Park in Grayson County. A $5 hunting fee applies. Also in Patrick County, Primland Hunting Reserve in Claudville, half an hour south of the Blue Ridge Parkway, is a well-known hunting preserve of 10,000 acres specializing in birds, deer and even sporting clays. Call Rick Hill at (703) 251-8012. Guides and dogs are available.

Westvaco Corporation, a huge paper and bleached board milling concern, also offers hunting and fishing permits on vast holdings of company land in Virginia and West Virginia. Westvaco's office is listed at the end of this chapter.

The most popular game are squirrel, grouse, bear, deer, bobcat, fox, duck, rabbit, pheasant and quail. For truly adventurous pioneers, muzzle-loading rifles, bow and arrow and other primitive weapons are allowed at various times.

The Blue Ridge is home to most of the record-setting areas for hunting in Virginia. Latest statistics single out Bedford County for having the highest turkey harvest, with 498 birds harvested. Bedford also came in second highest for deer, with 5,753. In 1993, the five North Central Mountain counties (Alleghany, Augusta, Bath, Highland and Rockbridge) harvested a whopping 15,640 whitetail deer.

Whether you're going on your own or signing up with a hunting lodge, you're going to need a valid license, which can be obtained by clerks of circuit courts and other authorized agents (see below). Licenses and permits are good from July 1 through June 30. Hunting seasons and bag limits are set by the Virginia Department of Game and Inland Fisheries and vary according to county. Some counties are off-limits to hunters of certain species, while others have liberalized hunting rules.

Take note that one outstanding hunting lodge is Fort Lewis Lodge in Millboro, Bath County. It's a mountain paradise; call John Cowden there at (703) 925-2314.

The best suggestion to assure you are hunting within the bounds of the rules and regulations is to send for the latest pamphlet from the Department of Game and Inland Fisheries, "Hunting in Virginia Regulations." The brochure lists everything you need to know about how and where to hunt in the Blue Ridge, or where to find specific game information. To obtain the brochure, write or call the Department of Games and Inland Fisheries, P.O. Box 11104, Richmond, Virginia 23230-1104, (804) 367-1000

For other information about where to hunt in the Blue Ridge, write or call the following.

Virginia State Parks, 203 Governor Street, Suite 306, Richmond, Virginia 23219, (804) 786-1712

Jefferson National Forest, 210 Franklin Road S.W., Roanoke, Virginia 24001, (703) 982-6270

George Washington National Forest, Harrison Plaza, 101 North Main Street, Harrisonburg, Virginia 22801, (703) 433-2491

Westvaco Corporation, Appalachian Woodlands, P.O. Box 577, Rupert, West Virginia 25984

Photo: Wintergreen Resort

Blue Ridge skiing can challenge any skier, from beginner to expert.

Inside
Skiing

Heavy snow only rarely blankets Virginia's Blue Ridge, but this hardly stands in the way of a good time at the region's four ski resorts. Some of the best snow-making systems in the country can be found in Virginia, making it possible to ski even after the first crocuses break ground in early March.

"We don't need natural snow — we like to think we can make it better and put it where we want it," quips Mark Glickman, president of the Virginia Ski Association.

All the state's ski resorts offer such a dizzying array of activities that there is no reason to leave your in-laws at home, even if they don't cotton to the sport. Swimming, golfing, hiking, horseback riding, aerobics, snowboarding, sleigh riding, dancing, dining and movie-going — the list goes on of things to do besides skiing at many of the resorts.

Wintergreen, The Homestead, Bryce Resort and Massanutten are all true year-round vacation spots. To learn more about their services and activities other than skiing, please refer to our Resorts chapter.

There are so many variables affecting the cost of a ski vacation that detailed price information is not provided by this book. Whether you

ski during the day or after dark, rent or bring your own skis, stay overnight or spend the night, take a private or group lesson — all are factors affecting the price. A range of cost-saving packages is available at every resort.

Of the four resorts, only the Homestead rents cross-country skis and has trails for the sport. But if you own your own, there's no place better for cross-country skiing than along the Blue Ridge Parkway or Skyline Drive after a heavy snow. In addition, the Mount Rogers National Recreation Area in southwest Virginia is a breathtaking place for cross-country skiing during much of the winter, thanks to its high altitudes. The Recreation Area does not rent skis or have ski trails per se, but there are miles of pathways on hiking trails and primitive fire roads where the adventurous can glide to their heart's content.

Shenandoah Valley Region

BRYCE RESORT
Rt. 263, Basye   *(703) 856-2121*
Hours: 9 AM to 10 PM

This intimate, family-oriented ski resort is a little more than an hour from the Washington Beltway and less than three hours from Richmond. Just a few miles off I-81, Bryce is tucked in the folds of the Shenandoah Mountains. It's owned by the 400-odd families who live on Bryce Mountain and utilize the facilities, which include a 45-acre lake, an 18-hole golf course, nine tennis courts, a swimming pool and a small airport for private planes.

Although most skiers at Bryce drive in from the Washington, D.C., metropolitan area, the resort has become a favorite spot for Valley residents, particularly on weekday evenings.

There's nothing quite like twilight skiing under the lights and afterward warming up with a hot-buttered rum inside the glass-walled Copper Kettle Lounge. Manfred Locher manages the resort, and his brother, Horst, directs the ski school, the ski area and an extensive racing program. Both have been at Bryce since the resort opened in 1965.

Bryce's most notable feature is its racing program. The resort is known for being one of the best places in the South for skiers of any age to improve their ski techniques in ways that are only possible through participation in a racing program. For 20 years Bryce has sponsored NASTAR races, starting a trend among Southern ski resorts. Every Saturday, Sunday and holiday at 3:30 PM, the NASTAR races begin, offering skiers the chance to test their abilities against the pros. The race is handicapped according to age and gender.

Bryce has seven slopes covering

20 acres, two double-chair lifts and two rope tows. The resort gets about 40 inches of snow annually but produces enough snow to cover all its slopes.

A broad beginners area is easily seen from the deck and huge picture windows of the two lodges at the ski slopes' base. One lodge houses the Copper Kettle Lounge and a restaurant that serves hearty breakfasts, lunches and dinner. The second lodge houses a cafeteria, ski rental and repair facility and a shop that sells everything from goggles and ski boots to flashy, fashionable ski wear.

The Horst Locher Ski School offers private and group lessons. On weekends and holidays children between the ages of 4 and 7 can attend the SKIwee Children's School, where games are used as a teaching tool to hold children's attention.

Many ski vacation packages are available at Bryce. Cheaper group rates for 20 or more people include lift tickets, equipment and lessons but are not offered on weekends or holidays.

In the summer, grass skiing at Bryce is the popular sport for local adventurers. Invented in Europe as a summer training method for skiers, grass skiing mimics snow skiing but substitutes short tread-like skates for skis. Rentals and lessons in grass skiing are offered in the summer and fall.

A variety of accommodations is available in condos, chalets and townhouses near the slopes for weekend rentals or longer-term stays. For lodging information and reservations, call (800) 296-2121.

The ski resort accepts MasterCard and VISA.

Directions: Bryce is only 11 miles from I-81. Take exit 69 at Mt. Jackson. Follow to Route 11. Turn right on Route 263 then follow straight to Bayse.

MASSANUTTEN RESORT

Harrisonburg (703) 289-9441
Hours: 9 AM to 10 PM

This ski resort is an easy two-hour drive from Richmond, Washington, D.C., or Roanoke. In the heart of the Shenandoah Valley, it sits atop Massanutten Mountain — once upon a time a haven for moonshiners.

The resort's 14 trails and 68 acres of skiing tower above an attractive, airy lodge at the base. Inside are a cafeteria, convenience store and glass-walled nightclub with a big dance floor. This place gets real lively on Saturday nights. Another feature of the enormous lodge which sets it apart from most other ski facilities in the state is a large windowed room with tables and chairs where guests can bring their own food, "camp out" during the day and watch the skiing without spending a dime.

The resort only gets about 34 inches of snowfall a year, but it has greatly expanded its snow making operations to bring about quicker recovery to the slopes when conditions are less than favorable. Massanutten was the first ski resort to open and the last to close last season. Diamond Jim, a 3,400-foot run with a vertical drop of 1,110 feet, brings a greater challenge for expert skiers at Massanutten. The resort's highest point is 2,880 feet, where the expert slopes Diamond Jim and Paradice start downhill. Both are lighted for night skiing and are served by Virginia's first quad chairlift.

Like other resorts, Massanutten is open for skiing night and day. No half-day tickets are sold on weekends or holidays. Children 5 and younger receive free lift tickets. For children 5 and older, the Ski Wee ski school provides lessons, rentals, lift tickets and lunch for $40 on weekdays and $45 on weekends and holidays. On Saturdays and Sundays, one trail is open exclusively for NASTAR racing.

An extensive program for the disabled is a special feature at Massanutten; instruction is offered for people with special needs on Tuesdays, Thursdays, Sundays and by appointment.

Plenty of special rates are offered, from coupon books that give you eight lift tickets for the price of

Call Ski Virginia at (800) THE-SNOW for the latest snow, snow-making and skiing conditions at Virginia's four ski resorts.

Insiders' Tips

five to ski passes if you plan to ski for at least five consecutive days. Special rates are also offered to groups of 20 or more.

Group lessons cost $15 a person for one and one-half hours for all ability levels; private, one-hour lessons are $30 for the first person and $20 for each additional skier. A weekday "Learn to Ski Guarantee" for beginners costs $30 and includes rentals, a lesson and beginner lifts.

Overnight lodging and ski packages are offered at Massanutten's chalets, villas and hotel rooms and at hotels in nearby Harrisonburg. The resort's supply of overnight accommodations is limited. Reservations should be made far in advance. For those who are lucky enough to stay "on mountain," as the locals say, a sports complex called "Le Club" offers indoor swimming, sauna, outdoor hot tubs, an extensive exercise gym, children's movies, ping pong and more. Call Massanutten for information on all accommodations and ski packages.

MasterCard, VISA and American Express are accepted, as well as most skier discount cards.

Directions: To get to Massanutten, take Route 33 east off I-81 in Harrisonburg. Go 10 miles to Route 644, where you'll see signs to the resort.

East of the Blue Ridge Region

WINTERGREEN

Rt. 664
Wintergreen   (800) 325-2200
Hours: 9 AM to 4:30 PM daily, 7 to 11 PM nightly. After Jan. 1, 12:30 PM to 11 PM Sun.-Fri.

Skiing magazine called Wintergreen "the South's single best ski resort" in 1991. Just 43 miles from Charlottesville, Wintergreen's accommodations, restaurants, shops and other amenities bring to mind some of the poshest ski resorts in the country. It features 10 slopes — ranging from a vast beginners area to the Highlands, a three-slope complex designed for advanced skiers only.

Skiers may be restricted from certain slopes, depending upon ability. To ski the 4,125-foot Wild Turkey run, for instance, skiers must first demonstrate their ability to make controlled, parallel turns down very steep slopes. The way Wintergreen carefully segregates slopes according to ability level keeps the more advanced slopes relatively uncongested. Safety on the slopes is a primary concern at Wintergreen. Its ski patrol was ranked tops in the nation in 1992 by the National Ski Patrol Association.

Free beginner lessons are offered to those who rent skis from Wintergreen. Children 5 and younger ski for free when accompanied by an adult. Wednesday is Family Day, when children 17 and younger ski for free when accompanied by an adult.

You can ski in the morning and golf at the Stoney Creek course in the afternoon for the price of a ski ticket.

A summit ski area, the resort's accommodations and facilities sit at the top of the slopes. Restaurants and condominium complexes offer extraordinary views up the spine of the Blue Ridge and off to each side. To the west is the Shenandoah Valley and to the east, the Piedmont.

The resort's headquarters is the Mountain Inn, where guests can check in, enjoy a drink or sandwich at the Gristmill Restaurant and browse at an array of shops selling everything from exquisite hand-knit sweaters to Blue Ridge Mountain crafts and quilts.

You can park your car for the duration of your stay. Shuttle buses serve all the lodging complexes day and night — a good thing since parking space is in short supply.

The Wintergarten sports complex features an indoor pool, a small exercise room, a sauna and whirlpool — all in a building with skylights and huge windows through which you can see the Blue Ridge. There are also several hot tubs on the deck outside, where you can soothe aching muscles while stargazing.

Dining at Wintergreen is exceptional. The Garden Terrace offers fine dining in the evenings, and children can eat for free from 5:30 to 6:30 PM. Wintergreen has seven other cafeterias and restaurants. The Confectionery delivers a surprisingly good pizza from 5 to 9

Photo: Massanutten Resort

Massanutten Resort offers several programs for racing enthusiasts including NASTAR, the Junior Race Team, the Massanutten Challenge Race and USSA racing.

PM, and the Blackrock Market grocery store stocks sandwiches, muffins and other quick food.

Programs for children at Wintergreen are outstanding — rated tops in the country by *Family Circle* and *Better Homes and Gardens* magazines. The Treehouse, which actually houses a real-live treehouse, is right next to where ski equipment and lift tickets are bought. This is the headquarters for child care for children from ages 2½ to 7 years old. It's also where day-long ski programs for children begin. "Ski and Splash" offers ski lessons, lunch, swimming and snacks to 8- to 12-year-olds on the weekends and holidays.

Wintergreen takes MasterCard, VISA and American Express credit cards.

Directions: From areas north or east of Wintergreen, follow I-64 west to Exit 107 (Crozet, Route 250). Take Route 250 west to Route 151 south and turn left. Follow Route 151 south to Route 664, 14.2 miles. Turn right and Wintergreen is 4.5 miles ahead on Route 664.

You can also get to Wintergreen from the Blue Ridge Parkway. Head south on the Parkway after leaving I-64 at the top of Afton Mountain at the Waynesboro exit. After roughly 12 miles, look for signs to Wintergreen at Reed's Gap.

Alleghany Highlands Region

THE HOMESTEAD

Rt. 220, Hot Springs
Hotel reservations   (800) 336-5771
Ski information   (703) 839-7721
Hours: 9 AM to 5 PM weekdays, 8 AM to 5 PM weekends; 6 to 10 PM Tues.-Sat.

This elegant hotel became the South's first true ski resort when it opened its slopes in 1959. Daniel Ingalls, the Homestead's board chairman, had dreamed for years of bringing the exciting sport to his already famed resort.

But Mother Nature needed some help before skiing could take off in Virginia's Blue Ridge, with its erratic snowfalls and occasional balmy winter days.

In the 1950s, northern ski resorts were experimenting with snow making to augment the real thing. Ingalls seized upon the chance to turn his resort into a four-season operation and hired some Yankee engineers to bring their snow-making technology to the Homestead.

He invested nearly $1 million to develop a 3,000-foot slope on Warm Springs Mountain, along with side trails, a ski mobile and a glass-walled lodge with a circular fire pit, ski equipment shops and a rental service. Since then, the slopes have grown 200 feet steeper and the runs more challenging and diverse. The four-wheeled ski mobile has been replaced with modern ski lifts. An Olympic-sized ice-skating rink sits at the base of the slopes, with instructors close at hand.

Sepp Kober, a native of Igls, Austria, was hired in 1959 to help design the slopes and develop what would quickly become a premier ski school. Known as the Father of Southern Skiing, Kober imports about a dozen young Austrian ski instructors each season to teach at his ski school. Kober offers group, private and children's lessons. Nine runs are open for both day and night skiing, and half day rates are also available.

All skiers who spend the night at The Homestead may, of course, take advantage of its many sporting facilities and services, from its historic spa (with aroma and massage therapy) to an 18-hole golf course and high tea in the afternoon. Some of the most exquisite dining in the Southeast is offered at The Homestead.

The nearby Cascades offers lodging packages and is an economical alternative to staying at The Homestead. There are other small inns, motels and bed and breakfasts nearby.

A range of ski packages is available, with extra savings for weekday stays. Discounts for skiing are available for groups of 15 or more. And on Sundays, church groups can even have religious services on the slopes when arranged in advance.

All major credit cards are accepted.

Directions: The Homestead is about 200 miles from Washington, D.C. Take the Bridgewater Exit (Route 257) off I-81; go south on Route 42 then west on Route 39 to Route 220 into Hot Springs. For a lengthier but highly scenic route, take I-64 west off I-81 near Lexington, then Route 39 northwest to Route 220 into Hot Springs.

Photo: Prince Michel Vineyards

Winemaking at Prince Michel encompasses ancient techniques, French traditions and high tech resources.

Inside
Wineries

America's first true connoisseur of fine wine was Thomas Jefferson, a Virginian born in the foothills of the Blue Ridge. And so it is fitting that the region is now home to so many fine wineries. In fact, with few exceptions, the state's most highly acclaimed wineries are in the foothills of the Blue Ridge. This is no coincidence. Higher elevations help ensure healthy growing conditions for grapes, minimizing summer heat and lengthening the growing season.

"Good Morning America's" Spencer Christian, the Virginia-born meteorologist and wine aficionado, compares the Shenandoah Valley, both climate- and soil-wise, with the Mosel Valley of Germany, a famous Riesling region. Christian also notes that the Piedmont of Virginia shares many of the same characteristics as the Bordeaux region of France.

Thomas Jefferson experimented for 30 years with grape growing and wine making at Monticello, believing that Virginia provided a suitable environment for wine making. But it wasn't until the 1980s that the wine-making industry really took off in the state. In 1973, Virginia had only 59 acres of grapes; by 1981, the total had grown to 581 acres. Today, there are 1,400 acres of vines and 43 wineries scattered across the commonwealth.

Just as the acreage has expanded, so have sales. Since 1992, sales of Virginia wines have grown by more than 20 percent annually. Generally speaking, Virginia wines sell best in Richmond and the Tidewater and Charlottesville areas but in recent years have caught on in the Northern Virginia suburbs.

The Blue Ridge is home to roughly 27 wineries, most concentrated in the gorgeous rolling farmland stretching from Culpeper to Charlottesville.

Most are small, family-owned and -operated establishments. They are located in mountain coves, on mountain tops and along rolling hills in the Shenandoah Valley. If you're lucky, you'll be in the area when one of the wineries hosts a festival or open house. Rebec Vineyards in Amherst County throws a big party in the fall with the Virginia Garlic Festival, for instance, and several wineries get together for the annual Montpelier Wine Festival on the grounds of James Madison's estate in May. Chateau Morrisette in Southwestern Virginia hosts summer and fall jazz concert series on its grounds, offering tastings, tours and gourmet lunches.

We recommend an excellent guide to Virginia's wineries that includes maps, complete directions and a calendar of events. It's available for free and updated annually. Just write to the Virginia Wine Marketing Program, VDACS, Division of Marketing, P.O. Box 1163, Richmond, Virginia 23209, or phone (804) 786-0481.

The following is a complete list of wineries of the Blue Ridge region, beginning with those in the Shenandoah Valley. Wineries are organized geographically, from north to south and east to west.

Shenandoah Valley Region

DEER MEADOW VINEYARD
199 Vintage Ln.
Winchester (703) 877-1919, (800) 653-6632

Owner Charles Sarle built his own winery and made his first commercial wines in 1987, after retiring from a career as a mechanical engineer. He had been a home wine maker for 10 years. He and his wife, Jennifer, operate the winery on their 120-acre farm southwest of Winchester. They make Chardonnay, Seyval Blanc, Chambourcin and "Golden Blush" — a wine from an American hybrid. They invite you to tour their winery and bring along a picnic lunch and a fishing pole. Deer Meadow Vineyard is open March through December. Tours are offered from 11 AM to 5 PM Wednesdays through Sundays and most Mondays.

NORTH MOUNTAIN VINEYARD & WINERY
Off Rt. 623
Maurertown (703) 436-9463

This winery and vineyard are situated on 20 acres in northern Shenandoah County that have been farmed since the late 1700s. The vineyard was established in 1982, when proprietor Dick McCormack planted some 8,000 vines of Chardonnay, Vidal and Chambourcin.

At the winery building, which was built in 1990 and modeled after a European-style farmhouse, you can taste some of his wines for free. The winery produces several table wines, including a spiced apple variety. North Mountain is open from 11 AM to 5 PM on weekends and holidays for tours and tastings.

SHENANDOAH VINEYARDS
Off Rt. 11
Edinburg (703) 984-8699

This is the Shenandoah Valley's first winery, growing Chardonnay, Riesling and some French-American hybrids, such as Chambourcin and Vidal Blanc. The winery itself is on the lower level of a renovated Civil War-era barn, which also houses a small gift shop and tasting room. Owner Emma Randel grew up on the Shenandoah County farm, where her mother was born in an old log cabin that still stands on the property. Free tastings are available, and leisurely unguided tours are encouraged. The winery is open from 10 AM to 6 PM every day except Thanksgiving, Christmas and New Year's Day.

GUILFORD RIDGE VINEYARD

Off Rt. 211
Luray   (703) 778-3853

Owners John Gerba and Harland Baker use hybrid grapes and Bordelaise methods to produce their Page Valley Red, Delilah (light red), Pinnacles (crisp white) and other wines. Call ahead to arrange a visit and purchases.

ROCKBRIDGE VINEYARD

Off Rt. 252
Raphine   (703) 377-6204

Shepherd and Jane Rouse are the new owners of this five-acre winery, one of Virginia's newest. Shep is the wine maker at Montdomaine, but here he is trying his hand on his own patch of land, located between Staunton and Lexington. The Rouses produce Chardonnay, Riesling and two blends called St. Mary's Blanc and Tuscarora. Call in advance for tours.

East of the Blue Ridge Region

WILLOWCROFT FARM VINEYARDS

Off Rt. 7
Leesburg   (703) 777-8161

Small but selective is perhaps the best way to describe this five-acre vineyard on top of Mount Gilead with its splendid vista of the nearby Blue Ridge. Owners Lewis and Cindy Parker create some of the Piedmont's finest Cabernet Sauvignon, Chardonnay, Riesling, Seyval and Aprés Midi. Each September, the Parkers invite the public to come out and help harvest grapes. It's a special, hands-on kind of experience that too few people have the opportunity to enjoy. The vineyard is open from noon to 5 PM on weekends year round. Special appointments can be made at other times by phone.

SWEDENBURG WINERY

Off Rt. 50
Middleburg   (703) 687-5219

Named after its proprietors, Wayne and Juanita Swedenburg, this vineyard contains more than 15,000 wine grape vines and is situated on the 130-acre Valley View Farm, which has been under continuous cultivation for more than 200 years. The winery produces European-style premium wines, including an outstanding Seyval and Rhine Blush. Swedenburg is also the site of the annual Vinifera Wine Growers Association Festival (last Saturday of August) featuring more than 20 Virginia wineries. There's plenty of room to stretch out here and have a picnic, and you may even want to bring your fishing pole and wet a hook in the farm's

---

Trek to the vineyards of the Piedmont and Shenandoah Valley during the fall harvesting season to sample some of the best wines being produced in the United States.

Insiders' Tips

pond. The vineyard is open from 10 AM to 4 PM daily.

MEREDYTH VINEYARDS
Off Rt. 628
Middleburg   *(703) 687-6277*

This gorgeous Fauquier County vineyard is among the most prized in Virginia, with excellent offerings of Seyval Blanc, Sauvignon Blanc, Riesling and Chardonnay. Meredyth is situated on a 56-acre farm outside of Middleburg along the edges of the Bull Run Mountains, foothills to the Blue Ridge that are also among the oldest mountains in the world. The Archie Smith family opens the vineyard for public tours every day of the year from 10 AM to 4 PM, except Christmas, Thanksgiving and New Year's Day. The vineyard store is open from 10 AM to 5 PM daily.

NAKED MOUNTAIN VINEYARD
Off Rt. 55
Markham   *(703) 364-1609*

This chalet-like winery is nestled on the east slope of the Blue Ridge, east of Front Royal in Fauquier County. A picnic area on the five-acre vineyard offers sensational views. Owners Bob and Phoebe Harper produce Chardonnay (one of the best in Virginia, according to some), Riesling, Sauvignon Blanc and Cabernet Sauvignon. They use traditional methods of wine making — including fermentation in French oak barrels. The winery has a spacious tasting room on the second floor surrounded by a deck. Tours are offered in January and February from 11 AM to 5 PM on weekends and holidays. From March through December, tours are available from 11 AM to 5 PM Wednesday through Sunday and holidays. For groups of 10 or more, call ahead for an appointment.

LINDEN VINEYARDS
Off Rt. 55
Linden   *(703) 364-1997*

Linden has 12 acres of vineyards and leases six acres at Flint Hill, producing about 4,000 cases a year of Chardonnay, Seyval, Cabernet, Sauvignon Blanc and Riesling-Vidal. The latter is a blend that does not require aging and produces a young, fresh wine, with 48 percent Vidal and 52 percent Riesling. The small, well-designed winery, which was started in the spring of 1987, includes a comfortable tasting room, which enjoys a view over the vineyards into the mountains. There are also picnic areas outdoors. Tours are offered on weekends in January and February. From March through December, the winery is open for tours from 11 AM to 5 PM on Wednesdays through Sundays. The winery is also open most Mondays, but it is closed to the public on major holidays.

OASIS VINEYARD
Hwy. 635
Hume   *(703) 635-7627*

This vineyard and winery is located on a spectacular stretch of land facing the Blue Ridge mountains. The winery produces Chardonnay, Riesling, Merlot, Gewürztraminer, Cabernet Sauvignon and two types of Champagne, using the traditional *methode*

PRINCE MICHEL
DE VIRGINIA

VINEYARDS & RESTAURANT

Just 10 Miles South of Culpeper on Route 29 South

Wine Museum, Shop & Restaurant
(703) 547-3707 or (800) 869-8242

Tours & Tastings Daily, 10-5, Free Admission
Restaurant: (703) 547-9720 or (800) 800-WINE

champenoise. Owners Dirgham Salahi and his charming, Belgian-born wife, Corinne, purchased the property in the mid 1970s and planted French hybrid grapes as a hobby. They soon learned that the soil was well-suited for wine grape growing, and the rest is history. Although much of Oasis' wine is sold at the winery, it is also carried by some independent wineries and served by many restaurants in Washington, D.C. Tours are offered daily from 10 AM to 4 PM, but sales are available until 5 PM.

FARFELU VINEYARD
Rt. 522
Flint Hill   (703) 364-2930

This is a small winery not far from Oasis Vineyard that is being revitalized. It was one of the first Virginia wineries to receive a commercial license as a farm winery and produced its first wines in 1975. Owner Charles Raney, a former United Airlines pilot, produces Cabernet Sauvignon, Chardonnay

and a couple of picnic wines. Tours and tastings are available from 11 AM to 5 PM daily, but Raney asks that visitors telephone in advance.

ROSE RIVER
VINEYARDS AND TROUT FARM
Rt. 33
Syria   (703) 923-4050

This is a 177-acre farm winery in Madison County that borders Shenandoah National Park on the east. There are picnic sites and hiking trails for guests to enjoy. The vineyards produce Cabernet Sauvignon, Chardonnay, Mountain Peach, Mountain Blush and other wines. Fresh or smoked trout is also for sale. Tours are offered March to November from 11 AM to 5 PM on Saturday and Sunday. The winery is open daily in October from 10 AM to 5 PM and at other times or days by appointment.

PRINCE MICHEL DE VIRGINIA VINEYARDS

Leon   (800) 869-8242,
                        (703) 547-3707

Just south of Culpeper, along Route 29, sits Prince Michel de Virginia Vineyards, the largest wine producer in the state. So popular are its wines that Prince Michel runs out every year.

Prince Michel is also the only Virginia winery with an extensive museum about wine and an exclusive restaurant with a French chef. The winery's owner, Jean Leducq, lives in Paris and made his fortune in the industrial laundry industry. His dream was to have his own winery, and he started one here in the Blue Ridge foothills in 1983.

The French influence can be felt in many corners at Prince Michel, which is located north of Charlottesville and about 70 miles southwest of Washington, D.C. All the employees receive French language instruction. The museum's diverse collection includes a series of photos showing the process of grape-crushing; some eye-opening photos taken in Burgundy show two naked men in a barrel with the grapes, stirring and ventilating them. (Rest assured, this is not a technique applied here at Prince Michel!) There is also a fascinating collection of every Mouton Rothschild label from 1945 to 1984 — many of which were designed by famous artists, such as Picasso, Salvador Dali and Georges Roualt.

The winery also has a special room for viewing a video documentary about the history of wine, the process of making it and about Prince Michel de Virginia Vineyards.

A self-guided tour takes visitors throughout the winery and features displays that describe the wine-making process.

The tour ends at the gift shop, which sells everything from elegant wine canisters to scarves, wine-related jewelry and, of course, the wine itself. Visitors can sample wine or drink it by the glass at an attractive bar inside the gift shop.

Prince Michel produces about 40,000 to 45,000 cases a year, while it has the capacity to produce nearly double that amount.

Some of the vineyard's award-winning wines include the 1992 Chardonnay, Cabernet Merlot Reserve, along with Rapidan River's (its sister winery) 1992 Semi-Dry Riesling and the 1992 Dry Riesling (Rapidan River Vineyards produces Rieslings and Gewürztraminer nearby in Orange County). Prince Michel also won a gold medal for its 1990 Barrel Select Chardonnay in the Virginia Governor's Cup Com-

Insiders' Tips

The Shenandoah Valley's climate and grape-growing conditions are similar to that of the famous Mosel Valley of Germany. Virginia's Piedmont, meanwhile, largely emulates the Bordeaux region of France.

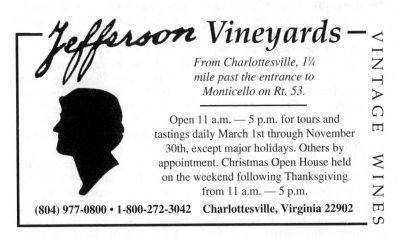

Jefferson Vineyards

From Charlottesville, 1¼
mile past the entrance to
Monticello on Rt. 53.

Open 11 a.m. — 5 p.m. for tours and
tastings daily March 1st through November
30th, except major holidays. Others by
appointment. Christmas Open House held
on the weekend following Thanksgiving
from 11 a.m. — 5 p.m.

(804) 977-0800 • 1-800-272-3042   Charlottesville, Virginia 22902

VINTAGE WINES

petition. And, this is just a sample of the awards won by this ambitious winery.

The Prince Michel Group owns 105 acres on site, 45 acres at the nearby Rapidan River property and 13 acres in the Napa Valley.

Prince Michel is open to visitors from 10 AM to 5 PM daily, except major holidays. The annual Fete des Vendanges harvest festival takes place in October — call for details.

And for more information about the fine Prince Michel Restaurant at the vineyards, please refer to our Restaurants chapter or call (800) 800-WINE for reservations.

The Rapidan River Vineyards are also located in Leon; for information, call (703) 547-3707.

MISTY MOUNTAIN VINEYARDS INC.
Madison   *(703) 923-4738*

According to *The Wine Spectator,* Misty Mountain's owner Michael Cerceo makes some of the state's best red wines. Cerceo, a physicist,

refurbished a 19th-century barn to make roughly 3,500 cases of wine a year from his 12 acres of vines. The winery produces barrel-fermented Chardonnay, Merlot, Cabernet Sauvignon and Riesling. Tours are offered from 11 AM to 4 PM Monday through Saturday and on Sundays by appointment. Tours are offered by appointment only November through January.

AUTUMN HILL VINEYARDS
BLUE RIDGE WINERY
Stanardsville   *(804) 985-6100*

This is a small, award-winning winery located on the plateau of a hill northwest of Charlottesville. Owners Avra and Ed Schwab left Long Island for Virginia in the mid 1970s — Ed had been head of an interior design firm and had grown weary of the rat race. They decided to grow grapes and make wine and planted the first stage of their vineyards in 1979. Their European-style wines include Chardonnay,

Riesling, Blush and Cabernet Sauvignon. They are open to visitors the last weekend of April and the first weekends of August and November.

BARBOURSVILLE VINEYARDS
Barboursville   *(703) 832-3824*

The giant Italian wine firm Zonin owns this winery outside Charlottesville, which includes a cattle farm and the imposing ruins of a mansion designed by Thomas Jefferson for Virginia governor James Barbour. The site is a registered Virginia Historic Landmark and has endless perfect spots for picnicking. The winery produces 10,000 cases of wine a year from 75 acres of grapes. According to *The Wine Spectator*, the whites are clean and crisp, while the reds are light and fruity in style. Wines include Chardonnay, Riesling, Sauvignon Blanc, Cabernet Sauvignon, Cabernet Blanc and Pinot Noir. The Malvaxia dessert wine is also popular. Barboursville was awarded the Virginia Governor's Cup for its Cabernet Sauvignon Reserve 1988. Tours are available on Saturdays from 10 AM to 4 PM. Tastings and sales are offered seven days a week from 10 AM to 5 PM.

BURNLEY VINEYARDS
Barboursville   *(703) 832-2828*

This is one of oldest vineyards in Albemarle County, producing Chardonnay, Cabernet Sauvignon, Riesling, Rivanna White, Rivanna Red, Rivanna Sunset (blush) and Daniel Cellars Somerset (dessert) wines. Lee Reeder and his father planted the first vines in 1976, the year after nearby Barboursville Vineyards opened. In 1984, father and son started their own winery. Today, they produce about 5,000 cases a year from grapes grown on both their own 20 acres and from Ingleside and North Mountain Vineyard. Tours are available and tastings offered in a room with a cathedral ceiling and huge windows overlooking the countryside. The winery is open March through December from 11 AM to 5 PM Wednesday through Sunday. In January and February the vineyards are open on weekends only. Group tours or evening visits can be arranged in advance.

JEFFERSON VINEYARDS LTD.
Charlottesville   *(804) 977-3042*

Near Monticello, this vineyard is situated on the same stretch of rolling land once owned by Filippo Mazzei, the 18th-century wine enthusiast who helped convince Thomas Jefferson to plant vines.

Italian viticulturalist, Gabriele Rausse, from the University of Milan, was hired to grow grapes and make wine here in the early 1980s. Rausse was also Barboursville's first wine grower and has worked with growers statewide for 15 years. Today, he produces Pinot Grigio, Pinot Noir, Cabernet Sauvignon, Chardonnay and Riesling at Jefferson Vineyards. Tours are available March through November from 11 AM to 5 PM daily, except major holidays. From December through February you must make an appointment. The schedule could change in 1994, so we recommend you call ahead. The winery

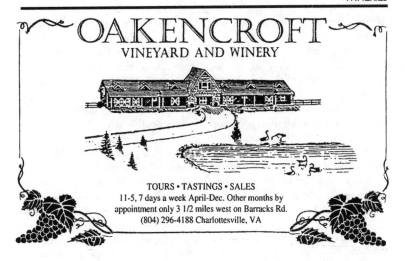

OAKENCROFT
VINEYARD AND WINERY

TOURS • TASTINGS • SALES
11-5, 7 days a week April-Dec. Other months by
appointment only 3 1/2 miles west on Barracks Rd.
(804) 296-4188 Charlottesville, VA

also has a small gift shop, tasting room and picnic area under a grape arbor.

Don't miss the market owned by the vineyard a few miles away on Route 53 (halfway between Monticello and Ash Lawn-Highland). It sells all the wines made at the vineyard, along with homemade breads, imported cheeses, crackers, cookies and fresh produce when in season.

OAKENCROFT
VINEYARD AND WINERY
Charlottesville   *(804) 296-4188*

Owner Felicia Warburg Rogan heads the Jeffersonian Wine Grape Growers Society — a group that won Charlottesville the title of Wine Capital of Virginia and initiated the annual Monticello Wine and Food Festival about 13 years ago. The winery is situated on a bucolic farm west of the city, with a lake in front and rolling hills behind. A big red barn houses the winery, tasting room and gift shop. The winery produces Chardonnay, Blush, Cabernet Sauvignon, Countryside White-Seyval Blanc, Sweet Virginia and Jefferson Claret. Tours are available April through December from 11 AM to 5 PM daily. From January through March you must schedule an appointment.

MONTDOMAINE CELLARS
Charlottesville   *(804) 971-8947*

Wine maker Shep Rouse's Bordeaux-type reds are among the best in Virginia, according to *The Wine Spectator* magazine. One of Virginia's largest wineries, Montdomaine produces Chardonnay, Cabernet Sauvignon and Merlot. It has become known for its Merlot, a difficult vine to grow in Virginia. Both it and the Cabernet are aged in French oak.

Montdomaine also has a new label, Horton Vineyards, whose first release is the Vidal Blanc — a light, fruity white wine with a slight oak accent.

Montdomaine's winery building is partially built into a hillside for natural cooling. Visitors are welcome year round for tours and tastings, and the place is only about 10 miles from the Thomas Jefferson Visitors Center off Interstate 64. Tours are given from 10 AM to 5 PM daily March through December. In January and February, tours times are 10 AM to 5 PM Thursday through Sunday.

TOTIER CREEK VINEYARD

Charlottesville   *(804) 979-7105*

This family-owned vineyard, located about 10 miles south of Charlottesville, has produced its first wine from grapes planted in 1982 and '83. The owners consider themselves growers and vintners of fine, premium wines. Jamie Lewis, owner and vintner, uses Virginia white oak barrels to age his wines, which include three types of Chardonnay, Merlot, Cabernet, Riesling and blush — a blend of Riesling and Merlot. Totier Creek's wine can only be purchased at the vineyard or at wine festivals.

The vineyard is situated in the Green Mountain range — a series of foothills east of the Blue Ridge. Tours and tastings are conducted 11 AM to 5 PM Tuesday through Saturday and noon to 5 PM on Sundays.

AFTON MOUNTAIN VINEYARDS

Afton   *(703) 456-8667*

This winery lies on a southeastern slope of the Blue Ridge at 960 feet, just minutes from the end of Skyline Drive and the beginning of the Blue Ridge Parkway near Afton, a village known for its antiques and mountain crafts. The vineyards — 9½ acres of vines that are among the most mature in Virginia — and winery offer magnificent views of the Rockfish River Valley and the mountains immortalized in Edgar Allan Poe's *Tale of the Ragged Mountains*. Wines available in 1994 and '95 include Chardonnay, Cabernet Sauvignon, White Zinfandel, Gewürztraminer, Riesling and Sweet Afton Semillion Apple Wine. Winter wines include Merlot and Pinot Noir. It's open Wednesday through Monday from 10 AM to 6 PM (5 PM during winter) and closed on major holidays.

CHERMONT WINERY INC.

Esmont   *(804) 286-2211*

This small winery in the rolling hills of southern Albemarle County was established in 1978 by Josh Sherman, a career pilot and retired Navy captain. Sherman planted 10 acres of Chardonnay, Riesling and Cabernet Sauvignon grapes over a period of three years, making his first wine in his basement in 1981. He has since built a winery with a large tasting room. The winery produces Chardonnay, Riesling (dry and semisweet) and Cabernet Sauvignon. Tours are offered noon to 5 PM Tuesday through Saturday most of the year. Tours January through March and on Sundays are by appointment only. The winery is closed on major holidays.

WINTERGREEN VINEYARD & WINERY
Rt. 664
Nellysford   (804) 361-2519

Located in the beautiful Rockfish Valley and adjacent tot he Blue Ridge Parkway, this Nelson County vineyard and winery offer spectacular views during all seasons of the year. Part of the original historic High View plantation built by the Rodes family, the land has been in agricultural use since the early 1800s, in turn producing tobacco, wheat, barley, hay, apples and now grapes. Award-winning wines include Chardonnay, Cabernet Sauvignon, Riesling, Blush, Three Ridges White, Governor Nelson White and Mill Hill Apple wine. The facilities are open for free tours and tastings daily from 10 AM to 6 PM (winter hours are noon to 5 PM). You are also invited to bring a picnic lunch; a gift shop is available. To get to the vineyard, exit Blue Ridge Parkway at Milepost 13, turning onto Route 664 E. The winery is four miles on the left.

MOUNTAIN COVE VINEYARDS
Lovingston   (804) 263-5392

Owner Al C. Weed II was the first in Central Virginia to plant grape vines, starting his operation in 1974. A native of Brooklyn, New York, Weed left his career in investment banking and moved with his family to the Nelson County farm in 1973. He planted French hybrid grapes, believing that they were more hardy and proliferous than vine. Today he produces several blends called "Skyline White," "Skyline Red" and "Skyline Rose." His peach wine is also popular. Weed built most of

the little log cabin tasting room and the winery himself. Tours are available April through December from 1 to 5 PM daily and January through March 1 to 5 PM Wednesday to Sunday.

REBEC VINEYARDS
Amherst   (804) 946-5168

This tiny, five-acre family-owned winery is about halfway between Charlottesville and Lynchburg on Route 29. Ella Hanson once could laughingly boast that her and her husband's winery was the smallest in Virginia, but that's no longer the case. Nor does size necessarily equate to quality. The Hansons produce white, blush, Chardonnay, Cabernet Sauvignon and Riesling. Rebec Vineyards hosted Virginia's first Garlic Festival in September 1991, and it was a rollicking success. The festival now takes place annually, usually in October, and features a garlic queen contest, a garlic-eating contest, live music, good food and lots of Virginia wine.

The Hanson home was built in 1742 and has been home to the descendants of three governors of Virginia: Thomas Nelson, William Crawford and William Cabel. Tours are available March 15 through December 15 from 10 AM to 5 PM daily. From December 15 to March 15, tours are by appointment only.

STONEWALL VINEYARDS
Concord   (804) 993-2185

This is a family-operated winery within easy driving distance from Appomattox and Lynchburg. Owners Larry and Sterry Davis produce Claret, Cayuga White, Chambourcin,

Vidal Blanc and Pyment, a medieval blend wine, honey and spices. Tours are offered March through December from 11 AM to 4 PM Wednesday to Sunday or by appointment. The winery also throws an annual celebration in early May featuring wineries, foods, crafts and live music. In mid-October, it holds a "Jazz on the Lawn" festival, with gourmet food, live music and, of course, plenty of wine. Call for the exact dates, because they vary from year to year.

CHATEAU MORRISETTE WINERY INC.

Meadows of Dan   *(703) 593-2865*

This winery is set on a hilltop on a 40-acre farm that borders the Blue Ridge Parkway in Floyd and Patrick counties. A French restaurant on the premises is reportedly fabulous. The Morrisettes' first wines were produced in 1983. They are made in a traditional European style, using stainless steel tanks for fermentation and French and American oak for aging. The winery, built of native stone and wood, resembles a miniature German castle. The wine cellar is underground, and a tasting room, deli and a large deck for picnicking are also part of the winery.

Chateau Morrisette also hosts the monthly "Black Dog" jazz concert series every summer, beginning in June and ending in October. Live jazz, tastings, tours and gourmet lunches make this an exciting event.

Tours, tastings and sales are available from noon to 5 PM daily except on major holidays.

Inside
Other Attractions

With so many and varied attractions to see in the Blue Ridge area as a whole, there are a few that deserve a chapter of their own: Covered Bridges, Zoos, Caverns and Spectator Sports.

Covered Bridges

Virginia's first covered bridges were built around 1820, and during the following century hundreds were erected across both wide and narrow rivers and streams. Since, they have nearly disappeared from the Virginia scene. Happily, a few picturesque covered bridges — favorite courting spots for couples of yesteryear — have been carefully preserved on Virginia's side roads to recall the past. Of the seven covered wooden bridges made accessible to the public, the Blue Ridge claims the bridge deemed the oldest and most unusual, Humpback Bridge in Covington, Alleghany County. Don't forget your camera! Here's a rundown of these beauties, from north to south.

MEEMS BOTTOM BRIDGE

North of Harrisonburg and less than a half mile from busy I-81, visitors can step back in time at

There are 43 species of exotic and native animals, including Ruby the Tiger, at the
Mill Mountain Zoo in Roanoke.

Photo: roanoke Convention and Visitors Bureau

Meems Bottom Bridge, a 204-foot, single-span Burr arch truss over the north fork of the Shenandoah River, two miles south of Mount Jackson on Route 11. It takes its name from the Meems family who owned the Strathmore estate west of the Shenandoah River. Rebuilt in 1979, almost three years after arsonists burned the original 1893 structure, the one-lane bridge still caters to automobiles on quiet Sunday drives. It previously was burned in 1862, when Stonewall Jackson went up the valley ahead of Union General John C. Fremont, prior to the battles of Harrisonburg, Cross Keys and Port Republic. Rebuilt, the bridge was again destroyed in a flood in 1870. Six miles south is New Market, a major tourist destination for Civil War buffs.

HUMPBACK BRIDGE

Known as the "Granddaddy of them all," Humpback is Virginia's oldest standing covered bridge and the nation's only surviving curved-span covered bridge. Built in 1835 as part of the Kanawha Turnpike, it is a graceful, 100-foot arched span with an eight-foot rise over Dunlap Creek in Alleghany County, within viewing distance of I-64, off the Callaghan Exit between Covington, Virginia, and White Sulphur Springs, West Virginia. Its hump-like design is unique in the western hemisphere. Only one other bridge, located in France, is similarly constructed.

During autumn, the Humpback Wayside, between Virginia's breathtaking Allegheny and Blue Ridge Mountains, is a popular picnic area.

Visitors can stroll through the bridge and wade in the shallow creek below to admire the bridge's hand-hewn oak timbers. Milton Hall, an historic bed and breakfast with gorgeous gardens, is close by.

SINKING CREEK BRIDGES

Near the beautiful Appalachian Trail in the New River Valley's Giles County stand two modified Howe trusses built across Sinking Creek, north of Newport. Built in 1912 and 1916, the 55-foot Link's Farm Bridge and 70-foot Sinking Creek Covered Bridge were left in place when a modern bridge was built in 1963. The Newport countryside is worth exploring for its quaint, country setting and is considered choice farm real estate by professors at nearby Virginia Tech. Northwest is Mountain Lake Resort, made famous by the movie *Dirty Dancing*.

Zoos

There are enough natural sites in this area to keep anyone happy, and when you add in the wonderful zoos, even the most avid naturalist has something to howl about.

NATURAL BRIDGE ZOO

U.S. Hwy. 11 off I-81 at
Exit 175 or 180   (703) 291-2420

Located next to Natural Bridge Village and Resort, this 25-acre zoo is also an endangered species breeding center. It has the largest petting area in Virginia and elephant rides for the kids. For two decades, the zoo has been raising generations of endangered species, including four generations of the Scarlet Macaw,

Siberian tigers and ring-tailed lemurs. For $2, on weekends, children can ride an 8-year-old African elephant. They'll get a real thrill mingling with llamas, ostriches and peacocks. The family also will enjoy large covered picnic pavilions and a well-stocked gift shop. Hours of operation are 9 AM to 6 PM seven days a week. Admission is $5 for adults and $3 for children ages 3 to 12.

MILL MOUNTAIN ZOO
Off Blue Ridge Pkwy.
Roanoke   *(703) 343-3241*

Located on top of Roanoke's Mill Mountain, off the Blue Ridge Parkway and alongside the famous star, is a 3-acre zoo operated by the Blue Ridge Zoological Society of Virginia. Its main star is Ruby the Tiger, who received local and national attention during a two-year fund drive to build a new habitat at the zoo, which was completed in 1992. Thanks to recent donations,

Ruby also has her own watering hole for use in the summertime. In addition to Ruby, 43 species of native and exotic animals are housed in the zoo. A popular attraction is the prairie dogs, who pop up and down out of their burrows, much to the delight of schoolchildren. Other residents are Japanese snow monkeys, tree kangaroos, red pandas and white-naped cranes. The zoo is open to the public daily (closed Christmas Day) 10 AM to 5 PM. Admission is $3.50 for adults, $2 for children younger than 12, and free to those under 2. The Roanoke Jaycees operate a miniature train with an additional fee. A concession and souvenir stand are open during peak season. Picnic facilities, a wildflower garden, and a breathtaking overlook view of Roanoke are located nearby. Access to the zoo can be taken from I-581; follow the signs off the Elm Avenue Exit to Jefferson Street and take a left on Walnut Avenue over the bridge.

FANTASYLAND

Off Route 746
Hobby Horse Farm Inc.
Bedford   (703) 586-7465

This isn't really a zoo, but it's an attraction so unusual that we've included it in this section for animal lovers. Located three miles from the city of Bedford, off Route 746, Fantasyland is open April through October. Picture real, live horses so small that even a tot can reach down and pet them. No kidding! That's the scenario at Fantasyland over at Hobby Horse Farm, just open last spring. Featuring the world's smallest horses, Hobby Horse Farm is the culmination of more than 20 years of selective downsize breeding by Bob and Jean Pauley. After having tons of visitors stop by in disbelief after hearing about the animals or spotting them from the road, the Pauleys finally decided to start charging admission for the curious.

Various breeds include miniature Clydesdale, Appaloosa, Arabian, Pinto, Draft and Buckskin. There are also miniature donkeys, goats, sheep, mules, pigs and Dexter bulls. Lots of other animals are on hand, including llamas, Tennessee fainting goats, prairie dogs, rabbits, peafowl, exotic chickens and goldfish. Bus tours and school groups are welcome. You'll also find a train ride, gift shop, picnic area, clean restrooms and refreshments for guests. Admission is $4.50 for adults and $3.50 for children. Seeing is believing. This place delights both old and young alike.

THE WONDERFUL WORLD OF MINIATURE HORSES THEME PARK

Off U.S. 29
Madison   (703) 948-4000

Imagine full grown horses (not ponies) shorter than a yardstick! That's what you'll find at Morgan and Georgeanna Gibbs' wonderland, just 25 miles north of Charlottesville in Madison County. These miniature horses dance, prance and show off for about 20,000 visitors a year. They all have mystical names, like Hercules and Thor. In the show, they follow Georgeanna's instructions and jump over obstacles that are wider than the horses are tall! Children can delight in riding the living carousel and petting these tiny animals. But the Gibbs have even more than these impressive horses. Some of the other exotic pets at Wonderful World are potbellied pigs, a breed of sheep dating to Biblical times and a monkey named Ooh! that rattles his cage.

If you find it difficult to tear yourself away from the horses, you can arrange to take one home. The park sells about 20 colts and fillies a year; prices start at $2,500 and can run up to several hundred thousand dollars.

The theme park is open on weekends from mid-April through Memorial Day, Wednesday through Sunday from Memorial Day to Labor Day and weekends from Labor Day through October. Hours are 10 AM to 5 PM Wednesday through Saturday and noon to 5 PM Sunday. Show times are at 11 AM, 1:30 PM and 3:30 PM. Admission is $5.75 for adults, $5 for senior citizens and

Photo: Wonderful World of Miniature Horses

Some of the smallest horses in the world can be found in Madison at the Wonderful World of Miniature Horses.

$3.50 for children. Group and birthday party reservations are available.

Caverns

America's history does not end at ground level. Just ask any cave lover. There is another world beyond, with a history 30 million years older than America. Exploring caves, or spelunking, can be a surreal experience — you're surrounded by an unearthly silence and ever-growing stalactite icicles and stalagmite gardens in year-round temperatures that average 54 degrees. A sweater is a good idea. Unlike our above-ground gardens, these require no sun, but mineral water is a must, enabling painstaking growth of only one cubic inch every 125 years. Under Virginia's soil are so many miles of caves that spelunkers themselves

say the end has never been found to some of them. The Blue Ridge of the Appalachians boasts the highest number of caves in North America. Six are easily accessible from major interchanges of Skyline Drive, I-81 or I-66.

As with most of the Blue Ridge, Thomas Jefferson also left his mark and was an early spelunker. He wrote about Madison's Cave (closed to the public) near Grottoes in his *Notes on the State of Virginia*.

How the caves were discovered is often one of their most interesting aspects. They often involve stories of Native Americans, soldiers and adventurous children with disappearing pets who become unsuspecting eyewitnesses to a netherworld directly under our own. Unfortunately, some caves show signs of vandalism from eager souvenir hunters. The Virginia Cave Act ensures that the Blue Ridge

Caverns endure for many more generations of the adventuresome. On a hot day, you can't beat the caverns for comfort while you gaze in awe at the world under our feet.

SKYLINE CAVERNS
Off I-66 at Exit 6
Front Royal   *(703) 635-4545*

Sixty-million-year-old Skyline Caverns, at the foothills of the Blue Ridge that border Skyline Drive, has a unique solarium entrance, where green shrubs border the cave to create a most attractive welcome. Three running streams traverse the core of the cave, unbelievably stocked with trout as an experiment in adaptation. Fat and thriving, they require chopped pork each week to make up for a lack of Vitamin D. Another unusual aspect is anthodites, called "orchids of the mineral kingdom," the only such rock formations known to exist in the world — and growing at a rate of one inch every 7,000 years!

Skyline is noted for its simulated scenes of reality, such as the Capitol Dome, Rainbow Trail and the Painted Desert. Kids enjoy the outdoor Skyline Arrow, a miniature train that carries them on a half-mile journey through a real tunnel. Skyline is also near the north entrance of Shenandoah National Park, where more fun awaits spelunkers. It's open year round; hours depend on the season. Admission is $9 for adults and $4 for children ages 6 to 12.

SHENANDOAH CAVERNS
Off I-81 at Exit 269   *(703) 477-3115*

Shenandoah Caverns, taking its name from the Native American word for "daughter of the stars," were discovered in 1884 during the building of the Southern Railway. The caverns are an estimated 11 million years old and are the closest major caverns located off I-81. They are also the only ones in Virginia with an elevator, a real boost to the handicapped, elderly and just plain tired. One formation, called Bacon Hall for its hanging slabs of striped iron oxide and calcite, was featured in *National Geographic*. Other incredible sights are Grotto of the Gods, Vista of Paradise and Rainbow Lake. Nearby attractions are plentiful, including Skyline Drive, New Market Battlefield and its two Civil War museums, Tuttle & Spice 1880 General Store and the Meems Bottom covered bridge. It is open year round; hours depend on the season. Admission is $8 for adults and $4 for children ages 8 to 14. Group rates are available upon request, and the caverns are wheelchair-accessible.

LURAY CAVERNS
U.S. Hwy. 211, 15 minutes off I-81
at Exit 264, Luray   *(703) 743-6551*

Luray Caverns, the largest known cave on the East Coast, is a colorful cathedral of natural beauty boasting the world's only Stalacpipe Organ. Stalactites are tuned to concert pitch and accuracy and are struck by electronically controlled, rubber-tipped plungers to produce music of symphonic quality. You must see this amazing instrument to appreciate it. An hour-long conducted tour transports you through nature's underground wonderland in vast chambers 140 feet high. Memorable formations include the Fried Eggs, the enormous Double Column and Pluto's Ghost. Placid, crystal-clear pools, such as Dream Lake, remarkably reflect the thousands of stalactites from above. One of the largest chambers, the Cathedral, has been the setting of nearly 250 weddings. A wishing well has produced nearly half a million dollars from tourists; proceeds are donated to charity. You'll also find a gift shop and restaurant. Outside, don't miss the Luray Singing Tower, a carillon of 47 bells, the largest weighing 7,640 pounds, the smallest 12. Recitals are given seasonally by Carillonneur David Breneman. A self-guided tour of the Historic Car & Carriage Caravan is included in your caverns admission. The central entrance to Skyline Drive in the Shenandoah National Park is only 15 minutes from the caverns, which are open year round. Hours are seasonal. Admission is $11 for adults and $5 for children ages 7 to 13. Ages 6 and younger are admitted free.

ENDLESS CAVERNS
Off I-81 at Exit 257
New Market   *(703) 740-3993*

On the first of October, 1879, two boys and their dog chased a rabbit up the slope of Reuben Zirkle's farm. The rabbit disappeared under a boulder. The boys moved the boulder, and before their astonished eyes appeared a great shaft of Endless Caverns. No end has ever been found to the labyrinth of winding channels and vast rooms, which now are lighted artfully and dramatically for visitors. Snowdrift and Fairyland are two of the most popular formations. Of all the caverns, Endless is the one that most seems as if you are venturing into uncharted, rugged territory, and its outdoor scenery is the most beautiful. Just as interesting are the historic native limestone buildings constructed during the 1920s. Relaxation is first class on the wide porches of the Main Lodge, where you are invited to rest, rock and relax a while as you enjoy Endless Caverns' breathtaking view of the Shenandoah Valley. The big, stone lodge is cooled in the summer and warmed in winter by pure, fresh air direct from Endless Caverns. Nearby, Endless Caverns Campgrounds is a beautiful facility at the foot of Virginia's Massanutten Mountains, adjoining George Washington National Forest. More than 100 campsites are available. Driving on I-81, you can't miss the sign for Endless Caverns — it's the largest outdoor billboard in the Eastern United States at 500 feet

Trips into the caverns may require some strenuous climbing. If there are elderly people, babies or small children in your party, call ahead for information.

Insiders' Tips

long and 35 feet high. It's open year round except Christmas. Hours from March 15 to June 14 are 9 AM to 5 PM; June 15 to Labor Day, 9 AM to 7 PM; after Labor Day to Nov. 14, 9 AM to 5 PM; and November 15 to March 14, 9 AM to 4 PM. Admission is $9 for adults and $4.50 for children ages 3 to12.

GRAND CAVERNS
Off I-81 at Exit 235
Grottoes   *(703) 249-5705*

Grand Caverns, within Grand Caverns Regional Park, is one of the oldest and most spectacular caverns you'll visit. The public has been coming here since 1806, including Thomas Jefferson, who rode horseback from Monticello to see the site. During the Civil War, Gen. Stonewall Jackson quartered his troops within this massive stone fortress after the Battle of Port Republic. Union soldiers also visited the cave. Their signatures still can be seen in pencil on the walls. In better times, the Grand Ballroom, which encompasses 5,000 square feet, was the scene of many early 19th-century dances for the socially prominent. Cathedral Hall, 280 feet long and 70 feet high, offers visitors a look at one of the largest rooms of any cavern in the East. Massive columns and the rare "shield" formations, whose origins are a mystery to geologists, are highlights.

Grand is a hauntingly beautiful cave, and its origins are equally mysterious. Its unique, vertical bedding is believed to be the result of Africa's collision with Virginia, millennia ago. It's open year round from 9 AM to 5 PM. Admission is $9

for adults and $6 for children ages 3 to12. Discounts are offered to AAA Auto Club, senior citizens and active military.

NATURAL BRIDGE CAVERNS
U.S. Hwy. 11 off I-81 at
Exit 175 or 180   *(703) 291-2121*

Here's a cavern with its own ghost! For more than 100 years, people have been hearing the plaintive voice of a woman, deep within the underground limestone formations. The first time it happened in 1889, men working in the caverns abandoned their ladders, fled and refused to go back. Their tools and lanterns were found in 1978. The last time the ghost was heard was as recently as 1988, when six people on the last tour of the day heard a distinct moaning sound, which continued throughout the guide's narrative. In all cases, it is documented that those present had an eerie feeling and fled the premises without hesitation. Located at the immensely entertaining Natural Bridge of Virginia complex, the caverns are enjoyed best when you take the guided, 45-minute tour 347 feet underground after you've seen awesome Natural Bridge and the Wax Museum above. Tours require some strenuous physical activity. The pathways are winding and steep in areas, so walking shoes are suggested. The Caverns Gift Shop is the largest in the Valley, with 10,000 square feet of space. It features some of the most unusual gifts in the Blue Ridge, including rock and mineral candy, sure to delight the young ones. Colonial-style Natural Bridge Hotel features sumptuous buffets. The cavern is open March through November, 10 AM to 5 PM daily. Admission is $8 for adults; $3.50 for children (ages 6 to 15); and a special combination ticket to see all three attractions at $13 for adults and $7.50 for children ages 6 to 15.

DIXIE CAVERNS
5753 W. Main St.
Salem   *(703) 380-2085*

Dixie Caverns' tour guides initially take you up the mountain, instead of down into it, where you will see a shaft of light from the outside. Your guide will point out where a pet dog fell down through the hole in the mountain, much to the astonishment of its owners, who discovered the cavern when they rescued their pet. They also found evidence that the Native Americans of Southwestern Virginia used the cave heavily for shelter and food storage. Some of the most popular formations are the Turkey Wing, Magic Mirror and Wedding Bell, where dozens of couples have been united as they dodged dripping water. On the outside, there's lots to do and see as well. The Dixie Caverns Pottery offers a huge display with thousands of gifts. There's a special basket shop and another shop named Christmas in Dixieland. Students love the Rock and Mineral Shop, with its famous polished-stone wheel. Campers enjoy a complete facility that has a new bath house. It is open all year for RVs and campers. For fishermen, there's the adjacent Roanoke River. Open year round from 9:30 AM to 5 PM daily, the adult admis-

sion is $5.50; children ages 5 to 12 cost $3.50. The cavern is located just south of Roanoke off I-81 Exit 132.

Spectator Sports

Believe it or not, some people do tire of watching spectacular sunsets on Virginia's mountains and yearn for something more to do. For them, the Blue Ridge offers fine college sports, ice hockey, baseball, Virginia's $12 million Horse Center and more. Here is a sampling:

College Sports

JAMES MADISON UNIVERSITY BASKETBALL
Harrisonburg   *(703) 568-DUKE*

Men's basketball is James Madison University's most prominent sport. The Dukes had their sixth season under Charles G. "Lefty" Driesell in the 1993-'94 season. Driesell, formerly head coach at the University of Maryland and Davidson College, won his 600th game in the 1991-'92 season. Games are played at the Convocation Center on the east side of Interstate 81.

UNIVERSITY OF VIRGINIA FOOTBALL, BASKETBALL AND OTHER SPORTS
Charlottesville   *(800) 542-UVAI*
                          (804) 924-UVAI

Football games at Scott Stadium have gotten so popular that it's hard to get tickets at the last minute. The Cavaliers boasted seven consecutive winning seasons as of 1994. For those reasons, orange-garbed UVA alumni are flocking to the games in record numbers, hollering "Wahoo-Wah!" at all the right moments.

Increasingly, season tickets are sold out well in advance, so if you're interested, call them NOW. For ticket information call: (800) 542-UVA1 (in state) or (804) 924-UVA1. The same numbers should be called for information and tickets to basketball, soccer and other games at UVA.

In the 1993 to '94 season, the men's basketball Cavaliers advanced to the final 32 of the NCAA tournament. The women's team won the Atlantic Coast Conference Championship in 1992. Under head coach Debbie Ryan, the women advanced to the final four in NCAA tournaments in the 1990, '91 and '92 seasons, advanced to the final eight in '93 and to the Sweet 16 in '94.. Basketball games are played inside the 8,864-seat University Hall.

If you're a soccer fan, you can watch the top team in the nation if you catch a home game at UVA. The men's soccer team won the national championships in 1991 and 1992 and the women's team advanced to the final four in 1991. The new Klockner Stadium for soccer opened in the fall of 1992. Klockner, a leading U.S. plastics firm, donated funds for the stadium.

Lacrosse is another winning sport at UVA, where the women's lacrosse team is No. 1 in the nation, having won the NCAA tournament in 1991 and 1993. They have advanced to the Final Four for the past four years — a record feat!

And for the more leisurely — but nevertheless competitive — sport of golf, UVA hosts the Cavalier Classic Golf Tournament every spring. Some of the top teams and players in the country come to Charlottesville to play in the tournament at the Birdwood Golf Course.

VIRGINIA TECH HOKIE BASKETBALL
U.S. Hwy. 460 Bypass, off I-81
Blacksburg   *(703) 231-6726*

A Division I NCAA team and member of the Metro Conference, Tech's had an illustrious basketball legacy in its 33rd season of play in Cassell Coliseum, having won 336 of 418 games played there. Needless to say, the Hokies have never had a losing season at home in 32 years, and Cassell is often packed to capacity. One of Tech's two all-time top scorers is All-American guard Dell Curry, who helped Tech to four post-season tournaments and finished his career with 2,389 points. Following his senior season in 1986, he was a first-round draft pick by NBA's Utah Jazz. The other Tech player to have his jersey retired was Olympian Bimbo Coles, who finished his collegiate career in 1990 as the all-time leading scorer in school and Metro Conference history, as well as having set a record high scoring mark for Division I players in Virginia. The route to Cassell Coliseum is well-marked.

VIRGINIA TECH HOKIE FOOTBALL
Virginia Tech
Blacksburg   *(703) 231-6726*

Virginia Tech Football is BIG in western Virginia — so big that if you want to catch a game, go as early as you can to avoid the traffic jams on the less-than-adequate roads leading off I-81 onto U.S.

Hwy. 460 to Lane Stadium (capacity 51,000). Thousands of tailgating fans will join you in the parking lot. It's simply the main event for this part of the Blue Ridge, with wild, roaring crowds and lots of pageantry and fun! For those interested in the game itself, be aware that Tech is in the Big East Conference. Its mascot is a turkey sporting maroon and orange. A 1990 game with the University of Virginia, the Gobblers' arch rival, set a stadium record of 54,157, the largest crowd ever to see a football game in the state. Famous Tech football player graduates include Bruce "The Sack Man" Smith, who won the Outland Trophy in 1984; George Preas with the Baltimore Colts; Ricky Scales with the Houston Oilers; Don Strock of the Miami Dolphins; and Bill Ellenbogen of the New York Giants. To get to Lane Stadium, get off I-81 to the Blacksburg Exit and take U.S. Highway 460. Just follow the crowd!

As one of the premier college football programs in the state, the Virginia Tech Hokies compete against the nation's top collegiate powers.

Polo

VIRGINIA POLO CENTER
Old Lynchburg Rd.
Charlottesville   *(804) 979-0293,*
                          (804) 977-POLO

It's not surprising that polo's a popular sport among the genteel society of Charlottesville. But students, as well, flock to the Virginia Polo Center—especially when their own Virginia Polo Team holds games on Friday nights during the school year.

From late May through September, the Charlottesville Polo Club also holds matches at 6:30 and 8 PM. Tickets are $3 per person.

Charlottesville resident and fiction writer Rita Mae Brown — author of *Rubyfruit Jungle* and other colorful works — played a key role in launching the Piedmont Women's Polo Team several years ago. The women's team holds games every Saturday at 6:30 PM in July and August.

ROANOKE
SYMPHONY POLO CUP
Green Hill Park   *(703) 343-9127*
Roanokers "Ponder the Ponies and Promote the Notes" at this fes-

tive fund-raiser for the Roanoke Symphony. Held in October at Green Hill Park in Roanoke County, the polo tournament not only provides a unique cultural experience but also allows patrons of the arts to enjoy good food and fun together. General admission is low (about $10) so that the revelry is accessible to everyone. However, you may rent tables for "tailgate" parties and tents for private groups. These costs range from approximately $170 to $1,450, depending on the size of tent or table you choose. Concessions are available during the activities. Tent and tailgate patrons have their names listed in the program as a gesture of appreciation.

Steeple Chase Races

FOXFIELD RACE COURSE
Garth Rd.
Charlottesville   (804) 293-9501

The Foxfield Race Course hosts exciting horse races twice a year, attracting a crowd of around 20,000 people from as far away as New Jersey. The races are held the last Saturday in April and the last Sunday in September. Usually about 75 horses compete in the event, which involves leaping over brush hurdles and timber fences. Races start at 1 PM, with horses taking off every half-hour.

Although hotdogs and soft drinks are sold at the course, sophisticated tailgate parties have become the norm. Increasingly, the scene looks like something straight out of *Town and Country* magazine, with women adorned in hats and smart outfits. It's not unusual here

to see folks sipping on champagne and feasting on pate by the light of a candelabra on the back of a BMW.

General admission costs $12 in advance and $15 at the gate, with an extra $5 for parking. Depending upon location, you can also reserve a parking spot for anywhere from $55 to $200, which includes four admission tickets.

The Foxfield Race Course is five miles west of the Barracks Road Shopping Center.

Foot Hunting

THE BOAR'S HEAD INN & SPORTS CLUB
Charlottesville   (800) 476-1988
                         (804) 296-2181

The Boar's Head Inn & Sports Club, west of Charlottesville, hosts this old English sport the Saturday after Thanksgiving every year. The Farmington Beagles and the Hunt Staff and Field Master at the Boar's Head Inn lead the foot hunt over 53 acres (many stray dogs and cats are scared out of hiding). After the hunt, the Inn serves a traditional Hunt Tea. On Thanksgiving morning, many of the hunters head to the age-old "Blessing of the Hounds" services at Grace Episcopal Church in Cismont. Afterwards, guests are welcome to watch the traditional fox hunt that takes place at a neighboring farm.

Horse Shows

VIRGINIA HORSE CENTER
Off I-64 W. at Exit 55
Lexington   (703) 463-2194

A showcase for the Virginia horse

industry and one of the top equine facilities in the United States, the $12 million World Class Virginia Horse Center hosted the 1988 Olympic Dressage Trials and is home to several premier national horse shows, as well as the annual Virginia Horse Festival. There are exciting horse events every month. The Indoor Arena Complex has 4,000 spectator seats and a 150-foot by 300-foot show arena. There are 610 permanent stalls, 110 portable interior stalls, two winterized barns, an enclosed schooling area, on-grounds restaurant and 48 camper hookups. The Outdoor Wiley Arena is lighted and has four all-weather dressage arenas, speed events ring and pavilion. Outside courses are pre-novice through preliminary cross-country, with a Hunter Trial Course of five miles of trails through the woods. The schedule of events here includes living history Civil War encampments, Jack Russell Terrier Races, Therapeutic Riding demonstrations and Fox Hound Demonstrations, along with the usual horsing events. Off I-81, take Lexington Exit 191, proceed on I-64 W. to Exit 55, then follow signs for only two miles to the Horse Center. Tours are offered but be sure to call beforehand.

Hockey

THE ROANOKE EXPRESS
HOCKEY ROANOKE INC.
4502 Starkey Rd. S.W.
Roanoke   *(703) 989-GOAL*

Roanoke has a new professional hockey franchise, thanks to a group of seven civic-minded business owners. The team replaces the 1992 to '93 season's Roanoke Rampage. The season runs from October through March at the Roanoke Civic Center on Tuesdays, Fridays and Saturdays, with a few exceptions. The team will perform in the East Coast Hockey League that includes 19 teams from nine different states.

Season tickets are available. Individual tickets are $4 to $8 a person. There won't be a lack of action, both on the ice and in the stands. Bring the entire family!

Baseball

SALEM BUCCANEERS
620 Florida St.
Salem   *(703) 389-3333*

A Class A team for the Pittsburgh Pirates, the Buccaneers live happily in the sports-crazed Roanoke Valley city of Salem. They were Carolina League champs in 1987. Beginning in April, 140 games are on the agenda until September, half at home at Salem Municipal Field. The Buccaneers are excellent Valley citizens and plan numerous promotions benefiting area charities. You can hear the Buccaneer games on WROV-AM 1240 Radio. General admission is $3, with seniors and children getting $1 off. Take Salem Exit 141 off I-81.

LYNCHBURG RED SOX
City Stadium
Lynchburg   *(804) 528-1144*

Lynchburg has had a baseball team in its midst for over 100 years. Since 1966, this group has been in the class A level of the Carolina League, along with other Virginia cities such as Salem and Woodbridge. The Lynchburg team has been affiliated with many different clubs along the way including the Chicago White Sox and the New York Mets. Since 1988, however, these "boys of summer" have been a part of the Boston Red Sox. The team, also know as the L-Sox, plays in City Stadium, which has a capacity of 4,200. They play 140 games per season, half of them at home. All games are broadcast on radio station WLLL-AM. General Admission is $3.75.

Race Car Driving

NEW RIVER VALLEY SPEEDWAY
Radford   *(703) 639-1700*

Once known as Pulaski County Speedway, this track now named the New River Valley Speedway. A NASCAR-sanctioned event, racing takes place on a paved, oval track that is four-tenths of a mile long. Every Saturday night from April to September, the Speedway packs in visitors from all over the New River Valley. The featured division is late model stock, but other divisions include limited sportsman, modified mini, mini stock and pure stock. A family atmosphere prevails, with over 2,000 children showing up each Saturday. And, no matter what your preconceptions about racing are, this is a sport for everyone to enjoy. Doctors, lawyers, farmers and schoolteachers all make the Speedway a part of their weekends! Admission is $8 for adults and $1 for children 12 and younger.

Inside
Annual Events

Not a season passes in Virginia's Blue Ridge and its foothills that some group isn't finding a way to celebrate it. You will have plenty to do each month all around the 14-county region: craft shows, antique sales, historic commemorations, agricultural fairs, horse shows and races, athletic competitions and some of the best fun you'll find anywhere in traditional holiday observances. Imagine the Shenandoah Valley sky ablaze with fireworks on Independence Day, or conjure up a sense of patriotic pride as this history-rich region celebrates the birthdays of such famous Americans as Thomas Jefferson, George Washington, James Madison and the South's famous generals, Robert E. Lee and Stonewall Jackson.

Let your tastebuds lead the way as folks gather around to sample their favorite foods served with a big helping of fellowship. The Virginia Chili Cook-off in Roanoke is one such event, and the Highland Maple Festival in Monterey (with

The world-famous Shenandoah Apple Blossom Festival is held each year on the first weekend of May.

Photo: Winchester-Frederick Co. Chamber of Commerce

• *175*

syrup-making demonstrations and plenty of maple-flavored goodies) is another. Other gatherings pay homage to such diverse edibles as garlic (and its humble brother, the ramp), apples in every form (especially apple butter!), wine, tomatoes, molasses, poultry and more. Fall festivals usually feature the entire harvest — so save up your calories.

Music is almost always on the program, running the gamut from hoedowns to symphonies. Don't miss the Old Fiddlers Convention — the original and largest such event — and other cultural extravaganzas. Many activities are held at the region's beautiful historic mansions, such as Montpelier, Monticello and Ash Lawn-Highland.

The list that follows is a sampling of some of the bigger events — and lots of smaller ones, too — that you can plan a weekend or longer around.

January

VIRGINIA SPECIAL OLYMPICS
Wintergreen   *(804) 325-2200*
Wintergreen Resort hosts this annual snow-skiing competition for mentally retarded athletes.

BIRTHDAY CONVOCATION
FOR ROBERT E. LEE
Lexington   *(703) 463-3777*
The venerable general is saluted on his birthday at Lexington's Lee Chapel.

BIRTHDAY CELEBRATION
FOR STONEWALL JACKSON
Lexington   *(703) 463-3777*
The South's second-greatest hero gets his due at this city-wide festival, beginning on the grounds of Washington & Lee University.

February

GEORGE WASHINGTON'S
BIRTHDAY CELEBRATION
Winchester   *(703) 662-6550*
This is an open house at George Washington's Office Museum. It is held every February on the weekend closest to Washington's birthday.

VALENTINE'S DAY WEEKEND
Wintergreen   *(804) 325-2200*
There are parties, special ski challenges and events for the kids to top off this annual festival at Wintergreen Resort.

March

HIGHLAND MAPLE FESTIVAL
Monterey   *(703) 468-2550*
This festival is celebrated across Highland County — that rugged, gorgeous region bordering West Virginia west of Staunton. During the festival, you can visit local sugar camps and watch the actual process of syrup-making. There's also an arts and crafts show, a maple queen contest and ball, dances, including the maple sugar hoedown, and plenty of opportunities to scarf down pancakes with maple syrup, maple donuts and fresh fried trout.

Charlton Heston and Peter Max in attendance at the American Film Fest, held every October in Charlottesville.

St. Patrick's Day Parade

Staunton   *(703) 885-8504*

Staunton shows its Irish roots at this popular event.

St. Patrick's Day Parade

Roanoke   *(703) 981-2889*

Downtown Roanoke "sports the green" during this weekend parade.

Whitetop Mountain Maple Festival

Mount Rogers National Recreation Area
(703) 388-3294

Usually held on two weekends in late March, this festive event features live country and western music, tours of maple tree tapping areas, arts and crafts and pancake dinners.

April

Historic Garden Week

Locations throughout
Virginia   *(804) 644-7776*

This late April event throws open the doors of more than 200 private homes and gardens throughout the Commonwealth for tours. Many Blue Ridge area cities participate in this statewide event, which is always held during the last full week of April. Charlottesville, Staunton, Harrisonburg, Roanoke and the Front Royal area always participate.

Old Town Easter Egg Hunt

Winchester   *(703) 665-0079*

Held on the Saturday closest to Easter, this egg hunt delights youngsters from age 2 to 7 on the lawn next to the Godfrey Miller Center in downtown Winchester.

CHAMPAGNE AND
CANDLELIGHT TOUR

Charlottesville   *(804) 293-9539*

This enchanting evening tour of the Ash Lawn-Highland home of President James Monroe is always held during Historic Garden Week. Period music is performed during tours of the Federal-style home and beautiful gardens, which are illuminated with 2,000 candles.

THOMAS JEFFERSON
BIRTHDAY COMMEMORATION

Charlottesville   *(804) 295-8181*

Admission to Monticello's grounds and gardens is always free on April 13, the birthday of Virginia's best known renaissance man — U.S. President, Secretary of State, scholar, architect, collector and horticulturist.

FOXFIELD RACES

Charlottesville   *(804) 293-9501*

This wildly popular steeplechase has also become one of Charlottesville's top social events.

THE DOGWOOD FESTIVAL

Charlottesville   *(804) 295-3141*

This popular community event features a queen's coronation, fashion show, fireworks, carnival, barbecue and, finally, a grand parade on Saturday. The attraction shows off Charlottesville at its springtime best. It's usually held in mid-April and lasts nearly two weeks.

EASTER AT WINTERGREEN

Wintergreen   *(804) 325-2200*

Every Easter weekend, Wintergreen Resort holds a variety of activities for families: Egg-Stravaganza games for kids, a Ukrainian egg decorating workshop, culinary workshop and an Easter morning worship service.

VIRGINIA HORSE FESTIVAL

Lexington   *(703) 463-4300*

This event showcases the state's horse industry with breed exhibits, a large equine trade show, terrier races, an equine art contest, a draft horse pull and more. It's held at the posh Virginia Horse Center, just outside Lexington on Virginia Route 39.

SPRING GARDEN SHOW

Lynchburg   *(804) 847-1499*

This is a gardener's field day in early April at the Community Market, where landscapers, florists and nursery operators display their products and where gardening techniques are demonstrated. There's also entertainment and food.

SPRING BALLOON FESTIVAL

Bedford   *(703) 586-9401*

Hot-air balloons fill the Piedmont sky during this colorful spring festival.

FRANKLIN COUNTY SPRING
ARTS AND CRAFTS FESTIVAL

Rocky Mount   *(703) 483-9542*

Mountain crafts, food and music are the star attractions here.

BRUSH MOUNTAIN
ARTS AND CRAFTS FAIR

Blacksburg   *(703) 552-4909*

Quilters, potters, weavers, decoy carvers and other artists show their wares at the juried festival held in this arty college town.

RIVER RUN AND BICYCLE RIDE
Narrows *(703) 921-1544*

Athletes face off against the rugged terrain found near Breaks Interstate park, on the Virginia and Kentucky border.

HONAKER REDBUD FESTIVAL
Honaker
Russell County *(703) 889-8041*

This tiny community of 1,000 celebrates spring every year with a month-long festival, featuring gospel singing, arts and craft shows, a canoe race down the Clinch River, car show, homecoming dinner, beauty pageant and parade. The redbud tree, indigenous to the Southwestern Virginia county, blossoms this month.

LONESOME PINE
ARTS AND CRAFTS FESTIVAL
Big Stone Gap *(703) 523-0846*

This community close to Kentucky is home to a wonderful annual celebration of mountain heritage. Here you will find craft-making demonstrations and the display and sale of homemade arts, crafts and food.

May

VIRGINIA GOLD CUP
The Plains *(703) 347-2612*

The Old Dominion's premier steeplechase event is always held the first Saturday in May, the same day as its big sister, the Kentucky Derby. Sometimes boisterous and oh, so preppy, this is a social event of major proportions in Virginia, with more than 50,000 onlookers during a typical year. Imagine a gigantic UVA frat party or, as one friend commented "A WASPy Woodstock," and you kind of get the idea of what this is all about.

OATLANDS SHEEP DOG TRIALS
Leesburg *(703) 777-3174*

This highly entertaining weekend fete (typically the second week of May) champions the herding instincts of border collies. It takes place at glorious Oatlands Plantation, just outside of Leesburg in the heart of the Virginia Hunt Country.

SHENANDOAH
APPLE BLOSSOM FESTIVAL
Winchester *(703) 662-3863*

This four-day celebration is a salute to the area's apple-growing industry. You'll find high quality arts and crafts shows, numerous parades, live music, a 10-kilometer race and a circus. Past festival queens have included presidents' daughters Lucie Baines Johnson and Susan Ford, as well as the daughter of Hollywood actress Dixie Carter.

SPRING FLY-IN
Winchester *(703) 662-5786*

This festival is always held the Sunday of Apple Blossom Festival. Aircraft owners compete for various prizes and share their aviation interests with the public. The festival is held at the Winchester Regional Airport.

ANTIQUE CAR SHOW
Winchester *(703) 869-7475*

Held always in May, this show, flea market and car corral draws hundreds to the Jim Barnett Park in Winchester. It is sponsored by the Shenandoah Region Antique Auto Club of America.

NORTH-SOUTH SKIRMISH

Gainesboro *(703) 888-7917*

This is the spring nationals event of the North-South Skirmish Association, held at Ft. Shenandoah in Gainesboro. It's always held in May.

VIRGINIA MUSHROOM FESTIVAL

Front Royal *(800) 338-2576*

Held usually the second weekend in May, this Main Street festival features arts and crafts, great food, wine tastings hosted by four or five area wineries, live music, clogging and open air theatrical performances.

WILDFLOWER WEEKEND

Shenandoah National Park
(703) 999-3482

This event celebrates the arrival of spring. Guided walks, exhibits, slide programs and workshops are held at the 195,000-acre park during the third weekend in May.

NEW MARKET HERITAGE DAYS

New Market *(703) 740-3432*

The Shenandoah Valley town salutes its pioneer and German, Scottish and Irish heritage at this weekend festival capped by a large parade.

VIRGINIA POULTRY FESTIVAL

Harrisonburg *(703) 433-2451*

The hoopla here, including cookouts, a parade and, yes, a poultry queen, celebrates Virginia's status as one of the largest chicken- and turkey-producing states.

MEMORIAL DAY HORSE FAIR AND AUCTION

Harrisonburg *(703) 434-4482*

The Memorial Day tradition is the largest horse auction in the Shenandoah Valley.

FOLK ARTS AND CRAFTS FESTIVAL

Weyers Cave *(703) 886-2351*

The focus here is on local artisans, many of whom exhibit solely at this festival.

ANNUAL KITE DAY

Charlottesville *(804) 293-9539*

At Ash Lawn-Highland, home of President James Monroe, the fields are open to children and the young at heart for kite flying. Both designs and flights are judged for prizes. It is usually held in early May.

SPRING WILDFLOWER SYMPOSIUM

Wintergreen *(804) 325-2200*

Every May, Wintergreen Resort invites prominent specialists to lead workshops, lectures and other educational programs about wildflowers. There are guided hikes, wildflower sales, photography displays and entertainment.

MEMORIAL DAY CELEBRATION

Wintergreen *(804) 325-2200*

Every year, the resort kicks off its summer season with the Stoney Creek Valley Parade, a kite festival, a Firemen's Ball and an opening day celebration at Lake Monocan.

MONTPELIER WINE FESTIVAL

Montpelier Station *(703) 832-2828*

Regional wines are showcased on the grounds of Montpelier every

May. The festival provides an opportunity to enjoy one of the state's premier products, its wine, as well as equestrian events, crafts, music and food.

DOLLEY MADISON'S BIRTHDAY
Montpelier Station   (703) 672-2728

This is an annual celebration at Montpelier, four miles from Orange on Route 20 S.

INTERNATIONAL
SPRINGTIME CELEBRATION
Staunton   (703) 332-7850

Four mini-festivals at the Museum of American Frontier Culture coincide with Europe's traditional May Day celebrations. Come dance a jig and munch on a meat pasty while watching baby lambs frolic in a nearby pasture. Activities at the museum's working German, Scotch-Irish, English and American farms include traditional dancing, music and foods. This happens on either the first or second Saturday in May.

OUTDOOR ART SHOW
Staunton   (703) 886-2351

This downtown Staunton event features local as well as national artists, including a large number of wildlife painters.

THEATER AT LIME KILN
Lexington   (703) 463-3074

Memorial Day begins the summer season at Lime Kiln, an outdoor theater that's nationally recognized for presenting original plays and musicals that relate to Virginia's culture and history. Plays and concerts are held under the stars in an enchanting setting — the ruins of an actual lime kiln built in the 1800s. Plays are performed Monday through Saturday until Labor Day. On Sunday nights, some of the best and brightest in the eclectic music business perform jazz, blues, folk and bluegrass music at Lime Kiln.

BASS BONANZA
Covington   (703) 962-2178

This is held every year at Lake Moomaw in the Allegheny Mountains. The elusive large-mouth bass is the featured attraction.

PIONEER DAY
Covington   (703) 962-8943

A downtown festival, it pays tribute to the brave souls who settled this rugged corner of western Virginia.

AN EVENING OF ELEGANCE
Lynchburg   (804) 847-8688

This annual fund-raiser for the Virginia School of the Arts is always

In vintage Virginia fashion, one of the state's largest sporting events is also its biggest social event — the Virginia Gold Cup in Fauquier County. Insiders arrive early, stay late and in between eat, drink, gossip and maybe watch a race or two.

Insiders' Tips

held in early May. Internationally acclaimed dancers perform with local students at the E.C. Glass Auditorium.

CHILDREN'S DAY AT THE MARKET

Lynchburg   *(804) 847-1499*

Also in early May, bring your kids to the Community Market to watch clowns and touch the animals at the petting zoo. You'll find lots of entertainment, games, food and an annual poster contest.

MAY FEST

Stonewall Vineyards
Concord   *(804) 993-2185*

This wine and food festival is held on a farm in the rolling hill country outside of Lynchburg.

THE VIRGINIA CHILI COOK-OFF

Roanoke   *(703) 981-2889*

Thousands of connoisseurs pour into Roanoke's historic farmer's market the first Saturday in May to indulge themselves. Don't forget to head down the block for some homemade strawberry shortcake at Community School's Strawberry Festival.

FESTIVAL IN THE PARK

Roanoke   *(703) 342-2640*

This is a two-week-long celebration beginning Memorial Day weekend. It hosts one of the East Coast's largest sidewalk art shows, a river race, concerts, fireworks, children's games, ethnic foods, bike and road races and a children's parade. During the second week, a carnival is held at the Civic Center.

VINTON DOGWOOD FESTIVAL

(703) 345-9616

This community next to Roanoke celebrates spring in early May every year with a parade, band competition, an antique car show, music, food, crafts, bike races, a long-distance run, an evening of country music and more.

ARTS AND CRAFTS FESTIVAL

Wytheville   *(703) 228-5541*

This is usually held around the first few days of May.

WINE AND CHEESE FESTIVAL

Wytheville   *(703) 228-3111*

This Virginia wine sampler also includes an auction.

PLUMB ALLEY DAY

Abingdon   *(703) 628-8141*

This arts and crafts jamboree is always held the Saturday of Memorial Day weekend.

MOUNT ROGERS RAMP FESTIVAL

Whitetop Mountain   *(703) 388-3294*

This is a tribute to the pungent wild mountain leek. Bring a bottle of Listerine to the festival if you plan to try some of the many ramp-laden foods. There'll be ramps in stews and salads, fried with trout and roasted with bear meat. Mountain crafts and quilts are on display, and bluegrass music keeps things hopping on the mountain top. This event is always held the third weekend in May.

MOUNT ROGERS NATURALIST RALLY

(703) 783-2125

This is a weekend retreat for discovering the natural history and wildlife of Southwestern Virginia. It features a naturalist speaker and hikes led by college professors. It is usually scheduled in mid-May to coincide with the Ramp Festival.

APPALACHIAN TRAIL DAYS
Damascus   *(304) 535-6331*

This three-day event in tiny Damascus draws AT hikers from far and wide, making it a standard reunion for many. The hikers stage an amusing parade and talent show. Arts and crafts shows, street dances, clogging demonstrations and live music keep little Damascus hopping for days. It's usually held in mid-May.

RALPH STANLEY
BLUE GRASS FESTIVAL
Coeburn   *(703) 395-6318*

This foot stompin' event, featuring local native and bluegrass music legend Ralph Stanley, is held on Memorial Day weekend in this community along the edge of the Jefferson National Forest in the far reaches of Southwestern Virginia.

BIG STONE GAP COUNTRY FAIR
(703) 523-4950

A traditional affair, it's always held on Mother's Day weekend at Bullit Park.

June

SHENANDOAH VALLEY
FARM CRAFT DAYS
Middletown   *(703) 869-2028*

Pottery, quilts, toys and other locally made items are features at this county event.

CONFEDERATE MEMORIAL SERVICE
Winchester   *(703) 662-1937*

This year marks the 128th annual program to honor the memory of the more than 3,000 Confederate soldiers buried in the Stonewall Jackson Cemetery. This is sponsored by the United Daughters of the Confederacy, Chapter 54. It's always held on a Sunday in June.

BLUEMONT CONCERT SERIES
Winchester   *(703) 665-0079*

This free outdoor concert series draws hundreds to the lawn of the old Frederick County Courthouse in Old Town Winchester. You can hear folk, Cajun, bluegrass and other types of acoustic music performed under the stars on Friday evenings in June, July and part of August. It's a relaxing way to end the work week.

COURT DAYS FESTIVAL
Woodstock   *(703) 459-2542*

This event, also held in mid-June, re-creates the days when the old-time County Judge came to town to settle cases. The festival features a dog show, pig roast, street dances, exhibits, live music, a bike-a-thon, 5-K run and more.

NATURAL CHIMNEYS JOUST
Mt. Solon   *(703) 350-2510*

Here's an anachronism if you've ever seen one. This is the National Hall of Fame Jousting Tournament, where "knights" hailing from several states congregate to joust for a shining ring. Bluegrass music fills the air, and the seven castle-like towers of Natural Chimneys form a spectacular backdrop. This happens the third Saturday in June and August every year.

NELSON COUNTY SUMMER FESTIVAL
Rt. 653 (804) 263-5392

Held in late June, this is a family-oriented, upscale festival on the lovely grounds of Oak Ridge Estate south of Lovingston.

SUMMER FESTIVAL OF THE
ARTS AT ASH LAWN-HIGHLAND
Charlottesville (804) 293-4500

This festival is a potpourri of music, with its opera and musical theater productions, a Music at Twilight concert series with traditional and contemporary musical performances and a Summer Saturdays family entertainment series.

ANNUAL SUN AND
SAND BEACH WEEKEND
Stuarts Draft (703) 337-1911

Held at Shenandoah Acres Resort, this is nonstop summer celebration — you'll need plenty of energy for this one. There's volleyball, minigolf, sand castle building contests, various water contests and a DJ dance on Saturday night. This is always held the third weekend in June.

RAIL ROAD DAYS
Clifton Forge (703) 862-2210

Celebrate the railroad heritage of the C&O with the Gandy Dancers, a train excursion, exhibits and all kinds of activities.

BLUE RIDGE MUSIC FESTIVAL
Lynchburg (804) 948-1639

Folk, classical or jazz concerts are held every evening during this week-long event in mid-June at Randolph Macon Women's College.

DINNER AT DUSK
Lynchburg (804) 847-1459

Dine with the crew members of the *James River Bateau* — the resurrected flat-bottomed boat that once hauled tobacco to Richmond and beyond before canals were built. Participants dress in full costume and tell tales of the river, perform folk music and celebrate the start of the Festival by the James.

FESTIVAL BY THE JAMES
Lynchburg (804) 847-1811

This is a downtown festival that celebrates the James River and its significance to the Lynchburg area. Always held in mid-June, it includes a foot race, exhibitions and demonstrations by costumed artisans, Civil War re-enactments, horse pulls, canoe races and more.

CONSERVATION FESTIVAL
Roanoke (703) 343-3241

This is held every year in mid-June at Mill Mountain Zoo.

ROANOKE VALLEY HORSE SHOW
Salem (703) 389-7847

Held in mid-June, this is one of the top all-breed horse shows on the East Coast. It usually attracts about 1,000 entries from across the United States.

MONTGOMERY COUNTY
HISTORICAL FESTIVAL
Blacksburg (703) 552-4061

The Smithfield Plantation hosts this annual event the second Saturday in June.

CAMBRIA
WHISTLESTOP ARTS FESTIVAL
Christiansburg   (703) 382-4251

This juried competition and festival showcases various Southwestern Virginia artists.

FESTIVAL AROUND TOWN
Pearisburg   (703) 921-1324

This beautiful town near the Appalachian Trail hosts this all-day arts and music fete.

CIVIL WAR WEEKEND
Newbern   (703) 674-4835

Held usually the third weekend in June, this event features an afternoon tea, living history demonstrations, marches, a church service and lectures. A battle re-enactment happens Sunday afternoon at Tabor Farm. Other events are held at the Wilderness Road Regional Museum.

RENDEZVOUS
Radford   (703) 639-3619

Appalachian folkways and mountain storytelling are the focus of this all-day festival on the fourth Saturday in June. Events are held at the Long Way Home Outdoor Theater.

CHAUTAUQUA FESTIVAL IN THE PARK
Wytheville   (703) 228-3111

This is the biggest annual event in Wythe County, with nine days and nights of entertainment. Other than arts and craft shows, there are antique sales, ballets and big band, bluegrass and classical music performances.

GRAYSON COUNTY
OLD TIME FIDDLER'S CONVENTION
(703) 655-4144

This is a precursor to the Old-Time Fiddlers Convention held in August in Galax.

BEST FRIEND FESTIVAL
Norton   (703) 679-0961

This event features music, games, arts and crafts and is always held on Father's Day weekend.

CRAFTERS FAIR
Waltons Mountain Country Store
(804) 325-2200

This fair is held in mid-June.

July

SAFE AND SANE
4TH OF JULY CELEBRATION
Winchester   (703) 465-5757

This is a midday party at the downtown pedestrian mall, with patriotic speeches, cake, balloons, carriage rides, a bike decorating contest and a parade.

The best place to watch July Fourth fireworks is in the Valley of Virginia, in places like Staunton, Harrisonburg and Roanoke, where the flashing evening sky silhouettes the mountains. The experience is unforgettable!

Insiders' Tips

FREDERICK COUNTY FAIR

Clearbrook   *(703) 662-9002*

The old-fashioned country fete is held at the county fairgrounds on Route 11 N.

4TH OF JULY CELEBRATION

New Market   *(703) 740-3432*

This Shenandoah Valley town hosts a big celebration for the whole family, with lots of food, games, children's rides, a parade and fireworks.

SHENANDOAH VALLEY MUSIC FESTIVAL

Orkney Springs   *(703) 459-3396*

Classical music is performed in a series of concerts running from July to September live under the stars in an outdoor pavilion next to the Orkney Springs Hotel, a massive pre-Civil War building. Get there early for the ice-cream socials that are held before every concert. Arts and crafts shows are also held those weekends.

SHENANDOAH VALLEY BICYCLE FESTIVAL

Harrisonburg   *(703) 434-3862*

This festival is usually held the last two weekends in July.

INDEPENDENCE DAY CELEBRATION

Charlottesville   *(804) 295-5191*

Held every year at McIntire Park, the celebration includes softball and baseball games, band concerts, children's rides and games, a picnic and, of course, fireworks.

INDEPENDENCE DAY CELEBRATION

Charlottesville   *(804) 295-8181*

About 50 new citizens from the Charlottesville area are naturalized each Fourth of July on the grounds of Thomas Jefferson's Monticello. A fife and drum corps provides music at this moving event, attended usually by nearly 1,000 people.

FOURTH OF JULY JUBILEE

Wintergreen   *(804) 325-2200*

At Wintergreen Resort you'll find greased watermelon races, clogging demonstrations, an arts and crafts show and a grand fireworks display.

PLANTATION DAYS FESTIVAL

Charlottesville   *(804) 293-9539*

At Ash Lawn-Highland, James Monroe's 535-acre estate, merchants, crafters, servants and soldiers are depicted in a celebration of early American life. More than 20 crafters and artisans in period costumes demonstrate and sell their work. Visitors can also enjoy 18th-century music and games and a dressage performance, "Dancing with Horses."

ANNUAL RAFT RACE

Stuarts Draft   *(703) 337-1911*

At Shenandoah Acres Resort, folks of all ages race around a measured course in inflatable rafts. Cash prizes are offered to winners. This always happens in late July.

HAPPY BIRTHDAY U.S.A.

Staunton

As corny as it sounds, this is an old-fashioned, flag-waving, apple-pie Fourth of July celebration spawned by Staunton's hometown heroes, the Statler Brothers. You can be sure to hear plenty of good

Photo: Virginia Div. of Tourism

The Bonnie Blue National, "A" rated for all divisions, is one of the most prestigious events held at the Virginia Horse Center just north of Lexington.

country music at this event, held at Gypsy Hill Park.

JULY 4TH CELEBRATION
Clifton Forge   (703) 862-4246

This is the largest Independence Day spectacle in the Alleghany Highlands.

INDEPENDENCE CELEBRATION
Lynchburg   (804) 525-1806

This is not your typical Fourth of July party. At Poplar Forest, interpreters will portray the lives of local citizenry during Thomas Jefferson's time. There will be early 19th-century craft demonstrations and lots of food.

JULY 4TH CELEBRATION
Bedford   (703) 586-7161

The Blue Ridge lights up under a blazing nighttime sky.

MUSIC FOR AMERICANS
Roanoke   (703) 343-9127

At Roanoke's Victory Stadium, this Fourth of July celebration features a performance by the Roanoke Symphony Orchestra, the community chorus and fireworks.

MISS VIRGINIA PAGEANT
Roanoke   (703) 981-1201

This annual event produces the state's Miss America contestant.

VINTON JULY 4TH CELEBRATION
(703) 342-6025

It is held every year at the Vinton War Memorial.

SALEM FAIR AND EXPOSITION
Salem   *(703) 375-3004*

This is an old-time country fair held at the Salem Civic Center, both indoors and outside. For nearly two weeks there are carnival rides, games, food, concerts and livestock judging. There's also a bake-off that attracts some of the best cooks in the Roanoke Valley.

FOURTH OF JULY CELEBRATION
Radford   *(703) 731-3677*

At Radford's Bisset Park there will be gospel music, craft shows, food vendors and fireworks. All events take place along the New River.

RIVERFEST
Radford   *(703) 639-2202*

Celebrate the great outdoors with a raft race down the New River. There's also a barbecue cooking contest, craft show and live music. It's always held the second Saturday following the Fourth of July.

NEW RIVER VALLEY HORSE SHOW
Dublin   *(703) 980-1991*

This is the largest such event in the New River Valley.

BLUE RIDGE HERITAGE FESTIVAL
Fort Chiswell   *(703) 228-3111*

This event represents Southwestern Virginia's 19 counties, with mountain music, arts and crafts, and representatives from the many attractions of the Blue Ridge and Highlands.

HOTTEST FUN
IN THE SUN BEACH DAY
Wytheville   *(703) 228-3111*

Every third Saturday in July, this event draws sun worshipers and water enthusiasts for a great family fun day.

CHILI COOK-OFF
& INDEPENDENCE DAY CELEBRATION
Marion   *(703) 783-3881*

Cooks and revelers from throughout the Southeast head to Marion for this annual Independence party with spice.

HUNGRY MOTHER STATE PARK
ARTS & CRAFTS FESTIVAL
Marion   *(703) 783-3161*

This event is always held the third weekend in July.

August

OLD TOWN HOE DOWN
Winchester   *(703) 665-0779*

Always held in August, this annual celebration of farming features displays of farm implements, live music, craft demonstrations, fresh produce and a petting zoo. It takes place in Old Town Winchester.

GREAT AMERICAN DUCK RACE
Winchester   *(703) 662-4118*

Held every August at Jim Barnett Park, this is an annual fund-raiser of the Winchester-Patrick County Chamber of Commerce. Games, music, refreshments and duck races attract a good crowd.

ROCKINGHAM COUNTY FAIR

Harrisonburg   (703) 434-0005

Virginia's largest agricultural county salutes its agrarian roots.

THOMAS JEFFERSON'S
TOMATO FAIR

Lynchburg   (804) 847-1499

This early August agrarian festival starts at 6 AM, with tomato and canned good competitions, live entertainment and handmade crafts. It's held at the downtown Community Market.

STEPPING OUT

Blacksburg   (703) 552-4061

This major downtown festival is always held the first weekend in August.

NEWPORT AGRICULTURAL FAIR

(703) 544-7469

One of the oldest agricultural fairs in Virginia, this Giles County community event features judged food and agriculture exhibits and livestock competitions, bluegrass music and horseshoe and jousting tournaments.

VIRGINIA HIGHLANDS FESTIVAL

Abingdon   (703) 628-8141

Beautiful, historic downtown Abingdon is the backdrop for this event that features one of the largest antique shows in the country. There are historic tours, workshops and fine arts and crafts. This is always held the first week in August.

OLD FIDDLER'S CONVENTION

Galax   (703) 236-8541

This is the real McCoy — the oldest and largest old-time music festival in the country. It's always held during the second week in August. You'll find bluegrass and folk bands, clogging and flatfoot dancing day and night.

VIRGINIA KENTUCKY DISTRICT FAIR

Wise   (703) 328-9772

This country fair in rural Wise County features Appalachian music, games, folklife exhibits and rides.

APPALACHIA COAL
AND RAILROAD DAYS

Appalachia   (703) 565-0361

This is a must-do for railroad and coal buffs. It's always held the second weekend in August.

September

APPLE HARVEST
ARTS & CRAFTS FESTIVAL

Winchester   (703) 662-4135

This fall festival offers apple butter-making and pie contests, live music and arts and crafts galore. It's held at Jim Barnett Park.

ANNUAL INTERNATIONAL
STREET FESTIVAL

Winchester   (703) 665-0079

Usually held in late September, this festival features costumes, native gourmet dishes and crafts and entertainments from around the world.

BOTTLE AND POTTERY
SHOW AND SALE

(703) 877-1093

This year marks the 21st annual show and sale of antique bottles, pottery, postcards and small collectibles by the Apple Valley Bottle Collectors Club.

ANNUAL HARVEST FESTIVAL
Edinburg (703) 984-8699

Shenandoah Vineyards hosts an all-day festival every September, giving you a chance to stomp on grapes, munch on barbecue, take a hayride, dance and, of course, sample some wine. There's also an arts and crafts exhibit.

EDINBURG OLE' TIME FESTIVAL
Edinburg (703) 984-8521

Bluegrass music and crafts are on tap at this Shenandoah County fest.

NEW MARKET
ARTS & CRAFTS SHOW
New Market (703) 740-3329

This is a show of high quality arts and crafts from the Blue Ridge and Shenandoah Valley region. It happens every year in late September.

ALBEMARLE COUNTY FAIR
North Garden (804) 296-5803

This is usually held the first few days of September.

CONSTITUTION DAY CELEBRATIONS
(703) 672-2728

Enjoy free admission to tour Montpelier, the home of President James Madison, the father of the Constitution. This is an opportunity to better understand the man who contributed so much to the founding of our government.

LABOR DAY SPECTACULAR
Wintergreen (804) 325-2200

Wintergreen Resort throws a huge weekend party around Labor Day, with a boat race, cookout with bluegrass, goofy talent show and family scavenger hunts.

TRADITIONAL FRONTIER FESTIVAL
Staunton (703) 332-7850

This is a good time to visit the Museum of American Frontier Culture, which hosts this festival the weekend following Labor Day every year. Come and enjoy traditional crafts, food and entertainment from Germany, England, Ireland and America at the museum's "living history" farms.

BUENA VISTA LABOR DAY FESTIVAL
(703) 463-5375

This is a huge event that usually attracts some of the state's leading politicians. There are band concerts, arts and crafts, tennis and horseshoe tournaments, amusement rides and more.

KALEIDOSCOPE
Lynchburg (804) 847-1811

This is Lynchburg's big annual fall festival that lasts nearly three weeks. It includes a children's festival on the third Saturday, major antique show with 100 dealers, riverfront music jamboree with barbecue, craft show, bike race and teddy bear parade. Thousands of runners participate in the 10-mile race.

FALL FOOD FESTIVAL
Lynchburg (804) 847-1499

Held on a mid-September weekend, this fest features the best in regional and seasonal fare.

Photo: Donald Roakes

The James River Bateau Festival is held every June in Lynchburg.

FINCASTLE FESTIVAL
(703) 473-8280
Historic Fincastle celebrates its Scotch-Irish roots at this day-long festival held downtown. Arts, music, games and merchant open houses await visitors.

HENRY STREET HERITAGE FESTIVAL
Roanoke *(703) 345-4818*
This is an annual celebration of African-American culture in a neighborhood close to downtown Roanoke. There are ethnic food, music, entertainment and children's activities.

OLDE SALEM DAYS
Salem *(703) 387-0267*
This is a downtown celebration held the second Saturday in September, the focus of which is antiques, crafts and health care.

WINE FESTIVAL
Smith Mountain Lake *(703) 721-1203*
On the last Sunday in September, nearly a dozen of Virginia's best wineries converge at Bernard's Landing and Resort for a festival on the beautiful lake. Chamber music, wine tastings and good food make this one of the area's more sophisticated festivals.

SEPTEMBERFEST
Radford *(703) 731-3656*
This is a two-day downtown festival with jazz, wine tastings, sidewalk sales and competitions with a variety of bands. Septemberfest always happens the second Friday and Saturday in September.

CLAYTOR LAKE ARTS AND CRAFTS FAIR
Pulaski County *(703) 980-7363*
This a popular Labor Day weekend event for the whole family.

DOCK BOGGS MEMORIAL FESTIVAL

Wythe County (703) 328-0100

This is always held the second weekend in September.

SALTVILLE LABOR DAY CELEBRATION

(703) 496-7038

Here you will find an 1800s fashion show and Civil War re-enactment. There will also be salt-making demonstrations, a street dance, parade and live entertainment.

GRAYSON HIGHLANDS FALL FESTIVAL

Mouth of Wilson (703) 579-7092

Held at the Grayson Highlands State Park, this is an old-time festival with apple butter and molasses-making demonstrations and presentations by a blacksmith. There is bluegrass and gospel music, barbecue chicken and other foods.

CHILHOWIE APPLE FESTIVAL

Chilhowie (703) 646-8213

This Smyth County celebration is always held the last weekend in September.

October

NORTH-SOUTH SKIRMISH ASSOCIATION FALL NATIONALS

Gainesboro (703) 666-7917

Civil War re-enactors fire old weapons at breakable targets in an original manner, wearing authentic uniforms. There is also a ladies' dress competition. This will be the 44th year of this event at Ft. Shenandoah.

ANTIQUE SHOW AND SALE

Winchester (703) 662-4996

This show is held in early October at the War Memorial Building.

BATTLE OF CEDAR CREEK LIVING HISTORY & RE-ENACTMENT

Middletown (703) 869-2028

This is a panorama of Civil War-era living history, including the only re-enactment held on an original battlefield of the Civil War. This takes place at Belle Grove Plantation on the weekend closest to October 19, the anniversary of the Battle of Cedar Creek of 1864.

HERITAGE FESTIVAL

Luray (703) 778-3230

This festival brings to mind the old-time county fair. There's country music, clogging shows, wagon rides, apple cider, home-cooked food, a steam and gas engine show and a Saturday Chili Cook-Off. More than 100 crafts workers also display their wares.

ELKTON AUTUMN DAYS ARTS & CRAFTS FESTIVAL

Elkton (703) 298-9370

This is an outdoor festival that's usually held during the best weekend for enjoying the brilliant colors of autumn.

BACCHANALIAN FEAST

Charlottesville (804) 296-4188

This evening feast at the Boar's Head Inn includes a seven-course meal with Virginia wines and entertainment. It's usually held on one of the first Fridays in October to kick off the Monticello Wine and Food Festival.

MONTICELLO WINE AND FOOD FESTIVAL

Charlottesville   (804) 296-4188

Held also at the Boar's Head Inn, this is a chance to taste many of the wines made in Virginia and view exhibits of the state's many wineries and vineyards.

VIRGINIA FESTIVAL OF AMERICAN FILM

Charlottesville
          (804) 924-FEST , (800) UVA-FEST

Film makers, scholars, movie stars and the public explore trends in American film making at this event, which usually happens around the end of October. In the past, such stars as Gregory Peck and Sissy Spacek have graced the festival. (See our Arts and Culture chapter for more information.)

VIRGINIA HERITAGE WEEKEND

Wintergreen   (804) 325-2200

Wintergreen Resort hosts this event the first weekend of October. There will be a country cookout and an outdoor bluegrass concert, Appalachian heritage crafts workshops, clogging demonstrations, folklore and storytelling.

APPLE BUTTER MAKING FESTIVAL

Nelson County   (804) 277-5865

This festival is held both at the beginning of October and in the middle of the month.

HALLOWEEN WEEKEND

Wintergreen   (804) 325-2200

Take the eerie Ghost Express chair lift; then share hair-raising stories around the campfire at Wintergreen this weekend. There's also

a children's haunted house, a costume contest and opportunities for families to carve pumpkins.

VIRGINIA FALL FOLIAGE FESTIVAL

Waynesboro   (703) 949-6505

This happens usually the first two consecutive weekends in October. This major event features a 10-K run, an arts and crafts show with more than 200 exhibitors, a chili cookoff and lots of good foods made with apples. It also includes a gem and mineral show.

OKTOBERFEST

Staunton   (703) 886-2351

German beer, Virginia wine, food and an Oompah Band playing traditional German music make this a special festival. There's also a Bach Bash presented by the Mid-Atlantic Chamber Orchestra and arts and crafts displays.

FALL FOLIAGE FESTIVAL

Clifton Forge   (703) 862-4969

The autumn glory of Alleghany County serves as an incredible backdrop for this arts, craft and food festival.

SORGHUM MOLASSES FESTIVAL

Clifford   (804) 946-5063

This little town east of the Blue Ridge salutes the dark, gooey sweet substance in October with a festival that includes a jousting tournament, country music, arts and crafts and a flea market. You can also watch molasses and apple butter being made.

VIRGINIA GARLIC FESTIVAL
Amherst (804) 946-5168

The five-acre Rebec Vineyards hosts this mid-October celebration. Several Virginia wineries participate, and there is wonderful food for epicures. A Garlic Queen dressed in a giant bulb with sprouts shooting from her head has been known to make an appearance.

JAZZ ON THE LAWN
Concord 804) 993-2185

Just east of Lynchburg is another winery, Stonewall Vineyards, which hosts this relaxing weekend event in mid-October. Enjoy live jazz, gourmet food and local wines.

HARVEST FESTIVAL
Lynchburg (804) 847-1499

This end-of-October festival features Virginia-made products and crafts, square dancing and country music. Children go crazy with the costume contests and community pumpkin-carving.

HARVEST FESTIVAL ON THE MARKET
Roanoke (703) 342-2028

Every October, folks pour into the streets of Roanoke's historic City Market for horse-drawn carriage rides, lessons in scarecrow-building, hot cider and live bluegrass.

ROANOKE RAILWAY FESTIVAL
Roanoke (703) 342-2028

The city celebrates its railroad heritage every year with a Columbus Day festival all weekend. You can take a ride on an old steam train then have a bite of pork at the pig roast. There's also nostalgic entertainment, a car show and a huge rail-related crafts show at the nearby Civic Center.

ANNUAL ZOO BOO
Roanoke (703) 343-3241

It's a Halloween party at the Mill Mountain Zoo.

HAUNTED CAVERNS
Dixie Caverns (703) 380-2085

This Halloween tour of Dixie Caverns will make your hair stand on end. Grinding chain saws, shrieks and lots of fake blood make this event a blast for those who thrive on horror.

SMITH MOUNTAIN LAKE FALL FESTIVAL
(703) 721-1203

Also on Columbus Day weekend, Smith Mountain Lake's six or so communities all host festivals — forming a virtual ring of festivals around the lake. There are arts and crafts shows, an antique car show, a flea market, traditional folkway demonstrations and more.

BLUE RIDGE FOLKLIFE FESTIVAL
Ferrum (703) 365-2121

Ferrum College hosts this annual event the last Saturday in October. Widely attended, the festival showcases regional traditions, with crafts workers showing time-honored skills, old-time musicians and traditional Appalachian competitions.

WHITETOP MOUNTAIN SORGHUM AND MOLASSES FESTIVAL
(703) 388-3294

This festival at Mount Rogers National Recreation Area features molasses and apple butter made the old-fashioned way. There are games, bake sales, arts and crafts and old-time gospel and bluegrass music.

MECC HOME CRAFTS DAYS
Big Stone Gap *(703) 523-2400*

Two days of arts and crafts at Mountain Empire Community College feature bluegrass and country music, clogging, whittling, broommaking and other mountain heritage displays.

November

OLD TOWN CHRISTMAS PARADE
Winchester *(703) 667-2409*

This parade is held in late November.

MONTPELIER HUNT RACES
(703) 672-2728

These famous races have been taking place on the beautiful grounds of Montpelier, home of James Madison, since 1934.. They feature two flat track and five overjump races, as well as a Jack Russell terrier race and the Dolley Madison tailgate competition.

THANKSGIVING AT WINTERGREEN
(804) 325-2200

If cooking for a crowd is not what you want, spend the weekend at Wintergreen. They'll deliver turkey and all the trimmings to the door of your rented condo. Or you can partake of traditional buffets and dinners at all the resort's restaurants. There's also a turkey trot square dance, a hayride sing-along and a musical revue cabaret.

CHRISTMAS AT THE MARKET
Lynchburg *(804) 847-1499*

Always held at the end of November at the downtown Community Market.

FRANKLIN COUNTY FALL ARTS AND CRAFTS FESTIVAL
Rocky Mount *(703) 483-9542*

This festival is usually held the weekend before Thanksgiving.

ARTS AND CRAFTS BAZAAR
Wytheville *(703) 228-3111*

This bazaar is usually held the weekend before Thanksgiving.

December

ABRAM'S DELIGHT CANDLELIGHT TOUR
Winchester *(703) 662-6550*

Take the tour at Abram's Delight, Winchester's oldest home.

CHRISTMAS OPEN HOUSE AT STONEWALL JACKSON'S HEADQUARTERS
Winchester *(703) 662-6550*

Members of the United Daughters of the Confederacy are your costumed hostesses at this Confederate Christmas.

FIRST NIGHT WINCHESTER
(703) 662-3884

This is an annual New Year's Eve celebration of the arts in town. More than 40 different artists perform at sites throughout Winchester in this family-oriented, alcohol-free celebration.

CHRISTMAS CANDLELIGHT TOUR
Middletown   *(703) 869-2028*

See Belle Grove Plantation decked in its holiday splendor.

ANNUAL YULETIDE TRADITIONS
Charlottesville   *(804) 977-1783*

These special events at Ash Lawn-Highland, historic Michie Tavern and Monticello are held throughout December. There are Christmas By Candlelight evening tours and historic re-enactments at Ash Lawn-Highland. Also at Ash Lawn is Gingerbread and Lace, a celebration with caroling, ornament making, tree trimming and refreshments. At Michie Tavern, an array of Christmas delicacies are served in the Ordinary for a Yuletide feast. Monticello holds a candlelight open house several evenings before Christmas, with refreshments and music. There's also a holiday wreath workshop at the Monticello Visitors Center. The first few days after Christmas there are afternoon holiday concerts at Ash Lawn-Highland.

FIRST NIGHT VIRGINIA
Charlottesville   *(804) 296-8269*

This is a family-oriented New Year's celebration of the arts in the downtown area from 6 PM to midnight.

APPALACHIAN MOUNTAIN CHRISTMAS
Wintergreen   *(804) 325-2200*

During Christmas week, the resort celebrates with horse-drawn carriage rides, ornament and Appalachian craft workshops, wandering minstrels, jugglers and clowns and an old-fashioned carol sing. You can also enjoy a candlelight Christmas buffet and grand lighting ceremony.

TRADITIONS OF CHRISTMAS
Museum of American Frontier Culture
Staunton   *(703) 332-7850*

Throughout the month there are opportunities to tour the museum's living farms by lantern at night and to learn about how America's early settlers and their kin in the old country prepared for Christmas. There are also gift-making workshops for children.

CHRISTMAS AT THE MANSE
Staunton   *(703) 886-2351*

The holidays add a special glow to the Woodrow Wilson Birthplace.

CHRISTMAS AT POINT OF HONOR
Lynchburg   *(804) 847-1459*

This is a celebration of the joyous season as it would have been in the 1820s. Held at Point of Honor, a mansion built by Patrick Henry's doctor, George Cabell, the event is an opportunity to revel in the color and aroma of festive greens and sing along with a local group performing 19th-century carols.

SCROOGE DAY
Lynchburg   *(804) 847-1499*

Always the last Saturday before Christmas, this is the day to take care of last-minute shopping at the downtown Community Market. You'll find handmade gifts, stocking stuffers, home-baked treats, wreaths, greenery and trees.

ROANOKE CHRISTMAS PARADE
(703) 981-2889

This is a festive outing for the whole family; it's always held the first Saturday in December.

DICKENS OF A CHRISTMAS
Roanoke   *(703) 342-2028*

Always the second Saturday in December, Roanoke's City Market is the place for carriage rides, chestnut roasting, ice carvings, hot cider and holiday music.

FIRST NIGHT ROANOKE

This is a nonalcoholic New Year's celebration in the downtown City Market area. There's ice skating for kids, holiday music, hot cocoa and a "Resolution Wall" where you can write your New Year's resolutions for the world to see.

DECK THE HALLS OPEN HOUSE
Newbern   *(703) 674-5888*

Visit the Wilderness Road Regional Museum for a rustic Christmas to remember.

CHRISTMAS CANDLELIGHT TOUR OF HOMES
Abingdon   *(703) 676-2282*

In mid-December, Abingdon's loveliest homes are open for tours. There are also holiday music parties, carolers and horse-drawn carriage rides.

CHRISTMAS AND FLOWER SHOW
Big Stone Gap   *(703) 523-1235*

The show is held on the first weekend in December.

Photo: Roanoke Convention and Visitors Bureau

Professional actors perform at Mill Mountain Theater year round.

Inside
Arts and Culture

Whew! For a relatively sparsely populated region, the Blue Ridge of Virginia offers abundant opportunities for arts and cultural experiences. Listing the best and brightest is a difficult task, since they're all backed by energetic people who believe strongly in the cause they promote.

The diversity of arts and culture is a pendulum of interesting events. Elvis Presley lives on in Roanoke, where he is honored by a private citizen at Miniature Graceland, while maple sugar is celebrated at its own museum in Highland County. Also in Highland, you can attend Bear Mountain Outdoor School and learn Blue Ridge country survival skills such as building a log cabin. In Alleghany County, there's one of the largest railroad archives in the United States, through the C&O Railroad Historical Society.

If music is your leisure salvation, you can choose Friday night flat-footing at Cockram's General Store in Floyd County, with fiddles, autoharps and a 1940 juke box that still works. Or, you can attend chamber music fests at Garth Newel Music Center in Bath County, where you may find yourself in an audience once graced by the late Jackie Kennedy Onassis or other New York City residents who jet into the Homestead Resort for the mountain ambiance in the beautiful hills of Bath.

Historically speaking, the Charlottesville area is one of the country's best-known tourist cities, with such attractions as Montpelier, Monticello and Ash Lawn-Highland, the former homes of three of our greatest presidents. Half a million visitors a year make the trek to the neoclassical mansion designed by the third president of the United States, Thomas Jefferson. Farther south, you can travel to Jefferson's summer getaway at Poplar Forest in Bedford County. In the hills of Pulaski County, you can stroll through an 1810 village in Old Newbern and see what life was like nearly two centuries ago.

History buffs shouldn't overlook an important source of information at our nation's libraries. In Lynchburg, Jones Memorial is one of the nation's foremost genealogical libraries and offers research and lending services by mail. Virginia Tech's Carol Newman Library has the fifth largest microforms collection in the United States and Canada.

Theater opportunities range from movies to live performances. Worldly chic Charlottesville, home to numerous movie stars and directors, hosts the biggest names in the movie business with its Virginia Festival of American Film. More than 20,000 people show up for the annual event. Here's a chance to view film classics and hobnob with celebrities, who usually attend the closing bash.

If historical drama is more to your liking, you can attend Virginia's only outdoor drama, *The Long Way Home*. This stirring true saga of Mary Draper Ingles' capture by Indians and escape home through nearly 1,000 miles of wilderness to Radford has been riveting audiences to their seats for 22 years.

It seems that, no matter how small, nearly every community in the Blue Ridge has its own performing theater group, some comprised of as few as a dozen people, as in, for example, sparsely populated Giles County. In small town Lexington, Lime Kiln Theater enjoys a national reputation for its open-air plays and musical performances in a magical setting. Staunton residents Robin and Linda Williams, from public radio's "A Prairie Home Companion" with Garrison Keillor and Lake Wobegon, are regulars.

If you're a museum buff, the range and quality of museums here are beyond belief for an area the size of the Blue Ridge. The Mennonite-influenced work of world-famous artist P. Buckley Moss, "the people's artist," whose annual revenues have been estimated at $11

million, can be seen in her private retreat and museum at Waynesboro.

There's probably not a small town in the United States with as many military museums as Lexington, with its VMI Museum, George C. Marshall Museum, Stonewall Jackson House and Lee Chapel.

In the Roanoke Valley, an international tribute to the millions of lives touched by the volunteer rescue squad movement, "To the Rescue," honoring the father of the movement, Julian Stanley Wise, can be seen in the Roanoke Valley History Museum.

Some museums honor a way of life we tend to forget about, such as the Cyrus McCormick Museum in Rockbridge County. It is dedicated to the inventor of the first successful reaper, which revolutionized agriculture. Each county seat seems to have its own museum for recording local history. One, in Botetourt County, records the history of a county seat that once was an English land grant stretching the whole way to the Mississippi River!

Not to be underestimated for the role they play in the region's arts and culture are the wonderful, diverse programs underwritten by colleges and universities. Enough cannot be said about the influence of academic giants such as Virginia Tech in Blacksburg and the University of Virginia in Charlottesville. Yet, the largest colony of artists in residence in the country, the Virginia Center for the Creative Arts (affiliated with Sweet Briar College), is located in the remote foothills of the Blue Ridge in Amherst County. And then there's tiny Ferrum College in Franklin County, which has taken upon itself to become the nation's most important repository of Blue Ridge Culture through its Blue Ridge Farm Museum, Institute and Folk Life Festival.

Education in the arts doesn't begin on the college level. Nearby, in culturally rich Lynchburg, is the Virginia School of the Arts, one of the few select secondary schools in the nation tailored for the study of the arts.

The cultures of many ethnic groups are celebrated here. African-American poet Anne Spencer was a celebrity in her time in Lynchburg, constantly entertaining a steady flow of world dignitaries at her renovated home and grounds, open to the public by appointment. In her meticulous garden, she chatted with Martin Luther King, Paul Robeson, Marion Anderson, Thurgood Marshall, Dr. George Washington Carver and Jackie Robinson. Congressman Adam Clayton Powell even honeymooned there. In Roanoke, the Harrison Heritage Museum for African-American Culture exists to celebrate and remind western Virginia of the rich contributions of its black citizenry.

Enjoy selecting attractions from our list below of the best and the brightest. Since many attractions are rural and some understaffed and underfunded, you may want to call ahead to be sure of hours. Admission prices, of course, also may change. Good luck if you're trying to see it all!

Shenandoah Valley Region

Winchester and Frederick County

THEATER

SHENANDOAH SUMMER MUSIC THEATRE

Shenandoah University
1460 University Dr.
Winchester   (703) 665-4569

Student actors, singers and dancers perform four lively musicals ev-

---

ery summer, Wednesday through Sunday nights, at the university.

WAYSIDE THEATRE

Main St.
Middletown *(703) 869-1776*

The second oldest professional theater in the state brings the best of Broadway to the valley from May to December. The company's professional actors from New York and around the country perform comedies, dramas and mysteries in an intimate downtown theater. The theater is in the middle of this little town, which you'll find by taking Exit 302 from I-81.

DANCE

MASSANUTTEN MOUNTAIN CLOGGERS

Harrisonburg *(703) 434-1251*

This small clogging group performs at such posh places as the Homestead, the Greenbrier and the Commonwealth Club in Richmond, as well as at local craft shows. They're looking for new members and will give lessons on the traditional dance form.

PLAINS PROMENADERS
SQUARE DANCE GROUP

Luray *(703) 743-6792*

This group of about 60 dancers meets for classes and workshops every Tuesday night September through May at the Plains Elementary School in Timberville. Some of the more advanced dancers also perform at special events around the area. The group's been around for about 20 years.

MUSEUMS

ABRAM'S DELIGHT MUSEUM

1340 Pleasant Valley Rd.
Winchester *(703) 662-6519*

This is the oldest house in Winchester, built in 1754 of native limestone with walls 2½ feet thick. There's also a restored log cabin on the lawn from the same period. Abram's Delight is beautifully restored and furnished with period pieces. It's open daily from 9 AM to 5 PM April 1 through October. Admission is $3.50 for adults, $3 for seniors and $1.75 for children ages six to 12. You can save by buying a block ticket for entrance to this museum and two other historic sites in town, Stonewall Jackson's Headquarters and George Washington's Office Museum. Block tickets cost $7.50 for adults, $6.50 for seniors and $4 for children.

KURTZ CULTURAL CENTER

2 N. Cameron St.
Winchester *(703) 722-6367*

Admission is free to this newest addition to Winchester's cultural life. The center is a short walk from the downtown pedestrian mall.

Downstairs in the building is a permanent interpretive exhibit called "Shenandoah — Crossroads of the Civil War." Numerous displays detail the Shenandoah Valley's major battles. Upstairs is an art gallery whose exhibits change regularly. The cultural center is open Monday through Saturday from 10 AM to 5 PM and Sundays noon to 5 PM.

WASHINGTON'S OFFICE MUSEUM
Braddock and Cork Sts.
Winchester (703) 662-4412
Part of this old log and stone building was used by Washington when he was colonel of the Virginia Regiment protecting the 300-mile frontier to the west. It's open daily from 9 AM to 5 PM April 1 through October. Admission is $2 for adults, $1.50 for seniors and $1 for children from ages six to 12.

OTHER CULTURAL ATTRACTIONS

BELLE GROVE PLANTATION
U. S. Hwy. 11
Middletown (703) 869-2028
Belle Grove (c. 1794) is an 18th-century plantation, working farm and center for the study of traditional rural crafts. It was the home of Major Isaac Hite, Jr. and his family for more than 70 years. Hite was a grandson of one of the first permanent settlers in the Shenandoah Valley. Thomas

Jefferson was actively involved in Belle Grove's design, thanks to some family connections. Hite married the sister of James Madison, who was a close friend of Jefferson. In fact, James and Dolley Madison spent part of their honeymoon visiting the Hites at Belle Grove.

Belle Grove hosts a variety of special activities throughout the year, from the Shenandoah Valley Farm Craft Days in early June to the Battle of Cedar Creek Living History Weekend in mid-October. There's also a very nice gift shop and quilt shop at the site.

The plantation is open to the public mid-March through mid-November from 10 AM to 4 PM daily and Sundays from 1 to 5 PM. Admission is $3.50 for adults, $3 for seniors and $2 for children ages six through 12. Belle Grove is one mile south of Middletown on U.S. Highway 11. Take Exit 302 from I-81, then head west on Route 627 to U.S. Highway 11.

STONEWALL
JACKSON'S HEADQUARTERS
415 North Braddock St.
Winchester (703) 667-3242

Jackson used the private home of Lt. Col. Lewis T. Moore as his headquarters during the Civil War from 1861 to 1862. Jackson's office is much as it was during his stay, and the house contains artifacts of Jackson, Turner Ashby, Jed Hotchkiss and other Confederates. The house is open daily from 9 AM to 5 PM April 1 through October. Admission is $3.50 for adults, $3 for seniors and $1.75 for children.

Shenandoah and Page Counties

VISUAL ARTS

JOHN SEVIER GALLERY
Congress St. and Old Cross Rd,
New Market (703) 740-3911

Set in a little log cabin in the heart of the downtown, this gallery specializes in watercolors and oil paintings by three local artists. It also sells locally made crafts such as woodwork, ornaments and stained glass windows, and fine photographs. One wall is set aside for an "Artist of the Month" display. The gallery is open seven days a week.

MUSEUMS

BEDROOMS OF AMERICA MUSEUM
9386 Congress St.
New Market (703) 740-3512

This sounds like a sleeper of a museum, but actually it's a fascinating place if you like old furniture and want to learn more about American antiques. There are 11 different rooms of authentic furniture showing every period of America's bedrooms, from William & Mary (c. 1650) through Art Deco (c. 1930). The rooms are also furnished with period accessories, bed coverings, curtains and wall coverings. The museum is housed in a restored 18th-century building that was used for a time by Confederate General Jubal Early as his headquarters during the Civil War. It's open daily from 9 AM to 8 PM from Memorial Day to Labor Day and the rest of the year from 9 AM to 5 PM. The museum is closed on Christmas Day. Admission is $2 for adults and $1.25 for children ages eight to 14.

STRASBURG MUSEUM
King St. (703) 465-3175

This museum was originally a steam pottery (c. 1891) and is a registered historic landmark. Strasburg was once famous for its pottery, and its old nickname, Pottown, can still be seen around town on various business signs. The museum displays blacksmith, copper and pottery shop collections and artifacts from Colonial farms, homes, barns and businesses. There are also Civil War and railroad relics. The museum is open daily from 10 AM to 4 PM May through October. Admission is $2 for adults and 50¢ for children.

TUTTLE & SPICE GENERAL
STORE MUSEUM

Four miles north of New Market at
Shenandoah Caverns Exit (703) 477-9428

The museum features nine shops set up to resemble a 19th-century country village. These include a tobacco store, doctor's house, haberdashery, millinery, apothecary shop and ice cream parlor. The items in the shops are museum pieces and not for sale, but there is a large gift shop. Admission is free, and the museum is open daily from 9 AM to 6 PM.

WOODSTOCK MUSEUM

137 West Court St.   (703) 459-5518

This downtown museum features artifacts of country life in Shenandoah County, including tools, pottery, hardware, linens and handmade furniture. Admission is free.

MUSIC

SHENANDOAH VALLEY
MUSIC FESTIVAL

Woodstock   (703) 459-3396

This 31-year-old outdoor summer music festival features symphony pops, classical masterworks, folk, jazz and big band music — all performed on the grounds of the grand, historic Orkney Springs Hotel. This was a popular spa and mineral springs resort at the turn of the century. Evening concerts are held on weekends from mid-July through Labor Day in a rustic open-air pavilion. Arts and crafts shows take place on the hotel's front lawn on the symphony concert weekends and feature handcrafts by artisans from the Shenandoah Valley and greater region.

Another festival tradition is the old-fashioned ice cream social held next to the pavilion prior to each concert. Admission prices and concert times vary. For information and a free season brochure contact the Festival's Woodstock headquarters. By the way, the Orkney Springs Hotel serves country-style buffet dinners on all concert nights. Reservations are required and can be made by calling (703) 856-2141. Lots of guests also like to picnic on the grounds before the concerts.

Those with a literary bent like to pay homage to Charlottesville, Virginia's poetry and prose capital, where they can sit in on symposiums and lectures sponsored by UVA's English Department, walk over to the campus's restored Edgar Allan Poe dormitory room, or hang out at the nearby Kafkafe with other soon-to-be Flannery O'Conners and William Faulkners.

Insiders' Tips

OTHER CULTURAL ATTRACTIONS

LURAY CAVERNS CAR AND CARRIAGE CARAVAN

U.S. 211 Bypass,
Luray (703) 743-6551

Right next to Luray Caverns is a car buff's haven — rooms full of all kinds of automobiles from the vehicle's first 50 years of existence. The museum grew out of the car collecting hobby of Caverns president H.T.N. Graves. You'll see Rudolph Valentino's 1925 Rolls Royce, a Conestoga wagon, an ornate sleigh, an 1892 Benz, one of the oldest cars in the country, and much more. All 140 items—cars, coaches, carriages and costumes— are fully restored. Admission is included in your ticket to Luray Caverns. The Caravan is open every day, beginning at 9 AM and closing 1½ hours after the last cavern's tour.

Harrisonburg and Rockingham County

VISUAL ARTS

DONOVAN'S FRAMERY

130 University Blvd.
Harrisonburg (703) 434-4440

This shop behind Valley Mall is the site of permanent exhibitions of the Rockingham County Fine Arts Association.

SAWHILL GALLERY

James Madison University (703) 568-6407

This gallery exhibits five or six shows of fine art a year. It's open during the academic year on weekdays from 10:30 AM to 4:30 PM and weekends from 1:30 to 4:30 PM. In the summer, it's open only on weekdays from noon to 4 PM. There is no admission charge.

MUSEUMS

JAMES MADISON UNIVERSITY LIFE SCIENCE MUSEUM

Burruss Hall (703) 568-6378

This museum displays Native American relics, sea shells, birds and butterflies from around the world. It's open during the academic year, and the hours vary, depending upon the schedules of student volunteers.

REUEL B. PRITCHETT MUSEUM

Bridgewater Community College
(804) 828-2501

A collection of rare artifacts here includes a three-volume Bible printed in Venice in 1482 and a medieval book of Gregorian Chants made and hand-copied by a monk. Admission is free, and the museum is open Tuesday through Thursday 2 to 4 PM.

SHENANDOAH VALLEY HERITAGE MUSEUM

115 Bowman Rd.
Dayton (703) 879-2616

This museum features a 12-foot electric relief map that depicts Stonewall Jackson's Valley Campaign of 1862. the map fills an entire wall and lets you see and hear the campaign battle by battle. The museum also displays many artifacts revealing different aspects of the Shenandoah Valley's history. It is open Monday through Saturday from May 1 through October from

OPERA ROANOKE

. . . bringing opera to life

1994 - 1995 Season!

Rigoletto   **Amahl**
Travels
world premiere

The Jefferson Center   **703-982-2742**

9 AM to 4 PM and Sundays from 1 to 4 PM. The rest of the year it is open only on weekends. Admission is $4 for adults and $2 for children ages six through 12.

THEATER

JAMES MADISON UNIVERSITY DINNER THEATER

Gibbons Hall   (703) 568-6740

Every summer the drama department puts on three plays seven nights a week. There's also a nice spread of food to enjoy while you're watching the light dramas.

LATIMER-SHAEFFER THEATRE

James Madison University (703) 568-6260

This theater presents dance, live music and plays throughout the academic year and in the summer.

OTHER CULTURAL ATTRACTIONS

THE DANIEL HARRISON HOUSE (FORT HARRISON)

Dayton   (703) 879-2280

This historic stone house (c. 1749) just north of Dayton was a natural fort to which Daniel Harrison added a stockade and an underground passage to a nearby spring. Loopholes for firing rifles at Native Americans may have been set in the house's stone walls, giving rise to the name Fort Harrison. Guided tours of the house are available, and there is no admission charge.

The site also hosts community events, such as a Family Craft Weekend the second weekend in June and the Dayton Autumn Festival the first Saturday in October.

The Daniel Harrison House opens in late May and closes the last Sunday in October. It is open for special events November to April.

Hours are 1 to 5 PM Saturdays and Sundays.

LINCOLN HOMESTEAD
Rt. 42, Harrisonburg

Abraham Lincoln's father, Thomas Lincoln, was born in Rockingham County, and his ancestors were buried here in a little cemetery 7.5 miles north of Harrisonburg on Route 42. The house now standing at the old Lincoln homestead is privately owned, so please respect that when you visit the cemetery.

Staunton, Waynesboro and Augusta County

VISUAL ARTS

THE FRAME GALLERY
21 N. Market St.
Staunton   *(703) 885-2697*

This small gallery inside a downtown frame shop displays paintings, prints, sculpture, tapestries and artifacts. It's open from 9:30 AM to 5 PM Tuesday through Friday and from 9:30 AM to 2 PM on Saturdays.

SHENANDOAH VALLEY ART CENTER
600 W. Main St.
Waynesboro   *(703) 949-7662*

This nonprofit cultural center provides a forum for artists of all diversities to exhibit their works. Located in a beautiful, old downtown house, the center holds art exhibits, music and drama performances, workshops and classes for children and adults. It is an affiliate of the Virginia Museum of Fine Arts. You'll also find readings of prose and poetry and even music appreciation lectures. The galleries are open 10 AM to 4 PM Tuesday through Saturday and 2 to 4 PM Sunday. Admission is free.

STAUNTON-AUGUSTA ART CENTER
1 Gypsy Hill Park   *(703) 885-2028*

An old pump house at the entrance to the beautiful Gypsy Hill Park in Staunton is headquarters for this art center, an affiliate of the Virginia Museum. It puts on 10 exhibitions every year, some of which are shows on tour from the Virginia Museum. It also displays art work by area elementary and high school students every May and exhibits works of local artists. In addition, the art center offers classes and workshops for children and adults throughout the year. An Outdoor Art Show is held on the third Saturday of May. During the holidays, there's an Art for Gifts Exhibit and Sale. It's open 9 AM to 5 PM weekdays and 10 AM to 2 PM Saturdays. Admission is free.

VALLEY FRAMING STUDIO & GALLERY
328 W. Main St.
Waynesboro   *(703) 943-7529*
(800) 821-7529

Valley Framing Studio is the area's most comprehensive art gallery, carrying the largest inventory of art and artists' work in the Shenandoah Valley. The gallery specializes in limited edition prints and represents nearly 100 percent of the major print publishers in the art world. Work from artists such as Bev Doolittle, Robert Bateman, Steve Lyman, Charles Wysocki and Charles Fracé is available here. And

Civil War or aviation art lovers will recognize Troiana, Kuntsler, Gallon, Harvey, Phillips and Kodera. Valley Framing also has an extensive inventory of local and regional artists' prints, bronzes and ceramics. The gallery is open year round from 10 AM to 5 PM Monday through Friday and 10 AM to 3 PM Saturday and by appointment.

WHARF GALLERY
125 S. New St.
Staunton (703) 886-0271, (800) 903-0122

This fabulous gallery is located in the historic White Star Mill building that once housed a steam generated flour mill. The mill operated for 83 years, from 1892 to 1975, and produced several varieties of flour. Today, variety is still available. The gallery displays a wealth of pottery (functional and decorative), prints, paintings, ceramics, jewelry and other crafts by local and regional artists. Admission to the gallery is free. There is also a framing shop with a wide selection of frames and mattings. Wharf Gallery is also in the process of expanding from the second floor of the mill onto the third floor. The shop offers art gallery qulity at affordable prices. Hours are 10 AM to 6 PM Tuesday through Thursday, 10 AM to 9 PM Friday, 10 AM to 7 PM Saturday and 1 to 5 PM Sunday. There are extended hours from August through November.

DANCE

SHENANDOAH CLOGGERS
Staunton Parks
and Recreation Dept.   (703) 245-5727

This group of about 26 dancers practices every Thursday night at Staunton's Gypsy Hill Park. They teach lessons to children and adults from 6 to 6:45 PM, then practice until 9 PM. The cloggers perform

Photo: Virginia Div. of Tourism

Traditional German dancing entertains visitors at the Museum of American Frontier Culture.

all over the place, from nursing homes and civic meeting halls to arts festivals and parades.

MUSEUMS

MUSEUM OF AMERICAN FRONTIER CULTURE

Exit 222 off I-81, then Rt. 250 W.
(follow signs)
Staunton (703) 332-7850

Somehow, museum doesn't seem an appropriate word for the living, breathing outdoor Museum of American Frontier Culture. Authentic farmsteads have been painstakingly brought from the Old World and reconstructed here. Original gardens, hedges, pastures and even road layouts have been duplicated, along with the old ways of survival. There are Scotch-Irish, 17th-century German and early American farmsteads, and an English farmstead is now under construction. The staff of knowledgeable, articulate interpretrs makes a visit truly exciting. All kinds of critters make their home at the museum, from lambs and chickens to cows and kittens, and this helps make for a thrilling day for children. Dozens of special events take place throughout the year, such as Lantern Tours at Christmas and the Traditional Frontier Festival in mid-September, with crafts, food and entertainment. Last year, the museum was awarded the coveted "Phoenix" from the National Travel Writers Association. That tells you just how special this plce is. The museum is open 9 AM to 5 PM daily. Hours are 10 AM to 4 PM December 1 through March 15; it is closed Thanksgiving, Christmas and New Year's Day. Admission is $5 for adults, $2.50 for children and $4.50 for seniors. Special rates for a group of 15 or more are available.

P. BUCKLEY MOSS MUSEUM

2150 Rosser Ave.
Waynesboro (703) 949-6473

The museum dedicated to this former resident of Augusta County resembles many of the large, tall houses built by early 19th-century settlers. Since the early 1960s, Moss has found her inspiration and much of her subject matter in Shenandoah Valley scenery and in the Amish and Mennonite peoples of the area. Although the artist was born in New York, she moved here in the mid '60s when her husband got a job at DuPont. Hers is a moving story. Born with what later was diagnosed as dyslexia into a family of high achievers, Moss was ridiculed and taunted as a child for her lack of academic prowess. She hid her childhood sorrow in her artwork, and eventually her family recognized her artistic genius. As a result, she now uses her foundation profits, guided by the worldwide Moss Society, to help needy children. Whenever she travels, she makes it a point to visit pediatric hospital centers to encourage children. She and her firt husband lived here for about 20 years. She married her English manager after her divorce. The museum's displays examine the symbolism in her work and her sources. Her mother works at the museum, and Moss often visits when she's not traveling. The museum and shop are located just

south of I-64 at the Waynesboro West Exit. The hours are 10 AM to 6 PM Monday through Saturday and 12:30 PM to 5:30 PM Sunday. Admission is free.

WOODROW WILSON
MUSEUM AND BIRTHPLACE
18 to 24 N. Coalter St.,
Staunton *(703) 885-0897*

This museum is a tribute to our nation's 28th president, who was born next door to a Presbyterian minister and his wife in 1856. The museum chronicles in detail Wilson's life as a scholar, Princeton University president, governor and statesman. Seven exhibit galleries include rare artifacts, photographs, personal possessions and a replica of Wilson's study at Princeton. The displays do not shy away from the controversies Wilson generated in his lifetime—from the way in which he alienated wealthy trustees and alumni as Princeton's president to his lack of support for women's

suffrage as U.S. president. Of course, the displays also highlight the reforms Wilson brought about as the nation's leader.

The museum houses Wilson's beloved Pierce-Arrow automobile, which is brought out yearly in the Happy Birthday USA parade down Main Street and also travels to the Pierce-Arrow Convention in California. His birthplace has been carefully restored to appear as it would have when he lived there as a child. Throughout the Greek Revival-style house are furnitur, silver and other personal items belonging to the Wilsons and period pieces typical of Presbyterian manses in the antebellum era. The museum and birthplace are open 9 AM to 5 PM daily in the summer months. Hours are 10 AM to 4 PM Monday through Saturday December through February except Thanksgiving, New Year's Day and Christmas. Admission is $6 for adults and $2 for ages

6 to 12, with AAA and Seniors discounts.

MUSIC

JAZZ IN THE PARK
Gypsy Hill Park
Staunton

Free jazz concerts are held in this beautiful park on Thursdays at 8 PM during the summer months.

MID-ATLANTIC CHAMBER ORCHESTRA
Staunton

This Washington, D.C.-based orchestra of professional musicians performs three or four times a year at the Robert E. Lee High School auditorium. For more information, call Bob Link at (703) 885-1232.

SHAKIN'
Staunton

All kinds of bands — from rock 'n' roll to country — perform downtown at Mary Baldwin College every other Friday during the summer months from 5:30 to 7:30 PM. This is another freebie!

STONEWALL BRIGADE BAND
Gypsy Hill Park
Staunton

This is reportedly the oldest continuously performing band, having thrown its first concert before the Civil War. The local musicians perform every Monday at 8 PM during the summer months. There's no admission charge.

THEATER

FLETCHER COLLINS THEATER
Deming Hall, Mary Baldwin College
Staunton   (703) 887-7189

Every academic year, the theater department at this women's college produces five plays, from musicals such as Gilbert and Sullivan to Shakespeare and new, modern plays.

OAK GROVE PLAYERS
232 W. Frederick St.
Staunton   (703) 885-6077

This amateur theater company produces five plays every summer in the middle of a grove of oak trees two miles west of Verona. Founded in 1954 by Fletcher Collins, the retired head of Mary Baldwin College's Theater Department, this is one of the oldest outdoor theaters in the country. Lots of patrons picnic on the grounds before the plays, which are mainly comedies. Admission is by season subscription only, although patrons are allowed to buy tickets for their guests from out of town. The Oak Grove Players were the first to perform "The Nerd," a play by the late Larry Shue, a native of Staunton.

SHENANARTS INC.
Staunton   (703) 248-1868

This is a not-for-profit performing arts company that produces all kinds of plays and musicals and hosts a retreat for playwrights every summer at the Pennyroyal Farm (c. 1808), just north of Staunton. Performances take place at the Pennyroyal Farm in warm weaher and in the winter at McCormick's Cabaret at Frederick and Augusta streets in downtown Staunton. The arts corporation also offers theater programs for youth — one of which led to a full-blown production of a rock opera, *The Wall*, in 1992. A touring company performs throughout Virginia and West Virginia. One of the traveling shows is a play about AIDS that's geared for teens, performed entirely by teenaged actors. The annual Shenandoah Vlley Playwrights Retreat has been going on

for 18 years and hosts writers from all over the world.

THEATER WAGON INC.

437 E. Beverley St.
Staunton, Va. 24401   *No phone*

Through this grant-funded program, Fletcher and Margaret Collins encourage the development f new plays and translations of old ones. Fletcher Collins headed Mary Baldwin College's theater department for 32 years and founded the local Oak Grove Players. He and his

Lee Chapel at Washington and Lee University was built at the request and under the supervision of Robert E. Lee.

wife critique new play scripts and occasionally produce them, using local talent, at their downtown historic home.

WAYNESBORO PLAYERS
Waynesboro
Contact: Bill Robson at (703) 885-4668

This is a nonprofit amateur theater group made up of actors from Waynesboro, Staunton and Augusta County. They perform three plays a year, in addition to some dinner theater offerings at Waynesboro-area restaurants. Most of the plays are performed at the Waynesboro High School auditorium.

OTHER CULTURAL ATTRACTIONS

STATLER BROTHERS COMPLEX
501 Thornrose Ave.
Staunton (703) 885-7237

The Statler Brothers, the world-famous down-home country singers, make their ome in Staunton and have their own museum and office complex in town. Their annual July Fourth concert brings 100,000 people into town, and rooms are reserved a year in advance. The last concert was set for 1994, so its future is in limbo. Tours are free and are given only at 2 PM on weekdays. You can see all kinds of Statler Brothers' memorabilia collected over their past 25 years of performing. A gift shop sells their albums, cassettes, compact discs, T-shirts, sweaters and other souvenirs. A tip from those in the know: If you really want to see the Statler Brothers in the flesh, hang out until after the museum closes. That un-usual tour time does serve a purpose.

SWANNANOA
Afton Mountain
Waynesboro (703) 942-5161

The romantic history behind the Swannanoa Marble Palace and Sculpture Garden is only one intriguing reason to visit this mountain-top estate, created as a railroad executive's monument to his wife. More than 300 artisans used the best materials of their time (c. 1905) to create this palace as a replica of the Villa de Medici in Rome. Gorgeous gardens and stunning artwork (including a 4,000-piece Tiffany stained-glass window) have been faithfully maintained.

Today, Swannanoa is also headquarters of a New Age school of transcendental thinking — The University of Science and Philosophy — founded by Walter and Lao Russell, who rented the mansion in the late '40s. The Russells believed the estate was perched atop a "sacred mountain" and reopened it as a center for their belief in the "Science of Man." Correspondence courses and seminars are offered.

In addition to the gardens and lower floors, the top three floors and towers of the palace are now open to the public. Hours are 9 AM to 5 PM daily, and admission fees start at $5 per person.

Lexington

VISUAL ARTS

ART FARM GALLERIES
Rt. 39 (near the Virginia Horse Center)
                    (804) 463-7961
Chinese artist and teacher Sing Ju started the Art Farm in 1975 as a "farm to raise young artists." A retired professor of art at the local Washington and Lee University, Dr. Ju conducts summer workshops in the traditional Chinese method of painting. Students come from all over the country to live for a week at the farm and learn from Dr. Ju. The gallery is on the first floor of a rambling house and displays the artist's paintings. Many are reasonably priced; all are astonishingly beautiful.

ARTISTS IN CAHOOTS
1 Washington St.   (703) 464-1147
A cooperative gallery for local artists and crafters, Artists in Cahoots offers local arts and crafts and has ongoing demonstrations. Browsing is encouraged, and artists are happy to take you for a tour. You'll find metalwork, jewelry, hand-blown glass, photography, sculpture, pottery and paintings.

HARBS' BISTRO
19 W. Washington St.   (703) 464-1900
Harbs' Bistro is a sophisticated cafe with walls adorned with paintings by artists from up and down the East Coast. The exhibits change every month or so. Gallery operator and painter Agnes Carbrey moved to Lexington a few years ago from New York City, and many of the shows are of New York-based artists. Carbrey also showcases the work of noteworthy artists from the local area, of which there are quite a few. Gallery openings are a great way to meet Lexingtonians, enjoy fine hors d'oeuvres and pay tribute to the artist or artists. Of course, it's also a great place to have lunch or dinner.

MUSEUMS

GEORGE C. MARSHALL
MUSEUM AND LIBRARY
VMI Parade Grounds   (703) 463-7103
The Marshall Foundation was founded in 1953 at the suggestion of President Harry Truman to honor the memory of Gen. George C. Marshall, the only military hero to win a Nobel Peace Prize, for his plan to reconstruct Europe following World War II. None other than Winston Churchill himself sai, "Succeeding generations must not be allowed to forget his achievements and his example." Marshall also was former Army Chief of Staff and Secretary of State and Defense.

Presidents Johnson and Eisenhower dedicated the museum in 1964. Visitors can see a stirring movie of Marshall and a striking photographic display. The stark, black and white photos of the faces of children of war-torn Europe will haunt you and remind you of why Marshall should be remembered forever for his humanitarian efforts that gave the United States its reputation as an upstanding, moral nation with a gigantic heart. Open from 9 AM to 5 PM March 1 through October 31, the museum closes one hour earlier November 1 through March 1. Admission is $3 for adults, $1 for children ages 7 to 18; a senior citizen discount is available. School groups and college students with a valid school I.D. are admitted free.

LEE CHAPEL AND MUSEUM

Washington & Lee University
Main St.   *(703) 463-8400*

Civil War buffs won't want to miss the beautiful Lee Chapel and Museum, the focal point of the campus where the great Confederate served as president for five years after the war. It contains the remains of Lee and the famous pose of the recumbent Lee, sculpted by Edward Valentine. It is open 9 AM to 5 PM Monday through Saturday from April through October and closes one hour earlier October through April. Sunday hours are 2 to 5 PM.

STONEWALL JACKSON HOUSE

8 East Washington Ave.   *(703) 463-2552*

Stonewall Jackson House is the only home that the famous Confederate general ever owned. Restored in 1979 by the Historic Lexington Foundation, the house is furnished with period pieces, including many of Jackson's personal possessions. The house, which is listed on the National Register of Historic Sites, is open to the public daily for guided tours of the rooms. In addition to tours and exhibits, the Stonewall Jackson House sponsors a variety of educational programs through the Garland Gray Research Center and Library located on the office level of the museum. Educational activities include in-school programs, internships, lectures, workshops and scholarly symposia.

It is open 9 AM to 5 PM Mnday through Saturday and 1 to 5 PM Sunday. Hours extend to 6 PM in June, July and August. The museum is closed on major holidays. Admission is $4 for adults and $2 for children ages 6 to 12.

VMI MUSEUM

VMI Parade Ground
N. Main St.   *(703) 464-7232*

The VMI Museum, on the lower level of Jackson Hall on the VMI Campus, brings to life our nation's history. Stonewall Jackson's horse, Little Sorrel, a wonder of state-of-the art taxidermy, probably is its most curious and popular display. Other displays and exhibits tell American history through the lives and service of VMI faculty. Both Gen. Stonewall Jackson and Gen. Robert E. Lee taught at VMI.

Open 9 AM to 5 PM Monday through Saturday and 2 to 5 PM Sunday, the museum is closed holidays.

MUSIC

LENFEST CENTER
FOR THE PERFORMING ARTS

Washington & Lee University
                          (703) 463-8000

W&L's Lenfest Center is the cultural heart of Lexington, offering lively arts from national concert performers as well as W&L's own University-Rockbridge Symphony Orchestra and other music department concerts. The center offers a Concert Guild Series, Theater Series and Lenfest Series featuring performances to appeal to all artistic tastes.

ROCKBRIDGE CONCERT-THEATER SERIES
(703) 463-9232

For 47 years, the Rockbridge Concert-Theater Series has continued to bring outstanding performers to the Rockbridge area community for both the public and local schools. Selections may include ballet, classical dance and popular ensembles.

THEATER

LIME KILN THEATRE
Lime Kiln Rd.
Box Office at 14 S. Randolph St.
(703) 463-3074

Performances at the outdoor Lime Kiln Theatre celebrate the history and culture of the Southern mountains. What makes the place unique and even enchanting is its setting in what was once a limestone quarry. Lime Kiln is best known for its annual musical, *Stonewall Country*, a rollicking tribute to local Civil War hero Stonewall Jackson. Robin and Linda Williams, favorites of Garrison Keillor's "A Prairie Home Companion," sometimes star in the performances. And if you've never heard the two sing together, you have not lived! Also to be performed this summer is *Glory Bound*, a play by a local drama professor, Tom Ziegler. You can also catch performances of *Romeo and Juliet* and a family Folktale Fest.

Lime Kiln's popular Sunday night concert series always offers an eclectic slate of musicians. This summer's schedule includes Leon Redbone, Robin and Linda Williams and the Nashville Bluegrass Band.

Lime Kiln has beautiful picnic areas with tables and grills and sells some food and drinks.

It began sponsoring an annual play-writing contest last year to encourage the creation of plays that are relevant to this region and that can be performed at Lime Kiln. Performances begin at 8 PM nightly on scheduled dates and are held rain or shine. There's a big tent with plenty of seating in bad weather. Call ahead for information.

OTHER CULTURAL ATTRACTIONS

HISTORIC GARDEN WEEK
April date changes yearly
(703) 463-3777

History and garden aficionados flock to Lexington in the spring for its incomparable Historic Garden Week. Each year, civic-minded residents open their historic homes and gardens to an appreciative public. Many are furnished with family heirlooms, gorgeous antiques and ornate gardens. We highly recommend it!

HOLIDAY IN LEXINGTON
December date changes yearly
(703) 463-3777

For one weekend in December, this 19th-century college town welcomes you to its historic downtown district with minilights and white candles. Events include tours of historic properties and homes, music, galas, theater and overall festivity. If you like Christmas in Williamsburg in eastern Virginia, try it western Virginia style.

HULL'S DRIVE-IN THEATRE

Rt. 5   *(703) 463-2621*

One of the last auto drive-in theaters left in Virginia, Hull's is worth a visit for nostalgia. From the well-groomed grounds to the syrupy snowballs, Hull's Drive-In is one of the premier mom 'n' pop operations anywhere. Nothing's changed since 1950. It's open weekends at dusk mid-March through November.

McCORMICK FARM

Steeles Tavern   *(703) 377-2255*

This is the home of world celebrity Cyrus McCormick, who invented the first successful mechanical reaper. A few miles north of Lexington, McCormick Farm is part of the Virginia Tech College of Agricultural and Life Sciences and a Virginia Agricultural Experiment Station. Visitors may tour the blacksmith shop, gristmill, museum and McCormick family home.

McCormick was 22 when he invented the reaper in 1831. The invention launched a new era in agriculture, an age of mechanization that not only changed life on the farm, but also made it possible for millions of people to leave the land and enter an industrial society.

The entire family will enjoy visiting McCormick Farm and learning about an invention that revolutionized the world. It is open 8:30 AM to 5 PM daily.

MOCK CONVENTION

Washington & Lee University
                          (703) 463-8460

This is an event worth waiting for every four years! It's a tremendous party and long, incredible parade straight from the '50s. Students try to outdo each other with outlandish floats. The 1992 extravaganza included an Elvis float with live donkeys in tow! It should be a mandatory event for all civics students. Held only during presidential lections, W&L's nationally known mock convention in spring attracts national politicians and celebrities. It is written up internationally as "the nation's foremost and most accurate predictor in presidential politics." The convention has earned this respect by correctly predicting the presidential nominee 14 times in 19 attempts since its inception in 1908. It has been wrong only once since 1948, when it predicted Edward Kennedy would receive the Democratic nomination in 1972. And once again, the students were right in 1992 with the selection of Bill Clinton. New York Gov. Mario Cuomo and former Speaker of the House Tip O'Neill were among the illustrious, inspiring speakers of the 1992 convention.

Botetourt County

MUSEUMS

BOTETOURT MUSEUM

Court House Complex
Fincastle   *(703) 992-8223*

Botetourt County (pronounced

A photograph from the To The Rescue national exhibition at Center in the Square.

Bot-uh-tot), named in 1770 for Lord Botetourt of England, once stretched the whole way to the Mississippi River, encompassing what is now parts of West Virginia, Kentucky, Ohio, Indiana and Illinois. Fincastle was the historic county seat. Today, thousands of people come to this historic town and its museum to seek and find fascinating historical information. The museum is sponsored by the Botetourt County Historical Society, an active group proud of the county's heritage. Programs, especially those dealing with genealogy, are open to the public. The museum plays an important role in Historical Fincastle's annual fall Old Fincastle Festival, one of the largest festivals in the Roanoke Valley. Museum hours are 10 AM to 2 PM Tuesdays and Thursdays, 2 to 4 PM Sundays and upon request.

Craig County

MUSEUMS

CRAIG COUNTY MUSEUM
Main & Court Sts.
New Castle   *No Phone*

Dedicated Craig County residents are lovingly restoring this old c. 1910, three-story brick hotel as a repository for Craig County's past. They've already restored a bedroom to just as it was in the old hotel and have established a genealogy library for those tracing their roots in this rural, scenic town. Operated by the Craig County Historical Society, which also sponsors the Craig County Fall Festival in October (the county's largest), the museum's potential as a first-class attraction is just beginning to be fulfilled. It is open Monday through Wednesday 1 to 4 PM.

Roanoke

VISUAL ARTS

THE ARTS COUNCIL
OF THE BLUE RIDGE
*Center in the Square, Center
on Church, Level I
20 East Church Ave.* (703) 342-5790

The heart and soul of the cultural community in the Roanoke region, this council provides services and information to its 75 organizational members and the many artists throughout the Blue Ridge region. Programs include a quarterly newsletter; City Art Show, a regional juried art exhibition held annually; Center Scholars, an arts program for high school students; Art in the Window, which offers free display space for artists and children; and the Perry Kendig Award for outstanding support of the arts. In 1994, the Council published "Blueprint 2000," the first community wide cultural plan in the region. Office hours are Monday through Friday 9 AM to 3 PM.

ART MUSEUM OF WESTERN VIRGINIA
*Center in the Square, Levels I & 2
One Market Square* (703) 342-5760

The Art Museum of Western Virginia is a gathering place for the large colony of Valley artists who migrate here both for the beauty and for the artistic opportunities. Permanent galleries emphasize American art of the 19th and 20th centuries. There are impressive collections of sculpture in the Sculpture Court. The folk art gallery features works by artisans of the southern mountains. Museum education programs feature dialogues, family days, tours, films, performances, classes and workshops. Its rotating exhibitions are of regional, national and international significance. There's also a store stocked with regional American crafts and folk art and Art Venture, an interactive art center for children. It is open 10 AM to 5 PM Tuesday through Saturday and 1 to 5 PM on Sunday.

MUSEUMS

HARRISON MUSEUM OF
AFRICAN-AMERICAN CULTURE
523 Harrison Ave. N. W. (703) 345-4818

A Roanoke showcase for African-American culture, the Harrison Museum of African-American Culture is on the Virginia Historic Landmarks Register as the first public high school for black students in western Virginia.

The museum's mission is to "research, preserve and interpret the achievements of African-Americans, specifically in western Virginia, and to provide an opportunity for all citizens to come together in appreciation, enjoyment and greater knowledge of African-American culture."

Since its opening in 1985, the museum has offered art and historical exhibits in its galleries and the Hazel B. Thompson Exhibition Room. The permanent collection of local artifacts and memorabilia has grown from a few objects to several thousand. Thanks to the generosity of donors, Harrison Museum owns an impressive African collection, which includes masks, bronze sculptures, paintings, furniture and textiles. Several traveling exhibits and displays may be borrowed by schools and organizations.

One of its most popular undertakings is the annual Henry Street Heritage Festival held on the last Saturday in September. It's a festive celebration of African-American heritage, usually held on the Henry Street site, which has relocated to Elmwood Park due to construction.

A recently opened Museum store and gift shop offers Afrocentric art, books, cards, jewelry and African art. Open 10AM to 5PM Monday through Friday and 1 to 5PM Saturday and Sunday. For group tours, contact the curator.

ROANOKE VALLEY HISTORICAL SOCIETY AND MUSEUM CENTER IN THE SQUARE, LEVEL 1 AND 3

One Market Sq. (703) 342-5770

The rich heritage of Roanoke unfolds before you in the galleries of the Roanoke Valley Historical Society and Museum, run by a dedicated group of preservationists. Prehistoric artifacts acquaint you with life in the Valley before Colonial settlement, through the frontier days into the boom days of the Norfolk & Western Railroad and n into the present. You will see a charming re-creation of an 1890 country store and intriguing fashions from the 1700s to the 1990s. Its changing exhibits are both resourceful, sensitive and relevant to the Roanoke Valley. They also are of national interest, with a recent D-Day exhibition, for example.

The museum membership con-

ducts tours of historic sites offered to the public. Its shop, Past Presents, on the first floor, offers handmade quilts, historical maps, genealogical charts and vintage toys. You can also buy the dogwood pattern china used at Hotel Roanoke. In addition, it's home to the national exhibition, "To the Rescue," on display through May 15, 1995.

Hours of operation are 10 AM to 4 PM Tuesday through Friday, 10 AM to 5 PM Saturday and 1 to 5 PM Sunday. Admission is $2 for adults, $1 for seniors and children ages 6-12, and free for those younger than 5.

THE SALEM MUSEUM
801 E. Main St.
Salem (703) 389-6760

The Salem Museum is found in the Williams-Brown House. That's easy. What was a little difficult for awhile was finding the Williams-Brown House! The 1840s house was slated to be torn down, but a group of Salem residents towed it from its original location to a safer destination just a quarter of a mile away.

Run by volunteers of the Salem Historical Society, the museum features topics ranging from the adventures and hardships of the Civil War to the leisure of a summer sojourn at the Lake Spring Resort Hotel. The Brown House serves to explore various aspects of local and Virginian history. A gift shop and a gallery for rotating historical exhibits are also on the premises.

Hours are 10 AM to 4 PM Tuesday through Friday and noon to 5 PM Saturday.

SCIENCE MUSEUM OF WESTERN VIRGINIA AND HOPKINS PLANETARIUM
Center in the Square, Levels 1, 4 and 5
One Market Sq. (703) 342-5710

The Science Museum teaches the wonders of science through hands-on experiences. Its enthusiastic volunteers play a special role in making the museum a fun experience for both adults and children. You can broadcast a weather report and see yourself on TV, enjoy the touch tank and Tot and Parent Learning Center and see the stars in the Hopkis Planetarium. You'll explore the reaches of the universe and then come back down to earth to enjoy lectures, movies and special events such as technology expos and wildflower pilgrimages. Children also like the first floor Science Museum Shop with real educational toy bargains that are so much fun kids don't have a clue that they're learning while they play.

Exhibits change frequently, ranging from roaring mechanical dinosaurs and real sharks to animated life-size animals of the future. Special attention is taken to provide exhibits teaching care of the environment, such as the Wetlands. The first-class planetarium has been filled wih everything from dancing laser shows to imaginative narratives on the creation of earth and the stars. It's a great way to spend an entire afternoon in Roanoke.

The museum is open 10 AM to 5 PM Monday through Saturday and 1 to 5 PM Sunday. Planetarium shows are Friday and Saturday from 6:30 to 9:30 PM. Admission is $4 for adults and $2.50 for ages 3 to 12. Call (703) 344-3007 for Planetarium and Laser times and prices.

CATHOLIC CHURCH MUSEUM
624 N. Jefferson St. (703) 362-2245

The history of the Catholic Church in the Roanoke area is shown by the artifacts and memorabilia maintained at the three-room museum in Saint Andrews Parish Center. A major Roanoke landmark, the stunning St. Andrews Catholic Church is more than 100 years old. The impressive Gothic-style cathedral looms above the commercial landscape downtown as a daily reminder of serene spirituality.

The museum is operated by the Catholic Historical Society of the Roanoke Valley and is open 10:30 AM to 2 PM Tuesdays or by appointment.

FIFTH AVENUE PRESBYTERIAN CHURCH WINDOW
301 Patton Ave. N. W. (703) 342-0264

After the Civil War, in 1903, the Rev. Lylburn Downing, pastor of Fifth Avenue Presbyterian, an African-American church, commissioned a stained glass window to honor Confederate Gen. Stonewall Jackson. The Rev. Mr. Downing had been a member of the Sunday School class Jackson had established for slaves at his own church in Lexington. Although the church burned down in the 1920s, the unusual window was spared and then included in the rebuilt church, where it serves today as a symbol of racial harmony.

The window may be viewed Tuesdays and Thursdays from 10 to 11 AM.

TO THE RESCUE
NATIONAL EXHIBITION
Roanoke Valley Historical Society and Museum
Center in the Square, Level 3
One Market Sq. (703) 344-5154

To the Rescue, the only permanent national exhibiion dedicated to volunteer lifesaving, brings an international spotlight to Roanoke as the birthplace of the rescue squad movement. As a nine-year-old Roanoker, Julian Stanley Wise never forgot standing helplessly by as two men drowned when their canoe capsized on the Roanoke River. He vowed then that he would organize a group of volunteers who could be trained in lifesaving. He did. In 1928, he and his crew of NW Railway workers became the first volunteer rescue squad in America to use both medical techniques and transport on victims. Later, they were the first to use iron lungs during the polio epidemics that struck the country. They pioneered the Holger method of lifesaving and modern day cardiopulmonary resuscitation.

The creation of the exhibit, which includes breathtaking, hands-on interactive videos and displays, was overseen by the famous museum expert Conover Hunt, a Virginia native whose last project was The Sixth Floor, the JFK Museum in Dallas. The quality and brilliance shows. The exhibit includes artifacts from 31 states and three countries. To the Rescue also houses the National Rescue Hall of Fame, which will recognize Emergency Medical Services heroes during National EMS Week the second May of each year. Additionally, the exhibit now houses the National EMS Memorial, recognizing 38 men and women from 14 states who gave their lives while saving others. This exhibit has the potential to make Roanoke the international center of EMS activities, and efforts to do so are underway.

Hours of operation are 10 AM to 4 PM Tuesday through Friday, 10 AM to 5 PM Saturday and 1 to 5 PM Sunday. Admission is $1.

VIRGINIA'S EXPLORE PARK
Headquarters
101 S. Jefferson St. (703) 345-1295

Virginia's Explore Park, a new park with an original style, offers a unique recreational and educational experience. This exciting park, located seven miles from downtown Roanoke, features numerous attractions, including a frontiersman who displays the survival skills of the earliest explorers, the Blue Ridge Settlement, where interpreters authentically demonstrate the lifeways of 18th-century pioneers, and a live exhibit on regional Native American culture, where visitor participation is encouraged. In addition, 10 miles of wilderness trails are available for visitors to wander independently or on guided nature hikes.

Special events, such as Militia Days, the Fall Foliage Festival, American Indian Heritage Weekend, classes and workshops take place throughout the year. Call for details on upcoming events.

The park is open 9 AM to 5 PM Saturday through Monday from spring through fall. Groups may make special appointments. Admission is $4 for adults and $2.50 for children ages 6 to 18.

VIRGINIA MUSEUM
OF TRANSPORTATION

303 Norfolk Ave.   *(703) 342-5670*

Roanoke proudly displays its railroad heritage with the Virginia Museum of Transportation, located in a restored freight station next to the Norfolk & Southern mainline. It chronicles the formation of transportation over the lives of generations. Here, you can come face to face with steam engines, vintage electronic locomotives and classic diesels. You can climb on board a caboose and stroll through a railway post office car.

Inside, you can walk down Main Street to see early autos, freight trucks, fire engines and carriages. You'll see the way passenger cars looked at their peak in the '40s, before the automobile took over as king of the highways. Everywhere, from posters and photographic displays, there's nostalgia for a time when life rolled along more smoothly on tracks to an unquestioned destination. Don't miss the fabulous carved wooden miniature circus with thousands of figurines to appreciate and the largest collection of museum rolling stock on the entire East Coast. "Making it Move," an exhibit on transportation, offers interactive entertainment. The gift shop offers unique prints, books and toys for railway buffs. The museum hosts many special events including the Roanoke Railway Festival.

The site is open 10 AM to 5 PM Monday through Saturday and noon to 5 PM Sunday. It's closed on Mondays in January and February. Admission is $4 for adults, $3 for senior citizens, $2 for students and $1.75 for children ages 3 to 12.

MUSIC

OPERA ROANOKE

111 W. Campbell Ave.   *(703) 982-ARIA*

Opera Roanoke produces operas of consistently high quality. The company engages up-and-coming professional singers in innovative new productions. General Director Craig Fields, who also serves as the music director of the Roanoke Symphony, enjoys a national reputation. The Opera offers season subscriptions with performances both in Roanoke and Salem. Perennial favorites such as Bizet's *Carmen*, Verdi's *Aida* and Lehar's *The Merry Widow* are showcased with top talent, who convincingly portray the passion, laughter, beauty and tragedy of life. Standing ovations are the norm.

Opera Roanoke takes the extra step, with English translation subtitles projected over the stage to ensure that opera goers can follow every twist and turn of the plot. Operatifs, on the order of intermissions features at the Met, are enlightening lectures for each opera hosted by Bond at the historic Radisson Patrick Henry Hotel. Opera Roanoke is the icing on the cake of Roanoke Valley culture!

THE ROANOKE SYMPHONY
ORCHESTRA

111 W. Campbell Ave.   *(703) 343-9127*

The Roanoke Symphony Orchestra continues to receive national fame for two reasons: first, for its successful, cleverly conceived community outreach, and second, for the success of its director, the diminutive but mighty media darling Victoria Bond. You'll find Bond and her symphony anywhere they can bring the joy of fine music to the people. She and her symphony made a recording with THE Ray Charles (Uh Huh!), who flew his entire entourage to Roanoke in 1992, and cavorted with country star Chet Atkins' magical flattop on stage at the summer series, "Picnic With the Pops." The Moody Blues shared the bill in the summer of 1994.

The Symphony was responsible for bringing competitive polo to the Valley through sponsorship of the Roanoke Symphony Polo Cup, where you can "Ponder the Ponies and Promote the Notes" each fall. There's a never-ending round of school performances, get-togethers and fun events in the name of the symphony. It goes without saying that the Roanoke Symphony Orchestra is the most popular and involved grassroots cultural organization in the entire Roanoke Valley. Having one of the wealthiest women in America, Marian Via, as a major benefactor enabled them to achieve this lofty status. Even with her unfortunate death a few years ago, the Symphony's popularity should ensure that its quality doesn't miss a beat in the years ahead.

THEATER

GRANDIN MOVIE THEATRE
1310 Grandin Rd.   *(703) 345-6177*
Daily Performances in multi-theaters
Yes, you CAN see a movie in a gorgeous movie theater like the ones that the wrecking balls have destroyed throughout America, thanks to Julie Hunsaker and the Lindsey family. Comedian Bill Murray of Saturday Night Live and *Ghostbusters* fame did a benefit for it recently, remarking that places like the Grandin should never be forgotten or destroyed. Classics and modern movies can be seen for the best prices in town, often with 99¢ specials. This cavernous, popcorn-scented architectural masterpiece will thrill everyone, especially children who have never seen anything quite like the tiled floors, mahogany candy cases and ornate decor of the Grandin. This is one of Roanoke's greatest cultural treasures.

MILL MOUNTAIN THEATRE & THEATRE B
Center in the Square, Level 1
Box Office   *(703) 342-5740*
A Roanoke institution that has been both burned down (when located on Mill Mountain) and flooded out (during the Flood of '85), Mill Mountain Theatre has been a Roanoke institution for 30 years, attracting cutting-edge visiting artists and scholars for the cultural enrichment of western Virginia.

Offered is the Main Stage, with productions featuring world premieres such as *All I Really Need To Know I Learned in Kindergarten*, adapted by Robert Fulghum; Norfolk Southern's Festival of New Works in the exciting Alternative Theatre B; Centerpiece, a lunchtime series of readings; and children's musicals. The theater offers a new play competition, drama enrichment programs, summer drama day camp, youth ensemble, guest speakers and jurors. Mill Mountain Theatre's dynamic presence in the Roanoke Valley makes it a cut above any theater group in the Blue Ridge and makes a visit to the Star City well worthwhile and guaranteed enjoyable.

Admission charges vary with each play, time and date of performance.

OTHER CULTURAL ATTRACTIONS

CENTER IN THE SQUARE
One Market Sq. (703) 342-5700

This complex is the home of: Art Museum of Western Virginia, the Arts Council of the Blue Ridge, Mill Mountain Theatre and Theatre B, Roanoke Valley History Museum, Science Museum of Western Virginia and Hopkins Planetarium. Resident organizations' hours vary. (See above).

In all the United States, only Roanoke has Center in the Square, visited by nearly 400,000 annually. That makes it the best-attended cultural center in western Virginia — more, even, than Richmond's Valentine Museum. Five resident organizations coexist in a restored 1914 warehouse that is the anchor of Roanoke's historic city market. A dramatic sculptural spiral staircase symbolizes how these five organizations have come together to create a richer cultural life in western Virginia. A confetti-like sculpture, a gift by the famed Dorothy Gillespie, hangs on one wall. In the heart of shops, galleries and restaurants,

Center in the Square is the binding cultural tie in the life of a growing, vibrant downtown and a "must see" while in Roanoke. The shopping in its three member stores is also terrific, with some real bargains in science, art and history.

JEFFERSON CENTER
540 Campbell Ave. S. W. (703) 343-2624

The Jefferson Center opened its doors in August of 1993, the result of the Center Foundation's fundraising efforts to efurbish Roanoke's grand old Jefferson High School, which had stood closed and empty for years. Located within is a wide variety of tenants: a Police Academy, Opera Roanoke, the Roanoke Symphony offices, Habitat for Humanity and more! The "J" Room is full of memorabilia, such as trophies, awards and annuals from Jefferson High's alumni. The Foundation even revived the school's old newsletter, the "Jefferson News," to carry information about reunions, scheduled events and more. This beautiful old building is definitely worth seeing.

MILL MOUNTAIN ZOO
Off Blue Ridge Parkway (703) 343-3241

Mill Mountain Zoo is a 3-acre habitat operated by the Blue Ridge Zoological Society, whose dedication is legendary. Its main attraction is Ruby the Tiger, who received national attention during a two-year fund drive to build a new habitat at the zoo, which was completed in 1992. Now, thanks to other donations, Ruby has a new watering hole, too, for use during the summertime.

Although this zoo serves the noble purpose of nurturing endangered species, small children best love the ordinary creatures, such as the pygmy goats and frisky prairie dogs, who pop in and out of their holes like a living calliope. A Zoo Choo-Choo train, operated by the Roanoke Jaycees, thrills the tiny tots. Picnic facilities, Roanoke's famous gigantic metal star and a breathtaking overlook view of Roanoke are also part of Mill Mountain's appeal. It makes for a very pleasant afternoon.

The zoo is open daily 10 AM to 5 PM (closed Christmas Day). Admission is $3.50 for adults and $2 for children ages 2 through 12.

See our Other Attractions chapter for moe information on the zoo.

MINIATURE GRACELAND
605 Riverland Dr.   *(703) 56-ELVIS*

The King lives! You'll find him in miniature in this Southeast Roanoke neighborhood, complete with an adoring audience of Barbie dolls seated in a miniature auditorium as he revolves on stage, under the light of the Mill Mountain star. This private collection of Kim Epperly and her husband, Don, has been visited by people from 14 countries and featured in foreign tabloids.

Epperly, editor of the international "The Wonder o You" newsletter, dedicated to the late Elvis Presley, is the heart and soul behind keeping the memory of the entertainer alive. Epperly's husband has crafted replicas of the entire estate and placed them in their side yard. The display is lighted nightly

and fans are invited to stroll through the grounds and hear an Elvis song wafting over the loudspeaker. A different musical tribute is featured each night.

Inside the basement of her home, Epperly maintains her own personal museum of Elvis artifacts, including "Love Me Tender" shampoo and conditioner, full-size mannequins sculpted with auto body compound to look like Elvis' features and newspaper clippings of when the King first visited Roanoke. Each year, the Epperlys add something new to the yard. Don Epperly does most of the construction from scrap wood, based on pictures or descriptions from his wife. Right now, they're finishing up his airport and a privacy fence. Soon, Sun Studios will be added and the Civic Center will be moved to the back. Last year, the Epperlys consented to show their private collection at an opening on January 10, Presley's birthday, at the Roanoke Valley History Museum. It was a blockbuster! There are two things you can't doubt — the popularity of Elvis and the sincerity of the tribute the Epperlys provide. Visitors are welcome anytime.

THE ROANOKE
VALLEY HORSE SHOW
Junior League of Roanoke Valley
     (703) 774-3242

Rated "A" by the American Horse Show Association, this show has been a national standout in horse-lovers' country for 21 years. Sponsored by the Junior League of Roanoke Valley and Roanoke Valley Horsemen's Association, it is held in June and attracts more than 1,000 entries nationwide for a purse of over $250,000 and grand prix of $75,000. It's the only indoor, air-conditioned show in Virginia and continues to be one of the top multibreed shows in the United States. This is a truly special community effort which, over the years, has plowed $1 million back into community projects.

East of the Blue Ridge Region

Washington and Sperryville

VISUAL ARTS

MIDDLE ST. GALLERY
Corner of Gay and Middle Sts.
Washington   (703) 675-3440
This is a nonprofit artists' cooperative featuring museum-quality paintings, photography and sculpture. Exhibitions change monthly, and classes are offered for adults and children. It's open from Friday through Sunday from 11 AM to 6 PM and by appointment.

SOUTHERN DRAWL ARTWORKS
Main St.
Sperryville   (703) 987-9333
This fine arts gallery features original works and limited edition prints on wildlife, nature, Civil War and aviation. Both regional and local artists are represented. "No bad white wine, stale cheese or pretentious conversation," reads its brochure. "Just fine art and good manners." The gallery is open Satur-

days from 10 AM to 5:30 PM, Sundays from noon to 5:30 PM and by appointment.

MUSIC AND THEATER

THE THEATRE AT WASHINGTON
Gay and Jett Sts.
Washington   (703) 675-1253
This is the site of cultural activities ranging from high quality films to plays and performances by gospel choirs, chamber music ensembles, folk rockers and other musical groups.

THE OLD TOWN HALL
Gay St.
Washington   (703) 675-1616
This is atually a performing arts center that serves as home to the Ki Theatre, a multimedia performance troupe made up of leaders in the fields of theater, dance, music, story telling and the visual arts. The artists create and perform original theatrical productions based on stories. They perform locally and tour across the country.

Formerly an old Methodist church, the building is also where virtually the entire community gathers the first weekend in December to see Christmas nativity plays. The *Shepherd's Play* and *Three Kings* are 14th-century Christian dramas performed by more than 30 members of the Washington community.

Ki Theatre (pronounced "kee") has cosponsored "Crossroads: Soul and Soil — the Arts and the Land," a Columbus Day weekend festival. Held the second weekend in October, the festival has celebrated farming and the arts with farm tours, performances at farms and workshops on growing and marketing produce.

Also at Old Town Hall is the popular exchange program, in which artists from across the coutry (and sometimes from other parts of the world) perform January through April on the third Sunday of the month. At the end of the shows, the audience always has an opportunity to converse with the performers.

Charlottesville and Surrounding Area

VISUAL ARTS

BETH GALLERY AND PRESS
Barboursvile   *(703) 832-565*

Artist Frederick Nichols Jr. has his studio and gallery here just off Route 33 in a renovated general store across from the railroad tracks. He calls his work "photo-impressionism." He does enormous colorful landscapes of Blue Ridge scenes using either oil paint or a silk-screen process. A friendly fellow, Nichols will give tours through the gallery and studio on the weekends and during the week when he's open. Nichols' career has taken off since he won top honors at a recent international print exhibition in Japan.

FAYERWEATHER GALLERY
Rugby Rd.   *(804) 924-6122*

This university gallery next to the Bayley Art Museum has regular exhibits by faculty and student artists, so it's naturally where the UVA Art Department likes to hang out. Admission is free, and it's open Monday through Friday from 9 AM to 5 PM.

FRANCES CHRISTIAN BRAND GALLERIES
111 Washington Ave.   *(804) 295-5867*

Call before you drop by this eclectic gallery, which is actually a private home containing the art collection of Frances Christian Brand, now deceased. Cynthia Brand, her granddaughter, lives here and likes to have people over for coffee while they admire the rooms full of pre-Columbian pottery, Mexican art, African masks and sculptures, and paintings done by Frances Brand.

McGUFFEY ART CENTER
201 Second St. N.W.   *(804) 295-7973*

This is an arts cooperative that began in 1975 with city support. It's located in a renovated elementary school within walking distance from historic Court Square and the downtown pedestrian mall. Its light, airy rooms have been transformed into more than 40 studios where you can sometimes watch artists work. There are also galleries and a gift shop. Exhibits, tours and gallery talks are available to the public year round. The center also offers classes for the public in children's art, printing, painting, drawing and more.

NEWCOMB HALL ARTS SPACE
University of Virginia   *(804) 924-3601*

This student-run gallery in the UVA Student Union building is open daily from noon to 9 PM and admission is free A recent exhibit, one of many in the ever-changing variety of art on display, included the heartbreaking AIDS quilt.

PIEDMONT VIRGINIA COMMUNITY COLLEGE

Rt. 20 and I-64 (804) 977-3900 Ext. 203

An art gallery here displays regular exhibits by student and professional artists. Admission is free, and the gallery is open from 8 AM to 10 PM weekdays.

SECOND STREET GALLERY

Inside the McGuffey Art Center

(804) 977-7284

This sophisticated gallery presents the work of regional and national artists — from paintings and prints to more avant-garde art forms, such as site-specific installations. The gallery hosts lively receptions, art talks, slide presentations, workshops and tours. It's free and open Tuesday through Saturday from 10 AM to 5 PM and Sundays from 1 to 5 PM.

DANCE

CHIHAMBA

(804) 296-4986

The Chihamba Dance Company of Dancescape celebrates and educates people about African cultures through music and dance. Programs include concerts, lecture demonstrations, workshops and African craft sessions. One six-week program offered last winter, called Discover Africa through the Arts, taught African beading, weaving, tie-dying, leather work, mask making and sand painting.

CONTRA CORNERS

(804) 295-1847

Contra Corners puts on a dance the second and fourth Sunday of every month at the Greenwood Community Center. A dance workshop happens from 5:30 to 6:30 PM and a dance from 6:30 to 9:30 PM.

DANCESCAPE

(804) 296-4986

Dancescape not only offers instruction in various African art forms (see Chihamba, above) but it also gives classes in flatfoot clogging, modern dance and jazz to adults, teens and children. One of the instructors hails from Guinea, West Africa. Mohammed Dacosta danced for several dance companies before moving to Charlottesville. Another instructor, Sheila Stone, apprentices with a 78-year-old flatfooter who lives near Elkins, West Virginia.

THE MIKI LISZT DANCE COMPANY

(804) 973-3744

Based at the McGuffey Art Center, this nonprofit company performs annual dance concerts, conducts workshops with guest artists and offers lectures and demonstrations in nursing homes, schools, hospitals, libraries and museums. The company also sponsors the annual Community Children's Dance Festival.

MUSEUMS

BAYLY ART MUSEUM

Rugby Rd. *(804) 924-3592*

This is the University of Virginia's own modern museum that has both a permanent collection of ancient pottery, sculpture and some paintings, along with special, short-term exhibitions. String quartets and other classical music groups perform certain times during the year. Admission is free, and it's open Tuesday through Sunday from 1 to 5 PM.

JAMES MADSON MUSEUM
129 Caroline St.
Orange *(703) 672-1776*

The downtown museum offers four permanent exhibits dealing with the life and times of Madison and his important contributions to the American political system. Artifacts include furnishings from his nearby home Montpelier, some of his correspondence when he served as president and a few of Dolley Madison's belongings. The museum is open weekdays from 10 AM to 5 PM and weekends from 1 to 4 PM March through November. The rest of the year, it's open only on weekdays from 10 AM to 4 PM. There's a nominal admission fee.

THE VIRGINIA DISCOVERY MUSEUM
East end of Downtown Mall (804) 293-5528

This is a dynamic place for children and their families, filled with hands-on exhibits, science programs, costumes in which the children can play "dress-up" and a real cabin from Rockingham County. Special exhibits change every few months. An art room, complete with all kinds of materials, invites children to create at their own pace, and a gallery space displays their creations for about three weeks.

The Discovery Dash children's race is held in May. There are many other special events, such as photo contests and a Halloween party.

It's open Tuesday through Saturday from 10 AM to 5 PM and Sundays 1 to 5 PM. Admission is $3 for adults and $2 for children up to age 13 and senior citizens. Parking is free at the Market Street Parking Garage or Water Street outdoor lots.

THE WALTONS MOUNTAIN MUSEUM
At the Schuyler Community Centr, Rt. 617
Schuyler *(804) 831-2000*

Earl Hamner, whose early years are chronicled in the heartwarming television series, grew up in tiny Schuyler. A new museum dedicated to Hamner and the Waltons opened to great fanfare several years ago in the same school where the Hamner youngsters learned their ABCs. The museum is actually a series of former classrooms that recreate sets from the TV program. You'll find copies of actual scripts, photo displays that juxtapose Hamner's real family with the television actors, and all manner of memorabilia.

Visitors can also sit back and watch a video documentary which shows interviews with Hamner, former cast members and episodes from one of the most endearing television series ever.

A $30,000 state grant and support from Hamner and community leaders have mde it all possible.

The school is on Rt. 617 in Schuyler, a stone's throw from the old Hamner homestead. Schuyler is half way between Charlottesville and Lynchburg, a few miles off Route 29.

Visiting hours are 10 AM to 4 PM, and admission is $3 for adults and $2 fochildren. The museum is open daily from the first Saturday in

March through the last Sunday in November, except major holidays.

MUSIC

ASH LAWN - HIGHLAND
(804) 293-9539
The restored home and gardens of President James Monroe host a chamber music series every summer, as well as three light operas. Other special events throughout the year bring pianists, singers and dancers who perform to 18th-century music.

CHARLOTTESVILLE AND UNIVERSITY SYMPHONY ORCHESTRA
112 Old Cabell Hall *(804) 924-6505*
Seventy musicians form this volunteer orchestra, which has received rave reviews. Professional principal musicians perform alongside outstanding student and community players. Concerts are held in the Cabell Hall auditorium located on the historic lawn at UVA.

CHARLOTTESVILLE GAMELAN ENSEMBLE
(804) 979-4818
This group performs traditional Javanese music as well as more contemporary "American Gamelan." The Ensemble includes around a dozen musicians performing on various bronze gongs and xylophone-type instruments.

MONTICELLO TRIO
(804) 924-3052
This is a professional chamber music trio that performs regularly in Charlottesville and also tours across the state and nation.

OLD CABELL HALL
UVA *(804) 924-3984*
Located at the south end of the lawn, this auditorium is the scene of all kinds of concerts throughout the year, from avant-garde jazz to internationally acclaimed chamber music. The Tuesday Evening Concert Series — a Charlottesville tradition for more than four decades — is held here every year and has presented such artists as Yo Yo Ma, the Tokyo String Quartet and the Juilliard String Quartet.

ORATORIO SOCIETY OF CHARLOTTESVILLE-ALBEMARLE
(804) 286-2150
This is Central Virginia's largest community chorus, performing major classical choral works in at least one concert annually.

PIEDMONT CHAMBER PLAYERS
(804) 973-2194
This is a local group of professional musicians that presents a concert series every year at Cabell Hall and also appears in schools and colleges throughout Central Virginia.

THE PRISM COFFEEHOUSE
214 Rugby Rd. *(804) 97-PRISM*
This nonprofit volunteer organization presents folk, traditional and acoustic concerts in a casual smoke-free, alcohol-free setting. Formed in 1966, the Prism is one of America's oldest surviving coffeehouses. Concerts are held on the weekends. The group holds its bimonthly meetings and jam sessions every second Monday at the Prism. Local song writers also meet there regularly, and a monthly percus-

sion jam session invites players at all levels of experience to make noise together. You can also occasionally hear azz and even African drumming performances here.

THE SWEET ADELINES
(804) 973-7203 (night), 924-0276 (day)

This a four-part harmony barbershop chorus for women only. They perform around town and compete in barbershop competitions nationally. All women interested in barbershop harmony are invited to attend.

THE WESTMINSTER ORGAN CONCERT SERIES
(804) 293-3133

Held every year at Westminster Presbyterian Church, this series of concerts offers a variety of organ music combined with other instruments and singers. Concerts are free.

YOUTH ORCHESTRA OF CHARLOTTESVILLE-ALBEMARLE
(804) 924-6505

This orchestra has been around for more than a decade, providing the best in musical direction and coaching for elementary and high school musicians. It includes a youth orchestra, jazz ensemble, string ensemble and the Evans Orchestra for younger musicians.

Theater

COMMUNITY CHILDREN'S THEATRE
(804) 971-5671

For 40 years this company has brought affordable family theater to the Charlottesville community.

Performances often sell out well in advance, but individual tickets, when available, are sold at the door an hour before curtain call and at other locations. Free children's workshops are offered in the winter. Performances are held at the Charlottesville Performing Arts Center.

FOUR COUNTY PLAYERS
(703) 832-5355

This theater company out of Barboursville produces Shakespeare, full-scale musicals and children's productions. In August, Shakespeare productions are staged in a most magical setting: the ruins of what was once the estate of James Barbour, governor of Virginia (1812 to 1814), Secretary of War and Ambassador to the Court of St. James. Thomas Jefferson, a friend of Barbour's, designed the house, but it was destroyed by fire on Christmas Day, 1884. Towering, overgrown boxwoods surround the ruins, adding to the air of enchantment about the place. The award-winning Barboursville Vineyards are located within walking distance.

In cooler months, Four County Players operates a dinner theater in conjunction with Toliver House in Gordonsville.

HERITAGE REPERTORY THEATRE
1 Culbreth Rd., UVA
Charlottesville   (804) 924-3376

The highly acclaimed Heritage Rep produces a series of plays every summer at the University of Virginia.

LIVE ARTS
609 East Market St.
Charlottesville *(804) 977-4177*

Located one block off the downtown mall, Live Arts is home to a resident theater company, the Live Arts Theater Ensemble (LATE). LATE produces everything from original avant-garde plays to well-known Broadway musicals. LATE started several years ago in Charlottesville and aims to become a professional theater. It also hosts poetry readings, music events and provides a space in which other groups may perform.

THE OLD MICHIE THEATRE
609 E. Market St. *(804) 977-3690*

This is home for theater and puppetry arts for children and teens in Central Virginia. A summer theater school offers weeks of instruction in drama, music, story telling, puppetry and clowning. The theater also produces summer musicals.

UNIVERSITY OF VIRGINIA DEPARTMENT OF DRAMA
(804) 924-3376

This is UVA's main student theater group, producing six major stage shows every academic year. TheUVA Spanish Theater Group also performs plays entirely in Spanish every spring. Productions have included *All My Sons* by Arthur Miller, *My Three Sisters* by Anton Chekhov and *Top Girls*, a contemporary satire by Cary Churchhill.

Other Cultural Attractions

ASH LAWN-HIGHLAND
Charlottesville *(804) 293-9539*

This 535-acre estate was the home of James Monroe, our nation's fifth president, who fought in the Rvolution under George Washington and went on to hold more offices than any other U.S. president.

As ambassador to France, Monroe negotiated with Napoleon for the Louisiana Purchase — an acquisition of western territories that doubled the size of the country. During his presidency, Monroe articulated the nation's first comprehensive foreign policy, later termed the Monroe Doctrine, to prevent further European colonization of the Americas.

Ash Lawn-Highland is just about 2½ miles from Thomas Jefferson's Monticello, off I-64. Visitors can tour the home that is full of Monroe possessions and stroll through the boxwood gardens, where magnificent peacocks strut around. Livestock, vegetable and herb gardens and Colonial craft demonstrations recall what life was like on the Monroe's plantation. Special events at the estate include summer opera performances sung in English, an early American festival, Plantation Days, on July Fourth weekend and Christmas candlelight tours.

Monroe purchased the 1,000-acre plantation in 1793 because he wanted to be closer to his friend and mentor, Thomas Jefferson. Monticello's property then bordered Highland. Jefferson had personally selected the site and sent his gardeners to start orchards for

Monroe. In lae 1799 Monroe and his wife, Elizabeth Kortright of New York, moved to their tobacco plantation, where frequent guests included James and Dolley Madison, who lived nearby at Montpelier.

Today, the Monroe estate is owned and maintained as a working farm by Monroe's alma mater, the College of William and Mary.

Ash Lawn-Highland is open daily from 9 AM to 6 PM March through October and 10 AM to 5 PM daily from November through February. Admission is $6 for adults, $5.50 for seniors and $2 for children ages 6 to 12. A special President's Pass costs $16 (children and adults) and gets you into Ash Lawn-Highland, Monticello and Michie Tavern. Groups of 25 or more receive a special rate.

MICHIE TAVERN

Charlottesville   *(804) 977-1234*
Historic Michie Tavern (pronounced "micky") is one of the oldest homesteads remaining in Virginia and was originally located along a well-worn stage coach route near Earlysville, about 17 miles away. To accommodate the many travelers seeking food and shelter at their home, the Michie family opened it up as a tavern in 1784. The tavern was dismantled piece by piece, moved to the present site and reconstructed in 1927.

Today, visitors to Monticello and Ash Lawn-Highland can stop by this tavern for a hearty Southern-style meal. It's located on Route 53 on the way to both attractions. Visitors can also see a fine collection of 18th-century Southern furniture and artifacts and learn about the tavern's lively history from both tour guides and audio recordings. Next door, a 200-year-old converted slave house, called The Ordinary, serves fried chicken, black-eyed peas, stewed tomatoes, cole slaw, potato salad, green bean salad, beets, homemade biscuits, cornbread and apple cobbler every day of the year from 11:30 AM to 3 PM.

Michie Tavern also features 18th-century craft demonstrations every weekend from April through October and houses the small Virginia Wine Museum in its basement.

Next door, the Meadow Run Grist Mill houses a General Store where visitors can buy Virginia wines, specialty foods, crafts and all kinds of gifts.

The Michie Tavern Museum is open year round from 9 AM to 5 PM except Christmas and New Year's. Admission to the museum costs $5 a person, unless you have lunch, in which case you get a $2 discount to the museum. Lunch costs $8.95, not including beverage, dessert and tax.

MONTICELLO

Charlottesville   *(804) 295-8181*
An important annual event is July Fourth at Monticello, which hosts festivities on the mountain top that are highlighted by a naturalization ceremony for new U.S. citizens.

Jefferson's wide-ranging interests made him an avid collector of sculpture, maps, paintings, prints, Native American artifacts, scientific instruments and fine furniture —

and these objects kept his house quite cluttered. With all the nieces and nephews and other relatives and visitors also filling his home, it's no wonder the man liked to escape to his wooded retreat, Poplar Forest, in nearby Lynchburg.

Jefferson, our nation's third president, author of the Declaration of Independence and international statesman, reportedly detested politics. He wrote to his daughter Martha in 1800, "Politics is such a torment that I would advise every one I love not to mix with it." But he refused to shirk his duty to his country and its fragile democratic system.

He began construction of Monticello in 1769 when he was just 26, and often longed to retire there during the most active part of his political career. Work on Monticello continued for 40 years thereafter, during which Jefferson made many alterations. Evidence of his interest in architecture, science, agriculture, the arts and much more can be found throughout the estate, which includes an eight-acre orchard, 1,000-foot vegetable garden and vineyard.

The Thomas Jefferson Center for Historic Plants sells historical plants and seeds at a garden shop at Monticello from April through October. There is also a fine museum shop at Monticello, offering a varied selection of brass, porcelain, crystal, pewter and silver gift ware, plus reproductions made exclusively for Monticello.

During the 1980s more than 5 million visitors toured Monticello. It's such a popular destination for tourists that long lines are inevitable during the peak season of summer and early fall, so it's advisable to start early in the day to avoid a long wait. A lunch stand selling good picnic food is open from 10:30 AM to 3:30 PM daily from April through October.

Monticello is located on Route 53, three miles southeast of Charlottesville. Take Exit 121 off I-64 and follow the signs. It's open daily from 8 AM to 5 PM March through October and from 9 AM to 4:30 PM the rest of the year. It's closed on Christmas Day. Written tours are available in foreign languages.

Admission is $8 for adults, $7 for senior citizens and $4 for children ages 6 to 11. As mentioned earlier, it's possible to save on the cost of adult admission to Monticello, Ash Lawn and Michie Tavern by buying a $17 President's Pass at the Charlottesville/Albemarle Convention and Visitors Bureau. This bureau is located at Route 20 S. and I-64, near Monticello.

THOMAS JEFFERSON VISITORS CENTER
Rt. 20 S.   *(804) 293-6789*

A permanent exhibition on Jefferson's domestic life here is an ideal introduction to nearby Monticello. Nearly 400 objects and artifacts, from his pocketknife to a porcupine quill toothpick, are on display, many for the first time. Also, an award-winning film entitled "Thomas Jefferson: The Pursuit of Liberty," is shown daily at 11 AM and 2 PM in the exhibition theater. The hours are 9 AM to 5:30 PM daily March through October and 9 AM to 5 PM the rest of the year. Admission is free.

MONTPELIER

Montpelier Station   *(703) 672-2728*

The gracious home of President James Madison and his beloved wife, Dolley, opened for public tours in 1987. The estate is in the early stages of restoration, and extensive archeological work and architectural research are ongoing. This is what makes Montpelier such an interesting, even exciting, place to visit. Someone touring the estate might hear about a new discovery on the 2,700-acre property the same day it happened! The staff is an enthusiastic, friendly bunch.

For these reasons, a tour of Montpelier is the perfect complement to a visit to Monticello. Unlike Jefferson, Madison did not document the fine details of his everyday existence, from his gardening techniques to his diet. So the process of uncovering (and literally, in some cases, unearthing) what Montpelier was like in Madison's time is slow and painstaking. Unlike Monticello, where lines form for hours and tours are rather regimented, you can dally at Montpelier and even brainstorm with a tour guide.

Montpelier was owned by the DuPont family for decades before it was bequeathed to the National Trust for Historic Preservation in the 1980s. The DuPonts built major additions to the home and planted elaborate formal gardens. The biggest challenge for Montpelier's new owners, the National Trust, was what to do about all the new rooms and interior changes. They considered doing away with the DuPont imprint and restoring the property to its original Madisonian form. But a compromise was struck, with the exterior and landscape keeping their 20th-century appearances, along with three DuPont rooms in the house. The rest of the mansion's museum is being reconfigured as Madison-period rooms, based on the results of research in progress.

The estate offers breathtaking views of the nearby Blue Ridge Mountains. Visitors are given guided tours of the main floor of the 55-room mansion and may also stroll throughout the grounds and see the barns, stables, a bowling alley and the garden temple Madison built over his ice house. The cemetery where a number of Madison family members are buried, including Dolley and James, may also be visited.

Montpelier's energetic and imaginative staff have big plans for the museum: a full-scale educational center for children to be in a renovated barn, a winery, extensive walking trails and displays in the mansion using the newest technology. For instance, you may one day see a hologram in a hallway, suggesting how the space used to look when it was Madison's bedroom.

Special events throughout the year include the famous Montpelier Hunt Races, which take place on the first Saturday in November.

Montpelier was first settled by Madison's grandparents in 1723. After the completion of Madison's second presidential term, Dolley and

• 237

James retired to Montpelier, where their legendary hospitality kept them in touch with world affairs. Madison was the primary author of the Constitution and one of the authors of the Federalist Papers. He was a proponent of freedom of religion and education in Virginia and served as second rector of the University of Virginia. Madison's public life spanned 53 years and included services as a delegate to the Continental Congress, member of the Virginia House of Delegates, U.S. Congressman, Thomas Jefferson's Secretary of State, and U.S. president for two terms.

Montpelier is about 25 miles north of Charlottesville near Orange. It is open daily from 10 AM to 4 PM, except Thanksgiving, Christmas, New Year's and the first Saturday in November. Admission is $6 for adults and $1 for children 6 to 12. years of age.

OAK RIDGE
Arrington   (804) 263-4168

This estate, more than two centuries in the making, is now open to the public. Located in the rolling hills of Nelson County, the estate was once the private kingdom of Thomas Fortune Ryan, one of the nation's 10 wealthiest men at the turn of the century. The estate once employed hundreds of people and boasted its own railroad station, dairy, race track, post office, 18-hole golf course, power plant and water system. Many of the outbuildings are stil standing, such as the rotunda greenhouse, carriage house, railroad station, dairy complex and spring house. Visitors can

tour the first floor of a 14,275-square-foot mansion and sections of the grounds. Many guests enjoy having a picnic lunch on the front lawn before or after their tour. The estate's owners, John and Rhonda Holland, want to put Oak Ridge and Nelson County on the map as a major tourist spot.

Oak Ridge is open for tours during the summer months from 10 AM to 4 PM Tuesday through Thursday. Tours cost $10 per person, with discounts for senior citizens, school groups and visitors to the nearby Walton's Mountain Museum.

OATLANDS
U.S. Hwy. 15 S.
Leesburg   (703) 777-3175

This breathtaking 261-acre estate and Classical Revival mansion was built by George Carter. The house was originally the center of a 5,000-acre plantation and was partially remodeled in 1827. Most of the building materials, including bricks and wood, came from or were made on the estate. The home is furnished with American, English and French antiques, and the surrounding formal gardens have some of the finest boxwood arrangements in the United States. The estate's fields are now used for equestrian races and shows.

THE ROTUNDA/THE UNIVERSITY OF VIRGINIA
                    (804) 924-7969

Free tours of Mr. Jefferson's "Academic Village" are offered daily from the Rotunda, which Jefferson designed after the classical Pantheon. Begun in 1819 and opened in 1825, the university is renowned for its magnificent and unique architectural design. In fact, in 1976 the American Institute of Architects voted Jefferson's design for the University the most outstanding achievement in American architecture.

Along with his authorship of the Declaration of Independence and the Statute of Virginia for Religious Freedom, the university was an achievement for which Jefferson wished to be remembered. He called it the hobby of his old age, but this is quite an understatement. Not only was he the principal architect, Jefferson also helped select the library collection, hire faculty and design the curriculum. He was also one of the major financial contributors and succeeded in securing public funding for the school.

It was his ardent lobbying for public education in Virginia that led to the establishment of the university in the first place. Jefferson had studied at the College of William and Mary in Williamsburg, but he felt the state, which then encompassed West Virginia, needed a major university. All of this he accomplished during his retirement at Monticello, from which he often watched the university's construction with his telescope. The magnificent Rotunda was completed in 1826, the year Jefferson died.

Tours are conducted daily from the Rtunda at 10 and 11 AM and 2, 3 and 4 PM, except for about two weeks around Christmas. The tour also includes a look at Edgar Allan Poe's old dorm room, which appears much the same as it did when Poe was a student in 1825. By the way, Poe had to leave the university prematurely after running up a huge gambling debt that he couldn't pay.

THE VIRGINIA FESTIVAL OF AMERICAN FILM
University of Virginia
Charlottesville   (800) UVA-FEST

This six-year-old festival held at UVA is dedicated to celebrating and exploring the unique character of American film. It lasts for four days, bringing leading actors, filmmakers, scholars and the public together to discuss American film in a serious way.

The event has attracted national attention by featuring special events that honor the history of American film. These have included a 50th anniversary "encore premiere" of *Mr. Smith Goes to Washington*, with its star, James Stewart, in attendance.

Other renowned actors and filmmakers who have participated in the festival include Gregory Peck, Sissy Spacek, Charlton Heston, Sidney Poitier, Robert Duvall, John Sayles and Robert Altman.

This is such a stimulating, exciting event — well worth planning your fall vacation around. Special discount hotel-and-event package rates are available. Call (800) UVA-FEST for more information.

SCOTTSVILLE ON THE JAMES
The Albemarle County seat until 1762, Scottsville is an old river town right on the James, about 20 miles from Charlottesville on Route 20. In and around the town are 32 authentic Federal buildings — one

of the four or five largest concentrations of Early Republic architecture in the state. The town also has a museum that was originally a Disciples Church built in 1846.

Lynchburg

VISUAL ARTS

ARTS COUNCIL OF
CENTRAL VIRGINIA
Greater Lynchburg Chamber of Commerce
(804) 847-1597

Coordinating the huge wealth of cultural events of Lynchburg and Central Virginia, the Arts Council serves as a clearinghouse for information about area artists, musicians, actors and dancers and offers calendars of their performances. It is active in preservation and advancement of the arts with a mission to make Lynchburg a model cultural center, a goal well within reach by the year 2000.

LYNCHBURG FINE ARTS CENTER
1815 Thomson Dr.   *(804) 846-8451*

An affiliate of the Virginia Museum of Fine Arts in Richmond, the Fine Arts Center has provided Lynchburg with an environment where the arts have flourished. Programs have included arts and music with opportunities for instruction or performance in dance and drama. Membership in FACination, the Center's pop chorus, is open to residents. The Regional Ballet Theatre is the Center's resident dance company. The Alliance for Visual Arts, the resident art organization at the Ceter, presents year round exhibits and classes. Professional instruction is available in all media. The Center's auditorium seats 500 and the costume shop is open to the public for costume rentals.

VIRGINIA CENTER
FOR THE CREATIVE ARTS
Amherst   *(804) 946-7236*

A surprising artistic treasure is located just outside of Lynchburg in Amherst County. It is the Virginia Center for the Creative Arts, the largest working retreat for professional writers, artists and composers in the country, who come seeking the solitude conducive to creative work. Artists who visit from abroad are often the leading artists in their own countries, and some of the most important exchanges between artists worldwide take place here. The Virginia Center for the Creative Arts is affiliated with an elite private women's college, Sweet Briar, known for its international programs, and is supported by the National Endowment for the Arts.

The V.C.C.A. is not frequently open to the public but does have exhibits at Camp Gallery, located in the renovated barn that aso houses the artists' studios. There are three different shows each summer with meet-the-artists receptions on Sunday afternoons. Special events are also open to the public, such as a summer exhibit by a Mozambican sculptor in residence. Many public events, such as poetry readings with Russian writers-in-residence, are cosponsored with Sweet Briar.

Camp Gallery hours are 2 to 4:30 PM Sundays during summer months only.

Photo: Theater At The Kiln

The Lime Kiln Theatre in Lexington.

MAIER MUSEUM OF ART
Randolph-Macon Woman's College
1 Quinlan St.   (804) 947-8136

Known for its collection of 19th- and 20th-century American paintings, the Maier Museum at prestigious Randolph-Macon is also the site of the Blue Ridge Music Festival, which brings a continuing rich and varied schedule of internationally recognized musicians to the area. This is a tremendous community asset well worth the visit for arts lovers.

It is open September through May from 1 to 5 PM Tuesday through Sunday.

MUSEUMS

LYNCHBURG MUSEUM AT OLD COURT HOUSE
Fifth St.   (804) 847-1459

Located in one of Virginia's out-standing Greek Revival civil buildings, the Lynchburg Museum is the headquarters for Lynchburg's fine museum system. The courtroom was restored around 1855. It traces Lynchburg's history through each successive period and is an outstanding collection for both scholars and history buffs, especially for the Civil War period.

Open from 1 to 4 PM daily, the museum is closed holidays. Admission is $3 for adult and $1 for students.

PEST HOUSE MEDICAL MUSEUM AND CONFEDERATE CEMETERY
Old City Cemetery
Fourth and Taylor Sts.   (804) 847-1811

In the 1800s, Lynchburg residents who contracted contagious diseases such as smallpox or measles were quarantined in the Pest House. Medical care and cleanliness were virtually nonexistent then, and most patients died and were buried a few yards away. By 1861, the Pest House was used for Confederate soldiers. Dr. John Jay Terrell, 33, volunteered to assume responsibility for the soldiers and changed their wretched conditions. His office shows the state of medicine during that era. You can see an 1860s hypodermic needle and one of the first chloroform masks ever used. This is a fascinating medical journey through history and a sobering reminder of humankind's mortality and just how far we've come in a little over 130 years.

Open sunrise to sunset, the facility offers guided tours by appointment.

MUSIC

BLUE RIDGE MUSIC FESTIVAL
Randolph-Macon Woman's College
(804) 947-8000

The Blue Ridge Music Festival has been created as a celebration of musical diversity. Now in its fifth season, the blue Ridge Music Festival continues to inspire and challenge music lovers of all ages and tastes with concerts of the world's great chamber music, jazz improvisation and folk music from Tex-Mex ballads to Appalachian melodies. An unparalleled week of concerts awaits you on this attractive campus.

COMMUNITY CONCERTS
E. C. Glass High School   *(804) 384-3184*

The 50th Anniversary of Lynchburg's Community Concerts will be held at the Lynchburg Civic Auditorium through an association with Columbia Artists Management. Many special events, ranging from singers, pianists, ballet and ethnic performances, are part of this special subscription series that is an asset to Central Virginia. No single tickets are sold.

POINT OF HONOR
112 Cabell St.   *(804) 847-1459*

In the afternoons, you can usually find Lynchburg's history elite, some of whom are from historical families themselves, at this restored 19th-century mansion. Lovingly restored by the Lynchburg Historical Foundation, the Garden Club of Virginia and the Katharine Garland Diggs Trust, Point of Honor shows today's families what life was like in the days of Dr. George Cabell Sr., Patrick Henry's personal physician. It also was home to Mary Virginia Ellet Cabell, one of the founders of the Daughters of the American Revolution. Its name comes from the gun duels fought on its lawn.

It is open daily 1 to 4 PM; closed holidays. Admission is $3 for adults and $1 for students.

THEATER

CHERRY TREE PLAYHOUSE
New Address Pending

A new theater, the Players is a group of artists, musicians, business people, directors, technicians and others who came together to advance the arts and theater in the Lynchburg area. There is an active children's and youth theater as well. The Players, who are currently relocating, are closed for the summer. Admission is $7.50 for adults; $6.50 for students. No children younger than age 6 may attend.

OTHER CULTURAL ATTRACTIONS

ANNE SPENCER HOUSE AND GARDEN
1313 Pierce St.   *(804) 846-0517*

Anne Spencer was an internationally recognized African-American poet of the Harlem Renaissance period in the 1920s. Her poems are included in the *Norton Anthology of Modern Poetry*. Behind her home is the garden and accompanying cottage, "EdanKraal," built for her by her husband as a place where she could write. The garden has been beautifully restored by Hillside Garden Club. Revered the world over for her brilliance and intellect, she entertained many great leaders and artists of her day, including Dr. Martin Luther King, Supreme Court Justice Thurgood Marshall, scientist Dr. George Washington Carver, sports legend Jackie Robinson, Congressman Adam Clayton Powell (who honeymooned there) and the legendary singers Paul Robeson and Marion Anderson. Her son, Chauncey, still lives in the family home, so hours ar by appointment only. Call him at (804) 846-0517.

JONES MEMORIAL LIBRARY
2311 Memorial Ave.   *(804) 846-0501*

The second oldest library in Virginia, Jones Memorial is also one of Virginia's foremost genealogical libraries. With 30,000 volumes specializing in genealogical, historical and Lynchburg holdings, the Jones is known for its vast records. These include Revolutionary War records, family histories, enlistments and Virginia county and state court records. Records from England, Ireland and Scotland include heraldry information. It offers research and lending services by mail. This gem is probably one of the most under-utilized treasures of the Blue Ridge.

The library is open 1 to 9 PM Tuesday, noon to 5 PM Wednesday through Friday, and 9 AM to 1 PM Saturday; it is closed Sunday and Monday.

RED HILL
Patrick Henry National Memorial
Brookneal   *(804) 376-2044*

Who can forget Revolutionary War hero Patrick Henry's speech, "Give me liberty or give me death!" Red Hill was home to the famous lawyer and his 17 children and is also his burial ground. The original plantation of nearly 3,000 acres showcases the largest collection of Patrick Henry memorabilia in the world, including the famous P. H. Rothermel painting, "Patrick Henry before the Virginia House of Burgesses." You can see Henry's home, original law office, kitchen and overgrown boxwood garden as they were before Henry's death in 1799.

The memorial is open 9 AM until 5 PM daily except November through March, when it closes at 4 PM. It is closed holidays. Admission is $3 for adults, $1 for students and children.

VIRGINIA SCHOOL OF THE ARTS
Columbia and
Rivermont Ave.   *(804) 847-8688*

Virginia School of the Arts, a

private residential secondary school, is dedicated to preparing young people for careers in dance, theater and the visual arts. It is one of only six such schools for the arts in America, and students come from throughout the United States. Its arts faculty includes prominent professional performers and artists who contribute greatly to Lynchburg's culture.

Smith Mountain Lake

OTHER CULTURAL ATTRACTIONS

SMITH MOUNTAIN
VISITORS CENTER & DAM

Rt. 908   *(703) 985-2587*

At Appalachian Power's Visitors Center overlooking Smith Mountain Dam, you'll enjoy both the view and learning how electricity is generated — the whole purpose of the creation of Virginia's largest lake by A.P.C.O. The entire experience provides insight into the relatively recent lake culture of western Virginia. An audiovisual presentation shows how the dam was constructed. You can spin zoetropes and watch how A.P.C.O. uses the water cycle to generate electricity. The ramp in the overlook offers a spectacular view of the dam and gorge. Picnic facilities are nearby.

It is open 10 AM to 6 PM daily and closed holidays.

SMITH MOUNTAIN LAKE
STATE PARK & VISITORS CENTER

Route 1, Huddleston   *(703) 297-5998*

In addition to camping and the only public swimming area on the lake Smith Mountain State Park offers a continuing variety of educational programs aimed at lake and nature lovers. The Visitors Center offers a schedule of programs and lectures. Hours are 8 AM to 10 PM daily.

Bedford County

MUSEUMS

BEDFORD CITY/COUNTY MUSEUM

201 E. Main St.
Bedford   *(703) 586-4520*

Visitors will enjoy a collection showing the story of Bedford, a charming Virginia city at the foot of the Peaks of Otter, a Blue Ridge Parkway attraction. It begins with early Native Americans and progresses through the mid 20th century. Here, you'll see Native American relics, Revolutionary War and Civil War artifacts, clothing, flags and quilts, among other interesting, well-displayed artifacts. Research assistance is available for genealogists outside Bedford.

Hours are 10 AM to 5 PM Monday through Saturday. Admission is $1 for adults and 50¢ for children. AAA discount is available.

OTHER CULTURAL ATTRACTIONS

ELKS NATIONAL HOME

Bedford   *(703) 586-8232*

A spacious retirement home used recently as a set in the Disney movie, *What About Bob?*, the Elks National Home for retired members of this fraternal organization is best known for its annual Christmas light display. Men from every state work all year to give western Virginia's children a Christmas show worth driving to see. The rest of the year, the beautiful grounds are open for visitors.

HOLY LAND
USA NATURE SANCTUARY
Rt. 6, Bedford   *(703) 586-2823*

This 400-acre nature sanctuary where the religious can imagine the journey and deeds f Jesus Christ is located in the beautiful Blue Ridge close to the Peaks of Otter. You have to use your imagination to envision the Biblical scenes outlined for Bible research and study, but many find inspiration from the visit.

POPLAR FOREST
Rt. 661, Forest   *(804) 525-1806*

Thomas Jefferson's summer home, Poplar Forest has been under renovation for several years now, and visitors are invited to watch the painstaking excavations and historical restoration. During Jefferson's time, Poplar Forest as a working plantation of nearly 5,000 acres tended by slaves who grew corn and tobacco. Although Monticello was Jefferson's pride and joy, Poplar Forest was where he came to get away from it all, riding three days from Charlottesville by horseback to reach it. As Mikhail Gorbachev said when he visited in the spring of '93, "This is the first Camp David!" Restoration of the main house has begun and is expected to take four years.

Jefferson himself designed the unusual building. History and Jefferson buffs will be fascinated with seeing his office, library and even two domed "necessaries" that were part of day-to-day life. July 4 is the best time to visit, since historical actors staff the home in period attire and speak the language of the day, transporting you right back to 1815. The event is free and takes place from noon to 5 PM. Picnicking is encouraged. Poplar Forest's huge, ancient boxwoods are incredible to see on the beautiful grounds. The staff's enthusiasm for this cultural treasure is highly contagious.

Open 10 AM to 4 PM Wednesday through Sunday April through November, it is also open on major holidays except Thanksgiving. (Please note that the last tour begins at 3:45 PM.) Group tours may be arranged year round. Admission is $5 for adults, $4 for senior citizens, $2 for college students and $1 for children 18 and younger.

SEDALIA CENTER
Rt. 638, Big Island   *(804) 299-5080*

The Sedalia Center for the art of living and the living arts is a regional, nonprofit organization offering programming in the arts, culture, environmental awareness, health and inner development. It offers classes, workshops, seminars and special events to ignite and nourish the creative process in each person, according to its mission — and it does it well. The center's modern building is set on seven acres of land at the foot of Flintstone Mountain near Big Island. Special events include dance, story telling, music festivals and a country fair. The Sedalia Coffeehouse is held every fourth Saturday, and contradancing is every second Friday. At least once a quarter, you'll find the Coffeehouse serving as an open jam, in keeping with Sedalia's mission to ignite and nourish the creative process in each person.

Here, you can take classes in everything from Cajun cooking and Tai Chi to "Introduction to Mountain Dulcimer and Fundamentals of Instrument Construction." Lectures may include "How Native American Indians Lived with Nature and How Some of Their Approaches Might Work for Us." A small but very dedicated group of creative people makes the Sedalia Center the heart of a special culture for people of the Blue Ridge foothills.

Franklin County

MUSEUMS

BLUE RIDGE INSTITUTE MUSEUMS
Ferrum College
Ferrum   *(703) 365-4416*
The Blue Ridge Institute of Ferrum College, the State Center for Blue Ridge Folklore, presents the folkways of the region and Virginia as a whole through two unique museum facilities. The Blue Ridge Farm Museum presents the history and culture of early Virginia settlements in the southwestern mountains of the state. There's an 1800 German-American farmstead with log house, oven, outbuildings, pasture and garden that reveals the daily life of colonists who came from the German settlements of Pennsylvania and the Shenandoah Valley. All buildings are authentic and

were moved from their original Blue Ridge locations. Heirloom vegetables flourish in the gardens, vintage breeds of livestock shelter by the barn, and costumed interpreters work at farm and household chores true to early life in the region.

Both historical and contemporary folkways engage the visitor to the Institute's Museum Galleries. Two rotating exhibits showcase the rich texture of Virginia folklife as found in music, crafts, art and customs. The Museum galleries are the only facilities in the Commonwealth dedicated exclusively to the presentation of traditional culture.

The Farm Museum is open weekends from mid-May through mid-August, Saturdays 10 AM to 5 PM and Sundays 1 to 5 PM. Admission is $3 for adults and $2 for children and senior citizens. Museum Galleries are open year round Mondays through Saturdays 10 AM to 4 PM. Admission is free.

THEATER

BLUE RIDGE DINNER THEATRE
Ferrum College, Sale Theatre
Schoolfield Hall
Ferrum   *(703) 365-4335*
Celebrating its 15th season at Ferrum College, the Blue Ridge Dinner Theatre operates on the three guiding principles of theater as discovery, wholesome family entertainment and celebration. It also serves up a great luncheon or dinner in combination with everything from murder mysteries to great historical masterpieces. Adjacent to the nationally known Blue Ridge

Institute, tours of this facility are also offered to theater-goers.

Performances are varied, with hours at 12:15 PM and 6:45 PM.

OTHER CULTURAL ATTRACTIONS

BOOKER T. WASHINGTON NATIONAL MONUMENT

Hardy (703) 721-2094

Booker T. Washington was born into the legacy of slavery. He spent the first nine years of his life in bondage on this small tobacco farm. It was from this unlikely beginning that Washington achieved international recognition as an educator, orator, unofficial presidential advisor, founder of Tuskegee Institute and race leader. Begin your tour of this famous African-American educator's birthplace by watching the slide show and seeing the exhibits at the Visitor's Center. This is the most famous attraction in Franklin County and with good reason. From the beautiful, restored farm and its animals to the hike up Plantation Trail, this monument offers a scenic, historic sojourn into a time in America when slavery was a way of life.

It is open daily 8:30 AM to 5 PM, except for Thanksgiving, Christmas and New Year's Day. Admission is free.

BLUE RIDGE FOLKLIFE FESTIVAL

Ferrum College
Ferrum (703) 365-4416

On the fourth Saturday of October, Ferrum College showcases the rich culture of regional folklife. This blockbuster festival is now in its 21st year. Visitors can experience the tastes, sights and sounds of western Virginia folk culture as demonstrated by local residents. More than 40 Blue Ridge crafters demonstrate and sell rugs braided by hand, baskets, shingles and other folk arts. The South's thriving auto culture is featured along with vintage steam and gas-powered farm machinery. Among the most popular events for spectators are the horse pulling contests and coon dog water races. Many of these demonstrations are getting to be extinct as the old-timers die, so if you want to see the Blue Ridge as it was make it a point to go to the festival. It's crowded, but lots of fun.

The festival is held from 10 AM to 5 PM. Admission, which includes a tour of the Farm Museum, is $4 for adults and $3 for students.

BLUE RIDGE INSTITUTE

Ferrum College,
Ferrum (703) 365-4416

It is often astounding to visitors that a small Methodist-related college in Franklin County, Virginia, has taken on the role of preserving a cultural heritage to the extent and level of visibility that Ferrum College has done. The result, the Blue Ridge Institute, along with the Blue Ridge Farm Museum and its Folklife Festival, paces Ferrum among the nation's most important colleges culturally. Its archives contain thousands of photos, videotapes, phonograph records, vintage books and manuscripts. The archive is recognized for its special holdings and documentations of Appalachian photos, Shenandoah Valley beliefs, Southwestern Virginia folktales and African-American and Caucasian folk music from throughout Virginia.

Ferrum's thater group, the Jack Tale Players, continues the legacy through acting out legends of the South. BRI Records, which presents the diverse musical heritage of Virginia's folk culture, has been nominated for several Grammys.

People of English, Scotch, Irish, African and German descent will especially be interested in the distinct identities reflected in Blue Ridge music, crafts, foods, beliefs and customs formed after emigrating from their homelands.

The institute is open Monday through Friday 8 AM to 4:30 PM. rchives are open by appointment.

New River Valley Region

Blacksburg

VISUAL ARTS

Virginia Tech features several art galleries with good reputations that are worth visiting.

ARMORY ART GALLERY
201 Draper Rd.   *(703) 231-4859*

Virginia Tech's Department of Art and Art History operates the Armory Art Gallery as an educational and outreach program. The gallery is located in the Old Blacksburg Armory and has 1,000 square feet of exhibition space. A year round rotation calendar features work by national or regional

artists, work by student artists and other shows of community interest.

PERSPECTIVE ART GALLERY
Squires Student Center   *(703) 231-5200*

Perspective Gallery offers a wide variety of styles and media by artists ranging from internationally known professionals to students. The gallery is a program facility of the University Unions and Student Activities. The showcase gallery provides a spotlight for special interest exhibits and works from selected artists. Gallery talks and receptions where the public can meet featured artists are also offered.

XYZ COOPERATIVE GALLERY
223 N. Main St., above College Inn
(703) 953-3435

A lively exhibitory gallery, XYZ sponsors continuing exhibitions of intriguing works of art. You'll enjoy the vitality of the changing exhibitions.

THEATER

THEATRE ARTS DEPARTMENT
Virginia Tech   *(703) 231-5615*

The New River Valley's cultural richness comes in great part from Virginia Tech's presence, and theater is no exception. The only Theatre Arts Department in Virginia to have both its graduate and undergraduate programs accredited by the National Association of Schools of Theatre, it has received more awards from the American College Theatre Festival than any other college or university in the Southeast. The Theatre Arts Department at Tech stages about 20 productions each year, including comedies, dramas, musicals and reviews. Virginia Tech hosts four subscription shows within the academic year. There are three theaters: Haymarket Theatre at Squires Student Center, Black Box Theatre in the Performing Arts Building and Squires Studio Theatre. All productions are open to the public. Don't miss Tech's Summer Arts Festival held throughout each summer.

Christiansburg

VISUAL ARTS

NEW RIVER VALLEY ARTS COUNCIL
(703) 381-1430

An active group which publishes an arts directory, a lively magazine and calendar of local artists, the New River Valley Arts Council is a complete source of information on the wide range of arts within the region. If you're planning a visit there and want to see what the area offers, give them a call first.

PALETTE ART GALLERY
Roanoke Rd., just off U.S. Route 11/460
(703) 382-8861

For 30 years, Palette Art Gallery has provided a showcase for Southwestern Virginia artists at its rambling building; it specializes in local art. Begun by Vance Miller, an 80-year-old Impressionist artist, the Palette has no pretense and is chock full of art, quaint and conservative. There's no indoor plumbing and a coal stove provides the heat. You'll find many of Miller's paintins in Virginia Tech offices. In addition to being a great source of art, the Gallery has returned nearly $100,000 back to the community for charitable causes since opening in 1961.

MUSEUMS

THE MONTGOMERY MUSEUM AND LEWIS MILLER REGIONAL ART CENTER
300 S. Pepper St.   (703) 382-5644

A Valley-wide project to promote Montgomery County's rich history and arts, this center is located in a mid 19th-century home of American and Flemish bond brick made from local materials, with hand hewn oak beams and rafters. A curious aspect of the manse portion of the house is a "step-up" feature in the back rooms, thought to be a carry-over design from Colonial days when it was believed that evil spirits bearing illness traveled the night air along floors. The house contains both historic and contemporary work including exhibits and shows of Southwestern Virginia artists and crafters. It also houses a

If you're planning to see a popular attraction, early morning is the best time. That way, you'll miss both the crowds and the heat.

genealogical research area, historic small press library and an archive.

It is open 2 to 5 PM weekends May through October or by appointment.

OTHER CULTURAL ATTRACTIONS

CAROL M. NEWMAN LIBRARY

Virginia Tech Campus (703) 231-6170

Virginia Tech's Carol M. ewman Library has a microforms collection of nearly 5 million, making it the fifth largest in the United States and Canada. Contained within this store of information are rare books and magazines, government documents, newspapers, Virginia Confederate Service Records and issues of the campus newspaper back to 1903.

SMITHFIELD PLANTATION

Virginia Tech campus, off U.S. Hwy. 460 Bypass onto Va. Rt. 314
(703) 951-2060

Built by Col. William Preston in 1772, Smithfield Plantation has been extensively restored and is a Virginia Historic Landmark. It was the birthplace of two Virginia governors, James Patton Preston and John Buchanan Floyd, and was briefly the home of a third, John Floyd Jr.

Hours are 1 to 5 PM Thursday through Sunday April 1 through Novemer 1. Admission is $4 for adults and $1.50 for children 12 and younger.

VIRGINIA TECH DUCK POND

Virginia Tech campus

If you took a poll of where many people went on their first date or fell in love in the New River Valley, it would be the Virginia Tech Duck Pond, hands down! It's a Tech landmark beside the golf course, where mothers take their babies, couples hold hands and picnic and the fattest ducks in the world hold court over bread crumbs and crackers. This place gives a whole new meaning to the cliche "Lucky Duck," and is the most popular stroll on campus.

Floyd

VISUAL ARTS

OLD CHURCH GALLERY

Rt. 221 (703) 745-4849

In this 1850 Greek Revival building, various art work exhibits are adjacent to the history room. A century-old copper still (used to make moonshine whiskey) is on display. There's an active quilter's guild, monthly literary group, arts and crafts workshop and children's programs in the summer.

NEW MOUNTAIN MERCANTILE HERE AND NOW GALLERY

114 N. Locust St. (703) 745-4278

For art and crafts definitely out of the ordinary, don't miss New Mountain Mercantile and its Here and Now Gallery. Located in the 100-year-old Boyd Store building, six miles off Milepost 165.2 at the Blue Ridge Parkway, this collage of colorful creations has a gallery in one corner that highlights the art of one individual each month. What looks like an ordinary building on the outside is extraordinary inside.

It's just down the block from Cockram's General Store.

It is open 10 AM to 6 PM Tuesday through Saturday and noon to 5 PM on Sundays.

THEATER

FLOYD THEATRE GROUP
Floyd   *No phone*

This theater group started with a Skit Night for locals and ended up an enthusiastic collection of folks who present outstanding plays. Skit Night is still an annual event. Productions are scheduled with tremendous community support and participation. It's yet another facet of the wide range of cultural activities in Floyd County.

OTHER CULTURAL ATTRACTIONS

COCKRAM'S GENERAL STORE
South Locust St.   *(703) 745-4563*

The culture of mountainous Floyd County doesn't get any better than this! At 7 PM Friday nights, folks start showing up with fiddles, harmonicas, banjos and guitars and what follows is a Floyd County tradition. The flat-footing begins, the old-timers reminisce, and the music that is the lifeblood of the Floyd County mountain spirit soothes the brow and heals the wounds of the work week. This is an endangered cultural species that is personally financed by Freeman Cockram, who believes Floyd Countians need such a place to gather. Don't miss this New River Valley landmark.

MABRY MILL
Mile 176, Blue Ridge Parkway
(703) 745-4329

Undoubtedly the most scenic and most-photographed place on the Blue Ridge Parkway, Mabry Mill has been called one of the most picturesque water mills in the entire United States. It still grinds flour for buckwheat cakes and cornpone and produces some of the most delicious cornmeal you can buy for Southern-style cornbread. Mabry Mill also is a workshop of live crafts, music and exhibits that shows a way of life a century ago. There's also arts, crafts and a restaurant. If you're traveling through Floyd County, don't miss it!

Giles County

VISUAL ARTS

THE MOUNTAIN LAKE SYMPOSIUM & GALLERY
Mountain Lake   *(703) 626-7121*

In the rarefied air on the second highest mountain in Virginia, Mountain Lake provides the picturesque setting each year for the Mountain Lake Symposium, begun by the Virginia Tech Department of Art and Art History, which has gained national recognition as an art criticism conference. Supported by the Virginia Museum of Fine Arts, it is yet another jewel in the culture of the Blue Ridge. While at Mountain Lake, also check out its Gallery, the home of the popular Bob Evans Knobbits make-believe creatures.

Alleghany Highlands Region Profile:
Stewart H. Bostic

Imagine yourself on a steam excursion 40 years ago. The air is crisp and the leaves are just beginning to show fall colors as you steam through the mountain passes in the railroad coach of the Chesapeake & Ohio, one of America's great passenger trains.

Listen to the echo of the big steam locomotive's chime whistle as it rounds a bend in the track that snakes through the breathtaking Alleghany Highlands. Waiting for you at the historic Clifton Forge Railroad station is a day of fun.

Days gone by?

Not really, thanks to Stewart H. Bostic, a rail fan supreme who makes history come alive each year with excursions and events through the Chesapeake & Ohio Historical Societies Archives and Rail Facilities. The group is one of the largest organizations in the world dedicated to the study of a single railroad, which traces its roots back to 1836.

The Societies publishes a monthly magazine and has a collection of historic passenger and freight cars covering the period of the 1920s to the 1950s.

Stewart H. Bostic

The collection includes more than 100,000 ink-on-linen engineering and mechanical drawings, 50,000 photos and thousands of publications about the railroad that made the sleepy Alleghany County town of Clifton Forge boom and bustle long ago. Much of the credit for this vast railroad treasure trove belongs to Bostic, who worked for the C&O from 1944, at the age of 17, until his retirement in 1985.

In between, he served his country in the U.S. Army Air Corps from 1945 to 1947 and stayed in the Army Reserves through 1958. Not one to stay away from railroads for long, however, Bostic then served as a railway consultant from 1987 to 1992.

Over many years, Bostic, 67, not only helped establish the C&O Railroad Historical Society but also has served as archive building manager, assistant archivist, operations officer for COHS passenger cars and assistant to the COHS president.

His latest endeavor is helping to restore the old C&O Freight House and developing a railroad museum, passenger car shop and display area for the coaches the society already has restored.

Bostic's wife, Ida Marie, a native of nearby Ronceverte, West Virginia, says her husband is never happier than when he's "tinkering and sweating" on restoring a bedraggled old railroad car with his friends.

Although that's sometimes difficult for Ida Marie to understand, nevertheless it's a romance that many others share. The C&O Railroad Historical Society now enrolls 2,500 members in 49 states.

Lest anyone think, however, that Bostic's interests are strictly historical, one need only look at his many other civic endeavors to enhance the quality of life in Alleghany County. A deacon at Temple Baptist, Bostic also belongs to the American Legion and is a Shriner.

Alleghany Chamber of Commerce Director Michelle Wright calls Bostic one of the county's "most active, best-known, tireless supporters for tourism." Chairman of its Ambassadors Committee, Bostic even arranged to have a railroad caboose donated to the Chamber for its promotional efforts.

For some, trains are a hobby. For others, trains are their life. Stewart Bostic says trains have helped to make his life both an education and enjoyable.

Sharing that love of the history of the iron horse has made the Alleghany Highlands a better community for thousands of residents and visitors.

NEW RIVER VALLEY ARTS AND CRAFTS GUILD

U.S. Hwy. 460, Pembroke (703) 626-3309

Handmade treasures in the mountain tradition are both made and sold in the New River Valley Arts and Crafts Guild in the heart of Pembroke. There's usually a quilt in the making, as well as rug weaving and other activities going on among the 60 artists who display and sell here.

Hours are 10 AM to 5 PM Tuesday through Saturday an 1 to 4 PM Sunday.

MUSEUMS

ANDREW JOHNSTON MUSEUM & RESEARCH CENTER

Main St.
Pearisburg   (703) 921-5000

Located next to the Post Office, this restored brick house is home to a genealogy library and historic Giles County displays.

It is open by appointment.

Radford

VISUAL ARTS

FLOSSIE MARTIN GALLERY

Radford University   (703) 831-5754

This state-of-the-art facility occupies 2,000 square feet of space on the beautiful Radford University campus. The combination gallery/museum features rotating exhibits of both regional and nationally known artists. In its short four-year history, the gallery has had on its roster such important guests and international figures as the avant-garde John Cage and Dr. Jehan Sadat, wife of the former leader of Egypt, who dsplayed her own personal Egyptian art collection. The gallery sponsors CLAY, USA, an annual survey of contemporary ceramics.

The gallery hours are 10 AM to 4 PM Monday through Friday, noon to 4 PM on Sunday and extended hours of 6 to 9 PM on Thursdays during fall and winter.

THEATER

THE LONG WAY HOME
OUTDOOR DRAMA
Ingles Homestead Amphitheater
(703) 639-0679

For 22 years now, the only outdoor theater drama in Virginia has been wowing audiences with the Earl Hobson Smith historic epic, *The Long Way Home*. This exciting drama focuses on local history, with a true heroic adventure depicting Mary Draper Ingles.

Ingles was captured after fleeing from a 1755 attack by Indians on the north fork of the Roanoke River, where she saw her mother and infant nephew murdered by the Shawnees. Forced to travel west 800 miles to make salt for the Shawnee, the story tells of her courageous escape and long trek back to Radford to warn of an upcoming attack. This breathtaking saga of honest, hard working pioneers who labored to tame the American frontier is re-enacted in the Ingles Homestead Amphitheater at her homesite and grave. There's overnight camper parking available. This is a "must see" production for theater and history buffs.

Performances are given June through Labor Day. Tickets are $6.50 for adults an $3 for children ages 1 to 12.

OTHER CULTURAL ATTRACTIONS

RADFORD UNIVERSITY COLLEGE
OF VISUAL AND PERFORMING ARTS
(703) 831-5141

The university offers the public solo music performances, theater, art exhibits, classical ballet, big band music, jazz and modern dance. Call the university for a schedule of culturally enriching events featuring students and nationally known guest artists.

Pulaski County

VISUAL ARTS

THE FINE ARTS CENTER
FOR THE NEW RIVER VALLEY
21 W. Main St.   *(703) 980-7363*

This is the cultural hub of the New River Valley, featuring contemporary works, music shows, private collections and amateur and professional artists. It is housed in a storefront building considered a prime example of Victorian commercial architecture. Built in 198, the center has been designated a Virginia Historic Landmark. This Center is also a prime example what can be accomplished when a community bands together to found and fund a grassroots fine arts center. Pulaski can be proud, indeed, of this facility.

OTHER CULTURAL ATTRACTIONS

HISTORIC OLD NEWBERN & WILDERNESS ROAD REGIONAL MUSEUM
New River Historical Society
(703) 674-4835

Nineteen original 1810 buildings comprise part of the 57 properties of the Old Newbern National Historic District, a neighborhood originally planned by early settlers. Newbern served as Pulaski County's seat from 1839 to 1893, when the courthouse was destroyed by fire. This interesting tour takes you through the historic buildings, some already renovated and some in the process, including a slave cabin, old jail, rose garden, pre-Civil War church, buggy shed and small weather-boarded barn. The museum contains artifacts of this era and sponsors a full annual agenda of everything from a Civil War Reenactors' Boot Camp and Civil War Weekend (Pulaski County was the site of the famous Battle of Cloyd's Mountain) to flea markets, dinners and holiday events.

Nearby are some great shops and restaurants, including Valley Pike Inn, Granny Swain's Country Store and PJ's Carousel Village, the world's largest manufacturer of carousel horses and animals, found at major amusement parks and fine gift shops around the world. With the tour, shops and restaurants, this makes for a wonderful day!

Hours are 10:30 AM to 4:30 PM Tuesday through Saturday; 1:30 to 4:30 PM Sunday.

Alleghany Highlands Region

Visual Arts

ALLEGHANY HIGHLANDS ARTS & CRAFTS CENTER
439 East Ridgeway St.
Clifton Forge   *(703) 862-4447*

The Galleries' changing exhibits feature works produced by Alleghany Highlands' and other artists. It is a not-for-profit volunteer organization that encourages creative experiences and appreciation of the visual arts.

It is open 10:30 AM to 4:30 PM Monday through Saturday during June, July and August and Tuesday through Saturday September through May.

THE HIGHLAND COUNTY ARTS COUNCIL
P. O. Box 175
Monterey 24465   *No phone*

The Highland County Arts Council provides artistic enrichment and enjoyable programming for all ages. H.C.A.C. has provided children's programs and also sponsored artists in residence who go into the schools. Other projects are a Maple Festival Crafts Booth, Highland Dance Classes and story telling. Various events are scheduled throughout the year.

Museums

BATH COUNTY
HISTORICAL SOCIETY MUSEUM
Courthouse Square   *(703) 839-2543*

Artifacts of Bath County and the Indian and Civil wars are prominent here. You'll see books, apparel and photographs. There's also a genealogy library. The group just published a history of Bath County for its 1991 Bicentennial.

It is open 8:30 AM to 4:30 PM Monday and Wednesday through Friday May through November. Tuesday hours are noon to 8 PM.

MAPLE MUSEUM
U.S. Hwy. 220, Monterey (703) 468-2550

In the land of Maples, there's a museum celebrating old-time sugaring. See a replica of a Sugar House, where there are sugar- and syrup-making demonstrations. Also on display are tools and equipment used by sugar makers throughout the years. Old-timers who can't otherwise get to the real sugar camps will find this especially interesting.

It is open daily.

Music

GARTH NEWEL MUSIC CENTER
Hot Springs   *(703) 839-5409*

From among the giant hemlocks, the hills of Bath County come alive with the sound of music, envied by music lovers the world over. The importance of the Garth Newel Center to the culture of the

Alleghany Highlands and western Virginia cannot be underestimated. Musicians, students and awe-inspired audiences come together in this unspoiled mountain area to hear beautiful music, such as Mozart, Haydn and Dvorak, in an enchanting mountain setting.

Featured are the Garth Newel Chamber Players and Garth Newel Piano Trio. Garth Newel provides an intensive residential Chamber Music Study Program for serious young musicians who receive a full scholarship. The architecture and acoustics of Herter Hall provide a wonderful ambiance for chamber music and create a unique sense of being outdoors while actually indoors! Before the performance, many visitors have made it a tradition to join friends for a picnic on the grounds. As thousands have discovered over the years, a concert here is more than just music — it's an experience. Garth Newel also sponsors holiday weekends that are a feast for lovers of chamber music, with gourmet meals, fine wine and convivial company. This is a Blue Ridge gem visited regularly by dignitaries the world over.

Other Cultural Attractions

BEAR MOUNTAIN OUTDOOR SCHOOL
Hightown   *(703) 468-2700*

Real mountain culture and crafts can be learned at Bear Mountain, located 4,200 feet up in Highland County. You can attain practical building skills, engage in rural living pursuits such as log cabin building, blacksmithing and stone masonry, and take natural history hikes. Or, perhaps organic gardening, beekeeping, mushroom cultivation or spinning and natural dyeing are your cup of herbal tea. Workshops are one-on-one and hands-on, stressing real projects. Students actually build a log cabin or timber frame. This is a place to experience country living, rather than being lectured to about it. The school centers around a modern lodge 560 acres up in the clouds. Here's everything about the Blue Ridge that is unique!

C&O RAILROAD
HISTORICAL SOCIETY
P. O. Box 79
Clifton Forge 24422   *No phone*

This organization in an historical railroad town is dedicated to preserving and interpreting the history of the Chesapeake & Ohio Railroad. It has one of the best archive collections of material pertinent to the history of a single railroad. It comprises over 100,000 ink-on-linen engineering and mechanical drawings, 50,000 photos and thousands of books and publications surrounding the industrial roots of the railroad that made this town boom long ago. The group publishes a monthly magazine and has a collection of historic passenger and freight cars covering the period of the 1920s to the 1950s. It has 2,500 members in 49 states and is one of the largest organizations devoted to the study of a single railroad that traces its roots from 1836. The railroad's logo, the Chessie cat, taken from its "Sleep Like a Kitten" ad campaign in 1933, is one of the most famous logos in America.

Photo: Harrisonburg Chamber of Commerce

A car isn't the only way to get to the Farmers' Market in Harrisonburg.

Inside
Shopping

Whether you're looking for antiques, handcrafts or outlet malls for bargains in clothing and housewares, the Blue Ridge region has it all. Of course, there are the usual shopping malls, Wal-Marts and Kmarts. But practically every town in the Shenandoah Valley, foothills or other regions of the Blue Ridge has at least one quaint little antique shop and a place that sells locally made handcrafts.

Some fine furniture makers in the region, such as E.A. Clore in Madison or Suter's in Harrisonburg, sell directly to the consumer. You must visit their showrooms to see what they make, because you won't find their beautiful furniture elsewhere.

This is also true for the shops selling fine handcrafts. Places such as the Blue Ridge Pottery on Route 33 near Skyline Drive and Limeton Pottery in Front Royal specialize in ceramics that are crafted literally right next door. Other shops, such as Forever Country in New Market and the Handcraft House in Madison, represent dozens of artisans whose creations also cannot be found in department stores.

Charlottesville is known for its fine downtown shops that sell crafts and other *objets d'art* from around the globe. There, you can just as easily find an African mask as a bar of American soap.

If you're visiting from out of state and want a Made-in-Virginia souvenir, there are plenty of shops specializing in such products. **Virginia Born and Bred** in Lexington is one fine example, selling beautiful brass and silver items as well as folk art, woven goods, peanuts, jams and jellies. Virginia Made in Staunton is another.

The following is a description of some of our favorite shops in the cities, towns and rural areas we've covered in this guidebook. This is in no way a comprehensive listing, and we may have inadvertently missed your favorite shop. Also, in the retail world, shops come and go, so call ahead if you have your heart set on a particular store. This seems especially true in the antiques trade. Drop us a line and give us your Insider's perspective if you know of one we've missed.

Shenandoah Valley Region

Winchester

One of the finest places in the region to find handcrafted jewelry, clothing, ceramics and home furnishings is Winchester's **Handworks Gallery**, (703) 662-3927, located in the Loudoun Street Mall (for pedestrians only). Around the corner on W. Piccadilly Street is the beautiful **Colonial Art and Craft Shop**, (703) 662-6513, which sells fine china, crystal and silver, elegant lamps and picture frames. **Kimberly's Antiques and Linens**, (703) 662-2195, is not too far away on N. Braddock Street. Located in historical Sheridan's Headquarters, Kimberly's sells early American and Victorian furniture, antique quilts and crochet spreads, fine bed linens and Civil War relics and literature. Virginia food products, such as honey, preserves and apple butter, are also sold here. **The Happy Goose**, (703) 662-0344, is one of several shops in Creekside Village, a Williamsburg-style shopping development on U.S. Highway 11. Here you will find Rowe Pottery, braided rugs, afghans, wreaths and other country-style items.

Strasburg

Strasburg considers itself the antique capital of Virginia. We don't necessarily endorse this claim, but we do agree that very fine antiques can be found here at fair prices. Whether you're a serious collector or someone who just likes to drool at beautiful things, you must visit the **Strasburg Emporium**, (703) 465-3711, a 65,000-square-foot downtown building that houses about 100 antique and art dealers. The building, right on N. Massanutten Street, used to be a silk mill. Along with high quality formal and country furniture, you'll find a lot of unusual items at the Emporium, such as old carnival horses, hobby horses, carriages, stoneware and iron beds. The Strasburg Emporium is open daily from 10 AM to 5 PM and has plenty of free parking.

Bits, Bytes & Books, (703) 465-4200, on W. King Street, has a vast collection of old and new mysteries, westerns, science fiction and children's books, locally crafted gifts and glass collectibles. The **Cedar Creek Relic Shop**, (703) 869-5207, a couple of miles away in downtown Middletown, claims to have the largest collection of authentic Civil War relics for sale in the Shenandoah Valley. If you're hankering for a sword, bayonet, musket or an artillery shell or two from that bloody war this is the place to shop.

Front Royal

The Limeton Pottery studio and gallery, (703) 636-8666, features locally made stoneware and earthenware pottery, along with note cards, baskets and other handcrafted items. One of downtown Front Royal's most interesting shops is the **Bizarre Bazaar**, (703) 636-6845, located in a 100-year-old home on Chester Street and open only on the weekends and some evenings. Here you'll find hand-made crafts, folk art, pillows, quilts, wall hangings and more. Across from the Visitors Center on Main Street is **Valley Crafters**, (703) 635-4699, a shop selling baby doll clothes, quilts and all kinds of country handcrafts.

Mount Jackson

Farther south, the little town of Mount Jackson off I-81 offers a number of quaint antique shops within walking distance of one another. **Wolftrap Antiques**, (703) 477-3250, situated in a pre-Civil War building on Main Street, specializes in walnut Victorian furniture. The **Widow Kip's Bed and Breakfast and Antique Shop**, (703) 477-2400, decorates its six rooms with antiques that are all for sale. It's located on Route 698, within walking distance of the downtown.

Luray

In downtown Luray, **Mama's Treasures**, (703) 743-1352, has an extensive collection of colorful glassware and old costume jewelry, along with some antique furniture and quilts. **Zib's Country Connection**, (703) 743-7394, on E. Main, features a unique collection of Victorian greeting cards, handcrafted gifts, collectibles and some antiques. Five miles east of Luray on Route 211, at the entrance to the

Photo: Virginia Dept. of Economic Development

Shoppers can find handmade Virginia crafts at one of the many craft shops in Abingdon.

Shenandoah National Park, sits the **Pine Knoll Gift Shop**, (703) 743-5805. This is an old-time store that's crammed with all kinds of Elvis and Hank Williams souvenirs, knives, quilts, baskets, coonskin caps, Native American moccasins and jewelry, jams and jellies, fireworks, great fudge and peanut brittle.

New Market

About two miles north of New Market on scenic U.S. Highway 11 are two showrooms of **Antiques by Burt Long**, (703) 740-3777. Long specializes in country, oak and Art Deco furniture and also peddles pie safes, iron beds, cupboards, pottery, baskets and other accessories.

New Market's downtown **Paper Treasures**, (703) 740-3135, is a fascinating place to browse through old books, magazines and prints. The last time we checked, the store was selling old copies of *Colliers Weekly*, *The Saturday Evening Post*, *Ebony, Life,* and old Civil War maps and books. The store also sells some of the best in contemporary children's literature.

Shenandoah Valley Crafts and Gifts, (703) 740-3899, on Congress Street (or Route 11), offers a variety: country furniture, fireworks, hand-loomed rugs, quilts and Virginia hams. Also on Congress Street is **The Christmas Gallery**, (703) 740-3000, which sells handmade crafts, wreaths, exquisite porcelain dolls and hundreds of kinds of ornaments, and **Quarter Creek**, (703) 740-4431, which specializes in 18th-century furniture.

Woodstock-Edinburg

Seven Bends Gallery, (703) 459-5525, in downtown historic Woodstock displays and sells original watercolors and photographs of the valley, along with stoneware pottery, hand-woven coverlets, stained glass lamps, wooden toys and other handcrafted items. Woodstock is also home to an **Aileen Stores Inc.** outlet, (703) 459-3077, that sells women's sportswear for up to 70 percent off retail.

Every Saturday and Sunday, a popular huge flea market takes place between Woodstock and Edinburg, offering antiques and collectibles both inside and outdoors. To get to **The Flea Market**, (703) 459-4723, take Exit 283 from I-81. It's on Route 11 on Landfill Road.

Richard's Antiques, (703) 984-4502, one mile south of Edinburg on Route 11, specializes in fine country and formal antiques and paintings.

Harrisonburg and Rockingham County

ANTIQUES

Nearly two dozen antique shops can be found throughout this area, which includes not just the thriving university city of Harrisonburg but also the little towns of Mt. Crawford, McGaheysville, Dayton and Elkton.

Chalot's Antiques, (703) 433-0872, is a mecca for lovers of fine old furniture. Right on Main Street in tiny Mt. Crawford, in a building nearly 200 years old, the shop deals in high quality 18th- and 19th-century furniture. There are hundreds of pieces of flow blue China in this shop, along with Victorian bric-a-brac, primitive accessories and old glassware.

The Antique Mart, (703) 289-MART, in McGaheysville is a restored old bank building that houses

25 shops of furniture and other collectibles. Farther east, in Elkton, is one of the area's finer antique shops, the **Curiosity Shop**, (703) 298-1404, where you'll find antique furniture, folk art, primitives, quilts and old tools for the most discriminating buyer.

Jeff's Antiques, (703) 879-9961, in Dayton specializes in oak and walnut furniture and also carries pottery, primitives, toys and oil lamps.

In the **Dayton Farmer's Market** you will find **Log Cabin Antiques**, (703) 434-8510, along with other shops selling freshly baked breads, candies, lace and handcrafted items. The antique store in the market specializes in primitives and painted country furniture.

Downtown Harrisonburg has several shops selling antiques and collectibles, most notably **James McHone Antique Jewelry**, (703) 433-1833. Here you will find exquisite estate and antique jewelry, sterling flatware and oil paintings. **Villager Antiques**, (703) 433-7226, sells painted country glassware and pottery, along with oak and walnut formal furniture.

HANDCRAFTS

The Mennonite-operated **Gift and Thrift Shop**, (703) 433-8844, in downtown Harrisonburg takes you around the globe with its selection of gorgeous weavings, ceramics, clothing and other crafts made in about 35 developing nations. Many of the craft makers are refugees, disadvantaged minorities or people with physical disabilities. The proceeds go toward the Mennonite Central Committee, the relief and development wing of the church. The prices are great, and spending money here helps people who are truly in need.

Suter's, (703) 434-2131, at 2610 S. Main Street has been around since the early 1800s, when Daniel Suter, a skilled Mennonite cabinet-maker and carpenter, settled in the Harrisonburg area and began making furniture. Today, William Suter and his daughter, Carol, are carrying on the family tradition of quality craftsmanship. The company makes gorgeous Colonial reproductions in cherry, mahogany and walnut, using the finest techniques. They have showrooms here and in Richmond, or you can send for a beautiful color catalog.

Tucked away in the **Skyline Village Shopping Center** on E. Market Street is an unexpected place to find unique handcrafted porcelain jewelry, pottery, wooden ware, rugs and other crafts. **The Bay Pottery**, (703) 432-1580, also has a store in nearby Broadway on S. Main Street.

The best shopping in Virginia can be found in the hidden nooks and crannies of the Blue Ridge, especially in the tiny mountain craft shops and antique stores of Shenandoah, Greene, Albemarle, Augusta, Bath and Floyd counties.

Insiders' Tips

It's definitely worth driving to the little town of Dayton, just south of Harrisonburg, for the **Dayton Farmer's Market**, (703) 879-9885, a place where the merchants are incredibly friendly. Inside the indoor market on Route 42, peddlers sell fresh poultry, seafood, beef, home-baked goods, fresh fruits and vegetables, cheeses, nuts and other dried goods. Specialty shops carry Early American tin lighting, pottery, quality antiques and handcrafts, clothes and even grandfather clocks. You can have a hearty, delicious lunch at **Huyard's Country Kitchen** inside the market. Nearby also in Dayton is the **Clothes Line**, (703) 879-2505, a fabric shop that also sells brilliantly colored hand-woven rugs and quilts. There's a hitching post out front where buggy-riding Mennonites tie their horses while they shop.

East of Harrisonburg in McGaheysville is the **Country Goose Gift and Craft Shop**, (703) 289-9626, that sells fine crafts made in the Shenandoah Valley. It's a short drive from Massanutten Resort on Route 996. Here you will find salt-glazed pottery, handmade country furniture, folk art, baskets, benches, pillows, quilt racks, weavings and much more.

OTHER UNUSUAL SHOPPING SPOTS

The central business district has some specialty shops worth a visit, such as **Touch the Earth**, (703) 434-2895, with its Native American clothing, African jewelry and other exotic gifts, and **Reminisce**, (703) 433-1889, which offers Victorian-era clothing and accessories.

North of Harrisonburg, around Timberville, is a great place to partake of the region's sweetest crop of all — apples. **Showalter's Orchard and Greenhouse**, (703) 896-7582, on Route 881 has its own cider mill and sells freshly pressed cider from late September through December 1. There are also many varieties of apples to choose from, available from mid-August through the winter. **Ryan's Fruit Market**, (703) 896-1233, on Route 613 northwest of Timberville, sells apples, sweet cider and pumpkins from the first of September to mid-November.

Locals flock to the **Green Valley Book Fair**, (703) 434-4260, which is held several weekends in the spring, summer, fall and winter at a warehouse near Mt. Crawford. Every spring and fall there is also a record fair, lasting only a single weekend. New books and records are sold at cut-rate prices.

Staunton and Augusta County

ANTIQUES

Historic downtown Staunton is full of interesting boutiques, including many antique shops — so many, that Staunton has just issued a new brochure just for antique shopping! Staunton has a treasure trove of architectural delights packed into five National Historic Districts, offering numerous places to hunt for antiques. Twenty-two shops are listed in the new brochure, many within walking distance of one another. One centrally located shop is the **Rose Street Interiors**, (703) 886-

0578, at 2 E. Beverley, which sells some exquisite furniture but mostly curios, lamps, pillows and other accessories.

Memory Lane, (703) 886-3649, is located just a few blocks away in the historic Wharf Area, at 112 S. New Street. Claude "Chick" Crawford offers a wide variety, from antiques and collectibles to arts and crafts items. The shop is open from 11 AM to 5 PM Monday and Tuesday and Thursday through Saturday.

Also at the renovated Wharf Area sits **Depot Antiques**, (703) 885-8326, a lovely shop featured in *Southern Living*, where you'll find country formal furniture, folk art and gifts. Across the street, you can get lost in the **Jolly Roger Haggle Shop**, (703) 886-9527, a collector's paradise with coins, jewelry, china, old money, weapons, Civil War and Native American artifacts and much more. And around the corner at 112 New Street, a quaint little shop called **Of Things Past** sells prints, jewelry, lamps and some furniture. The names of all of these shops are as much fun as looking in their doors. Another great place to buy antiques, where you can stay overnight, eat in a gourmet restaurant and enjoy a sophisticated nightclub is the **Belle Grae Inn**, (703) 886-5151, at 515 W. Frederick Street.

Just north of Staunton, **Dusty's Antique Market**, (703) 248-2018, houses more than a dozen dealers of oak and walnut furniture, tools, quilts, primitives and other old things, and the nearby **Rocky's Antique Mart**, (703) 234-9900, also is headquarters for dozens of dealers

selling lots of everything, including brass beds, china presses, gorgeous estate jewelry and sterling silver.

Also just north of Staunton is the **Verona Flea Market**, (703) 248-3532, which is open Thursday through Sunday. Thirty dealers sell a large variety of oak, pine, cherry, walnut and other antique furniture, along with quilts and linens, old books, china and more.

HANDCRAFTS

The Virginia Made Shop, (703) 886-7180, off Exit 222 from I-81, has an extensive collection of foods, wines, handcrafts and other souvenirs from the Commonwealth. It's located right next to **The Bacova Guild**, (800) 544-6118, famous for silk-screened handcrafts and Rowe's Family Restaurant, an excellent place to sample down-home regional cooking and a favorite hangout for the Statler Brothers. The cookies here are big, homemade and delicious, and the pies melt in your mouth.

Silver Linings on W. Beverley, (703) 885-7808, in the downtown is a popular shop with tourists and locals. You'll find jewelry, including exotic and hard-to-find beads, and folk art from around the world, along with clothes, pocket books and funky bric-a-brac. Across the street is the fascinating **Once Upon a Time Clock Shop**, (703) 885-6064, which sells antique wall clocks of every variety. It's "open by chance or by appointment."

Elder's Antique and Classic Autos, (703) 885-0500, on New Street, has a big window out front through which you can see the sleek old Rolls Royces and other beauties. Farther up New Street and across from the train station concourse sits **Naked Creek Pottery**, where you can watch Jim Hanger work at his wheel, if you're lucky. If you want to buy Jim's pottery, go across the street to the **Wharf Gallery**, which carries Naked Creek Pottery and other fine artwork. Read more about this wonderful, not-to-be-missed gallery in the Arts and Culture chapter.

OTHER UNUSUAL SHOPPING SPOTS

A brochure, "The Gift Connection," was produced last year to highlight 15 unique shopping experiences in the historic downtown district. Get your copy by calling the Visitor's Center at (800) 332-5219.

The first block of E. Beverley in downtown Staunton is a fun place to browse through shops and have lunch. **The Pampered Palate**, (703) 886-9463, sells gourmet sandwiches and also has an unusually good selection of Virginia, French and Italian wines. They do gift baskets, too. Next door, **Grandma's Bait Clothing Store**, (703) 886-2222, carries fine clothing for infants and children, and the **Golden Tub Bath Shop**, (703) 885-8470, sells everything for the bath, including elegant bath fixtures, soaps and towels. **Holt's China**, (703) 885-0217, at 16 E. Beverley, specializes in beautiful china, tabletop accessories, fine glassware and special occasion gifts and has a wide assortment of greeting cards. **The Emporium**, (703) 885-1673, 101 E. Beverley, features a large selection of toys and antique gifts. **Turtle Lane**, (703) 886-9313, at 10 E. Beverley, is a distinctive gift shop with antiques and other unusual gifts. **Arthurs**, (703) 885-8609, at 3 E. Beverley, has a dazzling collection of lamps and brass, pewter and silver items. And fanciers of odds and ends will want to browse through **Collector's Choice**, (703) 885-8572, at 18 W. Beverley. The downtown emporium has a wonderful selection of local handcrafts, sculptures, dolls, toys, collector's plates and figurines, among other curios.

Down by the train station, don't miss **Rails**, (703) 885-6575, 123 August Street, which bills itself as more convenient than a trip to Paris, Rome or Rio, with the same shopping experience. They have many unusual items, including some beautiful antiques and gifts, and chances are you won't leave empty-handed.

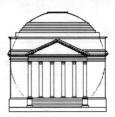

Waynesboro and Stuarts Draft

The **Waynesboro Village Factory Outlets**, (703) 942-2320, right off I-64, houses dozens of specialty shops carrying discounted brand-name clothing, shoes, luggage, home furnishings, lingerie and more. **Liz Claiborne**, **Royal Doulton**, **Dansk**, **Corning/Revere**, **Bass Shoes**, **London Fog** and **Bugle Boy** are but a few of the stores at this attractively designed outdoor mall. The center area is also popular for its quality arts and crafts exhibitors, who sell their work Thursday through Sunday from April through December.

The Antique Barn, (703) 943-3756, opened in the spring of 1992 at the Waynesboro Village Factory Outlets; it's open seven days a week.

Another special find in Waynesboro is **The Christmas Store**, (703) 943-6246, at 326 W. Main Street. They have Christmas collectibles, Snow Village, Heritage Village, Radko, figural ornaments, antique Santa reproductions and American Christmas folk art.

A number of Mennonite-operated businesses make shopping a real pleasure in the Stuarts Draft area. **Kinsinger's Kountry Kitchen**, (703) 337-2668, on Route 651, sells breads, cookies, cakes and pies made from scratch. The hummingbird cake and cheese herb bread are out of this world. About a half mile away on Route 608 is **The Cheese Shop**, (703) 337-4224, an Amish-Mennonite family business since 1960. The tidy little store in the back of a simple brick house sells more than 30 varieties of cheese at great prices, along with nuts, dried fruits and other dry foods in bulk. The Cheese Shop is closed on Wednesdays and Sundays.

The Candy Shop, (703) 337-0792, on Route 608 near U.S. Highway 340, sells a complete line of Hershey products, including reproductions of early tins and glass. There are no tours at the nearby Hershey plant in Stuarts Draft, but some of the items made there include Reese's Pieces, Whatchmacallits and Bar None. The Candy Shop also carries quilts, which they will custom make, along with handmade furniture.

Another shopping attraction based in Waynesboro is the **Virginia Metalcrafters Factory Showroom**, (703) 949-9432, at 1010 E. Main Street. Through an observation window, you can watch the age-old technique of pouring molten brass into molds and buy imperfects and discontinued items at reduced prices. You'll find handcrafted solid brass and iron candlesticks, lighting fixtures, fireplace equipment, wooden accessories and much more.

In downtown Waynesboro, meanwhile, you'll also find **The Olde Prospector**, (703) 949-5900, at 411 W. Main Street, featuring hand-crafted natural jewelry, museum-quality gemstones, more than 1,100 types of minerals and expert gem and mineral consultation. The store's catchy slogan, "We'll mine the world for you," speaks of its excellent customer orientation. Close by, at the **Valley Framing Studio and Gallery**, (703) 943-

7529, 328 W. Main, customers can select from the Shenandoah Valley's largest inventory of frame supplies, limited edition prints and bronzes, ceramics and other gifts. The white building next door at 326 W. Main is the **Christmas Store**, (703) 943-6246, which year round peddles the spirit of the yuletide season along with other arts, crafts and interesting curios.

Lexington

ANTIQUES

The Lexington Historical Shop, (703) 463-2615, at 9 E. Washington Street, is the only shop of its kind in Virginia. It specializes in Confederate-related original materials. Autographs, documents, books, prints, soldiers' letters, flags, belt buckles, uniforms and more will awe any Civil War buff. Owner Bob Lurate also offers Virginia-related histories, maps and other documents, along with antique quilts and other collectibles. If you can't make it to Lexington, call to receive a catalogue so that you can order by mail.

For one of the finest antique stores in the Rockbridge County region, visit **Old South Antiques Ltd.**, (703) 348-5360, in the charming village of Brownsburg, 15 minutes north of Lexington via U.S. Highway 11/710 or State Route 39/252. Old South specializes in New England, Pennsylvania and Southern antiques in original paint and refinished cherry, walnut and pine. The shop is recommended by *American Country South* for its country-style wares and known for its large selection of American Country furniture and accessories.

Braford Antiques on Highway 130 (291-2217) is another exquisite shop down the road from Natural Bridge. The Brafords have a fine collection of 19th-century American furniture and pieces from Asia.

GENERAL STORES

Enjoy a step back in time with the Lexington area's two real general stores, **The General Store**, (703) 261-3860, 2522 Beech Avenue in Buena Vista, and the **Old Country Store**, (703) 348-1300, located on Virginia Byway 39 in historic Rockbridge Baths. Both have been in business 100 years and, in many ways, actually are working museums. Don't miss the made-in-Virginia items and country crafts. Maury River even offers you the once-in-a-lifetime opportunity to visit an old-fashioned working outhouse! And next door is a swinging bridge across the river — a rare find in this day and age. In Buena Vista, visitors love The General Store, with its early farm and transportation exhibit and century-old display cases. Aromas waft through the old building, where you can find a bit of everything, including blue jeans, bulk seed, fabric and kitchenware.

HANDCRAFTS

Artists in Cahoots, (703) 464-1147, is a cooperative gallery of local artists and crafters downtown at 1 Washington Street. You'll find oil and watercolors, pottery, metalwork, hand-blown glass, photogra-

The University Corner

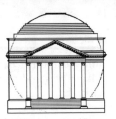

111 14 Street • (804)296-1115

101 14th St.,N.W.
(804)971-8088

109 14th St.,N.W.
(804)296-2233

SUBWAY

104 14th St.,N.W.
(804)295-7824

104 14th St.,N.W.
(804)977-1606

phy, sculpture, hand-painted silk scarves and porcelain jewelry.

OTHER UNUSUAL SHOPPING SPOTS

Downtown shopping is a panorama of boutique-type shops that will keep you browsing all day. For gifts, try **Fantasies**, (703) 463-7222, at 21 Nelson Street for the new, subtle and dazzling. **Virginia Born and Bred**, (800) 437-2452, at 16 W. Washington Street, is a sophisticated shop that is chock full of Old Dominion handcrafts, wine, fine brass work, linens and more. For sleek or funky dresses and exotic jewelry and accessories, don't miss **Pappagallo**, (703) 463-5988, at 23 N. Main. If new and used books are your idea of a perfect afternoon of browsing, go to the **Second Story**, (703) 463-6264, 7 E. Washington Street, or **The Bestseller**, (703) 463-4647, on Nelson Street.

T.G.I.F., (703) 463-9730, 30 S. Main, is a popular destination for Washington & Lee students, with its "seconds" from J. Crew, Tweeds and other fashionable clothing manufacturers.

If you're hankering for chocolate, head down to **Cocoa Mill Chocolates**, (703) 464-8400, on West Nelson Street. Hand-dipped, scrumptious confections are sold individually or by the box, and the owners also have a mail-order service.

In Rockbridge County, on Route 606 at Racine, Don Haynie and

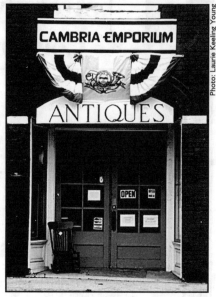

Photo: Laurie Keeling Young

Shoppers love the multitude of antique shops throughout the Blue Ridge.

Tom Hamlin welcome you to the wonderful world of herbs in a big way. They are the darlings of the local garden club set for the way they have renovated **Buffalo Springs Herb Farm**, (703) 348-1083, an extraordinary 18th-century stone house and garden open for herbal teas, luncheons and tours. These two perfectionists have a huge following for their herb workshops that always feature flawless food (such as hand-pressed herbal cookies) and decor. There is a gorgeous gift shop in a big red barn that sells herbal products, dried flowers and garden books. Their display gardens look like something out of Williamsburg. You'll see a culinary garden, springhouse tea garden and four-square heirloom vegetable and herb garden. To make a wonderful trip even better, Buffalo Springs is located next to historic **Wades Mill**, (703) 348-1400, a working water-powered flour mill that is listed on the National Register of Historic Places. The mill is open from April to mid-December and produces and sells all kinds of bread flours, corn-meal, cereal and bran. Gift boxes are also sold.

Botetourt County, Troutville and Fincastle

ANTIQUES

Many a Roanoker loves to take a trip out to the cool, crisp country-side in autumn, buy apples from the county orchards and go antiquing. The opportunities are numerous on U.S. Highway 11 heading into Troutville and on U.S. Highway 220 on the way to historic Fincastle. Both towns have more than their fair share of terrific little antique shops. In Troutville, the **Troutville Antique Mart**, (703) 992-4249, beside the Troutville Fire Station and Goodwill Tinker Mountain Industries, offers the best opportunity for browsing under one roof. Here, a dozen dealers display fine antiques and collectibles, and the prices are some of the lowest you'll find. How about a first-class 1890s leather and wooden trunk for $100? You can find it here.

HANDCRAFTS

A real gem in a rural area, **Amerind Gallery**, (703) 992-1066, Route 220 N., Daleville, features artwork of Native American and western artists. It is a member of the Indian Arts and Crafts Association and guarantees the authenticity of every Native American handmade item in the gallery. Amerind offers a unique cultural opportunity to learn about American art forms and cultures. Original works decorate the walls, and the art is superb.

Across town, in Troutville, there's a breath of fresh air in every gift at Al and Rachael Nichol's **Apple Barn**, (703) 992-3551, off Route 11. Located on a working apple farm, you can browse through country collectibles sipping a complimentary cup of hot, spiced cider and buy or pick your own bag of apples before you leave the picturesque orchard setting. Shopping at Nichol's is an experience for your spirit and soul in the fresh Botetourt County country air.

ORCHARDS

Botetourt County is apple orchard country. There's nothing more beautiful than the acres of delicate apple blossoms that signal the coming of spring in the Blue Ridge. The county has quite a few orchards, large and small. Probably the biggest and best known are **Ikenberry**, (703) 992-2448, and **Layman's**, (703) 992-2687, both on U.S. Highway 220 in Daleville. In addition to apples of every kind, you can buy such seasonal specials as pumpkins, sweet corn and peaches.

Craig County

Whatever your need, you'll find

it at **New Castle Mercantile**, (703) 864-5560, located at 325 Main Street. In this tiny mountain community, New Castle Mercantile fills the bill for seeds, animal feed, hardware, housewares and toys.

Roanoke

ANTIQUES

The Roanoke Valley is a treasure chest of top-notch, low-cost antiques. When movie star Debbie Reynolds' daughter, star and author Carrie Fisher, came to visit at her mom's Roanoke home, antiquing is the first thing she wanted to do — and she spent all day! What you'll find is a tremendous variety downtown. **Trudy's Antiques**, (703) 343-2004, 12 Wells Avenue N.E., specializes in old prints and advertising, dolls, jewelry and glassware. **Sandra's Cellar**, (703) 342-8123, 120 Campbell Avenue S.E., is a nostalgia trip specializing in vintage clothing, furniture and toys. **Bob Beard Antiques**, (703) 981-1757, is "open by chance or appointment" at 105 Market Street, and it's a find for the unexpected. **Russell's Yesteryear**, (703) 342-1750, 117 E. Campbell Avenue, has the slogan, "When you visit the Market, stop in and see us. If you don't, we both lose money." Lovers of Civil War antiques will want to visit historian Howard McManus' shop, **Magic City Station**, (703) 344-2302, at 11 S. Jefferson Street, to see his collection of memorabilia. McManus is an expert on the Battle of Cloyd's Mountain in Pulaski County and the war in Southwestern Virginia. For a complete list of antique shops in the Valley, call (703) 342-6025.

HANDCRAFTS

If fine handcrafts are what you're seeking, look no farther than the historic City Market. You will find the perfect gift and probably end up buying something for yourself, as well. **Gallery 3**, (703) 343-9698, 213 Market Street, offers the epitome of art for the kitchen, wood, glass, gifts and clothing. Gallery 3 is a favorite shopping spot for corporate art collectors, too, who will find works by both local and nationally known artists, including Wolf Kahn. On the first Fridays of each month, Gallery 3 offers Art By Night, featuring local artists and their work. Custom framing also is available.

Also located on the Market, at 206 Market Square, is **Studios on the Square**, (703) 345-4076, a second-floor studio where 18 working artists demonstrate and sell wares that include pottery, paper, fiber, wood, textiles, jewelry, baskets, stained glass, photography and fine paintings. The climb upstairs to this treasure house of arts and crafts stores is well worth it. You'll think you're in a loft in New York, and chances are you won't leave empty handed.

OUTLETS

Roanoke offers some interesting outlets for unusual items. On U.S. Highway 220 S., hunters and those who like the camouflage look won't want to miss **Trebark Outfitters**, (703) 774-9007, 3434 Buck Mountain Road. Jim Crumley, the inventor of Trebark camouflage, lives in Roanoke and offers good deals at his store. Hunting and fishing lovers and fans of the sporting life will also enjoy the **Orvis Factory Outlet**, (703) 344-4520, downtown at 21-B Campbell Avenue. Summers are an especially good time to shop, since you can get discounts of up to 80 percent on winter items offered in their national catalog and in the Orvis Retail Store just a block away. Other tremendous buys can be found at an **Emerson Creek Pottery** outlet (see Bedford shopping chapter), (703) (342-7656), gorgeous handmade pottery on the Market at 108 Market Street. Also downtown, but a little more difficult to find, is **Design Accessories**, (703) 344-8958, an outlet store for custom-made Austrian crystal jewelry. It's located on First Street. Again, you can find discounts of 70 percent or more on fascinating watches, jewelry and accessories featured in national bridal magazines. For household items, go to Crossroads Mall on Williamson Road to **Waccamaw Pottery**, (703) 563-4948.

SPECIALTY STORES

There are terrific specialty stores and boutiques throughout the Roanoke City Market. In the Market Building that anchors the shopping area, you will find surplus Army gear at **Sam's On the Market**, (703) 342-7300, 304 Market Street, and a shop just for people who like birds, **For the Birds**, (703) 345-9393, 303 Market Street, among other specialty stores. Other favorites of all

generations are branches of Blacksburg stores in the New River Valley. Don't miss **Mish Mish**, (703) 345-1020, at 14 E. Campbell, which specializes in art supplies; **Books, Strings & Things**, (703) 342-5511, 202 Market Square, a great place to browse among tapes and CDs, books, cards and calendars; and **The Children's Corner**, with its own little rocking chair, which endears parents who bring their prodigy to read and rock while they pick out their favorite oldies. The major malls in the area — Crossroads, Tanglewood and Valley View — also have some specialty stores of a more commercial nature.

East of the Blue Ridge Region

Washington

This tiny community of fewer than 200 residents boasts a number of sophisticated galleries, antique shops and places to buy fine handcrafted gifts.

Peter Kramer, (703) 675-3625, at Gay and Jeff streets has been making beautiful furniture for 25 years in this lovely old town. Each of his creations is one-of-a-kind, a hand-crafted creation made from native American wood. Some of the furniture is rather whimsical, while other pieces are more classical and austere. Kramer also has showrooms on Cape Cod.

The Rush River Company, (703) 675-1136, a crafts gallery on Gay

Street, displays and sells works of more than 20 artists. You'll find furniture, fabrics, photographs, paintings, pottery, jewelry, baskets and clothing here.

Country Heritage, (703) 675-3738, specializes in American folk art, quality handcrafts, country and primitive furniture and fine antiques. More than 100 craft makers are presented at this shop on Main Street.

Sperryville

Just south of Washington, in Sperryville, you'll find scores of antique and craft shops, including the **Trading Post**, (703) 675-3990, which sells Native American quilts, beadwork, jewelry, pipes and crafts, and the **Sperryville Emporium**, (703) 987-8235, a series of connecting buildings where you can find everything from antiques and apples to country hams and honey.

Faith Mountain Herbs and Antiques, (703) 987-8547, sells flowers, herbs, crafts and fashions for women, with many items priced well below retail. **The Church Mouse**, (703) 987-9106, is a charming, turn-of-the-century Gothic church that has been converted into a gallery and craft shop. **Springhouse Antiques**, (703) 987-3177, on Main Street specializes in country pine and oak antique furniture, flow blue china, quilts, linens and kitchen collectibles. **Elmer's Antiques**, (703) 987-8355, sells walnut, cherry and oak antiques and also sells apples and presses its own cider in season. **Country Manor** is the last shop on Route 211 W. before you get to Skyline Drive. Here you can browse for hours among carvings and baskets, including white oak baskets woven locally and grape vine baskets woven by the Manor's owner, Phylis Swindler.

Loudoun County

You won't find any monolithic mega-malls in beautiful Loudoun County, but that doesn't mean there's no place to shop. Grab your wallet and head for historic downtown Leesburg (intersection of routes 7 and 15), where more than 100 specialty retailers are housed along Market and King streets. The city's colorful **Market Station** (corner of Loudoun and Harrison streets) offers another 100 or so shops, and, if you still haven't had enough, more than 250 stores stretch along the Route 7 corridor up to the Fairfax County line. This route will take you through the communities of Ashburn, Sterling and Sterling Park.

Nearby in Middleburg, browse through more than 60 stores in the historic district. Most are along Washington and Madison streets, but wander down the cobbled side streets to find horsing attire and accessories, antiques, home furnishings, handcrafted gifts, clothing and art. **Middleburg Antiques Center** at 105 W. Washington Street is a haven for period furniture and assessories, fine estate items, rugs, lamps, silver and jewelry

North of Charlottesville — Greene and Madison Counties

ANTIQUES AND HANDCRAFTS

Two major rural highways intersect through this area, Route 29 and Route 33, and along both roads are dozens of shops chock full of antiques and handcrafts.

Starting in Madison, the **Bleak-Thrift House**, (703) 948-3645, is a restored old home (c. 1838) where you will find some antique furniture, glassware, primitives, lace and linens. English boxwoods surround the home, which is in downtown Madison on Main Street (Route 29 Business).

Madison is headquarters for **E.A. Clore Sons Inc.**, (703) 948-5821, makers of simple but handsome furniture since 1830. "We don't make any fancy furniture," says company president Edward Clore, "but we try to make it last . . . and, by golly, it does." Nestled in a hollow three-tenths of a mile from Route 637, E.A. Clore specializes in handmade Early American furniture from walnut, cherry, oak and mahogany. Clore sells directly from its factory to the consumer, and its showrooms are right next door.

Just to the north, in the tiny mountain town of Criglersville, sits the **Mountain Store**, (703) 923-4349, open only on weekends. It's a truly wonderful place that offers books, handmade crafts and an interesting selection of children's toys and jigsaw puzzles.

Two miles south of Madison on Route 29 are several shops worth visiting. **Spring Hill Farm Antiques**, (703) 948-4647, has dozens of quilts, ironware, blue and white stoneware, twig, tramp and folk art and old American "country" furniture. The store also has a fabric and upholstery service and a huge selection of lamp shades. Next door, the **Madison Antiques Center**, (703) 948-3428, represents about 55 dealers from around the country.

Handcraft House, (703) 948-6323, situated on Route 29, sells very fine crafts made by more than 300 artisans from across the nation. They feature Cat's Meow houses, rubber stamps and accessories, Byer's Choice Carolers and Yankee candles.

About seven miles south of Madison on Route 29 is **Country Garden Antiques**, (703) 948-3240, another fine store in a restored old home. This place sells exquisite antique furniture (both American and European): imported colorful tiles, old prints, old wrought iron gadgets, English lawn ornaments, antique jewelry and framed art work. The place also sells hard-to-find pillow covers from France that are copies of old tapestries.

When Route 29 arrives in Ruckersville, it intersects with Route 33 and forms a crossroads that bustles with activity for antique lovers. The three-story **Greene House Shops**, (804) 985-2438, houses at least 50 dealers of antiques, crafts, quilts and all kinds of gifts. It's open every day and even accepts credit cards. Across the road is the **Country Store Antique Mall**, (804) 985-3649, and the new kid on the block,

Antique Collectors, (804) 985-8966.

Lord Browne Antiques, (804) 985-7797, located on Route 29 about one-third mile south of this intersection, specializes in period Virginia mantles and accessories for the hearth.

Early Time Antiques and Fine Art, (804) 985-3602, also in Ruckersville, has a good reputation for its 18th- and 19th-century furniture, oil paintings and accessories.

Farther west on Route 33 toward Skyline Drive is a popular wayside called the **Blue Ridge Pottery**, (804) 985-6080, located in what was once the Golden Horseshoe Inn (c. 1827). The Inn, located along what was once called the Spotswood Trail, used to serve travelers making the difficult climb over the mountains. Gen. Stonewall Jackson reportedly stayed here during the war, using the inn as his temporary headquarters only a few weeks before he was killed. Alan Ward throws his stoneware pottery in a little studio right next door to Blue Ridge Pottery and welcomes visitors. His pottery, which is modelled after traditional Valley styles but painted with modern, vibrant glazes, is sold in the shop, along with locally made crafts, Virginia wines, apple butter and jams and Christmas decorations.

Closer to Stanardsville is the **Edgewood Farm Nursery**, (804) 985-3782, which stocks one of the largest selections of herbs and perennials in the state. You can walk to the nursery from **Edgewood Farm**, an elegant, hospitable bed and breakfast inn run by Eleanor Schwartz. Norman Schwartz, her husband, operates the nursery.

Charlottesville and Surrounding Area

ANTIQUES

There are at least two dozen antique stores in the Charlottesville area, and this does not count the dozens of "mini" shops that share a single roof.

You'll find several stores in the heart of the downtown: **Alley Antiques**, (804) 979-1554, and the **Downtown Charlottesville Art and Antique Center**, (804) 295-5503, on the Historic Downtown Mall, and **South Street Antiques**, (804) 295-2449, only a block away. You could spend hours strolling through the 16,000-square-feet Downtown Antique Center, which represents dozens of dealers in decorative accessories, period furniture, vintage clothing and more.

On the higher end of the scale, **Ann Woods Ltd.**, (804) 295-6108, on Route 250 W., specializes in 18th- and 19th-century English and American furniture and silver. Woods also offers an interior design service in her shop. Next door is another exclusive shop, **1740 House Antiques**, (804) 977-1740, which sells 18th-and 19th-century furniture and accessories.

DeLoach Antiques, (804) 979-7209, at 1211 W. Main Street, is a charming place to find stylish and unusual decorative objects and antiques at very good prices. An eclectic selection of Neoclassical, French, English and American pieces are displayed throughout a beautifully decorated townhouse that was built by one of Thomas Jefferson's master craftsmen in 1817.

If you're interested in either antique or new rugs from the villages of the Middle East, stop by the **Sun Bow Trading Company**, (804) 293-8821, on Fourth Street. Saul, the owner, has many a tale to tell about these tribal textiles and nomadic Oriental rugs and his journeys to find them, and will serve you a cup of Middle Eastern tea.

The **Greenwood Antique Center**, (703) 456-8465, is located about 15 miles west of Charlottesville on U.S. Highway 250. It sells fine old furniture, primitives, glassware, Chinese porcelain, works of art and jewelry. **Whitehouse Antiques**, (703) 942-1194, in nearby Afton, has a wide variety of American period pieces, from country to formal. The shop also caters to the dealer trade and has new inventory weekly. **Afton House Antiques**, (703) 456-6759, sells fascinating collections of antique furniture, arts, crafts, dolls and home furnishings.

Beltrone & Company, (804) 974-1861, at the Woodbrook Shopping Center sells original weapons and artifacts from the American Revolution to World War I.

If you're looking for out-of-print books, the **Daedalus Bookshop**, (804) 293-7595, on Fourth Street has three floors of them. The **Heartwood Bookshop**, (804) 295-7083, on Elliewood has an impressive rare book collection, with an emphasis on Americana and literature.

Finally, for a trip back in time, you must not miss **Tuckahoe An-**

Crafters' Gallery

"An abundant collection of functional and decorative contemporary American crafts"
6 miles from the Boar's Head Inn on Rt. 250 West
Open Tues.-Sat. 10 til 5, Sun. 1 til 5.
(804) 295-7006

tique Mall, (804) 361-2121, on Route 151 at Nellysford, near Wintergreen Resort. You could spend an entire day looking through the 50 shops — 10,000 square feet — of quality antique furniture, including oak, walnut and pine, plus collectibles, art and glassware. They're open Thursday through Sunday from 10 AM to 5 PM.

HANDCRAFTS

Charlottesville is known for having an abundance of shops that sell exquisite crafts from around the world. Many of the shops seem more like galleries, and some function as both.

The historic Downtown Mall is a good place to start exploring such stores. On the west end, close to the Omni, **The Nicholas & Alexandra Gallery**, (804) 295-4003, stocks dolls, rugs, toys, artwork and all kinds of other crafts made in Russia and other republics of the former Soviet Union. Right next door is

Renaissance Gifts, (804) 296-9208, an unusual shop selling rugs, pottery, masks and other items from Africa, South America and Asia. If you need spinning and weaving supplies, look no farther than **Stony Mountain Fibers**, (804) 295-2008, a stone's throw away.

Artworks, (804) 979-2888, centrally located on the mall, is another gallery of contemporary crafts that sells jewelry, art pieces and hand-woven clothing. **Paula Lewis**, (804) 295-6244, on Fourth Street and E. Jefferson, also has a splendid collection of old and new quilts, along with country folk art, Pueblo Indian pottery, quilting supplies and books.

The **McGuffey Art Center**, (804) 295-7973, is a renovated elementary school within walking distance of the Downtown Mall that houses a contemporary gallery and workshops and studios where more than 40 artists and crafts makers create their works of art. There are some very gifted artists at work here who are represented by galleries in New York City and other major cities. A small gift shop sells some of their creations. You'll find pottery, photography, prints, stained glass, sculptures, jewelry and much more.

At the Barracks Road Shopping Center is the **Peddler's Shop**, (804) (971-4847), another good source of fine hand-crafted gifts made all over the United States.

The Crafter's Gallery, (804) 295-7006, located nine miles west of Charlottesville on Route 250, specializes in selling contemporary crafts, glassware, pottery, ironware, silver, weavings and leather goods.

While you're heading west, it's worth a trip to Afton to visit **Blue Ridge Terrace Gifts Inc.**, (804) 949-0988, on Route 250 W., which sells traditional and mountain crafts made locally. The landmark building was constructed in 1925; it also houses antique and art galleries.

Lewis Glaser Inc., (804) 973-7783, at 1700 Sourwood Place specializes in hand-cut Colonial-style goose quill pens. Internationally known quill maker Nancy Floyd is the exclusive producer of quill pens used by the U.S. Supreme Court.

Just a short drive into the countryside, in downtown Nellysford in Nelson County, you'll find **Valley Green**, (804) 361-9316, a gem of a store specializing in arts, crafts and handcrafts made exclusively by Virginian artisans. Photography, jewelry, stained glass, porcelain dolls, collector-quality miniature furniture and wearable fiber art fashions are featured here.

UNIVERSITY CORNER SPECIALTY SHOPS

"On the Corner" is the local term for that tight little neighborhood of shops, cafes and restaurants only a half-block away from the Rotunda and original UVA campus. A number of specialty shops make the corner an interesting place to wander around for both guys and gals and even youngsters.

Derek's U-Spirit, (804) 977-1606, 104 14th Street, sells UVA sweatshirts, pants, hats, fraternity and sorority items and other college souvenirs. A short walk away on 14th Street is **Innovations**, (804) 971-8088, a hair salon catering to the university and professional

Shop Barracks Road

crowd. Some say you have to be a magician to get through four rigorous years at the demanding University of Virginia. No wonder **Magic Tricks**, (804) 293-5788, at 101 14th Street, is located conveniently nearby, selling a wide assortment of amusing tricks, gags, games and novelties.

Arnette's, (804) 977-8451, at University and Elliewood avenues has three floors full of unique gifts, cards, clothing and accessories. There's something for everyone in this charming family-run store — even a science and nature shop for kids.

Barr-ee Station, (804) 979-7981, on University Avenue is a great outlet store that sells brand-name, high-quality clothing for men and women at cut-rate prices.

The Phoenix, (804) 296-1115, on 14th Street is a unique women's boutique that sells exquisite and funky dresses, unusual T-shirts, exotic earrings, belts and other accessories. **The Garment District**, (804) 296-1003, on University Avenue caters to university women with its cute, fashionable clothing at reasonable prices.

For traditionalists, **Eljo's**, (804) 295-5230, at 3 Elliewood Avenue has been selling "preppie" clothes for more than 40 years, offering the best of Ralph Lauren, Southwick, Corbin and Gitman.

On the athletic front, the **"Go Pal" Bicycle Shop**, (804) 295-1212, on 14th Street specializes in mountain and road bikes, with a wide selection of Trek and Bianchi models. They are also licensed to repair all kinds of bikes. **Blue Wheel Bi-**

cycles, (804) 977-1870, at 19 Elliewood Avenue features fine bicycles at competitive prices, along with a good selection of accessories. This bike shop has been around for nearly 20 years. **Ragged Mountain Running Shop**, (804) 293-3367, on Elliewood Avenue has a huge selection of running and aerobic shoes at very competitive prices.

And for all your framing needs, head to **Freeman-Victorious Framing**, (804) 296-3456, at 1413 University Avenue. The shop also sells antique prints and posters, mirrors, and other fine gifts.

Heartwood Bookshop, (804) 295-7083, at 5 Elliewood Avenue also has a great collection of secondhand scholarly and popular books in both hardback and paperback. You'll find cookbooks, histories, literature, mysteries, nature, science fiction, an antiquarian collection and more. (See our earlier entry under Antiques for more information.)

Mincer's, (804) 296-5687, at University Avenue and Elliewood is open seven days a week and has been selling university sportswear for more than 40 years.

Also on University Corner is **Willie's Hair Design**, (804) 295-1242, for your hair styling needs.

HISTORIC DOWNTOWN MALL

We've already described some of the shops in the downtown pedestrian mall that specialize in exquisite handcrafts. There are also many other delightful specialty shops, most of which are owner-operated.

One of the most interesting

places to browse is the **Old Hard-ware Store**, (804) 977-1518, a block-long building that houses a restaurant and soda fountain, several specialty food bars and shops selling just about everything: gold and silver jewelry, games, wrought iron and more. The Old Hardware Store is aptly named. It operated from 1895 to 1976 and was once the premier hardware store in central Virginia. Not only did it sell rope and tools and other hardware, but you could also find fine china and silver there, along with everyday crockery and eggs and other staples. Just like the old days, the Old Hardware Store still has something for everyone. You can even get your hair trimmed and your shoes shined here.

Other outstanding specialty shops on the Downtown Mall include **Palais Royal**, (804) 979-4111, which has the finest in French designer linens, robes, towels and blankets, and **The Jeweler's Eye**, (804) 979-5919, an eclectic collection of jewelry dating from the 1700s through the 1900s.

K.M.H. Hightower, (804) 979-0136, on the east end of the Mall sells items by Caswell-Massey, producers of bath products and colognes for the world's fashionable elite since 1752.

Pewter Corner, (804) 971-3788, claims to stock the largest selection of pewter in the United States. There are also two fine Oriental rug shops right on the Mall: **Purcell Oriental Rug Co. Ltd.**, (804) 971-8822, and **T.S. Eways**, (804) 979-3038, right next door.

The Williams Corner Book-store, (804) 977-4858, just a couple of doors down from the Old Hardware Store, is considered by some to be the best book store in town.

BARRACKS ROAD SHOPPING CENTER

Located at Barracks Road and Emmet Street, this is a unique & worthwhile shopping destination because there are dozens of wonderful specialty shops and a few department stores within walking distance (just watch the traffic).

For a vast selection of ladies' shoes, check out **Scarpa**, (804) 396-0040, where the styles range from collegiate casual to formal, with all the top brands including Anne Klein and Ralph Lauren. Ladies' dresses and accessories, including beautiful formal wear, can be found at nearby **Talbott's** (other location: Roanoke) (804) 296-3580, offers a premiere selection of classic apparel & accessories in a comfortable, residential atmosphere. This store is especially popular with the community and UVA population. **Les Fabriques**, (804) 296-0757, with its designer and bridal fabrics, buttons and other accessories including top-brand sewing machines.

Speaking of youngsters, **Shenanigans**, (804) 295-4797, is a great place to find children's books, toys, stuffed animals, dolls from around the world and children's music — including sing-along videos. True to its name, **Whimsies**, (804) 977-8767, has fanciful and spunky children's wear, including clothes for infants and toddlers. It's next door to Shenanigans.

The Book Gallery, (804) 977-2892, also has a great selection of

children's books, along with other books on topics ranging from Thomas Jefferson and Virginia history to home decorating and sports.

For those who answer to the call of the wild, head to **Blue Ridge Mountain Sports**, (804) 977-4400, for all your camping, backpacking, hiking and outdoor outfitting needs.

Virginia's best is showcased in **The Virginia Shop**, (804) 977-0080, located on "the Island" behind Ruby Tuesdays Restaurant. A great selection of gifts, food, wine, books, music and much more — all with the Old Dominion mark of quality — are for sale here seven days a week.

Nature by Design, (804) 977-6100, is a fascinating shop for folks of all ages, selling such variety as polished rocks for less than a dollar and driftwood water fountains at $1,300. You will find jewelry, bird feeders, garden accessories, chimes, agate bookends, puzzles, games and more — and all with a touch of nature.

Keller & George, (804) 293-5011, is where you'll find the popular Jefferson cup, along with fine jewelry and distinctive and unusual gifts.

Plow & Hearth, (804) 977-3707, sells beautiful outdoor ornaments and furniture made of wrought iron, cedar and other sturdy materials.

Art Needlework Inc., (804) 296-4625, has a large selection of needlepoint and knitting patterns and supplies, including Persian, Appleton, Medici, silk and metallic yarns in every color. The unique shop also sells hand-dyed yarns in wool, cotton, silk, mohair and angora.

For women's clothing, **Krissia**,

(804) 295-9249, sells exquisite lingerie, chic swim wear and fine hosiery and slippers. **Levy's**, (804) 295-4270, sells gorgeous, sophisticated sportswear and bathing suits downstairs and formal wear and snappy business suits on the upper level.

Nearby **Seminole Square** is a very fine furniture store that has been furnishing homes in Central Virginia since 1926. **Gilmore, Hamm and Snyder Inc.**, (804) 973-8114, sells quality furniture by such manufacturers as Henkel Harris, Henry Link and Hickory Chair, along with hand-woven Oriental rugs, lamps, pictures, mirrors and window treatments.

Lynchburg

ANTIQUES

A phenomenal array of antique stores — nearly 20 in all — can be found in this historic and cultural city. For a list of them all, contact the Visitor's Center at (804) 847-1811.

For a quick downtown whirl, try **Redcoat Antiques**, (804) 528-3182, 1421 Main Street, and **Sweeney's Curious Goods**, (804) 846-7839, 1220 Main Street. There's also a concentration near River Ridge Mall off Candlers Mountain Road.

HANDCRAFTS

Virginia Handcrafts Inc., (804) 846-7029, part of The Farm Basket shopping complex at 2008 Langhorne Road, will keep you wandering around all day. It's a casual shop where browsers and their children are welcome. The spacious store features a collection of American crafts, including kaleidoscopes, game boards, pottery and jewelry. These are displayed among paintings, planters, fountains, lamps, rugs and much more than can possibly be described here. One room is devoted to crafts made by Virginians. The atmosphere is just plain fun! If you're looking for a relaxed, casual and friendly atmosphere, you'll find it at Virginia Handcrafts.

Adjoining it is The **Farm Basket Shop**, (804) 528-1107, where you can browse through rooms of carefully chosen gift items from around the world. Children can entertain themselves with an imported wooden train in a toy department that also overflows with stuffed animals, dolls and baby gifts. Custom invitations and announcements can be created with a calligraphy computer. A mail order catalog is available. Have a cucumber sandwich at the best homemade-food restaurant in the area, located within the complex. The Farm Basket's fruit stand produce is locally grown in their own mountain orchards. This is a Lynchburg landmark not to be missed!

OUTLETS

There are 14 terrific outlets and discount stores in Lynchburg. A complete list is available from the Visitor's Center, (804) 847-1732.

The granddaddy of them all, the first shoe company south of the Mason-Dixon line (founded 1888) and the most famous, is **Craddock-Terry Shoe Factory Outlet**, (804) 847-3535, at 601 12th Street. Select from 300,000 pairs of shoes in stock from the national Masseys catalogs and get up to a whopping 70 percent off. You'll see the billboards with the gigantic plastic pairs of red high heel pumps as you come into town on major roads. The store specializes in hard to find sizes and widths, from 3-13, AAAA to EEEE. Shoe lovers will recognize national brand names, such as Rockport and American Gentleman. It's worth an overnight stay for an average family just to buy seasonal shoes and see the sights of Lynchburg at the same time. Another fine shoe outlet is **Consolidated Shoe Store**, (804) 237-5569, 10200 Timberlake Road.

For clothes and accessories, there's **Carolina Hosiery**, (804) 846-5099, at 525 Alleghany Avenue, and **Tultex Mill Outlet**, (804) 385-6477, at Forest Plaza West Shopping Center. For the largest Tultex collection, known world wide, go to Martinsville, home of Tultex. It borders the Blue Ridge and also offers furniture outlets.

SPECIALTY SHOPS

For both specialty shopping and terrific eating, go to the **Community Market**, (804) 847-1499, Main at 12th Street, established in 1783. You'll find homemade crafts, Virginia-made goods and baked goods. Something is always going on, and the Market is the hub of Lynchburg activity, as it was in the days of Thomas Jefferson, who scared Lynchburg citizens by biting into a tomato, long thought to be a poisonous fruit. This market and the one in Roanoke are centerpieces of Blue Ridge life and a joy to behold.

Smith Mountain Lake

GENERAL AND SPECIALTY
STORES AND SERVICES

There are two major areas for shoppers at Smith Mountain Lake: Bridgewater Plaza on Route 122 at Hales Ford Bridge, where the official Smith Mountain Lake Partnership Visitors Center is located, and Village Square, at Route 122/655, Moneta.

Hales Ford is the very center of lake life. Here, you'll find enough interesting little shops to see while the kids play miniature golf at **Harbortown Golf**, (703) 721-1203, or ride the carousel. On summer weekends, entertainment is offered. And the rest of the year, the steady seasonal stream of boats and visitors from around the world are often entertainment enough.

Bridgewater Plaza's anchor, in addition to the miniature golf course, is **Bridgewater Marina and Boat Rentals** and **Bridgewater Para-Sail,** (703) 721-1639. The *Virginia Dare*, a dinner cruise ship, also leaves port from here.

Lovers of fine art will enjoy **The Little Gallery**, (703) 721-1596. You can find one-of-a-kind treasures and enjoy the works of well-known artists, as well as emerging local ones.

Gifts Ahoy, (703) 721-5303, will delight children and has the lake's most unique collection of gifts and greeting cards. The Plaza also has the great restaurant, **Schooner's** (see the Restaurants chapter), with terrific pizza and hamburgers fresh-ground daily, and the refreshing **Ice Cream Cottage**, (703) 721-1305, where your family can get such cooling fare as flavored shaved ice or your favorite ice cream in a waffle cone.

At Village Square there's **Village Accents**, (703) 297-7751, a collector's showcase featuring figurines such as Emmett Kelly, Jr., clowns and Native American sculpture. **Needlecrafter Custom-made Sweaters**, (703) 297-6334, offers everything for the handcrafter, and **Smith Mountain Flowers**, (703) 297-6524, has gifts, candy, fruit and flowers for any occasion.

Beyond these two centers, other shops are either general or specialized and far flung. **Classic Collections**, (703) 297-2804, on Route 122, north of Hales Ford bridge, has quilts, pottery, baskets, customer designed flags, teddy bears, bird carvings and oak rockers. **The Old Country Store and Deli**, nearly four miles north of Hales Ford bridge, has souvenirs, balloons, food, fishing and hunting equipment and just about anything else you need while enjoying the lake.

Bedford County

ANTIQUES

There are nearly 20 antique stores within a close radius in Bedford County. In downtown Bedford, there's **Bridge Street Antiques,** (703) 586-6611, at 201 N. Bridge Street, specializing in furniture, tools, silver and primitives. Books, toys and Virginia antiques can be found downtown at **Hamiltons,** (703) 586-5592, at 155 W. Main. Farther out of town, you'll find **Old Country Store**, (703) 586-1665, a mile west of Bedford on Route 460. Twelve dealers do business at **The Peddler Antiques** (804) 525-6030, on Route 854 between routes 811 and 221. You'll find many shops between Lynchburg and Bedford. For a complete list, call the Bedford Area Chamber of Commerce at (703) 586-9401.

OUTLETS

If you love pottery and seeing how it's made, it's worth a trip to Bedford to visit **Emerson Creek**'s factory in Bedford County. The company's product line can be found in all 50 states and is becoming widely collected as a fine art. The retail shop, (703) 297-7884, provides tour schedules and directions to their stores. If you're going just to shop, the seconds shop is located in an 1825 log cabin next to the factory on Route 727 E., 10 miles from Bedford. A new renovated showroom houses a permanent display of the pottery's 14-year-old private collection. Emerson Creek Pottery is known for its designs featuring fields of wildflowers dancing in a spectrum of pastel and vibrant hues. Each pot is hand-decorated. The line consists of earthenware pottery, including vases, coffee mugs, pitchers, lamps, creamers and sugars, flower pots and lotion bottles, in more than a dozen colors and patterns.

Franklin County

GENERAL STORES

If you're in Franklin County, the one stop you must make is **Boone's Country Store,** (703) 721-2478, a few miles from the intersection of Route 122 at Burnt Chimney and Route 116 at Boone's Mill — the winding mountain road to Roanoke. Run by German Baptists, the store has the most heavenly sticky buns, pies, cakes, rolls and homemade entrees this side of Amish country. There are also country items and piece goods. If you want to take home an authentic reminder of German Baptist country, don't miss Boone's.

HANDCRAFTS

For a tremendous buy on hand-smocked children's items and clothing, as well as good quality children's consignment clothing and juvenile accessories, travel the main road between Roanoke and Rocky Mount, U.S. Highway 220, and stop at **Kids Kastoffs**, (703) 483-2496. You'll find the same quality as in specialty stores, at about a third of the cost. Downtown Rocky Mount is the location of **From the Heart**, (703) 489-3887, 178 Franklin Street, a store with a unique assortment of gift items, local art, toys, pottery, linen and antiques.

OUTLETS

Southern Lamp & Shade Showroom, (703) 483-4738, on U.S. Highway 220, near Wirtz, has a great selection of lamps and shades at below retail prices. It's well worth visiting if you're shopping for lighting. In Rocky Mount, **Virginia Apparel Outlet**, (703) 483-8266, 721 N. Main Street, has a fine selection of clothing for the entire family at outlet prices.

New River Valley Region

Blacksburg

ANTIQUES

Antique stores are spread out all over the New River Valley, especially in the Blacksburg area. Downtown, there's **Grady's Antiques,** (703) 951-0623, at 208 N. Main Street, **Other Times LTD**, (703) 552-1615, at 891 Kabrich Street, and **Heirloom Originals**, (703) 552-9241, 609 N. Main. You'll find a good selection of collectibles and decorative antiques at all of these shops.

OUTLETS

There are two good clothing outlets in the downtown area that cater to the Virginia Tech crowd. **T.G.I.F. Outlets**, (703) 951-3541, on N. Main sells returns and overstock for clothing catalogs with sporty clothes. You'll find J. Crew, Clifford & Wills, Smythe & County and Lands End. On S. Main, in the Blacksburg Square Shopping Center, there is **Virginia Apparel Outlet**, (703) 961-2889, which manufactures and retails for major catalog companies including L.L. Bean, Vanity Fair, Bugle Boy and Botany 500.

SPECIALTY SHOPS

In the downtown, a very special store that started out as a hole in the wall several decades ago has since grown to be one of the most popular art supply and overall "neat stuff" stores in western Virginia. Everyone "in the know" in the New River Valley (and Roanoke, where there's a second store) knows this is **Mish Mish**, (703) 552-1020, which probably should be renamed Hodge Podge. It's located at 204 Draper Road. Shoppers of any age could spend the entire day there looking at everything from the finest art supplies and watercolors to a rainbow of Silly Putty. Sixty specialty shops and **Peebles Department Store** are among the stores at **New River Valley Mall**, (703) 381-0004, on 782 New River Road off U.S. Highway 460 in Blacksburg. The specialty stores, along with Peebles, really are a cut above those you find in other western Virginia shopping malls. The mall also wins your heart with free wheelchairs, high chairs in the food court, strollers and special programs.

Christiansburg

ANTIQUES

Cambria Emporium, (703) 381-0949, at 596 Depot Street in Christiansburg, is the best place in Montgomery County to find tiny antique treasures and surprises. The big, red, three-story building in the historic Cambria area of the county is a landmark in itself, constructed in 1908 and recently renovated as an antiques mall housing 20 dealers. Here, among 20,000 square feet, you can find every antique imaginable in a pleasant, old-time setting that will remind you of the good old days. It's open, airy and uncluttered. You'll find broad categories of glassware, furniture, dishes, quilts, vintage clothing and fine china. Along with those, you'll run across small reminders of the past that will make you ooh and ahh! For the antique lover, Cambria Emporium is definitely worth an overnight in this charming town. The Oaks bed and breakfast inn nearby is the perfect place to stay. Don't forget to go upstairs to see **Casey's Country Store**, a room laid out like a c. 1900s general store. A counter sign reads, "If it ain't priced, it ain't for sale, folks!" That's the spirit of Cambria Emporium.

OUTLETS

Both irregular and first quality fashions from chic brand-name Donkenny's women's wear can be purchased at a savings at the **Donkenny Fashion Outlet**, (703) 382-8538, on N. Franklin Street You can buy irregular clothing for up to $6.25 (yes, that's what we said!) and regular clothing for up to $45. Don't miss it if you want top fashion for few dollars. For castoffs of every kind, stop at **Big Lots**, (703) 381-5124, at the Northgate Village Shopping Center at 1695 N. Franklin on U.S. Highway 460. It's one of a chain packed with discontinued merchandise and overstocks from insurance claims, buyouts and bankruptcies. You can get unreal prices if you hit the store at the right time, but constant vigilance is the key that pays off!

Floyd County

GENERAL STORES

Without a doubt, counterculture Floyd County has the most diverse, interesting shopping of any area in the New River and, some might say, the entire Blue Ridge. **Cockram's General Store**, (703) 745-4563, is the epitome of that fact. For more than 75 years, Cockram's has been the center of Floyd County entertainment, night life and culture. It has become famous not only for its merchandise but for its famous Friday Night Flatfooting Jamboree (see our Arts and Culture chapter). Cockram's is dedicated to keeping traditions alive, but nearly died itself last year when owner Freeman Cockram found himself in debt after people who owed him money came upon rough times. The community rallied in support of the cultural institution, in a way reminiscent of old-fashioned note burnings and barn raisings, and Cockram's is still in business. As a general store, Cockram's offers a plethora of merchandise, including potted possum and bib overalls, sold from an old-fashioned candy counter. If you need it, you'll find it at Cockram's!

Down the road a piece, there's another interesting general store, **Poor Farmers Market**, (703) 952-2670, a combination grocery store, deli and gift shop, on U.S. Highway 58 in Meadows of Dan, just off the Blue Ridge Parkway. It's a hub for locals and tourists alike. The store began when owner Felecia Shelor told a local farmer she'd buy his produce and then peddle it wholesale. The idea boomed, and the store has grown 10 times its original size since 1983. Its deli serves great lunches, with such favorites as fried apple pies and the Hungry Hillbilly sandwich. The owner's life story is as interesting as the store: She rose from a life of poverty as a bride of 15 to a store owner with 15 employees. You'll love this place, and the prices are great!

HANDCRAFTS

When you're traveling the Blue Ridge Parkway looking for a unique Blue Ridge gift, don't miss **New Mountain Mercantile**, (703) 745-4ART, a shop at 114 Locust Street, six miles from Milepost 165.2 in Floyd. It's filled with many handmade items. Browse through stunning clothing (tie-dyed and batik), dolls, pottery, jewelry, Native American handcrafts, perfume made of essential oils, candles (both herbal and decorative), stained glass, quilts, field guides and books on subjects such as herb gardening

and gift making. You'll also find music, instruments and hand-tuned wind chimes. The store is run by three sensitive, savvy women, Theresa Cook, Kalinda Wycoff and Christine Byrd, who know great buys when they see them. Their store also serves as a Floyd County Information Center of sorts. Their **"Here and Now" Art Gallery** features new exhibits monthly. New Mountain Mercantile rates as one of the outstanding handcraft stores in the entire Blue Ridge. They also have a branch store at the Virginia Explore Park and at Tanglewood Mall in Roanoke. You never know which Bluegrass artist will be performing out front to lure you in.

SPECIALTY STORES

A direct contrast to a simple country mountain way of life, **Chateau Morrisette**, (703) 593-2865, the sixth-largest winery in Virginia, is a delightful stop, not only to buy wine and baked goods at wholesale prices, but as a terrific gourmet place for lunch (see the Restaurants and Wineries chapters).

Wintergreen Farm Sheepskin Shoppe, (703) 745-4420, specializes in sheepskin products, of course, but also has fine American handcrafts, antiques and unique walking sticks. While there, visit the turn-of-the-century Farmstead Museum and Woodwright Blacksmith Shop. It's located on Highway 221, two miles south of Floyd.

Another uniquely specialized, interesting place is **Brookfield Christmas Tree Plantation**, (703) 382-9099, on Route 8, which sells trees by mail across the United

States. Fresh wreaths, pine roping and other gifts are also available, or you can make your own in workshops. Trips to the 800-acre farm are encouraged. Free hayrides and preselection of your tree are offered every weekend in October and November. It's a wonderful story book outing for the whole family and a memory children will never forget! Also in the spirit of the holidays is **County Christmas House**, (703) 745-3565, on Route 615. Formerly the Possum Hollow School House, it will have everything to decorate your tree and home.

Bluegrass and old-time music lovers won't want to miss seeing the largest distributor of such music in the world, **Country Records**, (703) 745-2001, on Main Street. Request come in from the four corners for their old-time fiddle music and gospel albums.

OUTLETS

Better than an outlet store, with more fabric than you could ever find in any retail store, **School House Fabrics**, (703) 745-4561, on Locust Street, is a cloth addict's dream. An old three-story-high school house has been renovated and filled with everything from specialty fabrics to buttons and beads. What is amazing is how organized and well-grouped this massive mania of yard goods is for shoppers. Each room is arranged according to fabric. For example, downstairs there is a large room devoted to bridal fabrics, lace, veils, beading and wedding goods. Out back, an extra building contains large reels

of upholstery fabric, tapestry and some remnants. Don't expect to leave without buying enough fabric and notions to last well into the year 2000.

Giles County

ANTIQUES

You can't miss **White Horse Antiques**, (703) 726-7021, at U.S. Highway 460 between Pearisburg and Narrows. There's a huge, plaster white horse in the window. You'll find a wide range of quality and prices: sets of Florentine dishes priced up to $100 and china plates for a dollar. Another interesting antique store is **Woodland**, (703) 921-1600, in tiny downtown Pearisburg. You can find some real gems among the rural offerings.

HANDCRAFTS

The New River Valley Arts and Crafts Guild operates a dynamic **Fine Arts Center Shop**, (703) 626-3309, in the Old Pembroke School on the main drag, U.S. Highway 460. More than 50 categories of handcrafts are available from 60 working artists, with such original works as snake canes and Knobbits. In addition to a huge variety of first-class items for sale, the Guild has a floor loom in operation, on which beautiful rugs can be woven from old rags and discarded clothing. The service is open to the public for a small fee. There's also a year-round Christmas Corner.

Radford

ANTIQUES

Some dandy antique shops can be found in Radford, including **Grandma's Memories**, (703) 639-0054, 237 First Street, and **Collector's Corner**, (703) 639-9185, 327 First Street. **Uncle Bill's Treasures**, (703) 731-1733, at 1103 Norwood Street, rounds out a great selection of antique stock.

SPECIALTY SHOPS

The combined **Norwood Art Gallery and Encore Gift Shop**, (703) 639-2015, 1115 Norwood Street, is the best place in the city to find unique gifts and original fine art Their offerings range from the very unusual to the very trendy. Discover eclectic folk art, Toys that Touch the Senses and truly unique cards, gift items and packaging. After you're done shopping, have some artfully prepared cuisine in a casual gallery setting at Gallery Cafe.

Pulaski County

Pulaski County and Main Street Pulaski offer the most tremendous shopping surprises of anyplace in the rural Blue Ridge. It's a Blue Ridge town, where time seems to have stood still just for the benefit of tourists. While the Pulaski County's unusual shops have been established for some time, newcomers to Downtown Pulaski within the past two years will think they're dreaming when they see what has happened to a formerly neglected downtown area.

Roscoe Cox, a Pulaski native and retired executive, took up the town's languishing Main Street program and, within eight months, had 20 new stores and restaurants within two blocks of the town's newly rebuilt courthouse, which burned down a few years ago. You'd have to see it to believe it! A former military man who gets paid $5 an hour to work 20 hours a week (and works 60 to 70), Cox literally has become a one-man downtown revivalist.

Some stores already there even before the revival are worth the trip in themselves. Theda and Rudolph Farmer of **Theda's Studio**, (703) 980-2777, have been in the portraiture business for more than 55 years, and a visit to their shop is like taking a trip through time, from the original tin-roofed ceilings to the arresting pictures of brides from the '50s and '60s. With an outside barber pole that still turns, **Sani-Mode Barber Shop**, (703) 980-6991, is like looking through the window into a Norman Rockwell painting. The prices of haircuts are a throwback to that time, as are the lines of barber chairs from the '40s and '50s. This is a priceless — we repeat, priceless — experience that may not be on the Americana landscape for much longer.

You can find handmade Oriental rugs, art and antiques at **Old World Carpets**, (703) 980-2669. **R.P. Collectibles**, (703) 994-0812 has a wide selection of antique clocks, Depression-era glass creamer sets and hundreds of knives. **Pulaski Antique Center**, (703) 980-5049, has two full floors of quality antiques and post-1900 furniture, as well as a large selection of glassware and artwork. The shop, located at 80 W. Main St., also houses one of the South's largest selection of quality antique wicker.

New stores include specialty ones, such as **C&S Galleries**, (703) 674-0232, an authorized P. Buckley Moss dealer; **The Colony of Virginia Ltd.**, (703) 980-8932, specializing in items hand crafted in Virginia; and **New River Fine Arts Gallery**, run by the Fine Arts Center for the New River Valley, (703) 980-7363, which has been serving the arts and culture of the New River Valley for 15 years. In this spacious setting, you'll find furniture, glassware, rugs, quilts, baskets and jewelry. Nationally known artists Annie Moon and Pam Tyrell are represented here. Also, don't miss **Upstairs, Downstairs**, handpainted furniture downstairs and a series of small boutiques upstairs. You'd find furniture like this for four times the cost in the metropolitan areas.

Nearby is **The Count Pulaski Bed & Breakfast and Gardens**. The Renaissance Restaurant, at 55 W. Main Street, is a nice place to stop for lunch with a terrific selection of sandwiches, salads and entrees.

Main Street Pulaski's main thrust, however, is attracting first-class antique stores. It has succeeded wildly in this area. The list is long and still growing. By the time you ready this, who knows how many first-class, unusual stores Roscoe Cox will have attracted to Main Street Pulaski!

GENERAL STORES

Pulaski County offers some unusual specialty shopping in unique settings. **Draper Mercantile**, (703) 980-0786, on Route 658, two minutes off I-81 at Exit 92, is a revitalized 1880s general store, doctor's office and fire station in what was old Downtown Draper. Now, it's a discount place to buy, among other things, the largest display of Ridgeway brand grandfather, wall and mantle clocks in Virginia. You also can buy, at a 40 to 60 percent discount, High Point, North Carolina, showroom furniture, gifts, crafts, floral arrangements, reproduction toys and Christmas ornaments. If you can't take it with you, the gracious owners, Lee and Katie LaFleur, will arrange to have it shipped to your home.

SPECIALTY STORES AND OUTLETS

Christmas store buffs, don't you dare miss the opportunity of a lifetime at the trio of **PJ's Carousel Collection Christmas** stores at Newbern in Pulaski County, (703) 674-4300; Fort Chiswell, (703) 637-NOEL; and Wytheville, (703) 228-ELFS. The latter two are in Wythe County, and all are just off I-81. **PJ's Carousel Village** in historic Newbern is the original home of the famous full-size and miniature Carousel horses — right next to the factory where they are manufactured. Factory seconds are available. The Carousel Village is 3,500 square feet of fun! Be sure to have some ice cream in the old-fashioned parlor. The stores down the road offer the world's only Christmas carousel (Wytheville) and a 150-

year-old Christmas House (Fort Chiswell).

Alleghany Highlands Region

ANTIQUES

You'll find many charming little shops in quaint downtowns, as well as in unexpected, out-of-the-way country roads in the counties of Alleghany, Highland and Bath. It's a junket you're bound to enjoy, whether you're hunting for top-quality antiques or just out enjoying the scenery.

Special items can be found at **Always Roxie's**, (703) 862-2999, 622 Main Street, Clifton Forge, Alleghany County, which specializes in dollhouses and miniatures. Their slogan is, "We can help make your mini house a mini home." You can find railroad items, crocks, jewelry and glassware.

Lovers of quilts and high quality, unusual quilted gifts and handcrafts won't want to miss**Quilts Unlimited**, (703) 839-5955, a Homestead Resort shop located on Cottage Row in Bath County. They handle both new and antique quilts, along with a fine selection of regional handcrafts.

In Highland County, visit **High Valley Antiques and Collectibles**, (703) 474-5611, located in a pre-Civil War era log home, and the **Woodlane Craft Shop**, (703) 499-2230, Route 84, which offers antiques, crafts and "junque."

GENERAL STORES

Over in McDowell, just off Route 250, there's **Sugar Tree Country Store and Sugar House**, (703) 396-3469, a 19th-century country store featuring maple products, apple butter, pottery, baskets and some antiques. Located in the scenic Bullpasture Valley, the store is of special interest during the annual Highland Maple Festival, when they have demonstrations of old-time methods of making maple syrup in iron kettles.

HANDCRAFTS

In Alleghany County, visit the **Highlands Arts & Crafts Center**, (703) 862-4447, in downtown Clifton Forge, located off I-64. You can see displays of fine arts, handcrafts, antiques and collectibles. The Center is a not-for-profit volunteer organization that encourages creative experiences and appreciation of the visual arts. Included for sale are pottery, wooden wares, jewelry, stained glass, needlework, quilts, fiber arts and watercolors and oils.

In Bath County, shops in The Virginia Building at **The Homestead** offer country crafts. You can buy dolls, rugs, candles, baskets, tin and pottery.

Highland County's **Gallery of Mountain Secrets**, (703) 468-2020, on Main Street in Monterey, is a treasure of traditional arts and fine crafts. It's a very special store, down from the historic Highland Inn, that offers jewelry, pottery, wooden and quilted items and decorative accessories. In the Highland Inn, the **Glass Slipper**, (703) 468-2143, features finely crafted stained-glass gift items, along with other quality handcrafts. Also on Main Street, **Highland County Crafts**, (703) 468-2127, gives a touch of country to all its gifts. It offers a Christmas corner and maple syrup and homemade preserves and pickles.

OUTLETS

It's worth a trip to the Alleghany Highlands just to shop at the **Bacova Guild Factory Outlet**, (703) 839-2105, on Main Street in Hot Springs in Bath County. You've seen the Bacova Guild's wide variety of silk-screened gifts, including mailboxes and doormats, in leading outdoor catalogs such as Orvis and L.L. Bean. Every family in Bath County received a silk-screened mailbox free of charge from the Bacova Guild's owners, a county trademark undoubtedly unmatched in the United States and perhaps the world! The wildlife-motif items are made in Bacova, a charming village built in the early 1920s as a lumber mill company town. In 1965, the village was completely restored by philanthropist Malcolm Hirsh, whose brother, Philip, owns Meadow Lane Country Lodge in Warm Springs. A complete line of decorative, yet useful, gift items are

at least 20 to 40 percent off regular prices. Summer shopping can yield an incredible Christmas gift bonanza!

SPECIALTY STORES

Across the Alleghany County border in Greenbrier County, West Virginia, shops at the **Greenbrier Resort** will remind you of New York City. They include a toy store and fabulous boutiques.

Bath County's Homestead Resort offers a great array of shops including **Ashleys**, (703) 839-3286, located just off the main lobby, with products from Crabtree & Evelyn. Other Homestead shops are **The Captain's Cabin**, (703) 839-5447, **Bootery**, **Men's Shop**, **Tower Shop** with logoed items and linen and children's shops.

Highland County has the unique **Ginseng Mountain Farm**, (703) 474-5137, storefront off U.S Highway 220, with erratic hours. Call ahead for an appointment for choice spring lamb cut to your specification, sheepskin products, stoneware, maple syrup and stove and fireplace bellows. Another great place is **The Personal Touch**, (703) 468-2145, Main Street, Monterey, that carries country fabric art, lampshades and stained glass.

Photo: Wintergreen Resort

Mountain biking is a popular sport in the Blue Ridge.

Inside
Resorts

Rare is the region anywhere in this country where such a variety of famous and soon-to-be famous resorts can be found. They range from two ultra-posh Mobil four- and five-star resorts within a half hour's drive of each other — the world-famous Homestead and Greenbrier — to mile-high Mountain Lake that the movie *Dirty Dancing* made famous . . . along with Patrick Swayze's biceps. Another resort, Bernard's Landing on Smith Mountain Lake, was the site of Bill Murray's zany hit, *What About Bob?*

To visit most of these resorts is to experience a lush lifestyle, your every wish the command of staffs that may provide a two-to-one guest ratio. European royals such as the Duke and Duchess of Windsor and Prince Rainier and Princess Grace were "regulars" at the Greenbrier. Most of America's Presidents have been regulars at the swankier resorts, including The Homestead. Prepare to drop big bucks at some of them; others are surprisingly affordable.

The listing below, from north to south and east to west, tells you a little about the resorts' histories, amenities and what sets each apart in the realm of accommodations.

Shenandoah Valley Region

BRYCE RESORT

Basye   (703) 856-2121
Directions: Bryce Resort is located 11 miles west of I-81, Exit 273 on Va. Rt. 263. From Washington, D.C., area, take Beltway to I-66 W., to I-81 S., to Mt. Jackson exit. Take Rt. 263 W. to Basye and Bryce Resort. Sky Bryce Airport is a five-minute walk away.
AX, MC, V

Bryce Resort, built amidst the beautiful mountains of the Shenandoah Valley, offers a wide range of family recreation with modern, privately owned studio condominiums, townhouses and chalets to please individual tastes. All units offer interesting decor and many reflect the history of this colorful and friendly valley. Many are furnished with kitchenettes.

Bryce is especially attractive to the golf and outdoor lover. Popular as a winter skiing recreation getaway (see the Skiing chapter), it is also unique for its grass skiing (yes, we said "grass," in which participants glide down the resort's hills on Rollerblade-type skis during the summer months), for athletes 12 years and older.

Bryce's golf course is a par 71,

18-hole championship course, 6,175 yards in length. Facilities include a driving range, putting green, club and cart rentals, professional instruction, individual club storage and a fully stocked golf shop. Greens fee is $27 Monday through Thursday and $37 weekends and holidays. A great golf package is offered for three days, including 18 holes of golf with cart per day and two dinners.

While Mom and Dad are on the course, the children can enjoy Lake Laura, a 45-acre man-made private lake with its own sandy beach, offering swimming, boating, windsurfing and fishing. Beach admission is $3. Windsurfing is taught at a certified school, on a dryland simulator, before you head for the water. The beginning package costs $30.

Horseback riding is another family outing at T. J. Stables, open Memorial Day Weekend to Labor Day and, weather permitting, afterwards. Pony rides are available for children ages three to six.

Mountain biking and rollerblading are new sports at Bryce Resort. "Diamond Back" mountain bikes can be rented at the ski shop for $13 for up to 3½ hours and rollerblades for $10 for the same amount of time. Tennis is another favorite activity, with lighted outdoor courts and a well-stocked pro shop. Court time per hour is $10 with light tokens $3.

Lodging prices vary according to accommodations. Condos on the ski slopes, with a great fireplace, bedroom and bath, rent for $95 nightly (there's a three-night minimum during ski season); two-bed-room townhouses on the golf course rent for $115 nightly; and scattered chalets range from $250 to $700 for a two-night stay. No out of state checks are accepted.

MASSANUTTEN

Harrisonburg (703) 289-9441
Directions: From I-81, take Exit 64, turn right on Rt. 33 E., go 10 miles to Rt. 644; the entrance is on the left.

AX, MC, V

Massanutten bills itself as "More than a Mountain, Your Place in the Fun . . ." with 5,300 acres of unspoiled beauty and unequaled recreation. The Massanutten experience can't be said any better than that! Massanutten is probably known best for its superb skiing and winter recreation (see the Skiing chapter) and also for its exchange program with Vail and Beaver Creek Resort in Colorado.

Golfing is probably what Massanutten is second-best known for, with its semiprivate, 18-hole PGA Championship golf course and its scenic splendor. Greens fee is $20, with $22 per cart.

Guests also enjoy Massanutten's multimillion dollar sports complex, Le Club, which provides a full gym, fitness center, racquetball and everything you need to stay in top physical condition. Year-round swimming is available. Tennis buffs will enjoy lighted outdoor courts at no fee.

Kids like putt-putt at $2.50 and pond fishing for free. There also is a host of programs geared to children, including tubing, canoeing, nature hikes and arts and crafts.

Mountain bikes are available for $5 per hour.

Dining opportunities are sparse, with a cafeteria-style restaurant located in the sports complex. Nearby Harrisonburg, however, home of James Madison University, offers a bonanza of great restaurants.

It is best if you call (703) 289-9441 for current rates, since they were being restructured at our press time.

WINTERGREEN

Wintergreen   (800) 325-2200
Directions: The resort is 43 miles southwest of Charlottesville, bordering the Blue Ridge Pkwy. Off I-81, west or east, on Rt. 250, take Rt. 250 east to Rt. 151 south; turn right. Follow Rt. 151 south to Rt. 664, 14.2 miles. Turn right; Wintergreen is 4.5 miles ahead on Rt. 664.

AX, MC, V

Wintergreen, an 11,000-acre resort along the solitary spine of the Blue Ridge, enjoys a reputation as one of the most environmentally conscious resorts in the Blue Ridge.

The resort embodies the idea that conservation is good for development, and the philosophy has paid off. Wintergreen was the recipient of the National Environmental Quality Achievement Award in 1987.

Wintergreen's name also appears on the list of "Top 50 Favorite Family Resorts" by *Better Homes and Gardens* and "Top 10 Family Mountain Resorts" in the country by *Family Circle* magazine. Furthermore, *Golf Digest* rated the resort's Stoney Creek course as one of the best new resort courses in the country in 1990, while the same year, *Tennis* magazine selected Wintergreen as one of its "Top 50 Tennis Resorts."

Needless to say, recreational amenities are legendary. Wintergreen is known as a great place to ski and golf on the same day (see the Skiing chapter to read about its 10 slopes). In addition to Stoney Creek, there's Devils Knob,

Wintergreen's 18-hole championship golf course, with the highest altitude of any course in Virginia. The course rate is $60 and the cart fee is $20 per single player.

Tennis buffs have their pick of 20 composition clay and five all-weather hard surface courts. The court rate ranges from $12 to $28, and tennis clinics, workouts and ball machine rentals are available.

Swimmers can take advantage of a superb indoor pool at Wintergarden Spa and five outdoor pools. Water enthusiasts also have 20-acre Lake Monocan for swimming and canoeing. Mountain bikes can be rented by the hour for $8, $50 daily, and there is a 25-mile network of marked hiking trails. Horseback riding and pony rides are offered seasonally, with new lessons on vaulting, the European sport of horseback gymnastics. And, after all that activity, you might want to take advantage of their therapeutic and sports massages at $35 a half hour.

Special events, such as the Spring Wildflower Symposium, are featured throughout the year and include holiday celebrations such as the spectacular Appalachian Mountain Christmas, with horse-drawn carriage rides and candlelight dinners.

Babysitting services are available. In summer, a special children's program is offered that introduces youngsters to the beauty and wildlife of the Blue Ridge.

Dining out is no problem with the resort's six full-service restaurants. There are Cooper's Vantage, The Garden Terrace and the Grist-mill for casual dining and The Copper Mine for continental cuisine. Rodes Farm Inn offers country and family-style meals while the Verandah specializes in regional cuisine. There also are seasonal restaurants, following the golf and skiing schedules, and three lounges, one with live entertainment.

Wintergreen offers 350 rental homes and condominiums, ranging from studio-size to seven-bedroom. Most have fireplaces and fully equipped kitchens, and many have spectacular views. Rates range from $100 to $455 nightly out of season to $130 to $550 in season. Various packages are available, including golf, tennis, family, sports and romance getaways. Personal checks are accepted.

NATURAL BRIDGE OF VIRGINIA

Natural Bridge   (703) 291-2121
                               (800) 533-1410
Directions: Natural Bridge is 13 miles from the Blue Ridge Pkwy., minutes off I-81, 12 miles from I-64 and 39 miles north of Roanoke. Traveling up or down I-81, you can't miss it.
                     All major credit cards

One of the seven wonders of the natural world, Natural Bridge Resort isn't posh in the same sense as some of the other great five-star resorts of the Blue Ridge, but it's definitely worth seeing and staying at overnight because of its unique character. Many make the trip just for the unique sunrise services, as well as for the nightly Dramas of Creation, a spectacular light and sound show. Both are held under the 23-stories-high, 90-foot-long structure.

The story of Natural Bridge, a

36,000-ton limestone arch carved millions of years ago, is a historian's delight. Early on, the bridge was worshipped by the Monocan Indians. Thomas Jefferson was the first American to own the bridge, which he purchased from King George III in 1774. George Washington surveyed the bridge as a lad. In fact, you can still see the spot where he carved his initials. Colonists made bullets by dropping molten lead off the bridge into the cold creek water below. During the War of 1812, soldiers mined the nearby saltpeter cave to make explosives.

Additional attractions are the 34-stories-high caverns (it is said they are haunted with ghostly voices still heard as late as 1988), and the Natural Bridge Wax Museum, which houses lifelike figures including a gallery of American presidents. A huge gift shop, featuring everything from homemade fudge to candy made to look like rocks, along with fine gifts. For lunch or a snack, a deli featuring several fast food stations is located in the gift shop. For recreation, the tennis courts, indoor heated swimming pool and new 18-hole Mini-link Indoor Golf Course are popular features. Each attraction costs $7 per adult and $3.50 per child (ages six to 15); special combination rates are $13 per adult and $7.50 per child to visit all three attractions.

Accommodations feature 180 rooms in the newly refurbished hotel, Annex and cozy Hillside Cottages. Room rates range from $46 to $88, to $195 for a three-room suite. Personal checks are accepted for advance deposits only.

East of the Blue Ridge Region

THE BOAR'S HEAD
INN & SPORTS CLUB

Charlottesville   (800) 476-1988
Directions: From I-64, take the U.S. Hwy. 250 W. exit. Go west 1½ miles and turn left into the Inn. Amtrak and major airlines service Charlottesville.

All major credit cards

Built to perfection in Old English tradition, this inn is any Anglophile's delight. In case you didn't already know, the boar's head symbolized festive hospitality in the days of Shakespeare's England. A beautiful old grist mill symbolizes the Boar's Head Inn's link with Virginia's proud past. If visiting Jeffersonian Country or the University of Virginia, this Mobil Four-Star, AAA Four-Diamond complex is the place to stay! The Boar's Head is also for tennis lovers, being rated one of the top 50 tennis resorts by *Tennis* magazine. Unique to Blue Ridge resorts is its hot air balloon flight over the Blue Ridge countryside, which is almost *de rigueur*.

A quarter-century ago, Boar's Head's president, John B. Rogan, brought the old mill to its present spot from near Thomas Jefferson's historic Monticello home. Today, the 1830s mill is the resort's main dining and social room, called, in quaint understatement, the "Ordinary." Public rooms are furnished with antiques brought from England, and guest rooms contain custom-designed period furniture. Gardens feature traditional southern flowers and greenery.

Within this 43-acre country-estate atmosphere are 175 guest rooms and suites, 12 meeting rooms, a grand ballroom, five dining rooms, specialty shops and a sports club. Resort facilities include three indoor Grasstex tennis courts, 10 Lee Fast-Dry clay courts and six all-weather courts, along with two platform tennis and four squash courts. Golf (18-hole), swimming, fishing and horseback riding are available nearby.

Three public dining rooms are located in the Inn — The Old Mill Room, Garden Room and the Tavern, the latter of which is open nightly for live entertainment. The real highlights of the year are the traditional Thanksgiving and Christmas celebrations, the most unique of any Blue Ridge resort. The Thanksgiving feast is preceded by the "Blessing of the Hounds" of the Keswick Hunt, at Grace Episcopal. A Hunt Tea is held after the hunt. The Merrie Olde England Christmas Festival is a pageant of

English yuletide celebrations in days of yore. Unique is the "Feast Before Forks," the bringing in of the boar's head, wassailing and torchlight parades.

The Boar's Head resort is a true historical spectacle of America's past and a great place to bring visitors from foreign lands for an experience they'll never forget!

Boar's Head offers a variety of packages, ranging from bed and breakfast at $99 during value season (November through March) to bed, breakfast and ballooning at $375 during high season (April through October). There are accommodating specials, including the traditional golf and tennis packages, but the special ones unique to Jeffersonian Country are the Historic Tour and Bacchanalian Feast packages.

KESWICK HALL

701 Country Club Dr.
Keswick   *(804) 979-3440*
              (800) ASHLEY-1
Directions: From Charlottesville, go east on Bypass 250, east on Rt. 22 and right onto Rt. 744 until you reach a stop sign. Keswick is directly ahead from the stop. From Washington, D.C., travel on Rt. 29 S. to Charlottesville and follow directions above. From Richmond, take I-64 W. to Shadwell/ 250 Exit. Follow directions from Charlottesville.

For the absolute ultimate in pampered living, outstanding service and gorgeous surroundings, you must come to Keswick, "a fine estate drawing on the best traditions of English County Life." Sir Bernard Ashley, co-founder of Laura Ashley company, founder of Ashley House Inc. and owner and devel-

Photo: The Homestead

The well-known Homestead Resort in Hot Springs.

oper of Keswick Estate, is adding his distinction to the long and fascinating history of Keswick. Broad Oak, a pre-Civil War mansion, once stood here, replaced by Villa Crawford in 1912. Twice the location of the Virginian State Open, it became a country club in the 1940s. Now it is the 600-acre Keswick Estate, a magnificent backdrop for Keswick Hall, a country house hotel; Keswick Club, exclusive traditional golf and leisure club; and attractive residences for the person of discriminating taste. (See our chapter on Real Estate for more information.)

The word "luxury" may come to mind, but there's no glitter or brashness to be found at this hotel. Sir Bernard wants visitors to feel as if they were house guests in an old English house with a butler and a maid. Phyllis Napier, the Ashley House interior designer, has made each of the 48 rooms distinctive, and no two are alike. The elegant chambers are decorated with antiques from Ashley's collection and, of course, Laura Ashley fabrics in the familiar flowery prints and more sophisticated styles. All the suites have themes, and great emphasis is placed on the little details: pure cotton sheets, fluffy bathrobes and other amenities to pamper you.

Public rooms around the house can be found to suit any mood. There is a library, pretty chintz sitting room for English afternoon tea (with scones and jam), the inviting morning room with fireplace and piano and the snooker room for an after-dinner game. Informal meetings or functions can easily be held in these comfortable, naturally lighted rooms. The Keswick Board Room is perfect for very private high-level meetings and prestige seminars.

Dining is a central part of the Ashley House experience. The dining rooms have views over the regal mature woodland surrounding Keswick. Chefs create dishes using a combination of European classic recipes and the best of modern cooking, using fresh produce from the community and the Estate's own herb garden. An extensive cellar of wines from both the Old World and the new are all "little extras" that make a stay so special. Outside, the vine-covered terraces and lovely gardens offer superb views. The grounds are impeccably maintained.

For those wishing for a little more vigorous "R and R," there is plenty of activity on the grounds. The Keswick Club is an elite private club and the ethos of quality, service, exclusivity and discretion of the English private club are paramount. Membership is strictly limited and access is by invitation only.

However, residential guests at Keswick Hall can secure House Membership. The golf course is an 18-hole championship Arnold Palmer signature course, designed to offer an exciting round for the professional and an enjoyable challenge for the amateur. The Pavilion furnishes an indoor/outdoor pool, exercise room, spa, sauna and clay courts. Regular aerobics classes are held and beauty and massage treatments are available. The Pavilion Pub is presented as an Old English tavern with wooden floors and leather chairs.

Nearby attractions include Monticello, Ash Lawn-Highland, Montpelier and the University of Virginia. Skyline Drive and Shenandoah National Park are both splendid in all seasons.

Room tariffs begin at $195 per night for a house room and range to $645 for a master suite. A 10 percent discretionary service charge is added to accommodation services. Keswick Hall promotes a no-tipping policy throughout. A cash deposit equal to one night's cost will be confirmed in writing. Reservations are strongly recommended.

BERNARD'S LANDING

Moneta   *(800) 572-2048*
Directions: It is 45 minutes from either Roanoke or Lynchburg. From Roanoke, take Rt. 220 south to a left on Rt. 697 at Wirtz. Follow Rt. 697 to its intersection with Rt. 122; turn left. Continue for approximately seven miles, then turn right on Rt. 616 at Central Fidelity Bank. Drive seven miles, then turn left on Rt. 940, which will dead end at Bernard's. From Lynchburg, take Rt. 460 west to Rt. 122 and drive about 25 miles to Rt. 616. Turn left and follow above directions to Bernard's.

All major credit cards
Bernard's Landing is a relatively new resort on relatively new Smith Mountain Lake. The largest in Vir-

ginia with 500 miles of shoreline, it has become a water playground getaway for people from all over the East Coast. Known as a piece of paradise, this resort's majestic view and magnificent sunsets sinking into the crystal clear water have drawn artists from around the world.

Bernard's Landing was built in 1981 on what was once a prosperous farm worked by slaves of the Parker family. A descendent, Phyllis Parker, manages sales and marketing for the resort today. The family home, an original brick plantation house, still stands at the center of Bernard's activity. Appalachian Power filled the lake in 1966, submersing 22,000 acres and making many Franklin, Bedford and Pittsylvania county farmers instantly

wealthy. Bernard's was built on the widest part of the lake and is one of few places where you can see the magnificent view of the seven-mile-long Smith Mountain Lake.

Walt Disney Productions searched the entire United States for a lake resort with just the right combination to portray Lake Winnipesaukee, New Hampshire, an out-of-the-way vacation spot that still had luxurious amenities. In 1990, a staff of 100, including Bill Murray and Richard Dreyfuss, stayed nearly half a year for the filming of *What About Bob?* Many were so impressed with the pristine beauty of the lake that they stayed even longer. That's because Bernard's has become known as the place where people come to get

Photo: Boar's Head Inn

The Boar's Head Inn and Sports Club in Charlottesville.

away from it all. Although friendly, Franklin County residents grant you privacy, whether you're sailing, swimming or just drinking in the silence.

The well-planned waterfront community sits on its own peninsula and is designed to take advantage of its natural surroundings of mountains reflected by the sparkling lake. As you drive up, the resort impresses you with its huge expanse of lawn that separates the buildings. This could be a premier location for an international kite-flying competition. There are sandy beaches for swimming and sun bathing and an Olympic-size swimming pool. The plantation home serves as a clubhouse. A health club with exercise equipment, indoor handball courts and six tennis courts complement the recreational activities. Clearly, the draw is the water. But if you want more than a splendid view, there's plenty to keep you entertained.

Smith Mountain is an angler's paradise. Nationally known for its striped bass fishing, the lake boasts the state's record striper — weighing 44 pounds, 14 ounces. If you're into fishing (see Fishing under our Recreation chapter), Bernard's operates a marina and rents fishing, pontoon and ski boats right at the dock. The Virginia Commission of Games and Inland Fisheries manages and maintains an adjoining 5,000 acres for hunting enthusiasts.

The resort's restaurant, The Landing, serves gourmet meals, packs many a picnic lunch for boaters and consistently earns *Roanoker*

magazine's "Best Restaurant on the Lake" award. Probably every resident at the lake has enjoyed Bernard's sumptuous Sunday brunch, truly worth a tasting trip. The savory omelets are the most requested item. Prices are reasonable for great sandwiches at the dockside restaurant or evening entrees.

Bernard's rental facilities run from one- to three-level townhouses to single-level homes or one- to three-bedroom condos. They feature fireplaces, decks, skylights and cathedral ceilings. Nightly rentals in peak season range from $105 for a one-bedroom condo to $195 for a three-bedroom townhouse.

Alleghany Highlands Region

THE HOMESTEAD RESORT

Hot Springs   *(703) 839-5500*
Directions: From I-81, take Mt. Crawford-Rt. 257 Exit west to Rt. 42. Take Rt. 42 south to Millboro Springs, then Rt. 39 west to Warm Springs and U.S. Hwy. 220 south to Hot Springs. There is ground service from Roanoke Regional Airport. Ingalls Field, Hot Springs, is located nearby, serving private and corporate aircraft.

All major credit cards

The Homestead, one of the South's major resorts, is grandly situated on 15,000 acres in the Allegheny Mountains. It has held the Mobil Five-Star Award for more than 30 years. It's as "homey" as its name and is famous for its afternoon teas in its long, wide lobby. Washington and Jefferson strolled these grounds, and Lord and Lady

Astor honeymooned here. The most unusual "guests" of all began their visit December 29, 1941, three weeks after the attack on Pearl Harbor, when 363 Japanese diplomats, along with many Japanese citizens in the United States, were placed at The Homestead for a three-month internment.

The Homestead has been pampering guests since the late 1700s, when the aristocracy of Virginia went to the mountains, with their refreshing springs, instead of enduring the lowland heat with the common folk. In those days, it was fashionable to move from one mountain spring to another, virtually en masse, in a group composed of high society. Originally valued for medicinal purposes by Native Americans, the springs around The Homestead became centers of social activity.

Hot Springs, where The Homestead has stood for more than a century, was one of the most prominent springs in Virginia. The lineage of The Homestead as a resort and its tradition of "taking the waters" can be traced back to 1766. The spa of today was built in 1892, the dream of M. E. Ingalls, great great-grandfather of the owner who sold it last year to Resorts International of Dallas, Texas. Designed with the grandeur and technological expertise of today, the spa treatments are still one of the most popular services. The two covered pools and the sheltered "drinking spring" have been preserved in their natural condition. Eleanor Roosevelt's special chair is still at one of them.

There are still legions of visitors who swear by the springs' curative properties. The magnificent, ornate indoor pool is fed continuously by waters of the Octagon Pool, which can be viewed in front of the spa. The most popular spot is where the natural mineral waters come rushing out under the see-through canopy. There are two outdoor pools as well.

This year, the Homestead is undergoing approximately $12.5 million worth of improvements, including refurnishing and plumbing in guest rooms, refurnishing hallways in the East Wing and redecoration of the Great Hall and dining room.

Today, it is often the golfers who swear by the Homestead's magical abilities to renew youth and vigor. And no wonder! Golf is king at this resort. There is championship playing on three 18-hole courses, one of which has been the site of the U.S. Amateur and boasts the oldest first tee in continuous use in the United States. *Golf Digest* and *Golf* magazine rank the Cascades Course among the top in the nation. John D. Rockefeller used to spread his wealth here by tossing shiny dimes into the pool of water in back of the first tee for the caddies to fight over. President William Taft nearly created a scandal by playing the "frivolous" game of golf on the Fourth of July holiday here at the turn of the century. Golf carts are included in the rates, which range from $76 to $101 for the champion course.

Tennis is also superb at The Homestead, with 19 courts, including four all-weather ones. Singles are $10 per person and doubles are $7.50 per person, per hour.

Fishing is another favorite sport (permits cost $20), as is skeet and trap at The Shooting Club, where a round of 25 birds costs $20. Hiking and horseback riding are other popular activities, with carriage rides in fringe-topped surreys on scenic trails a pleasant option. Bowling and movies are indoor activities guests enjoy.

Winter brings a whole new round of sports with skiing (see the Skiing chapter), considered some of the best in the South, and ice skating. Half-day skating sessions cost $5.50 weekends and holidays. There are fabulous winter weekends priced for the budget-minded pocketbook. Bring the kids!

The Homestead is a classic. Six hundred spacious guest rooms are offered at the sweeping Colonial-style building, topped by a modern high-rise clock tower. Inside are white Corinthian columns, high-ceiling rooms and turn-of-the-century crystal chandeliers. Daily room rates in high season, November through April, are $258 to $308 for double occupancy; in value seasons, $218 to $268. Children younger than 12 may share their parents' room with no charge. Prices include breakfast and dinner in the main dining room or in the casual atmosphere of Sam Snead's Tavern in the Village. The new owners have expansive renovation plans to make the resort even grander!

THE GREENBRIER

White Sulphur Springs, W.Va.

(800) 624-6070

Directions: Take White Sulphur Springs Exit off I-64. Turn right onto Rt. 60 and travel two miles; the entrance is on the left. The Greenbrier's entrance is across the street from Amtrak Station, a stop for the luxurious American-European Express Railway Train Deluxe, a match for the Orient Express. Accessible by air from Roanoke Regional Airport, the resort is two hours away by limousine.

All major credit cards

"Monumental" is the first word that comes to mind about this five-star National Historic Landmark set in 6,500 acres of breathtaking scenery. Both its history and its current style, as well as its star-studded guest list, have enchanted people for two centuries. The Greenbrier has hosted world summits and celebrities in the midst of the sleepy little town of White Sulphur Springs. One never knows when TV star Bill Cosby or former British Prime Minister Margaret Thatcher will be seen on the grounds. In 1981, when the U.S. government wanted the ultimate in rest and recreation for its former Iranian hostages, it chose the Greenbrier.

Its history has been nothing short of incredible, beginning in the 18th century when aristocratic Southerners came to drink the mineral waters, stroll and chat while avoiding the summer sun. Twice during wartime, the U.S. government took over and used the resort as a hospital, first in 1861, when the Confederacy also claimed it as its military headquarters. It came perilously close to total destruction during the 1864 occupation by Union troops, when it was ordered burned. Only a plea from a U.S. senator saved it. Later, Gen. Robert E. Lee used it as his summer home. During World War II, former guest Gen. George Marshall (for whom the museum in nearby Lexington, Virginia, is named) turned it into a 2,200-bed hospital named Ashford General. According to locals, many a wounded soldier, upon awakening, thought he had died and gone to Heaven.

After the war, again a resort, The Greenbrier was refurbished and redecorated. Its interior designer used over 30 miles of carpeting, 45,000 yards of fabric, 40,000 gallons of paint, 15,000 rolls of wallpaper and 34,567 individual decorative and furniture items on the job. The outstanding results still stand today.

In 1992, the Pentagon confirmed that a secret underground bunker large enough to house the president, his cabinet and Congress, was constructed here during the nuclear attack threat of the Cold War. Locals have known of its existence for years, but it's a fact the Greenbrier wouldn't discuss. However, this year, resort officials requested that the bunker be declassified. The Green-brier would like to open a 100,000 square foot gambling casino within the facility.

Staff outnumber the guests, with 1,600 employees and a 1,200-guest capacity. There are 650 guest rooms (no two of them furnished alike), 69 cottages (some come with use of a Cadillac), 51 suites, 30 meeting rooms, three championship golf courses, 20 tennis courts and a $7 million spa. To ensure you are adequately fed, there are 120 chefs (no kidding . . . 120!) to serve you six-course dinners in The Greenbrier's acclaimed combination of classical, Continental and American cuisine, in six different settings. The list of culinary awards is endless. The Greenbrier is acclaimed for its own cooking school, La Varenne.

Adjacent is the world-famous Greenbrier Clinic, a diagnostic center where CEOs can have a checkup in the morning and play golf in the afternoon on a course designed by Jack Nicklaus.

Golf also gets a lot of attention at this resort. Sam Snead was the club's pro and played his best game ever here, setting a PGA record of 59 in the third round. Bob Hope, Bing Crosby, Arnold Palmer and the Prince of Wales were regular golf-

The difference between the high season (May through October) and the rest of the year will make large differences in your resort vacation pocketbook. You may pay up to five times more in June than January at the major luxury resorts.

Insiders' Tips

ers. In 1979, the course served as the site of the International Ryder Cup matches. Golf is complimentary during winter months, with the fee ranging from $40 in the off season to $80 in peak season; the golf cart is extra at $34.

For the tennis set, 15 outdoor Har-Tru courts and five indoor Dynaturf courts await play. Doubles are $42 per hour indoors. Recreational offerings are rounded out with croquet, indoor and outdoor swimming, bowling, billiards, trout fishing, hiking, horseback riding, carriage rides, biking, cross-country skiing, trap and skeet shooting and shopping in a large gallery of wonderful stores. For a touch of heaven, give yourself a gift of one (or more) of the 18 different treatments of the new spa and have your own nutritionist and exercise trainer design an individual program for you. A five-day spa package costs $2,300.

You won't miss a meal at The Greenbrier. Nobody does. The Greenbrier's food is so excellent that just this year, First Lady Hillary Clinton spirited away The Greenbrier's head chef to work at the White House. French food lovers were aghast, but the new First Chef has been knocking them dead with fine American cuisine ever since.

Rates are based on a Modified American Plan, which includes breakfast and dinner in the main dining room. Nowhere else is The Greenbrier's Southern heritage more apparent than at the breakfast table, with fresh brook trout, hominy grits, Virginia ham and ba-con, cornbread and biscuits. Dinner of six courses is truly an event. A string ensemble provides music, and dinner is served with candlelight and chandeliers. The vichyssoise is a favorite of Greenbrier regulars, along with its famous peaches and cream for dessert. In 1989, The Greenbrier delivered 10,000 of its famous handmade chocolate truffles for former president George Bush's inaugural dinner.

The Greenbrier's multitude of accommodations are available in a variety of packages, including golf, tennis and family. Its tariff schedule ranges from $132 per person nightly November through April on the Modified American plan to $166 per person April to October.

You don't have to stay overnight to enjoy the Greenbrier. Dessert and beverage for two can be had for about $20. Have a snack and then tour the President's Cottage Museum or visit the Miniature Gift Shop, a little dollhouse that sells only miniatures. Then, save your dollars to experience the total experience!

New River Valley Region

MOUNTAIN LAKE RESORT

Mountain Lake   *(800) 346-3334*
Directions: Take U.S. Hwy. 460 Bypass around Blacksburg to Rt. 700. Follow Rt. 700 for seven winding, scenic country miles to Mountain Lake.

All major credit cards
If you saw the great, nostalgic sandstone lodge in the hit movie

Dirty Dancing, you saw Mountain Lake Resort. The majestic beauty of this grand old hotel was forever captured in 1986 after filmmakers, searching for a gentle, romantic circa-'60s resort, saw an ad for Mountain Lake in a magazine. The rest is history. Dirty Dancing Weekends sell out quickly, and everyone wants to know where Patrick Swayze slept when he stayed there.

But there's far more history than that to Mountain Lake, one of only two natural freshwater lakes in Virginia and one of the highest natural lakes in the East. It was formed when a rock slide dammed the north end of the valley, creating a 100-foot-deep lake fed by underground streams that rarely allow the water temperature to rise above 72 degrees.

The first report of a pleasure resort here was in 1857, and the first hotel was wooden. In the early '30s, William Lewis Moody of Galveston, Texas, purchased the property and built the present huge hotel from native stone. His elder daughter, Mary, who died in 1986, loved to sit under the great stone fireplace in the lobby, which still says "House of Moody." Since her death, Mary's foundation has contributed $200 million to charitable organizations, and Mary ensured her beloved Mountain Lake, where she stayed each summer, would keep its 2,600 acres of natural paradise in perpetuity.

Mountain Lake's motto is "We'll Put You On Top of the World." And they do. When you stay at Mountain Lake and sit on the great stone front porches in a rocking chair overlooking the lake, you can't help but feel refreshed and renewed. Summer offers the opportunity to relax in cool mountain air, and in the autumn, few fall foliage vistas can compare to Mountain Lake's.

A year-round resort, its winter cross-country skiing and horse-drawn sleigh rides are incomparable. The other seasons offer a variety of boating, fishing (guests must furnish own equipment), hiking, tennis, swimming and lawn games. A health club is equipped with a whirlpool, exercise equipment and sauna. There is a Recreation Barn with games and snacks and several shops featuring Appalachian arts and gifts. Mountain Lake is also known for its special weekends, with themes such as Dirty Dancing, Mardi Gras, Appalachian Culture and Murder Mysteries.

The food is always superb in the newly decorated, stone dining room, where guests lucky enough to get window tables will see a panorama of bluebirds, canaries and redbirds scolding spoiled squirrels awaiting guests' handouts. Deer are common visitors to the grounds, and other wildlife is prevalent. Jacket and tie is suggested for evening meals, which are a gourmet's delight and unbelievably priced for such fare in a beautiful setting. Brunch is $13.95; lunch entrees range from $6.95 for Orange Roughy with Lemon Pepper Glaze to $11.95 for broiled New York strip. This includes rolls and a choice of soup, salad or vegetable du jour. Many nearby (17 miles away) Virginia Tech parents make the trip just for the meal, which can be booked with a reservation.

Accommodations include the 50-room hotel, whose room amenities may include fireplace and whirlpool; the 16-room Chestnut Lodge; and 15 wooden cottages with fireplace. Prices for couples range from $125 nightly to $175 in the lodge, with a small additional charge for each child. Most guests stay on the Modified American Plan, which includes lodging, breakfast, dinner and use of all facilities and equipment. Personal checks are accepted. The air is rare, and so is the experience!

Southwestern Virginia Region

DOE RUN LODGE
RESORT AND CONFERENCE CENTER
Mile 189 Blue Ridge Pkwy.
Hillsville   (703) 398-2212,
                    (800) 325-M189
            All major credit cards

Just across the border of Floyd County, in Patrick County, Doe Run Lodge Resort and Conference Center and its High Country Restaurant are nestled in the most beautiful part of the Blue Ridge Parkway. With Groundhog Mountain as the midpoint on this road of pastoral beauty, your senses will be overwhelmed by what this year-round resort has to offer. Azaleas, rhododendron, dogwood and mountain laurel are in the air in spring and early summer. The foothills below reveal a burst of color from apple, peach and nectarine orchards and grape vineyards. You may hear animals of the forest — deer, fox, hawks, eagles, groundhogs and raccoons — scampering through the woodlands.

Doe Run Lodge Resort and Conference Center was built to fit the beauty of this environment. The chalets are constructed of stone and wood beams. Floor-to-ceiling windows allow magnificent views. These large suites have a fireplace, two bedrooms, two full baths and a living/dining area — a real buy for the money! The chalets, townhouses and single-family residences are furnished and have complete kitchens. Millpond Hideaway, designed for use by executives or honeymooners, has a whirlpool tub, luxury shower and steam cabinet, full-suite stereo and TV, fireplace and enclosed garage. To realize the true value of these accommodations, share a chalet with another couple or with your family, as it can accommodate up to six people, with two bedrooms and two full baths.

High Country Restaurant offers a unique menu of seafood, steak and other regional recipes, including venison, duck, fresh rainbow trout from their stocked pond, pheasant and country ham. Picnic lunches are packed to go. This lovely resort is the best the Parkway has to offer — pay a visit and let the magic of the Blue Ridge happen!

Inside
Bed and Breakfast Inns and Country Inns

Isn't it time you got away from it all? Slip into the tranquility of country life at an old stagecoach inn on the Valley Turnpike in Woodstock, linger for a while at the Inn at Narrow Passage or get closer to heaven at the Bent Mountain Lodge that sits high in the Blue Ridge. No matter what your interest, you can find the perfect place to relax.

Each of these grand old bed and breakfast inns and country inns has its own distinct charm, with histories as varied as the decor. How many of us dream of spending the night in a real mansion? Experience just that at Lynchburg's Man-

sion Inn. You may stay on the former site of an ancient Native American village at Silver Thatch Inn in Charlottesville. Or you may be swept away by the beauty of bubbling springs at Meadow Lane in Warm Springs, on land that has remained in the Hirsh family for over three generations.

You'll find that Blue Ridge innkeepers are among the most cordial hosts in the world — genuinely concerned about your well-being and comfort. And these antique country manors can convey to you a sense of tranquility hard to find anywhere else. The soothing coun-

Photo: Prospect Hill

The front porch of Prospect Hill near Charlottesville.

tryside and warm hospitality of the Blue Ridge's bed and breakfast inns are the perfect remedy for the headaches of modern living.

Reservation Services

The following services are available to assist you in selecting a bed and breakfast or country inn and making reservations. Most inns have similar price ranges of between $50 and $100 dollars per night.

BED & BREAKFAST
ASSOCIATION OF VIRGINIA
P.O. Box 791
Orange 22960   (703) 721-3951
BLUE RIDGE BED & BREAKFAST
Rt. 2, Box 3895
Berryville 22611   (703) 955-1246
GUEST HOUSE BED & BREAKFAST
Charlottesville   (804) 979-7264
PRINCELY BED & BREAKFAST INC.
Alexandria   (703) 683-2159
SHENANDOAH VALLEY
BED & BREAKFAST RESERVATIONS
P.O. Box 634
Woodstock 22664   (703) 459-8241
SHENANDOAH VALLEY
LODGING SERVICES
Rt. 3, Box 119F
Luray 22835   (703) 743-2936

Shenandoah Valley Region

Woodstock

COUNTRY FARE
402 Main St.   (703) 459-4828

You'll travel the historic Lee Highway (Route 11) to find this small-town bed and breakfast inn.

A half acre of glorious magnolia, boxwoods and Japanese cherry trees encircle the home. Proprietor Bette Hallgren greets the road-weary traveler at the door with soothing, old-fashioned hospitality, inviting you into a home that exudes Old Country charm and history. Country Fare was built in the late 18th century; a section was added in 1840. From 1861 to 1864, the building served as a hospital. An old log cabin, the original dwelling, was an auction house for years. The house has been restored and is now as beautiful as ever.

The three guest rooms are furnished with antiques and country collectibles. Each has been hand-stenciled in original designs. The master bedroom has a private shower, another room has twin beds and a Boston rocker, and the double room has its own fireplace. A continental breakfast is served each day. Sit by the inviting fire in the common room and eat homemade breads, or have your coffee on the brick patio.

After breakfast, take a walk into the village of Woodstock to explore the town's history. George Washington presented the town's charter to the Virginia House of Burgesses on March 31, 1761. The 8th Regiment emanated from Woodstock during the Revolutionary War. The courthouse, designed by Thomas Jefferson in 1792, is the oldest building of its kind still in use west of the Blue Ridge Mountains. There are also attractions of natural beauty, such as Shenandoah National Park, Skyline Drive, Luray Caverns and various vineyards. Visit

Inns to Bed & Breakfasts

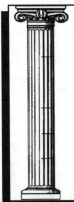

New Market Battlefield, Belle Grove Plantation and Wayside Theater. Seasonal activities include the Shenandoah Music Festival and the Shenandoah County Fair each summer. A deposit is required with reservations.

THE INN AT NARROW PASSAGE
I-81 and U.S. Hwy. 11 S.   (703) 459-8000

This log inn overlooking the Shenandoah River has been welcoming and protecting travelers since the 1740s, when it was a haven for settlers against Indian attacks. Later, this historic building would become a stagecoach inn on the Valley Turnpike and headquarters for Stonewall Jackson during the Civil War's Valley Campaign. Travelers today will still find The Inn at Narrow Passage to be an inviting and warm place to relax and revive their energy. Ed and Ellen Markel have taken great care in restoring this landmark to its 18th-century look that entices guests with its charming Early American character.

The interior is decorated with gorgeous antiques and Colonial reproductions. Each bedroom has all of the comforts of home and more. Some rooms have wood-burning fireplaces for a cozy evening. For your comfort, the inn is centrally heated and air conditioned. Join other guests in the Colonial dining room for breakfast in front of a cheery fire. For a calm, soothing day, you can rest by the massive limestone fireplace in the living room or sit on the porch and view the beautiful lawns that slope down to the river. However, there is no lack of activity. Hiking and fishing are options right at the inn itself. Nearby, you'll find historic battlefields, wineries, caverns and skiing at the famous Bryce Resort. The Markels will be happy to suggest a day's activities for you, or you can just sit on the porch and chat as the sun sets across the Valley.

Stanley

JORDAN HOLLOW FARM INN
(703)778-2209, (703)778-2285

Jordan Hollow Farm Inn is a beautifully restored Colonial horse farm that has been converted into a country inn. The farm has 45 acres nestled in a secluded hollow surrounded by the Shenandoah National Park and the George Washington National Forest. Marley and Jetze Beers have personally created the inn and say that, "Jordan Hollow is the kind of place in which we

Inns to *Bed & Breakfasts*

The Inn at the Crossroads

Approx. 12 miles from the Blue Ridge Pkwy and 9 miles from Charlottesville.
Rt. 2 Box 6, North Garden, VA. 22959 (804) 979-6452

Heritage House, Inc.
BED & BREAKFAST

Main Street • P.O. Box 427 • Washington, Virginia • 22747
Telephone: (703) 675-3207

most want to live." The buildings, except for Rowe's Lodge, are the original farm buildings, renovated to provide cozy but modern facilities. There is an overall family farm environment that is nurtured by the Beers. The property is a blend of rolling hills, lush meadows and fragrant woods.

In the spring and early summer, foals and kittens can be seen soaking up the sunshine and frolicking in the fields. The sun deck surrounding Rowe's Lodge is perfect for overseeing all of the farm's activities. This lodge was named for Rowe Baldwin, a relative who came to help for a few weeks and has been there ever since! There are 16 beautiful guest rooms, decorated with country antiques and artifacts. All have private baths and some have fireplaces and Jacuzzis. You'll enjoy meals in the Colonial farmhouse four dining rooms (two 200-year-old log cabin rooms and the 100-year-old Fox and African ones).

The food is described as "country cosmopolitan," and it is outstanding. The flavor is good old home cooking with a bit of French flair and a unique touch of African and Mideastern seasonings. There is a large selection of dishes, including quail, chicken, veal, steak, fish and pasta. You'll also enjoy homebaked bread, a garden salad and fresh vegetables. Top off your meals with tasty desserts and a fine selection of wines and beers.

For indoor entertainment, visit the library, cable TV lounge and pub named The Watering Trough that was originally a stable. There is live entertainment on Friday and Saturday nights, and you may find yourself challenged to a game of pool or chess by Jetze. A stable on the property can accommodate riding for the beginner or expert, as well as pony rides for children younger than 8. Other nearby activities include swimming, hiking, canoeing, fishing, skiing, museums, antiques and craft shops. The farm is a short drive from Lake Arrowhead, Luray Caverns, Shenandoah National Park and George Washington National Forest. Room reservations must be guaranteed by the equivalent of one night's stay. Limited boarding facilities are available for pets. You need to let them know if you are bringing children prior to making your reservations.

Harrisonburg

JOSHUA WILTON HOUSE
412 S. Main St.   (703) 434-4464

Roberta and Craig Moore will welcome you to the Joshua Wilton House in historic Harrisonburg. Their inn is located in an elegantly restored Victorian home right in the heart of the Shenandoah Valley. Restoration efforts have preserved much of the original architecture.

The Moores will spoil you with complimentary wine and cheese, and their gourmet breakfast, including homemade pastries, fresh fruits and a delicious pot of coffee, is enough to summon anyone out of bed in the morning. The bedrooms are furnished with period antiques to give them the charm of the 1880s. You can choose from three dining

Inns to Bed & Breakfasts

rooms, a sun room or an outdoor terrace and dine on food that is famous across the Shenandoah Valley. All five of the bedrooms have private baths and reading areas.

The Wilton House is within walking distance of James Madison University and fascinating downtown Harrisonburg. There is also a variety of athletic activities, such as golfing, biking, hiking, swimming and skiing, accessible from the inn. This old mansion is "an oasis of quiet charm and gracious living," as its brochure indicates, surrounded by the Blue Ridge Mountains.

Penn Laird

HEARTH N' HOLLY INN

Rt. 33   *(703) 434-6766*

After a day of skiing or sightseeing, you'll love coming back to this gracious old inn, ideally located midway between Massanutten Ski Resort and James Madison University, both just 10 minutes away. Innkeepers Doris and Dennis Brown have provided for your every comfort, with amenities that will make your stay memorable. The inn, a combination of Colonial and Victorian styles, is situated on 15 acres that offer magnificent views of Massanutten Mountain.

Relax away the morning in the sunroom, where the scent of fresh flowers and aroma of fresh-brewed continental coffee are irresistible. Breakfast sittings are at 7 AM and 9 AM. Afterwards, take a stroll up the country lane and into the wooded areas — all on the Hearth N' Holly grounds — where the fresh country air and tranquil surroundings are soothing to the senses.

Nearby, you can enjoy the theater, arts and sports events at JMU, or spend your time at Massanutten Four Seasons Resort (a great place to golf or ski). For more gorgeous scenery, take the Skyline Drive and Blue Ridge Parkway, or recall the area's rich history at New Market Battlefields, where occasional Civil War re-enactments are big draws. And the caverns are a must-see! Endless, Grand and Luray caverns are all easy drives and a cool way to spend a hot summer day.

The Inn has three guest rooms, all with queen-sized brass beds and charming decor. One has a private bath, and the others share a bath. Each room as a special fireplace for those chilly evenings. Rates range from $65 to $75 per night, breakfast included.

One night's deposit is required to hold a reservation. Sorry, pets are not allowed, and the Inn is a nonsmoking establishment. The Inn is located off I-81, Exit 247A, about five miles east on Route 33.

Staunton

ASHTON COUNTRY HOUSE

1205 Middlebrook Ave.   *(703) 885-6819*
(800) 296-7819

With 24 beautiful acres surrounding this country retreat, it's hard to believe that the center of town is a mere mile away. A c. 1860 Greek Revival manor house, Ashton has been owned since 1991 by Sheila Kennedy and her husband, Stanley Polanski, a professional jazz pia-

Inns to Bed & Breakfasts

The Hummingbird Inn

circa 1853

P.O Box 147 • Goshen, VA 24439
Phone: (703) 997-9065 or (800) 397-3214

hearth 'n

HOLLY
INN

Rt. 2 Box 325, Penn Laird, VA 22846
(703) 434-6766

Make Your Trip Perfect!

Visit one of these great

Blue Ridge

Bed and Breakfasts!

nist. The 40-foot center hall hints at the manor-house stylings you'll find throughout, including the rosewood grand piano. No detail is overlooked in their guests' comfort, including flannel sheets in the winter and cool cotton chambray in the summer — plus four plump pillows. Ah, luxury!

A generous breakfast includes scones, scrambled eggs, hash browns . . . all the comfort foods of home prepared with a professional touch by Sheila, a graduate of the New York Restaurant School. Three porches overlook the expansive grounds, populated by several dogs, numerous cats and a pair of genteel goats. Lovely English country-style furnishings, immaculate housekeeping and gracious common rooms enhance your stay. Four double guest rooms and one suite are available, all with private bath or shower (or both). Four of the rooms have a fireplace and one features a balcony.

The inn can accommodate children 16 and older, and will accept pets only in certain situations. Rates range from $85 for the suite to $70 for a single. Credit cards are not accepted. Wheelchair access and a specially equipped bathroom are available.

The inn is open year round.

BELLE GRAE INN

515 W. Frederick St.   (703) 886-5151

This authentically restored 17-room inn built in 1870 will please you with its luxurious rooms and appetizing menu. It is named for two of the surrounding mountains,

Betsy Belle and Mary Grae. The Scotch-Irish settlers in the area, reminded of their homeland, named the mountains for Scottish landmarks. Belle Grae sits atop a hill in the historic town of Staunton. Wicker rockers invite relaxation on the veranda; white gingerbread decorates the porch of the main, original building. You will be mesmerized by the four stained glass panels in the double entrance door — engraved inside a crystal oval is the inn's name. Period reproductions and antiques, which are for sale, are found throughout the dining rooms, bistro, lounge and other lovely rooms. The bedrooms are each furnished a little differently, but all fit the period. You can sit in front of your cozy fireplace and sip complimentary sherry from long-stemmed glasses. Many of the rooms have private baths, with such amenities as English herb soap, shampoo, moisturizer, toothbrush and herb bath foam. The annex features rooms furnished for corporate clientele. They feature desks, dressing rooms, phones, queen-sized beds and color televisions.

The popular chef at this fine establishment will get you going for a day of business or sightseeing with his delicious, full American breakfast. Or, if you prefer to relax, a continental breakfast and newspaper will be delivered to your room. Private parties and weekend dining get a special flair from live entertainment and candlelight meals. An extensive dinner menu will keep even the most refined palate happy. Select from cream of asparagus soup, charcoaled sword-

Inns to Bed & Breakfasts

fish, tenderloin of beef covered with backfin crab or bourbon carrots. Homemade breads and desserts, such as Amaretto mousse, chocolate peanut butter pie or smudge pie, complete the meal.

Activities in the area include walking tours through gorgeous historic Staunton, shopping at a gigantic antique warehouse or chess and backgammon in the quiet of the inn's sitting room.

FREDERICK HOUSE

Frederick and New Sts. (703) 885-4220

Three stately old townhouses were rescued from demolition, to be transformed into Frederick House. These Greek Revival buildings have been restored and the rooms inside graciously appointed with antiques and paintings by Virginia artists. The oversized beds add an extra touch of comfort. Each of the 14 rooms and suites has its own private bath, cable TV, telephone, radio, air conditioning and private entrance. A full, delicious home-cooked breakfast is served each morning in Chumley's Tea Room.

One activity we recommend is a relaxing stroll through the town to photograph Staunton's gorgeous architecture. Woodrow Wilson's birthplace is only two blocks away, and Mary Baldwin College is right up the street. Cycling, hiking and touring are perfect activities for the surrounding Blue Ridge and Allegheny mountains. Hosts Joe and Evy Harman will point out places of interest and provide a bit of history as well. Ask the Harmans to help you plan a day on the town to suit your curiosity and show the great beauty of this fair city.

KENWOOD

235 E. Beverley St. (703) 886-0524

Kenwood, a beautifully restored turn-of-the-century Colonial Revival home, is located in the historic section, next door to the Woodrow Wilson Museum and Birthplace and within walking distance of Staunton's finest restaurants and shops. Filled with period furniture and antiques, the bed and breakfast inn offers comfortable accommodations in a relaxed atmosphere. A full Shenandoah Valley breakfast is included with your stay.

Guests have their choice of four upstairs bedrooms. Two have queen-sized beds and private baths. The other two are great for families. One has a queen-sized bed, and the other has a twin bed and double bed. These two rooms have an interconnecting bath.

Your hosts, Liz and Ed Kennedy, can suggest many ways to spend your days in the area, many within a short walk or drive of the inn. Take the Staunton Walking Tour, visit Mary Baldwin College and Stuart Hall and see the exhibits at the Museum of American Frontier Culture and the Statler Brothers' Museum. Stroll along picturesque East Beverley to see the antique shops or have a gourmet meal. Wintergreen Resort, Harrisonburg, Lexington and Charlottesville are about 30 minutes away, and Skyline Drive and Blue Ridge Parkway are only 15 minutes away.

Inns to *Bed & Breakfasts*

THE SAMPSON EAGON INN
238 E. Beverley St.

(703) 886-8200
(800) 597-9722

This elegant inn is located in the historic Gospel Hill section of Staunton, adjacent to the Woodrow Wilson Birthplace and Mary Baldwin College. The property's original owner, Sampson Eagon, was a Methodist preacher who actually held services on the grounds here during the 1790s.

Don't expect any preaching today, however: The inn is tailor-made for privacy, with five distinctive guest rooms, each furnished with beautiful period pieces, a queen-sized canopied bed, cozy sitting area and modern bath. Private TVs with VCRs are also standard in the rooms, and the inn even has a fax machine, just in case you can't get away from the office completely. In the morning, enjoy a full gourmet breakfast in the formal dining room (although the accent is on casual), where you'll be greeted with such entrees as pecan Belgian waffles, Grand Marnier souffle pancakes and an array of egg dishes.

Last year, *Country Inns Magazine* calls the Sampson Eagon Inn one of America's "Best Inn Buys," and *Gourmet* magazine writes that proprietors Frank and Laura Mattingly "take the second 'B' in B&B seriously." This indeed is a memorable retreat in a unforgettably historic setting.

THORNROSE HOUSE
531 Thornrose Ave.   (703) 885-7026

Otis and Suzanne Huston are the innkeepers at this beautiful bed and breakfast inn in the heart of Staunton's historic Gypsy Hill area. The moment you step into the grand entranceway, you will begin to discover the charm of this Georgian Revival brick home. The Huston's have redecorated the entire house since they moved into the home, expanding to five lovely guest rooms, each with its own private bath.

After a good night's sleep, you'll love waking up to the smell of a hearty breakfast. After you've satisfied your tastebuds, it's time to venture out and see the sites that make Staunton so special. Nearby attractions include the P. Buckley Moss Museum, Monticello, Grand Caverns and the Museum of American Frontier Culture. Across the street is the 300-acre Gypsy Hill Park, where you can play golf, tennis (rackets and balls provided) or swim. Watch for the mama duck and her ducklings as they waddle from their nest under a shade tree in the front yard of Thornrose to the park, where they might meet up with a peacock, swan or even some deer. Thornrose House also has beautiful gardens gracing its one-acre grounds. The wraparound veranda with rocking chairs is perfect for a lazy chat in the company of fellow rockers. And the sitting room, with its fireplace and grand piano, is inviting. Thornrose House is a magnificent place to stay while visiting this town.

Rates range from $55 to $75, and one night's deposit is required to confirm reservations. School-aged children are welcome. Regret-

Inns to *Bed & Breakfasts*

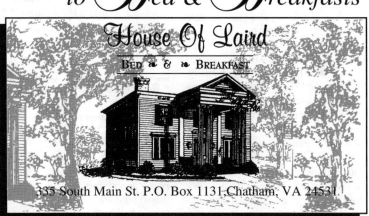

House Of Laird
BED & BREAKFAST

335 South Main St. P.O. Box 1131 Chatham, VA 24531

THE
ASHBY INN
& RESTAURANT

One of the "20 best inns in North America" — *The Washington Post,* in 1993. Ten guest rooms reflect their early heritage. A first-rate restaurant — featured *Gourmet* magazine— whose daily menus is guided more by tradition than trend. Gravlaks of salmon. Jumbo lump crabcakes. Duck with turnips. Goose and oyster gumbo.

John and Roma Sherman, Innkeepers • Route 1/Box 2A, Paris, VA 22130 • 703/592-3900

Looking Glass House
Bed and Breakfast
circa 1848

A gracious
English country
Farmhouse

VA Highway 151 Rt. 3, Bx. 138 Afton, VA. 22920-9407
(800) 769-6844/(703) 456-6844

tably, no provisions for pets are available.

Swoope

LAMBSGATE

Rts. 254 and 833   *(703) 337-6929*

A restored 1816 vernacular farmhouse located six miles west of Staunton invites you to a comfortable, cozy lodging, a bountiful Southern breakfast and spectacular mountain views. Dan and Elizabeth Fannon invite you to relax in their home on the Middle River, surrounded by seven pastoral acres — a working sheep farm. You can hike or bike the back roads or watch the day-to-day activities of life on a farm. Children are welcome, and they would especially enjoy the animals and a garden behind the house that grows everything from spices to grapes. Fishing fans can set out for the nearby river (poles provided).

Or just relax on the porch swing and enjoy the scenery.

A delicious breakfast, often featuring Dan's bran muffins and homemade peach and strawberry preserves, gets the day off on the right foot. Breakfast orders are taken the evening before; the daily newspaper and plenty of coffee greet guests at the day's first light. Wooden floors, solid furniture and warm quilts handmade by Mrs. Fannon, as well as the sheepskin rugs at your bedside, are touches of the "coming home" feeling the home is well-known for.

Lambsgate is open all year, offering three double guest rooms, with a maximum of six sharing a bath. Smoking is not permitted and no credit cards are accepted. A double room is $48, a single $37, including tax and service. An extra child is $10 more, and a crib is provided.

Rockbridge and Lexington

BRIERLEY HILL

Borden Rd.
Lexington   *(703) 464-8421*

This bed and breakfast inn opened in October 1993 and is already receiving return visits by guests who rave about the wonderful food and beautiful accommodations — not to mention the breathtaking views from the large veranda. Situated on eight acres of hillside farmland, the inn is quiet and romantic, and the hospitality is second to none. Owners Barry and Carole Speton enjoy the finer things in life and want to share them with their guests. Barry is a former lawyer and is interested in antique books, prints and furniture. Carole is the former director of the Canadian Figure Skating Association. She enjoys gardening, quilting and cooking.

The inn is decorated entirely with Laura Ashley wall coverings, fabrics and linens. There are five guest rooms available, all with elegant beds (four canopy beds and an antique brass bed), private bathrooms and sitting areas. The Deluxe King Room has an additional day bed, fireplace and TV. The inn is fully air conditioned and a cozy fireplace in the dining and living rooms warms the winter chill.

Photo: Richmond Newspapers

A view from the Skyline Drive.

A full country breakfast is served each morning between 8 and 9:30 AM. You can dine on Grand Marnier French toast, buckwheat banana pancakes, French scrambled eggs with cream cheese and herbs, eggs Benedict and Belgian waffles with strawberries and sour cream. Also included is juice, fresh fruit and ham, bacon or sausage. Afternoon tea is served from 3 to 5 PM with homemade cakes, breads, scones and cookies. Advance notice is required for dinner and it is worth it! Fresh herbs and vegetables from the garden are featured. Choose from entrees like boneless salmon steak with red wine and mushroom sauce, rib eye roast with herbs and red wine sauce and spicy stuffed chicken breast with sundried tomatoes.

You can relax in the serenity at Brierley Hill by lounging on the veranda or strolling down a country road. If you're up for a little more adventure, you can go sightseeing in historic Lexington. Special packages are offered for theater, horseback riding, winter getaways and specials for mid-week stays. Reservations must be secured by a deposit equal to one night's lodging. They accept all major credit cards and personal checks. Children over 14 years of age are welcome. Smoking is restricted to the veranda or garden. No pets are allowed.

THE KEEP BED AND BREAKFAST
116 Lee Ave.
Lexington   *(703) 463-3560*

This bed and breakfast inn sits on a quiet corner in the heart of Lexington's historic residential district. Owners Bea and John Stuart opened the gorgeous Victorian home to guests a few years ago, offering two suites and a double-

The Looking Glass House in Afton.

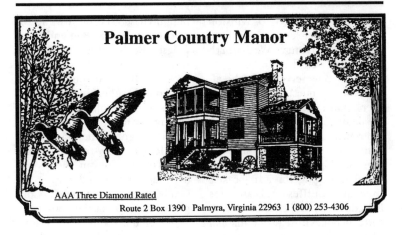

Palmer Country Manor

AAA Three Diamond Rated

Route 2 Box 1390   Palmyra, Virginia 22963 1 (800) 253-4306

bedded room, all with private baths. Don't expect a lot of frou-frou here; the decor is elegant and understated. The Stuarts put on a lavish breakfast, complete with linens on the table, and also serve dinner upon request. At tea time, the owners are always happy to share tea, coffee or sherry with their guests. "We like to spoil nice people," says Bea Stuart.

Summertime travelers to Lexington will be grateful for the central air conditioning at The Keep, which is a short walk from museums and shops in downtown Lexington. The inn does not allow children younger than 12 but does welcome small, well-behaved pets on a request basis. Rates are $75 a night for the double room and $100 for the suite.

THE INN AT UNION RUN

Rt. 674, Lexington   (703) 463-9715
A friendly, down-to-earth couple,

Roger and Jeanette Serens opened their inn just a few years ago and have won rave reviews for the service and enticing cuisine they offer. The inn is situated on roughly 12 acres about four miles from town and is bordered by a bird sanctuary. Union Run Creek, named for the Union Army that camped on the grounds in June of 1963, winds through the property. The Federal-style home was built in 1885. There an adjacent carriage house with four rooms, all with private baths. The main house has a small dining area, living room and den for guests downstairs and three rooms with private porches upstairs. Two of those rooms are equipped with Jacuzzis. American and Victorian antiques fill the rooms in both the carriage house and the main building. Other interesting collectibles include an array of Toby mugs dating from 1755, a walnut desk that belonged to Winston Churchhill, Meissen porcelain figurines and Henry Wadsworth Longfellow's clock.

The Serens serve tea in the afternoon, if requested, and wine or beer upon arrival. A full gourmet breakfast features such specialties as French toast made with English muffins and topped with fresh strawberries, whipped cream and powdered sugar, gingerbread pancakes, specialty souffles and an eggs Benedict-type of dish with spinach and artichokes instead of Canadian bacon. They also offer gourmet meals to guests and the public in a romantic dining room. For more details, refer to our Restaurants chapter.

Rates are $85 a night for a room with a Jacuzzi and $75 a night for all other rooms. The Serens offer special packages for guests who want to combine their stay with fox hunting, horseback riding or a trip to see a play or concert at the outdoor Lime Kiln Theater nearby.

SEVEN HILLS INN

408 S. Main St.

Lexington   (703) 463-4715

This inn's seven guest rooms are named after the seven historic estates in Rockbridge County that are connected to the Grigsby family who settled here in the 1700s. The estates themselves are as magnificent as any plantation home to be found in Virginia, and the Seven Hills Inn reflects this grandeur. It's a southern Colonial-style home that was actually built by a Washington & Lee fraternity in 1928. It passed through several hands before be-

ing purchased several years ago by its current owners, Ben and Carol Grigsby. Ben's mother, Jane Daniel, is the executive innkeeper.

All of the guest rooms are furnished with either the family's antiques or with 18th- or early 19th-century hand-crafted reproductions. A gorgeous handmade needlepoint rug from Portugal graces the living room, and decorative items purchased during the family's trips to the Orient are displayed throughout the house.

All of the rooms have private baths except for Liberty Hill and Cherry Hill, which share an enormous connecting bathroom. Those rooms are often used as a suite by families. Speaking of families, the inn welcomes well-behaved children. Rates are from $75 to $95, depending upon the size of the room. Rates are based on double occupancy; a third person costs an extra $15. Included in the cost are a deluxe continental breakfast and afternoon tea, upon request. Guests can watch television, read or play games in the Chapter Room in the basement where the fraternity used to hold its meetings.

LLEWELLYN LODGE AT LEXINGTON

603 S. Main St.

Lexington   (703) 463-3235
                         (800) 882-1145

This charming 53-year-old brick Colonial home is located in the heart of Lexington, within walking distance of all the city's historic sights. Ellen and John Roberts are your hosts at this lovely home. She's a gourmet cook who has been a part of the airline, travel, hotel and restaurant industries. John is a Lexingtonian who will be happy to share his knowledge of the surrounding area.

The friendly atmosphere is noticeable from the start as you are met at the front door with refreshments. The comfortable living room has a large fireplace — a perfect setting for good conversation. There is a separate television and telephone room. And, for your comfort, the lodge is air-conditioned the summer. The six bedrooms are distinctly different from one another and designed to meet the needs of a wide variety of guests. All have extra-firm beds, ceiling fans and private bathrooms. Room 1 has a pencil post queen-sized bed; the bath has a tub/shower. Room 2 has wicker furniture, a queen-sized bed and stall shower. Room 3 has an oak spindle queen-sized bed, easy chair and stall shower. Room 4 has a king-sized bed, sitting area, television and tub/shower. Room 5 has two brass double beds and a stall shower (great for a family). And Room 6 has two four-poster twin beds and a tub/shower. This last room is located on the first floor and can accommodate handicapped persons who do not require a wheelchair.

A gourmet breakfast awaits you each morning. You can feast on fantastic omelets, Belgian waffles, French toast, Virginia maple syrup, homemade muffins and breads, bacon, sausage, ham, juice, coffee and teas. After breakfast, take on the great outdoors! There is hiking on the Chessie Trail, bicycle riding, canoeing on the Maury River, tubing at Goshen Pass and golf and tennis at Lexington Golf and Country Club. (You might even find that John is willing to share his "secret" fishing spots with you.) In the summer, you can visit the drive-in movie theater or the Lime Kiln Arts Center, featuring regional historical dramas and concerts.

Rates range from $70 to $85 and include breakfast. A one night's deposit is required to hold a reservation. Smoking in the guest rooms or dining room is not permitted, nor are pets of any kind. The Lodge is designed with adults in mind, although children age 10 and older are welcome.

FASSIFERN

Rt. 39, Lexington (703) 463-1013

Visitors to the Virginia Horse Center pass right by Fassifern. It's a place of striking beauty: tall weeping willows surround a small pond, and bright flowers abound when the weather is warm.

Fassifern is situated on 3½ acres, just across the road from the Art

Farm, a gallery with summer workshops that teach the traditional methods of Chinese painting. On the other side of the Art Farm is the Horse Center.

This bed and breakfast inn's main building is a beautiful old home, built in 1867. There's also the "dependency," which used to be an ice house and servants' living quarters and now houses two guest rooms.

Owners Ann Carol and Arthur Perry assumed ownership of Fassifern in July, 1989, and they live on the property in their own separate quarters. Guests need not feel they must tiptoe around someone's private home, because this house is set up for guests and their needs. The guest living room is elegant but cozy, furnished with an old pump organ and piano, a stuffed leather chair and sofa and lots of magazines and books.

The beautifully decorated dining room is the setting for a hearty continental breakfast that includes freshly squeezed orange juice, homemade granola, fresh fruit, croissants and other breads, country ham spread and hot chocolate, coffee and tea.

All five guest rooms are air-conditioned and have private baths. The Austrian Room is furnished with gorgeous European antiques, while the Country Room is more casual, with golden oak furniture and bright reddish print wallpaper. The three other rooms are also beautifully furnished and appear to be very comfortable. There are two other private sitting areas in the house besides the living room.

Rates range from $79 to $87, which include breakfast. Children ages 8 and older are welcome. The owners recommend calling as far in advance as possible to make reservations.

THE HUMMINGBIRD INN
Wood Lane off Alt. 39
Goshen   (703) 997-9065

This unique Victorian villa has operated on and off as an inn since it was built in 1853. Its new owners, Jeremy and Diana Robinson, opened it again last spring to overnight guests and have done a beautiful job redesigning the interior. Its four guest rooms, furnished with antiques, are colorful and spacious and all have private baths. Full breakfasts include country bacon or sausage, homemade bread and foods unique to the area. There are wraparound verandas on the first and second floors, original pine floors of varying width and a rustic den, solarium and music room.

During Goshen's boom days in the late 1800s and early 1900s, the inn was directly across from the town's railroad station, and the steps from the tracks to the inn's private road are still in place. Trains still roll through several times a week, but never at night to disturb guests' sleep.

In the 1930s, the inn played host to Eleanor Roosevelt (one of the rooms is named after her) and Ephraim Zimbalist Sr., among other notables.

A wide trout stream defines one of the property lines, and only five minutes away is the gorgeous Goshen Pass, a popular spot for

200
South Street
A VIRGINIA INN

Charlottesville, Virginia 22902
804-979-0200
800-964-7008

kayaking, picnicking and sunbathing in warm weather. This place is not to be missed when the rhododendron are in bloom!

Guests can also enjoy a relaxing float in inner tubes along Mill Creek, which flows behind the inn. Historic Lexington is only 20 minutes away, offering fine restaurants and shops, the Virginia Horse Center, George Marshall Museum, Stonewall Jackson House and Cemetery and other historic sites.

The Robinsons offer a prix-fixé four-course dinner for $25. Among their varied specialties are chicken with wild mushrooms, salmon filet with dill sauce and rabbit a la Diana. Rates are between $60 and $75 November through March and $70 to $95 April through October. All include the sumptuous breakfast.

LAVENDER HILL FARM

Rt. 631, Lexington   (703) 464-5877
                      (800) 446-4240

Cindy and Colin Smith have re-

stored a 200-year-old farmhouse on about 20 acres of beautiful land a few miles outside Lexington. The house is situated on the banks of Kerrs Creek and has three light, airy guest rooms with private baths. One of the queen-sized rooms can be rented as a suite; it connects to a second room with a double bed.

What makes this bed and breakfast inn unique is the chance it offers to combine an overnight stay with horseback trips led by Virginia Mountain Outfitters. Packages are offered for riders of all levels of experience and are focused around such activities as trail rides and riding workshops.

The inn was designed with animal lovers in mind. Sheep, cows and friendly Nubian goats roam over the land that surrounds the farmhouse, and a border collie and cat stay close by.

Colin Smith is a gourmet chef who loves to cook with fresh herbs that are grown on the farm. In fact, his first book on cooking with herbs is scheduled to be out soon. Four-course dinners cost $20 per person and are optional. A sample menu: cream of black and white mushroom soup, a Greek salad, an entree of boneless loin of pork with green peppercorn sauce and a chocolate raspberry tart for dessert.

Rates for two at the farm range from $60 to $70 per night, which include a full country breakfast.

The Horse Lovers Holiday package costs from $225 to $245 per person, based on double occupancy, and includes a two-night stay, breakfast, dinner and picnic lunches both days, along with the use of horses, tours and all instruction.

Special theater packages are offered during the summer months, when the local Lime Kiln Theater puts on its outdoor plays and Sunday night concerts. The Smiths will purchase tickets and pack a gourmet picnic dinner to take along to Lime Kiln, where the bucolic grounds are conducive to sipping wine and feasting.

The Smiths don't allow pets or smoking inside the house. But, quips Cindy, they do welcome children accompanied by "well-behaved adults."

Waynesboro

THE IRIS INN
191 Chinquapin Dr.   *(703) 943-1991*

The charm and grace of Southern living in a totally modern facility, nestled in a wooded tract on the western slope of the Blue Ridge . . .

that's what will welcome you when you arrive at the Iris Inn. This architecturally interesting brick-and-cedar inn was built in 1991 and is ideal for a weekend retreat, business accommodation or tranquil spot for the tourist. Its focus is on comfort and the casual elegance of a contemporary home, further highlighted by spacious guest rooms in nature and wildlife motifs, each with private bath.

The main building has six guest rooms, each furnished with 18th-century reproductions, family pieces and antiques. Some of the many room themes are Deer Room, Wildflower Room, Pine Room, Bird Room and Duck Pond. The bright and airy rooms all have king- or queen-sized beds (some have a day bed for a third person). One room is equipped for the handicapped. A seventh guest room — the Hawk's Nest — is an efficiency unit, complete with kitchenette and sitting area, ideal for longer stays and a favorite of honeymooners.

The Great Room, in addition to being the breakfast room, provides a gathering place around the high stone fireplace where guests may relax and enjoy the woodland views. Beverages are available at the check-in, and the "bottomless" cookie jar is located on the sideboard. A balcony library overlooks this beautiful room, providing panoramic views of the Shenandoah Valley. Wraparound porches on both floors and a three-story lookout tower (a hot tub is on its first floor!) are popular with guests.

A full breakfast is served at 8:30 AM and includes homebaked

Prospect Hill
ca. 1732

The *Virginia Plantation Inn*
ca. 1732

The Sheehan Family Innkeepers • *Telephone* (800) 277-0844

breads, juice and fruit, fresh-brewed coffee and an entree that changes daily. After this hearty meal, travel to nearby sites and attractions, including Waynesboro's Virginia Metalcrafters and P. Buckley Moss Museum, the historic Monticello and Ash Lawn near Charlottesville, and Skyline Drive, Blue Ridge Parkway and the Appalachian Trail.

Rates range from $75 to $95; corporate rates are available, with meeting space for 10 to 12. Reservations are confirmed by phone with Mastercard or VISA or by receipt of check. Children can be accommodated by special arrangement only; there are no facilities for pets. Smoking is not permitted.

Roanoke and Salem

THE MARY BLADON HOUSE
381 Washington Ave. S.W.
Roanoke   *(703) 344-5361*
This 1890s Victorian home is nestled in the heart of the Old South-

west neighborhood in Roanoke. Bill and Sheri Bestpitch want The Mary Bladon House to be your home away from home as you explore the beautiful Roanoke Valley. The Rococo Revival, Renaissance Revival and Eastlake-style furnishings, antique English china, original brass light fixtures and even the Victorian playing cards on the writing table in the parlor combine to recapture the charm of "a time when elegant comfort was a way of life," say the Bestpitches. Guests will feel the spirit of the Victorian age while relaxing in the rocker in their room or on the swing on the wraparound front porch.

The guest rooms are decorated with crafts and period antiques. Families travelling with children are welcome in the roomy suite. For your comfort, modern conveniences, such as air conditioning and a 24-hour telephone answering service, are provided.

A delicious breakfast will help

you start your day. The meal features the cook's choice of eggs, pancakes, waffles or French toast served with bacon, ham or sausage. Home fries, hot and cold cereals, juice, coffee and tea are also available. With advance notice, the cook will be happy to accommodate special dietary requests.

Afterwards, spend the day in downtown Roanoke. Visit the restored Farmers' Market and Center in the Square, an arts and entertainment mecca. The home is also only five minutes from the Blue Ridge Parkway. You'll also find easy access to Natural Bridge, Dixie Caverns, Mabry Mill, Smith Mountain Lake, Peaks of Otter and more! After a busy morning, return to the inn for afternoon tea, served from 4 to 6 PM. And, with advance reservations, you can savor a terrific dinner in the dining room.

Pets cannot be accommodated. Smoking is permitted on the verandas only. Rates range from $62 to $130, and a deposit is required. Long-term and business rates are also available.

THE INN AT BURWELL PLACE
601 W. Main St.,
Salem (703) 387-0250

Michel Spence Robertson is the innkeeper of this turn-of-the-century mansion at the southern end of the Shenandoah Valley. The magnificent front porch allows for a panoramic view of the Blue Ridge Mountains and the Roanoke Valley. Each of the five bedrooms is decorated with queen-sized beds, period furniture and antiques, and each has a private bath. A large

suite with fireplace and whirlpool is perfect for families with children or for couples desiring privacy and romance.

After a large country breakfast of eggs, French toast or pancakes, fresh fruit, home fries, muffins and more, visit the sights of Salem. The historic downtown area is full of antique shops. Roanoke College and Salem's Farmers' Market are within walking distance. A short drive away are Dixie Caverns, the Blue Ridge Parkway, Mabry Mill, Peaks of Otter, Natural Bridge and historic downtown Roanoke. Return after a day's exploring to afternoon tea on the porch.

Pets are not permitted, and smoking is not allowed inside the inn. One night's deposit is required with reservations.

WALNUTHILL
436 Walnut Ave. S.E.
Roanoke (703) 427-3312

Before coming to Roanoke, innkeeper Alexandra Condron commuted between her homes in Montreal and Florida. During her drives along Interstate 81, she fell in love with Virginia. While staying in Roanoke, Condron saw a huge three-story yellow brick house for sale. She knew that this was where she wanted to settle and open her bed and breakfast inn.

The house, built in 1916, was obviously meant to last, as it was reinforced with steel beams. The front door has windows of leaded glass with beveled panes. The formal living room and foyer are decorated with a blend of American antiques, as well as modern and conti-

nental styles. The family room features a sectional sofa, TV, stereo with classical music and a collection of books. The guest rooms are bright and airy, with queen-sized beds. One room has a contemporary bed with lighted-mirror headboard, a Louis XIV reproduction desk and chair, Victorian lace curtains and a large Persian rug. Another room is furnished with a replica of a French bedroom suite, with a triple dresser, antique tilt-top table, two stuffed rocking chairs and Oriental rugs. The third room is very private and features white wicker furniture, a day-bed and queen-sized bed, sitting area with TV and Aubusson rugs. All rooms have private baths. One of the bathrooms is a converted sun porch that has a wall of windows and a hot tub. Occasionally, Condron will open her apartment to guests when the other rooms are full.

The dining room is decorated

simply but with elegance. A long table covered with a Belgian lace tablecloth seats up to 10 people. The china matches an antique cobalt German chandelier that Condron picked up at an auction. A full gourmet breakfast is served on antique serving dishes by Rosentahl and Meissen. Choose from secret-recipe pancakes, Virginia ham, bacon or sausage, homemade biscuits with sausage gravy or eggs. Also a favorite is Walnuthill's special homemade fig syrup.

After breakfast, the large veranda is a great place to relax, with seating areas for guests, who may also choose to lounge in one of the two hammocks. Or, head for adventure in historic downtown Roanoke. Children are welcome, as are well-behaved pets. No smoking is allowed. Rates are very affordable, ranging from $49 to $59.

East of the Blue Ridge Region

Paris and Hunt Country

ASHBY INN

Rts. 701 and 759   *(703) 592-3998*

Yes, Virginia, there is a Paris in the Piedmont, and it's one of the prettiest villages in the Commonwealth. Adding to the story book charm of this Fauquier County hamlet is the Ashby Inn, a home dating back to the 1820s that now serves as one of the region's finest inns and restaurants. Six well-appointed guest rooms are furnished with Early American pieces, and the four dining rooms range from a rustic pub to a formal room. Testament to the inn's gracious hospitality and fantastic cuisine is the fact that one of its regular customers is neighbor Willard Scott of NBC's "Today Show" fame.

Sperryville and Washington

BLEU ROCK INN

U.S. Hwy. 211
Washington   *(703) 987-3190*

This cozy country inn is situated on 80 rolling acres in Rappahannock County. The gorgeous scenery will have you calling this place home in no time. Lush green meadows, a clear pond and tall shade trees are all surrounded by majestic mountains. There are seven acres of carefully cared for vineyards, where the inn grows grapes for its wine. The farmhouse has been renovated into an inn with

five guest bedrooms, each with private baths. You can enjoy dining fireside in one of the three dining rooms or relax in the lounge. The open-air terrace overlooks the vineyards of Cabernet Sauvignon, Chardonnay and Seyval grapes. At the large pond, you can try your hand at catching bass, catfish and blue gill. Or stroll through the open grazing lands and watch the horses run free. There is plenty of adventure to be found in Rappahannock County. Try skiing, bicycling, canoeing, golfing, hiking and caving. There are also historic sites and wineries for you to tour and explore.

Bernard and Jean Campagne are the owners and operators of Bleu Rock Farm and Inn. Jean, a Master Chef, has been honored with the Medals of Merite Agricole de France, Academie Culinaire de France, Cordon Bleu and Maitre Cuisinier de France. But you won't need his credentials to tell you that the food here is delicious. Breakfast, which is only served to overnight guests, is spectacular. It begins with fresh orange juice and coffee served with hot biscuits, croissants and muffins. Next is a fruit plate, no doubt full of fruit picked from their own orchards. Then the main course is served. It could be an omelet of ham, shiitake mushrooms and cheddar cheese, or Santa Fe French toast served with maple syrup and creme fraiche. Both are accompanied by a spicy pork sausage, made in house, and sauteed apples. This breakfast will really knock your socks off. Their dinners are equally superb.

Photo: The Oaks B&B

The Oaks Bed & Breakfast in Christiansburg.

Children older than 10 years are welcome, but supervision by an adult is requested when they are outdoors near the pond or horses. Pets are not allowed. One night's deposit is required with reservations.

THE INN AT LITTLE WASHINGTON
Middle and Main Sts.   *(703) 675-3800*

If you want to be pampered beyond your wildest dreams and eat food more delicious than you thought possible, then The Inn at Little Washington should certainly be No. 1 on your list. This inn, located in a cozy, quiet town in Rappahannock County, is the only *Mobil Travel Guide* five-star inn in the United States. Its praise has come from far and wide, and it has been written about in *USA Today*, *People* magazine, *The New York Times*, *The San Francisco Chronicle* and *Hemispheres* (United Airline's magazine).

All of that, and there isn't even a sign over the door.

Reinhardt Lynch and Patrick O'Connell are the owners of this heaven on earth. Lynch takes care of the day-to-day operations at the Inn . . . you know, little stuff, such as making sure that the 3,000 requests for Saturday night dinner are narrowed down to 65. O'Connell is the cause for all of the commotion. His culinary masterpieces are the main reason Inn at Little Washington is in business. The dinners are prix-fixé, which means that there's a fixed price no matter what you order. The evening meal consists of cocktails, wine, five to six courses, and after-dinner drinks. Normally, when a restaurant has a fixed price, the cost remains high, but your selection is minimal. Not true at Little Washington. There are 11 entree choices and 15 desserts. Not bad, eh? The only problem is choosing among such devilish delights as peppered tuna and swordfish grilled rare, local rockfish, salmon and sea scallops with a sautee of silver queen corn, and veal medallions with purees of black olives, sundried tomatoes and pesto. Desserts include warm custard bread pudding with Wild Turkey sauce and white chocolate mousse in passion fruit puree. It will make your mouth water just reading about it.

The rest of the Inn should not be shadowed by the success of the restaurant. The consistently excellent service and the luxury of the rooms are certainly entitled to praise. There are only 10 guest rooms, and each is spectacular enough to stand on its own. The rooms are filled with antiques, overstuffed reading chairs and canopied beds and elegantly decorated with faux bois woodwork and draped fabrics. The scent of freshly cut flowers mingles with that of potpourri and drifts across the room. Old-fashioned silhouettes hang on the wall. Colorful pillows form a mountain of comfort on the bed. But do not succumb to them yet. First, soak in a tub of pine-scented bubbles in the marble-and-brass bathroom. Pamper yourself with the heated, fluffy towels, then wrap yourself in the plush white robe and watch the fountain from your balcony. You will pinch yourself to see if you're still awake. The Inn is very popular, so advance registration is a must.

HERITAGE HOUSE

Main St.
Washington   (703) 675-3207

Jean and Frank Scott's elegant inn dates back to 1837 and is said to have been used by Confederate Gen. Jubal Early as a command center during the Civil War. It's located in the heart of "little" Washington, a minute's stroll away from various shops and historic landmarks. The great outdoors are at your back door here, including Shenandoah National Park and Skyline Drive. Not far away are the Rapidan, Rose and Thornton rivers and other well-known trout streams.

Four gracious guest rooms are all air-conditioned and each has a private bath. A gourmet breakfast is served at 9 AM, and is a seated meal, with hot entrees, fruit, home-baked fruit breads, juice and a variety of coffees and teas to start your day. All day long, guests can continue to enjoy the fresh-baked treats and tea, coffee and cocoa in the living room or snacks in their rooms.

The rooms have individual themes. The Suite, for example, allows you to view the magnificent Blue Ridge from its sitting room/ sun porch. It has a queen-sized bed and full bath. You may also choose from the Lace Room, with its blue-flocked wall coverings, crystal lamps and antiques, or the Amish Room, decorated with a simple antique double bed, rag dolls and an original Thomas Palmerton landscape. Charles Dickens' *Old Curiosity Shop* and the city of London create the theme of the British Room, featuring David Winter cottages and castles.

Room reservations are confirmed upon deposit of one night's tariff. Deposits may be made by check, Visa or MasterCard. Accommodations are adults-only, no pets and nonsmoking.

Culpeper

FOUNTAIN HALL BED & BREAKFAST
609 S. East St.   *(703) 825-8200*

George Washington, the first County Surveyor of Culpeper, referred to Culpeper as "a high and pleasant situation." And this bed and breakfast inn in Culpeper County is no exception to that rule. Fountain Hall is built on land with a long and interesting history. It was originally part of a large tract owned by Virginia's Royal Governor, Sir Alexander Spotswood. In 1923, the house was sold to Jackson Lee Fray, founder of the local telephone company. Fray hired an architect to build the Colonial Revival house from the older, Country Victorian structure.

Steve and Kathi Walker are the hosts of the home today. They take special pride in the fact that Fountain Hall became the first bed and breakfast inn in Culpeper. The guest rooms are all elegantly decorated and named, in order to make each truly unique. Rooms range from a single with shared bath to a two-room suite with private bath and porch. All rooms have individual telephones.

Fountain Hall can accommodate board-style meetings or small receptions with equal grace. Pets are not allowed and smoking is permitted in designated areas only. Guests are required to send a deposit of one night's rate.

THE INN AT MEANDER PLANTATION
James Madison Hwy., Rt. 15
Locust Dale   *(703) 672-4912*

Cradled in the heart of

Jefferson's Virginia, The Inn at Meander Plantation offers a rare opportunity to experience the charm and elegance of Colonial living at its best. This historic country estate, built in 1766 by noted Virginian Joshua Fry, allows guests to return to an earlier, more romantic time when hospitality was a matter of pride, and fine living was an art practiced in restful surroundings.

The stately Colonial mansion, sitting majestically on 40 acres of rolling pastures and woods, was converted to a country bed and breakfast inn in 1993. The sun-drenched bedrooms, each with private bath, welcome you with elegance, warmth, romance and comfort. Four-poster queen-size beds piled high with plump pillows beckon you to snuggle beneath down comforters.

Throughout the house, you'll discover plenty of private nooks for reading, writing or quiet contemplation. Guests often gather in the parlor that was often visited by Thomas Jefferson and Gen. Lafayette. A baby grand stands ready for impromptu concerts.

A full country gourmet breakfast is served daily in the formal dining room or under the arched breezeway on sun-warmed mornings. Fresh-baked muffins topped with homemade apple butter or fruit preserves complement tantalizing and creative entrees that vary with the seasons and mood of the morning. Full dinners and take-along picnic baskets can be prepared, with advance notice. The graceful rooms and gardens are available for special events.

Outdoors, white rockers line both levels of the expansive back porches, providing peaceful respites for sipping afternoon tea. Boxwood gardens are dotted with secluded benches and a hammock for spectacular views. Croquet, volleyball, badminton and horseshoes can be played on the lawns, while wildlife and birds abound in surrounding woods and fields. Trail rides and English riding lessons are offered at the stables.

Innkeepers are Suzanne Thomas and Suzie Blanchard; Suzie's husband, Bill; and their daughter, Kelly. Suzanne, a former newspaper writer, continues a dual career in historic preservation and food writing. She writes a weekly food column for 40 newspapers and welcomes a chance to share recipes from her collection of 400 cookbooks. Bob loves sharing his passion for classical music and rehabilitating old houses, while Kelly most often can be found in the stables. Their golden retriever, Honey, and Bojo, the sociable Siamese, offer their own special greetings to guests.

The inn is located in the bend of the scenic Robinson River in Madison County, nine miles south of Culpeper and six miles north of Orange. The best of the countryside is close at hand, including wineries, antique shops and history sites. The inn features a smoke-free environment.

Stanardsville

EDGEWOOD FARM BED & BREAKFAST
Rt. 2   *(804) 985-3782*

A quiet and secluded 130-acre farm at the foothills of the Blue Ridge is the site of this bed and breakfast inn in Greene County. The murmur of nearby streams provides solace for the weary traveler, and the surrounding woods are the perfect place for exploring the natural beauty of the area.

The home itself is a step back in time. Originally built in 1790, the house was doubled in size in the 1860s. Restoration of the glorious old building began in the mid 1980s. The period-decorated bedrooms come complete with fireplaces and private baths. (Bathrooms are furnished with pleasantly scented goat's milk soap, lotion and shampoo made in nearby Charlottesville.) Upon arrival, Norman and Eleanor Schwartz, your hosts at Edgewood Farm, will greet you with refreshments and smiles. Each morning, you will be treated to a big country breakfast, including an unbelievably generous array of homebaked muffins, coffee cakes and other breads, and an exotic fruit compote.

But before you even head downstairs for breakfast, open your door and you'll find an urn of fresh, hot coffee on a beautiful silver service with fresh flowers and linen.

Gardeners and nature lovers alike will love the plant nursery that specializes in herbs and perennials. An abundance of historical and natural attractions are within a 30-mile radius of the farm. Skyline Drive, Monticello, Montpelier, Ash Lawn-Highlands and the University of Virginia are only a few. There are also vineyards and antique and craft shops close by. Special arrangements can be made for meals other than breakfast, so call ahead. A deposit is required with reservations.

Orange County

NORFIELDS FARM BED & BREAKFAST
Gordonsville   *(703) 832-2952*
                                  (703) 832-5939

This is a moderately priced, but perfectly charming and comfortable bed and breakfast inn that's nestled on 500 acres in the foothills of the Blue Ridge. Norfields is in its fourth generation of dairy farming, and the inn dates back to 1850. Green pastures with 250 holstein cows and wildlife make this an especially ideal retreat for city folk. There is a two-bedroom suite downstairs with a private bath that holds an old clawfoot tub. The suite is perfect for a couple with children. A large, sunny living room is available for reading, relaxing or watching television (with cable). It's separated from the dining room by French doors. The kitchen is also quite enticing, with antiques and stenciling. Two more country-style bedrooms are upstairs. All the rooms are air-conditioned.

A complete country breakfast is served every morning, at the guest's convenience. Proprietress Teresa Norton invites her guests to relax on the front porch swing, take a long walk or fish in the well-stocked pond. Whether for business or pleasure, enjoy the quiet seclusion and warm hospitality at Norfields Farm, located 30 minutes from Charlottesville and one hour from Richmond. Rates are $65 to $75, a night based on double occupancy. The cost of a single room is $50. Children are welcome, and so are pets, by prior arrangement. Norfields is a nonsmoking home.

TIVOLI
9171 Tivoli Dr.
Gordonsville   *(703) 832-2225*
(800) 840-2225

Tivoli is a unique three-story 24-room hilltop Victorian mansion in the heart of Virginia's historic and scenic Piedmont region. Framed by its 14 massive Corinthian columns, the house commands views of the Blue Ridge Mountains in the distance and its own surrounding 235-acre working cattle farm. Four carefully restored bedrooms, two with private bath, two with shared bath, and each with its own working fireplace are available for overnight guests. Owners, Phil and Susie Audibert, pride themselves on their easygoing hospitality and their trademark "don't leave hungry" breakfasts, featuring big brown fresh-off-the-farm eggs.

With its ballroom (complete with a Steinway grand piano), 12-foot-high ceilings, state-of-the-art kitchen and antique-filled living and dining rooms, Tivoli also offers ample space for wedding receptions, private parties, small conferences and seminars. Wineries, Civil War battlefields, Monticello, Montpelier, gourmet restaurants, amateur theatre and Shenandoah National Park are all within easy driving distance.

Guests are also encouraged to walk the farm's rolling pastures and miles of wooded trails.

Rates are $75 to $125, and VISA and Mastercard are welcome. Smoking is restricted, and the inn cannot accommodate children younger than 12. One night's deposit is required in advance, with a seven-day cancellation policy for a refund.

HOLLADAY HOUSE
155 W. Main St.
Orange   *(703) 672-4893, (800) 358-4422*

Pete and Phebe Holladay run this friendly bed and breakfast inn in their restored 1830 Federal-style home in downtown Orange. Guest rooms are spacious, comfortable and furnished with antiques. Phebe is an artist, and many of her works decorate the walls, along with an interesting collection of prints by other artists. The living room is an especially inviting place to sit and read.

Fine china and silver are used for breakfast, which is served in the privacy of guests' own rooms. The bountiful breakfasts include juice and coffee or tea, homemade muffins, fresh fruit and a main course, such as eggs and bacon.

There are five rooms and one suite available, and rates range from $75 to $185, including the full breakfast.

The Holladays welcome families with children and are happy to talk to guests about the Orange

County area's many things to see and do.

Holladay House is only a 10-minute drive from James Madison's Montpelier and within easy walking distance of the James Madison Museum. Two wineries, Barboursville and Burnley, are also nearby.

WILLOW GROVE INN

14079 Plantation Way
Orange   *(703) 672-5982*
         (800) WG9-1778

If you want to live and breathe history while you're staying overnight in Orange County, consider this antebellum mansion with formal gardens and sloping lawns.

Willow Grove Inn is listed on the National Register of Historic Places. It was built by the same craftsmen chosen by Thomas Jefferson for work on the University of Virginia.

The mansion, the exterior of which is a prime example of Jefferson's Classical Revival style, fell under siege during the Civil War. You can still see trenches near the manor house, and a cannonball was recently removed from its eaves.

Nestled on 37 acres, the mansion retains its original Colonial atmosphere, carefully preserved by its owners. Fine American and English antiques decorate the manor house, and English boxwood, magnolias and willows grace the lawns.

But don't let this intimidate you. Owners Richard Brown and Angela Mulloy have figured out just how to help their guests wind down and truly enjoy their visit. For example, there is no checkout time — you can sleep until noon and have a full breakfast at 2 or 3 PM, if you like. A newspaper and pot of fresh coffee will be at your door in the morning, along with fresh-baked muffins, if you want something before the hearty breakfast.

Several dining rooms offer distinct atmospheres: Clark's Tavern is dark, cozy and casual, while the Dolley Madison Room is formal and resplendent in delicate china and crystal.

Antique furnishings, wide pine flooring and original fireplace mantels preserve the traditional character of each of the inn's seven bedrooms. You'll also find fresh flowers in the rooms; for extra comfort, your hosts have provided long down pillows and comforters. Coconut milk baths await guests in private bathrooms.

By the way, Chef Warren Volk prepares the most exquisite food you will find in any restaurant for many miles around. This is THE place to dine in Orange County. A pianist and vocalist provide romantic background music many nights.

As with virtually all bed and breakfast inns in the area, rates aren't cheap. They range from $95 to $155, which includes breakfast. But a special deal on Sundays and Thursdays allows guests to enjoy a five-course meal, stay the night and eat breakfast for only $55 per person, plus tax.

SLEEPY HOLLOW FARM

16280 Blue Ridge Tpk.
Gordonsville   *(703) 832-5555*

This is a cozy 18th-century house filled with nooks and crannies and bedrooms that feel like private hideaways. Flower and herb gardens surround the house, and the broader surroundings are woods and rolling fields where cattle graze. Beverley Allison and her daughter, Dorsey Allison-Comer, run the inn, which has been the Allison family home for decades.

The atmosphere here is casual and comfortable. Three dogs and two cats serve as the palace guards, quips Beverley Allison. In their rooms, guests find a welcome basket stocked with Virginia peanuts, fruit and a homemade chocolate chip cookie. If this isn't enough to snack on, a freshly baked cake awaits the hungry at all times in the sitting area. The formal dining room is one of the prettiest you'll find anywhere, and it overlooks the herb garden and distant rolling hills.

All of the rooms have private baths, and one has a working fireplace and whirlpool. A beautiful pond on the grounds can be used for swimming or for fishing for catfish, bass or brim. Ducks and their babies can be seen gliding around the pond much of the year. Speaking of babies, Sleepy Hollow is one of the few bed and breakfast inns in the area that caters to children. A baby crib and playpen are available, and there are two suites that are popular with families.

Rates range from $60 to $95 and include a full country breakfast and afternoon tea, if requested. Private dinners are also offered by prior arrangement. The owners like to hold wine tastings, if there are several guests who stay more than more night.

Another plus at Sleepy Hollow is the late checkout time — 1 PM. Skyline Drive is only a 20-minute drive away, and the Massanutten Ski Resort only 45 minutes away, across the mountain by way of Route 33.

THE SHADOWS
BED AND BREAKFAST INN
14291 Constitution Hwy.
Orange   (703) 672-5057

Barbara and Pat Loffredo are the innkeepers of this restored 1913 stone house. The inn is surrounded by old cedars on 44 acres in Orange County. If you want to relax and forget about the hassles of modern life, stay at the Shadows. You can curl up in front of the large stone fireplace with a cup of hot cider or enjoy a good book from the library. Relish the romance of holding hands on the porch swing and chat with other guests while enjoying the ritual of afternoon tea in the gathering room.

The four artfully decorated guest bedrooms are individually named and creatively appointed, each with its own special charm. In addition, the Loffredos had the good fortune to discover two cottages a few steps away from the house; these, too, have been lovingly restored. The two-room Rocking Horse Cabin is decked in country crafts, while the two-room Cottage, a former cook's quarters, sports it own deck, for a quiet view of the country retreat. The Blue Room has a queen-sized pre-Civil War walnut bed and a day bed. The natural cedar bathroom features a lady's vanity, clawfoot tub and pedestal sink. The Rose Room is full of frills and lace, with a full-sized antique high-back oak bed and a private upper deck. The Peach Room is an Art Deco delight, with twin burled walnut beds and a private hall shower. The Victorian Room, with a full-sized iron and brass bed and ruffled bed and window dressings, has a private hall bathroom with a tub/shower and pedestal sink. A hearty country breakfast is served each morning.

The Shadows is conveniently located near Montpelier, Civil War battlefields and local wineries. Pets are not allowed. Reservations are accepted with one night's deposit.

Charlottesville Area

CLIFTON — THE COUNTRY INN
Va. Rt. 729
Shadwell (804) 971-1800

Clifton is winning rave reviews around the country for its elegance, comfort, wonderful amenities and gourmet dining. So outstanding is this inn that *Country Inns* magazine called it one of the top 12 in the nation. And Judith Martin, Miss Manners herself, listed Clifton as one of her four favorite hotels in the world in her latest book, *Miss Manners Guide to the Turn of the Millennium.* Clifton is an imposing 18th-century manor house with pillared veranda and a clear view to Monticello when the trees are not in bloom.

Clifton was built by Thomas Mann Randolph, husband of Thomas Jefferson's daughter, Martha, on land that once adjoined the Shadwell Plantation, Jefferson's birthplace. It is believed to have been built as an office for Randolph, but it became his home in his later years. Clifton offers overnight guests a gracious escape from the here and now, a chance to slip away to a less hurried Jeffersonian life. At Clifton, decisions become no more demanding than whether to play a few wickets of croquet, read a long-awaited book by the fire, float around the lake on an inner tube or practice a Chopin prelude on the grand piano.

Innkeepers Craig and Donna Hartman set the mood at Clifton with their obvious and genuine affection for people. They will greet you with a willingness to help with luggage, an explanation of all the options for filling your time and even a tour of the house, if there is time. Tea is served at 4 o'clock every afternoon, complete with gourmet teas, fresh fruits and freshly baked treats. Every room has its own fireplace, and they aren't just for show. Firewood is freshly laid in each guest's room in the cool season, ready for the strike of a match. Guests are also warmed by down comforters on each of the antique beds. All the rooms and suites have private baths, as individual and unusual as the rooms themselves. One of the most popular rooms, the Martha Jefferson, features walls, bed hangings and a rug the color of rich vanilla ice cream. The carriage house is a spectacular guest suite featuring a stair railing and other architectural artifacts from the recently dismantled Meriwether Lewis home. This seems especially fitting because Martha and Thomas Randolph's affection for Lewis was such that they named their fourth son after him.

Outside, flower beds surround a manicured croquet court. Down the lawn from the enclosed veranda is a spacious gazebo, and a little farther is a tennis court and lap pool for serious swimming. All of this is surrounded by 45 acres of dense forest, through which a short walk brings you to a dock on the private, pristine lake. This is the perfect point from which to begin a swim or a lazy float in an oversized inner tube. The cost of a stay at Clifton ranges from $143 to $193 per night for two. Some of the suites have sofa beds, and children may share their parents' accommodations for no extra charge. Pets are not allowed, nor is smoking. Full breakfasts are included in the price of a room and feature fresh fruit, sausage or bacon, a lavish entree, juice and coffee or tea. Clifton also operates a restaurant that serves gourmet dinner to the public Wednesday through Sunday. Exquisite meals consist of four or five courses, and are prepared by Craig Hartman and assistant Ron Miller, both award-winning chefs and graduates of the Culinary Institute of America. Light refreshments — from fresh-baked cookies to a self-serve refrigerator stocked with wine, sodas, beer and water — are also always available for guests. Clifton is also happy to prepare luncheons and private dinners to order.

Clifton is just off Route 250 E. It is only four miles from Charlottesville and three miles from Monticello.

THE 1817 ANTIQUE INN
1211 W. Main St.
Charlottesville   *(804) 979-7353*

If you suspect this inn in a historic townhouse might be too stiff and formal for your fancy, consider: the friendly black lab sitting quietly in the hallway, so happy for a scratch behind the ears; or, the fact that owner Candace DeLoach Wilson, in her early 30s, loves nothing more than for her guests to sit back and relax in the living room and munch on the M&Ms she keeps in a big bowl.

Eclectic decor makes this place unique in tradition-bound Charlottesville. For instance, the living room is decorated with items as disparate as Biedermeier chairs, American Empire chests, Venetian tables and a big zebra skin rug. The total effect is exciting, but comfortable.

This is precisely the aim of Candace, who grew up in Savannah, attended college in South Carolina and then moved to New York, where she worked as an interior designer for 10 years.

She met her husband, Jon, a fellow Southerner, in New York and the two married and moved to Charlottesville for his industrial engineering position in 1992.

In the spring of 1993, Candace opened DeLoach Antiques in a townhouse that adjoins the inn. Most all the antiques and furnishings in the inn are for sale — and at reasonable prices for the Charlottesville area.

Both buildings were built in 1817 by one of Thomas Jefferson's master craftsmen, James Dinsmore of

Northern Ireland. Dinsmore was the principal carpenter at Monticello and several original dormitories at the University of Virginia.

Along with another master builder, Dinsmore was Jefferson's principal carpenter for the Rotunda, which is only a few blocks from The 1817 Inn.

Prices are reasonable at the inn, given the luxurious surroundings and the bountiful breakfast. Rates range from $89 for a double room, $129 for a king and $179 for a suite. Breakfast includes hearty muffins, granola, yogurt, piles of fresh fruit, juice and coffee.

The inn's convenient location makes it a popular destination for parents of UVA students. Within easy walking distance is The Corner — a block or two of restaurants, clothing stores and other shops across from campus. Some of Charlottesville's most appealing restaurants are along Elliewood Avenue in this neighborhood.

Back to the inn: All the bedrooms evoke a romantic mood, whether it be the spacious Mattie Carrington room, with French antiques and a glass chandelier, or the exotic Lewis and Clark room, with an African cowhide rug, fur pillows and English hunt pictures. The Sleeping Porch is also enchanting, furnished with two antique iron double beds draped with mosquito netting canopies and made up entirely in cream linens.

Our favorite is Mrs. Olive's Room in the back, with its many white-shuttered windows hung with silk balloon valances and love seat, chair

and tufted ottoman that make for a comfortable place to read and write letters.

The Tea Room Cafe is a delightful addition to The 1817. Here, you can enjoy gourmet lunches at a reasonable price. Lunch is also served in the solarium and on back porch.

Perhaps most appealing are the warm, unpretentious personalities of Candace and Jon and the inn's manager, Sarah Landon. You will be left alone as much as you like at The 1817 Inn, but you will also be treated like a welcome friend.

INN AT THE CROSSROADS

North Gardem   *(804) 979-6452*

Located in the countryside nine miles south of Charlottesville, Inn at the Crossroads commands spectacular vistas of the nearby Blue Ridge and is centrally located to many of the regions's finest natural attractions, including Crabtree Falls, Devil's Knob Mountain, the James River and Sherando Lake National Recreation Area. The aptly named inn and one-time tavern, built in 1820, sits at the crossroads of two old Colonial roads, a north-south route linking Charlottesville with Lynchburg and an east-west pike connecting the James River with the Shenandoah Valley. Four comfortable bedrooms, all with private baths, await guests, as do two common rooms stuffed with books, antiques and local curios.

INN AT MONTICELLO

Hwy. 20 S.
Charlottesville   *(804) 979-3593*

Carol and Larry Engel invite

you to, "Spend the day at Thomas Jefferson's beloved Monticello. Spend the night with us." This country manor house was built in the mid 1800s and is cradled in the valley of Thomas Jefferson's own Monticello Mountain. The gorgeous grounds are full of dogwoods, boxwoods and azaleas and feature a lush, manicured lawn and beautiful Willow Lake. The croquet set is set up neatly on the lawn and a lazy hammock summons you for a mid afternoon nap.

Inside, there are five elegant bedrooms, each furnished with period antiques and reproductions. The beds are made with crisp cotton linens and down comforters. Some have special features, such as a working fireplace, four-poster canopy bed or private porch. Every room has a private bath. For your comfort, a smoke-free environment and central air conditioning are provided.

Let the aroma of freshly brewed hazelnut coffee lure you from your warm bed. Breakfast each morning includes fruits and juices, hot tea and coffee, sugar and cream. Their changing menu of such delicious entrees as Crab Quiche and Orange Yogurt Pancakes provides for the best of seasonally available specialties.

You will never run short of things to do or see here. Within moments, you can visit Monticello (the home of Thomas Jefferson), Michie Tavern, Ash Lawn-Highland (the home of James Monroe) or Montpelier (the home of James and Dolley Madison). There are also vineyards and wineries, recreational activities and a long list of seasonal events. Your visit to historic Charlottesville will definitely be more memorable with a stay at the Inn at Monticello. A two-night minimum stay is required on certain "peak season" weekends.

PALMER COUNTRY MANOR
Rt. 640, Palmyra   *(800) 253-4306*

One hundred and eighty acres of wooded wilderness await you in this country paradise, once a part of a 2,500-acre ranch known as "Solitude." Palmer Country Manor has had a widely varied list of owners through the years. Perhaps the most interesting was Richard McCary, a mason who built the Palmyra Stone Jail, Carysbrook Plantation and the house which is now know as Palmer Country Manor. McCary prospered quickly, and within 20 years he and his wife owned 583 acres. However, in 1858, Richard was arrested for murder and put in the jail he built. On September 16, 1858, he was forced to sell the entire plantation.

Eventually, the land was bought by Kathy and Greg Palmer from the estate of a previous owner. They opened the Palmer Country Manor in July of 1989, and its tradition of excellence has been growing since. The furnishings and the ambience reflect an 1834 plantation house. Amenities include a library, parlor and screened porch. You can stay in the historic plantation house, which is decorated to fit the period, or in one of the private cottages. Each air-conditioned cottage comes complete with a fireplace, king- or queen-sized bed, color television, full bath and large private deck.

Each room can accommodate as many as four people. A complimentary breakfast is served every morning, and a lavish dinner is available every night. Adventurous types can find all they need to whet their appetites minutes away, such as white water rafting in the James River. You can also hike, picnic, fish or relax in the nearby woods. Or, if you are feeling a little romantic, take a champagne balloon ride at sunset. Everything you could want in a vacation or weekend retreat is awaiting you here.

PROSPECT HILL INN

Trevilians *(703) 967-0844*
    (800) 277-0844

A graceful English tree garden shades the manor house and a boxwood hedge lines the entrance way to this 1732 mansion. A few steps away are the slave quarters, the overseer's house, slave kitchen, smoke house and carriage house. A large open lawn rolls on for a quarter mile. This is Prospect Hill, a plantation that is more than 2½ centuries old. You will begin to feel the country spirit the moment you breath the sweet, clean air. Michael and Laura Sheehan are the innkeepers today, but the tradition of hospitality began long before their time.

After the end of the Civil War, the son of the plantation owner returned to find Prospect Hill overgrown and run down. In order to make ends meet, he was forced to take in guests from the city. In 1880, he built an addition to Prospect Hill and remodeled the old slave quarters for guest bedrooms. This renovation created an interior as beautiful as the extraordinary magnolias, tulip poplars and giant beeches in the yard. The slave quarters have beamed ceilings and warm, crackling fireplaces. The rooms in the manor house are adorned with antique furnishings and lovely quilts and most have a fireplace. A private veranda offers a view over the hillside. There are 11 guest rooms in all, each with modern bathrooms (some equipped with Jacuzzis to soak your cares away.)

A full country breakfast is served in bed or at a table in your room. Dinner is served as well; a bell will ring to announce it. The Sheehans keep the tradition of serving their guests the same meal they have made for their family. There are three candlelighted dining rooms for your five-course feast. The blessing is given and then leisurely dining begins. Dishes are basic country-style with a French Provincial twist. Tea time is a ritual at Prospect Hill, and you can also enjoy a glass of Virginia wine before dinner while you are curled up next to the fireplace. There is plenty to do and see from here.

The inn is located in the Green Springs Historic District of Louisa County, so there is plenty of natural beauty around. Try hunting, biking, hiking swimming or driving along Skyline Drive and the Blue Ridge Parkway. Or you can visit Monticello, Ash Lawn, University of Virginia, Montpelier, the Barboursville Vineyards or Oakencroft Vineyard and Winery. A deposit of one night's lodging is required.

SILVER THATCH INN

3001 Hollymead Dr.
Charlottesville   (804) 978-4686

Built in 1780 by Hessian soldiers, the Silver Thatch Inn's central house brings to mind the architecture of Colonial Williamsburg. It is an immaculately restored white clapboard building with beautiful landscaping, including dogwood, magnolia and pine trees all around.

The Hessian soldiers, who were captured during the Revolutionary War in New York, had been marched south to Charlottesville. They built a two-story log cabin on the site of a former Native American settlement. This section of the inn is now known as the Hessian Room. In the 19th century, the inn served as a boys' school, then a tobacco plantation and after the Civil War, a melon farm. A wing was added in 1937, and a cottage was built in 1984 to complement the main building.

Owners Vince and Rita Scoffone stand firm on their promise of providing a smoke-free environment. Smokers are welcome to go outside to smoke, but no exceptions are made indoors.

Telephones and a television are available in common areas of the Inn. The idea here is to withdraw from the rat race, to rest and recuperate.

The interiors are decorated with early American folk art, quilts, reproduction furniture and antiques. Each of the seven guest rooms are named for Virginia-born presidents, with the "star" room being The Thomas Jefferson, of course — complete with a pencil-post queen-sized canopy bed and fireplace. The remaining six rooms are elegantly decorated but not overly formal. All have private baths and several have fireplaces. Guests will find scrumptious homemade cookies waiting for them in their rooms.

The Silver Thatch Inn has a restaurant with three dining rooms, a sun room and a bar, where guests can enjoy a complimentary glass of wine or beer before dinner.

Chef Gordon Carlson changes the gourmet menu frequently, but always includes a vegetarian special and some entrees, such as grilled filet mignon, to satisfy conventional tastes. Two of the more exotic items on one winter menu this year included roasted quail Sonoran (served with a Southwestern sauce of tomatoes, onions, olives, bacon and garlic) and lamb chops Fez (grilled with Merguez sausage, Moroccan tomato sauce and couscous). Homemade desserts will surely tempt the most stoic of dinner guests: a hazelnut/brown sugar tart with Frangelica cream and flourless chocolate cake with pecans, sat on a platter with a other equally tempting desserts.

Silver Thatch is only a short drive from UVA, Monticello, James Madison's Montpelier and Ash Lawn-Highland. Both Skyline Drive and the Blue Ridge Parkway are about a half-hour's drive away. Athletes of all ages can use an outdoor swimming pool and tennis courts near the inn, when weather permits. A two-night minimum stay is required on weekends.

Advance deposits are required for reservations. Rates range from

$105 to $125 and include a generous continental breakfast

200 SOUTH STREET

South St.
Charlottesville   *(804) 979-0200*

200 South Street is comprised of two restored houses in historic downtown Charlottesville. The restoration was completed in 1986, and every detail of the Inn was meticulously recreated or renewed, including the classical veranda and a two-story walnut serpentine hand rail. The larger of the two buildings was completed in 1856 for Thomas Jefferson Wertenbaker, son of Thomas Jefferson's first librarian and close friend, and remained a residence until the 20th century. In the following years, the building was believed to house a finishing school for girls, a brothel and then a boarding house before it was transformed into the Inn.

The rooms are decorated with lovely English and Belgian antiques. If you wish, you may have a room with a whirlpool bathtub, a fireplace, a canopy bed or a private living room suite. Every room has a private bath. The Inn's main gallery houses an ongoing exhibition of Virginia artists and a part of the private collection of Holsinger photos (of historic Charlottesville). A complimentary continental-style breakfast, afternoon tea and wine are available to tempt your tastebuds each day. And, if you are looking for action, you'll find it in Charlottesville. 200 South Street is only blocks from the finest restaurants, shops and entertainment in the area. It is also less than five miles away from both the University of Virginia and Monticello. Of course, if you prefer to relax, you can curl up with a book in the Inn's library or sitting room, daydream in the upstairs study or lounge on the veranda or garden terrace. Innkeepers Brendan and Jenny Clancy will make your stay memorable and delightful. Come here to get away from it all without leaving any luxury all behind.

Afton and Nellysford

ACORN INN

Rt. 634, Nellysford   *(804) 361-9357*

Kathy and Martin Versluys have done their fair share of traveling and know how great it can be to find those off-the-beaten-path wonders along the way. They have also experienced the pleasure of finding truly accommodating hosts in these places, as they did while touring South America, snapping photos for a Dutch publishing company. These are among the reasons why the couple decided to open their own bed and breakfast inn in Nelson County, in the gorgeous Blue Ridge. The Acorn Inn is a unique stop for vacationers or simply a relaxing weekend getaway. You have a choice of three different lodging styles, including the Inn itself (which is a remodeled horse stable), the Acorn Cottage and the Farmhouse. The rooms in the inn are decorated to be comfortable and contemporary. Each of the 10 sunny guest rooms has a double bed, wardrobe, desk, large window and the original stall door.

A large continental-plus breakfast is available each morning, featuring fresh fruit, coffee, teas and a variety of homebaked breads. After enjoying this ample meal and the friendly conversation that accompanies it, most guests take off to explore the area — and there's plenty to choose from to keep everyone happy. There are crafts festivals, local vineyards and beautiful golf courses. If you bring your bicycle, you can follow a bike route mapped out by Mr. Versluys. Or, in the winter, you can swoosh down the famous ski slopes at Wintergreen. After a long day, we suggest that you come back and relax around the Finnish soapstone stove amid the Mexican decor of the A-frame room. You may even get to sample the delicious cookies that Mr. Versluys makes. Then, it's time to retire to your inviting room and let the countryside sing you to sleep.

Economy and convenience are only two of the many reasons to stay here. No matter what adventure you choose, the Acorn Inn is the place to stay. One night's deposit or 50 percent of the anticipated bill is required at time of reservation.

LOOKING GLASS HOUSE
Va. Hwy. 151
Afton   (703) 456-6844, (800) 769-6844

This beautiful farm house near the Blue Ridge Parkway in Nelson County was built in 1848 and today has been restored into an English country-style inn that takes its name from a popular Lewis Carroll tale. The inn is within a half-hour's drive of Charlottesville, Monticello and several gorgeous sites along the Parkway, including Wintergreen Resort.

Innkeeper Mary Haviland has decorated each of her four guest rooms with distinct touches and antiques she brought back from her travels in England. Vintage linens are used on all guest beds, and each room contains a private bath. Other amenities include two wicker-filled porches for relaxing views of the countryside and a library and formal drawing room, comfortable settings for reading a book, playing parlor games, conversing with friends or watching a favorite video. Refreshments are offered to guests each afternoon.

Breakfast, a culinary delight, includes fresh-baked muffins or breads and juice followed by a second course of seasonal fruits and then the main entree, which could be heart-shaped waffles, puffed pancakes or baked egg fittatas. Victorian silver, linen and antique serving pieces provide a welcome touch at the morning meal, served on ever-changing china patterns in the formal dining room. For early risers, coffee and tea are served at 7 PM from the antique hutch outside the rooms.

Fresh-cut flowers from the garden grace the inn's interior, and guests may stroll through the rose garden or see the plantings along the two stream banks for a more private experience.

A deposit of one night's stay (by check, Visa or MasterCard) within seven days confirms your reservation. Certain holidays or weekends may require a two-night minimum. Children are welcome, but pets are

Photo: Hummingbird Inn

The Hummingbird Inn in Goshen, only a 20 minute drive from historic Lexington.

not. Smoking areas are provided on the porches.

THE MARK ADDY
Rt. 151 S. and Rt. 613 W.
Nellysford(804) 361-1101, (800) 278-2154

Beautifully restored and lovingly appointed, the Mark Addy offers the richness and romance of a bygone era. Charming rooms and luxurious suites, all with magnificent views of the Blue Ridge Mountains, await guests. The inn is the result of faithful restoration of an estate house, Upland, that was begun as a four-room farmhouse in 1884 and expanded to its current size by 1910.

East guest room has a unique theme, among them the Oriental, English, Victorian and military-style Colonel's Room. Each has a private bathroom with either a double whirlpool bath, double shower or an antique claw-foot tub with shower. For those relaxing moments, choose one of their five porches or the hammock or spend your time outdoors — the inn sits on 12.5 acres — to take advantage of the serenity of the country setting. Public rooms include a dining room, parlor, sitting room (with cable TV, VCR, games and phones) and a library.

A bountiful breakfast is served, and a decanter of liqueur is placed in each room.

Nearby attractions include Skyline Drive, Monticello, wineries, Wintergreen Resort and all the shops, museums, restaurants and social activities of the university city of Charlottesville. For those who are happiest when browsing through curiosity shops, Tuckahoe Antique Mall and Jordan's, are just a few miles away, and for the more adventurous of spirit, canoeing, hiking and rafting are only minutes away.

Reservations are accepted with a deposit of 50 percent of the cost of the total stay, and may be made by check, Mastercard or Visa. Smoking is restricted to the porches.

THE MEANDER INN
AT PENNY LANE FARM

Rts. 612 and 613
Nellysford   *(804) 361-1380*

The Rockfish Valley in Nelson County is the setting for this country farmhouse on 50 acres of horse-grazed pasture and woods. Rick and Kathy Cornelius are the innkeepers of the Meander Inn, an 80-year-old Victorian home in the heart of the foothills of the Blue Ridge Mountains. Hiking trails and the Rockfish River distinguish the land. The five guest rooms are tastefully decorated with Victorian or country antiques and four-poster beds. You'll wake each day to the gorgeous sight of the morning sun on the breathtaking mountains. If you rise early enough, you can help fetch the morning eggs from the hen house and give the horses their breakfast grain. Or you can just wake in time to savor a scrumptious country breakfast prepared for all of the guests.

Leisurely afternoons can be spent taking tea on the porch or watching the guinea hens play in the brush. As the name suggests, you can "meander" along Skyline Drive and behold the spectacular scenery. If you are an adventure lover, choose from the many activities offered on the farm or minutes away. There are skiing, canoeing, horseback riding, tennis, golf, fishing, hiking, swimming, biking and more! Then, after a fun-filled afternoon, enjoy a glass of Virginia wine and sit around the wood stove listening to the antique player piano. A trip to Meander Lane and Penny Lane Farm is a great escape from the hustle and bustle of every day life.

REDWOOD LODGE

Rt. 250, Afton Mountain
Afton   *(703) 943-8765*

This lodge on Afton Mountain features private tourist suites and apartments, each with its own entrance, bath and balcony. Stunning views of the Shenandoah Valley and accessibility to the Blue Ridge Parkway and Skyline Drive are the big selling points here, along with a fine breakfast served to guests in the lodge's dining area.

Amherst, Monroe and Lynchburg

DULWICH MANOR

Rt. 60, Amherst   *(804) 946-7207*

Flemish bond brickwork and fluted columns adorn the outside of this late 1880s English-style manor house. Nestled in the countryside and surrounded by the Blue Ridge Mountains, Dulwich Manor is abounding with beauty and country appeal. You will know your journey is over when you turn onto the winding country lane and see the inviting porch of this estate, set on five secluded acres in Amherst County. Hosts Bob and Judy Reilly will be there to welcome you into a world away from the hassle of every day life. Period antiques decorate the rooms, and there are large fireplaces to relax by in the living room and study. The six bedrooms are reminiscent of an English country home. The beds are canopied brass or antiques. You can choose a room with a fireplace or window seat for relaxing afternoons or evenings. The Scarborough Room also offers a whirlpool tub and a canopied queen-sized bed.

Each day begins with a full country breakfast, including fresh fruits and juices, inn-baked muffins and breads, country sausage, herb teas and hot coffee. Take a stroll after breakfast and see the natural beauty of the Washington and Jefferson national forests. The nearby Blue Ridge Parkway is a perfect place for hiking, picnicking or photographing the view. Natural Bridge and Caverns, Peaks of Otter and Crabtree Falls are all wonderfully scenic spots for a lunch. This area of the country is also full of history: Washington, Jefferson and Patrick Henry were all born near here. The Appomattox Courthouse, Monticello, Ash Lawn and Poplar Forest are all within a short distance of Dulwich. Bob and Judy ask you to, "Leave it all behind for a brief sojourn into a turn-of-the-century world of pampering and comfort."

FAIRVIEW BED & BREAKFAST

Rt. 778, Amherst   *(804) 277-8500*

Casual living and friendly conversation are staples of living at Fairview. Surrounded by green pastures and rolling fields, this Italian-influenced home is the perfect place to forget all of your cares. There are cats, dogs, burros, llamas and cows roaming the pastures, and Sara, the black Lab, oversees all. Judy and Jim Noon enjoy their porch whenever possible because of the beautiful view and crisp, clean air. The home is the only one in Amherst County with a tower. The Italian influence can be seen in the architecture of the house: the woodwork, ell and dentil moldings and oculus windows. The inviting rooms have high ceilings and large windows to preserve the feeling of the Victorian age. The handmade bricks were fired right on the property, and the dining room window pane is inscribed, "This house was built in 1867, Fairview July 22 in 87."

The three guest bedrooms, each with a private bath, are filled with antiques, but the Noons maintain that these are to be used and enjoyed by all. All of the bedrooms have fireplaces and large windows overlooking the mountains. A fourth room, known as The Duck Room, is available for children or a third person. The entire house is air-conditioned for your comfort.

A full breakfast is designed for guests' needs and wishes. Juice, coffee or tea, homebaked muffins or bread and fresh fruit compote is served wherever you wish — in your room, on the porch or in the dining room. There is plenty of activity around, as Fairview is only 15 miles from the Blue Ridge Parkway, 22 miles from Wintergreen, and minutes from Sweet Briar College.

Advance reservations are suggested. A 50 percent security deposit is required along with reservations. Children are welcome, and well-behaved pets are invited to play with the other animals. Smoking is allowed, with consideration for other guests.

"ST. MOOR" HOUSE
BED & BREAKFAST
High Peak Mountain Rd.
Monroe   *(804) 929-8228*

Warm Virginia and British hospitality will greet you at this lovely house. It sits among large trees facing majestic High Peak Mountain in Amherst County. The nature lover will enjoy strolling along the acres of fields and woods and seeing the pastures, horses, cows and the clear, cool pond. The sight is even more breathtaking when the peach and apple orchards on the adjacent land are in full bloom. You may also sit on an outside deck and enjoy the birds and landscapes. The home's interior is every bit as lovely as the vistas outside. The old chestnut post-and-beam architecture makes "St. Moor" House unique. A cathedral ceiling, handmade brick fireplace and plenty of gorgeous antiques and Orientals make the atmosphere inside warm and inviting. For the comfort of the guests, the building is centrally air-conditioned, and private or semi-private baths are available.

The aroma of a delectable breakfast will wake you each morning.

The serenity of this getaway will be perfect for afternoons spent reading a favorite book, wandering across the meadows or chatting on the porch. Nearby are the natural wonders of the Blue Ridge Parkway, Natural Bridge and the James River. Advance registration is required. Children are welcome, but pets are not allowed.

LANGHORNE MANOR
313 Washington St.
Lynchburg   *(804) 846-4667*

Share in the comforts and heritage of this 27-room classical mansion, built c. 1850 for the Langhorne family. It stands today in the heart of Lynchburg's historic Diamond Hill neighborhood. Antebellum architecture, mahogany and walnut furnishings and crystal and brass chandeliers decorate the interior of Langhorne Manor. The three bedrooms and two suites are full of massive antique furniture and Langhorne family heirlooms. Each has a private bath, most with clawfoot tubs, and all are air-conditioned for your comfort. A delicious homemade breakfast is served in the gorgeous oak-panelled dining room. Ask about romantic dinners, late night snacks and picnic lunches. The gallery displays changing exhibitions of sculpture and other works by Virginia artists.

Proprietors Jaime and Jaynee Acevedo will be happy to point out the history in this home, on the National Register since 1979, and the others in the quiet neighborhood. There are beautiful mountains, orchards and antique shops all around. Whether strolling through the neighborhood or traveling to such places as Poplar Forest, Fort Early, Natural Bridge and Crabtree Falls, you are sure to find entertainment to suit your interests. You will never run out of things to do here in the heart of Lynchburg!

Reservations are accepted with the receipt of one night's fee. Smoking is not permitted on the upper floors, and pets are not allowed. Call to discuss children before bringing them along.

Lynchburg Mansion Inn Bed and Breakfast

405 Madison St.
Lynchburg   *(804) 528-5400*
                        (800) 352-1199

"Welcome to the Lynchburg Mansion Inn Bed and Breakfast, where you can return to a finer yesterday." This quote from its brochure sets the stage for a memorable experience. Built in 1914 for James R. Gilliam Sr., this 9,000-square-foot Spanish Georgian Mansion is located on a half acre in the Garland Hill Historic District. A six-foot-high iron fence surrounds the main house and carriage house. Three separate entrance gates are anchored in massive piers, and guests drive under the columned porte-cochere upon arrival. Large concrete front steps lead to the six-columned entry portico. The front door opens onto the 50-foot grand hall with its restored cherry columns and wainscoting. There are 219 spindles in the cherry and oak staircase.

Bedrooms here are the ultimate in luxury. Some rooms have fireplaces, and all beds are king- or queen-sized. Every room has a full, private bathroom, plenty of storage space, air conditioning, padded satin clothing hangers, color television, telephone and even a night light. Decor varies from the Victorian-style Gilliam Room, with mahogany four-poster bed with steps, a rose strewn comforter, plump pillows and billowing lace, to the light and airy Country French Room that's done in crisp Laura Ashley prints, with a bleached four-poster bed and armoire.

Each morning, the newspaper is delivered to your door along with a freshly brewed pot of coffee and a pitcher of juice for those who would like to wake up privately before venturing forth. A full breakfast is served in the dining room, with fine china, crystal and silver. There is an information center in the back hall that has brochures and newspapers on local events, so you can plan your outings. Go for a fun-filled day of sightseeing and shopping and then retire to the elegant living room and sink into an overstuffed fireside chair. The Lynchburg Mansion Inn aims to satisfy your every need. One night's deposit is required for reservations. Smoking is permitted only on the veranda. The request is for well-behaved children and no pets.

The Madison House Bed & Breakfast

413 Madison St.
Lynchburg   *(800) 828-MHBB*

The Madison House, c. 1874, is the ultimate in comfort and style. The mansion was built by Robert C. Burkeholder for wealthy tobacco-nist George Flemming. It is a brilliant example of Italianate and Eastlake Victorian architecture, located in the historic Garland Hill District of Lynchburg. The elaborate New Orleans-style cast iron porch welcomes you to a world apart from modern hassles and hustles.

Irene and Dale Smith will greet you and invite you into this ornate home. For more than a century, the interior floor plan has remained untouched. Crystal chandeliers hang delicately from the ceiling. An intricate peacock stained-glass window and numerous fireplaces and original woodwork are only a few of the details that make The Madison House distinctive. You'll find antique-filled parlors and a library of books from as far back as the late 1700s.

Each bedroom is individually decorated and features a mixture of antiques and modern conveniences, such as telephones. A lush, soft robe is provided in your room so that you may relax in total comfort. The Gold Room has a bay window, a king-sized brass bed, sitting area and antique vanity. The Madison Suite has a private sitting room with TV and writing desk and a bed chamber with a queen-sized canopy bed. The Rose Room has an 1840s hand-carved mahogany antique bed with matching dresser and armoire and a fireplace. The Veranda Room features a screened-in sitting porch with Victorian-style white wicker. Each has a private bath, two of which feature original bathroom fixtures from the turn of the century. Bed linens and bath towels are all 100 percent cotton,

and the rooms are centrally air-conditioned.

A leisurely breakfast in the dining room can consist of such tasty treats as freshly perked cinnamon coffee, a fresh fruit cup, homemade muffins and bread, spinach quiche, French toast or Eggs Benedict. Afternoon tea is served, as well.

After breakfast, you can visit some of the fascinating historical sights in and around Lynchburg, such as Poplar Forest, Old Western Hotel, the Old Court House Museum and Appomattox Court House. The Blue Ridge Parkway, Skyline Drive and underground caverns are also close by. Check with the Smiths about walking-tour brochures and points of interest.

Smoking and pets are prohibited. Children are discouraged, although some exceptions may be made. Reservations are strongly recommended; a deposit is required.

WINRIDGE BED & BREAKFAST
Corner of Rts. 675 and 795
Madison Heights   *(804) 384-7220*

Winridge Bed and Breakfast, 14 miles off the Blue Ridge Parkway, offers a panoramic view of the Blue Ridge Mountains and the simple elegance of country living. The Colonial Southern home is a 14-acre country estate built in 1910 by Wallace A. Taylor, president of the American National Life Insurance Company of Richmond. LoisAnn and Ed Pfister are the hosts now, and the landmark has been restored to its original grandeur. The outside of the home is gorgeous, with four massive columns adorning the entry portico. Grand windows are in abundance so that the beauty of the surrounding countryside is visible from anywhere in the home. The three guest rooms are furnished with your comfort and privacy in mind. The Habecker Room has a queen-sized four-poster bed and private bath with ceramic-tiled shower. The Walker Room has a queen-sized cannonball bed, and the Brubaker Room has two twin beds. The Walker and Brubaker Rooms share a hallway bath with footed tub and brass and porcelain shower.

A delicious, hot breakfast is served every morning in the lovely old dining room. There is plenty of entertainment to be found on the estate. Explore the meadows, swing under the big shade trees or relax on the porches. The library and living room are full of books, magazines and games for your amusement. Or, if you prefer to venture off of the grounds, the Blue Ridge Parkway, National Historical Park at Appomattox Courthouse, Poplar Forest (Thomas Jefferson's summer home) and several colleges are all within a short drive. There are also sites of engrossing natural beauty, such as Crabtree Falls, the Peaks of Otter and Natural Bridge and Caverns.

A deposit equal to one night's stay is required to hold a reservation. Smoking is permitted only outside. Children are welcome and are invited to play with the Pfister children.

Chatham

HOUSE OF LAIRD
(804) 432-2523

Built in 1880, this Greek Revival house has been totally, lovingly restored and professionally decorated with antiques, quality reproductions, Oriental rugs, imported draperies, wall coverings and moldings.

The House of Laird is most remembered for its romantic Library Suite — two working fireplaces, antiques, Oriental rugs, Irish-estate canopy bed with 40 yards of material, roses, chocolates, bath with heated towels, cable TV and gourmet breakfast in front of the fire. Luxurious and private, the suite affords and ideal setting for renewing or beginning important relationships. The Empire Room, although not a suite, is every bit as grand with its 100-year-old canopy Empire bed and working fireplace, and it's made plush with a Chinese Oriental rug, Belgium-imported draperies and hand-screened French wallpaper in the bath. The Empire Room is the best of the Victorian era with its aura of muted pink hues complemented with rich mahogany woods.

The Lairds are famous for their hospitality that culminates in a gourmet breakfast of traditional southern foods creatively served on antique china, silver and damask table linens.

Three blocks from the Colonial-era village of Chatham, named after the Earl of Chatham, who sided with the American revolutionaries, the house sits in a garden surrounded by 200-year-old oaks. This setting is a short distance from historical houses and battlefields, vineyards, seasonal festivals, antique auctions, fine dining, scenic mountain drives, horseback riding, hiking, fishing and boating.

For discerning guests wanting superior lodging in which no detail has been overlooked, the Lairds offer the ultimate bed and breakfast experience. The House of Laird has earned an AAA three-diamond rating. They offer week-day business discounts and host small weddings and meet-the-author literary weekends.

One guest said it best: "Here we discovered and unexpected haven from the banal, the coarse and the frantic. Your charm and courtesy stoked the fire of our faith that some people still will do things right. Thanks!"

Rocky Mount and Wirtz

THE CLAIBORNE HOUSE
BED AND BREAKFAST

119 Claiborne Ave.
Rocky Mount   *(703) 483-4616*

English-style gardens surround the 1895 Victorian Claiborne House, an elegant turn-of-the-century home in Franklin County. This tranquil getaway is nestled between the Blue Ridge Parkway and glorious Smith Mountain Lake. In the spring, you will be enchanted by the colorful azaleas and dogwoods in the yard. And in the cooler months, the beauty of the autumn colors will leave you breathless. The best place to be for enjoying the scenery is the 130-foot wraparound porch, complete with white wicker furniture in the Southern tradition.

Inside, the lovely Victorian-era furnishings are celebrations of days past. The bedrooms are no exception to that beauty: Each room comes with a king-, queen- or twin-sized bed and private bath. A full gourmet breakfast is served each morning and may include fresh berries or other home-grown fruits in season or homemade bread. Specialties are eggs Benedict, blueberry crepes, spinach souffles and sourdough pecan waffles. A special service provided guests is fresh hot coffee each morning outside their doors as they prepare for a romantic candlelight breakfast. The table colors change daily to accent a different set of china.

Many guests spend their day reading a book from the lending library. Or you can watch the house cat, Rascal, spend his day by the goldfish pond. Margaret and Jim Young are your hosts, and they will be pleased to help you plan a day's excitement. If you're looking for adventure, visit Smith Mountain Lake. There are a variety of activities for all ages on its 500 miles of shoreline. Year-round activities include fishing, golf, tennis and biking. Booker T. Washington National Monument is just moments away. Ferrum College and its Blue Ridge Farm Museum, Mabry Mill, Peaks of Otter, Mill Mountain Zoo and Roanoke's historic Farmer's Market are all within a short drive.

Well-behaved children are welcome. Sorry, no pets are allowed. Smoking is restricted to the outside only, and advance reservations are requested, with a one-night deposit required.

THE MANOR AT TAYLOR'S STORE
Rt. 122, Wirtz   *(703) 721-3951*

In 1799, Skelton Taylor first established Taylor's Store as a general merchandise trading post at this site in Franklin County. It served the community and travelers alike for many years. Later, the building functioned as an ordinary and a U.S. Post Office. The original manor house was built in the early 1800s as the focus of a prosperous tobacco plantation. The present-day home, once featured in *Southern Living*, has emerged as a lovely blend of the periods in which it has been restored. Lee and Mary Tucker are your hosts at this 120-acre utopia. The manor itself features several common areas, a formal parlor with a grand piano, a sunroom full of plants and a great room with a large fireplace. You may also enjoy the billiard room, guest kitchen or the fully equipped exercise room. The home is furnished with period antiques that lend a romantic atmosphere.

There are several types of bedrooms to choose from, each with its own unique decor and ambience. You can stay in the Castle, Plantation, Victorian, Colonial or English Garden suites. The Toy Room is decorated with antique toys, quilts and an extra-high queen-sized canopied bed with bed steps. The Christmas Cottage is ideal for families with children. Three bedrooms, two baths, a fully equipped kitchen, den with stone fireplace and a large deck with gorgeous views of the six ponds and wilderness area are enough to take anyone's breath away. All guest rooms have private baths, and some have a private balcony or kitchen.

After a fresh gourmet breakfast, plan your day. The estate offers hiking, picnicking, canoeing and fishing in one of its spring-fed ponds. There are also swimming docks, a gazebo and even a resident flock of geese! If you prefer to relax, soaking in the hot tub or lounging on the sun decks seem to be the best methods. Nearby are Smith Mountain Lake, Booker T. Washington National Monument, the Blue Ridge Parkway and all of Roanoke's sights.

Smoking is not allowed in the Manor house, and pets are not allowed in the house or the cottage. Children are welcome in the cottage. Advanced reservations are important, and a one-night deposit is required.

Scottsville

HIGH MEADOWS
Off Rt. 20, Scottsville   *(804) 286-2218*

High Meadows, just outside Charlottesville, is a terrific restoration of a 1832 Federalist-Victorian home that is a Virginia Historic Landmark and National Historic Home, as well as a full-service country inn. High Meadows offers the discriminating guest a rare opportunity to look at both 170 years of architectural history and more than 10 new and exciting years of viticultural happening. The inn's management offers today's guests the same hospitality, service and warmth that travelers experienced at its opening — for more than a decade, the hallmark of comfort and good food owned and operated by the Suska/Abbitt team.

There are 12 guest rooms, three with whirlpools and seven with fireplaces, all furnished with period antiques. Guests will enjoy the copious flower gardens and pinot noir grapevines, with charming footpaths leading to ponds and creeks. Guests are welcomed with champagne and stay in uniquely appointed rooms that are furnished with period antiques and art. Each has a private bath.

Expect a four-course breakfast and dinners by candlelight or gourmet picnic baskets on request. Dining is a sensuous experience. Breakfast might be gourmet egg dishes, scones or freshly squeezed orange juice. All foods are prepared for the health conscious, yet appeal to the palate with such variety as Alaskan smoked salmon, crusty breads, tenderloins of pork and venison, homemade ice-cream pies and sinful chocolate desserts. The multicourse dinners offer distinctive cuisine featuring northern European and Mediterranean dishes.

To confirm reservations, a deposit of one night's lodging is required.

New River Valley Region

Blacksburg

BRUSH MOUNTAIN INN
3030 Mount Tabor Rd.   *(703) 951-7530*

Former Virginia Tech administrator and Bronze Star Vietnam War veteran Mode Johnson welcomes you to his "cottage-inn-the-woods" that specializes in personalized service. This 20-acre site is situated at the foot of Brush (or Brushy) Mountain. From the vantage point of a room-side deck, you can watch deer bound by or a large red-tailed hawk soar across the sky. Squirrels, chipmunks and the powerful screech owl are also neighbors living in the towering Jefferson National Forest trees.

The cottage, built of laminated cedar and pine logs from Montana, features a timber-framed great room with a 20-foot stone fireplace, knotty pine walls, a wood stove, large whirlpool and an outdoor balcony off each bedroom. Normally, only two guest rooms are available, but special arrangements may be made to accommodate more guests. The Sunrise Room faces east, and the Forest Room is a suite located on the first floor. TV, telephone and refrigerator are available for guest use. Munchies, bottled water and magazines are little extras that make lounging around the woodstove even more comfortable.

A game room provides darts and puzzles for indoor fun, while outdoor activities include croquet and horseshoes. The surrounding forest is perfect for hiking. Mode keeps a stock of blaze orange apparel for guests to use during fall hunting season. Just six miles away is the Audie Murphy Monument, which marks the site where the most decorated World War II hero and movie star died in an airplane accident.

Brush Mountain Inn is a great getaway for families. While many bed and breakfast inns will not allow children, here kids of all ages and pets are all welcome (with notice). Unique treats can be planned for honeymoon, anniversary, birthday or other special weekends. A one-night deposit is necessary to confirm reservations. Smoking is restricted to decks and balconies.

L'ARCHE

301 Wall St.   *(703) 951-1808*

An elegant 1907 Federal Revival-style home takes you away from it all — right in the heart of downtown Blacksburg. This renovated landmark, located just a block from Virginia Tech, was opened by Vera Good in 1993. Six comfortable rooms are traditionally decorated with fluffy comforters and handmade quilts. Each features a private bath, queen-sized beds, fresh flowers and bedside tables. One room is accessible to the physically challenged. The Country Room will accommodate a family with two children.

The drawing room is perfect for reading, chatting or relaxing, and the two cavernous dining rooms overlook the gardens. Share a table for two on the wide porch or sit under the Jeffersonian gazebo, which sometimes provides the setting for weddings. The gardens are for your enjoyment and exploration. And there are many recreational opportunities close at hand. Try white water rafting on the New River, boating at Claytor Lake State Park or picnicking by Cascades Waterfall. Horseback riding, horse shows and carriage rides are found at Dori-Del Equine Center. Nearby Virginia Tech and Radford University provide endless cultural and athletic events to choose from.

Breakfast at L'Arche is a special event! The inn serves fresh fruit, homebaked breads, muffins and cakes, homemade granola and spiced teas. The morning repast may also include French toast, fluffy omelet or pancakes and waffles. Special dietary needs can be accommodated. Dinner may be served upon request.

Reservations are strongly encouraged. One night's lodging deposit is required. A two-night minimum stay is necessary on football weekends, commencement, parents' weekend or other special events. Smoking is permitted outside on the grounds. Gift certificates are available.

THE SYCAMORE TREE

(703) 381-1597, (800) 381-1598

Charles and Gilda Caines welcome you to share their custom-built home, situated on 126 beautiful acres at the foot of Hightop Mountain. The Caineses have decided to make Virginia their home after living in Alabama, Kansas and New Jersey during Charlie's career. The Sycamore Tree is designed to give guests an "unforgettable experience in a peaceful country setting," said the hosts.

The bed and breakfast inn features six light, airy rooms decorated with furniture from the famous Hotel Roanoke. One room has a skylight, and all feature a connecting private bath, central heat and air conditioning. A room is specially designed for use by physically challenged guests. Relax in the parlor and look out on the mountain skyline and gorgeous wildlife. The family room has a fireplace for cozy fireside chats.

The Sycamore Tree pampers you with nature, but for a little city life you can travel to nearby downtown Blacksburg, just six miles away, or historic downtown Roanoke, 25 miles away. There are plenty of cultural activities to be found, from theater to summer festivals. Virginia Tech, Radford University and Roanoke College provide various academic and athletic events. For adventure, you can try hiking on the Appalachian Trail or take the two-mile walk to the Cascades. And, the Caineses will be sure to start your day off right with a delicious breakfast.

Advance reservations are required, with a deposit of one day's lodging necessary within seven days of the request. Football games, parents' weekends, graduation and large family groups require a minimum two-night stay. Pets, smoking and alcoholic beverages are not allowed. Children older than 12 are welcome.

TWIN PORCHES

318 Clay St.   *(703) 552-0930*

Kelly and Susan Mattingly bought an old, rundown boarding house in 1991 and transformed it into the inviting Twin Porches bed and breakfast inn. The Mattinglys had been students at Virginia Tech years before and decided to move back to the Blacksburg area after experiencing life in Northern Virginia. Susan loved this "diamond in the rough" because of its special little features — gingerbread trim, the ornately carved front door and porches on both levels. Just before they opened in 1992, Twin Porches won a civic beautification award as part of Blacksburg's 10th anniversary awards ceremony.

Comfortable guest rooms are decorated with antiques and quality reproductions. Queen- and full-sized beds are provided, and private baths in two rooms are equipped with original clawfoot and pedestal tubs. The kitchen was renovated to make a lovely formal dining room, where a full breakfast is served each morning. The parlor offers a stereo and cable television.

For the sports lover, Lane Stadium is located just 500 yards away. Virginia Tech is a terrific source of entertainment and diversion year round. Downtown Blacksburg is within walking distance for shopping and fine dining. Huckleberry Trail, a walking and cycling path built on the bed of the Huckleberry rail line, is just a block away.

One night's lodging is required to confirm reservations. Special weekday and corporate rates are available. Smoking is not permitted.

Christiansburg

THE OAKS

311 E. Main St.   *(703) 381-1500*

Massive oak trees, believed to be 300 years old, surround this majestic estate in Christiansburg that holds a three-star rating from Mobil, three diamonds from AAA and four crowns from the American Bed and Breakfast Association, the top rating in its category. A rich green lawn stretches for what seems like miles. The home itself stands like a fairy-tale castle. Major W.L. Pierce built the magnificent buttercup-yellow Queen Anne Victorian for his family. Construction was complete in 1893. The home remained in the Pierce family for almost 90 years.

Margaret and Tom Ray have recently converted The Oaks into a country inn. The luxurious manor is well-suited for both leisure and business travelers. Guest rooms feature queen- or king-sized canopy beds with Posturepedic mattresses, fireplaces and window nooks. The private baths in each room are stocked with plush towels, fluffy terry robes and toiletries. The garden gazebo houses a new Hydrojet hot tub. A small, separate cottage has a sauna, efficiency kitchen and bathroom with shower.

Tragically, The Oaks' grounds suffered under the cruel snow and ice storms that arose this past winter. The garden, gazebo, fountain and fish pond were all severely damaged. But the Rays are optimistic, saying that things should be back in shape by the summer.

Each morning, guests awake to freshly ground coffee and a newspaper. Breakfast is a real pleasure at The Oaks, with a menu that is varied and features such delicious specialties as curried eggs, shirred eggs in spinach nests, rum raisin French toast or whole wheat buttermilk pancakes in praline syrup. Sausage, bacon, ginger-braised chicken breasts and oven-fresh breads are all favorites. A bounty of fresh fruits and juices are available in season.

Take some time after breakfast to lounge on the wraparound porch with Kennedy rockers and wicker chairs. Investigate the books and games in the parlor or study. Or have a nice chat in the sunroom. Cable television and a VCR are also provided, but considering the attractions in the surrounding area, you probably will feel guilty turning the TV on. You'll want to consider hiking on the Appalachian Trail and boating or fishing on Claytor Lake. The historic Newbern Museum, Long Way Home Outdoor Drama, Mill Mountain Theatre, Center in the Square, Smithfield Plantation and Chateau Morrisette Winery are all only a short drive away. Don't miss The Oaks' Victorian Christmas each December!

Gift certificates are available. Advance payment and a two-night minimum are required for special-event weekends at local universities.

Pulaski

THE COUNT PULASKI BED & BREAKFAST AND GARDENS

821 North Jefferson Ave.   (800) 980-1163

The move to 821 N. Jefferson was Florence Byrd Stevenson's 63rd — and last! She, along with her husband William H. Struhs, established the first bed and breakfast inn in Pulaski in this house that is more than eight decades old. The four-story brick home has three stairways and three upper guest rooms. The American Room has a canopied four-poster bed that is so high off the floor you have to climb into it using a stepstool! The room is decorated in Colonial blue, yellow and copper and features a small gas log fireplace. A crested plate on the door to the Polish Room represents the royalty of the Polish count for whom Pulaski is named. There are twin beds that come together to make a king-sized bed. Hand-decorated wooden pieces around the writing desk show fairy stories. James Michener's *Poland* lies on the desk, a gift given to Stevenson as a child. The French room is decorated with lithographs of Parisienne scenes. The seats of its two rosewood chairs were done in needlepoint by Stevenson's mother.

All of the rooms have private baths. The rest of the house is decorated with furnishings from her life in Europe and Asia, along with family antiques. A 1912 Steinway baby grand sits in the living room and a Vietnamese temple bell sits on the mantle. It is customary for guests to ring the bell when they come downstairs for breakfast in the morning. A Byrd clock, which has been in the family for more than 100 years, also shares the mantle. Ceiling fans, air conditioning and fireplaces are all features found throughout the house. Start the day with a full breakfast in the dining room or on the porch. Then explore Pulaski's revitalized Main Street, famous for its antique shops. Florence and William will be happy to tell you about the many other activities close at hand, including museums and national and state parks. Later, you could try a lunch or dinner cruise aboard the *Pioneer Maid*.

Reservations are suggested and will be held with a MasterCard or Visa. Rates are $75 to $95 plus tax. Young children and pets can't be accommodated. The Count Pulaski is a smoke-free establishment.

Floyd County

BENT MOUNTAIN LODGE

Off U.S. 221 (Bent Mountain Rd.)
Copper Hill   (703) 929-4979

The views are heavenly — in beauty and proximity — from this beautiful lodge overlooking the Blue Ridge Parkway from 3,200 feet up. Imagine waking up in the morning, sitting in a big rocking chair on your deck and gazing at the gorgeous mountains and rolling countryside. Innkeepers David Wood and Michael Maiolo get to do it every day! Wood has been a teacher, a textbook salesman, director of food services for the Texas Rangers baseball club and a real estate agent who writes literature for young people. Maiolo is a former high school English teacher with a passion for Faulkner. Their only wish for guests is that they can be happy and relax. There are no planned activities, just areas for you to explore. The beauty of nature is emphasized a great deal. They have cut back the trees so that the wildflowers can be appreciated in their abundance. There are black-eyed Susans, daisies, fire pinks, sundrops and many more. Nature trails wind through the woods.

The lodge is decorated with country elegance. There are five guest rooms and one two-room suite. All have private baths with Jacuzzis and plush carpets. You may find a quilt covering your bed, and some of the rooms have high ceilings. The large dining room is oak-paneled and constructed with hand-hewn timbers. There are bookshelves that run from the floor to nearly the 20-foot-high ceiling. A glass wall of French doors opens onto the 3,000-square-foot deck. A huge fireplace rounds out the room. The entire lodge is air-conditioned.

The lodge serves three meals a day to its guests. Their specialty is a country dinner with pot roast, chicken or country ham and fresh vegetables, bought from local farms, when available. Virginia wines are featured as well. The restaurant is only open to non-guests from 5:30 to 9 PM Friday and Saturday and noon to 3 PM Sunday, but they will serve breakfast or lunch to a group of 10 or more.

Many weddings and conferences have been held here. Bent Mountain Lodge is also a great place for small weekday business meetings. These are generally held in the lounge, which has a fireplace and a bar from the former Floyd Mercantile store. Whatever the reason for your stay, Wood and Maiolo want you to feel at home. For that reason, they place few restrictions on their guests. Children and pets are welcome, smoking is OK and there is no minimum stay. So, relax and enjoy the view. The Lodge is closed from January 2 through April 15 each year.

Alleghany Highlands Region

Clifton Forge and Covington

FIRMSTONE MANOR
BED & BREAKFAST
Longdale Furnace Rd.
Clifton Forge   (703) 862-0892

Stone gates welcome you to Firmstone Manor's grounds. The winding drive is lined with flowering plum trees, while closer to the house there are multitudes of flowers and exotic shrubbery. Marko and Danica Diana Popin will give you a warm greeting in the magnificent entrance hall. The Popins are avid antique and art collectors, and Firmstone is full of their treasures. The rooms are decorated with furnishings and fabrics selected by Diana. Laurel-leaf embellishment enhances the 11-foot ceilings. Embossed iron door hinges and brass carbide chandeliers with etched-glass globes can be found throughout the house. There are hand-painted marble fireplace mantels on each of the eight fireplaces. Floor-to-ceiling windows provide for a view that will leave you breathless. The nine bedrooms are decorated in Victorian, European or Southwestern decor. Newlyweds or second-honeymooners will love the romance of a private suite furnished in white wicker and muted peach and grey tones.

A delicious English or continental breakfast is served each morning in the dining room or in individual rooms. Picnic lunches are available. In the best English tradition, guests may take afternoon tea in the garden. There is plenty to do at Firmstone. Children can romp in the play yard while their parents enjoy croquet beneath century-old shade trees. The nature lover will like strolling on the manor's 12 acres. The grounds are rich with wildflowers, deer and songbirds. If you decide to venture away for the day, Longdale National Recreation Area offers hiking tails and a sandy beach along a mountain lake for swimming. The North Mountain Trail is perfect for photographers who won't want to miss this view of the Shenandoah Valley's southern tip and the Blue Ridge. Daytrippers can soak in the mineral waters at Hot Springs, Warm Springs and Sweet Chalybeate Springs. Then, after a day's adventures, you can return to Firmstone for a tasty four-course dinner. You'll be able to savor fresh herbs and vegetables from the gardens outside and crisp watercress from a nearby stream. Weddings and social gatherings can be accommodated.

MILTON HALL
BED & BREAKFAST INN

207 Thorney Ln.
Covington   *(703) 965-0196*

The Honorable Laura Marie Theresa Fitzwilliam, Viscountess Milton, built this manor in 1874. Lord Milton was ill and Lady Milton hoped that the peace and tranquility of the countryside and beautiful mountain scenery would help return him to health. Today, Milton Hall still stands on 44 acres just west of Covington, in the community of Callaghan. Surrounded by the Allegheny Mountains, the house presents an exotic contrast to its rustic surroundings. There are many gables, buttressed porch towers and Gothic trimmings, which suggest the design came from across the Atlantic. However, the inside of the house is not as ornate. It is spacious, but more of a large country home than a mansion. It is believed that the plain interior was purposely executed by Lady Milton, due to her sensitivity and graciousness, in perhaps not wanting to overwhelm the local residents with the elegance and affluence to which she was accustomed.

A roomy living area and equally large dining room each have two sets of French doors that open to the gardens in the south lawn. The guest bedrooms have private baths. The one exception is the center bedroom with the oriel window that has become the Milton Hall logo. Addition of a bathroom would require a drastic change in the original floor plan, and no one advocates that. There are rooms with a queen-sized bed, fireplace and private bath. The second-floor master bedroom suite has a private bath, queen-sized bed and sitting area. One of the original bedrooms in the servants' quarters has been converted into a bath suite complete with whirlpool and fireplace. Some rooms have telephones, and a central hall phone is available to all guests.

Every morning, guests have the choice of a full English breakfast or a continental breakfast, which can be served in your room. Complimentary afternoon tea is provided, as well. Picnics or elegant basket lunches are available to sightseers. Dinner may be served by special arrangement. There are plenty of attractions in the area: Lake Moomaw, national forests and state wildlife management areas are just a few. There is also the famous Humpback Bridge, Virginia's oldest standing covered bridge, within walking distance. The bridge is the nation's only surviving curved-span covered bridge.

Children are welcome, with proper supervision. Pets that are accustomed to an environment such as Milton Hall are also welcome. Smoking is not regulated but left up to the guests to give their opinion. A one-day's deposit is required with reservations.

Hot Springs

CARRIAGE COURT

Rt. 220   *(703) 839-2345*

Jim and Patricia Poling are hosts at this lovely getaway, located on Maple Ridge Farm. The inn is surrounded by beautiful pastures and wooded mountainsides, and the area is well-known for its natural warm and hot springs. Carriage Court is a group of five old farm buildings that have been remodeled and converted into a country inn and restaurant. The restaurant is in a converted two-story cow barn. Lunch and dinner are served in the downstairs dining rooms or on umbrella tables on the outside deck. On the second floor, the Coach Room & Pub provides a pleasant spot to enjoy a cocktail or a candlelight dinner.

There are four spacious guest rooms offered, all with their own distinct decor. On the first floor, you may choose from Number One, which has a king-sized bed and a queen-sized convertible sofa, a large bathroom, tiny refrigerator, ceiling fan and a French door that opens to a deck with table and chairs, or Number Two, with two full-sized beds, sitting area, full bath, ceiling fan, tiny refrigerator and a French door leading to a deck. Number Three has a private stairway leading to the multilevel suite on the second floor. It has a separate dressing room, queen-sized brass beds, sleeper love seat and an Old World-style restored bathroom. Number Four is actually a two-room apartment. An outside stairway leads to the accommodations, which include a living room, dining area, kitchenette, bedroom with a queen-sized bed, two large closets and a bathroom. The latter two can be joined together as a large apartment to accommodate up to six people. Cable TV is provided in each room, and an ice machine is located in a common lobby. Full maid service is available upon request for $5 per room during the winter season.

There are plenty of activities in the area to keep you busy all day long! Just one mile away is the world-famous Homestead Resort. You'll find golf, skiing, skating, riding and hiking trails and hunting and fishing areas. Or, if you prefer shopping, there are many fine businesses and restaurants nearby. Jim and Patricia make your stay enjoyable and will even add a special touch for occasions such as anniversaries and birthdays by delivering champagne, flowers and breakfast or dinner for two or more. Rates range from $58 for a double room to $120 for the large apartment.

Millboro and Warm Springs

FORT LEWIS LODGE

Rt. 625, Millboro   *(703) 925-2314*

In 1754, Col. Charles Lewis built a stockade to protect the southern pass of Shenandoah Mountain from Indian raids. This frontier outpost became a vast 3,200-acre farm, situated deep within the Allegheny Mountains. For more than 200 years, this area has remained virtually unchanged. The spectacular scenery and rushing mountain streams are enough to take your breath away. About 15 years ago, John and Caryl Cowden moved from Ohio to manage and operate the farm. Today, they are your gracious hosts at this mountain paradise. They have restored the old red-brick manor house and the Lewis grist mill, dating back to 1850. They have also taken the time to build a new guest lodge. A large gathering room, framed with massive beams of oak and walnut, will invite you to relax with a cup of coffee and enjoy a chat with the Cowdens. A gorgeous view "in the round" of the grounds can be obtained from an observation tower, made of an enclosed stairway leading to the top of an adjoining silo, also the site of three additional bedrooms. The 12 bedrooms are decorated with wildlife art and handcrafted walnut, cherry, red oak and butternut furniture. Much of the furniture was made by local craftsmen from wood cut right on the property. All of the guest rooms have a private or semiprivate bath.

Venture out to the 19th-century grist mill for a scrumptious feast. Three meals are included in the room rate, and all dishes are handmade and delicious! A full country breakfast includes freshly baked breads, eggs, sausage, bacon, fruits and French toast with locally made maple syrup poured over top. Lunch is served in the lodge, or you may opt to take a boxed lunch along with you. The buffet dinners offer fresh vegetables from the farm's garden. The outdoor activities are abundant here. There are more than two miles of the meandering Cowpasture River flowing through this fertile valley, which provides for swimming, tubing and sport fishing (catch and release) for smallmouth bass and trout. Several state-stocked trout streams are nearby. There are miles of marked trails and old logging roads for you to stroll along or explore. Camping is another special option at Fort Lewis. With advance notice, the lodge will outfit overnight campouts anywhere along the property. Deposit of one night's stay is required.

MEADOW LANE LODGE

Rt. 39, Warm Springs　　*(703) 839-5959*

"A little jewel of a country inn, set in meadows and mountains . . . ," Meadow Lane Lodge is unquestionably the keystone jewel in the crown of heritage tourism country inns. You will know it from the moment you lay eyes on Meadow Lane. The estate cannot be seen from the road. You must wind your way up a narrow road, between meadows and woods. Finally, you will emerge upon a large clearing — and there it is. A three-section white frame house with green and yellow trim beckons you. The stone dairy house and the old ice house are right out of the days before refrigeration. The deck, out behind the 1920s barn, is an overlook with a most impressive view. From here, guests can observe a nature preserve that has almost any plant or animal native to Virginia. Two miles of the crystal clean Jackson River flow through the property. One and a half miles up the river is a limestone spring, the origin of Meadow Lane's water supply. Across the lawn you'll see some unusual animals: peacocks, a pet duck and Japanese Silkies (a type of chicken with black skin and white feathers) roaming the grounds. There is even a half-breed cat, part domestic and part bob.

The history of Meadow Lane is just as impressive as the scenery. The land was part of the original grant given to Charles Lewis, an early Virginia settler, by King George III. An old log cabin, built in 1750, is visible from the west side of the Jackson River. A stockade built around the cabin during the French and Indian War eventually became known as Fort Dinwiddie. Today, Philip and Catherine Hirsh are the owners and innkeepers, with Meadow Lane having been in the Hirsh family for three generations.

The guest rooms are decorated for a combination of modern comfort and antique grandeur. There are double rooms, suites with fireplaces and private cottages. Some rooms have surprising little extras, such as a 19th-century walnut dropleaf table, engravings or a private porch. The Common Room has a fireplace at each end. The Breakfast Room serves you from a 1710 oak sideboard. A full Southern breakfast is served each morning.

The Bacova Guild showroom is nearby, as are the Garth Newel Music Center, The Homestead and Lake Moomaw. But many guests just like to stay put and play croquet on the lawn — it's the house specialty! The 1,600-acre expanse allows for hiking, fishing, canoeing and "creative loafing." Children older than 6 years are welcome. No pets are allowed without prior approval. A deposit is required with reservations.

Save With Ramada In Virginia

15% Off

RAMADA FOUR-FOR-ONE

When traveling with family or friends, the Ramada 4-for-1 program helps to minimize expenses. Participating Ramada locations allow as many as four people to pay the single rate when sharing the same room. Rollaways are slightly extra. Advance reservations are recommended but are not required.

PARTICIPATING PROPERTIES

Ashland
(I-95S, Exit 92)
Harrisonburg
(I-81S, Exit 243)
Lexington
(I-81, Exit 195)
Lynchburg
(Hwy. 29 Bypass,
Main St. Exit)
Newport News
(I-64E, Route 17)

Norfolk Newton Road
(I-64, Exit 80B)
Petersburg
(I-95S, Exit 52)
Richmond North
(I-95S, Exit 82)
Richmond South
(I-95S, Exit 64)
Richmond West
(I-95S to Parham Rd.)
Virginia Beach Oceanfront
(I-64E to 44E to 57th St.)

Virginia Beach On the Beach
(I-64E to 44E to 6th St.)
Williamsburg Historic
(I-64E, Exit 242A, L on
US 60)
Williamsburg West
(I-64E, Exit 234, R on
646, L on US 60)
NORTH CAROLINA
Nags Head Beach
(Ocean front at Mile
Post 9½)

RAMADA LIMITEDS•INNS•HOTELS•RESORTS•PLAZA HOTELS

FOR RESERVATIONS CALL

1-800-2-RAMADA

(1-800-272-6232)
OR YOUR LOCAL TRAVEL PROFESSIONAL

Present the coupon in the back of this book at check-in
to receive your discount.

Inside
Other Accommodations

After you've had a great day and are looking for an equally great place to stay, the Blue Ridge of Virginia has a wide selection of comfortable, pleasing general accommodations to top off your sightseeing. In this chapter, we provide a good cross section of accommodations in the region — motels, hotels and resorts. Since the Blue Ridge region is so large, we are not including every option available to travelers. Also, don't forget that this is a guide, not a directory, so we want to point you toward some of our favorites, not just what's there. But, the properties we are presenting here will more than get you started in your search for the perfect place to lay your head. And, there are some truly perfect spots to be found.

Room rates vary throughout the Blue Ridge, since some accommodations are in small towns and some are in the larger cities. Some are simple motels, and others are posh hotels. Most rates range from $30 on up for a double. We've categorized the rates for each property

Photo: Abingdon Convention and Visitors Bureau

The Martha Washington Inn in Abingdon offers Four-Star, Four-Diamond accommodations.

we've included so you'll have a good idea of what to expect. Here's what our dollar signs mean, for two people to a room per night:

$30 to $40	$
$41 to $60	$$
$61 to $85	$$$
$85 and up	$$$$

Now that your pocketbook is taken care of, let's explore the vast array of accommodations that will take care of the rest of you.

Shenandoah Valley Region

Strasburg

HOTEL STRASBURG
201 Holliday St.   (703) 465-9191
$$$ and up   All major credit cards

This white clapboard structure was built after the Civil War as a hospital. Its Victorian history and charm is evident — from the antique furniture in the rooms to the unique second-story balcony porch. The public rooms have been decorated with period furniture and the walls are covered with folk and fine art. Hotel Strasburg is perfect for a short, romantic getaway or a longer vacation.

The 25 cozy guest rooms feature private baths and are decorated with period furniture, Victorian wall and floor coverings and classic window treatments. Other special touches are toiletries, fresh flowers, basketed greenery, telephones and big, fluffy towels. Suites and staterooms also include a sitting area.

This grand old hotel is located

near Strasburg Emporium (see Shopping), Hupp's Hill Battlefield Park, Wayside Theatre and Half Moon Beach. A variety of golf packages is also offered.

Front Royal

QUALITY INN SKYLINE DRIVE
10 Commerce Ave.   (703) 635-3161
          (800) 228-5151
$$ All major credit cards

Located at the beautiful northern entrance to Skyline Drive, Quality Inn will give you excellent service and attractive accommodations. Each of the 107 rooms comes equipped with cable television, including HBO. Guests can enjoy meals in the dining room; banquet and conference rooms are available with advance notice. Ask about discount rates.

Basye

The most frequently recommended accommodation in Basye is the Bryce Resort, (703) 856-2121, described in detail in the Resorts chapter

New Market

NEW MARKET BATTLEFIELD DAYS INN
9360 George Collins Pkwy.
          (703) 740-4100, (800) 325-2525
$$ All major credit cards

On May 15, 1864, Union Troops occupied Manor's Hill. Confederate Troops were south on Shirley's Ridge. The Confederate troops enlisted the help of young cadets from

Hotel Strasburg

A Victorian Experience Of The 1890's
For The 1990's

Rehearsal Dinners
Corporate Retreats

Wedding Receptions
Romantic Getaways

In Historic Strasburg 1-800-348-8327
Antique Capitol of Virginia

Virginia Military Institute and pushed the Yankees north. Ninety percent of the battle and casualties occurred here. Today, the New Market Battlefield Days Inn stands in that very spot on Manor's Hill. The New Market Battlefield Park Hall of Valor & Military Museum, dedicated to the cadets of VMI, is adjacent to the hotel. Other attractions in the area include Shenandoah and Endless Caverns, New Market historic district and championship golfing. A short drive away are Shenandoah National Park, Skyline Drive, Luray Caverns and Bryce and Massanutten ski resorts.

The 92 guest rooms feature king-sized or double beds and remote control color cable TV. Complimentary coffee and danish are served to guests each morning. An outdoor pool is on site and handicap facilities are available. Groups and buses are welcome.

QUALITY INN SHENANDOAH VALLEY
(703) 740-3141, (800) 228-5151
$$ *All major credit cards*

The Johnny Appleseed Restaurant and Apple Core Village Gift Shop are special attractions of this motel. You will be treated like a VIP with red carpet service and complimentary sunrise coffee and sunset cider. The 100 spacious rooms have free in-room movies, and the outdoor pool and sauna are perfect for relaxing afternoons. Or, you can enjoy the game room and miniature golf course. The property is located near Historic New Market, Luray Caverns, New Market Battlefield and more. AAA and AARP discounts are offered.

THE SHENVALEE GOLF RESORT
9660 Fairway Dr.   *(703) 740-3181*
$$ *All major credit cards*

This lovely lodge is a golf lover's delight! Motels are located right along the golf course. Or, for those not here to enjoy the links, there are poolside motels. The 18-hole PGA golf course features a practice driving range and a fully equipped pro shop. Three regulation tennis courts, a large swimming pool, fishing pond and hair salon are located at the resort for your pleasure and convenience. Take your meals in the dining room or visit the Sand Trap Tavern for a casual evening.

Luray

SKYLAND LODGE
Shenandoah
National Park   (703) 743-5108
$$$ MC, V

Skyland Lodge is located in the gorgeous Shenandoah National Park. Known as "Virginia's Mountain Playground," the park will awe a first-time visitor or a seasoned mountaineer. From every window and doorway of this lodge there are incredible views of the surrounding Shenandoah Valley. And Skyland knows how important it is to educate the public on the need to care for this land. Naturalist programs are conducted so that guests can learn how to keep this stunning vista clean and attractive.

The multi-unit lodge provides 186 rooms. There are no telephones and few televisions in the rooms or lodge units. However, a TV lounge and public phones are located on the premises. A full-service restaurant, taproom featuring nightly entertainment and a mountain craft shop are located at the Lodge. A 50 percent advance deposit is required eight weeks prior to your stay.

Harrisonburg

HOLIDAY INN HARRISONBURG
1 Pleasant Valley Rd.   (703) 434-9981
                            (800) HOLIDAY
$$ All major credit cards

This beautiful, two-story roadside hotel is found in the heart of historic Harrisonburg. From here, Massanutten Ski Resort, Skyline Drive, New Market Battlefield and Museum and Shenandoah and Endless caverns are only a short trip away. There are 130 rooms, all with air conditioning and color TV with Showtime.

Special group services are available with advance notice. These include complimentary bus parking, group meals and preregistration for groups with keys in envelopes. A full service restaurant, the River Mill Cafe, is located on the site. Holiday Inn is handicapped-accessible, and pets are allowed.

MASSANUTTEN RESORT
                            (703) 289-9441
This popular resort is detailed in our Resorts chapter.

Staunton and Waynesboro

BUDGET WEST LAWN MOTEL
2240 W. Main St. (Hwy. 250 W.)
Waynesboro   (703) 942-9551
$$ MC, V

Budget West Lawn is tucked into the heart of the Shenandoah Valley, just seven miles from the Blue Ridge Parkway and Skyline Drive. This American-owned and -operated motel provides a touch of home in clean, spacious and quiet rooms. Each of the 20 rooms provides comfortable double or queen-sized beds, cable TV and telephone. Nonsmoking rooms are available, and all rooms are equally accessible. There are 20 restaurants nearby for casual or fine dining.

HOLIDAY INN STAUNTON
Rt. 275 and I-81 Exit 225
Staunton   *(703) 248-6020*
$$$ *All major credit cards*

Historic downtown Staunton is less than five minutes away from this luxurious hotel. Holiday Inn is only three miles from Woodrow Wilson Birthplace and the Museum of American Frontier Culture, among other attractions. There are 112 spacious rooms available, some for nonsmokers and handicapped persons. A full-service restaurant located in the hotel serves international cuisine, and the lounge features weekend entertainment. Amenities include tennis courts and an indoor/outdoor heated pool. A 30-day advance deposit is required.

Lexington

BEST WESTERN
KEYDET-GENERAL MOTEL
U.S. Hwy. 60 W.   *(703) 463-4715*
$$ *All major credit cards*

Best Western is located 1½ miles

from the Lexington Visitor's Center and is close to Virginia Military Institute, home of the Keydets. This hotel offers a few conveniences not found at all other hotels. For example, they will accept pets, and many rooms have refrigerators and wet bars. There is also air conditioning and a television in each room. A restaurant is located on the property. Senior citizen discounts are available.

COMFORT INN
I-64, Exit 13
(U.S. Hwy. 11 S.)   *(703) 463-7311,*
    (800) 228-5150
$$ *All major credit cards*

Conveniently located near the Virginia Horse Center, Comfort Inn offers a complimentary continental breakfast. You'll find an indoor pool, enclosed corridors, glass elevator and free local calls. Children younger than 18 stay free. Several restaurants are nearby.

HOLIDAY INN LEXINGTON
I-64 and
U.S. Hwy. 11 N.   *(703) 463-7351,*
    (800) 465-4329
$$ *All major credit cards*

Located 1½ miles from the Lexington Visitor's Center, the 72 rooms at this Holiday Inn come complete with air conditioning and

Often, for less than the price you would pay for a room at a hotel chain, you can book a unique local accommodation. Be prepared for surprises — mostly pleasant ones — with characteristics of the area.

Insiders' Tips

televisions. There are nonsmoking and handicapped-accessible rooms available. A full restaurant and pool are located in the hotel. Pets are allowed. Ask about the senior citizen's discount.

HOWARD JOHNSON LODGE AND RESTAURANT

I-64 and I-81, Exit 53
(U.S. Hwy. 11)   (703) 463-9181,
                        (800) 654-2000
$$ All major credit cards

This mountain-top hotel is located near Washington & Lee University, Virginia Military Institute and Natural Bridge. Good for smaller business and social functions, its meeting room can hold up to 135 people. There are 88 regular rooms, 10 nonsmoking and two handicapped-accessible rooms. All have complimentary HBO.

There is an on-site restaurant and guest laundry. The gift shop features local hand-crafted items. AAA and AARP discounts and group rates are available.

RAMADA INN

I-81 at U.S. Hwy. 11   (703) 463-6666,
                         (800) 228-2828
$$ All major credit cards

The business traveler as well as families and tour groups will appreciate the convenience and comfort of this hotel, located near Washington & Lee University, Virginia Military Institute and historical sites. There are 80 guest rooms and three suites. The suites or double bedrooms are ideal for families with children. Two of the guest rooms are handicapped-accessible, and there are 12 nonsmoking rooms.

Rockbridge Restaurant (see Restaurants), a full service restaurant and lounge, is located within the Ramada. Other amenities include an indoor swimming pool and cable TV. The banquet facilities can accommodate up to 200. AAA and AARP discounts are available.

Natural Bridge

NATURAL BRIDGE OF VIRGINIA

U.S. Hwy. 11   (703) 291-2121
$$ All major credit cards

Natural Bridge of Virginia, containing the Natural Bridge Hotel, Annex and Hillside Cottages, is detailed in the Resorts chapter of this book.

Roanoke, Troutville and Salem

COMFORT INN — ROANOKE/TROUTVILLE

U.S. Hwy. 11 S.   (703) 992-5600,
                         (800) 228-5150
$$ All major credit cards

Seventy-two guest rooms are available, each equipped with satellite television. Other amenities include nonsmoking rooms, an outdoor pool, enclosed corridors and a gift shop. Senior citizen discounts are honored.

HAMPTON INN

3816 Franklin Rd. S.W.
Roanoke   (703) 989-4000
                 (800) 426-7866
$-$$ All major credit cards

Just three miles from downtown, close to Roanoke Memorial Hospital and across the road from

Tanglewood Mall, the Hampton Inn offers an expanded continental breakfast, HBO and ESPN, VCRs, direct-dial phones, copier and FAX service, meeting room, hair dryers, refrigerator/freezer and microwave, and nonsmoking rooms in its 59-room motel. Hospital and commercial rates are offered.

TRAVELODGE — ROANOKE NORTH
2444 Lee Hwy. S.
Roanoke   *(703) 992-6700*
                     (800) 255-3050
$$ *All major credit cards*

Travelodge wants you to feel at home, so they provide a free continental breakfast, free coffee, tea and popcorn and free local calls. Rooms offer attractive furniture, cable TV (with CNN and Showtime), executive work areas and direct-dial telephones. Children younger than 18 stay free when sharing a room with their parents. Efficiency rooms are available for relocating personnel or longer-term visitors. Pets are welcome, and rooms for the physically impaired and non-smokers are available.

COLONY HOUSE MOTOR LODGE
3560 Franklin Rd.
Roanoke   *(703) 345-0411,*
                     (800) 552-7026
$$ *All major credit cards*

Colony House is situated just two miles north of the Roanoke entrance to the spectacular Blue Ridge Parkway. This small, quiet inn specializes in personal service. The 67 rooms are air conditioned and carpeted and have direct-dial phones, cable TV (with HBO and ESPN) and king-, queen- or double-

Knights Inn

1300 Seminole Trail
Charlottesville, Va. 22901
804-973-8133

sized beds. There are a few suites available. You're close to great restaurants, terrific shopping, the interstate highway and downtown. Colony House is a wonderful base for business travelers and tourists. Call for special discounts and rates.

FRIENDSHIP INN
526 Orange Ave.
Roanoke   *(703) 981-9341,*
                     (800) 327-5887
$ *All major credit cards*

Access to the Roanoke Civic Center is about as simple as it gets from this hotel, since it's located just across the street! The Friendship Inn is also less than one mile away from Center in the Square, the historic Farmers Market and the Virginia Transportation Museum. Free coffee is offered each morning. The guest rooms have cable television with HBO. FAX service and shuttle pick up are available. Ask about group, discount and seasonal rates.

HOLIDAY INN HOTEL TANGLEWOOD
4468 Starkey Rd.
Roanoke   (703) 774-4400
$$ All major credit cards

This hotel's 196 guest rooms are traditionally furnished. Each comes with climate control, color TV (with Showtime, CNN and ESPN), AM/FM radio and two vanity dressing areas. Starkey's Bistro, located in the hotel, serves continental breakfast or regional cuisine. For some excitement, try the Elephant Walk lounge (see Nightlife), which takes its atmosphere from a safari decor. The hotel offers outdoor swimming and tennis. Complimentary limousine service to the airport is available, as well as rental cars, private limos and taxi service.

INNKEEPER MOTEL
815 Gainesboro Rd.
Roanoke   (703) 982-0100,
                    (800) 822-9899
$$ All major credit cards

The Innkeeper Motel knows that it's the little touches that make a stay more pleasant. Guests at this hotel are treated to a complimentary continental breakfast, coffee, newspaper and ice. Their 98 rooms feature firm, extra-length beds for a sound night's sleep. Each room has sofas, desks, AM/FM clock radios, electronic fire alarms and a remote-controlled color television with cable. There are nonsmoking rooms and handicap facilities available. Some rooms come with Jacuzzis. An outdoor pool is located on the grounds for guest use.

THE JEFFERSON LODGE
616 S. Jefferson St.
Roanoke   (703) 342-2951,
                    (800) 950-2580
$$ All major credit cards

The Jefferson Lodge is located in the heart of downtown Roanoke. A walk of only a few blocks will have you at the main public library, city and federal government buildings, hospitals and shopping. It is only three blocks to the City Market and Center in the Square.

One hundred newly decorated rooms await guests. Free parking, coin-operated laundry and color TV are all provided for your comfort. An outdoor swimming pool and family dining room are on the property. Special group rates are available.

THE RADISSON PATRICK HENRY HOTEL
617 S. Jefferson St.
Roanoke   (703) 345-8811,
                    (800) 833-4567
$$ and up   All major credit cards

On November 12, 1925, the Patrick Henry Hotel opened its doors for the first time. Its 11-story exterior was already a wonder, but visitors and guests were astounded by the beauty of the interior. Today, the hotel has been restored to its previous splendor, and it is the only operating landmark hotel in Roanoke.

The guest rooms are more than spacious. Each has been modernized, but in a way that reflects the historic heritage. Rooms have their own separate kitchenettes. Airport transportation, free parking, smoking and nonsmoking floors and a

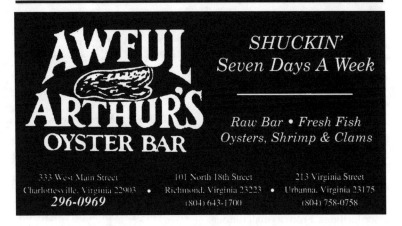
restaurant are all a part of this hotel's special charm.

ROANOKE AIRPORT MARRIOTT
2801 Hershberger Rd. N.W.
Roanoke   *(703) 563-9300*
$$$ *All major credit cards*

The Roanoke Airport Marriott has been chosen as a AAA Four Diamond award winner, and the reasons are easy to see. The elegant lobby welcomes you. Sounds of casual conversation float over from Whispers, the lobby bar. You catch the scent of some delicious dish being served to a guest in Lily's or Remington's (see Restaurants). Soon, you open the door to your lovely room, one of the 320 guest rooms and suites available here. You will find all of the comforts of home and more. Every guest room has individual climate control, AM/FM radio, remote-controlled color cable TV, two direct-dial telephones with message lights, video messages and complimentary personal care products. Twenty-four hour room

service, valet service, airport transportation and free parking are just a few more of the benefits here.

There are indoor and outdoor pools, a fitness center, sauna, whirlpool and two lighted tennis courts. Or, if you feel like finding some action, try Charades, the entertainment lounge (see the Nightlife chapter).

The Marriott's Grand Ballroom, Shenandoah Ballroom and six meeting rooms can accommodate groups from 20 to 900. There is a total of 17 conference rooms available, with more than 12,800 square feet of flexible space. Special rates include Two For Breakfast Weekends, Honeymoon Packages, Super Saver and longterm rates.

SHERATON INN ROANOKE AIRPORT
2727 Ferndale Dr. N.W.
Roanoke   *(703) 362-4500*
     (800) 325-3535
$$$ and up   *All major credit cards*

Indoor/outdoor pools, tennis courts, volleyball and golf are available at this outstanding hotel. For more adventure, there is a piano bar and a club, Miami's. Oscar's Restaurant will provide an extraordinary dining experience in the heart of this elegant hotel. Each of the 150 guest rooms and four suites is equipped with satellite TV, two phones, individual climate control, radio and two double beds or a king-sized bed. Pets are allowed in the room with a $25 deposit.

Sheraton has more than 7,200 square feet in meeting and conference facilities. From a small dinner of 20 to a banquet of 350 people, the Main Ballroom will easily house your guests. A conference center and luxurious hospitality suites are perfect for business, meeting and social functions. AAA and AARP discounts are available.

QUALITY INN — ROANOKE/SALEM
I-81 Exit 41 and Rt. 419
Salem   (703) 562-1912,
                         (800) 228-5151
$$ *All major credit cards*

Quality Inn is great for families with children. At the Quality Park here, kids can swing, play games and enjoy other activities or swim in the children's pool. The 120 rooms have cable TV with HBO, and pets are allowed to stay with you. The dining room, Back To Berkeleys, serves tempting meals from breakfast through dinner. BTB's lounge features live entertainment.

East of the Blue Ridge Region

Madison County and Syria

GRAVES' MOUNTAIN LODGE
Syria   (703) 923-4231
$$$ and up (meals included)
                         All major credit cards

Graves' Mountain Lodge is a family-owned resort tucked away in the beauty of the Blue Ridge Mountains. This is a complete resort, with recreational facilities to please the whole family. Choose from swimming, tennis, softball, volleyball and ping pong. Or you can try horseback riding, fishing, hunting and hiking. Visit the gift shop to see mountain crafts, Native American and folk carvings and jewelry. The recreation lounge has books, magazines, games, a piano and a television set.

Stop in at the old-time country store, Syria Mercantile Company, where you can buy groceries, dry goods and other everyday needs. If you decide to venture off the farm, the surrounding area has plenty to offer. You can enjoy sight seeing at Luray Caverns, tour gorgeous Skyline Drive or observe authentic full-time farm operations at R.S. Graves' Bros. Farm.

There are 10 different accommodation styles for you and your family to choose from. Ridgecrest Motel has 22 rooms and two conference rooms. Hilltop Motel has 16 rooms, some with TV sets. The Old Farm House has seven rooms with half baths and a portico to the shower house. Also, nine cottages are located near or in the vicinity of the lodge.

Charlottesville

BEST WESTERN CAVALIER

105 Emmet St.	(804) 296-8111
	(800) 528-1234
$$	All major credit cards

The 118-room Cavalier is located centrally in Charlottesville, right near the University of Virginia. The accommodations options include two suites, three handicapped-accessible rooms and 18 for nonsmokers. A swimming pool is located on site. Continental breakfast is served each morning. Up to 150 people can be accommodated in one of the three meeting rooms. Two-day and special meeting packages are offered.

THE BOAR'S HEAD INN

| Rt. 250 W. | (804) 296-2181 |
| $$$ | |

This is a charming place to stay. It is detailed in the Resorts chapter of this book.

COURTYARD BY MARRIOTT

1445 Seminole Tr.	(804) 973-7100
	(800) 321-2211
$$	All major credit cards

Shopping, historical sites and the University of Virginia are all close to Courtyard by Marriott. The 142 rooms feature color televisions with HBO and ESPN and free in-room coffee. The hotel has 75 nonsmoking and two handicapped-accessible rooms, along with 12 suites. The indoor pool, whirlpool and exercise room are perfect for keeping up with your normal daily routine or just relaxing. A restaurant and lounge complete the amenities.

HOLIDAY INN
NORTH-UNIVERSITY AREA

1600 Emmet St.	(804) 293-9111
	(800) HOLIDAY
$$	All major credit cards

This historic getaway will please you with its personal service and contemporary rooms which, along with the rest of the hotel, have been handsomely decorated. They provide you with all of the comforts of home and feature air conditioning and color TV with Showtime. An exercise room features a treadmill, universal gym and sauna, and the large outdoor pool and landscaped courtyard are both relaxing and

If you plan to visit the mountains of Virginia during the gorgeous autumn tourist season, book your lodging reservations early — like four to six months in advance — to assure that you'll have a place to stay during this busy and beautiful time of year.

Insiders' Tips

pleasing to the eye. The Holiday Inn is located just one mile from the University of Virginia.

HOWARD JOHNSON

1309 W. Main St.   (800) 654-2000
$$ All major credit cards

Adjacent to the University of Virginia and University Hospital, Howard Johnson is designed to offer guests every convenience. It also offers easy accessibility to the sports complex and stadium. The Charlottesville historic district, shopping and restaurants are within walking distance. The rooms here are decorated with comfort in mind. Studio rooms offer a large living area tastefully decorated for private parties. For the business person, roomy accommodations provide a large work area in a relaxed atmosphere. Studio rooms have adjacent areas that provide a conference table for either working or relaxation. Tourists and business people alike will find everything they need at this fine facility.

KNIGHTS INN

1300 Seminole Tr.   (804) 973-8133
$$ All major credit cards

This edition of the clean and comfortable national motel chain is conveniently located right off of Route 29, close to shopping malls, restaurants and shops and within a five-minute drive of the University of Virginia. Knights Inn's 115 rooms cater to a largely tourist crowd, along with UVA alums who flock to Charlottesville in the fall for football games and special events at the university. It's an affordable option, but you should be sure to book early if you plan on staying during weekends any time of the year.

SHERATON INN CHARLOTTESVILLE

2350 Seminole Tr.   (804) 973-2121
$$$ All major credit cards

This 240-room palatial accommodation on 20 acres offers everything you need for rest and relaxation after seeing the sights in Charlottesville. That includes a casual restaurant, Treetop; a formal restaurant, Randolph; and a great nightclub, Dooley's. There are also two indoor and outdoor pools. A great place to relax!

HOLIDAY INN
CHARLOTTESVILLE/MONTICELLO

I-64 and Fifth St.   (804) 977-5100
     (800) HOLIDAY
$$ All major credit cards

Located two miles from downtown Charlottesville and four miles from various historical attractions, this hotel is in a great central location for tourists and businesspeople alike. The high-rise building has 130 rooms and one suite. Meeting and banquet facilities are available for up to 150 people.

OMNI CHARLOTTESVILLE HOTEL

235 W. Main St.   (804) 971-5500
     (800) THE-OMNI
$$$$ All major credit cards

This spectacular hotel has been AAA four-diamond rated. There are facilities for cocktail parties for 30 or a conference of 600 people. An indoor/outdoor pool, whirlpool, sauna, health club and restaurant are available for your enjoyment. The 208 grand rooms are decorated with elegant furnishings. There are 36 nonsmoking rooms

HOWARD JOHNSON

available, six suites and three handicapped-accessible rooms.

WINTERGREEN

(804) 325-2200, (800) 325-2200

Wintergreen is another fine resort in the Shenandoah Valley region offering a myriad accommodation alternatives. See our Resorts chapter for full details.

Lynchburg

COMFORT INN

*Rt. 29 Expressway
at Odd Fellows Rd.*   *(804) 847-9041*
$$ *All major credit cards*

A comfortable and clean room or suite awaits every Comfort Inn guest. Take advantage of the free shuttle from the airport, just a few miles down the road. A free continental breakfast is offered each morning and a VIP floor, meeting rooms and FAX machines are available as well. Located within five miles of Liberty University, Lynchburg College and Randolph Macon Woman's College, this hotel is a convenient choice for visiting parents or those doing business with the colleges.

DAYS INN

*3320 Candler's
Mountain Rd.*   *(804) 847-8655,
(800) 325-2525*
$$ *All major credit cards*

There are 131 spacious guest rooms available, each featuring remote-controlled television with HBO and in-room safes. The 20 King executive rooms come with recliners for ultimate relaxation. The hotel also provides complimentary transportation to the airport and local businesses, valet/laundry service, 24-hour guest wake-up calls and fax service.

The DayBreak Restaurant, situated within the hotel, provides a discount to hotel guests wishing to take their meals here. A gift shop, pool and playground are also provided. Ask about the audio/visual equipment in the meeting rooms.

HILTON — LYNCHBURG

2900 Candler's
Mountain Rd.   (804) 237-6333,
                         (800) HILTONS
$$$$ All major credit cards

Families with children should consider the Lynchburg Hilton. Not only do they offer adequate amenities and prompt service, but children of any age stay for free when they occupy the same room as their parents. The 168 attractive guest rooms and suites are furnished with large, comfortable beds, color satellite TV and direct-dial telephones. Suites also feature wet bars, refrigerators and double, full-length, mirrored closets. Wake-up service, a gift shop, a newsstand and a courtesy van are other comforts offered. An exercise room, heated indoor pool, spa and sauna are located on the premises.

Johnny Bull's Restaurant serves some of the finest cuisine in Lynchburg. There is a wide assortment of American, continental and regional foods on the menu. Share a cocktail and conversation with friends in The Imbibery.

HOLIDAY INN

Rt. 29 and
Odd Fellows Rd.   (804) 847-4424
                         (800) 465-4329
$$ All major credit cards

Writing desks, sleep sofas, direct-dial telephones with computer jacks and remote-controlled color television are all provided. If you are enrolled in Holiday Inn's Priority Club, you will also receive a steaming cup of morning coffee and newspaper delivery service. The on-site restaurant, The Seasons, offers an interesting menu for breakfast, lunch and dinner, and the luncheon buffet appears to be a hit! Meeting and function space is available. AAA and AARP discounts are offered.

Graves Mountain Lodge, a family-owned resort, is located in Syria.

Howard Johnson Lodge

Rt. 29 N. (804) 845-8041
(800) 654-2000
$ All major credit cards

There are 72 rooms available, all with oversized beds, plush lounge chairs, a writing desk and an extra vanity. Guests enjoy free in-room movies and cable television. Private patios and balconies will allow you to relax while viewing the breathtaking Blue Ridge Mountains. Next door is a Howard Johnson restaurant, which is open 24 hours a day.

Innkeeper Lynchburg

2901 Candler's
Mountain Rd. (804) 237-7771
(800) 822-9899
$$ All major credit cards

The Innkeeper offers a free continental breakfast and comfortable, clean accommodations. The guest rooms feature extra-length beds, remote-controlled color TV (with cable and HBO), custom-made desks, sofas and direct-dial touch-tone phones. Also for your comfort, nonsmoking rooms and handicapped facilities are available. Whirlpool baths or shower massages and swimming pools tempt guests to relax. Children younger than 16 stay free, and roll away beds are complimentary. Corporate, senior citizen and tour/group rates are available.

Smith Mountain Lake

BERNARD'S LANDING
Moneta   (703) 721-8870,
$$$$ (800) 368-3142

Bernard's Landing, a leading resort, is an excellent choice to accommodate travelers. See the detailed description in the Resorts chapter of this book.

Bedford County and Bedford

PEAKS OF OTTER LODGE
Bedford   (703) 586-1081
$$$ All major credit cards

This lodge is like no hotel you've ever seen! Located at milepost 86 on the Blue Ridge Parkway, Peaks of Otter is surrounded by the natural beauty of the Blue Ridge Mountains, a gorgeous lake and unbelievably green countryside. The interior of the lodge is decorated to reflect that setting, with natural woods and subtly blended textures, tones and colors.

The 59 rooms offer double beds and private baths. Three large suites are also available. Each room opens onto its own private balcony. From here you will be able to view the magnificent mountain range. There are no telephones in the lodge, so you may truly unwind and relax away from the "modern world." Guests are welcome in the cocktail lounge and dining room for friendly conversation and delicious dining. Call ahead for seasonal rates.

Rocky Mount

COMFORT INN
950 N. Main St.   (703) 489-4000
$$ All major credit cards

Beautiful Smith Mountain Lake is just 14 miles away from this lovely hotel. The 60 rooms feature cable TV with HBO and AM/FM radios. A complimentary continental breakfast is served each morning, and sunrise coffee and sunset cider are available to all guests at no extra charge. There is an outdoor pool on the property.

New River Valley Region

Blacksburg

BEST WESTERN RED LION
900 Plantation Rd.   (703) 552-7770
       (800) 528-1234
$$ All major credit cards

This hotel is situated on 13 acres of beautiful wooded land. The perfect site for a meeting or banquet, the inn features facilities able to accommodate up to 400. There are 104 rooms available, including two suites and one handicapped-accessible room. Enjoy hearty meals in the dining room or relax with friends in the lounge, where there is nightly entertainment. Three tennis courts are located on the property for working off tension.

BLACKSBURG MARRIOTT
900 Prices Fork Rd.   (703) 552-7001
$$$ All major credit cards

The Blacksburg Marriott offers

148 outstanding rooms in the heart of the city, right across from Virginia Tech. Included are one suite, two handicapped-accessible rooms and 20 nonsmoking rooms. The rooms are comfortable and stylish, with in-room movies and HBO. There is an indoor/outdoor pool, tennis courts and a putting green. A health club is located within the hotel for your convenience. Enjoy elegant meals in the restaurant downstairs or drinks and conversation in the lounge. Banquet facilities are available.

HOLIDAY INN OF BLACKSBURG
3503 S. Main St.   (703) 951-1330
     (800) HOLIDAY
$$ All major credit cards

Nostalgics will love this hotel for its railroad theme restaurant! The 98 lovely rooms have all of the conveniences you'll need. There is one suite, one handicapped-accessible room and 10 nonsmoking rooms. Banquet and meeting rooms can accommodate up to 500. A lounge, coin-operated laundry, game room, pool and satellite cinema are available for guests.

Radford

BEST WESTERN RADFORD INN

1501 Tyler Ave.   (703) 639-3000
                         (800) 528-1234
$$ All major credit cards

Hunters Restaurant and Dux & Company Lounge (see Restaurants) make Best Western the place to come in Radford. The restaurant serves delicious food for breakfast, lunch and dinner. Dux & Co. draws a crowd from all over the New River Valley. The deluxe guest rooms are decorated in Colonial Williamsburg colors. Each has a color television with satellite, two touch-tone phones, a wall-mounted hair dryer and full bath amenities. King or double and nonsmoking rooms are available.

A gazebo-style indoor pool area with whirlpool, sauna and exercise facilities is provided for guest enjoyment. Free parking, ice and vending machines, babysitters, baby cribs and safety deposit boxes add to a list of amenities that make this an especially great choice to traveling families. Weekend and honeymoon packages are available, along with AAA and AARP discounts.

EXECUTIVE MOTEL

Rt. 11 W.   (703) 639-1664
$ All major credit cards

This small motel is clean and comfortable — and very affordable. Its location near St. Alban's Hospital and shopping provides added convenience. The 26 rooms feature two double beds, refrigerators, air conditioning, direct-dial telephones and satellite color televisions.

SUPER 8 MOTEL

1600 Tyler Ave.   (703) 382-5813
                         (800) 848-8888
$ All major credit cards

Super 8 provides excellent amenities: The rooms feature cable television with the Movie Channel. Waterbeds are available upon request. There is 24-hour desk and wake-up call service, and you will be treated to free coffee each morning. Nonsmoking rooms and business singles are available upon request.

COMFORT INN RADFORD

1501 Tyler Ave.   (703) 639-4800
$$ All major credit cards

Families, business travelers and tourists alike will appreciate the comfort and convenience of Comfort Inn. Thirty-two large, spacious rooms with color cable television and tasteful furniture await you. An indoor pool, meeting rooms and an on-site restaurant are available for guest use. The hotel is near Radford University, historic Radford Mainstreet, an antiques mall and Virginia's only historic outdoor drama, *The Long Way Home*. AAA and AARP discounts are available.

Pulaski County/Dublin

COMFORT INN

Off I-81 at Exit 98
Dublin   (703) 674-1100,(800) 221-2222
$$ All major credit cards

A special feature of this hotel is the Emily Virginia's Restaurant located on the property! Motor coach groups will enjoy the special red carpet greeting, apple cider reception and fresh apple farewell. Each of the 100 rooms has individual temperature control, satellite color TV, AM/FM clock radio and direct-dial touch-tone phones. Some rooms feature Jacuzzi. The conference room has a wet bar, and a private banquet room is also available. AAA and AARP discounts are offered.

Patrick County

DOE RUN LODGE
RESORT AND CONFERENCE CENTER
MP 189, Blue Ridge Pkwy.
Hillsville   *(703) 398-2212,*
     (800) 325-M189
$$$ *All major credit cards*

Just across the border of Floyd County, in Patrick County, Doe Run Lodge Resort and Conference Center and its High Country Restaurant are nestled in the most beautiful part of the Blue Ridge Parkway. With Groundhog Mountain as the midpoint on this road of pastoral beauty, your senses will be overwhelmed by what this year-round resort has to offer.

Doe Run Lodge Resort and Conference Center was built to fit the beauty of this environment. The chalets were constructed of wood beams and stone; floor-to-ceiling windows allow magnificent views. Each large suite has a fireplace, two bedrooms, two full baths and a living/dining area. The chalets, townhouses and single-family residences are furnished and have complete kitchens. Millpond Hideaway, designed for executives or honeymooners, has a whirlpool tub, luxury shower and steam cabinet, full-suite stereo and TV, fireplace and en-

closed garage. To realize the true value of their accommodations, share a chalet with another couple or with your family, as it can accommodate up to six people, with two bedrooms and two full baths.

High Country Restaurant offers a unique menu of seafood, steak and other regional recipes, including venison, duck, fresh rainbow trout from their stocked pond, pheasant and country ham. Picnic lunches are packed to go.

Alleghany Highlands Region

Alleghany County and Covington

THE ARBORGATE INN
I-64 to Rt. 220, Exit 5
Covington   *(703) 962-7600*
     (800) 722-7220
$$ *All major credit cards*

This motel is conveniently located within a two-block radius of shopping and fine restaurants. The 75 rooms (including several suites) come with amenities such as air conditioning, color TV with HBO and direct-dial phones. A conference room is available with advance notice.

COMFORT INN
Mallow Rd., Covington   *(703) 962-2141*
     (800) 228-5151
$$ *All major credit cards*

A free continental breakfast is served each morning for all guests of Comfort Inn. Also, for your pleasure, coffee is available 24 hours a day. All of the 67 rooms are equipped with air conditioning, satellite TV with the Movie Channel and Showtime (VCR available) and direct-dial phones — local calls are free. Laundry service is available. Relax in the outdoor pool, Jacuzzi, sauna or health spa. A full service restaurant is located in the hotel, and there's great shopping within a two block radius of the hotel.

HOLIDAY INN COVINGTON

Rts. 220 and 60
Covington   *(703) 962-4951*
     (800) HOLIDAY
$$ *All major credit cards*

Come to Holiday Inn and enjoy its wonderful restaurant or visit the lounge for nightly entertainment. The rooms are equipped with air conditioning, color TV with HBO and direct-dial phones. Ten non-smoking rooms are available. The outdoor pool and nearby shopping facilities are convenient amenities.

Highland County and Monterey

HIGHLAND INN

Main St., Monterey   *(703) 468-2143*
$$ *MC, V*

Michael Strand and Cynthia Peel-Strand are innkeepers of this cozy spot, found in Monterey (fondly referred to as "Virginia's Switzerland"). This Victorian home was built in 1904 to serve the lodging needs of tourists escaping from the summer heat of nearby cities. Eastlake porches with gingerbread trim and rocking chairs are so inviting you will want to stay indefinitely.

All 20 guest rooms have their own private baths and are decorated with antiques and collectibles. Choose a standard room (double bed), deluxe room (king-sized bed or two beds) or a suite (two rooms). A complimentary continental breakfast is provided each morning, with lunch and dinner served in the Monterey Room. The Black Sheep Tavern offers beer and wine every day but Sunday.

Inside
Restaurants

If you think dining in the Blue Ridge means just country ham, biscuits, fried chicken and apple pie, think again. Sure, there are plenty of old-fashioned restaurants offering hearty, conventional Southern fare. But there are also dining rooms whose chefs have won national and even international reputations for their innovative cuisine.

The latter tend to be concentrated in the Charlottesville area and northern foothills region east of the Blue Ridge. These highly acclaimed restaurants include the Inn at Little Washington and the Bleu Rock Inn, both just an hour from the "big" Washington beltway; the C and O Restaurant and Memory & Company in Charlottesville; and The Homestead in Hot Springs.

Some of the region's finest restaurants are tucked away inside beautifully renovated country inns, the Joshua Wilton House in Harrisonburg, Prospect Hill in Trevilians and the Valley Pike Inn in Newbern. Others sit smack in the middle of downtown districts and others along the major artery of the Blue Ridge, Interstate 81.

Photo: Laurie Keeling Young

Bogen's Restaurant in Blacksburg is a favorite for Virginia Tech students.

In this vast region, you will find mountain-top restaurants with magnificent views from your table — especially Peaks of Otter Lodge in Bedford, Chateau Morrisette in Floyd County and the historic restaurants inside Shenandoah National Park.

If you have a hankering for exotic ethnic cuisine, try the Maharaja or Saigon Cafe in Charlottesville or one of the fine Brazilian restaurants in Roanoke, such as Carlos' in the downtown market area. Or, if organically grown vegetarian food is your preference, head to the Wildflour at Roanoke's Towers Mall.

The healthy, home-cooked food at Lynchburg's The Farm Basket is wildly popular, with people lining up as early as 11 AM for lunch at one of the few tables. The lunch spot grew out of a fruit stand and vegetable garden; it's famous for its cucumber sandwiches on dill bread and gouda cheese biscuits.

Many restaurants throughout the region take pride in relying primarily on local products for their cuisine. The Highland Inn in Monterey specializes in fresh local trout and desserts concocted from Highland County maple syrup.

Many of Charlottesville's restaurants seem to be competing with one another for first place in offering the very finest, freshest and most innovative cuisine. This writer would hate to be the judge of such a contest, because there are so many mouth-watering places to dine in and around town.

We didn't include the franchise and fast-food restaurants in this chapter. However, you'll find just about every kind of national chain represented in every section of the Blue Ridge. For example, in Charlottesville, a college town that's always on the go, Subway, the fresh-sandwich favorite for reasonably priced food, caters to the collegiate crowd from its location on 14th Street, near the UVA campus.

Because of the vastness of the region we have attempted to cover in this guide, we were unable to list every good restaurant in every city, town and village. We hope your favorite is included. But if it is not, drop us a line with your suggestions. We update this book every year and may add your favorite to this list.

Readers may also be able to challenge our pricing guidelines for the restaurants listed below. Personal choices and menu changes will prove us wrong in some cases. Still, we hope to provide you with a basic idea of what you can expect to pay for dinner for two (no fancy desserts, wines or other alcoholic beverages). Price guides also do not include sales tax and gratuities. Here are the guidelines:

Less than $20	$
$21 to $35	$$
$36 to $50	$$$
More than $51	$$$$

Note also that this chapter does not include restaurants in the Shenandoah National Park; those are listed in our chapter on the Blue Ridge Parkway and Skyline Drive.

The restaurants profiled in this guide are listed alphabetically under regional sections, then big cities, such as Charlottesville,

Lynchburg and Roanoke. Others are listed according to their geographical location. As in other chapters of the book, we begin with the northern stretch of the Blue Ridge and work our way south, zigzagging east and west over the mountains and Shenandoah Valley.

Bon appetit!

Shenandoah Valley Region

White Post

L'AUBERGE PROVENÇALE
(703) 837-1375
$$$ All major credit cards

Perhaps Virginia's most celebrated French restaurant, L'Auberge is but an hour's drive west of Washington, D.C., in the gentle rolling hills of the northern Shenandoah Valley. Expect superb authentic cuisine fashioned from the Provence region of France. An excellent wine selection, including vintages from local vineyards, adds to the upscale experience.

Winchester

CAFE SOFIA
2900 Valley Ave.   (703) 667-2950
$-$$ All major credit cards

This lovely restaurant serves the only Bulgarian food in the Shenandoah Valley. They are open for lunch and dinner.

EL DORADO
1919 Valley Ave.   (703) 662-6488
$ All major credit cards

The Mexican owners aren't shy with their use of hot chili peppers. You can expect generous portions of hearty, spicy food. Four-cylinder salsa and tortillas arrive at your table before the meal. The atmosphere is casual — laminated tables and chairs and walls hung with pinatas, Mexican hats and travel posters of the home country. Local Mexicans frequent this place, a good sign that the food is authentic and good.

THE OLD POST OFFICE RESTAURANT & LOUNGE
200 N. Braddock St.   (703) 722-9881
$-$$ All major credit cards

This is a relatively new restaurant situated inside an original Winchester Post Office building, which was built in 1910. Lunch selections include gourmet sandwiches, salads and pasta, and dinner offerings include fresh veal, pasta and seafood.

Middletown

WAYSIDE INN
7783 Main St.   (703) 869-1797
$$-$$$ All major credit cards

An elegantly restored 18th-century inn is the setting for a great dining experience. Regional American is cuisine served in seven antique-filled dining rooms, including the old slave kitchen. Peanut soup, spoon bread and country ham, along with a variety of game and seafood dishes and homemade desserts, make this a special place to dine.

Strasburg

HOTEL STRASBURG

201 S. Holliday St.   (703) 465-9191
$$ All major credit cards

Victoriana abounds in this wonderfully restored and converted 1895 hotel. The tables, chairs and paintings are supplied through the nearby Strasburg Emporium, and every item is for sale, so the furnishings are always changing. The restaurant has a strong following in the northern Shenandoah Valley and is known for its generous portions, courteous service and delicious meals. Dinner specialties include Chicken Shenandoah — chicken breast sauteed with country ham, peanuts, apples and an apple brandy cream sauce. The Strasburg salad combines greens and vegetables with pecans, blue cheese, artichoke hearts, eggs and croutons. Reservations are recommended on the weekends.

Front Royal

OLIVER'S

108 S. Royal Ave.
(U.S. 340 S.)   (703) 635-3496
$$$ D, MC, V

The menu changes weekly at this popular restaurant, situated in a renovated Victorian house. Four dining rooms are decorated with old Fiesta china and fresh flowers, and background music hails from the '30s and '40s. A typical entree is

the pan-roasted beef tenderloin with a confetti of sweet potato, Smithfield ham and celery. Desserts include a dark chocolate mousse cake and creme brûlée. Children are always welcome. Oliver's is closed on Mondays and Tuesdays.

Woodstock

THE SPRING HOUSE

325 S. Main St.   (703) 459-4755
$$ All major credit cards

Word has it there used to be an underground spring on this property, and town folk came to fetch spring water from the lady who lived here. Folks still come here for refreshment, though the spring is now closed. Breakfast, lunch and dinner are served seven days a week. Specialty entrees include Eleanor's Delight (a creamy seafood mixture on an open kaiser roll, with tomato and cheese). Dinners come with a complimentary glass of apple cider, homemade walnut rolls with honey butter and a trip to a huge salad bar.

Luray

PARKHURST RESTAURANT

U.S. Hwy. 211 (two miles west
of Luray Caverns)   (703) 743-6009
$$$-$$$$ All major credit cards

This place is extremely popular with golfers who flock to Luray's great courses in the spring, summer and fall. The atmosphere is casual, although tables are set with cloth napkins, crystal, china and candles. Some of the specialties are escargots, tomato shrimp bisque, fettuccine with shellfish and veal Oscar. Every meal comes with a wonderful relish tray, served with a fresh, light garden dip, homemade breads and more. Dinner is served every night, and children are welcome. Reservations are suggested.

New Market

SOUTHERN KITCHEN
U.S. Hwy. 11   (703) 740-3514
$ MC, V

If you're up for traditional Southern food, nothing fancy, this is the place. There's peanut soup—which some say is the best made anywhere — Lloyd's fried chicken, barbecued ribs of beef and much more.

Lacey Springs

BLUE STONE INN
Rt. 11, take Exit 251
from I-81   (703) 434-0535
$$ No credit cards

This is a popular restaurant with professors from James Madison University, and people are willing to stand in long lines for a table. It specializes in tender steaks and fresh fish, such as Lacey Spring Trout.

Harrisonburg

EL CHARRO
1570 E. Market St.   (703) 564-0386
$$ MC, V

This is a good Mexican restaurant with locations also in Covington and Fredericksburg. The staff is fast and courteous.

HUYARD'S COUNTRY KITCHEN
Hwy. 42, Dayton   (703) 879-2613
$ No credit cards

You really shouldn't miss this place. Owner David Huyard and his cooks serve up ham, beef, chicken and vegetables buffet-style. The food is homemade and very tasty — more than likely nothing comes out of a can. The "kitchen" is inside the Dayton Farmer's Market, where you can shop for kitchen items, lace, fudge, antiques, fresh cheese, homemade breads and much more.

JOSHUA WILTON HOUSE
412 S. Main St.   (703) 434-4464
$$$$ All major credit cards

The restaurant inside this beautifully restored Victorian home serves the most exquisite food in town. It's no exaggeration to say

So what exactly is Blue Ridge cuisine? Insiders claim it's everything made in, intended for and consumed by Virginians. Virginia country ham is a good place to start, but you can also get Virginia peanut soup, Virginia applewood smoked turkey, chicken, pheasant and trout and, of course, succulent pork barbeque like that prepared by the Pig 'N Steak near Charlottesville.

Insiders' Tips

this is one of the best restaurants in Virginia. Hard to believe the place was once a frat house for James Madison University students.

Craig and Roberta Moore gutted the whole building and renovated it, and now it is a beautiful, romantic place to have dinner and spend the night.

A selection of about 140 wines includes a wide variety of American and French wines at very reasonable prices. Appetizer choices range from a salmon and scallop mousse to a confit of duck. The smoked-duck salad features carrots, walnuts, raspberries, an artichoke bottom and Boston bib lettuce. Entrees range from trout with a country ham cream sauce to grilled smoked beef tenderloin with smoked oysters. Lamb, quail, pork, veal, duck, salmon and tuna are also offered, prepared in creative ways. Among the many freshly prepared desserts is the creme brûlée — absolutely the best we've tasted anywhere. Reservations are suggested. (For more information on an overnight stay here, see our Other Accommodations chapter.)

L'ITALIA RESTAURANT AND LOUNGE
815 E. Market St.   (703) 433-0961
$$ D, MC, V

Owner Emilio Amato runs a marvelous restaurant right off I-81 in Harrisonburg. The pasta and sauces are all homemade, and many of the entrees are prepared with a light touch for those who need to keep their cholesterol levels down. We highly recommend the gnocci (tiny dumplings made with ricotta cheese and topped with a tomato and meat sauce) and the ravioli stuffed with meat.

THE VILLAGE INN
U.S. Hwy. 11 S.   (703) 434-7355
$ All major credit cards

The dining room at this small, family-owned motel serves simple, delicious meals prepared by Mennonite cooks. The Inn, which has a gorgeous view of the mountains, has a three-diamond rating by AAA.

Waynesboro

CAPT'N SAM'S LANDING
Rt. 250 W.   (703) 943-3416
$$

If you love seafood, come dine with the captain. Surrounded by a unique nautical decor, you can indulge in fish, crab, oysters, scallops, clams and more, prepared in a variety of delicious ways. Or, if you prefer, select steak or chicken. All entrees are served with a trip to the salad bar (or one hot vegetable) and a choice of french fries, baked potato or rice. Don't miss the weeklong Shrimp Feast (held either the first or second week of every month) for "all the shrimp you can eat prepared nine delicious ways." It's served with unlimited salad bar, baked bread and fried potatoes.

For just relaxing, stop at the separate pub for free fresh-popped corn and a special menu. Capt's Sam's is open Monday through Thursday from 5 to 9 PM and Friday and Saturday from 5 to 10 PM.

THE FOX AND HOUNDS
PUB & RESTAURANT

533 W. Main St.   *(703) 946-9200*
$$ *Most major credit cards*

The Augusta County Court records of March 7, 1798, mentioned the present site of The Fox and Hounds as being located on, "The First Main Street in a new town called Waynesborough." In 1837, a house was built on that site by John and Catherine Long; during the Civil War, it was used as a hospital for both Confederate and Union troops during the battle of Waynesboro. Today, this historic building is the second oldest structure still standing in Waynesboro. In 1987 the home was elegantly renovated to open its doors as the Fox and Hounds, given three stars by the Mobil Guide.

It's the perfect place to escape for great food. The traditional English decor will raise your spirits, and the menu will tempt your tastebuds. It includes such favorites as filet mignon, fresh salmon, chuckling oysters and nutty trout. Desserts, such as chocolate mousse, cheesecake and the famous Fox and Hounds Hot Fudge Swan, end your relaxing meal. Only the freshest ingredients are used in dishes which are continental and American in style. Lighter dining and a wide variety of imported and domestic beverages (over 30 beers and five single-malt Scotches) are available in the warm and welcoming atmosphere of the Pub. The Fox and Hounds is open Monday through Friday for lunch 11:30 AM to 2 PM; dinner is served Monday through Saturday 5 to 9:30 PM. It is closed Sundays.

SCOTTO'S ITALIAN
RESTAURANT AND PIZZERIA

1412 W. Broad St.   *(703) 942-8715*
$$

Come join in the casual, family atmosphere at Scotto's, where the owners take great pride in their Italian heritage and in the art of true Italian cooking. Enjoy their homemade dishes and gourmet pizzas, all at reasonable prices. You can also take out or have your food delivered. Beer and wine are served. Lunch and dinner are served from 11 AM to 11 PM Monday through Thursday, 11 AM to midnight Friday and Saturday and 11:30 AM to 11 PM on Sunday.

SOUTH RIVER, AN AMERICAN GRILL

2910 W. Main St.   *(703) 942-5567*
$

Now, here is a family restaurant that means business! Open seven days a week for lunch and dinner, South River offers 20 feet of vegetarian salad bar (with homemade salads and fresh fruit!) and a hearty menu to please all palates. They feature prime rib, St. Louis-style barbecued ribs, hand-patted burgers, homemade soups and a children's menu priced at $2.99. South River's atmosphere is pure Blue Ridge, with large picture windows, lots of plants, a fireplace and a full-sized hang glider suspended from the ceiling. The restaurant also offers banquet facilities for up to 100 and does off-premises catering. Hours are Sunday through

Thursday 11 AM to 10 PM and Friday and Saturday 11 AM to midnight.

WEASIES KITCHEN
130 East Broad St.   *(703) 943-0500*
$ *No credits cards*

You'll find "nothing fancy" here, according to the owner, but if down-home cooking in a laid-back setting is what you crave, Weasie's is the place for you. Join the many regulars and tourists who flock every morning to the kitchen of Mary Eloise Roberts, known as "Weasie" to her many friends and customers. During the past seven years, Weasie has turned the former Dairy Queen at the bottom of Afton Mountain into the major morning hangout in Waynesboro. Breakfast is the big draw, with homemade biscuits and gravy requested most. Desserts are also popular, all homemade. At lunch, which can be bought for $3.50, pies, puddings and cake all have Weasie's special homemade goodness. On weekends, Weasie's is open 24 hours a day. Otherwise, restaurant hours are 5:30 AM to 9 PM Mondays through Thursdays and 5:30 AM to 4 PM Sundays.

Staunton

THE BEVERLEY
12 E. Beverley   *(703) 886-4317*
$ *MC, V*

This restaurant has been around for a long time and is known for its luscious homemade pies and generous afternoon teas. It's a small, family-owned place where you can also get real whipped potatoes and country ham on homemade bread.

Traditional English tea is served from 3 to 5 PM on Wednesdays and Fridays and includes sandwiches, cake, cheese, fruit, scones and other pastries. It's open Monday through Friday from 6:30 AM to 7 PM and Saturday from 12 PM to 5 PM.

THE DEPOT GRILLE
Staunton Train Station   *(703) 885-7332*
$$ *Most major credit cards*

Located in the old freight depot portion of the restored C & O Train Station, this popular dining destination includes a 50-foot antique oak bar. The menu features fresh fish, Black Angus sirloin for two, crab cakes, seafood combination platters, salads and a "lite bites" selection. Daily specials, tasty desserts and a children's menu round out the choices. The Depot Grille has a full bar, including a selection of beers and wines from around the world. The restaurant is open seven days a week for both lunch and dinner. Hours at 11 AM to 10:30 PM Monday through Friday and 11 AM to 11:30 PM on weekends.

J RUGLES RESTAURANT
18 Byers St.   *(703) 886-4399*
$ *All major credit cards*

Situated amid the historic warehouse row, J Ruggles is a fun spot for food in Staunton. The lively pub and outdoor patio (open May through October) are favorties of both local businessmen and college students. The upstairs booths offer a more intimate dining area. The menu features sandwiches, pizzas, pasta, steaks and seafood. Food specials, beveral promotions and special events, such as the (summer only) jazz-on-the-patio series, keep the atmosphere festive nightly. The restaurant is open for dinner from 5 PM to midnight seven days a week.

PAMPERED PALATE CAFE

26 to 28 E. Beverley   (703) 886-9463
$ MC, V

This is another great watering hole smack in the middle of the most interesting shopping area in the downtown. Here you will find gourmet deli sandwiches, such as roast beef and brie on French bread, bagels, stuffed potatoes, iced strawberry tea and luscious desserts. For cappuccino lovers, don't miss "Cappy Hour," 2:30 to 4:30 PM Monday through Saturday, for cappuccino served with luscious Italian cookies and pastries. Continental breakfasts are served on the second level. The place also sells a lot of wines, including the best Virginia ones, as well as gourmet coffees, gift baskets and imported candies. Wine tastings are available. It's open Monday through Saturday from 9 AM to 5:30 PM and Sundays from 11 AM to 2:30 PM; hours are extended during the tourist season.

THE PULLMAN RESTAURANT

Staunton Train Station   (703) 885-6612
$$$ All major credit cards

Step back in time as you enter this authentically restored turn-of-the-century train station that includes a Victorian ice-cream parlor. The building is furnished throughout with antique fixtures and advertising signs from yesteryear. The menu features updated versions of old-time railroad dining car fare, including a wide variety of steaks, seafood, sandwiches and lighter meals. A lunch time soup and salad bar is offered six days a week, along with an elegant Sunday brunch buffet. Sit along the train station Concourse and watch as the trains pass by (Amtrak stops six times a week), and be sure to visit the elegantly appointed bar room. The Pullman is open for lunch and dinner seven days a week from 11 AM to 10:30 PM.

Greenville

EDELWEISS GERMAN RESTAURANT

U.S. 11 and 340 N. (Exit 213
off I-81)   (703)337-1203
$ MC, V

Edelweiss offers authentic German cuisine in the rustic setting of a log cabin. Ingrid Moore is hostess at this two-diamond AAA and two-star *Mobil Travel Guide*-rated restaurant. Dinner menu specialties include several German favorites. Choose from dishes such as Sauerbraten (sliced roast beef), Knackwurst (German beef frankfurter), Rahmschnitzel (thinly sliced pork fillets) and Hackbraten (German-style sausage meatloaf). fresh vegetables are served family style. But save room for dessert! The house specialty is Schwarzwalder Kirschtorte (black forest cake), and they also serve cheese cake, apple cake and tortes — all German-style, of course! If you enjoy beer with your meal, you'll find that there is a nice selection of imported light and dark beers.

Edelweiss provides catering for

all occasions, including formal events, such as weddings and banquets, and friendly get togethers — especially Oktoberfest parties. You can also arrange to reserve the restaurant for tour groups.

Hours are 5 to 9 PM Tuesday through Saturday and 11:30 AM to 3 PM Sunday; they are closed on Monday. A half-price children's menu is available for kids 12 and younger. Casual attire is welcome. Reservations are requested but are only necessary for groups of six or more.

Nelson County

LOVINGSTON CAFE

Off Rt. 29
Lovingston   *(804) 263-8000*
$ *All major credit cards*

This unpretentious cafe in the heart of Lovingston serves up an array of good, old-fashioned American eats, including great burgers, chicken and soups. It's a nice place to unwind on your way to or from Charlottesville, just a few miles to the north. The restaurant is open 11 AM to 9 PM daily.

Lexington and Rockbridge County

HARBS' BISTRO

19 W. Washington St.   *(703) 464-1900*
$ *No credit cards*

The sophisticated atmosphere, food and service at this bistro and gallery make it a popular lunch spot and evening watering hole for students and other locals. Harbs' really lives up to the definition of a bistro: an intimate, unpretentious

club atmosphere. The cafe's walls are covered with art, and its restroom signs are modeled after a bull and the Statue of Liberty.

During the day, choose from the menu of hearty sandwiches, salads, desserts and other specials. Their hero sandwiches are served on freshly baked loaves. The dinner menu changes frequently, but you can count on fresh, delicious bistro fare. Reservations aren't necessary, but you may wish to call ahead for prompt lunchtime service. It opens at 8 AM Monday through Saturday (9 AM Sunday) and is open until 8 PM Monday and Sunday and 9 PM the rest of the week.

THE INN AT UNION RUN

Rt. 674   *(703)463-9715*
$$ *All major credit cards*

The Inn at Union Run is located on 12 acres of beautiful property outside of Lexington. Dining here is a real treat. The romantic dining room seats 22 to 25 guests by candlelight at antique tables. There is truly great ambience here. You sit among gorgeous furniture and such interesting items as Toby mugs dating back to 1755 and 16th-century wine glasses.

The restaurant serves American regional cuisine created with local herbs and vegetables, when available. Executive Chef Jim Stewart and his wife, Higgins, are both graduates of Johnston & Wales University in Rhode Island, a top cooking school. The relatively young couple has a great deal of experience in country inn and gourmet cooking. *Gourmet Magazine* is after many of their recipes! The inn is famous for its breakfasts, which feature such specialties as ginger-bread pancakes and French toast made with English muffins and topped with fresh strawberries. But the dinner menu is just as desirable. Try an appetizer of the inn's own Union Run country pate, unique because it is made with pork. Fruits de mer abbink is one of the chef's specialties and consists of scallops, shrimp and salmon with homemade fettuccine and a saffron cream sauce. Also select from grilled quail with homemade roast garlic sausage and julienne vegetables, grilled beef fil-let, braised Greek-style lamb shank and Virginia leg of lamb stuffed with homemade sausage. For des-sert, the inn offers homemade sorbets, French vanilla and cappuccino ice creams and hazelnut torte. The mouth-watering Musician's Pie, loaded with nuts, has guests calling weeks in advance to make reservations with it in mind. A full wine list is available, and in 1993, the inn won the Governor's Wine Award for outstanding sales and promotion of Virginia wines.

The restaurant is opem from 5 to 9 PM Tuesday through Saturday and on Sunday and Monday by chance. (Learn more about The Inn at Union Run in our chapter on Bed and Breakfast Inns and Coun-try Inns.)

JASBO'S AT RAMADA INN
I-81 and U.S. Hwy. 11 N.
　　　　　(703) 463-9655,(703) 463-6666
$$　　　　　Most major credit cards
The savory foods served here have been praised as unusually good for a hotel restaurant. The chef presents fresh, contemporary dishes for lunch and dinner every day. The restaurant has a comfortable atmosphere, and the quality of the food far exceeds the prices. Choose from such dishes as grilled tuna Mediterranean, New Orleans on-ion bloom, Shrimp Creole and grilled salmon. The pecan-coated chicken with orange sauce is pep-pery and delightfully rich. There is also a list of American wines that includes several Virginia varieties. It is open seven days a week from 6:30 AM to 2 PM for breakfast and lunch and 5 to 10 PM for dinner.

SOUTHERN INN
37 South Main St.　　　(703) 463-3612
$$　　　　　　　　　　AX, MC, V
This charming historical restau-rant has been a tradition in Lexing-ton since the 1940s. Located in the heart of the downtown, the inn spe-cializes in Virginia wines. Visit this family restaurant for traditional Southern-style cooking, sandwiches or Greek and Italian dishes. It's also open for breakfast. The restaurant is open seven days a week from 10:30 AM to 11 PM.

WILLSON-WALKER HOUSE
30 N. Main St.　　　　(703) 463-3020
$$$　　　　Most major credit cards
The beautiful architecture of this 171-year-old, Greek Revival townhouse sets the perfect scene for an elegant dinner or brunch. But you are welcome, whether you're wearing coat and tie or shorts and loafers. The interior of the house is decorated with elegant antique furniture and artwork. Opening off of the foyer are the two

dining rooms, each with a fireplace with a faux-marble mantel and two portraits, c.1840.

The menu offers such tempting favorites as medallions of venison stuffed with cherries, apples and currants; broiled Norwegian salmon with pink and green peppercorn sauce; and mushroom pate with homemade walnut bread. Afterward, enjoy such scrumptious desserts as amaretto-pumpkin cheesecake and frozen chocolate-and-peanut butter mousse. There's also a children's menu. Second-floor banquet rooms are available for private parties. The restaurant serves lunch from 11:30 AM to 2:30 PM and dinner 5:30 to 9 PM Tuesday through Saturday. (Lunch is not served on Saturday from January to March). Reservations are recommended for lunch and dinner.

LEE HI TRUCK STOP RESTAURANT

U.S. Hwy. 11 N.   (703) 463-3478
$ Most major credit cards

You'll enjoy substantial, hearty fare that is appreciated both by locals and the trucking crowd at this friendly spot. Order the daily special and go away happy. They're open 24 hours a day.

MAPLE HALL

U.S. Hwy. 11 N.   (703) 463-4666
$$$$ Choice, MC, V

Come to Maple Hall for fine dining in an elegant atmosphere. This antebellum mansion is full of gorgeous antiques and restorations. Their seasonal menu allows for the freshest and most delicious cuisine imaginable. It's open seven days a

week (for dinner only) from 5:30 to 9 PM. Reservations are required.

NATURAL BRIDGE
RESTAURANTS

U.S. Hwy. 11 S.   (703) 291-2121
The Colonial Dining Room
$$ AX, MC, V

A wonderfully adequate oasis of good family food, the Natural Bridge Village restaurants are as popular with the locals as they are with visitors at this gigantic tourist attraction. Known for their Friday night seafood buffet and Sunday brunch, the Colonial Dining Room serves quality food. It's open Sunday through Thursday from 6 to 8:30 PM and on Friday and Saturday from 6 to 9:30 PM. They are also open in the mornings for breakfast and from noon to 3 PM on Sundays.

Roanoke, Salem and Catawba

ALEXANDER'S

105 S. Jefferson St.   (703) 982-6983
$$$ MC, V

Excellent food and renowned service make this restaurant well worth the trip into downtown Roanoke. Along with such tempting dishes as Chicken Scampi, Grilled Breast of Duck with Raspberry Butter and Veal Alexander, you can find homemade bread and desserts. Lunch is served Wednesdays 11 AM to 2 PM. Dinner is served Thursday, Friday and Saturday from 5 to 10 PM. The restaurant is also open for private parties seven days a week. Dinner reservations are recommended.

Roanoke Restaurants

IN THE MARKET

102 Salem Ave. S.E.
Roanoke, Virginia 24011

(703) 342-3937

309
First Street

Lunch
11:30-2:45 M-Sat.
Dinner
5-10 T-Thurs., 5-11 F&S
Closed Sunday
**309 Market Street
downtown Roanoke
(703) 343-0179**
Voted Best Market Restaurant

Carlos
BRAZILIAN
INTERNATIONAL
C-U-I-S-I-N-E

*Brazilian • French
Spanish • American
food at it's best.*
Lunch 11:00-2:00 Mon.-Sat.
Dinner 5:00-10:00 Mon.-Thurs.
5:00-11:00 Fri.-Sat.
312 Market St.
(703) 345-7661

VANUCCI'S

Lunch
11:00-2:00 M-Sat.
Dinner
5:00-10:00 T-Thurs.
5:00-11:00 F&S
Open Sunday
4:00-9:00

315 Market St.
(703) 981-0000

**Come To The Place Where
Traffic Isn't What Jams!**

Corned Beef
& Co.
BAR and GRILL

107 Jefferson Street
(703) 342-3354

MEDITERRANEAN ITALIAN
& CONTINENTAL CUISINE

127 Campbell Ave,S.E.
(703) 345- 5668

ON THE MARKET DOWNTOWN

ASIAN FRENCH CAFE

32 Market Sq.   *(703) 345-5593*
$$ AX, MC, V

If you are looking for the best Vietnamese cuisine in the Roanoke Valley, then look no farther. This cafe, located in the food court in historic Market Square, has a versatile menu of tempting dishes, thanks to the chef's two separate kitchens. You can choose from Asian-, French- or American-style cuisine, such as Grilled Sesame Chicken, Quiche Lorraine or fresh fruit plates with honey dip. You can also choose to eat in either the elegant dining room or the large, neon star-decorated food court. The dining room is open from 11:30 AM to 2:30 PM and from 5 to 10 PM Monday through Saturday. However, if you're just hopping in for a quick bite, the cafe operates two counters in the food court as well from 10 AM to 6 PM Monday through Saturday. Reservations for the dining room are suggested on Friday and Saturday.

BILLY'S RITZ

102 Salem Ave. S.E.   *(703) 342-3937*
$$ All major credit cards

Housed in a century-old hotel building, this traditional American grill is just one block away from Roanoke's historic Farmer's Market. Join the happy-hour crowd at a wonderful oak bar and dine in casual elegance in any one of four unique rooms amid a beautiful collection of art and antiques — or enjoy your meal in the open air courtyard for a truly special dining experience.

Although known for its great steaks, grilled fish and teriyaki dishes, Billy's Ritz excels at a variety of other food that keeps people waiting in line at Wildflour and added even more to the menu. You'll find the old standards, including Evie's Red Beans and Rice, but you'll also find dishes as diverse as Dragon's Tooth (fresh eggplant dipped in parmesan cheese and grilled with veggies and spicy salsa), Hummus and Polenta with Roma Tomato Sauce. Everything is strictly homemade.

The staff is very friendly, considering how packed the place is, especially on weekends. There's a local flavor to everything, including their own brand of coffee from Mill Mountain Coffee and Tea and steaks fresh from Mason & Hannabass Meats on the Roanoke City Market. For dessert, there's strawberry shortcake, huge brownies or other sinful temptations. With all the Roanokers eating there, tourists will know they've hit the culinary jackpot when they stop at Buck Mountain Grille. The restaurant also serves alcoholic beverages. It's open for lunch and dinner six days a week (closed Mondays). Hours are 11 AM to 9 PM Tuesday through Thursday and Sunday and 5 to 10 PM weekends.

CARLOS BRASILIAN INTERNATIONAL CUISINE

312 Market St.   *(703) 345-7661*
$$
All major credit cards

Hundreds of faithful feijao preto (black bean) lovers come from all over the Shenandoah Valley to partake of the magic that is Carlos Amaral's international cuisine. Carlos' time spent working in

cuisine, as well. The Pasta Raphael is sure to please, and don't miss the prime rib on weekends — we think it's the best in town. If you're in town for just the day, lunch with the downtown business crowd on delicious homemade soups, hearty sandwiches and a wide variety of salads. Enhance your meal with a bottle of wine from an extensive list or choose from the ever-changing selection of premium wines by the glass. And don't pass on dessert. The ice cream cakes are really something special.

This local favorite is definitely worth a stop on your visit to Roanoke. Lunch is served 11:30 AM to 2:30 PM Monday through Friday and dinner from 5 to 10 PM Sunday through Wednesday, 5 to 11 PM Thursday and 5 PM to 12:30 AM Friday and Saturday. Reservations are recommended for large groups.

BUCK MOUNTAIN GRILLE

Rt. 220 S., off Blue Ridge
Pkwy. Exit 121 S. (703) 776-1830
$$ DC, MC, V

They've done it again! Another smashingly successful restaurant even bigger and better than The Wildflour at Towers Mall is now open just off the Blue Ridge Parkway at the old Parkway Restaurant. Doug and Evie Robison have duplicated the delicious, home-cooked

28 different restaurants has manifested itself in a menu quite unlike anything even lovers of Brazilian food have seen. What Carlos does with simple fare, such as black beans and angel hair pasta, spiced with international flavor, packs the place for both lunch and dinner on Roanoke's bustling city market. He and his sister, Iima, co-owner of Carlos, have become some of the best-known supporters of the market's continuing renovation. Carlos is open 11 AM to 2 PM Mondays through Saturdays, reopening from 5 to 9:30 PM Mondays through Thursdays. Weekends, hours are 5 to 10:30 PM.

CORNED BEEF & CO.

107 Jefferson St.	(703) 342-3354
$$	AX, MC, V

Probably the most successful deli operation in town, Corned Beef & Co.'s hearty fare, served up by three former frat brothers who graduated from Roanoke College, is known both for its great food and downtown atmosphere. The name says it all — don't look for anything pretentious here. What you will find is good, basic deli sandwiches served quickly in a first-class atmosphere. These guys know what Roanokers want, and their success shows it. They're open from 11:30 AM to 10 PM Monday, Tuesday and Wednesday and 11:30 AM to 2 AM Thursday, Friday and Saturday.

EL RODEO MEXICAN RESTAURANT

4301 Brambleton Ave.	
Roanoke	(703) 772-2927
260 Wildwood Rd.	
Salem	(703) 387-4045
4017 Williamson Rd.	
Roanoke	(703) 362-7919
$	AX, MC

This popular family restaurant will whisk you away to Mexico with its south-of-the-border decor, Mexican food servers learning English who rarely get your order totally correct (but who cares, it's all good!) and ethnic foods. The menu lists each dinner with an individual list of ingredients for those unfamiliar with Mexican food. These special dinners are created to give you a taste of Mexican cuisine — on the mild side! Choose from fajitas, Taquitos Mexicanos, La Chicana, Enchiladas de Polo (chicken enchiladas) and much more. There are vegetarian and children's menus as well. You will find the service to be excellent, the food kept hot and the chef always willing to accommodate your substitutions. There is a special "lunch only" menu served from 11 AM to 2:30 PM Monday through Saturday. Dinner is served from 4 to 11 PM.

THE HOMEPLACE

Catawba	(703) 384-7252
$$	MC, V

A grand old farmhouse situated just outside of Roanoke is the site of The Homeplace. Their slogan is "Down home cooking that makes you want to eat all your veggies," and you would have to agree. This family-oriented establishment is the perfect place for a Sunday dinner. The delicious home cooking is served family-style in bowls placed right at your table. Fried chicken, mashed potatoes and gravy, pinto beans, baked apples and hot biscuits are the staples of the menu here. A neighborly and courteous staff will make you feel right at home. Always plan on a wait of at least 20 minutes, since Roanokers pack the place on weekends. But you won't mind it on the big front porch, where you can pet the farm felines while you wait. Dinner is served Thursday through Saturday 4 to 8 PM and Sunday 11 AM to 6 PM.

LA MAISON DU GOURMET

5732 Airport Rd.   *(703) 366-2444*
$$$-$$$$ *All major credit cards*

Here, close to the Roanoke Regional Airport, is elegant dining in a gracious 1929 Georgian mansion. La Maison has been voted Roanoke's "Favorite Restaurant for Special Occasions" and "Best Restaurant Interior and Exterior" by readers of *Roanoker Magazine*. This is a popular spot, where business deals are closed and special events in the Southern tradition are held. Proprietor Rance Marianetti prides himself on ensuring that everything is prepared as if it were for his own family. Outdoor weddings are popular here among the lovely landscaped boxwood garden. Inside, the mansion atmosphere continues. You may sample superbly prepared cuisine along with private label wines from the Barboursville Vineyard. Homemade Virginia seafood sausage is a house specialty.

Lunches are popular among the business crowd, with fresh fruit salads and a flaming spinach salad prepared at your table. Lunch also features all your favorite sandwiches. Entrees include Maryland crab cakes, beef peppercorn and catch of the day.

Dinner is exquisite. Appetizers might be fettuccine carbonara or escargot a la Bourguingnonne. Onion soup grantinee is a favorite, and lobster citrus salad with brandy mayonnaise could be the start of your meal. Specialties du Maison include roast rack of lamb for two, Chateaubriand Bouquetiere for two, a trio of beef, lamb and veal, Steak Diane and gourmet seafood. For dessert, expect a tempting array of pastries, Baked Alaska, Cherries Jubilee or sorbet with fresh fruit. At a place such as this, you expect fine service, and you get it. It's open for lunch and dinner Monday through Friday from 11 AM to 9 PM and Saturday for dinner only, 4 to 9:30 PM.

THE LIBRARY

3117 Franklin Rd., S.W.   *(703) 985-0811*
$$$$ *All major credit cards*

One of the most elegant and exclusive restaurants in the Roanoke Valley, The Library is known for its memorable dining experience. The *AAA Travel Guide* rates The Library one of the seven top restaurants in Virginia. Dine on delicious French cuisine by candlelight from a menu that includes such classics as Veal Princess, Beef Admiral and English Dover Sole. The decor of the restaurant is that of a well-stocked library. Dinner begins at 6 PM Monday through Saturday. Reservations are recommended.

LILY'S

At the Roanoke Airport Marriott
I-581 at Exit 3-W   (703) 563-9300
$$ *All major credit cards*

This casual, family restaurant is located in the Roanoke Airport Marriott. Lily's features a full range of moderately priced menu items, as well as popular buffets and children's menus. Prime rib is featured Friday and Saturday nights and champagne brunch on Sundays. Reservations are suggested; it's open daily.

LUIGI'S

3301 Brambleton Ave.   (703) 989-6277
$$ *AX, MC, V*

This Italian gourmet restaurant was established after the tradition of Mama Leone's restaurant in New York City. Naturally, the spaghetti is wonderful, and coupled with the other pasta selections, it's an Italian gourmet's delight. Some of their special treats include Veal Luigi's, Shrimp Scampi and the popular Cappuccino L'Amore, made with a blend of gin, brandy, rum, creme de cacao and Galliano liquor topped with a cinnamon stick, clove and whipped cream.

Homesick Northerners can get real Italian desserts, too, such as cannoli and spumoni ice cream. Luigi's is definitely a cut above any other Italian restaurant in town, both for food and service. Each dish is prepared by your special order, so count on a leisurely dinner with lots of attentive service. Hours are 4 to 11 PM Sunday through Thursday and 4 PM to midnight Friday and Saturday.

MACADO'S

120 Church Ave.   (703) 342-7231
$$ *All major credit cards*

The decor is as interesting as the food at Macado's, where both keep the restaurant packed with a younger crowd. A big hot-air balloon drops from the ceiling, and pictures and keepsakes from local or nationally known bands decorate the walls. You'll see the Three Stooges riding in an airplane, a section of a real classic car on the wall, old toys, posters, nostalgic collectibles and antiques. The extensive menu could take your entire lunch hour to read. It specializes in a delicious array of hot and cold deli sandwiches. The salads and chili are exceptional, too. The owner of the Macado's restaurant chain lives in Roanoke but has restaurants throughout the area, including Blacksburg, Charlottesville, Harrisonburg, Salem and Radford. Hours are 9 to 1 AM Monday through Thursday, 9 to 2 AM Friday and Saturday and 9 to 1 AM Sunday.

MEDITERRANEAN ITALIAN & CONTINENTAL CUISINE

127 Campbell Avenue S.E. (703) 345-5668
$ *All major credit cards*

A Turkish touch by owner Ihsan Demirci has turned this out-of-the-way place on the Roanoke City Market into one of the busiest restaurants on the block. Pasta is the main attraction. It is delicious, plentiful and inexpensive. Lovers of Fettuccine Alfredo and Stuffed Shells will be delighted to see their favorite Italian dishes prepared just right. Health food lovers also are treated to a wide array of pasta dishes with fresh vegetables, seafood and chicken. The Chicken Saltimboca, a tender breast of chicken with proscuitto and mozzarella cheese smothered in a light sauce of Marsala wine and onions, makes watching your weight bearable in this den of delights. Veal dishes are another attraction, especially the Veal Frances, tempting filets of veal dipped in a light eggs batter and pan-browned in white wine and lemon sauce. Spaghetti is the side dish, of course. The Mediterranean is open Mondays through Thursdays from 11 AM to 2:30 PM. They reopen at 4:30 PM and serve until 10 PM. Weekend hours also are 4:30 to 10 PM.

REMINGTON'S

At the Roanoke Airport Marriott
I-581 at Exit 3-W   *(703) 563-9300*
$$$$ *All major credit cards*

Remington's features a superb menu of distinctive American cuisine, complemented with superior service and fine selection of wines. Rated four-diamond by AAA, it serves dinner Monday through Saturday evenings; reservations are recommended.

THE ROANOKER RESTAURANT

Colonial Ave. at I-581
and Wonju St.   *(703) 344-7746*
$$ *MC, V*

For more than 50 years, this restaurant has held high standards for itself. And the results show. It's busy day and night, every day of the week — filled with loyal customers whose parents and grandparents ate here. Run by the Warren family

all these years, The Roanoker is frequented by customers have come to expect quick service and farm-fresh quality food served by people who truly care when they ask how you're doing.

The Roanoker was voted "Best Place to Eat With Your Mother," and it is! Breakfasts are the real highlight, and the same people can be seen every day enjoying it. Don't miss the red-eye gravy and ham with biscuits and grits. It's open Monday through Thursday 7 AM to 9 PM, Friday and Saturday 7 AM to 10 PM and Sundays 8 AM to 10 PM.

ROANOKE WEINER STAND

25 Campbell Ave.   *(703) 342-6932*
$ *No credit cards*

In 1916, when prohibition caused the decline of Salem Avenue by forcing its saloons to close their doors, brick-paved Campbell Avenue took over as Roanoke's main thoroughfare. The road was exciting and new, with streetcars and electric street light. The Municipal Building on Commerce Street and Campbell Avenue opened to the public. And, the "Roanoke Hot Weiner Stand" opened for business at the location where it would remain for more than 75 years. Harry Chacknes opened the stand with a six-burner stove, a kitchen that measured 13 feet by seven feet (including counter space) and six stools. And, right in the heart of the "Magic City," you could get a steaming, plump hot dog for just a nickel. Friendly smiles and neighborly conversations awaited every lunchtime customer.

Almost eight decades later, times

have changed. What once cost you five pennies now runs you $1.05.. The original six stools increased to 19 in 1988 when the Weiner Stand became a part of Center in the Square. They even traded up for a more modern stove after using the old one for 72 years. But some things haven't changed a bit. The stand is still in the Chacknes family. Harry's wife, Elsie, ran it in the 1960s. Now his nephew, Gus Pappas, is the owner. Elsie's nephew, Mike Brookman, works in the kitchen. And, while John Liakos is not actually a blood relative, he is certainly a part of the family after working here for over 30 years. You can still get that delicious, plump hot dog. And we don't think the friendly conversation and warm, honest smiles will ever leave the kitchen of the Roanoke Weiner Stand. Its hours are 7 AM to 7 PM Monday through Friday; 7 AM to 6 PM on Saturday.

SUNNYBROOK INN RESTAURANT

7342 Plantation Rd.   (703) 366-4555
$-$$ MC, V

Howard and Janet Schlosser wanted to purchase a place that created an atmosphere to fit their "home cooking" style. And they found it. In 1983, the Schlossers bought Sunnybrook Inn. This large farmhouse, built in 1912, was the home of the owners of a 150-acre dairy farm. Each day, the Schlossers bake homemade pies, cakes and rolls in their kitchen. Their menu is a compilation of recipes from all over western Virginia, some 100 years old. Their special Peanut Butter Pie is a legend at the Inn. Diners also love their oysters, fresh from the Chesapeake Bay and served year round. Every Friday and Saturday, there's a spectacular seafood buffet, with crab legs and fried oysters. There are separate children's prices. The restaurant is open 7 AM to 8 PM Monday through Thursday, 7 AM to 9 PM Friday and Saturday and 7 AM to 7 PM on Sundays. Reservations are required for large groups.

TEXAS TAVERN

114 W. Church Ave.   (703) 342-4825
$ No credit cards

As soon as you open the door to this 64-year-old white brick Roanoke landmark, the scent of hamburgers and hot dogs cooking on the grease-coated grill hits you. You will notice that the countertop is dented and dull, and some of the stools are long overdue for attention. Sometimes it seems as if the floor hasn't been swept for weeks. Men in industrial-white T-shirts, work pants and aprons shout "hello" to newcomers over the popping grill, bubbling chili and chattering customers. The staff is neighborly and will "shoot the breeze" with you — that is, if they have the time. But don't try to rush another customer or break ahead in the line. Texas Tavern frowns on such impolite behavior, and they might just tell you so! They proudly display a sign that reads, "We serve 1,000 people ten at a time." No, you certainly won't be pampered here. But what you'll find is some of the best chili this side of Texas!

The Tavern is the perfect place for a quick, hot lunch or a midnight snack. They serve all of the favorite standards: hot dogs, hamburgers and, of course, chili. And if you order a nice cool drink, you won't get a Styrofoam cup or even an aluminum can. Only glass soda bottles and straws found here. Texas Tavern is conveniently located near three (pay) parking lots, which is a bonus, since they have little parking space of their own. It is also just a few blocks away from the Farmer's Market and Center in the Square. The restaurant is open 24 hours a day, seven days a week.

THREE O NINE FIRST STREET

309 First St.   *(703) 343-0179*
$$ *Major credit cards*

Dining at Three O Nine First Street is like having your favorite meal with an old friend. If there's one thing that stands out about this place, it's the repeat business it seems to do as a downtown Roanoke favorite on the historic City Market. It's undoubtedly one of the top choices for lunch by downtown professionals.

With a pleasant, contemporary atmosphere and excellent service, lunch and dinner are served in sunny dining room under a skylight filled with green plants. Each day offers a menu special, such as their famous Seafood Salad and Chicken Fingers. A popular choice is one of the gourmet hamburgers, which include the Burgundy Burger, a daily special with a hint of fine wine; a Tex-Mex Burger, well-seasoned with Jalapenos, hot sauce and cheese; or First Street Favorite, a top-of-the-line gourmet burger with bacon and Swiss.

Dinner selections include traditional favorites, such as filet mignon, as well as Chicken Teriyaki and Sauteed Seafood Supreme (a delightful combination of fish, crab, scallops and shrimp sauteed in herbs and butter). Also available to please the vegetarian taste is a popular Ratatouille and Vegetable and Rice Medley. All dinner selections include hot bread and butter, fresh steamed vegetables or seasoned rice, and baked potato, onion rings or fries. Three O Nine will stay first in your mind after you've dined here. They're open for lunch 11:30 AM to 3 PM Monday through Saturday. Dinner is served from 5 PM to 2 AM Tuesday through Saturday.

VANUCCI'S ITALIAN CUISINE

315 Market St., S.E.   *(703) 981-0000*
$ *Major credit cards*

There's nothing better than inexpensive, fine Italian eating. That's what visitors to Roanoke's historic market will find at Vanucci's Italian Cuisine, a restaurant with masterfully prepared and beautifully presented Italian dishes complemented by excellent service and a warm, welcoming atmosphere. Host Walter Vanucci offers daily lunch and dinner specials at unbelievably low prices. Emphasis is on the northern Italian white sauce dishes. Pollame (poultry) might be Pollo Donatello, a breast of chicken topped with thin slices of eggplant and mozzarella cheese with house marina sauce, all for $5.25. Carne (beef) could be a succulent Veal Piccato sauteed in white wine, capers and lemon, for the same inexpensive luncheon price. Frutti Di Mare (seafood) features Seafood Pasta, a butterfly pasta with shrimp, fresh basil and mushroom cream sauce, also for $5.25. House salad and bread is served with each entree. Zuppa di Conchiglie (clam chowder) for $1.95 and Zuppa Di Granchi (crab soup) for $2.95 are popular favorites with the lunch and dinner crowds, along with a delicate Caesar Salad.

From the ample entrees to the excellent coffees, Vanucci's offers a memorable dining experience with each visit. Lunch is noon to 2 PM Tuesday through Saturday and dinner is served 5 to 10 PM Tuesday through Thursday and 5 to 11 PM Friday and Saturday. It is open Sundays from 4 to 9 PM.

WARD'S ROCK CAFE

109 S. Jefferson St.   *(703) 343-CAFE*
$ *MC*

Shake it up, baby! Roanoke's latest addition to the night scene is Ward's Rock Cafe, featuring such groups as Cows in Trouble and Big Idea, as well as Magician Travis Winkler and his traveling magic show. Ward's is helping to make a Jefferson Street section of restaurants become THE hangout for young Roanokers. It features a rooftop section where the latest hot groups are featured. Ward's promise is to serve appetizing food made from the freshest ingredients available, with an entertaining atmosphere and service with a smile.

Rock 'n' roll's greatest stars provide the theme. You may choose from Costello's Chicken Salad (a tangy concoction of all white chicken

breast with walnuts, red onions and tarragon) or The Orbison (roast turkey with Swiss cheese, Thousand Island dressing, cole slaw and spicy mustard on whole wheat). Other greats whose names are affixed to food are Ringo, Elvis and Mick Jagger. This must be a watering hole for Democrats, since Al Gore and Bill Clinton have their own sandwiches named for them, too! Dessert might be homemade brownies or buttermilk spice cake. A full range of beverages also is served, from healthful juices to hot chocolate and domestic and imported beer.

The goal at Ward's Rock Cafe is to become the home of the best food, greatest music and most fun in the Roanoke Valley. Ward Holland and his family are well on their way to making this dream come true. It's open 9 AM to 3 PM Monday and Tuesday, 9 AM to late in the evening Wednesday through Saturday.

WILDFLOUR CAFE AND CATERING

Towers Mall   *(703) 344-1514*
$$ *MC*

If you're going to eat at Wildflour, which everyone in Southwest Roanoke off Interstate 581 at the Colonial Avenue Exit appears to do, be sure and get there before 11:30 AM. A small operation with limited seating, what has been called the best food in Roanoke (by those who like healthy and homemade), is made from scratch early, so the smell of fresh baking bread lures in people who've been thinking about eating there since morning. It keeps getting more and more popular, and the only liability is that it's too small for the throngs who haven't seen food prepared like this since their organic '60s days. Each day, the breads du jour are arranged in a flower pot at the cash register for all to smell and admire. The best red beans and rice in the world comes out of this place — you could eat it every day and not tire of it. To top it off, the young owners take the time to chat and get to know everybody, yet run an extremely efficient operation. Hours are 11 AM to 5 PM Monday through Saturday.

East of the Blue Ridge Region

Loudoun County

THE GREEN TREE
15 S. King St.
Leesburg   (703) 777-7246
$$$

This famous watering hole, surrounded by the enchanting homes, historic buildings, shops and museums of Leesburg, specializes in authentic 18th-century recipes and does its own baking. Try a house specialty, such as Robert's Delight or the Jefferson's Delight, while listening to 18th-century music.

THE RED FOX TAVERN
2 E. Washington St.
Middleburg   (703) 687-6301
$$$ All major credit cards

The Red Fox serves up delicious traditional Virginia dishes, such as peanut soup, pheasant and crab,

along with continental seafood and beef dishes. The tavern, believed to be the oldest continuously operating dining establishment in the Old Dominion, sits in a lovely 18th-century stone building in the middle of Middleburg, Hunt Country's premier antiquing and equine center. Their hours are 11 AM to 4:30 PM and 5 to 9 PM Monday through Friday, 11 AM to 4 PM and 5 to 9:30 PM on Saturday and noon to 8 PM Sunday.

WINDSOR HOUSE
2 W. Washington St.
Middleburg   (703) 687-6800, 478-1300
$$$

This country pub, with its Old English decor and outdoor dining, has the elegant flavor of Virginia's Hunt Country and is the perfect place to dine after a walk through Middleburg's historic district. Specialties include fresh fish, steak and pasta.

Rappahannock County

BLEU ROCK INN
U.S. Hwy. 211
Washington   (703) 987-3190
$$$$ AX, MC, V

Owned by brothers Jean and Bernard Campagne, who also operate La Bergerie in Alexandria, the Bleu Rock Inn is situated on 80 acres about an hour from the Washington, D.C., beltway. The Inn's three dining rooms have fireplaces, and in warm weather, the terrace is a wonderful place to have dinner, drinks or dessert. From November through April, Chef Scott Carr offers a five-course, fixed-price menu on the weekends and a three-course, less expensive dinner on Wednesday and Thursday nights. The rest of the year, the restaurant serves dinner a la carte Tuesday through Sunday nights. The duck foie gras on a crisp potato cake has received rave reviews, as have the grilled sea scallops, blackened grouper, loin of lamb with Madeira and rosemary sauce and desserts. Reservations are suggested. For more information about an overnight stay at the Inn, see our Bed and Breakfast Inns and Country Inns chapter.

FOUR & TWENTY BLACKBIRDS

Rts. 522 and 647
Flint Hill (703) 675-1111
$$$ MC, V

This wonderful restaurant is on the border of the Shenandoah Valley region and East of the Blue Ridge, a short drive from Front Royal down Route 522 S. Owners Heidi Morf and Vinnie DeLuise prepare creative American cuisine at reasonable prices. The menu completely changes every three weeks so that the cooks can take advantage of the best available seafood and local produce. The first-floor dining room is small but offers privacy for romantics; the tables are in nooks with screens of lace or floral prints.

The restaurant serves brunch on Sunday and lunch and dinner Wednesday through Saturday. For dinner, guests can select from four appetizers, seven entrees and three desserts. Appetizers might include corn crepes filled with morels and shiitake mushrooms and served with a smoked red pepper sauce. One acclaimed entree is the beef filet kebabs in a red wine sauce sparked with blue cheese and walnuts and served with lemony sauteed potatoes and snow peas. Morf is the former dessert chef at the highly acclaimed Inn at Little Washington, and her work is sensational. Chocolate pecan tart, mango mousse, pecan shortcakes with sauteed apples and maple cider cream are a few of her creations. Reservations are suggested for dinner.

THE INN AT LITTLE WASHINGTON

Middle and Main Sts.
Washington (703) 675-3800
$$$$ MC, V

This highly acclaimed country inn is a favorite of Washington, D.C., media stars and politicians, being only a little more than an hour's drive from the city. Be prepared to spend big money here for exquisite regional American cuisine. The Mobil Five-Star restaurant has been praised by Craig Claiborne, the dean of food writers and restaurant critics, and in numerous publications, including the *Relais & Chateau*, a sort of Bible for the sophisticated European traveler. The menu changes daily, and guests are served a seven-course meal for a fixed price. Here's what one Richmond food critic rhapsodized over: the "fragrant, plump, explosively juicy little rabbit sausages" and the filet of salmon, wrapped in strudel pastry flavored with mushroom duxelle and accompanied by a delicate watercress butter.

On Saturday nights, dinner costs $88 per person, not including tax, tip, or wine. On weekday nights, the price drops to $78 per person. It's open for dinner daily except Tuesdays. But from June through October, the busiest season, dinner is served daily. Reservations are required. See our chapter on Other Accommodations for information about the inn.

Madison County

THE BAVARIAN CHEF

Madison	(703) 948-6505
$$-$$$	AX, MC, V

This restaurant a few miles north of Charlottesville serves huge portions of German cuisine, family-style. The food is extraordinary, especially the Sauerbraten and homemade desserts, which include a Bavarian nutball and Tiroler apfelstrudel with vanilla sauce. You can also enjoy conventional American seafood dishes. Reservations are suggested. The restaurant serves dinner from 4:30 to 10 PM Wednesday through Saturday and 11:30 AM to 10 PM Sunday.

BERTINES NORTH

Rt. 29, Madison	(703) 948-DINE
$$-$$$	No credit cards

After 10 years on St. Martin's Island, Bernard and Christine Poticha launched this Caribbean restaurant in, of all places, rural Madison County. This popular spot features such dishes as blackened shrimp and swordfish, Steak on a Hot Rock and Veal Mustard. Don't miss Christine's famous chocolate mess pie with a hint of Amaretto. Bertines is open Wednesday through Sunday from 3 to 9 PM.

PRINCE MICHEL RESTAURANT

Rt. 29, between Culpeper	
and Madison	(800) 800-WINE
	(703) 547-9720
$$$$	Most major credit cards

The owners of Prince Michel de Virginia, the state's leading winery, opened this exquisite French restaurant about two years ago. Its fixed-price menu emphasizes contemporary versions of traditional French cuisine and includes a choice of several imaginatively presented dishes for each course.

The restaurant offers the extraordinary cuisine of Alain Lecomte, a Frenchman who took first place in the prestigious Concours National de France des Chefs de Cuisine in 1990. Re-creating his highly acclaimed French specialities using local products and pairing these dishes with Prince Michel and Rapidan River wines has been exciting for the chef.

Lunch is $20, or $30 for the gourmet version, which offers an extra appetizer course and more choices for the entree. Dinner is $50 per person, exclusive of wine, spirits, taxes and gratuity. Reservations are recommended.

Guests enter through Prince Michel's wine shop where they may taste wine at the attractive wine bar. The stairway leading to the restaurant sets the stage for a unique experience. Styled by Parisian designer Ariane Pilliard in collaboration with local artist Marie Taylor, the decor focuses on trompe l'oeil effects, including floor-to-ceiling murals that transport guests to the Bordeaux region of France. Opulent table settings with French linen add to the atmosphere of elegance.

The restaurant is open from noon to 2 PM for lunch seating and 6 to 9 PM for dinner seating Thursday through Saturday. Lunch only is served on Sundays.

Travelers coming from the north will find the Prince Michel Restaurant ideally situated at the gateway to approximately 20 of Virginia's 40-plus farm wineries. The smart dinner guest will arrive early to tour the winery and enjoy the fascinating displays of its wine museum.

Orange County

WILLOW GROVE INN
14079 Plantation Hwy.
or Rt. 15 N., Orange   (800) 949-1778
(703) 672-5982
$$$-$$$$ No credit cards

Limoges china, crystal chandeliers, Chippendale chairs . . . get the picture? This elegant plantation home, built in 1778, is now a bed and breakfast inn with quite a restaurant. The regional American cuisine of Chef Warren Volk, formerly of the Boar's Head Inn, is the most contemporary thing about this magnificent place. The menu changes frequently, depending upon the season, but last winter's included such items as baked chevre with toasted brioche and red pepper conserve and grilled aged tenderloin of beef with fines herbes butter. Truly scrumptious desserts include dark chocolate cake with mocha creme and warm chocolate sauce, French lemon tart and white chocolate praline mousse.

One of the most inviting things about this place is the friendly (and handsome) bartender who helps guests select an appropriate wine for their dinners. The menu also suggests a particular wine for each entree and offers a full range of dessert wines, after dinner liqueurs and dessert coffees. This is the ideal setting for dinner after a full day of touring Montpelier and other Orange County sites. Reservations are recommended. Dinner is served Thursday through Sunday, with brunch also offered on Sunday.

Charlottesville

ABERDEEN BARN
2018 Holiday Dr., across from
Holiday Inn North   (804) 296-4630
$$-$$$ Most major credit cards

This is a well-established restaurant known for its roast prime rib and charcoal-grilled steak. But you can also have Australian lobster tail, crab cakes, shrimp scampi and other seafood delights here. The atmosphere is intimate, with candles on every table, and the Sportsman's Lounge features live entertainment nightly. Reservations are suggested. Dinner is served Monday through Saturday starting at 5 PM and on Sunday from noon to 9:30 or 10 PM.

AWFUL ARTHUR'S
333 W. Main St.   (804) 296-0969
$ AX, MC, V

This casual seafood restaurant down the street from the UVA campus specializes in fresh seafood and a has an awesome raw bar. It also features an English basement with billiards and darts. Awful Arthur's also serves brunch on Saturdays and Sundays. Reservations are accepted.

BAJA BEAN CO.

1327 W. Main St.   *(804) 293-4507*
$ *MC, V*

Found near the Rotunda, in The Corner, this California-style Mexican restaurant serves up lighter meals than your typical Tex-Mex fare. When owner Ron Morse moved here from San Diego, he brought the healthier California sensibility with him. The vegetarian specialities for lunch and dinner are especially popular. A full bar features 12 different kinds of Mexican beer and 15 different brands of tequila. Everything is made fresh, including both hot and mild salsa. The festive restaurant is decorated with banners and T-shirts from Puerta Vallarta, Cancun, Cozumel and other Mexican hot spots. Baja Bean Co. is open seven days a week, 11 AM to 2 PM, with live music every night except Sunday and Tuesday.

BILTMORE GRILL

Elliewood Ave.   *(804) 293-6700*
$-$$ *Most major credit cards*

One of the most attractive things about this restaurant is the beautiful, thick, wisteria-covered arbor

Memory
and
Company

*Dinner is Served
Tues-Sat beginning at 6pm
213 Second Street SW
Charlottesville, Virginia
(804) 296-3539*

that covers an outdoor dining area during the warmer seasons. A popular restaurant for UVA students, the place serves creative pasta dishes and other entrees, white gourmet pizza, unusual and hearty salads and much more. You'll find a wide selection of imported and domestic beer and an outdoor bar. The dessert menu includes such yummy items as apple maple pecan tart and the great American chocolate brownie.

The Biltmore is open Monday through Saturday from 11:30 to 2:30 AM, but they stop serving food at 10:30 PM. They open at 11 AM Sundays.

If you're allergic to cigarette smoke, call ahead before you make reservations at Blue Ridge restaurants. This is Virginia, a tobacco-growing state, and you'll find more smaller restaurants without the smoking restrictions or separate nonsmoking areas than in other parts of the country.

Insiders' Tips

BLUE RIDGE BREWING COMPANY

709 W. Main St.   (804) 977-0017
$$ AX, MC, V

If this place smells like a brewery, that's because it is one. A friendly, casual restaurant, its home brews are named for Blue Ridge mountain peaks, such as Humpback (stout), Hawksbill (golden lager) and Afton (red ale). The eclectic menu includes such dishes as bourbon steak, smoked trout wontons, pesto lasagna, Thai pork chops and blackberry cobbler. The bar's open every night until 2 AM, and reservations are suggested.

BLUE BIRD CAFE

625 W. Main St.   (804) 295-1166
$-$$ MC, V

Enjoy the "Best Food in C'ville" in a casual atmosphere at this charming cafe, located near the historic downtown area. Whether you choose to dine outdoors on the patio or inside, you'll find the experience enjoyable! A diverse menu includes fresh seafood, hand-cut prime beef, veal, poultry and pasta dishes. This is the home of the "World Famous Blue Bird Crabcakes." Fine French, American and Virginia wines are served, as are domestic, imported and microbrewery beers. Full bar service and cappuccino and espresso complement your meal, which simply *must* include one of the delicious desserts, baked on the premises. Lunches start at $3.75 daily and are served from 11:30 AM to 3 PM. Sunday brunch is from 11 AM to 3 PM. Dinner is served from 5 to 10 PM Sunday through Thursday and 5 to 11 PM Friday and Saturday.

Dinner reservations are recommended. Ample parking is available on the premises.

THE BOAR'S HEAD
INN AND SPORTS CLUB

Rt. 250 W.   (804) 296-2181
$$$$ (Old Mill Room)
$$ (The Tavern)   All major credit cards

The Boar's Head Inn's Old Mill Room used to be an actual grist mill. Now it's a formal establishment — one of the few places in the area that requires men to wear jackets in the evenings. Some of the chef's specialties are roasted striped bass with wild greens, crab with a sorrel sauce and grilled Madison County veal with country ham, leeks and fried tomatoes. A popular dessert is the chocolate pecan tart with bourbon ice cream.

The less formal Tavern offers an old English pub-type atmosphere. Reservations are required in the Old Mill Room for dinner and are suggested for lunch. If you want to have lunch or dinner in The Tavern, reservations are suggested. Sunday brunches here are impressive, offering a spread of food that includes omelets and Belgian waffles made to order, pastries, breads, cheeses, smoked fish, breakfast meats and egg dishes.

BRASA RESTAURANT AND TAPAS BAR

215 W. Water St.
next to Omni Hotel   (703) 296-4343
$$-$$$ All major credit cards

This newcomer to the Charlottesville restaurant scene specializes in Mediterranean cuisine, an amalgamation of Spanish, French and Italian influences with

Our chef has several degrees. 852° to be exact.

Wood-fired Mediterranean Cuisine
(804) 296-4343 215 West Water Street Charlottesville, Virginia 22902
Adjacent to Omni Hotel - Free Parking

an emphasis on wood-cooked seafood and beef dishes. (You haven't lived until you've tried wood-fired grilled shrimp!) Although intended to be appetizers, the delicious beef, chicken and seafood tapas also make for a meal on their own. Brasa, named for the embers of its wood-fired brick oven, is owned by the same folks who run Boston's L'Espalier Restaurant, so you know they know a thing or two about fresh seafood. The restaurant is open for lunch 11:30 AM to 2 PM daily and for dinner 5:30 to 10 PM. On weekends, the tapas bar stays open until midnight, if there is enough demand.

C AND O RESTAURANT

515 E. Water St.   (804) 971-7044
$$$$ (upstairs dining room)
$$ (Bistro)   MC, V

"I can confidently assure you that not since Jefferson was serving imported vegetables and the first ice cream at Monticello has there been more innovative cooking in these parts than at the C and O Restaurant," said William Rice, editor-in-chief of *Food and Wine Magazine*.

This celebrated restaurant is proudest of its upstairs dining room, with a menu that features such French cuisine as Coquilles St. Jacques au mangue and smoked duck breast with apricots. Dessert offerings on a typical Saturday night include mint chocolate cheesecake and lemon strawberry torte. Reservations are required upstairs but not in the downstairs Bistro. While more casual, the Bistro's menu also leans toward French cuisine, offering beef tornados with red wine mushroom glaze and sea scallops steamed with grapefruit dijon cream sauce. Hundreds of wines, including some very old ones, are available both upstairs and downstairs.

THE COUNTRY INN

Off 250 E., on Rt. 729   (804) 971-1800
$$$$ AX, MC, V

This elegant, historic inn also has a restaurant that serves a prix-fixé dinner on Wednesday through Sunday nights to some of the most demanding palates in the area. Craig Hartman and Ron Miller, award-winning chefs and graduates of the Culinary Institute of America, are considered masters in the kitchen. Craig's reputation, in fact, earned him an invitation to prepare dinner as guest chef at the famous James Beard House in New York City last March.

A typical winter dinner might start with smoked duck, move on to a soup of pureed winter vegetables and salad of organic greens, continue with a passion-fruit ice and choice of either rack of veal with wild mushrooms or grilled swordfish and end with a chocolate terrine.

Reservations are required.

THE COFFEE EXCHANGE

120 E. Main   (804) 295-0975
$ MC, V

This bakery/cafe on the downtown mall is an elegant place to hang out, sip coffee and read the paper or spy on attractive grad students. Coffees from around the world are served all kinds of ways, from cappuccino to frozen mochaccino. This is also a popular lunch spot, serving what some say is the best potato soup money can

Michie Tavern's "The Ordinary," a 200-year-old converted log house, is a restaurant specializing in Southern cuisine.

buy. The cafe also has salads, sandwiches, light meals, beer, wine and desserts. Unfortunately, it is often short on cookies and pastries in the evenings (the demand is clearly as high as this establishment's reputation) — just when you want something to nibble on with that coffee — so go earlier in the day to buy your goodies then hoard them until you have time to sit and drink your java.

COLLEGE INN
1511 University Dr.   (804) 977-2710
$$ All major credit cards

This University Corner landmark serves up a wide assortment of continental, Greek, Italian and American dishes. As the name suggests, it's a popular dining spot and watering hole among the university set but also caters to a loyal following of Charlottesville natives and tourists alike. The restaurant is open daily from 7:30 to 1 AM except

Sunday, when it opens at 8:30 AM and closes at midnight.

COURT SQUARE TAVERN
Fifth and Jefferson Sts.   (804) 296-6111
$ No credit cards

This bar on historic Court Square is a watering hole for lawyers and other professionals in town. No wonder — it has more than 130 imported bottled beers and Bass, Guiness, Sam Adams and Spaten on tap. You can also enjoy roast beef chili, grilled bratwursts and homemade cheesecake. The British pub atmosphere features antique mirrors and engravings, a stained-glass window and copper-topped bar.

COUPE DE VILLE'S
9 Elliewood Ave.   (804) 977-3966
$ No credit cards

This is a hip place that attracts scores of UVA students. The food is inexpensive but sophisticated. The restaurant serves fresh pasta that's made locally, along with sandwiches, seafood and homemade soups. An acoustic rock band pumps up the volume at 10 PM, except on Wednesday nights, when a country music singer performs (and there's never a cover charge). You can dine indoors or outdoors on the garden terrace (even in the rain, since there's an awning) Coupe de Ville's is open every night until 2 AM but closed on Sundays.

DURTY NELLY'S PUB

2200 Jefferson Park Ave.   (804) 295-1278
$ No credit cards

This is a great place for sandwiches. One of the tastiest is the Lady Godiva, a pita stuffed with turkey, bacon, Muenster, lettuce, tomato, onion and pepper-parmesan dressing. The pub also serves beer, wine and champagne. Their hours are 11 to 2 AM Monday through Friday (the deli's open until 10 PM), 11 to 2 AM Saturday and 11 AM to midnight Sunday.

GREENBERRY'S COFFEE AND TEA

Barracks Road Shopping Mall
$

On the island in the popular Barracks Road Shopping Mall is an oasis for the weary traveller. Greenberry's Coffee and Tea is a new company that has swiftly secured its place in the affections of both locals and visitors to this beautiful town. Serving the finest coffees and teas from around the world, Greenberry's offers new and exciting products to tempt even the most jaded connoisseur. Particularly memorable are the tea brick from China and the delightful pottery

imported from the Republic of Ireland. The most enduring memory after a visit to Greenberry's, however, is the coffee. The exquisite aroma of the freshly roasted beans greets you at the door, and the drinks, from a simple cup of "joe to go" to the scrumptious iced specialties and the incomparable cappuccino, never disappoint. This is coffee lovers' heaven, and you *can* take it with you . . . Greenberry's will gladly ship their wonderful beans.

GREENSKEEPER RESTAURANT

1517 University Ave.   (804) 984-4653
$-$$ All major credit cards

A popular college and "townie" hangout (it's open until 2 AM every night), the Greenskeeper defies categorization. The menu is all over the map, from pita-pocket sandwiches and grilled eggplant to pastas and burgers on whole-grain buns. Live musical entertainment keeps the place buzzing on the weekends. The restaurant opens at 2 PM.

THE HARDWARE STORE RESTAURANT

316 E. Main St.   (804) 977-1518
$-$$ MC, V

The Grand Old Hardware Store Building, a city landmark since 1895, houses this restaurant that offers an astounding variety of foods to suit every palate. You enter the restaurant from either the downtown mall or Water Street. Inside the central dining area, you'll see the same ladders and shelves that belonged to the old hardware store, which operated continuously from 1895 to 1976. This was the original sales area. On the Water Street end of the restaurant, the hardware store's offices have been transformed into dining rooms, and you can see the original typewriters and adding machines used by the store's clerical workers decades ago.

The restaurant is known for its generous portions, whether in beverages, sandwiches or salads. The menu's backbone is its array of marvelously concocted sandwiches, such as the Pavarotti, a robust hoagie stuffed with several types of ham, Genoa salami, provolone, onions and peppers. The restaurant also serves barbecued ribs, pasta, mesquite-grilled meats and a variety of crepes. If you simply want to satisfy your sweet tooth, there is a vast selection of pastries to choose from, or you can order a malt from the old-fashioned soda fountain. There are many other luscious desserts to choose from.

You'll find plenty of free parking at the Water Street door. For more information about the shops in the Hardware Store building, see our Shopping chapter.

HOT CAKES

37-A Emmit St.   (804) 295-6037
$-$$ No credit cards

No, it's not a pancake hose. Hot Cakes, located in the Barracks Road shopping Center, serves up an array of homemade breads, pastries, pies and cakes. The bakery also has gourmet lunch and dinner offerings, including tasty pasta dishes, and a full catering service. Hot Cakes is open 9 AM to 8 PM Sunday through Thursday and 9 AM to midnight Friday and Saturday.

**TRADITIONAL ITALIAN CUISINE
IN A CASUAL ATMOSPHERE**
Lunch/ Dinner/ Take-Out
**1252 Emmet St.
971-9308**
Visa/MC/Amex/Diners/Disc.

KAFKAFE

20 Elliewood Ave.   (804) 296-1175
$-$$ MC, V

This airy place is a sophisticated restaurant-cafe-bookstore in one. You could also almost consider it a gallery, with its changing exhibits of works by local artists. You can dine indoors or out on the patio and order as little as a cappuccino or an appetizer. For the latter, we highly recommend the rich, creamy pate served with olives, capers, cornichons, red onions and French bread. Salads are both creative — combining meats and diverse vegetables, nuts, cheeses or fruits — and generous, a rare combination. One of the most popular entrees is the chicken satay and Szechuan shrimp served with a hot peanut sauce. Desserts are made daily and include English trifle, Kahlua cheesecake, carrot cake and lots of wicked treats made with Callebaut chocolate from Belgium. The Chocolate Regal, a rich, dense cake served on a pool of raspberry puree, will make your toes curl, it's so devilish.

Daily newspapers from Madrid, London, Hamburg, Frankfurt and other great cities of the world are also available here. Kafkafe also holds fiction and poetry readings at night on a regular basis.

LITTLE JOHN'S

1427 University Ave.   *(804) 977-0588*
$ *No credit cards*

Be it lunchtime or the middle of night, Little John's is the place to go if you've got a hankering for a New York style deli sandwich. It's open 24 hours a day, Little John's is conveniently located on The Corner, a short walk from the Rotunda at UVA. Don't miss the Nuclear Sub, with cold slaw, turkey, barbecue and mozzarella, or the Baby Zonker, a bagel with cream cheese, bacon, tomatoes and onions.

MACADO'S

1505 University Ave.   *(804) 971-3558*
$ *AX, MC, V*

Like its sister restaurants in Roanoke, Farmville, Radford and elsewhere, this is a casual place to have a sandwich and beer or sundae made with Haagen-Dazs ice cream in the candy shop. It's on The Corner, close to campus and UVA Hospital. Hours are 9 to 1 AM Monday through Thursday and Sunday and 9 to 2 AM Friday and Saturday

MAHARAJA

Seminole Square   *(804) 973-1110*
$$ *AX, MC, V*

If spicy, rich Indian cuisine is your desire, this is the place to dine.

Located in the Seminole Square shopping center near Barracks Road, the restaurant has a cozy but spartan atmosphere. "Curry and spice and everything Indians think nice can be found on this restaurant's extensive menu," wrote one local critic. You'll find a variety of curries and chicken, shrimp and fish tandoori (which means it's marinated in herbs and spices and grilled in a clay oven) and more. Ginger, garlic, onions, cilantro, lemon, tamarind, cashews, almonds and yogurt are some of the ingredients that are blended together and served with meats, fish or vegetables, making this cuisine exciting to the palate. You can ask for your food to be chili hot, medium or mild. Reservations are suggested for dinner.

MAIN STREET GRILL

1329 W. Main St.   *(804) 977-4885*
$ *No credit cards*

This is a diner for the '90s, with pastel colors and modern art on the walls but with good old classic American cooking. Word has it they serve the best grilled cheese sandwiches anywhere. It's open from 7 AM to 2 AM, the grill welcomes families, with plenty of high chairs and booster seats for children. Its desserts alone are worth a visit: homemade key lime pie, hot fudge sundaes, mousse cake and cheesecake imported from the Bronx. The Main Street Grill has live music Thursday through Sunday nights and serves brunch on Saturdays and Sundays. It's open seven days a week.

RoCoCo's

PIZZA AND PASTA

(804) 971 7371

Mesquite Grilled Seafoods
Cappucino
Extensive Wine List

Corner of Hydraulic Rd. &
Commonwealth Drive in the
Village Green

Brunch, Lunch, Dinner • Serving All Day

MARTHA'S CAFE

11 Elliewood Ave.	(804) 971-7530
$	No credit cards

This is a highly popular place on The Corner, and it's no wonder. The food is homemade, interesting and reasonably priced, and the atmosphere is casual but never boring. Martha's has been around since 1976 and served cappuccino long before it was in vogue in this city. The menu emphasizes chicken and fish, and nothing is deep fried. It's known for its crab cakes, but other popular items are barbecued shrimp, jambalaya and spinach lasagna. All the desserts are made at the restaurant, and they include white chocolate mousse with Frangelica and chocolate decadence cake. Children's portions are available, and children and babies are welcome. The cafe is situated in an old house with an enormous elm tree out front. You can dine indoors, or, in spring or summer, outside on a cobblestone patio under the elm tree.

Inside, weavings from around the world and musical instruments hang from the walls. There's a fireplace and bathtub full of goldfish in the front room. Owner Ken Waxman loves to play old jazz on the stereo system. Though the cafe is within walking distance of the UVA campus, it does not necessarily cater to students. The clientele is older — lots of grad students, doctors and professors. As with most of the restaurants on crowded Elliewood Avenue, you need to park in the centrally located parking garage. Personal checks are accepted.

MEMORY AND COMPANY

213 Second St. S.W.	(804) 296-3539
$$$	MC, V

Founded as a cooking school in the early 1980s, Memory and Company continues as one of the finest restaurant traditions in the city. The restaurant is situated in a historical landmark, c. 1840, within walking distance of downtown Charlottesville. Executive Chef and Owner John Paul Corbet trained at the California Culinary Academy in San Francisco and has extensive wine, food service and culinary experience. He has catered to the likes of Robert Mondaui, Silver Oak Cellars and Iron Horse Vineyards, just to name a few from the California wine country.

A choice of dining rooms is available, including an exhibition cooking/dining area, a quaint and quiet dining room with wine racks and art displayed by local artists and, when weather permits, outside seating in their herb garden or patio area.

The menu, which changes seasonally, features country French and classical Italian, with accents of Southwestern and California cuisines. The four-course prix-fixé meal includes a selection of appetizers, entrees and desserts, all created daily from fresh ingredients. Dinner is served Tuesday through Saturday, beginning at 6 PM.

MICHIE TAVERN

Thomas Jefferson Pkwy.

(804) 977-1234

$ *AX, MC, V*

At Michie Tavern, a 200-year-old converted log house called The Ordinary serves fried chicken, black-eyed peas, stewed tomatoes, cole slaw, potato salad, green bean salad, beets, homemade biscuits, cornbread and apple cobbler every day of the year from 11:30 AM to 3 PM. Lunch costs $8.95, not including beverage, dessert or tax.

OREGANO JOE'S

1252 Emmet St.   *(804) 971-9308*

$-$$ *MC, V*

This is a popular, informal Italian restaurant one block north of Barracks Road shopping center. Owners Carl and Victoria Tremaglio and Roberta Corcoran use fresh local ingredients and imported Italian products, making all sauces, soups and dressings from scratch. Daily specials feature fresh, seasonal ingredients and often include such seafood as salmon, swordfish, tuna and red snapper. Cappuccino, espresso and international coffees are served, along with Virginia and Italian wines and domestic and imported beer. Children are welcome and so are take-out orders. Oregano Joe's also serves lunch on weekdays. Tremaglio's catering business, Festive Fare, handles everything from formal wedding receptions to picnics and business meetings.

RISING SUN BAKERY

109 14th St. N.W.

$ *No credit cards*

This family-owned full-service bakery with deli has been serving freshly made goodies to a faithful clientele since 1977. Everything is homemade from natural ingredients, which makes for delightful lunches and dinners in this relaxed, family-oriented atmosphere. Coffee and pastries are popular in the morning hours, and an espresso bar (open from 8 AM to 8 PM) draws the true coffee lovers in. Also try their fantastic cakes — seven different kinds! — that were voted "Best in Charlottesville" three years in a row. They're open seven days a week.

Rococo's

Hydraulic and Commonwealth Rds.
in the Village Green (804) 971-7371
$$ AX, MC, V

This elegant but casual Italian restaurant features homemade ravioli, fettuccine, stromboli, calzone, gourmet pizza and more. Some of its specialties are white cheese and pesto pizza and mesquite-grilled half chicken marinated in balsamic vinegar and rosemary. Another favorite is chocolate toffee ice-cream pie. The restaurant has an extensive wine list and a full-service bar. It's open for brunch on Saturdays and Sundays, and the full menu is available for take-out orders. The restaurant accepts reservations for parties of five or more, except on weekends after 6 PM, after which no reservations are made.

Saigon Cafe

1703 Allied Ln. (804) 296-8661
$ MC, V

The atmosphere is relaxed and comfortable at Charlottesville's first and only Vietnamese restaurant. Some of the specialties of the house are the Vietnam egg rolls, grilled lemon chicken and shrimp Saigon-style. The soups are especially noteworthy.

Silver Thatch Inn

3001 Hollymead Dr.
at Rt. 29 N. (804) 978-4686
$$$$ MC, V

The menu changes every six weeks or so at this exquisite restaurant in a beautiful old inn, c. 1780.

TASTINGS
OF CHARLOTTESVILLE

RESTAURANT
AMERICAN GRILL
WINE BAR &
RETAIL SHOP

293-FOOD **971-WINE**
(3663) (9463)
502 E. Market St.
Charlottesville, VA 22902

The Silver Thatch serves regional American cuisine, with an emphasis on fresh produce. Two typical entrees are the peppered and charred veal carpaccio with asparagus and mushroom compote and grilled lamb chops with minted apple and roasted corn relish. The wine list is All-American, with an emphasis on California and Virginia. Desserts are all homemade, beautifully presented and mouthwatering. Enjoy intimate dining by candlelight. Reservations are recommended. Dinner is served from 5:30 to 9 PM Tuesday through Saturday. Sunday is reserved for lodgers, and they are closed Mondays.

The Smokehouse

16½ Elliewood Ave. (804) 977-3024
$ No credit cards

Stop here for quick, delicious sandwiches piled with freshly smoked meats. The casual atmosphere attracts lots of tourists and students, who eat outdoors on picnic tables in warm weather. Their sandwiches and barbecue are considered the best in town.

SOUTHERN CULTURE

633 W. Main St.   *(804) 979-1990*
$$ *MC, V*

This is a hip cafe and restaurant with delicious food that leans toward the Cajun variety of Southern cuisine. Fettuccine Claire, with artichoke hearts, green chilies, red peppers, ricotta and roasted pecans, is a real hit here, along with crab and corn chowder and sweet potato fries. The atmosphere is dark and artsy — an exciting place for dining and chatting with good friends or a loved one. The bar appears to be a lively gathering place for intellectuals and artists of all sorts. It's open seven days a week from 5 to 10:30 PM and for drinks until 1:30 AM.

ST. MAARTEN CAFE

1400 Wertland Ave.   *(804) 293-2233*
$$ *AX, MC, V*

This is a favorite of UVA students — a place to forget your troubles and imagine you're far away on a tropical island. It has a late night menu until 1 AM. The cafe serves lots of fresh seafood and burgers. All the soups are made from scratch, and the cheesecakes are also made on the premises. It's open every night until 2 AM and every day for lunch. St. Maarten is on The Corner, near the college campus and hospital.

STAR HILL CAFÉ

320 W. Main St.   *(804) 295-4456*
$$$$ *All major credit cards*

This is an intimate restaurant with a country French atmosphere. The cuisine is mainly classic French, with specialties that include beef Wellington, chateaubriand, crepes Suzette and Caesar salad. Reservations are recommended, and jackets are required. They serve dinner from 6 to 10 PM Tuesday through Saturday and brunch on Sunday from 10 AM to 3 PM. They're closed Monday.

TASTINGS

502 E. Market St. (next to downtown parking deck)   *(804) 293-3663*
$$-$$$ *MC, V*

This restaurant, wine bar and wine shop combined is run by William Curtis, who also owns the popular Court Square Tavern nearby. You can stop first at the bar and sample a wine to order with your dinner, or simply drink and munch on a few crackers.

The wood grill adds a delicate flavor to meats and fish. Foods are straightforward, fresh and deeply satisfying. All year-round entrees include crabmeat casserole, grilled salmon with bearnaise sauce and herb-crusted rack of lamb, and in the summertime, strawberry rhubarb pie is the seasonal favorite. Select your dinner wine from more than 1,000 in the shop. Or you can order a half or full glass from a list of between approximately 125 wines. Better yet, have Curtis prepare a "flight" of three wines to sample during dinner.

Their wine list received the "Best of Excellence" award for 1993-'94 from *Wine Spectator* magazine.

Reservations are recommended.

THE TEA ROOM CAFE AT THE 1817

1211 W. Main St.   *(804) 979-7353*
$ *No credit cards*

For a sunny setting, try lunch at the Tea Room Cafe. It's located in the solarium (overflowing onto the gallery-style back porch) of the beautifully appointed 1817 Antique Inn. Gourmet dishes are served, and the prices are reasonable.

THE VIRGINIAN

1521 W. Main St.   *(804) 293-2606*
$$ *Most major credit cards*

A tradition since 1921, The Virginian is open daily across from the UVA campus. The emphasis is on healthy American food, including grilled steaks, seafood, pasta, burgers, homemade breads and desserts. Lunch and dinner are served from 11 AM to 11 PM, and they have late-night hours until 2 AM.

Other Restaurants near Charlottesville

PROSPECT HILL

Trevilians   *(800) 277-0844*
$$$$ *MC, V*

This historic plantation inn, located 15 miles east of Charlottesville, houses a beautifully decorated, candlelighted restaurant. Classic French cuisine is served here, with Provençale and American accents. A spring dinner menu listed, among its many entrees, tenderloin of beef tornados served with a port wine, sun-dried tomato and morel sauce. Or, for a lighter dinner, you could have tried the Volaille Farcie au Provence — a chicken breast stuffed with spinach and

---

Lovingston Cafe and Pizzeria

Steaks, Seafood, Veggie Specials, Homemade Soups & Desserts, Casual Atmosphere, Exotic Beers, Fine Wine, Sandwiches, Lunch & Dinner 7 Days a Week

Front Street, Lovingston
Nelson County, Virginia 263-8000

---

boursin cheese and served with Provençale sauce. Desserts are also French and include a chocolate cappuccino mousse and classic mille feuille, which means "a thousand layers."

The fixed-price, five-course dinners cost $40 a person, not including wine, taxes or gratuities. With advance notice, the chef will cater to people whose diets are restricted. Innkeepers Michael and Laura Sheehan invite dinner guests to arrive a half hour earlier for a glass of wine or cider and to stroll the grounds or sit by the crackling fire. Reservations are required.

PIG 'N STEAK

17 Valley St.
Scottsville   *(804) 286-4114*
Washington St.
Madison   *(804) 948-3130*
$ *No credit cards*

The *Southern Farmers Almanac* lists Pig 'N Steak as one of the top 50 barbecue places in the South and one of the top five in Virginia. You can also get real hickory pit-smoked ribs and steaks, hamburgers and tons of french fries. By the way, this is the home of the original Dew Drop Inn mentioned in "The Waltons" television show. Remember the place? It's where Jason Walton used to play the piano. The Pig 'N Steak is open every day except Monday.

RODES FARM INN

Off Rt. 151
Nellysford (804) 325-2200
$-$$

The red brick farmhouse run by Marguerite Wade as an inn and restaurant (see our Bed and Breakfast Inns chapter) is legendary in these parts for serving up some of the finest country fare south of the Mason-Dixon Line. The accent is on hearty: roast beef with gravy, fried chicken, pork chops, country ham, fresh garden vegetables, homemade biscuits, pies and cobblers. The down-home atmosphere attracts some pretty sophisticated palates. Past guests here include such notables as the Earl of Hanover, former President Gerald Ford, Alan Alda, Mick Jagger and John Lennon. Lunch is served daily from noon to 2 PM. Dinner "sittings" are at 6 and 8 PM Tuesday through Saturday and 12:30 and 2:30 PM on Sunday. Reservations are strongly suggested.

Lynchburg

BATEAU LANDING

Main at 12th St. (804) 847-1499
$ *No credit cards*

Lynchburg's historic community market, Bateau Landing, offers a vast array of country fare — fresh eggs, country ham and homemade jams and jellies with breakfast and lunch. Produce changes seasonally. After having a piece of homemade cake, pie or a cookie, browse the market and whet your appetite for shopping. This is truly a fun place for the whole family, with ever-changing vendors and seasonal goods. The market is open 7:30 AM to 2 PM Monday through Saturday.

CAFE FRANCE

3225 Old Forest Rd. (804) 385-8989
$$$ *AX, MC, V*

Jazz music helps to create an upbeat atmosphere in this cafe. From the Art Deco design to the wine bar, this restaurant is fresh and original. Both the lunch and dinner menus are extensive. Lunch calls for sandwiches, soups and burgers. An additional menu is available with the day's specials, which could include a French dip, soft shell crab sandwich or seafood au gratin. There is also a soup, dessert and coffee du jour. The dinner menu is even more varied. Delicious entrees such as Jamaican Prime Rib and Cornish Game Hen are available on the standard menu. A special dinner menu with the night's specials is offered, as well. Some of their more popular dishes are Rack of Lamb with Pommery mustard and seasoned bread crumbs and Virginia Jumbo lump and backfin crabmeat served with buerre blanc sauce. A deli take-out menu is available, as well. Lunch is served Monday through Friday from 11:30 AM to 3 PM. Cafe France is open for dinner Tuesday through

Saturday from 5:30 to 10 PM. Deli take-out is available on Monday from 11 AM to 3 PM and Tuesday through Saturday from 11 AM to 5:30 PM. Reservations are suggested for dinner.

CHARLEYS

3405 Candler's
Mountain Rd.   (804) 237-5988
$ AX, MC, V

There is always something special going on at Charleys. A new calendar comes out each month with a long list of special happenings. There's live entertainment every Wednesday. Every Tuesday is seniors day and all persons 55 and older receive 15 percent off of their entree. There is also a special 99¢ children's menu every Sunday through Thursday. The menu is just a varied as the entertainment. You can choose from such favorites as fajitas, seafood fettuccine, chicken cordon bleu and beef stroganoff, all homemade. Dining is available in the greenhouse dining room or in the more elegant back room. The restaurant is open 11:30 AM to 10 PM Sunday through Thursday and 11:30 AM to midnight Friday and Saturday. Reservations are suggested for parties of six or more.

CLAYTON'S

3311 Old Forest Rd.   (804) 385-7900
$ MC, V

Clayton's is a casual table service-style restaurant. A friendly staff serves up a delicious breakfast and lunch daily and dinner twice a week. Choose from chicken Tina, grilled marinated shrimp, grilled vegetable sandwich or one of their other tasty sandwiches. There are two hot specials daily. The restaurant is open for breakfast and lunch from 6 AM to 3 PM daily. Dinner is served on Wednesday and Friday from 5 to 9 PM.

EMIL'S

Boonsboro Shopping Ctr.
$$ (cafe)   (804) 384-3311
$$$ (rotisserie)   All major credit cards

Whether you dine in the informal surroundings of the cafe or in the more elegant rotisserie, Emil's is an excellent choice for fine dining. Each area has its own special menu and atmosphere. The cafe is casual and bright with plenty of green plants. Its menu is full of dishes such as G'Schnatzlets, roestis, seafood au gratin and crabmeat imperial. The rotisserie is elegant, with candlelight and a white setting. Here you can enjoy Veal Zurich, roast rack of lamb, chateaubriand maison, Norwegian salmon and entrees flambeed tableside. There is also a special lunchtime menu. Indulge yourself and try one of the many delicious desserts made in their in-house bakery. Emil's open Monday through Saturday from 10 AM to 10 PM.

THE FARM BASKET

2008 Langhorne Rd.   (804) 528-1107
$ No credit cards

Don't miss The Farm Basket while you're in Lynchburg! Regardless of your age or nature, it's the kind of place that will fascinate you for hours with its shopping opportunities. Then it will amaze you once again with its tiny restaurant that's always packed with locals and others who keep coming back for the homemade food prepared by cooks who look like your Grandma. They're famous for their cucumber sandwich on dill bread that melts in your mouth, Gouda cheese biscuits and Brunswick stew. Have a dessert of lemon bread with cream cheese and then go shopping! Lots of Lynchburg matrons stop by this beautiful neighborhood to get boxed lunches to go. It's open daily except Sundays 10 AM to 5 PM.

THE LANDMARK
STEAKHOUSE AND LOUNGE

6113 Fort Ave. (804) 237-1884
$$ *Most major credit cards*

The Landmark allows you to have an elegant dinner in a casual atmosphere. The rustic decor will make you feel at home, while special touches such as linen tablecloths will enhance your dining. Their steak and ribs have a terrific flavor because they are cooked over hickory charcoal. You can also choose from chicken and seafood dishes. The restaurant holds an ABC license, and you'll find a full bar and an extensive wine list. A nonsmoking section is also available. The Landmark is open for lunch from 11:30 AM to 2 PM Monday through Friday. Dinner is served from 5:30 to 10 PM Sunday through Thursday and 5:30 to 10:30 PM on Friday and Saturday. Reservations are suggested on weekends and during busy seasons, such as Christmas and prom time.

RED LOBSTER RESTAURANT

3425 Candler's
Mountain Rd. (804) 847-0178
$$ *Most major credit cards*

A nautical American theme perfectly matches the name of this seafood restaurant, which also has a Roanoke Valley location. Although the restaurant is casual, it is still well-suited for business, banquets or special occasions. A traditional array of fine seafood is offered. However, after dinner you may like to try some very creative desserts. Try their Sensational 7 Cake, made with seven different chocolates; the Fudge Overboard, a brownie pie topped with French vanilla ice cream, whipped cream and Hershey's chocolate syrup; or Key Lime Pie. It's open 11 AM to 10 PM Sunday through Thursday and 11 AM to 11 PM on Friday and Saturday. Reservations are not accepted, but call-ahead seating is available.

TEXAS STEAK HOUSE

4001 Murray Pl. (804) 528-1134
$ *Most major credit cards*

A real Texas dinner awaits you at this steak house, where a casual setting and a Texas theme set the stage for a delicious dinner. There is a vast variety of delicious foods, but steaks dominate the menu with 7 and 9 ounce filets. Try a Yellow Rose of Texas or a Hershey Brownie for dessert. It's open 11 AM to 10 PM Monday through Thursday, 11 AM to 11 PM Friday, 4:30 to 11 PM Saturday and 4 to 9 PM Sunday. Reservations are not accepted, but call-ahead seating is offered.

Smith Mountain Lake Area

BERNARD'S LANDING RESTAURANT

Rt. 940, Moneta   *(703) 721-3028*
$$ *All major credit cards*

If you want the finest dining and best view on the lake, Bernard's Landing Restaurant has it all! It's truly a special place, well worth the 45-minute drive from Roanoke or Lynchburg. Everything on the menu is a delight. Whether you want a sandwich (try the chicken salad) or a seafood platter of shrimp, scallops, flounder and deviled crab, you can expect a gourmet twist to your order. The Friday night seafood buffet is special, and there probably isn't a soul on the lake who hasn't been to Sunday brunch, with waffles and fluffy omelets served to your precise instructions.

If you're going to the lake to experience it the way lake fanatics do each weekend, don't miss this dining opportunity. You'll feel like you're in another world, with the lake breeze, service by waiters and waitresses dressed in nautical garb, boat decor indoors or outside dining in the soft breeze. It's open 11 AM to 10 PM Tuesday through Saturday and 11 AM to 3 PM Sundays.

PADDLE WHEEL CRUISES

20 Bridgewater Pl.
Moneta   *(703) 721-7100*
$$$ *All major credit cards*

Glide across gorgeous Smith Mountain Lake while enjoying some of the best food around. You can ride on the luxurious *Virginia Dare*, a 19th-century side wheeler, or on the *Blue Moon*, a 51-foot motor yacht perfect for smaller groups. Bask in the sun on an afternoon cruise or relax with a cocktail or favorite wine while watching the sun set across the lake. Seafood buffets and gourmet food make up the tempting menu. Many trips feature live entertainment to create a festive atmosphere. The cruises run year round, but times vary. Call the company for specific information. This is a wonderful experience for lake lovers. Reservations are required.

COOPERS CORNER

Rt. 608 and 626
Huddleston   *(703) 297-7104*
$$ *MC, V*

A pleasant restaurant specializing in German fare, Coopers Corner offers substantial family dining with a complete salad bar, special seafood and country and breakfast buffets. Angel hair pasta selections and chicken dishes are the specialties. It's open weekdays from 7 AM to 9 PM and weekends 7 AM to 10 PM.

DUDLEY MART & RESTAURANT

Rt. 670 and 668, Wirtz   *(703) 721-1635*
$ *No credit cards*

This revamped country school built in 1931 is now home to one of Smith Mountain Lake's most delightful dining surprises. The homemade barbecue and roasted chicken are worth the trip here, and it's a great place for a quick meal while you're touring the lake. Stop by Monday through Thursday from 6:30 AM to 9 PM, Friday and Saturday from 6:30 AM to 10 PM and Sundays from 7 AM to 9 PM.

SAL'S PIZZA RESTAURANTS
Fairway Village Shopping
Center   (703) 721-8904
South Lake Plaza
Union Hall   (703) 576-2263
$ MC, V

Homesick Northerners will feel right at home at one of the best restaurants on the lake. Sal's is a family restaurant that you just seem to keep coming back to, whether you order the Italian family's spaghetti and pasta specialities or come for the fantastic salad bar. Naturally, the pizza is just what you'd expect from authentic Italian cuisine. There's an adequate wine list to complement your meal. Kids enjoy their own separate menu and can choose from their favorite pasta dishes at a reduced price. When you visit on weekends, don't miss the $5 breakfast buffet for a tasty value. It's open seven days a week from 10 AM to 11 PM.

SCHOONERS RESTAURANT
Rt. 122 at Hales Ford Bridge
Moneta   (703) 721-1752
$ No credit cards

Whether you're driving down Route 122 or cruising across the beautiful lake, Schooners is a casual and friendly stop for lunch or dinner. You can dine inside or sit outdoors under sun umbrellas until their loudspeaker announces your order is ready. This little nook near Hales Ford Bridge is often chock full of locals and visitors. In addition to Greek foods and rib eye steak, this restaurant makes some of the best pizza and hamburgers known to the Blue Ridge. Their hamburger meat is ground fresh and pattied daily, so you never get frozen burgers. Their mouth-watering pizza is created from scratch at the time of your order, and the fresh tomatoes on the cheese pizza add a special touch you can't find anywhere else on the lake. It's open seven days a week from 7 AM to 11 PM.

Franklin County

OLDE VIRGINIA BARBECUE
108 Meadowview St.
Rocky Mount   (703) 489-1788
$ MC, V

Come discover the most succulent pork, beef ribs and chicken barbecue in the county. This restaurant, a local landmark, has created its own Olde Virginia Barbecue Sauce and is a favorite hangout for the Franklin County crowd. You've just never tasted better barbecued chicken and ribs anywhere else, and people who don't even like coleslaw can't believe how Olde Virginia's tastes — real Southern coleslaw that's irresistible! Children have their own menu as well, with $3.95 specials. It's open seven days a week from 11 AM to 9 PM.

New River Valley Region

Blacksburg

ANCHY'S
1600 N. Main St.   (703) 951-2828
$ AX, MC, V

A relaxing family atmosphere surrounds you as you dine in this college-town favorite. The menu consists of Euro-Asian favorites and treats such as fresh seafood and steaks. It's open 11 AM to 10 PM Tuesday through Friday, 4 to 11 PM Saturday and 10 AM to 9 PM Sunday. Reservations are suggested.

BOGEN'S
622 N. Main St.   (703) 953-2233
$ All major credit cards

Probably the most popular restaurant with both the college crowd and business people, Bogen's slogan is "Casual with Class." You can enjoy inexpensive food served in a great atmosphere. The menu features gourmet sandwiches, char-broiled steaks, spicy barbecued ribs and chicken and tempting seafood. To top it off, get cappuccino and one of their outrageous ice cream desserts — sky high and wonderful! It's open 11 AM to 12 AM Sunday through Wednesday and until 1 AM Thursday through Saturday.

HOLIDAY INN BLACKSBURG
3503 S. Main St.   (703) 951-1330
$$ All major credit cards

Dine in Vicker's Switch while visiting the beautiful Holiday Inn Blacksburg. Conveniently located, this restaurant has a comfortable atmosphere and friendly staff to make dining a pleasure. Taste their St. Louis barbecued pork, prime rib or bacon-wrapped scallops. They're open Monday through Saturday 11:30 AM to 2 PM and 5 to 10 PM and Sunday 6:30 AM to 2 PM and 4:30 to 10 PM. Reservations are suggested on special dates.

JACOB'S LANTERN
At the Marriott
900 Price Fork Rd.   (703) 552-7001
$$ All major credit cards

Fine dining and excellent tableside service can be found at Jacob's Lantern. Whether you are having a light meal or a complete dinner, you'll find both the food and service consistently good. It's open for breakfast and lunch from 6:30 AM to 2 PM and dinner from 5 to 10 PM seven days a week.

PEKING PALACE RESTAURANT
235 N. Main St.   (703) 552-4400
$ MC, V

For authentic Chinese cuisine in an elegant setting, you can't beat this restaurant in the heart of Blacksburg. Sample some of their delicious dinners, such as Hunan Double Delight, Dragon & Phoenix, General Tso's Chicken and Orange Beef. Also available on the menu are special selections for health-minded diners, prepared in compliance with the guidelines of the American Heart Association. These designated dishes, which are lower in fat, cholesterol and calories and contain no MSG, include Hawaii Chicken, Sizzling Triple Delight and Honolulu Scallops. The restaurant is open 11:30 AM to 10 PM on weekdays and 4 to 10 PM on weekends. Reservations are necessary for large groups.

SUNRISE HOUSE CHINESE RESTAURANT
1602 S. Main St.   (703) 552-1191
$ AX, MC, V

Another top notch Chinese restaurant in Blacksburg, the Sunrise has a relaxing atmosphere that makes for an enjoyable experience. Feast on Crabmeat Lagoon, General Tso's Chicken, Triple Delight and Hawaii Five "O." Prices are very reasonable. It's open seven days a week from 5:30 to 10 PM. Reservations are accepted but not necessary.

Christiansburg

THE FARMHOUSE

Cambria St.   (703) 382-4253
     (703) 382-3965
$$$ Most major credit cards

Exceptional service is a trademark of this authentic farmhouse-turned-restaurant. The farmhouse was part of an estate built in the 1800s. It was opened as a restaurant in 1963, and an old train caboose was added in the early 1970s for an even more unique dining experience. The staff provides their famous southern hospitality to all types of customers: families, corporate executives and college students. The rustic setting, decorated with both antiques and country furnishings, lends the perfect atmosphere to a first date or a 50th anniversary. The menu is full of such country-style favorites as prime rib, jumbo-size ocean shrimp cocktail, steak and their famous Farmhouse onion rings. A separate children's menu is available. The Farmhouse is open Monday to Friday 11:30 AM to 2:30 PM for lunch. Dinner is served from 5 to 11 PM Monday through Saturday and Sunday from noon to 9 PM.

THE HUCKLEBERRY

2790 Roanoke St.   (703) 381-2382
$$$ Most major credit cards

Convenient and luxurious, this restaurant is located near I-81 and several hotels in the Christiansburg area. Two lounges, Whispers and Sundance, offer top-40 and country and western entertainment. Their succulent barbecued items are slow-cooked in "the finest hickory-smoking oven money can buy." The restaurant also guarantees the high quality and freshness of its beef. Choose from baby back ribs, dijon chicken, filet mignon and broiled lobster tail. There is also a special children's menu. Senior citizens receive a 15 percent discount on all entrees. It's open daily 6:30 AM to 10 PM.

STONE'S CAFETERIA

1290 Roanoke St.   (703) 382-8970
$ No credit cards

A longtime favorite with locals and tourists alike, Stone's gives you real country food as fast as you can go through the cafeteria line to get it. Lovers of dishes such as fried chicken, greens, mashed potatoes and pinto beans will be in their glory, both when they taste and when they pay. It's open 6 AM to 7:30 PM Monday through Saturday.

THE OUTPOST

U.S. Hwy. 460 and Rt. 11
off I-81   (703) 382-9830
$$$ All major credit cards

Since 1960, lovers of Lebanese food have been flocking to The Outpost every Wednesday for Lebanese Night. Other nights, The Outpost is full of people ordering their chicken, seafood, spaghetti and real Italian pizza. Imported beer, wines and cocktails top off a fine meal with excellent service. It's open 4:30 to 11 PM Tuesday through Saturday.

Radford

BEST WESTERN RADFORD INN

1501 Tyler Ave.   *(703) 639-3000*
$$ *All major credit cards*

Hunter's Restaurant is a warm, pleasant experience, with fireside dining and delicious food. It is open daily for breakfast, lunch, dinner and cocktails. Dux & Company Lounge is the gathering spot for the New River Valley. Enjoy live entertainment over generous cocktails and tasty hors d'oeuvres. The lounge is open nightly from 4 PM until everyone goes home. The restaurant is open for breakfast and lunch from 6:30 AM to 2 PM Monday through Friday and from 7 AM until 2 PM on Saturday and Sunday. Dinner is served from 5 to 9 PM daily.

GALLERY CAFE

1115 Norwood St.   *(703) 731-1555*
$$ *MC, V*

Radford's trendiest restaurant, Gallery Cafe attracts crowds of professionals and students who enjoy artfully prepared international cuisine served in a casual and memorable gallery setting. With a recent renovation from an old department store, what once was the Gallery Cafe Restaurant is now divided into Gallery Cafe, Books and More and Hot Chilies Restaurant and Bar.

There's a variety of fresh ground and brewed gourmet coffees, as well as pastries, fancy foods and a great selection of magazines and books. Downstairs, Hot Chilies has a southwest accent with an eclectic flair. The menu features selections by a vegetarian chef and owner Charlie Whitescarver, a three-time winner of the Virginia State Championship Chili Cookoff contest. Each table has three types of hot sauces on it to challenge the meek or satisfy the bold.

The Norwood Room is elegantly appointed, and the Garden Room is an open area with soft music, serving a buffet lunch Monday through Friday. Soups, salads and sandwiches are available. It's the perfect place for a relaxing lunch — a haven from the rat race. It's open for lunch Monday through Saturday from 11:30 AM to 3 PM. Dinner is served from 5 to 9 PM on Wednesday and Thursday and from 5 to 10 PM on Friday and Saturday. Brunch is served on Sunday.

MACADO'S RESTAURANT
AND DELICATESSEN

510 Norwood St.   *(703) 731-4879*
$$ *Most major credit cards*

One of a chain of family-owned restaurants at various locations in the Blue Ridge, including Roanoke and Blacksburg, Radford's restaurant offers a fun alternative to other types of dining in the New River Valley. Macado's is popular both with students and professionals for its overstuffed sandwiches and unique, antique and collectibles-filled decor. Gourmet items from many nations are available, including cheese, wine and fine candies. It's open 9 AM to 1 AM Sunday through Thursday and 9 AM to 2 AM Friday and Saturday.

Giles County

MOUNTAIN LAKE
Rt. 700, Mountain Lake
(703) 626-7121, (800) 346-3334
$$$ All major credit cards

If dining in absolutely gorgeous surroundings is your idea of a great evening, as many from nearby Virginia Tech do, then you should drive seven miles up the winding mountain — the second highest in Virginia — to Mountain Lake. This 2,600-acre paradise is the home of the movie *Dirty Dancing*, and that glorious scenery wasn't designed in the prop room. For miles, all you will see are tall trees, rolling hills, beautiful wildflowers and a clear mountain lake. And as if that weren't enough, the dining is out of this world.

The elegant atmosphere matches the outstanding cuisine, which changes daily and may include chilled blackberry soup, sauteed shiitake mushrooms, London broil Madeira or red snapper with pecan butter. Breakfast could be a Giles County Platter of country favorites or Appalachian buttermilk pancakes. Call ahead to find out what culinary pleasures await you. Reservations are important, since guests dine there, too, as part of their resort stay.

Floyd County

BLUE RIDGE RESTAURANT
113 E. Main St.
Floyd   (703) 745-2147
$ No credit cards

Lunchtime regulars and those just passing through will find plenty of friendly faces here. Generous servings and honest-to-goodness REAL food are awaiting discovery at this hometown restaurant in the heart of town. They boast real mashed potatoes, not instant, and pinto beans that are always soaked, dried beans, not canned. Choose from such delicious country-style as hotcakes, country ham, grilled tenderloin and fried squash. There is also a special children's dinner plate at a reduced price. It's open Monday through Saturday 5:30 AM to 8 PM and Sunday 7:30 AM to 8 PM May to October.

CHATEAU MORRISETTE
Meadows of Dan   (703) 593-2865
$$ All major credit cards

World-class Virginia wines are produced from this small, family-owned winery in the Rocky Knob growing district. Founded in 1978, this winery is small enough to remain in the family and yet large enough to produce several different varieties of award winning wines. At the restaurant at Chateau Morrisette, called Le Chien Noir, you can dine on both American and international cuisine in an elegant Old World atmosphere. Their special Jazz on the Lawn events are reminiscent of a Monet painting of a French picnic, and the price is right at $5 a plate. Visitors are welcome to tour the facilities, sample the wines and enjoy a light meal surrounded by the magnificent Blue Ridge Mountains. It's open for lunch from 11 AM to 2 PM Wednesday through Saturday and 11 AM to 3 PM on Sunday. Dinner is served on Friday and Saturday evenings from 6 to 9 PM Reservations are requested.

PINE TAVERN

Floyd   *(703) 745-4482*
$$ *No credit cards*

Live music and theater are reasons enough to lure you to Pine Tavern. Dinner theater is performed on Tuesday evenings for a price of $4, which is added to the price of your meal. Dinner is served before the show, and dessert and coffee are available during intermission or after the show. Special nonsmoking evenings are set aside for those who would not be able to attend otherwise. Live music is played in the dining room on Saturday evenings, featuring bands from the area. The Dave Figg Quartet plays jazz here several times a month. The menu is full of delectable dishes, including lasagna, eggplant parmigiana, Szechuan tofu and baby ganouj. Organic and locally grown vegetables are used whenever available. Vegetarians may select from a special menu that includes vegetable stir-fry, black bean chili and French onion soup, all made with meatless recipes. The chef even uses separate cutting boards for vegetables and a separate deep fryer with vegetable oil for veggies only. It's open Wednesday through Friday 5 to 10 PM,

Saturday at noon for lunch and 5 to 10 PM for dinner and Sundays 2 to 9 PM. Reservations are suggested on Fridays, Saturdays and holidays.

THREE LEGGED COW CAFE

110 N. Locust St.   *(703) 745-2201*
$ *All major credit cards*

The name might be a little odd, but there's nothing strange about the rave reviews for this Floyd restaurant. As the proprietors say, "We're Udderly Delicious!" Located in nostalgic downtown Floyd, Three Legged Cow Cafe features seafood, steaks, burgers, pizza, vegetarian choices and even escargot. They also have ethnic Cajun and Mediterranean foods. The Buffalo Room upstairs is done in Art Deco and reminiscent of an old ice cream parlor. There is an original soda fountain amidst the bright colors. From 5 PM to midnight Thursday through Saturday there is live music. Every second Saturday, the cafe hosts a coffeehouse in the main restaurant. Hours are 11 AM to 9 PM Monday, Tuesday and Thursday and 11 AM to 10 PM Friday and Saturday. They're closed on Wednesday.

Pulaski County

NEW RIVER CRUISE COMPANY

Howe House Visitor's Center Dock
Claytor Lake   *(703) 674-9344*
$$$ *MC, V*

Take a ride on the *Pioneer Maid* across stunning Claytor Lake and enjoy authentic foods made with recipes from our colonial past. Due to its size — 60 feet long by 18 feet wide — this vessel can provide a fully enclosed deck and an open starlight one. Each day, the boat departs from the Visitor's Center dock and cruises down the New River at approximately five miles per hour. A narrative of historical points along the world's second oldest river enhances your trip. Lunch cruises feature deli sandwiches and fresh salads. The Moonlight Dinner/Dance cruise is called "Virginia is for Lovers," with local talent performing for dancing under the stars. The dinner menu features such items as George Washington Ham, Thomas Jefferson Fried Chicken, cooked greens with garlic and tomato and Virginia Spoon Bread. The cruises are two relaxing hours of drifting through the fantastic Blue Ridge Mountains. Office hours are 9 AM to 5:30 PM Tuesday through Sunday. Reservations are required.

THE RENAISSANCE

55 W. Main St. (703) 980-0287
$ MC, V

Part of historic downtown Pulaski and its beautifully revitalized Main Street, The Renaissance offers fine dining in a casual atmosphere. The restaurant's specialties include prime rib, seafood, chicken, pasta and steak. There is a full-service bar as well. Not only is the restaurant convenient to sightseers and visitors (its located directly across from the old courthouse) but it's also notorious for its terrific atmosphere and service. Hours are 11 AM to 9 PM Monday through Thursday, 11 AM to 10 PM Friday and Saturday and 11 AM to 3 PM Sunday.

VALLEY PIKE INN

Old Wilderness Tr.
Newbern (703) 674-1810
$ MC, V

The charm and history of this beautiful old inn is reason enough to come visit. Built before 1839, this stagecoach inn and tavern was a welcome stop for weary travelers on the Old Wilderness Trail. This center of hospitality was once known as the "Famous Haney Inn," named after its owners, John "The Jolly Irishman" Haney and his wife, Cornelius. At the turn of the century, this hotel was a home. It was purchased in 1974, renovated and renamed. Then, in 1989, Marilyn Rutland, a prominent Louisiana belle, fell in love with the area and purchased the home, which she decorated with sconce lights, a chandelier and dried Virginia wildflowers. Church pews were used to make the tables, and all of the doors and windows are from a structure built in 1834.

All meals are prepared and cooked from scratch, and the menu includes fried chicken, roast beef, country ham, spiced apples and homemade biscuits. You can also sample delicious Virginia wines with your meal. Summer hours (May through October) are 4:30 to 9 PM Thursday, Friday and Saturday and 11:30 AM to 6 PM on Sunday. Winter hours (November through April) are 4:30 to 8 PM Thursday and Friday, 4:30 to 9 PM Saturday and 11:30 AM to 6 PM Sunday.

Alleghany Highlands Region

Alleghany County

THE CAT & OWL
STEAK AND SEAFOOD HOUSE

Low Moor Exit off I-64   *(703) 862-5808*
$$ *All major credit cards*

Antiques create the scene as you dine in this beautifully remodeled home. This steak and seafood restaurant has a Victorian atmosphere that will please the eye and a wide selection of tasty dishes that will delight the palate. Popular selections are charbroiled shrimp, filet mignon and fresh tuna steak. Finish off your meal with delicious banana fritters. The restaurant is open Monday through Saturday 5 to 10 PM. Reservations are suggested.

DOUTHAT PARK RESTAURANT

Rt. 1, Clifton Forge   *(703) 862-5856*
$ *No credit cards*

This historic landmark is a vision of rustic beauty. The casual dining area has high beamed ceilings and a large gorgeous fireplace. A big porch overlooks a beautiful clear lake. Try their sandwich menu for lunch or their special buffets for dinner. You can enjoy a luscious Italian buffet on Wednesday nights or a tasty seafood buffet on Friday nights. It's open seven days from 11 AM to 8 PM.

EAGLE'S NEST RESTAURANT

Rt. 311, Crows   *(703) 559-9738*
$$$ *MC, V*

At Eagle's Nest, established in 1930, you can enjoy gourmet dining on a deck overlooking a waterfall. You'll feel like you're dining in Frank Lloyd Wright's private home! The nature lover and adventurous tourist will love this place, located in the middle of practically nowhere (about two hours from Roanoke west, 20 minutes from White Sulphur Springs, West Virginia, east) and one of the most intriguing in the entire Blue Ridge. In an ancient log cabin decorated with antiques, beside that breathtaking waterfall outlined in purple irises and a pool filled with trout and ducks, you'll see overstuffed felines (the restaurant's charity cases) roaming the mountain crags 70 feet straight up. The scenery alone makes this place one you won't forget. But, nothing about the food is forgettable either!

Served on country-blue speckled metal plates, dinners may be international in flavor one day, with a cucumber and mint salad, or fresh brook trout the next. Salads may be mandarin orange with pecan and the soup may be cream of leek. A full complement of house wines is available. The service, by fresh-faced country waitresses, is impeccable. This isn't just dining, it's an experience anyone in love with the Blue Ridge shouldn't miss it. Fidgety children might not do well here, since nobody is in a hurry. The restaurant is open daily 5 to 10 PM and Sunday from 3 to 9 PM.

HOLIDAY INN
Rt. 60 and 220
Covington   (703) 962-4951
$$ All major credit cards

A relaxing atmosphere and top-notch service accompany a meal at this restaurant. Choose from steak, seafood and other American favorites. It's open seven days a week from 6 AM to 10 PM.

IMPERIAL WOK
348 W. Main St.
Covington   (703) 962-3330
$ MC, V

A Chinese restaurant of high caliber, Imperial Wok is a favorite of Covington residents and is known for its quality for miles around. The more popular dishes include the Seafood Delight, chicken and shrimp combo and mixed vegetables with shrimp. Another favorite is the Happy Family meal, which is made with chicken, beef, pork, shrimp and fresh vegetables. It's open from 5 to 9 PM all week.

JAMES BURKE HOUSE EATERY
232 Riverside St.
Covington   (703) 965-0040
$ MC, V

Stop in here for breakfast or lunch. They serve soups, sandwiches, salads and desserts and are open from 9 AM to 3 PM daily (closed Sunday).

MARION'S CAFE
804 S. Highland Ave.
Covington   (703) 962-5022
$ No credit cards

Marion's serves terrific home-cooked meals in a comfortable atmosphere. Their specialties are homemade pies and German dishes. The cafe is open from 5 AM to 10 PM Monday through Saturday and Sundays 5 AM to 8 PM.

Bath County

CAFE ALBERT
Cottage Row
Hot Springs   (703) 839-5500
$$ AX, MC, V

Come discover this small, intimate cafe in Hot Springs. Continental breakfasts and light lunches are offered, as well as a wide assortment of freshly baked breads, pastries and cookies from The Homestead kitchens. You can start off your day with fresh berries, sliced banana with cream or melon. Then try the scrambled eggs Western Style with cheddar cheese and fresh fruit, served with toast. Or sample the Cafe's Crepe Albert, paper-thin crepes with fluffy scrambled eggs and tomato butter sauce served with smoked, sugar-cured ham.

Cafe Albert's lunch menu is just as wonderful as the breakfast. While waiting for your lunch, the cafe offers you its own Strawberry Spritzer or Virginia Apple Cider Cooler. You have a choice of sandwiches, such as hot corned beef or chicken salad, all served on rye, white, whole wheat, brioche or croissant, according to your preference. You will also receive your choice of macaroni, potato, fruit or tortellini salad, cole slaw or cottage cheese. Their lunch entrees include Spinach Salad Supreme with mushrooms, chopped bacon, egg, croutons and nuts; Virginia's Highland County smoked beef frank with chili, sauerkraut and relish; and the Cafe's

Shenandoah Croissant, a thinly sliced breast of turkey with spinach leaves on a Homestead croissant, with watercress spread, pepper jelly and potato salad. Top off a great lunch with something tasty from the dessert menu, perhaps a soda float or banana split. The cafe is open year round 11 AM to 5 PM; outdoor service is available in warm weather.

CASCADES CLUB RESTAURANT
Cascades Golf Course
Rt. 220   (703) 839-7997
$ AX, MC, V

You don't even have to be an Arnold Palmer wannabe to appreciate the beautiful scenery at the Cascades. You'll be dining in the clubhouse of this 18-hole masterpiece, rated as one of the top 30 golf courses in the United States. Light lunches and sandwiches are prepared from April through October, 11:30 AM to 6 PM daily.

THE CASINO
Homestead Grounds
Hot Springs   (703) 839-5500
$$$$ AX, MC, V

Dining out on the lawn in view of the beautiful tennis courts, or indoor dining are both options at this elegant restaurant. You can treat yourself to the buffet luncheon, sandwich service or a champagne brunch while relaxing in style. It's open April through October, the buffet luncheon is served from noon to 2 PM, sandwich service is from 2:30 to 5 PM, and beverages are served noon to 6 PM. Sunday champagne brunch is served 11 AM to 2:30 PM.

THE GRILLE
The Homestead
Hot Springs   (703) 839-5500
$$$$ AX, MC, V

If you're wanting to get "all dressed up and go" — coat and tie are required — you'll appreciate the fabulous setting and gourmet dining found at The Homestead. Delicious dishes for lunch, dinner or late supper are served. From April through October, lunch is served from noon to 2 PM, dinner starting at 7 PM and late supper from 10 PM until midnight. Reservations are required.

THE HOMESTEAD DINING ROOM
The Homestead
Hot Springs   (703) 839-5500
$$$$ AX, MC, V

Exquisite dining and dancing with dinner are featured at the world-renowned Homestead. Ladies and gents are expected to dress for dinner, which is served from 7 to 8:30 PM; reservations are required. Breakfast is from 7:30 to 9:30 AM.

SAM SNEAD'S TAVERN
Main St., Hot Springs   (703) 839-7666
$$ AX, MC, V

For a taste of colonial Virginia, visit this tribute to Hot Springs' living legend and native son. An historic old bank building houses the tavern where lunch and dinner are served to a golf theme. The menu lists the foods as Chip Shots (appetizers), From the Halfway House (sandwiches, burgers and light offerings), Water Hazards (fish), The Main Course (meat entrees), Handicaps (desserts) and From the 19th Hole (beverages).

Appetizers include lump crabmeat cocktail, spinach salad and chili con carne. For light fare, select a seafood taco salad, the "Sam" burger or a delicious golden-fried breast of chicken sandwich. Fresh Virginia Allegheny Mountain rainbow trout from Highland County and fresh swordfish steak are examples of the fish menu. Try the medallion of veal, a tender loin of veal sauteed and dressed with lemon butter sauce, or the Tavern's hickory smoked barbecued spareribs and chicken. The tempting dessert menu will have you asking for more parfait creme de menthe, fudge fantasy (a freshly baked brownie with vanilla ice cream and hot fudge sauce) or a chocolate nut sundae. Then, you'd better hit the course for real . . . walking, not in the cart! Seasonal entertainment is offered. Homemade meals are served daily. Call ahead for times.

THE WATERWHEEL RESTAURANT
The Inn at Gristmill Square
Warm Springs (703) 839-2231
$$$ D, MC, V

Continental cuisine is served in the setting of an old mill here. This area, composed of restored 19th-century buildings, is full of rustic beauty. The restaurant's delicious fresh trout is a favorite. Visit for dinner Sunday through Thursday 6 to 9 PM and Friday and Saturday 6 to 10 PM or for brunch on Sunday 11 AM to 2 PM.

Highland County

HIGHLAND INN
Monterey (703) 468-2143
$$ MC, V

This historic inn is a wonderful setting for a delicious dinner in casual elegance. Formerly known as the Hotel Monterey, this three-story landmark is one of the few mountain resorts of its size still in operation in Virginia. Lace curtains, candlelight and classical music set the mood for your evening of dining. Choose from a variety of tempting dinners, including local fresh mountain trout and grilled Brace of Quail. But be sure to leave room for their Maple Pecan Pie, made rich with Highland County maple syrup — simply delicious. The Inn is open for dinner 6 to 8 PM Wednesday through Saturday and for brunch from 11:30 AM to 2 PM on Sunday.

Inside
Nightlife

People don't come to the Blue Ridge of Virginia for the nightlife. Instead, they come to get away from big crowds, hustle and bustle and smoke-filled rooms. A survey of community leaders pretty much bears this out. Nobody seems to miss "night prowling" too much because there's so much to do and see during the daytime. Those who do miss it have moved or are thinking about moving to Washington, D.C., or Charlotte, North Carolina.

There are those who would argue with this premise, however, and indeed there is one chatty, trendy monthly publication, *V Magazine*, that covers the nightlife in the middle Blue Ridge area. You'd do well to get a copy by calling (703) 343-5138 before visiting Charlottesville, Lexington, Roanoke, Richmond, Staunton, Lynchburg or the New River Valley. You'll also find *V* at most all the "in" places.

The exceptions to this in-bed-at-a-reasonable-hour syndrome are the clubs in the college towns of Charlottesville and the New River Valley, metropolitan areas of Roanoke and Lynchburg and big

Photo: Wintergreen Resort

Night life at Wintergreen Resort.

resorts such as The Homestead, The Greenbrier and Boar's Head Inn, which offer something for everyone. Another exception would be Cockram's General Store in Floyd County, where everybody from miles around comes on Friday nights for a real hoedown.

Shenandoah Valley Region

Harrisonburg

We'll start our meandering journey in search of the big thrill and bright lights in Harrisonburg. **Clayborne's**, (703) 432-1717, at 221 University Boulevard, is decorated with palm trees, waterfalls and skylights. This restaurant and bar with a dance floor is a popular night spot for James Madison University students. Occasionally, live bands perform. On Main Street you will also find several popular spots, such as **Joker's**, (703) 432-6333, a downtown nightclub with live music and dancing, and **JM's Pub and Deli**, (703) 433-8537, with a big dance floor and either a DJ or a live band.

In the Sheraton Hotel on E. Market Street you'll find **Scruple's**, (703) 433-2521, (that is, if you're behaving . . .) This lounge offers disc jockey-guided music every night except Thursday night, when it hosts a popular comedy club. **Tully's Restaurant & Pub**, (703) 433-5151, located behind the Valley Mall, is a restaurant known for its baby back ribs and for attracting the 25-to-40 crowd on the week-

ends for music and dancing with a DJ. College students flock to the place on Wednesdays, which is both Ladies Night and Karaoke Night. If you're not yet familiar with this form of entertainment, it's when common folk like us get to stand on stage and make fools ourselves singing solo to popular hits. Tully's also has live music on Thursday nights.

Staunton

Heading down to Staunton, night prowlers will find that the action takes on a more refined air — which is just fine with most of us . . . most of the time. For a relaxing drink in an equally relaxing atmosphere, the **Belle Grae Inn** on Frederick Street, (703) 886-5151, a restored Victorian mansion, is a popular choice. The lounge in this historic downtown inn and restaurant has classical and jazz music on occasion. The decor is sophisticated, and so is the service. We can't say enough about the Belle Grae — you'll have to experience this gem for yourself. For more action, come to **McCormick's Pub and Restaurant**, (703) 885-3111, on Augusta and Frederick streets. This restaurant has a small dance floor and occasional live music. During the winter, it becomes a cabaret with dinner theater performances by ShenanArts, a local theatrical group. The piano lounge at the **Sheraton Hotel**, (703) 248-6020, offers light background music for relaxing entertainment. Then, in the downtown area, try the **Mill Street Grill**, (703) 886-0656, with an open mike on Fridays. Mill Street Grill is located in the heart of the renovated downtown. It's a cozy restaurant in an enchanting old converted grist mill, the historic White Star Mill Building. The second floor houses the Wharf Gallery.

Lexington

In Lexington and Rockbridge County, local night owls like **The Palms**, (703) 463-7911, a rowdy downtown bar and restaurant with a big screen TV and juke box. This is a popular college hangout, but locals also feel at home here.

A quieter, more sophisticated alternative is **Harbs' Bistro**, (703) 464-1900, on W. Washington Street, which serves wine, beer, cappuccino and extraordinary desserts (as well as a full menu). The patio is a perfect place to sip a cool drink on a hot summer night.

These days, a younger crowd flocks to **Sharks**, (703) 463-7005, on E. Nelson for a night of pool.

Without question the most exciting nightlife in Lexington in the summer happens at the outdoor **Lime Kiln Theater** (see our Arts and Culture chapter). The Sunday Night Concert Series draws huge crowds to hear reggae, bluegrass or folk music. Most every other night, Lime Kiln Theatre stages a play

whose theme relates in some way to the culture of the Southern Mountains. Lime Kiln has great picnic spots for dining before the performances.

Visitors should also check with the Lexington Visitors Bureau to find out about other plays and concerts at Washington & Lee's Lenfest Center and other sites around town.

Roanoke Valley Area

Things definitely start getting livelier if you drive an hour south to the Roanoke Valley. Forget the bedroom communities of Botetourt and Craig counties, though — everybody's home with their families, sleeping or else moved here to get away from noise. However, you can find others with insomnia, rub shoulders with young people on dates or meet the newly single seeking to be double at a variety of nightspots in this area.

A real gem, unique to the Blue Ridge, is **Roanoke Comedy Club**, (703) 982-5693, a comedy club that has hosted some of the biggest names in comedy since it opened a decade ago. Located in downtown Roanoke on the City Market, it is a really fun place to go to get rid of the week's stress. Every Thursday night is ladies night, and the club

One of the places Insiders like to see — and be seen at — on New Year's Eve, or, for that matter, any evening of the year, is the luxurious Homestead Resort. Removed, yes, but always, always "in."

Insiders' Tips

has a show for nonsmokers every Friday night.

If you're going bar hopping in Roanoke, you'll find some nicely appointed ones, such as **Charades**, (703) 563-9300, at the Marriott off I-581 on Hershberger Road, an action lounge with dancing, promotions and a hungry-hour buffet. **The Elephant Walk**, (703) 774-4400, at 4368 Starkey Road, close to Tanglewood Mall, is also very popular. **Scooch's**, (703) 362-4065, 5010 Williamson Road, is one of Roanoke's oldest rock 'n' roll bars; it's close to Hollins College. (But fellas, you can forget about picking up a Hollins girl here, because most of them are at private fraternity parties at the all-male enclaves of VMI or Washington & Lee and Hampden Sydney.) They have a karaoke contest every Thursday. Jazz lovers congregate at **Lowell's Restaurant and Lounge**, (703) 344-4884, at 2328 Melrose Avenue N.W. At Lowell's, you'll think you're in New York City when you hear the R&B, soul and jazz, with a DJ to spin out the music on Friday and Saturday. For real atmosphere, don't miss the **Iroquois Club**, (703) 982-8979, at 324 Salem Avenue downtown. There's a real variety of music and foot stomping or slam dancing. Big counterculture names are frequently booked here. It's a

truly interesting place, considered to be one of the most "hip" in town with the younger set. Another new addition to the downtown Roanoke area is **Ward's Rock Cafe**, (703) 343-CAFE, at 109 S. Jefferson Street. College students and other fun seekers have been known to line up around the block just to get in! And **309 First Street**, (703) 343-0179, found at 309 Market Street, is popular with the artsy crowd downtown. Here you can catch such local favorites as Anastasia Moon and Cows in Trouble (great names, eh?).

You can enjoy a quiet, inspirational moment (no children allowed) at the **Third Street Coffeehouse**, located in Old Southwest at the lower level of Trinity Methodist Church, Third Street and Mountain Avenue. It's a throwback to the coffeehouses of the '60s, and you'll find many people from that era soaking up the good Karma amidst guitar plucking and poetry readings.

In Salem, you can go to **Cheers**, (703) 389-4600, at Route 419 and Braeburn Drive, voted "Roanoke's Best Bar." If country and western dancing is your thing, wear your two-step boots to **The Top Rail**, (703) 389-0917, at 1106 Kessler Road. You also can go country at **Spurs**, (703) 344-0500, at 1502 Williamson Road N.E. Also try **Val-**

ley **Country**, (703) 344-6510, 3348 Salem Turnpike, Thursday through Saturday for dancing the two step!

East of the Blue Ridge Region

Charlottesville

Lots of restaurants in town bring in musicians on the weekends and some weekday nights and usually don't charge admission. These include the popular **Biltmore Grill**, (804) 293-6700, on Elliewood Avenue, the **Blue Ridge Brewing Company**, (804) 977-0017, on West Main, the **Tavern at the Boar's Head Inn**, (804) 972-2231, on Route 250 W., **Coupe DeVille's**, (804) 977-3966, on Elliewood (definitely an undergrad hangout), **Eastern Standard**, (804) 295-8668, on the Downtown Mall, **Fellini's**, (804) 295-8003, on W. Market, **Macado's**, (804) 971-3558, on the Corner and **Durty Nelly's**, (804) 295-1278, kind of a dive on Jefferson Park Avenue that serves great sandwiches. Schedules often change with the seasons, so we won't commit to print exactly when these restaurants turn into hopping nightspots. But, you can call if you're headed their way.

Other places where you'll find action at night in Charlottesville include **Dooley's**, (804) 973-2121, in the Sheraton on Seminole Trail. On Wednesday nights, Dooley's hosts the only live comedy show in town, bringing in stand-up comics from across the nation. The club opens its floor to a dance contest on Saturday nights.

Katie's Country Club, (804) 974-6969, on Route 29 N. by Office America, is a hard-drinking place with live country music on the weekends and some weekdays. It's popular with the Greene County locals and the 29 North suburban crowd. It's even been known to host wrestling matches.

Miller's, (804) 971-8511, in the Downtown Mall, is an excellent jazz club and restaurant with live music many week nights and always on the weekends. You'll also hear blues and country here. There's a big outdoor patio that can be nice in the summer if the heat isn't too withering.

We talked about the **Prism Coffeehouse**, (804) 97-PRISM, on Gordon Avenue in our Arts and Culture section but mention it again here because it is such a great place to hear live bluegrass, folk and other acoustic music. The coffeehouse sometimes brings in nationally known musicians, but it also provides a forum for the area's top folk, acoustic and traditional musicians to perform.

Two large nightclubs are back to back in the building at 120 11th Street S.W., close to campus: the country-oriented **Max** and rock 'n' roll hot spot **Trax**. Max, (804) 295-MAXX, boasts the largest dance floor in central Virginia. It has DJs on weekday nights and live country music on the weekends. Students pour in Thursday nights for country line dances and Wednesday night for lessons in two step. Trax, (804) 295-TRAX, is the hot spot in town to listen and dance to some nationally known and popular regional artists. A broad mix of acts in early '94 included the reggae sounds of Pato Banton and Yellow Man, plus the popular Soul Hat, out of Texas, and even some hip hop from Public Enemy. There's live music virtually every night here.

If a calmer, more intellectually stimulating evening is your preference, several places around town offer poetry and fiction readings from time to time. Contact the **Williams Corner Bookstore**, (804) 977-4858, on the Downtown Mall. **Kafkafe**, (804) 296-1175, a chic restaurant/cafe/bookstore on Elliewood Avenue, or the **UVA Department of English**, (804) 924-7105, to find out about upcoming readings.

New River Valley Region

Traveling south yet another hour, you'll hit College Town, USA — the New River Valley. If you feel self-conscious around the young and tanned with perfect bodies and no wrinkles, stay in Roanoke, where the crowd is older. If you don't, head for Blacksburg pronto! There are two major universities, Virginia Tech and Radford, within cruising distance of each other. Where to start? How about Blacksburg, home to 23,000 students, half of whom are likely to be the opposite sex.

If you want to do something with your hands other than hold a drink, how about a stopping at a sports bar. **Champions Italian Eatery and Cafe**, (703) 951-2222, 111 N. Main Street in Blacksburg, features dart lanes, pool tables, food and drink and some live music. If you're not into the sporting scene and just want to dance, go to **Buddy's**, (703) 552-6423, 130 Jackson Street, where there are bands, comedy and karaoke. **The Balcony**, (703) 953-2837, 217 College Avenue, also has live bands, as does **South Main Cafe**, (703) 951-8202, 117 Main Street. You'll hear such bands as SCUM, Not Shakespeare, Baby Igor, Yams from Outer Space and The Rhinoz. For more sedate music (and band names), try **Jacob's Lounge**, (703) 552-7001, at the Marriott, 900 Prices Fork Road.

If watching a loud, live band isn't your mug of beer, there's always the landmark **Carol Lee Doughnuts**, (703) 552-6706, at 133 College Avenue, a nice, quiet place for terrific, fattening donuts. But who cares? You wouldn't be doing the night life scene in Blacksburg with the college crowd if you had to worry about calories, right?

Actually, there is a place in Radford, a half hour south, where you can get nonfattening, super broiled seafood: the **East Coast Raw Bar**, (703) 731-0100, a downtown watering hole for "old salts" that features everything from stuffed fish to surfers. If you want to dance in Radford, **Sackett's**, (703) 731-0647, Norwood Street, is the self-proclaimed most popular bar in southwestern Virginia. It has a good-sized dance floor.

If you want to just sit and chat, and you like espresso and glorious desserts, try **Radford's Gallery Un-**

derground, (703) 731-1555, a cozy downtown pub located under the Gallery Cafe at 1115 Norwood Street. It's a favorite of university professors.

If country music is your thing, you'll fine plenty of it, good and loud, at **The Walton House**, (703) 731-1922, on Route 663, with first-class country groups who sing with the best of them to leave you crying in your beer.

In Floyd County, you'll do your rollicking and rolling country style at the legendary **Cockram's General Store's**, (703) 745-4563, Friday night hoedowns on Locust Street or at **The Pine Tavern**, (703) 745-4482, where anybody who's anybody hangs out on Saturday night to be entertained. The Pine Tavern, on U.S. Hwy. 221 N., also has dinner theater Tuesdays in June and offers nonsmoking performances part of the time. **Ray's**,

(703) 745-2501, also on U.S. 221 N., is another popular hangout for country and western and bluegrass.

Alleghany Highlands Region

Traveling to the western limits of the Blue Ridge, in the Alleghany Highlands, the night life is limited to the great Homestead and Greenbrier resorts. **The Homestead Club**, (703) 839-5500, offers cocktails and entertainment at the prestigious resort. The Tuxedo Junction Orchestra entertains with dance music nightly starting at 9:30. Just as elegant a club life awaits you at The Greenbrier's **Old White Club**, (304) 536-1110, where you can dance under sparkling chandeliers to live bands of the contemporary or big band variety. At either resort, it will be a night to remember.

The Colonnades is a Marriott community in Charlottesville.

Inside
Real Estate and Retirement

An outstanding quality of life is available in a great variety of neighborhoods, farms, second homes and retirement getaways in the Blue Ridge. They offer nearby schools and shopping, with property prices for every budget. Frequent is the story of visitors who just happened to be passing through the Blue Ridge, spied the small town, home or property of their dreams and moved without even having jobs. Finders' fees offered for Blue Ridge farmland, often held for generations, are not unusual.

Home sites in the Blue Ridge can be found to fit every taste. You can choose from secluded, architecturally spectacular modern homes nestled on mountain ridges such as Bryce, Wintergreen and Massanutten or tin-roofed Victorian homes in Salem or Edinburg, although these seldom reach the market. If you're looking for a farm spread, consider the gorgeous Catawba Valley near Roanoke or isolated country estates in Allegheny, Highland or Bath counties. If living near the water is your wish, you don't have to travel to the ocean. A visit to Smith Mountain Lake's Bernard Landing's condominiums or the townhomes at Mallard Point along Claytor Lake's white sand beaches will convince you you're already there. If New York City's old brownstones are your ideal, visit downtown Lexington or Lynchburg. If what you want is a primitive log cabin to fix up yourself, go to Franklin or Floyd counties.

Virginia's history as the first, largest and wealthiest of the British colonies in America and the Blue Ridge's reputation for historic preservation have resulted in the state's having more historic homes than all other states combined. The pleasant result is that Virginia has avoided having its prized structures — many of which are located in the Blue Ridge — overrun by burgeoning industry and population, as has happened in many states. Nearly 100 are open for visitation, and they do change hands. Several of the Realty companies that specialize in historic homes are Mead Associates in Historic Lexington, an affiliate of Sotheby's International, and McLean Falconer in Charlottesville, the chosen city of movie stars and millionaires, who often favor such houses. Also, *The Charlottesville Area Real Estate Weekly*, issued by the Charlottesville Area Association of Realtors, is a helpful, comprehensive guide to real estate in the seven-county area. Pick one up at any of its 420 locations or receive a copy in the mail by calling (800) 845-4114 or (804) 977-8206.

Lucky visitors may stumble upon their dream homes, but your best bet is to let local Realtors know that you're looking, since some homes, such as those in Charlottesville, South Roanoke and Lexington, are sold by word of mouth before they ever see the marketplace. Realtors can also offer guidance on the location of the best schools, favorite shopping areas and level of satisfaction you might have in neighborhood you're considering.

Local boards of Realtors are your best resource to answer questions about major developments and fair market prices. In this chapter, we've included information about these boards for each region, as well as local homebuilder's associations, in case you decide to remodel or build and want reputable contractors. Finally, we offer the average price of a home in each region, as provided by the Multiple Listing Service of the Virginia Association of Realtors. The following organizations can assist you in making regional or state-wide comparisons or answer questions about purchasing or building a home.

Home Builders Association of Virginia, 1108 E. Main Street, Suite 700, Richmond 23219-3534, (804) 643-2797

Virginia Association of Realtors, P.O. Box 15719, Richmond 23227, (804) 264-5033

Shenandoah Valley Region

Winchester

The east end of this northern Shenandoah Valley city and the southern part of Frederick County are growing rapidly. This is in part a result of the westward migration of Washington-based workers — people willing to commute an hour or so to their jobs to live in an area that is less crowded and costly. But the Winchester area also has a good number of industries that keep the real estate market healthy.

Much of the historic city's beauty comes from the graceful old homes along tree-lined streets and row houses built before and during the Civil War era. Many of these row houses, which are a short walk from the pedestrian-only Downtown Mall, are being restored and remodeled. You'll also see a lot of old homes that were built partially of stone.

In Winchester, the average price of a home on the market in June 1993 was $114,700. In Frederick County, where there are many developments of modestly priced homes on small lots, the average price of a home was $132,400.

Just to the east, in Clarke County, prices were even higher in June 1993. The average asking price of a home in that beautiful, rural county was $154,200. Also in Clarke, one estate in the country was selling for $1.1 million. Clarke County boasts quite a few 19th-century manor homes surrounded by rolling pastures, and these have attracted some of the county's wealthiest newcomers — Washingtonians willing to make the long commute to work or wanting a second home for the weekends. Oliver North is one of these new residents.

estate in Winchester, Front Royal and Warren, Frederick and Clarke counties, contact:

Blue Ridge Board of Realtors, 181 Garber Lane, Winchester, 22602, (703) 667-2606

Top of Virginia Building Association, 18 E. Piccadilly Street, Winchester 22601, (703) 665-0365

Front Royal and Warren County

Many federal employees and retirees have moved into this area, attracted by the beauty of the land and relaxed pace. The most prized properties here are those with a sense of privacy and clear views of the Shenandoah River or the mountains. While vacation homes on the river or in the mountains could be bought for as little as $68,900 in the summer of '93, prices were as high as $350,000. An historic estate in the spectacularly beautiful county can cost in the millions, but it is rare when one comes on the market. Spacious new homes on the county's two golf courses — Shenandoah Valley Golf Club and Bowling Green — cost as much as $400,000, but the average price of a home up for sale in Warren County is $114,700.

For more information on real

Shenandoah and Page County

Shenandoah County encompasses several quaint, historic towns, including Woodstock, Edinburg and New Market, along with the Bryce Resort community in Basye. Page County is more rural, with much of its land tucked between Massanutten Mountain and the Blue Ridge range farther east. A growing number of retirees and young couples out of Washington, D.C., seeking weekend retreats are buying property in both counties. The average price of a home is around $100,000, but prices are much lower in Page County, where the average cost is closer to $85,000. Riverfront property is usually more expensive and hard to come by (the south fork of the Shenandoah River runs through Page County, and the north fork winds through Shenandoah County).

The price of land in the Blue Ridge is considerably less than other parts of the country, especially the Northeast and West Coast. With a few exceptions, such as Charlottesville and the large estates of Hunt Country, you can expect to purchase more than what your dollar bought in other areas.

Insiders' Tips

For the most part, architectural styles are simple — this is a rural, no-frills kind of region. You will find are some interesting old homes, but brick ramblers, Cape Cods and modest, plainly built homes are more the norm.

Bryce Resort in western Shenandoah County is an entirely different real estate market. The year-round resort community features chalets, condominiums and townhouses near the resort's ski slopes, lake and other facilities. Prices range from $30,000 to $300,000, depending upon the size of the property and its proximity to the slopes.

There are four timeshare developments at Bryce Resort, but only one, Chalet High, is still selling. Managed by Alexander Properties, Chalet High is a development of chalets and townhouses on the northern end of Bryce Resort's golf course.

For more information about real estate in Shenandoah and Page counties, contact:

Massanutten Board of Realtors, 129-C S. Main Street, Woodstock 22664, (703) 459-2937

Shenandoah County Homebuilders Association, c/o Harris Thompson, Route 1, Box 1, Edinburg 22824, (703) 984-4136

Harrisonburg

In the heart of the Shenandoah Valley, Harrisonburg is a thriving university city that is also the seat of Virginia's leading agricultural county, Rockingham. Housing prices in this area accelerated during the 1980s but began levelling off in 1990 and '91. In 1992, the average price of a home was about $96,000. That year, you could buy a starter home for as low as $65,000 or a more luxurious house for anywhere between $100,000 and $350,000.

It's increasingly difficult to find nice, historic properties in many areas of the Blue Ridge but not in Harrisonburg and Rockingham County. There is still a good supply of old homes, some needing renovation and others already restored. It is also fairly easy to find farm properties; dairy and poultry farming are the leading agricultural industries.

Massanutten Village, a year-round mountain resort community, is a 15-minute drive east of Harrisonburg. You will find chalets, condominiums and townhouses near the resort's ski slopes, golf course, tennis courts and swimming pools. A property owners association maintains the roads, runs a police department and manages the entire 600-home development. There are hundreds of lots still for sale.

A total of 300 villas and condominiums at Massanutten are timeshares. The units cost anywhere from $8,000 to $16,000 for one week per year at the resort. Owners can also swap that week for one at a condominium in Germany, Key West, the Bahamas or any timeshare development that participates in an exchange program of Resort Condominiums International.

For more information, contact:

Harrisonburg-Rockingham Association of Realtors, 633 E. Market Street, Suite B, Harrisonburg 22801, (703) 433-8855

Shenandoah Valley Builders Association, 245 Newman Avenue, Harrisonburg 22801, (703) 434-8005

Staunton, Waynesboro and Augusta County

Augusta County is growing by leaps and bounds — especially in the Stuarts Draft area close to Waynesboro. A number of industries have built plants there over the past several years, including Hershey and Little Debbie Bakery, and this has led to a boom in housing. Farther west, more and more people from Washington, D.C., New York and other Northern states are retiring in the Staunton area, drawn to its rich history, pastoral beauty and vibrant downtown.

While the average price of a home in quiet, historic Staunton is about $65,000, it is closer to $85,000 in the Stuarts Draft area. In Waynesboro, a city that's home to such industries as Dupont and Genicom, homes sell for an average of $75,000.

There continues to be a great demand from newcomers to the county for big old homes and farmhouses, but both are in short supply. It isn't that they don't exist — they just rarely come on the market.

Two major developments in Staunton are worth mentioning. Ironwood, a private community next to the Staunton Country Club, is characterized by spacious, red cedar homes with private gardens. Baldwin Place is a planned community in Staunton's north end, where the homes, streets and even flora are reminiscent of early American villages. There are also many small, well-maintained developments throughout the county with five to 20-acre parcels.

Interest in Staunton's downtown area is definitely on the rise, as it is being developed into a major tourist area worthy of many repeat visits. Developers and families have happily embraced the charming, architecturally sound commercial buildings and homes. They're being snapped up quickly, but this is an area where you still can make a difference and be in on the cutting edge if you hurry!

For more information contact:

Staunton-Augusta Board of Realtors, 1023 N. Augusta Street, Staunton 24401, (703) 885-5538

Waynesboro Board of Realtors, 531 W. Main Street, Suite 15, Waynesboro 22980, (703) 949-4904

Augusta Homebuilders Association, P.O. Box 36, Waynesboro 22980

Lexington

In Lexington, known for its historic downtown and rolling pastures, the average price of a home is estimated at $87,000, according to local Realtors. Naturally, there are wide disparities in the cost of farmland estates, which can run anywhere from $200,000 to a cool million, to the historical homes downtown that can go for $370,000 on Marshall Street. Forty percent of Rockbridge County is farmland.

Lexington's historic downtown long has been popular for filming period movies. In 1938, Lexington's Virginia Military Institute was the site for parts of *Brother Rat*, and in the summer of 1992, dirt was poured on the streets for the Civil War movie *Sommersby*. Lexington has numerous buildings and homes that represent most of the architectural styles prevalent in American communities during the 19th century. You will find Victorian cornices and stoops on Main Street, turreted Gothic buildings at VMI, Roman Revival, slender Tuscan columns and bracketed pediments. There is even an Italianate villa at 101 Tucker Street, which dates to the late 1850s; a central bell tower surmounts its bracketed overhanging roof. Many of these gems are open for a Christmas holiday tour and again in the spring during Historic Garden Week.

Lexington's proximity to the state's Virginia Horse Center has attracted many would-be gentleman farmers, whose presence has driven up the price of farms. A restorable 1820 brick residence and cottage on 82 acres sold for about half a million dollars, but small family farms are still available for $100,000 (no house). With a house, you'll probably pay at least $50,000 more. Many such homes are sold by Mead Associates, Realtors located in the historic Jacob Ruff House at 21 N. Main Street.

Average family developments may be found in Lexington at above-average prices. Homes in the suburban, family-oriented neighborhoods of Birdfield, Mt. Vista and Country Club Hills start at $100,000, with many $150,000 and up. If you're looking for something in the price range of $80,000 to $100,000, neighboring Buena Vista offers some nice neighborhoods.

For more information, contact:

Lexington-Buena Vista-Rockbridge Board of Realtors, P.O. Box 311, Buena Vista 24416, (703) 261-2176

Roanoke Valley

The average price of a home in the Roanoke Valley runs $80,000. In the nearby Smith Mountain Lake area, populated by retirees and second-home owners, the average price is determined by whether or not a home is waterfront. Lake homes easily averaging $200,000. The nearby growing bedroom community of Botetourt County averages $73,500, and finders' fees are often offered for farmland. Others choose to live farther out in rural Craig County and the Catawba Valley, where a wide variety of homes averaging $50,000 and large spreads are easier to find.

Roanoke's neighborhoods are well defined, often bound together by civic leagues and The Neighborhood Partnership, an energetic organization uniting neighborhoods for the past dozen years, encouraging pride and fellowship. Popular areas of town range from pricey Hunting Hills in Southwest Roanoke County, with an average sales price of $270,000, to up and coming Wasena, where an average family home in a nice neighborhood can be purchased for $55,000. South Roanoke remains a favorite, with miniscule turnover in homes ranging from $90,000 to $350,000. More affordable but equally nice are such family favorites as Raleigh Court and Penn Forest, where neighborhood block parties and nightly strolls are the norm. Nearby Salem offers everything from downtown-area, tin-roofed Victorian-style homes with stained glass that can cost as much as the highest bidder offers (and we mean on the high side, not low!) to Beverly Heights, where young families congregate in ranch homes valued from $70,000 to $100,000. The adjoining town of Vinton offers pricey subdivisions such as Falling Creek, with homes costing more than $150,000, and charming downtown wonders you can still buy for less than $50,000.

For more information, contact:

Roanoke Valley Association of Realtors, 4504 Starkey Road S.W., Roanoke 24014, (703) 772-0526

Roanoke Regional Home Builders Association, 1626 Apperson Drive, Salem 24153, (703) 389-7135

East of the Blue Ridge Region

Heading south from Front Royal along the eastern side of the Blue Ridge Mountains, you will see some of the most gorgeous, rolling land anywhere on the East Coast. Between Front Royal and Charlottesville, there are four counties: Rappahannock, Madison, Greene and Albemarle (home of Charlottesville).

Generally speaking, prices are higher in Rappahannock County because of the growing number of relatively affluent residents who commute to Northern Virginia to work. Prices drop farther south in

Madison County, then rise again in Greene County, which is becoming a bedroom community for fast-growing Charlottesville and overall Albemarle County. Orange County — just to the east of Greene and north of Albemarle — is also a popular area for people who want to buy property in the Charlottesville area but want a better buy for their money.

In this entire region, some of the most beautiful historic properties have been transformed into bed and breakfast inns. Some say their number has more than doubled in 10 years.

In Rappahannock County, the minimum requirement for developing land is 25 acres. Madison County's rules are more relaxed: Three acres is the minimum. The median price of a home in Madison County was $90,000 in 1992; in Rappahannock County, it was closer to $125,000.

It is difficult to find historic Victorian or Colonial homes on the market in Madison and Rappahannock counties. Instead, the predominant styles are the brick rambler and simpler homes with vinyl siding.

The real estate market in Orange County, home of James Madison's Montpelier and the Barboursville Winery, is more upscale. You will find a diversity of residential properties and prices that are generally lower than in Albemarle County. But the gap is closing. The median price of a home in Orange County is roughly $100,000. Generally, the homes are scattered across the county, because the local government does not allow the growth of residential neighborhoods.

More than 95 percent of Orange County is zoned agricultural, and land cannot be subdivided into more than four parcels in any five-year period of time. Thus, it is practically impossible to rezone agricultural land to residential. This is precisely what makes it such a desirable place to live for people who can afford the prices of some of the stately old estates.

For more information about real estate in Rappahannock, Madison, Orange and, farther east, Culpeper counties, contact:

Piedmont Association of Realtors, 810 S. Main Street, Culpeper 22701, (703) 825-3789

Charlottesville

Charlottesville has the dubious distinction of being one of the most expensive areas in Virginia in which to live, second only to Northern Virginia. People of great wealth are drawn to the area, captivated by the beauty of the land, its sprawling historic estates and the city's cosmopolitan atmosphere. Plus, the many hospitals in the area mean lots of doctors. And jokes abound about the number of lawyers per capita — graduates of UVA who refuse to leave the area. In short, there's a lot of money floating around, and the real estate market has risen to the occasion.

This is especially true in that stretch of land west of the city along Barracks Road and toward Free

Union and east of the city at the new Keswick development. In that western area near Free Union, new homes on three- to six-acre lots in a subdivision named Rosemont cost $600,000 and up. Near the Farmington Country Club, also west of the city, stately homes run anywhere from $500,000 to more than $1 million. Inglecress is another exclusive development along Barracks and Garth roads, where homes on three to five acres cost anywhere from $750,000 to $1 million.

Architectural styles of most of these new homes are not terribly innovative; white columns and symmetrical porticos abound. Jefferson's Monticello and University of Virginia are architectural models — at least on the exterior. But inside many new homes you'll find contemporary features such as vaulted ceilings, skylights and open spaces.

Back to Keswick — this development east of the city gives new meaning to the term "exclusive" in Charlottesville. Sir Bernard Ashley, co-founder of Laura Ashley company and founder of Ashley House Inc., is also owner and developer of the 600-acre Keswick Estate. This is an elite, private, gated community with a maximum allowable density of approximately 100 homesites in two- to 3½-acre parcels. Amenities include Keswick Club, a private membership golf and leisure club with an 18-hole Arnold Palmer signature golf course and Keswick Hall, a 48-room country house hotel (see our chapter on Resorts). Community services are the Keswick Estate Homeowners' Association, Keswick

Estate Design Review Board, Bespoke Home Service, underground utility services (central water and sewage, electricity, natural gas, telelphone and cable television), fire and police protection and a rescue squad. Sympathetically-applied architectural controls ensure that all homes will be developed to the same high standards of design and construction. Future residents are free to supervise the construction of their Keswick home, though it is certainly not necessary. The Keswick House, a Bespoke Homes show house, is an example of the high standards set for the exclusive community. The example of the high standards set for the exclusive community. The $1.45 million price tag, which includes two leisure memberships and a full golf membership, is at the high end of the price scale. Lots may also be purchased for personal development under the guidance of Keswick Estate Owners' Association. Lots are priced at $185,000 to $295,000.

Nearby, Glenmore, a new development off Virginia Route 250 east of town, has become a destination for many Charlottesvilleans wanting to relocate. Apparently, the glut of houses on the market this year is largely due to the local residents wanting to move into Glenmore. The development surrounds a nice golf course and country club; prices range from $300,000 to $500,000 for a house and lot.

More than 100 homes in the Charlottesville area were built between the early 1700s and the Civil War era. Wealthy families, often using royal land grants, began migrating west from Richmond in the early 1700s. Such estates as Plain Dealing, Estouteville and Edgemont are registered historic landmarks. Because there are so many historic homes in the area, one or two may be on the market at any given time.

Estates with names posted on signs at the road are not limited to rich historic properties. It's become the fashion to name your abode — no matter how new. This is an English tradition, of course. It started when many early settlers in the area (who were either from England or whose parents were from England) gave their new homes a name that often linked it somehow to their ancestral home in the old country.

In the city, where there is no more room for development, there are some beautiful neighborhoods. Gracious old homes are concentrated in the Rugby Road area, but there are also more modest, rambler-type homes and Cape Cods in that neighborhood close to the university. Within a two-block range of Rugby Road, you can find homes that sell for anywhere from $300,000 to $1 million.

In the city, the median price of a home in early 1993 was $90,000 — including condominiums and townhouses. In the county, median prices ran anywhere from the upper $120,000s to the mid $130,000s — not including farms and estates.

Albemarle County is very restrictive in allowing for growth. The local government has targeted Crozet and the Ivy area, a few miles west of the city, as growth areas and is allowing some higher-density development. But the Free Union area

and many other parts of the county are to remain as rural as possible, with minimum requirements of one residence per 20 acres.

For some other important numbers:

Charlottesville Area Association of Realtors, 2321 Commonwealth Drive, Charlottesville 22901, (804) 973-2254

Blue Ridge Homebuilders Association, 2330 Commonwealth Drive, Charlottesville 22901, (804) 973-8652

Wintergreen Resort

Nestled in the mountains and foothills of Nelson County are two private communities that belong to the four-season Wintergreen resort: Stoney Creek, a year-round valley development, and Wintergreen Mountain Resort, primarily luxury condominiums but also many single family homes.

Wintergreen is secluded from encroaching development, bordered on the west and north by the Blue Ridge Parkway and a 2,400-acre federal preserve and on the south by the George Washington National Forest. More than half of Wintergreen's 11,000 acres have been set aside as permanent, undisturbed wilderness.

Homes and condominiums are situated on ridges for spectacular views of the valley and mountains and along private drives in Stoney Creek near the golf course. The community has its own pre- and primary school and private police force. Property owners receive benefits and privileges that include special lift lines at the ski slopes and preferred reservations for golf tee times and tennis courts.

Condominiums cost anywhere from $60,000 to $360,0000, homes from $125,000 to more than $1 million and land from $20,000 per lot to $280,0000 per lot. The posh resort is about a half hour's drive from Charlottesville.

For more information, call (800) 325-2200 or (804) 325-2500.

Lynchburg

"In the Blue Ridge Mountains of Virginia" is a well-known ballad in Central Virginia, particularly in the Lynchburg area. Certainly, the mountain view is one reason people choose to live in the City of Seven Hills, where the average price of a home is $79,000.

Lynchburg, along with surrounding Bedford County, is one of the most rapidly growing regions in the state. According to Realtor Alice Smith of Smith & Thurmond Inc., spokesperson for the Lynchburg Realtors, the average selling time for a home is only 115 days.

Among the areas of growth are Ivy Hill, a planned community around Ivy Lake and Ivy Hill Golf Course; Poplar Forest, a neighborhood of fine homes on wooded lots carved out of Jefferson's land surrounding his home; Meadowwood, just outside the city on lots averaging 2 to 3 acres; and Meadowridge, homes on 2- to 3-acre lots close to the mountains. Prices in these areas range from $125,000 to $350,000.

Campbell County, which is west and southwest of Lynchburg, continues to stretch out into previously agricultural areas. The largest and best-known subdivision is Wildwood, with mostly wooded lots ranging from a half to one acre and prices in the $100,000 to $125,000 range.

In Lynchburg, you'll love the tree-lined streets filled with two-story brick colonials with well-manicured lawns. Among the most prestigious and desirable are Peakland Place, Linkhorne Forest, Link Road, Rivermont Avenue and Boonsboro Forest. New growth west of the city is due to developable land there.

Lynchburg is proud of its designated historic areas, where many turn-of-the-century homes are being renovated into glorious show-cases. Neglected for years, many are being restored to their original condition: high ceilings, winding staircases and beautiful fireplace mantels, among other original features. The most advanced of these historic districts are Diamond Hill and Garland Hill. Close behind are Federal Hill, College Hill and Daniels Hill.

Lynchburg homes sell well, according to Smith, because of overall good economic conditions, availability of land for new construction, the variety of neighborhoods and wide price ranges (from $40,000 for a small, two-bedroom home to $1 million dollars for the larger homes). She also emphasizes outstanding scenery, the lowest interest rates in 20 years, available mortgage financing and, of course, a warm and friendly atmosphere.

For more information, contact:
Lynchburg Association of Realtors, 3639 Old Forest Road, Lynchburg 24501, (804)385-8760

Builders & Associates of Central Virginia, P.O. Box 216, Forest 24551, (804) 385-6018

New River Valley Region

The average price of a home in the New River Valley runs $85,000. In both Montgomery County, Blacksburg and Radford, well-paid university professionals have driven up the price of homes and land, especially premium farmland in Floyd and Giles counties. The New River area is considered one of the

five major growth areas of Virginia, according to noted Realtor E.R. Templeton of Raines Real Estate of Blacksburg. Requests for "finders" are often found posted on bulletin boards in little towns such as Newport.

Potential homeowners will most likely find Christiansburg and Pulaski the least expensive places to buy a home, according to the local Board of Realtors. The average price of a home was $20,000 higher in nearby Blacksburg.

The downtowns of Blacksburg and Radford offer true small-town atmospheres conducive to leisurely evening strolls, breathtaking parks (especially Radford's Bisset Park along the New River) and the likelihood of meeting others who enjoy an academically stimulating lifestyle. They also are packed with apartment complexes and townhouses for the thousands of students here. The majority of apartments are well-kept, and the students are pleasant and add immensely to the area's quality of life and diverse culture.

Popular family developments near Blacksburg are Foxridge, Heathwood, Toms Creek Estates and Westover Hills, where the average price of a home ranges from $90,000 to $95,000. In Christiansburg, the same type of development home will cost between $70,000 and $85,000. Some of Christiansburg's better known developments are Craig Mountain, Diamond Point, Victory Heights and Windmill Hills. In Radford, a family can buy a home in Sunset Village for a price on the low end

($40,000 to $70,000) and in the newer developments of College Park and High Meadows for $100,000 to $150,000.

Many New River Valley residents opt to live in the environs of Giles, Floyd and Pulaski counties, where rural living is prevalent. Farms still aren't inexpensive, since lots of professionals also like to live out in the country. The quality of farmland varies in each county and is scarce, due to the area's beauty and proximity to the Blue Ridge Parkway. It probably is least expensive in Pulaski County, where good farmland sells for about $1,000 an acre. Much of the land there is devoted to dairy farms and raising cattle and hogs.

Numerous second homes have been built in Pulaski County's Claytor Lake area. A recent development, Mallard Point, near Dublin, is a luxurious waterfront community of gracious townhomes unique to the popular water playground. The spacious two- and three-bedroom units offer amenities such as whirlpool, individual lighted boat slips and a private tennis court.

Downtown Pulaski is definitely on the rise, due to its dynamic Main Street Program. Professionals from Washington, D.C., and other metropolitan areas are renovating some of the Prospect Street mansions, notable for their witches' caps and winding front porches. An area short on bed and breakfast inns, Downtown Pulaski probably has more old mansions that would lend themselves to this cause than any other place in the New River Valley. It's the next hot spot of New River Valley tourism!

If you're looking for a nice family development, consider Mountain View Acres or Newbern Heights, with houses priced from $70,000 to $120,000. Oak View is more expensive at $80,000 to $160,000 but considerably more affordable than a similar development in neighboring Montgomery County.

For more information, contact:
New River Valley Association of Realtors, 811 Triangle Street, Blacksburg 24060, (703) 953-0040

New River Valley Home Builders Association, P.O. Box 2010 , Christiansburg 24068, (703) 381-0180

Smith Mountain Lake, Bedford and Franklin Counties

The average price of a home in this area varies greatly as you consider waterfront golf communities, second homes and retiree getaways. Most waterfront homes list for $150,000 to $200,000. Some of the more popular communities are Chestnut Creek, Waters Edge and the Waterfront and Waverly. Condos prices start in the low $80s at Bernard's Landing and the $60s at Striper's Landing.

It's worth a boat trip around Smith Mountain's 500 miles of shoreline just to see the architectural, custom-built splendor of some of the homes. One of the most noted builders of cedar lake homes is Smith Mountain Cedar Homes, perennially a high-volume performer, along with its parent company, Lindal Cedar Homes.

Rural farmsteads and homes in Bedford and Franklin counties are more affordable and available than in any of the other Roanoke bedroom communities. The average price of a home is less than in Roanoke, at around $63,000. Naturally, the cost of lake property brings up the median, but some real rural bargains still can be found.

For more information, contact:

Builders & Associates of Central Virginia, P.O. Box 216, Forest 24551, (804) 385-6018

Roanoke Regional Home Builders Association, 1626 Apperson Drive, Salem 24153, (703) 389-7135

Alleghany Highlands Region

There is no organized local board of Realtors in this area. No Multiple Listing Service records are kept on the average price of a home, but local Realtors say most homes typically sell for a fourth less than their urban counterparts. Another rule of thumb, from Highland County's Building Permits Office, is that the cost of building a new home there is $32 per square foot compared to $65 in Northern Virginia.

The area also is unusual in that much of the rural, mountainous property is owned by people who don't live there. For example, half of Highland County, the least-populated county in Virginia, is owned by people who live elsewhere but come to vacation in the highest county east of the Mississippi.

The real estate is prized for its proximity to The Homestead, the Potomac and James rivers and hunting and fishing preserves. Here, one can buy farms with miles of split rail fences on emerald-green pastures, maple sugar orchards, wooded tracts, trout farms and cattle farms. It's obvious to visitors that the sheep outnumber the human population five to one. So, for those looking for seclusion, the Alleghany Highlands region is a perfect choice. Many look to this area for retirement.

Retirement

Determining the perfect retirement location takes planning. Individual tastes and personal needs must be taken into account if you're one of the 25 percent of seniors who decide to move after retirement. Too many seniors move to a retirement spot sight unseen. The Blue Ridge, however, offers numerous agencies and contacts to help you determine where you would be happiest. Here is a list by region of agencies or programs that can be helpful for area retirees. They can offer you tips about broad, comprehensive service, personal care programs and local perks (such as Cox Cable Roanoke's free cable TV installation for seniors, "Enjoy the Prime Time of Your Life"). Also check with local hospitals, county health departments and social service departments, since many offer ongoing senior services, programs and seminars.

Shenandoah Valley Region

Agencies

SHENANDOAH AREA AGENCY ON AGING
15 North Royal Ave.
Front Royal 22630   (703) 635-7141

ROCKINGHAM COUNTY PARKS AND RECREATION DEPARTMENT
602 County Office Blg.
Harrisonburg 22801   (703) 564-3160

AUGUSTA COUNTY PARKS AND RECREATION DEPARTMENT
P.O. Box 590
Verona 24482-0590   (703) 942-5113

AMERICAN ASSOCIATION OF RETIRED PERSONS (AARP)
(703) 942-4282

WAYNESBORO DEPARTMENT OF PARKS AND RECREATION
413 Port Republic Rd.
Waynesboro 22980   (703) 949-6505

THE VALLEY PROGRAM FOR AGING SERVICES INC.
325 Pine Ave.
Waynesboro 22980   (800) 868-VPAS

SENIOR CORPS OF RETIRED EXECUTIVES (SCORE)
(703) 949-8203, (703) 434-3862

VOLUNTEER MEALS ON WHEELS — HARRISONBURG
(703) 833-5395

ALZHEIMER'S SUPPORT GROUP
(703) 885-8818

HOSPICE OF THE SHENANDOAH INC.
(703) 943-6886

MEALS ON WHEELS — STAUNTON
(703) 886-1219

AMERICAN ASSOCIATION
OF RETIRED PERSONS
Glasgow/Rockbridge Chapter(703) 463-1661

FAMILY SERVICE
OF ROANOKE VALLEY
3208 Hershberger Rd. N.W.
Roanoke 24017 (703) 563-5316

LEAGUE OF OLDER AMERICANS
706 Campbell Ave. S.W.
Roanoke 24016 (703) 345-0451

Retirement Communities

BALDWIN PARK
21 Woodlee Rd.
Staunton (703) 885-1122
This retirement community close to downtown Staunton has studio and one- and two-bedroom apartments with window boxes and patios or balconies.

BRANDON OAKS
3807 Brandon Ave. S.W.
Roanoke (703) 989-1201
A variety of spacious floor plans is available, plus dining, housekeeping, 24-hour security and on-site professional health care. The community has 172 units offered as one- and two-bedroom sizes and two-bedroom cottages.

ELM PARK ESTATES
4230 Elm View Rd.
Roanoke (703) 989-2010
Elm Park Estates is conveniently located near hospitals, medical facilities and shopping (Tanglewood Mall is across the street.). Amenities include a craft room, library, beauty salon and daily activities. Studios and two-bedroom apart-

ments are available, and pets are permitted.

ROANOKE UNITED
METHODIST HOME
1009 Old Country Club Rd. N.W.
Roanoke (703) 344-6248
Several types of facilities and levels of care are available to people of all faiths. There are social rooms, a chapel and a library on the premises. Guest rooms are available.

THE PARK-OAK GROVE
4920 Woodmar Dr. S.W.
Roanoke (703) 989-9501
Seven spacious designs are available, varying in size from studios to one- and two-bedrooms units. A first floor art gallery has been the scene of numerous exhibits, part of The Park-Oak Grove's ongoing Visual and Performing Arts Series. Inquiries are welcomed. Guided tours and complimentary lunches are easily arranged by calling during regular business hours.

East of the
Blue Ridge Region

Agencies

THE JEFFERSON AREA BOARD FOR
AGING (JABA)
2300 Commonwealth Dr.
Charlottesville (804) 978-3644

THE SENIOR CENTER, INC.
1180 Pepsi Pl.
Charlottesville (804) 974-7756

ALZHEIMER'S DISEASE AND RELATED DISORDERS SUPPORT GROUP
(804) 973-6122

WIDOW/WIDOWERS SUPPORT GROUP
(703) 974-7756

MEALS ON WHEELS
(804) 978-3644

CENTRAL VIRGINIA AREA AGENCY ON AGING (SERVES BEDFORD CO.)
2511 Memorial Ave.
Lynchburg   (804) 528-8500

CITY OF LYNCHBURG DEPARTMENT OF PARKS & RECREATION
301 Grove St.
Lynchburg   (804) 847-1640

SOUTHERN AREA AGENCY ON AGING (SERVES FRANKLIN CO.)
433 Commonwealth Blvd.
Martinsville   (703) 632-6442

Retirement Communities

VALLEY VIEW
1213 Long Meadows Dr.
Lynchburg   (804) 237-3009

Services include meals, housekeeping, transportation, wellness programs and a community center with hot tub and visiting nurse, which are included in the monthly rental fee. There's a country store, barber/beauty shop, games and crafts area and exercise room.

WESTMINSTER CANTERBURY
501 VES Rd.
Lynchburg   (804) 386-3500

Apartments are in eight different styles. Service includes beauty/ barber shop, individual climate control, no-scald water control, housekeeping and your choice of dining arrangements (either in your apartment or in the central area).

New River Valley Region

Agencies

NEW RIVER VALLEY AGENCY ON AGING
143 Third St. N.W.
Pulaski   (703) 980-7720

Retirement Communities

WARM HEARTH VILLAGE RETIREMENT COMMUNITY
2607 Warm Hearth Dr.
Blacksburg   (703) 961-1712

Located on a 220-acre wooded site, Warm Hearth has 46 one-level townhomes, apartments in three low-rise buildings and apartments for assisted living in a licensed home for adults.

Alleghany Highlands Region

Agencies

LEAGUE OF OLDER AMERICANS
(Serves Alleghany)   (703) 345-0451

VALLEY PROGRAM FOR AGING SERVICES INC.
(Serves Bath & Highland)   (800) 868-VPAS

Inside
Airports and Bus Lines

With its beautiful scenic mountains and interesting historical sites, Virginia is second only to Florida as the most popular tourist destination in the South. Airports are an important means for out-of-state tourists to conveniently visit the area.

More than 300 airports serve travelers in Virginia. These range from grass landing strips to large international facilities. Commercial airports generate 35 percent of the air industry's economic impact in Virginia, while general aviation airports account for only 7 percent. Yet, the importance of general aviation in the Blue Ridge is recognized by a constant upgrading of the existing air transportation system.

Of the existing system in the Blue Ridge, three large airports — Charlottesville, Roanoke and Lynchburg — receive varied commercial passenger service. They also provide a wide range of general aviation services for corporate and private aircraft. Others, such as Shenandoah Valley Regional and Ingalls Field, next to The Homestead Resort in Bath County, have limited scheduled flights. The majority of Blue Ridge airports are designed to accommodate the single-engine and light twin-engine aircraft that represent more than 90 percent of Virginia's fleet.

Below, the commercial airports are listed, north to south, with the remaining scheduled service and general aviation airports following.

Commercial Airports

CHARLOTTESVILLE-ALBEMARLE AIRPORT
201 Bowen Loop   (804) 973-8341

The Charlottesville-Albemarle Airport is located eight miles north of the City of Charlottesville in Albemarle County. It is accessible via U.S. Highway 29 and State Route 649 and is served by four major airlines: American Eagle, Comair, The Delta Connection, United Express and USAir Express. These carriers provide 31 departures per day to six major hub airports, including Raleigh/Durham, Charlotte, Pittsburgh, Greater Northern Kentucky/Cincinnati, Baltimore/Washington and Washington/Dulles international airports. From these points, connections are available to an additional 175 domestic and international destinations. USAir Express also provides daily nonstop service to and from New York's LaGuardia Airport.

The terminal consists of a

60,000-square-foot building with four airline ticket counters, six airline gate areas, baggage claim space, a 500-space daily parking area, 61-space hourly parking lot and an on-site travel agency.

Ground transportation is available from Avis, Budget or Hertz, and on-call taxi service is also provided. A number of hotels provide courtesy shuttle van service to and from their properties.

A food vending court and cafe-deli are also available.

The Charlottesville-Albemarle Airport's market area includes the cities of Charlottesville, Staunton, Harrisonburg and Culpeper, as well as the counties of Albemarle, Greene, Madison, Culpeper, Orange, Louisa, Fluvanna, Nelson, Augusta and Rockingham.

General Aviation services are provided by Corporate Jets of Pittsburgh, with aircraft fueling, hangaring, maneuvering and flight instruction services available. Navcom Aviation Inc. provides aircraft repair services. Auto rental service is provided at Corporate Jets through Avis, and courtesy vehicles are also available.

MAJOR AIRLINES:

American Eagle	(800) 433-7300
Comair	(800) 354-9822
United Express	(800) 241-6522
USAir	(800) 428-4322

CAR RENTALS:

Avis	(804) 973-6000
Budget	(804) 973-5751
Hertz	(804) 973-8349
Parking:	(804) 973-5145

LYNCHBURG REGIONAL AIRPORT
4308 Wards Rd.   (804) 582-1150

The Lynchburg Regional Airport is located six miles south of Lynchburg in Campbell County. It is accessible via U.S. Highway 29 and is served by two major airlines, USAir Express and United Express. These provide 21 departures per day to four major hub airports, including Charlotte, Pittsburgh, Baltimore/Washington and Washington Dulles international airports. From these points, connections are available to an additional 175 domestic and international destinations.

The facilities at the airport consist of a 35,000-square-foot terminal building, built in 1992, with one airline ticket counter, six airline gate areas, second-level boarding capabilities, a 400-space daily parking area and on-site travel agency.

Ground transportation is available from Avis, Budget and Hertz, and on-call taxi service is also provided. A number of hotels provide courtesy shuttle van service to and from their properties. A restaurant, lounge and gift shop also are available.

The Lynchburg Airport's west central Virginia market area includes the cities of Bedford and Lynchburg and the counties of Amherst, Appomattox, Bedford and Campbell.

General aviation services are provided by Virginia Aviation, with aircraft fueling, hangaring, maneuvering as well as flight instruction services available. Virginia Aviation also provides aircraft repair services, aircraft rentals and charter services, parking and tie-down.

MAJOR AIRLINES:

United Express	(800) 241-6522
USAir	(800) 428-4322

GENERAL AVIATION:

Virginia Aviation	(800) 543-6845

CAR RENTALS:

Avis	(800) 239-3622
Budget	(800) 527-0700
Hertz	(800) 654-3131

PARKING:

Republic Parking Systems	(804) 239-7574

TAXI/LIMOUSINE:

Airport Limo	(804) 239-1777

ROANOKE REGIONAL AIRPORT

5202 Aviation Dr., N.W.   (703) 362-1999

Roanoke Regional Airport is located three miles northwest of Roanoke. It is accessible via I-581 and is served by six major airlines: USAir, USAir Express, United Express/Air Wisconsin, Comair, The Delta Connection, The Delta Connection/Atlantic Southeast Airlines and Nashville Eagle. These airlines provide 52 departures per day to 12 major hub airports, with nonstop or direct service to 27 cities. From these points, connections are available to an additional 150 domestic and international destinations.

Its $25-million terminal opened in 1989. The dramatic glass-fronted, 96,000-square-foot building features four Jetway loading bridges, a modern baggage handling system and a panoramic view of the Blue Ridge Mountains. There are 772 daily and 227 hourly parking spaces, an on-site travel agency and a First Union Bank ATM.

Ground transportation is available from Avis, Dollar, Hertz and National. Three on-call limousine services are provided. A number of hotels provide courtesy shuttle van service to and from their properties.

A snack bar, restaurant and gift shop, video game room, lounge and conference center and nursery with diaper-changing table are also provided. There is a telephone hotel reservation system.

The Roanoke Regional Airport's market includes the cities of Roanoke and Radford and the counties of Alleghany, Bedford, Botetourt, Craig, Franklin, Floyd, Giles, Montgomery, Roanoke and Pulaski.

General aviation services are provided by Piedmont Aviation, including aircraft fueling, hangaring

The larger airports have excellent ground service to area accommodations, many provided by major hotels. And the major metropolitan bus lines offer fine transportation. Call ahead for ground service information and bus schedules.

Insiders' Tips

and maneuvering and flight instruction services. Piedmont also offers aircraft maintenanceas, as does Executive Air Inc. and Roanoke Aero Services. Air charters are offered by Piedmont, Executive Air, Hillman and Saker flying services.

MAJOR AIRLINES:

American Eagle	(800) 433-7300
Delta Connection (ASA)	(800) 282-3424
Delta Connection (Comair)	(800) 354-9822
United Express	
(Air Wisconsin)	(800) 241-6522
USAir	(800) 428-4322
USAir-Express	(800) 428-4322

CAR RENTALS:

Avis	(703) 366-2436
Dollar	(703) 563-8055
Hertz	(703) 366-3421
National	(703) 563-5050

PARKING:

APCOA	(703) 362-0630

GROUND TRANSPORTATION:

Blacksburg Limousine	(703) 951-3973
Cartier Limousine	(703) 982-5466
Roanoke Airport Limo	(703) 345-7710
Yellow Cab	(703) 345-7711

General Aviation and Scheduled Service Airports

WINCHESTER REGIONAL AIRPORT
491 Airport Rd.   (703) 662-5786

This airport is located two miles south of Winchester and 42 miles northwest of Washington-Dulles International. The airport and a U.S. Customs Service are open 24 hours a day. All-weather access

(AWOW III, Localizer approach, Pan Am Weathermation) is available to pilots, and there is a lighted runway. Executive fax, secretarial services and conference room with audiovisual equipment make business travel easier. There's on-demand air charter/taxi, overnight hangars, aircraft rentals and flight instruction. Crew car and courtesy vans provide transportation to nearby hotels and golf course. There's a $5 nightly tie-down fee for single-engine aircraft, $8 for larger aircraft.

FRONT ROYAL-WARREN COUNTY AIRPORT
Rt. 4, Front Royal   (703) 635-3570

Located four miles west of Front Royal, this facility has a new terminal and hangars. A Duat weather system is available for pilots. Local car rental, cab service and maintenance are available. Parachuting trips are also offered. Tie-down is $3 overnight.

SKY BRYCE AIRPORT
County Rd. 836, Off Rt. 263
Basye   (703) 856-2121

This unmanned airport with a 2,300-foot runway is within walking distance of Bryce Resort, a large, family recreational spot offering a myriad of activities. There is no fuel. Do-it-yourself, no-fee tie-down is available.

LURAY CAVERNS AIRPORT
County Rd. 652
Luray   (703) 743-6070

The 3,300-foot paved, lighted runway at the Luray Caverns Airport sells fuel and charges no fees for incoming craft. Located between the world famous Luray Caverns and the Caverns Country Club Resort, this facility offers free transportation to all Luray Caverns facilities.

NEW MARKET AIRPORT

Rt. 617   *(703) 740-3949*

This airport outside historic New Market and the Shenandoah Valley Travel Association Visitors Center, the largest in the Valley, features radio-operated lights, fuel (cheapest in the state at $1.54 a gallon, says the owner), tie-down at $3.50 nightly and cab service. There is a flying school and a $10 charter fee.

BRIDGEWATER AIR PARK

Hwy. 727   *(703) 828-6070*

Operated by K&K Aircraft and close to Bridgewater College, this airport sells fuel and has limited overnight tie-down sites at no fee. Hours of operation are 8 AM to 5 PM weekdays, 9 AM to 4 PM Saturday and Sundays noon to 4 PM. Taxi service is available from Harrisonburg.

SHENANDOAH VALLEY REGIONAL AIRPORT

Rt. 771 (Airport Rd.)
Weyers Cave   *(703) 234-8304*

Renovations are underway to expand this 10,000-square-foot terminal building, which offers a restaurant and Hertz and Avis car rental services. A general aviation terminal has fixed-base services, including fuel and maintenance. There are air charter, corporate management services and two flight training schools. Information on

hot-air ballooning, sky diving and sail planes is available. Parking is free. There are no pilot fees. Free use of Weathermation, Duat and other flight-planning facilities is offered.

EAGLES NEST

Rt. 5, Waynesboro   *(703) 943-3300*

Close to Wintergreen Resort, Eagles Nest offers fuel, car rental and mechanical service, with three mechanics on the field. Tie-down fee is $3 nightly. A flying school, rides and glider plane rental are available.

VIRGINIA TECH AIRPORT

1600 Ramble Rd.
Blacksburg   *(703) 231-4444*

Adjacent to the Virginia Tech Corporate Research Center and one mile from the main 24,000-student campus, this airport is situated on the Eastern Continental Divide at 2,134 feet above sea level. The runway is lighted and complemented by full-instrument approach capabilities. Tech Airport offers a full line of maintenance services and refueling. Flight instruction is offered and Ground School students can earn three academic credits from Tech. Hard-surface tie-downs cost $5. Hangar space has a three-year waiting list. Two rental car services (Holiday Ford and Rent-A-Wreck) are located nearby, and taxis are available.

NEW RIVER VALLEY AIRPORT

Rt. 100 N.
Dublin   *(703) 674-4780*

Two miles north of Dublin, New River offers fuel, maintenance and tie-down at $4 nightly. Hangar space is available. One plane is available for rental. A flight school also operates from here.

FALWELL AVIATION INC.
4332 Richmond Hwy.
Lynchburg (804) 845-8769
Located within the city limits of Lynchburg, Falwell offers fuel, maintenance, hangar, charter, flight instruction, rental and air ambulance. No landing or parking fees are charged, but there is a $5 tie-down for overnight.

NEW LONDON AIRPORT
Rt. 1, Forest (804) 525-2988
Located between Lynchburg and Smith Mountain Lake, this airport offers fuel and minor maintenance. There is no tie-down fee.

BROOKNEAL-CAMPBELL COUNTY AIRPORT AUTHORITY
Brookneal (804) 376-2345
This unattended rural airport has a pay phone on the field. Rental cars are available nearby, and there is no tie-down fee.

SMITH MOUNTAIN LAKE AIRPORT
Rt. 1, Moneta (703) 297-4500
Adjacent to Virginia's largest lake, with 500 miles of shoreline, Smith Mountain offers fuel, sightseeing charters, limousine and car rental. Tie-down is $5 nightly.

INGALLS FIELD
Va. Rt. 703
Hot Springs (703) 839-5326
Gateway to the world-famous Homestead Resort, Ingalls Field might have no planes one day and look like O'Hare the next, depending on which conventions are meeting. Two round trips daily to Washington/Dulles are offered by a commuter, and other trips are on demand. Rental cars and limo are available to Hot Springs, Warm Springs and other Bath County points of interest. Overnight tie-down is $3, and there's no landing or parking fee.

Metropolitan Bus Lines

Public transportation plays a vital role to major cities in the Blue Ridge. It provides an alternative to tourists or those with their own transportation and also provides the elderly and disabled with a means of getting around town.

Due to increased concern over energy consumption, ozone pollution and other critical issues facing the world today, public transportation is no longer just an alternative but an environmentally responsible way to travel. Major cities in the Blue Ridge offer bus transportation that is clean, accessible and inexpensive.

For a guide to public transportation in Virginia, call the Virginia Division of Tourism at (804) 786-4484. You'll receive an easy-to-read map prepared by the Virginia Department of Transportation.

Roanoke

VALLEY METRO GREATER ROANOKE TRANSIT COMPANY
12th and Campbell Aves. S.E.
(703) 982-0305

Valley Metro is Roanoke's regional transportation system, which tries hard to accommodate everyone from eager tourists to the disabled, who are given special consideration with STAR service. It also oversees the city's five downtown parking garages. This year, the company added 18 new motor coaches.

Valley Metro serves more than 5,000 passengers daily with its fleet of 40 buses. The modern main terminal, Campbell Court, is in the heart of the shopping district, located across from First Union Bank on Campbell Ave.

Riders may send for a bus guide in advance. Exact fare or your ticket should be ready since bus drivers carry no change. No smoking, eating or drinking is permitted. The bus operator should be signaled a block before you want to get off.

Charlottesville

CHARLOTTESVILLE TRANSIT SERVICE
104 Keystone Pl.　　(804) 296-6174
UNIVERSITY TRANSIT SERVICE
1101 Millmont St.
Charlottesville　　(804) 924-7711

The City of Charlottesville's Transit Service and University Transit work together to provide dependable, efficient, convenient and safe transportation.

Riders may send for a bus guide in advance. When they ride, they should have exact fare or ticket. Designated transfer points and routes are clearly marked on the guide in various colors. Eating, drinking and smoking are not permitted.

Two front seats may be reserved for senior citizens or those with disabilities.

Lynchburg

GREATER LYNCHBURG TRANSIT COMPANY
Memorial Ave.　　(804) 847-7771

Greater Lynchburg Transit serves both the City of Lynchburg and parts of Amherst County, carrying 3,500 to 4,000 passengers daily. Its fleet of 26 buses radiate from a main terminal at Plaza Shopping Center, the only transfer point, located between Memorial Avenue and Lakeside Drive. New bus guides, marked with colored routes, are available by mail. Exact fare or a pass is required.

Quality live-in child care...

with a special European *flair*.

- carefully screened European au pairs
- about $170/week for any size family
- AuPairCare counselors in your area

800-4-AUPAIR

A U.S. Government-designated program.

AuPairCare

Inside
Education

Some of Virginia's finest colleges and universities can be found in the Blue Ridge region — foremost being "Mr. Jefferson's University" in Charlottesville. Both the School of Law and the Colgate Darden Graduate Business School at the University of Virginia consistently rank in the top 15 nationally, and UVA's undergraduate program also wins top ratings. Virginia is also known for its respected college preparatory schools. Several in the Charlottesville area include St. Anne's-Belfield, Woodberry Forest in nearby Orange County, and the Miller School of Albemarle — a military boarding school for boys.

Farther south in the foothills region, Lynchburg is home to five colleges and two business schools, drawing over 15,000 students each year.

In addition, several college preparatory schools are located in the region, including Virginia Episcopal School, (804) 384-6221, in Lynchburg, one of the top independent schools in the southeast, and Seven Hills School, (804) 847-1013, a private, coeducational day school that stresses leadership, self-discipline and responsibility.

West over the mountains, every major city in the Shenandoah Valley has at least one college or university. There are also several college preparatory, parochial and military boarding schools.

Harrisonburg, the seat of Virginia's leading agricultural county of Rockingham, bustles with academic activity. James Madison University, Eastern Mennonite College and Seminary, and Bridgewater College are all located within a few miles here.

Farther south in historic downtown Staunton are Mary Baldwin College, a Presbyterian-affiliated school for women, and Stuart Hall, (703) 885-0356, the oldest Episcopal preparatory school for girls in Virginia.

Washington and Lee University and the embattled Virginia Military Institute sit in quaint, historic Lexington. As of August 1994, VMI remained the only public all-male college in the nation, but a pending court challenge could force the cadets to study, drill and sweat side by side with women.

A strict regime is also a way of life at two military boarding schools in the valley: Fishburne Military School in Waynesboro, (703) 943-1171, and Massanutten Military Academy in Woodstock, (703) 459-2167.

We've already mentioned Mary Baldwin College, but several other esteemed private women's colleges are nestled in the mountains and foothills of the Blue Ridge, including Hollins College in Roanoke, Randolph Macon Women's College in Lynchburg and Sweetbriar College in Amherst. South of Roanoke, the New River Valley is home to Virginia Tech and Radford University, two of the most popular choices in Virginia higher education.

The following list concentrates on the four-year colleges and some of the better preparatory schools in the Blue Ridge region. There are many two-year community colleges throughout the area, and information on them is available from the State Council on Education, (804) 225-2628. Call the numbers listed for each college or prep school to get information on the ones that interest you. Schools are listed in geographic order.

Shenandoah Valley Region

SHENANDOAH UNIVERSITY
Winchester   (703) 665-4581

This small university sits on 62 acres on the southeast edge of Winchester. It offers eight undergraduate degrees, the Bachelor of Music being one of the most popular. The school also has a lively music theater program. Graduate degrees are offered in business, music and physical therapy, among others. Tuition at the Methodist Church-affiliated institution is $10,000. The school has a satellite campus in Loudoun County.

CHRISTENDOM COLLEGE
Front Royal   (800) 877-5456

This is a tiny college founded in 1977 to inspire and educate Catholic students for church lay leadership. It has about 150 students and is projecting a stabilized student body of around 450, to retain a close community life. The college is situated on a 150-acre campus of gently rolling land surrounded by the Blue Ridge Mountains. The Bachelor of Arts degree is awarded in English, history, philosophy, political science and theology. The college also offers a two-year Associate of Arts degree. Tuition and fees run about $8,500.

EASTERN MENNONITE COLLEGE AND SEMINARY
Harrisonburg   (800) 368-2665
                              (703) 432-4000

Christian values and global concerns are integrated with the learning process at this private college, which was founded in 1917 to serve the educational needs of the Mennonite Church. There is an average of 1,000 undergraduates and around 100 seminary students. The most popular majors are business, education, biology, nursing and social work. Current tuition is $9,300.

JAMES MADISON UNIVERSITY
Harrisonburg   (703) 568-6211

This is a comprehensive public university that offers a wide range of courses on both the bachelor's

Lynchburg *is* Lynchburg's College

Offering undergraduate degrees in 47 fields in the liberal arts and professional studies with graduate degrees in business, personnel management, education and counseling.

A selective, independent, coeducational, residential college founded in 1903 as one of Virginia's first coeducational institutions.

LYNCHBURG COLLEGE
IN VIRGINIA

and master's levels. The strongest academic area include the arts, education, communication and health and human services. The beautiful 472-acre campus in the heart of the Shenandoah Valley is within walking distance of downtown Harrisonburg. Average enrollment is 11,000. Tuition and fees run around $4,000 for Virginia residents.

BRIDGEWATER COLLEGE
Bridgewater   *(703) 828-2501*

This private, Church of the Brethren-affiliated college is located seven miles south of Harrisonburg. Its average enrollment is 1,000 students, and the most popular majors are business and the general sciences for pre-med students. Founded in 1880, Bridgewater was the first coeducational college in Virginia. Current tuition and fees are $10,900.

MARY BALDWIN COLLEGE
Staunton   *(703) 887-7023*

This private women's college enrolls about 950 students, and more than half are Virginians. The students represent 42 states and eight foreign countries. Tuition for the 1994-95 school year is $11,200. Forty major and minor courses of study are offered, but the top five seem to be the Art, Psychology, Sociology, Business and Education programs. Also popular is a program of study known as the "independent major." This is a focused, individualized program combining studies from more than one academic discipline. Chemistry and biology majors in premed programs at Mary Baldwin maintained a 100 percent acceptance rate at medical schools. The beautiful, rolling campus is within walking distance of downtown Staunton.

WASHINGTON AND LEE UNIVERSITY

Lexington   *(703) 463-8400*

Washington and Lee University in historic Lexington was founded in 1749 and enrolls about 1,600 undergraduates and 400 law students. *U.S. News and World Report* has rated W&L as one of the top bargains for a quality private school education in America. The university offers both bachelor's and juris doctor (law) degrees.

Its history is rich with historic names. In 1796, George Washington contributed 100 shares of canal stock in the James River Co. to Liberty Hall Academy, a Presbyterian seminary. The grateful trustees changed the school's name to Washington Academy in 1798 and to Washington College in 1813.

Decades later, General Robert E. Lee rode into town on his horse, Traveller, in 1865 and became the college's president until his death in 1870. While there, Lee established the nation's first journalism program and its School of Law. W&L's gracious campus is designated a National Historic Landmark, with neoclassical brick buildings dating back to the generosity of Washington. Students still worship at Lee Chapel on the tree-lined colonnade. Lee designed the beautiful chapel and is buried there.

Although the student body is more diverse than ever, it is largely made up of the sons and daughters of wealthy Southerners and Easterners.

W&L is a charter member of the 14-college Old Dominion Athletic Conference and is a member of NCAA's Division III. Tuition is $13,750, with a total average cost of $20,300, including expenses.

VIRGINIA MILITARY INSTITUTE

Lexington   *(703) 464-7000*

Virginia Military Institute joins W&L in Lexington as a national treasure of tradition. Lt. Gen. Thomas J. Jackson, the immortal "Stonewall," taught here 10 years before leaving to heed the call of the South in the Civil War. It boasts one of the wealthiest alumnae per-capita giving groups in the United States and has some of the most famous military leaders in the world as graduates, including Gen. George C. Marshall, Class of 1901, author of the Marshall Plan to reconstruct Europe after World War II. A museum in his honor is next to the 12-acre parade ground.

This is the school that was portrayed in Ronald Reagan's film, *Brother Rat*, about VMI's infamous "Rat Line." However, tradition is being tested in the federal courts, since state-supported VMI doesn't want to admit women, but the U.S. Justice Department does. Twice, a sympathetic judge has ruled that VMI may remain all-male as long as nearby Mary Baldwin College offers women a similar leadership program. Nobody's expecting the Justice Department to leave things as they are, so the fight for males-only status undoubtedly will continue to be tested in the highest courts in the land.

VMI's 1,300 cadets are offered a baccalaureate degree in 13 disciplines and must also take four years of ROTC. They are encouraged to sign a formal contract during their

last two years, which normally leads to a commission. Degrees offered are in biology, chemistry, civil engineering, computer science, economics and business, electrical engineering, English, history, international studies, mathematics, mechanical engineering, modern languages and physics. Tuition is $3,010 in Virginia, $9,000 out of state. There are 13 intercollegiate athletic teams in NCAA Division I.

HOLLINS COLLEGE

Roanoke   *(703) 362-6000*

Founded in 1842, Hollins College was the first chartered women's college in Virginia. Enrollment is 1,030, with 842 undergraduate women and 188 coed graduate students. Hollins awards a bachelor's of arts degree with 25 majors and offers graduate programs in five disciplines: English/creative writing, children's literature, psychology, liberal studies, teaching and certificate of advanced studies.

It is known internationally for its clinic for stutterers, the Hollins Communications Research Institute, and also has a clinic for head injury patients, the Hollins College Rehabilitation Research Institute. Hollins has worked hard to facilitate valuable community outreach programs through its adult studies, the Women's Center and summer programs for women and rising juniors and seniors in high school.

Hollins enjoys a strong liberal arts focus, with nationally recognized programs in creative writing. Three Pulitzer Prize winners graduated from Hollins: Annie Dillard, Henry Taylor and Mary Wells Ashworth. Other notable alumna include *Time* publisher Lisa Valk Long and ABC News correspondent Ann Compton. In 1992, Hollins created the first graduate program for the writing and study of children's literature. Hollins is also noted for its international concentration.

Nearly half of its graduates study abroad. Hollins' sports programs are also well-known in the NCAA Division III and Old Dominion Athletic Conference. Its Riding Center is popular for women who like to take their horses to college with them. No wonder, since its riding team often wins first place at the Nationals. Tuition will be $13,470 for 1994-95.

ROANOKE COLLEGE

Roanoke   *(703) 375-2500*

This Lutheran-affiliated college, the second-oldest such American college supported by the Lutheran religion, celebrated its 150th anniversary in 1992. It enrolls 1,700 students and offers bachelor's degrees in 28 majors with a strong commitment to liberal arts and church-related values. For the fifth year in a row, *U.S. News and World Report* has named Roanoke College the number one "Up and Coming Liberal Arts College in the South." Famous Roanoke College gradu-

ates include Henry Fowler, former secretary of the treasury under Lyndon Johnson. Roanoke has 12 sports in the NCAA Division III. Tuition is $12,625 annually.

East of the Blue Ridge Region

THE UNIVERSITY OF VIRGINIA

Charlottesville   *(804) 924-0311*

"Mr. Jefferson's University" is central to the Charlottesville community. With its neoclassical buildings, white porticos and graceful landscapes, the university's grounds are considered among the most beautiful in America.

A fall 1992 survey by *U.S. News and World Report* hailed UVA as the second-best public institution in the nation (next to University of California-Berkeley). In the magazine's "best buys" category, UVA ranked fourth in the nation among both public and private universities.

It should be added here that the university has pretty much succeeded in shaking its reputation of being a party school, notorious among *Playboy* readers and others for its annual Easter parties and infamous mud slide near Fraternity Row. This is due in part to the increasingly stiffer entrance criteria; the number of applications far exceeds the space available for undergraduates. About half of all in-state applicants get in, and roughly two-thirds of the student body is made up of Virginians. But they are smarter, more studious and harder-working than ever.

> Nestled in the heart of the New River Valley
> is one of Virginia's outstanding universities.
>
> From September through May
> we offer numerous concerts, lectures, exhibits and plays.

RADFORD UNIVERSITY

A World of Difference

◆ **Top-notch cultural entertainment, including national and international groups:**
College of Visual and Performing Arts, (703) 831-5141.

◆ **Popular entertainment, lectures:**
Heth Student Center Information, (703) 831-5420.

◆ **Exhibits and outdoor sculpture court:**
University Art Galleries, (703) 831-5754.

◆ **See the exciting action of NCAA Division I Highlander and Lady Highlanders:**
Ticket and information office, (703) 831-5211.

◆ **Elderhostels, adult learning program:**
Office of Continuing Education, (703) 831-5483.

◆ **Tours for students and parents:**
Office of Admissions, (703) 831-5371.

For further information about Radford University, call or write:

Office of Public Information
P.O. Box 6916
Radford, VA 24142
(703) 831-5324

COME VISIT AND ENJOY OUR CAMPUS.

Total enrollment is about 18,000 graduate and undergraduate students. Current tuition and required fees for Virginia residents is roughly $4,500 per year.

The University of Virginia is especially noted for its schools of Law and Medicine and for the Colgate Darden Graduate School of Business Administration.

It's also known across the state for its Center for Public Service, which helps localities by collecting demographic and economic data for use in developing public policy. The university's relatively new Center for Liberal Arts provides continuing education for classroom teachers from across the state.

SWEET BRIAR COLLEGE

Sweet Briar   (804) 381-6100

Sweet Briar College is a nationally ranked, highly selective independent college of the liberal arts and sciences for women, offering the bachelor of arts or the bachelor of science degree. It is located 12 miles north of Lynchburg in Amherst County, on 3,300 rolling acres in the foothills of the Virginia Blue Ridge. The college is known for its laboratory-based and equipment-intensive program in the sciences. Its program in international education, which includes study-abroad in France, Spain, Germany, England and Scotland, attracts students from colleges across the country. Mary Oliver, Pulitzer Prize and National Book Award-winning poet, and celebrated writer John Gregory Brown form the core of the college's distinguished creative writing program. Sweet Briar's all-level

riding program, which regularly snags national championships, boasts one of the best on-campus facilities in the country. About 600 women from more than 40 states and 15 foreign countries choose from Sweet Briar's 40 majors, including interdepartmental and self-designed majors. For women older than 25, the college offers the Turning Point Program. Tuition is $14,500 annually.

LYNCHBURG COLLEGE

Lynchburg   (800) 426-8101

Lynchburg College, an independent, coeducational institution related to the Christian Church (Disciples of Christ), is one of America's top 50 liberal arts schools, according to the *National Review College Guide*. The school serves approximately 2,000 undergraduates and 500 graduate students. Tuition is $12,450 annually.

Two teaching innovations at Lynchburg College are the Lynchburg College Symposium Readings course and the Senior Symposium. LCSR incorporates classical reading selections across the curriculum, while in the Senior Symposium, students read selections from the classics and attend weekly lectures to discuss major themes addressed in the readings. Small classes and one-on-one interaction with professors are among the many benefits of an education at Lynchburg College.

Master's degrees are offered in business, personnel management, education and counseling. The Adult Center for Continuing Education and Special Services (AC-

CESS) program for adults who want to earn an undergraduate degree is specifically designed to address the special needs of persons age 25 and older. Services include admission, enrollment, advising, transfer arrangements, faculty contacts and program planning. The nursing program offers advanced degrees and specialization.

LIBERTY UNIVERSITY

Lynchburg *(800) 522-6225*

Liberty University is a Christian, comprehensive, coeducational university committed to academic excellence. Liberty serves more than 10,000 students from 50 states and 31 nations at the undergraduate and graduate levels. The school was founded by Dr. Jerry Falwell, the TV evangelist who is also founder of the Moral Majority. Liberty is accredited by the Southern Association of Colleges and Schools and offers 75 areas of study. Liberty Baptist Theological Seminary offers master's degrees in Christian education, divinity, counseling and theology.

Liberty's facilities include a 12,000-seat football stadium and the 9,000-seat Vines Convocation Center, which are used by the Flames athletic teams, who compete on the NCAA Division I level. Prospective students or anyone interested is encouraged to visit. For a free video tape, call the number above. Tuition is $6,000 annually.

RANDOLPH-MACON WOMAN'S COLLEGE

Lynchburg *(804) 846-7392*

Randolph-Macon Woman's College, a four-year liberal arts college affiliated with the United Methodist Church, serves 725 women from 42 states and 20 countries. It is located on 100 acres near the Blue Ridge and offers a 100-acre riding center nearby. For more than a century (the school turned 100 in 1993), the school has prided itself on giving women the edge for a multifaceted life. Many graduates pursue advanced degrees in science and medicine, a particularly strong area academically. Approximately 30 major courses of study, as well as minors in computer science, economics and business, are offered. The Across-the-Curriculum Writing Program ensures every student has strong writing skills. The Prime Time program is offered for women of nontraditional college age.

One of the school's most famous graduates is renowned author Pearl Buck. Several study abroad pro-

The cost for a Blue Ridge education differs widely. Some admissions offices quote a combined cost for tuition and room and board, while others list them separately. When comparing costs, be sure to ask which cost-quoting formula they use.

Insiders' Tips

grams are offered, including junior year in England. Tuition is $13,970 annually, although the $6,110 room and board fee should be noted because most students are required to live on campus while attending Randolph-Macon.

FERRUM COLLEGE

Ferrum   *(703) 365-4290*

More than any college in the Blue Ridge, Ferrum celebrates its ties to the local culture and brings national attention to Virginia, Franklin County and a nearly extinct way of life. Located on 800 acres in Franklin County, near Smith Mountain Lake, Ferrum is a private, coeducational, liberal arts United Methodist Church affiliate. Founded in 1913, Ferrum offers bachelor's degree in 31 majors to 1,200 students. It is nationally renowned for its Blue Ridge Institute and Blue Ridge Folk Festival each autumn. There, Coon Dog Trials and Jumping Mules are part of the program that brings thousands each year to Ferrum.

While educating students for success in modern society, Ferrum has remained attuned to those cultural traditions which give the region its sense of place and identity. In the early 1970s, the Blue Ridge Institute was established to document and interpret that heritage through research, fieldwork and educational outreach. Ferrum even was nominated for a Grammy Award for a recording series exploring Virginia folk music. Concerts have brought together traditional musicians, tale tellers and craftspeople. A Blue Ridge Archive preserves photos, recordings and printed materials important to Virginia folk culture.

Tuition is $13,600 annually. The college is in NCAA Division III. Baseball and football are popular sports at Ferrum.

New River Valley Region

VIRGINIA TECH

Blacksburg   *(703) 231-6000*

Virginia's largest and most diverse university, Virginia Tech has a pervasive presence in western Virginia as the largest employer in Southwestern Virginia. The school employs 5,900 full-time employees and has an annual payroll of $250 million. Virginia Tech enrolls nearly 24,000 undergraduate and graduate students and has 76 undergraduate and 124 graduate degree programs. There are eight colleges: Agriculture and Life Sciences, Architecture and Urban Studies, Arts and Sciences, Business, Education, Engineering, Human Resources and the new College of Forestry. All 50 states and nearly 100 foreign countries are represented in the student body.

Tech's 2,600-acre main campus is located in a town of 32,000 residents, in the scenic Blue Ridge Mountains. As you would expect, many students can't bear to leave Blacksburg after graduation, and legions of them stay to make it a top-notch, stimulating university town. Additional facilities include a 120-room conference center, 800-

acre research farm, Equine Center, graduate centers in Roanoke, Hampton Roads and the Washington, D.C., metro area and 12 statewide agricultural experiment stations. Plans are underway to convert Hotel Roanoke in the City of Roanoke, 36 miles away, into a conference/continuing education hotel, expected to open April 1, 1995.

U.S. News and World Report has ranked Virginia Tech in its top 50 national universities. It also ranks in the national top 20 with National Merit Scholars and top 50 nationally in annually sponsored research. Its Corporate Research Center is one of the best-known in the South. As a land-grant university with a statewide mission, Tech is responsible for Virginia's Cooperative Extension, which is carried to 107 Virginia communities. Tech is also a leader among universities in the United States in the use of communications technology. The entire campus is connected with the town of Blacksburg and the world through the unique Blacksburg Electronic Village. The school has gained quite a bit of fame through this bold use of the electronic superhighway. It also is famous for its traditional Cadet Corps.

Tech is a member of the Big East Conference and has a 51,000-seat stadium, offering some of the most popular spectator sports in the Blue Ridge. Be prepared for hour-long traffic jams when the Hokies play football at home. Tuition is $3,951 in state and $10,404 out of state annually, fees included.

RADFORD UNIVERSITY
Radford   *(703) 831-5371*

The New River Valley's other major state-supported educational institution, Radford University enrolls nearly 9,300 students in this residential community of 14,000. Radford is located 45 miles southwest of Roanoke in the Blue Ridge Mountains. In addition to the Graduate College, there are five colleges offering bachelor's degrees: Arts and Sciences, Business and Economics, Education and Human Development, Nursing and Health Services, and Visual and Performing Arts. Special pre-professional programs are offered in law, pharmacy, physical therapy, veterinary medicine, sports medicine, medicine and ROTC. The University is also planning a new program in Global Studies, to begin in 1997. As with Virginia Tech, many students elect to stay to live and work in this beautiful college town beside the scenic New River. Tuition in state is $3,034, out of state, $7,206 annually. Radford belongs to the Big South Conference and NCAA Division I and offers 17 varsity sports.

Southwestern Virginia Region

EMORY & HENRY COLLEGE
Emory   *(703) 944-4121*

This historic (1836), private, liberal arts college enrolling 850 was recently cited by *Money Guide* magazine as "One of the 100 Best Educational Buys in the U.S." Tuition is $7,900 annually. Emory & Henry offers 20 majors and special programs, including Appalachian Studies, premed and pre-law. It also ranks with the top one percent of U.S. colleges and universities in alumnae giving. In addition to a small, intensive setting for education, it is ideal if you are interested in spectacular mountains and easy access to the recreational opportunities they afford, including mountain climbing, hiking and bicycling. It is close to the historic town of Abingdon. Six varsity sports are in NCAA Division III, with membership in the Old Dominion Athletic Conference.

Preparatory Schools

THE MILLER SCHOOL OF ALBEMARLE

Charlottesville   *(804) 823-4805*

This is a college preparatory and academic military school located on 1,600 beautiful acres 14 miles from Charlottesville. There are only about 114 students a year, with the majority enrolled in the Upper School for grades nine through 12. The rest of the students are in fifth through eighth grade. The Upper School is organized as a Cadet Squadron of the Civil Air Patrol, the official auxiliary of the U.S. Air Force. All students wear uniforms and are expected to conform to "modified" miliary procedures. Both girls and boys attend school, but only boys board there.

The Victorian-style buildings at the school are National Historic Landmarks, and the campus covers farmland, orchards, forests, a pond and a 12-acre lake for swimming, fishing and canoeing.

Eighty-three percent of the school's 1994 graduates were accepted by colleges and universities, with most entering schools in Virginia.

Current tuition and other costs will range from $8,550 for a five-day boarding program for younger students to $12,000 for new students in grades 11 and 12. This includes room and board, student services, uniforms and laundry. Financial aid is available; the average award is $4,500.

ST. ANNE'S-BELFIELD SCHOOL

Charlottesville   *(804) 296-5106*

Formed in 1970 by the merger of St. Anne's School, a girls' boarding school founded in 1910, with the Belfield School, a coed elementary school established in 1955, St. Anne's-Belfield is in its third decade of providing an excellent education for boys and girls from preschool through 12th grade. The accredited school is located the the University of Virginia on two campuses totaling more than 60 acres.

A five-day boarding program is offered for students in grades seven through 12. In a nutshell, the school's guiding philosophy is: "Although we expect our graduates to be prepared for the nation's finest colleges and universities, our true purpose is to create a challenging yet charitable atmosphere where students gain skills necessary for both creative and disciplined thought. . . . The transmission of knowledge, encouragement of curiosity and the development of responsible, honorable behavior are the great ends of education."

The school maintains a student body of about 800, and limits the residential program to 40 students to maintain a family-like atmosphere. A full range of advanced placement and honors courses are offered for upper level students, while younger children study basic subjects as well as French, art, drama, computers and physical education. Graduates advance to enroll in some of the nation's finest universities every year.

Tuition and fees range from $4,600 for a half-day session for preschool to $7,850 for grades 11 and 12. The five-day boarding fee is an additional $7,600. Financial aid is available to families who demonstrate need. About 28 percent of the students receive financial assistance.

WOODBERRY FOREST

Woodberry Forest
Madison County   (703) 672-6008
This is a prep school for boys on 1,400 rolling acres in Madison County, about 30 miles north of Charlottesville and 70 miles south of Washington, D.C.

Independent and nondenominational, the school prepares students for successful performance at some of the best colleges and universities in the country. This past year's graduates were admitted to 91 colleges and universities, including seven Ivy League schools.

Woodberry Forest offers a comprehensive Advanced Placement program and a curriculum that includes rigorous requirements in English, math, foreign language, history and science, plus art, music and religion.

About 400 boys from 31 states and 12 foreign countries attend the school, with the majority coming from Virginia and North Carolina.

The school was founded in 1889 by Robert S. Walker, a captain in the Confederate army who wanted a school to educate his six sons. Thomas Jefferson drew the floor plan for the headmaster's residence for his friend, William Madison, brother of James Madison.

The average class contains about 12 students. Professors also live on campus and more than two-thirds have master's degrees, including four with doctorates.

The campus is gorgeous. Fine recreational facilities include an Olympic-size pool and a golf course. There are many teams in every sport, so each student has a chance to compete against other boys of similar athletic ability.

Current annual tuition and fees are $15,000. One student in four receives tuition assistance.

Photo: Abingdon Convention and Visitors Bureau

White's Mill, the oldest water-powered commercial grist and flour mill in Southwestern Virginia.

Inside
Southwestern Virginia

The mountain culture of Southwestern Virginia, comprised of 14 uniquely different counties, is a challenge to highlight in just one chapter. This area is so close to the Blue Ridge Mountains and offers such a refreshing cultural point of view that a visit is an enticing daytrip and easily much more!

Time-wise, don't let the map of Southwestern Virginia deceive you, however. A mountain mile can take considerably longer to navigate than the speedy miles on the efficient interstate highways of the Blue Ridge of Virginia. Besides, there's lots of rugged mountain scenery to enjoy as you go, so leave ample time to get to your destination.

Mountains formed the culture of this land that has more miles of trout streams than roads. In the pioneer days, this beautiful mountainous country was the western frontier, romanticized with the legends of Daniel Boone. In 1775, Boone opened up the route to the west by carving out the Wilderness Road through the Appalachian Mountains.

Today, visitors can stand at various mountainous vantage points at 20,000-acre Cumberland Gap National Historical Park and see why Boone's route through the Gap soon caught on with so many adventurous spirits. Or, they may visit the Kentucky border's "Grand Canyon of the South," Breaks Interstate Park, where a five-mile-long, 1,600-foot-deep gorge prevented even the trail-blazing Boone from selecting this particular passage as the gate to the promised land.

Hardy, adventurous souls still practice and cherish a culture born and nurtured by isolation from outside influences. This is evidenced by the area's famous bluegrass music and hallowed arts and crafts passed on by generations of self-sufficient natives who learned to eke out a living from the land, either by farming or coal mining.

The area's people, known for their genuine friendliness, are glad to share their culture with "outsiders" at special events throughout the region. Probably the most famous is the Old Fiddler's Convention, held for 59 years in the city of Galax on the second weekend in August, sponsored by Galax Moose Lodge 733. At this internationally known event, string music, folk songs and clogging entertain visitors from around the world while contestants compete for thousands of dollars in prizes.

The area's other major attraction is the world-famous Barter Theatre, the oldest professional repertory theater in America, in the town of Abingdon (an attraction in itself). Founded during the Great Depression, the Barter began when a hungry young actor offered local residents theater tickets in exchange for food. Although the Barter now offers cash to its young actors, some of the country's best, for performances, it still continues its barter tradition, as well.

Another popular attraction, the outdoor drama, *Trail of the Lonesome Pine*, is also related to the mountains. Based on the famous novel of a proud mountain people by Big Stone Gap native John Fox, Jr., the drama is performed here each summer to show how the coming of modern civilization changed life for the local mountain folks, especially a romantic young girl, June Tolliver.

As you may expect, the highest mountains in Virginia are here. The steepest peak is 5,730-foot-high Mount Rogers, which sets the scenic stage for the vast acreage of this remote area. Not far behind in stature is lofty 5,520-foot-high White Top, host to both maple and ramp festivals. Driving up either is an adventure you'll never forget, and don't be surprised to still see snow on the ground as late as April and May! When you're headed for the high country, expect at the least a 10-degree temperature drop.

Virginia's mountains are home to numerous state and national parks, including Hungry Mother, near Marion; Breaks Interstate on the Kentucky border in Coal Country; and Natural Tunnel, an 850-foot-wide limestone tunnel winding its way through the Southwest Blue Ridge Highlands. Hunting, fishing, swimming, hiking, canoeing and, of course, mountain climbing, are popular pastimes for adventurous visitors.

What some say is the most beautiful stretch of the Blue Ridge Parkway also winds along the western edge of Patrick County. The picturesque landmark, Mabry Mill, is located nearby, with beautiful accommodations such as scenic Doe Run Lodge for the Parkway's many visitors.

The area's culture is carefully preserved by many institutions, among them the Southwest Virginia Museum and Historical State Park in Big Stone Gap and the Carter Family Fold, named for the famous Carter singing clan (June is married to singer Johnny Cash) and located between Gate City and Bristol, near the Tennessee border.

As one travels farther up the winding Appalachians, Coal Country is all around in the counties near the tip of Virginia. America's black gold grips not only the history but also the future of everyone living in the area. From the coke ovens of Buchanan County to the Harry Meador Coal Museum in Big Stone Gap, photos and equipment give you an understanding of a way of life that has long centered around a boom-or-bust economy. These days, tourism, happily, is quickly taking hold as the isolated land's alternative industry.

While sampling the best attractions the area has to offer, you won't be at a loss for places to eat, stay or

Far Southwest Region

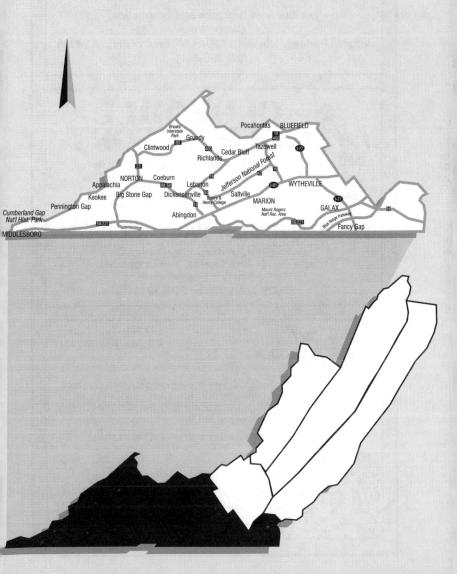

Breaks Interstate Park

Pocahontas   BLUEFIELD

Grundy

Clintwood   Cedar Bluff   Tazewell

Richlands

Jefferson National Forest

NORTON   Coeburn

Appalachia   Lebanon

Keokee   Big Stone Gap   Dickensonville   Saltville

Pennington Gap   Emory & Henry College   WYTHEVILLE

MARION   GALAX

Cumberland Gap Nat'l Hist. Park   Abingdon   Mount Rogers Nat'l Rec. Area

MIDDLESBORO   Blue Ridge Parkway   Fancy Gap

Southwestern Virginia Profile:
Ralph Stanley, Bluegrass Legend

Nobody embodies the rugged spirit of Southwestern Virginia quite like bluegrass-music legend Ralph Stanley. The 67-year-old musician, one of perhaps a half-dozen seminal figures in bluegrass and country music, is the architect of the "high lonesome" sound, a musical genre that's part angelic harmony, part primitive gospel and a whole lot Appalachian heartbreak. And indeed, Stanley classics such as "Rank Strangers," "Little Maggie" and "Mountain Girls Can Love" are the by-products of high times and low times, simple pleasures and deep pain.

They're a soundtrack of sorts to the landscape and lifestyle that define this remote and economically-strapped wedge of land between Kentucky, Tennessee, North Carolina and West Virginia — a surreal region teetering between breathtaking beauty and environmental neglect.

Dickenson County, Stanley's lifelong home, is in the heart of Virginia coal country, a place where no amount of land reclamation or economic stimuli will probably ever bring its quality of life up to that enjoyed by residents of the markedly more prosperous Blue Ridge.

Ralph Stanley

But it is, nevertheless, a land of immense pride and a wellspring of creative energy that has produced more than its share of great folk artists and musicians.

For more than 50 years, Stanley and his banjo, an instrument he learned from his mother, have been preaching the gospel of the "high-lonesome," recording more than 200 songs and 130 albums. He began his career playing and touring with older brother Carter (who died of alcohol-related complications in 1966), an equally masterful musician. After Carter's death, Ralph hooked up with the Clinch Mountain Boys, a group of local musicians, and together they still tour about 50 weekends a year — road trips that take them from the smoky honkytonks of the Appalachians to the grand music halls of

Germany and even an occasional stop at the Kennedy Center in Washington, D.C.

While the road has been good to Stanley, bluegrass is still largely considered a music that is "too regional" and a "hillbilly stepchild" of traditional country music. Consequently, Stanley has never become a household name. But that might be changing. Last year, he released the critically acclaimed "Saturday Night & Sunday Morning," a compilation of original gems that feature such accompanying artists as George Jones, Dwight Yoakam, Ricky Skaggs, Emmylou Harris, Vince Gill and Alison Krauss. The record proved that Nashville was willing to reexamine its roots and pay homage to one of its great grandfathers.

Don't expect Stanley to ever "go Nashville," however. He's ingrained in the haunting beauty and dark mystique of Southwestern Virginia, and that's where he will always remain. And you can join him in his homeland every Memorial Day weekend at the Ralph Stanley Bluegrass Festival outside of Coeburn, Va.

shop. There are plenty. The four-star Martha Washington Inn in Abingdon reigns supreme as the area's foremost accommodation, while many quaint bed and breakfasts offer an alternative way to relax. Restaurants such as Mosby's, in Norton, are eager to please. Shopping can range from quaint shops offering hand-crafted items, such as the Appalachian Peddlar, also in Norton, to the vast shopping outlets offered at Wytheville, at the crossroads of two busy interstate highways, 77 and 81.

With far too much interesting information to give ample justice to Southwestern Virginia's unique culture, we offer you a synopsis of the best and brightest of attractions in these 14 counties, along with the names of tourism groups who are eager to send you enticing material so you'll visit and stay awhile.

These counties are, for the most part, parallel. In keeping with the rest of the book, the listing will go from north to south and east to west, starting with Patrick and ending with Lee. Some are grouped together, since they market themselves as one entity for visitation. Others have so much going on that they stand well on their own. The 14 counties of Southwestern Virginia are: Patrick, Carroll, Grayson, the independent city of Galax, Bland, Wythe, Tazewell, Smyth, Buchanan, Russell, Washington, Dickenson, Wise, Scott and Lee.

Patrick County

Unspoiled, pristine and sprawling Patrick County, wedged between the Blue Ridge Mountains and the Piedmont, has always been a vibrant area where cultures collide. In the past, that included Iroquoian Cherokees versus Siouan Indians;

then Indians versus pioneers, trappers and settlers; and mountaineers versus planters.

The area still is as diverse today, offering attractions that range from archaeological artifacts to zoological exhibits and art to zithers. Named for the great orator Patrick Henry, the county has a wealth of American history from Colonial times to the present. Stuart, the county seat, was named in honor of a native son, dashing Confederate Cavalry Gen. J.E.B. Stuart.

Patrick County is home to one of the most beautiful sites on the Blue Ridge Parkway, Mabry Mill, at Milepost 176.1, made famous by artists and photographers the world over. The Parkway runs the length of Patrick County's western border. Its spectacular natural beauty, wildlife and foliage is highlighted by trails, waterfalls and sweeping overlooks of mountain ranges and valleys. At Fred Clifton Park, located off U.S. Highway 58, you can picnic with a view of five counties from several scenic overlooks.

The eastern part of the county boasts Fairystone State Park, named for the small fairystone crosses found there. The crosses are much sought after as good-luck charms. Legend has it that the crystalline stones are teardrops that angels and fairies shed when Christ was crucified. Camping and cabins are available at the park, and there's a lake with a beach. Rocky Knob at Milepost 174 also has cabins with electric kitchens. Other nice campgrounds are Deer Run, Dominion Valley, Lenglad, Round Meadow and Daddy Rabbit's.

With two-thirds of the county covered with woodlands, Patrick County is an outdoor-lover's delight. The "Top of the Mountain," a 3,000-foot plateau, is home not only to Lovers Leap and Fred Clifton Park, but to numerous shops in charming Meadows of Dan, with picnic spots and dining ranging from hot dogs to multicourse masterpieces at several fine restaurants, including Chateau Morrisette Winery, Doe Run Lodge and Restaurant and Woodberry Inn near Mabry Mill. Five minutes from the Meadows of Dan juncture is yet another restored, operating mill, Cockram Mill, where you can picnic beside the placid mill pond or browse through the souvenir shop.

Other scenic points of interest include Mayberry Trading Post at Milepost 180, built in 1892. This white frame general store is stocked with wonderful food and aromas, including apple butter, each fall. Nearby is Mayberry Presbyterian Church, founded in 1924 and a magnet to artists who come to paint or photograph the picturesque rock landmark.

Visitors also enjoy the Reynolds Homestead, the ancestral home of R.J. Reynolds, founder of the tobacco company bearing his name. It sits in restored elegance on the Reynolds Plantation in Critz. The original house and contemporary Continuing Education Center, now an extension of Virginia Tech, welcome visitors for numerous annual events ranging from a Victorian Christmas celebration to art shows, live theater and concerts.

Patrick County also is a

sportsman's delight. It is known for Primland Hunting Preserve, a private, 10,000-acre hunting reserve stocked with thousands of game birds, with hunt packages available for family outings and larger groups. Fishermen also will find the mountain streams sparkling with native and stocked trout at Philpott Reservoir, a man-made lake that stretches 15 miles and has a 100-mile shoreline with hundreds of campsites and a sandy beach.

The county has two of only a dozen covered bridges remaining in Virginia. Bob White, built in 1922, is located off Virginia Route 8 near Woolwine. Jack's Creek Covered Bridge was built in 1914 two miles south of Woolwine on Virginia Route 610. Both are beautiful examples of preserved Americana.

Next door to Patrick County is Henry County, home to Martinsville, an industrial center of textiles and furniture as well as the Virginia Museum of Natural History, which is the state's center for research, collection and exhibits in the natural sciences. It features stimulating visuals and hands-on exhibits. Outlet shopping is excellent at Tultex Clothing and Stanley Furniture, and the Martinsville Speedway packs them in for NASCAR races.

For more information on Patrick County, there are two groups to contact: the Blue Ridge/Piedmont Cultural Consortium in Martinsville at (703) 632-3221 and the Patrick County Chamber of Commerce at (703) 694-6012.

City of Galax, Carroll County and Grayson County

Carroll and Grayson counties and the City of Galax are bound together both by lay of the land and location.

City of Galax

An independent city, Galax is nestled in the Blue Ridge between Carroll and Grayson counties and serves as the commercial hub of the area.

Galax is a Main Street community with a charming downtown and is home to the oldest (since 1935) and largest fiddlers' convention in the world the second week of August, sponsored by the Galax Loyal Order of Moose Lodge 733.

Each year, about 30,000 people gather in Felts Park to enjoy the original music of pure American culture performed by a wide variety of nearly 2,000 talented artists who compete for thousands of dollars in prize money. The program includes folk song, fiddle, guitar, bluegrass banjo, clawhammer banjo and mandolin. Outside of the big festival, you can enjoy the Galax Mountain Music Jamboree the third Saturday of each month (except August) at 7 PM. May through October, the jamboree is held outdoors at Grayson Street Stage; November through April, it moves indoors to the Rex Theatre on Grayson Street.

If you're in town, also stop by at

Barr's Fiddle Shop at 105 S. Main Street for an impromptu jazz session. This is a unique music shop offering the musician a large selection of instruments and recorded music. Call Tom Barr at (703) 236-2411.

Galax also is a major center of Virginia's furniture manufacturing industry. Textiles and clothing are other important industries, and Consolidated Glass and Mirror Corporation operates one of the most modern, efficient mirror plants in the world.

For shopping, don't miss Rooftop of Virginia Cap Crafts, where you'll find everything from a cake of lye soap to the finest of handmade quilts. At 206 N. Main Street, you'll find a cathedral-type setting where the local community action agency and native craftspeople cooperate to bring to the public a wide selection of authentic handmade crafts. The center is open from 9 AM to 5 PM year round.

Another interesting Galax shop is Buckhorn Art and Antiques, 115 W. Grayson Street, featuring nationally acclaimed sporting artist Alice Taylor and outdoor writer and free-lance photographer Russ Sharrock. You'll find sporting collectibles and naturalist collections among the shelves of antiques and gourmet foods. Call (703) 236-2626. Also go to The Framer's Daughter Gallery to see limited edition prints of P. Buckley Moss, Civil War art, Alice Taylor prints and originals and other local southwestern Virginia scenes. Call (703) 236-4920. Gallery 109 at 109 N. Main Street is

another favorite showcase for local artists. Call (703) 236-3478.

If you enjoy log cabins, visit the Jeff Matthews Memorial Museum at 606 W. Stuart Drive, adjacent to the Vaughan Memorial Library. This is a glimpse into the past, with full authentic reconstruction. Don't miss the 58 cases full of Indian artifacts collected in the area. Visits are free. Call (703) 236-7874 for seasonal hours.

Also visit Harmon's Museum, Highway 58 and 221 in Woodlawn. Associated with Harmon's Clothing Outlet, the museum features a quaint collection of items, including an impressive Civil War collection. Call (703) 236-4884 for seasonal hours.

For a nice place to stay while nearby, try Riverview B&B in Independence. Call Ken and Rebecca Ogle at (800) 841-6628 for information about their inn, which overlooks the New River. It's private, with 90 acres. Rates range from $50 to $70 a night. Also popular is The Inn at Orchard Gap, at Fancy Gap, near the Blue Ridge Parkway. Call John and Barbara DeRemer at (703) 398-3206 about their spectacular mountain views seen from wide front porches. Rates range from $55 to $70 a night.

Carroll County

Carroll County is a rich agricultural area noted for fruit and vegetable production. The area, with its gently rolling hills and well-tended farms, has become a well-known destination for tourists and retirees, especially along the Blue Ridge Parkway.

Carroll sports numerous facilities for camping, swimming, fishing, horseback riding and hiking. You'll find an 18-hole golf course, Olde Mill, just off the Blue Ridge Parkway.

The county's most famous event is the annual Hillsville Gun Show and Flea Market, in its 27th year, conducted each Labor Day Weekend by VFW Grover King Post 1115. Join the 250,000 people who drive every year to this show. You'll spot cars lined up for miles before you get to the 100-acre-plus site, where more than 2,000 vendors offer every type of collectible imaginable. It's called the "Best Show in the South" — where the collectors collect. Call Melvin Webb about the guns at (703) 728-9810 and Ernest Martin about the flea market at (703) 728-7188.

Grayson County

Grayson County is rapidly becoming the recreational destination of Southwestern Virginia. It is home to Mount Rogers, the highest peak in Virginia, with its 60-mile-long Mount Rogers National Recreation Area; Grayson Highlands State Park; and New River Trail State Park, Virginia's only linear state park (a continuous park 57 miles long), featuring hiking, bicycling and horseback riding. All around are Fraser firs, the "King of Christmas Trees," which sell for $100 each in big cities. Christmas trees are overtaking cattle as the area's biggest business.

Mount Rogers National Recreation Area is the real draw, with its 154,000 acres of beautiful, unspoiled land set in the Jefferson National Forest. People, many hiking the Appalachian Trail, come to the area, isolated by altitude and climate, to return to another era and see a fragile ecosystem through its alpine meadows and spruce-crowned summits. The town of Damascus is famous for its mid-May party during Appalachian Trail Days, when hikers are invited to join in a parade with the towns-people, indulge in barbecued chicken at the fire station and square dance in the post office parking lot.

A visitors center provides information on outdoor facilities. The rugged setting is described by many visitors as the closest thing they've seen to terrain in Wyoming and Montana. Mount Rogers' Rhododendron Gap probably is one of the stiffest parts of the Appalachian Trail, but experienced hikers who make it to this point say the profusion of the wildflowers makes the effort worthwhile.

Family camping is available at sites that include Beartree, Comers Rock, Grindstone, Hurricane, Raccoon Branch, and Raven Cliff. Horse camping can be found at Fox Creek Trailhead, Hussy Mountain and Raven Cliff.

Favorite picnic spots are Beartree, Comers Rock, Fox Creek, Raven Cliff, Shepherd's Corner and Skull Gap. The most popular trails in addition to the Appalachian are Iron Mountain, Virginia Creeper and Virginia Highlands Horse Trail. Favorite hikes are to Mount Rogers Summit, Rhododendron Gap and Deep Gap.

Rangers warn visitors not to embark into the highlands wearing only light jackets and tennis shoes. When fog, cold rain or darkness fall, it's easy to get lost in the isolation. Most of the careless wanderers make it out of the wilds with just a cold, but there have been some tragic exceptions.

The Mount Rogers park stretches from the New River near Ivanhoe westward along the south side of Interstate I-81 to Damascus. Major access is off I-81 to Virginia Route 16 south from Marion and Virginia Route 600 south from Chilhowie. Headquarters for the area is on Virginia Route 16, south of Marion, and can be called at (703) 783-5196. Maps are available here for $3.

Grayson Highlands State Park contains 5,000 acres and provides facilities for camping, picnicking, swimming, horseback riding, hiking and nature study. To the delight to all visitors, several hundred ponies roam freely through the park. Each fall, on the last weekend of September, they are herded up and auctioned off at the park. Although the sale doesn't have the same visibility as the pony roundup at the Eastern Shore's Assateague and Chincoteague islands, locals say their event is better, with a higher quality of pony.

The New River Trail State Park, the state's linear park, offers 57 miles of trails. Much of it parallels the scenic New River, the second-oldest river in the world.

For more detailed information, directions, points of interest, brochures and maps of the area, contact: the Galax-Carroll-Grayson Chamber of Commerce, (703) 236-2184); Mount Rogers National Recreation Area, (703) 783-5196; Jefferson National Forest, (703) 982-6270; or Virginia's Division of State Parks, (804) 786-2132.

Town of Wytheville, Wythe County and Bland County

The Town of Wytheville and Wythe and Bland counties pride themselves on being the "Crossroads of America," with a convenient location at the intersection of I-81 and I-77 that brings in thousands of tourists for shopping and dining.

Town of Wytheville

Wytheville cuts a sharp contrast between the scenic beauty of the rolling peaks and valleys of the Allegheny Mountain Highlands and the bright, modern, new construction of motels, restaurants and industry. The area is a refreshing, welcome respite for a weary traveler.

Motorists enjoy the beauty of Bland and Wythe counties' forested lands for as far as the eye can see as they travel down the interstate highways. Pioneers heading west were so impressed that they settled here on a high, level plateau that became a natural crossroads for trappers and hunters making their way through Big Walker Mountain and Fancy Gap.

First called Wythe County Courthouse, the town later was named Wytheville for George Wythe, the first law professor at the College of William and Mary and designer of Virginia's state seal. The "Father of Wytheville," as he is called, was Col. Thomas Jefferson Boyd. A museum stands in his honor today, a project of the Wythe County Historical Society. Edith Bolling Wilson, wife of President Woodrow Wilson, was born here in 1872, daughter of the judge of the Court of Wythe County.

Wytheville played a significant role during the Civil War because of its location and the fact that lead mines and the only salt mine in the South were nearby. It was the site of constant clashes between the North and South. Although many homes were burned, the stone house of the area's first resident physician, Dr. John Haller, was spared. Old Rock House, a National Landmark, is now a museum full of handcrafts and mementoes.

Wytheville Community College, an accredited two-year institution, is located in Wytheville. The town also has a modern library and a well-established community center. Wythe County Community Hospital is located here. Along with Blacksburg, Wytheville was named one of the nation's best places to retire; Asbury Center at Birdmont, a multilevel retirement community, is located here. Two charming parks

are situated in the center of downtown.

Culturally, Wytheville is known for its recently revived Chautauqua Festival, held the third week in June and gaining in recognition yearly for its celebration of music, education and the arts. During the 1920s, Wytheville was a regular stop on the "Chautauqua Circuit," a series of tours featuring lectures, plays and concerts originating from the Chautauqua Institution near Buffalo, New York. An important forum for adult education, the tent Chautauquas flourished until the development of radio, which made them a thing of the past.

Events take place in the Elizabeth Brown Park. Wytheville's charming downtown offers several walking tours in an old-fashioned and thriving business district. It is known for numerous shopping opportunities, from local crafts to outlet bargains. Another popular shopping site is Snooper's Antique and Craft Mall, where 50 local craftspeople display their work. Here, you will find a wide selection of antiques, quilts, hand-blown glass and pottery. Snooper's is located on the I-81 frontage road eight miles north of Wytheville. Ten miles north at Fort Chiswell is Factory Merchants Outlet Mall, featuring an array of discount shopping for everything from kitchenware to toys.

The most unique shop in the Wytheville area is P.J.'s Christmas Carousel, where children can ride a carousel of Christmas animals. P.J.'s offers hand-crafted holiday decorations and gifts. It's next to Snooper's.

While you're shopping, remember that there are 14 motels and 35 restaurants in Wytheville. Wytheville offers some very nice places to stay, including the Holiday Inn Wytheville, Best Western, Ramada Inn and Days Inn. Wytheville also has the Boxwood Inn Bed & Breakfast. This inn is a lovely Georgian Colonial home located in the heart of scenic, historic Wytheville just off I-77 and I-81. There are eight spacious guest rooms, each tastefully furnished with a blend of traditional, period and antique furniture. Each has a private bath.

Some of the most memorable restaurants are Scrooge's, just off I-81, the Log House Restaurant on Main Street downtown and Words and Music Irish Cafe. Scrooge's is fashioned on the theme of the famous Charles Dickens story, *A Christmas Carol*. Also at Scrooge's, you'll find Tiny Tim's assortment of novelties and an ice cream parlor. The Log House was built in 1776 and features an old-fashioned menu that features an Appalachian flavor. Words and Music offers a taste of Ireland for both the palate and soul, with homemade apple dumplings and imported beverages served with eclectic live performances every other Saturday.

Wytheville also offers something for those hungry for outdoor beauty. The city is midway between Claytor Lake State Park in Pulaski County and Hungry Mother State Park in Smyth County. The area also offers fishing, boating and swimming in nearby Bland and Wythe counties. A great KOA campground is located there with Kamping Kabins, outdoor sports, farm animals for the kids and a large, heated swimming pool.

Wythe County

Agriculture and manufacturing are Wythe County's leading industries, but tourism in the great outdoors is quickly gaining, since the county is a mecca for recreation. A large portion lies within the Jefferson National Forest. The Appalachian Trail crosses the county, and part of Mount Rogers National Recreational Area lies in the southwestern corner.

Rural Retreat was the second town incorporated in Wythe County and offers a haven of natural beauty, especially at Rural Retreat Lake and Campground, located between Rural Retreat and Cedar Springs on Virginia Route 749. The 90-acre fishing lake offers picnicking, boat rental and a Junior Olympic swimming pool.

Anglers have it made in Wythe County. Trout fishing is popular at Cripple and Peak creeks. Hale Fishing Lake is 3,000 feet up Iron Mountain, south of Speedwell, just off U.S. Highway 21. Part of the Jefferson National Forest, the lake is stocked regularly with trout. Cedar Springs Sportsman's Lodge, near Cedar Springs on Cripple Creek, is a popular place for fishermen to catch their limit. Wytheville State Fish Hatchery is located on Route 629, near Fort Chiswell. Visitors are encouraged to see the grounds and displays.

The county is home to one of the most unique landmarks in the world, the shot tower at Shot Tower Historical Park, located where U.S. Highway 52 crosses New River at the Poplar Camp Exit on I-77. The 70-foot tower, the only one of its kind known in the world, was built in the early 1800s to make shot for the firearms of frontiersmen and settlers.

The tower is now the center of Virginia's newest state park, most of which is located in Wythe County. Its New River Trail offers the outdoor enthusiast opportunities for hiking, biking, horseback riding, canoeing and primitive camping.

Another great outdoor site is Big Walker Lookout, located between Wytheville and Bland on U.S. Highway 52. There are a chairlift, swinging bridge, cabin, gift shop and an observation tower 3,600 feet up that offers a view of five states,

Wythe Raceway also is nearby, a few miles from Rural Retreat. The oval clay track seats 5,000 fans who like late model and mini-stock racing, bike races and tractor pulls.

Bland County

Formed in 1861, Bland County is nearly 80 percent forest and has a population of 6,500. It was named for Richard Bland, a prominent Virginia patriot of the Revolutionary War. Thomas Jefferson called Bland "the wisest man south of the James River." Situated on the West Virginia border, Bland County is close to the Bluefields of Virginia and West Virginia.

The "Blizzard of '93," which dumped 32 inches of snow in the nearby New River Valley, brought snow drifts of 10 feet with it, stranding nearly 2,000 travelers. Bland County High School, churches and homes opened up to the surprised travelers. Three hundred were forced to spend the night in Big Walker tunnel. Needless to say, Bland County deservedly got a national reputation for hospitality after the "Blizzard of the Century."

Bland County's population, though sparse, is heavily engaged in agriculture, with 350 farms encompassing nearly 100,000 acres. Beef and dairy cattle and sheep are what most farmers raise. In fact, 95.9 percent of the land is used for agriculture, conservation and recreation, with only 1 percent used for industrial purposes.

As you'd expect, hunting and fishing are popular; deer, turkey and brook and rainbow trout are the main attractions.

Hunters of beautiful scenery and those wanting a refreshing alternative to interstate driving will want to travel Big Walker Mountain Scenic Byway, 16.2 miles of road, most of which passes through Bland County. The Byway takes travelers over some of the area's most scenic land, which is beautiful year round. There is camping, hiking, hunting and picnicking in the Jefferson National Forest along this route. To get on the Byway, take the intersection of Route 717 and I-77, about five miles north of Wytheville. Go west on Route 717. Landmarks along the way include Stony Fork Creek, Seven

Sisters Trail and Big Walker Lookout, where you can see several states.

Big Walker Mountain and Bland County offer a recreational activity unmatched in the Blue Ridge — llama hiking! With advance reservations, Bob and Carolyn Bane of Virginia Highland Llamas, (703) 688-4464, will lead you and your party, along with a herd of llamas, up Big Walker's old Appalachian Trail section. On special saddles, the llamas will carry a picnic lunch you can enjoy after hiking through lush green meadows up to a beautiful vista. The hike is about three hours up and 2½ hours down. An eerie aspect of the journey is listening to each llama hum in different monotones. Why do they hum?

"Because they don't know the words," says Carolyn Bane. Actually, humming is how the llamas communicate.

Golfers preferring a more predictable and traditional pastime will enjoy Wolf Creek Golf Club in Bastian, an 18-hole, par 70 public golf course open year round. It is on Route 614, five miles west of I-77 Bastian Exit. Golfers can look forward to a wonderful day at the Draper Valley Golf Club. A championship 18-hole course, Draper Valley players enjoy panoramic views of the Blue Ridge Mountains while playing. A putting green and driving range are also open to the public. This golf course is located on the I-81 service road between exits 86 and 89.

For some good country fun, try the Bland County Fair and Horse Show in August or the Bland County Lord's Acre Sale in October. Visitors are made to feel welcome by members of this friendly agricultural community.

Shoppers can find some good antique stores on Main Street in Bland, especially Heritage House Antiques and Imagine That!, whose motto is, "Bring your imagination and have a vision!"

If you're looking for a nice place to stay, blizzard weather or not, Bland County's Willow Bend Farm bed and breakfast is located just off I-77 and the Big Walker Mountain Scenic Byway. Rates range from $55 to $75, including breakfast. Call (703) 688-3719 for more information.

For more information on Wytheville and Bland and Wythe counties, contact: the Wytheville Convention & Visitors Bureau, (703) 228-3211, and the Wythe Ranger District of the Jefferson National Forest, (703) 228-5551. For regional tourism information, you also may call (800) 446-9670 or write the Virginia Highlands Gateway Visitor's Center at Drawer B-12, Max Meadows, Virginia 24360.

Smyth County

If you love the outdoors, breathtaking scenery and retracing the steps of soldiers in one of the most important counties in the Civil War, by all means visit gorgeous Smyth County (population 33,000) and enjoy all the natural beauty and rich history it has to offer, along with a host of good country restaurants and inexpensive places to stay.

Smyth County was formed in 1832 and named for Gen.

Alexander Smyth. The county's important towns are the county seat, Marion, named for Revolutionary War hero Francis "Swamp Fox" Marion; Chilhowie, apple capital of the state's southwest, whose Native American name means "Valley of Many Deer"; and Saltville, named for the salt ponds that have yielded mastodon bones with spear points embedded in them and nicknamed "Salt Capitol of the Confederacy." During the Civil War, there were 38 furnaces in operation, and in 1864 alone, 4 million bushels of salt were produced. In addition to providing table salt and salt for animals, the salt ponds' most important function was providing salt to preserve meat in the days before refrigeration.

Saltville's copious salt production brought an attack from the North on October 2, 1864. You still can see the trenches and fortifications from which the outnumbered Confederates nevertheless successfully defended the town's saltworks. One of the historic cannons stands at the entrance of Saltville's Elizabeth Cemetery, where some Confederate defenders are buried. The Saltville Historical Foundation, which restored some of the Confederate fortifications, also has various battle relics on display in the Saltville Museum and at Virginia Highland Community College. Visitors also can see a reconstruction of the historical, rough-hewn Madam Russell House, home of Patrick Henry's sister. All tours begin at the Saltville Museum, located in the center of town behind the post office.

The week before Labor Day, Saltville residents observe Salt-Making Week. They heat up some of the town's old salt kettles and boil down the brine, just as their ancestors did several hundred years ago. Then, on Labor Day, they celebrate with four days of music and fun.

Other historical attractions have equally interesting origins. The area's leading recreational area, Hungry Mother State Park, was named for Hungry Mother Creek. The park is located five miles from Marion, off I-81. As legend has it, pioneer Molly Marley and her small child were caught in an Indian raid that killed her husband. After eating only berries for many days, she collapsed at the foot of the mountain known as Molly's Knob. Her child, unable to rouse her, wandered down the creek and finally found a group of houses. The only words he could say were "hungry" and "mother." A search party found the child's dead mother, and the creek took its name from this sad tale.

On a more upbeat historical note, Smyth County's town of Troutdale was journey's end to the famous author Sherwood Anderson, who helped shape the modern short story and wrote the famous *Winesburg, Ohio*, and other literary gems. The Sherwood Anderson Short Story Competition is sponsored annually, and recognition is awarded to aspiring authors. Ripshin, Anderson's home, is open by appointment; call Tom Copenhaver at (703) 783-4192. Professor Charles Modlin at Virginia Tech, (703) 231-8447, is also knowledgeable about Anderson and his impact on Southwestern Virginia's literary riches.

In addition to lots of history, Smyth County offers many ways to have fun. Marion and Saltville each have town pools. Boaters and swimmers also can choose from Hungry Mother and Beartree lakes. Hungry Mother offers 2,000 acres of lovely, unspoiled Virginia countryside. You can hike or rent and ride horses through its miles of trails, swim, rent rowboats or paddleboats or fish on its 108-acre lake. Or, you can relax in the sun on its beach and enjoy the sunset from the porch of one of its cabins. For cabin reservations, call early in the season at (703) 783-3422. Hungry Mother Campground, a mile south of the state park on U.S. Highway 16 in Marion, also offers an especially nice camping area. Call (703) 783-2046. Other recommended campgrounds are Houndshell in Troutdale, (703) 655-4639, and Interstate, (703) 646-8384, off I-81 at Seven Mile Ford.

Each July, dozens of artists and craftspeople display their work at the Hungry Mother Arts and Crafts Festival. The festival lasts three days and offers leatherwork, handmade clothing and arts and crafts from throughout the Eastern United States.

Another popular event is Marion's July 4th Celebration and Independence Day Chili Championship. Cooks spend all morning preparing pots of their best chili, launching a day of games and concerts, topped off by fireworks.

Mount Rogers Recreation Area (See Grayson County section) is ac-

cessible from the Chilhowie Exit. Headquarters for Mount Rogers Recreation Area is at Highway 16 S. in Marion. Call (703) 783-5196.

Hunters and fishermen can pursue their dreams in gorgeous Tumbling Creek wild water and the Clinch Valley Mountain Wildlife Area, which includes a 300-acre mountaintop lake set aside for fishing, hunting and primitive camping. For more information, call (703) 944-3434 or the Virginia Commission of Game and Inland Fisheries at (804) 257-1000.

For those who don't want to rough it, a very nice bed and breakfast, Clarkcrest, is located at Chilhowie on Highway 607. The four large guest rooms are offered at $60 per double occupancy. Owners Doug and Mary Clark may be called at (703) 646-3707 or 646-3737. Another nice bed and breakfast is the Pendleton House Inn, owned by Mary Ann and Russell Martin. It has four beautifully appointed rooms with a gorgeous view of the mountains. Rates are $55 per night for one or $60 for two. Call (703) 646-2047 for reservations. General accommodations can be found in Chilhowie at Econo Lodge, (703) 646-8981; Budget Host Inn, at Marion, (703) 783-8511; or the Marion Holiday Inn, (703) 783-3193.

Visitors staying at Chilhowie may be lucky enough to catch its Apple Festival each September. This three-day celebration includes a huge parade and other festivities.

The area boasts many nice restaurants, including House of Hunan, (703) 783-2186, on Highway 16 S. at Marion, and Corner Downtown Cafe, (703) 783-7668, in Marion,

For more information, call the Smyth County Chamber of Commerce in Marion at (703) 783-3161.

Washington County and Abingdon

Washington County

Washington County, home of historic Abingdon, the oldest town west of the Blue Ridge, is alive with history, arts, music, education and Southern hospitality. It is indisputably the cultural center of Southwestern Virginia.

The area's pristine mountain streams and plentiful camping also attract outdoor lovers from all over. The Mount Rogers National Recreation Center is located here, its 115,000 acres offering breathtaking panoramic views, trails and cross-country skiing.

South Holston Lake, a large Tennessee Valley Authority reservoir, forms part of Washington County's southern border, where you can enjoy boating, swimming and fishing. The national Virginia Creeper Trail, which gently climbs from Abingdon to Whitetop Mountain, once was a Native American trail and then a railway. Many hikers, horseback riders and cross-country skiers tackle the former railroad bed's 34 miles for a dose of relaxation and nature watching. The Virginia Creeper Trail Club will send

you information if you write them at P.O. Box 2382, Abingdon, Virginia 24210.

Another county landmark is White's Mill, a Virginia Historic Landmark and one of the few remaining water-powered working mills in the country, located 3½ miles north of Abingdon. With much of its original machinery still in place, the two-story structure is an excellent example of 19th-century milling. There's also a trout-stocked mill pond and an early 20th-century general store. For more information, call (703) 676-0825.

Washington County is also home to Emory & Henry College, a private, four-year liberal arts school that is consistently rated among the top small colleges and most enjoyable colleges to attend in the Southeast. Virginia Highlands Community College is here, too.

Abingdon

What truly makes Washington County a premier vacation destination is Abingdon, beautifully and vitally alive with attractions of nationally known theater, arts, music, shopping, trendy restaurants, a four-star hotel and historic bed and breakfast inns.

Founded in 1778, Abingdon was once the most important town in western Virginia. The first Englishmen used Abingdon as a distribution point for mail and supplies on the Great Wilderness Road. It is now a community of friendly people with historic homes, quaint shops and galleries, who hope you'll stay awhile and partake of their hospitality.

The two unequalled stars in Abingdon's multifaceted crown are the Barter Theatre, celebrating its 61st anniversary, and the Martha Washington Inn, a lovingly restored classic hotel known for hospitality, gourmet food and fine service. Traditionally, people from around the world come to see the Barter Theatre's acclaimed plays, stay at the Martha Washington or an area bed and breakfast and then take their pick of the town's multitude of cultural offerings.

The Barter, the state theater of Virginia, was founded in 1933, during the Great Depression. It started when Robert Porterfield, an enterprising young actor, returned to his native Washington County with an extraordinary proposition: How about bartering fruits and vegetables for tickets to see a play? The idea of "exchanging ham for Hamlet" proved successful. The bounty of produce from the farms and gardens of Southwestern Virginia provided food and work for professional Depression-era actors. At the close of the first season, the company cleared $4.35 in cash, two barrels of jelly and a collective weight gain of over 300 pounds.

In keeping with the system of barter, the theater exchanged Virginia's famous country hams for royalties to produce the works of such playwrights as Noel Coward, Thornton Wilder and Bernard Shaw. Shaw, a vegetarian, returned the ham and requested spinach. The Barter obliged him. As time passed, Barter earned a reputation for top plays performed by top professionals. For an upcoming schedule of playbills, call the Barter at (800) 368-3240.

The Martha Washington Inn matches the historical charm and elegance of the year it was founded, 1832. The original home was built for Col. Francis Preston. After his death, it became the Martha Washington College for Women. After the college merged with Emory & Henry, the inn was used as a boarding house for actors at the Barter. In 1935, it opened as an inn. Its present owner, United Coal Company, spent more than $6 million on its renovation in 1992. The inn offers a restaurant, a nightclub, private club and gift shop.

For more information on the inn or to make reservations, call (800) 533-1014.

You will also be very pleased with your accommodations at any of the area's super bed and breakfasts, Victoria and Albert Inn, (703) 676-2797; Silversmith Inn, (703) 676-3924; Cabin on the River, (703) 628-8433; Maplewood Farm, (703) 628-2640; River Garden, (800) 952-4296; and Summerfield Inn, (703) 628-5905. All are charming . . . but not guaranteed to be ghost-free, unlike the Martha Washington Inn in Abingdon.

There's also camping at Washington County Park, WolfLair Campground, Riverside Family Campground and Lake Shore.

For a descriptive brochure of all the bed and breakfasts and attractions in the area, call the Abingdon Visitors & Convention Bureau at (703) 676-2282. You may want to take in the rest of Abingdon's sights on its scenic historic walking tour. A map is available by calling (703) 628-8141.

If shopping is your passion, try the Cave House Craft Shop, operated by the Holston Mountain Arts and Crafts Cooperative, located three blocks from the Martha Washington and a National Historic Site. It features the work of Southwest Virginia artisans. Another interesting shop is the Abingdon General Store, which also houses the Plum Alley Eatery, at 301 E. Main Street. Abingdon Mercantile and Frame Gallery and Antiques gathers together three stories and 12,000 square feet of wares of 19 antique dealers. Dixie Pottery, off I-81, five miles south of Abingdon, offers worldwide shopping under one large roof.

A very special shop that attracts a large following is the Antique Orchid Herbary, a few miles outside the town. You can experience everything from herbal barbecues to nature walks with an herbal picnic supper. Classes are held in fresh herb and flower bouquet making, summer party planning and gardening. For a list of delightful and unusual offerings, call (703) 628-1463.

If you're hungry, in addition to the Martha Washington, also try the downtown restaurants of PJ Brown & Company, Hardware Company Restaurant and the modern Starving Artist Cafe.

The cultural heritage of the area has been celebrated since 1948 at the annual Virginia Highlands Festival, held the first two weeks in August. The popular event serves up such fun as hot air balloons, live entertainment, art and crafts. Other popular festivals are the Washington County Fair and Burley Tobacco Festival, held in the fall, and the Damascus Appalachian Trail Days Festival, held every year in May to celebrate the famous trail.

The King William Regional Arts Center keeps art alive with exhibitions of national and regional interest, art camp, special events, and workshops and studios for adults and students. Call for a schedule of events at (703) 628-5005. If this interests you, you'll also want to go to The Arts Depot, where you'll see working artists in their studios, gallery exhibits, a performing arts series and an Appalachian Center for Poets and Writers. Call (703) 628-9091.

Each Christmas, Abingdon also conducts a charming candlelight tour of its historic homes. For information, call (703) 676-2282.

Tazewell County

Tazewell County, in the heart of mountainous Southwestern Virginia, is a center of education, commerce, medical care and travel. Its terrain encompasses the eastern edge of Virginia's Coal Country. Tazewell's combination of rustic beauty and bustling commerce has attracted 50,000 residents.

The county includes one of the twin Bluefields of Virginia and West Virginia. It's also noted for the scenic Burke's Garden, known as "The Garden Spot of the World," where the spurned railroad tycoon,

Cornelius Vanderbilt, originally wanted to build his famous Biltmore Estates. He later settled for Asheville, North Carolina, after local residents wouldn't sell. Asheville might have millions of tourist dollars, but Tazewell still has this breathtaking spot!

Stories of the fiercely proud, independent people of Tazewell abound. Legend has it that Vanderbilt wasn't the only tycoon who didn't impress the locals. Auto magnate Henry Ford, in the company of inventors Thomas Edison and Harvey Firestone, couldn't get a check cashed by the locals while on a camping trip.

Tazewell County became famous in 1842 when Dr. Thomas English wrote the poem, "Sweet Alice, Ben Bolt," while visiting the county. The poem later became a world-famous hit song inspired by Tazewell's beauty.

Tazewell is known as a regional medical center, with two hospitals providing state-of-the-art medical care for the area's residents. Opportunities for higher education also are here, with Bluefield College, a private, four-year institution; Southwest Virginia Community College; and National Business College.

Recreation abounds. The Jefferson National Forest and Clinch Valley Wildlife Preserve provide excellent year round hunting and fishing. You'll also find a number of horse stables and gun clubs nearby.

The Bluefield Orioles offer minor league baseball action at Bowen Field in Bluefield. Snow skiing is available within a one hour's drive, and several recreational lakes are nearby.

Tazewell County has a rich mountain past. Native Americans lived an agrarian life-style in Tazewell. Later, the Cherokee and Shawnee tribes hunted here. The first pioneers to explore Tazewell County in the 1700s were hunters, surveyors and land speculators. The Burke's Garden area, about 50 square miles of rich, beautiful farmland encircled by a continuous mountain range, was the site of the county's first land survey in 1748. As the land west of the Blue Ridge Mountains was developed, pioneers of German, Scotch-Irish and English origins began building settlements and farming in the 1770s. The county was formed in 1799.

The town of Tazewell, the county seat, was founded in 1800. Beautiful homes were built in the early 1800s, including the Bowen home in The Cove and the Gose house in Burke's Garden.

Burke's Garden, a National Historic District, is the largest rural historical district in Virginia. Those wishing to see the fabled area at its best, with produce, arts and crafts, should attend the September fall festival sponsored by the Burke's Garden Community Association. Call (703) 963-3385 for more information. To stay in the lovely valley, call the James Burke Inn B&B at (703) 472-2114.

Other important towns are Richlands, Bluefield, Cedar Bluff and Pocahontas. One infamous town is Frog Level — so tiny, it's hardly on the map. But Frog Level Yacht Club T-shirts sell briskly around the world and at the Frog Level Service Station. This tiny spot on the road is so packed with action on Friday night that lines form out onto the road.

Richlands was named for the fertile land along the section of the Clinch Valley where the town lies. The town was designed by Clinch Valley Coal & Iron, which envisioned Richlands as the "Pittsburgh of the South." Bluefield's name stems from a species of chicory that grows in abundance in the county. In the spring of 1993, the Tazewell County Board of Supervisors voted to make poke salad the county's official native vegetable. Poke salad was honored, according to one supervisor, "because the community couldn't be starved out" during tough times for coal miners. Along with coal mining, the railroad led to Bluefield's growth, and there is a city with an identical name across the border in West Virginia. Cedar Bluff's name sprang from the profusion of cedar trees nearby. A resort and woolen mill aided in its growth. Pocahontas, with a glorious past as a coal-mining boom town, retains that image and has its own exhibition coal mine for visitors.

Tazewell also saw lots of action in the Civil War as a route to Wytheville's lead mines and Saltville's saltworks. One young soldier, "Devil Anse" Hatfield, and his kin from the Tug Fork region of West Virginia, traveled to Tazewell, harassing Union troops. Later, Hatfield had his own war back home

to contend with, thanks to the neighboring McCoy family. Who hasn't heard of the infamous West Virginia "Hatfields and McCoys?"

The history of Tazewell County and Southwestern Virginia is chronicled from prehistoric to present times at the Historic Crab Orchard Museum and Pioneer Park in Tazewell. The park, with its eight log and two stone structures and a building housing horse-drawn equipment, is representative of the life-style of early pioneers. Call (703) 988-6755 for more information.

Another interesting historical area is Paint Lick Mountain, where Native Americans left their writing, pictures and artifacts.

The Bluefields, situated in two shallow valleys, offer scenery, shopping, commerce and the national reputation as "Nature's Air-Conditioned City." In 1939, Chamber of Commerce officials started serving free lemonade when the temperature hit 90 degrees, a promotion that still gets national airtime today, especially from Willard Scott of the "Today Show."

Visitors to Bluefield can enjoy Graham Recreational Park and the Bluefield Area Arts and Crafts Center at 500 Bland Street, the original City Hall and now on the National Register of Historic Places. Located here are artists' studios, a crafts shop, the Paine Art Gallery and Summit Theatre. Call (304) 325-8000 for more information.

Bluefield's Craft Memorial Library is the repository for the Eastern Regional Coal Archives, southern West Virginia's research facility dedicated to collecting, preserving and making available the heritage of the coal fields. It's a fascinating collection of films, diaries, company records, scrip, rare books and railroad memorabilia. Call (304) 325-3943 for more facts. As the self-proclaimed documenter of the coal fields, the Bluefield Chamber hosts a Coal Show, called the "Best in the East," every two years. Call the chamber at (304) 327-7184 for dates.

Downtown Cedar Bluff, originally known as Indian, Virginia, was founded in 1800 and is host to the historic district of the Old Kentucky Turnpike, as well as being the birthplace of Gov. George C. Peery. The town was also home to the C.E. Goodwin Sons' Woolen Mills, later known as the Clinch Valley Blanket Mills. The Goodwins began weaving coverlets in 1907, which was the beginning of one of the largest collections of blanket patterns in the world.

Water-ground meal was manufactured by Cedar Bluff Milling Company. This grist mill has been extensively renovated and is one of the region's major heritage tourist attractions. Another unusual attraction is the Wittle League Hall of Fame, built in 1980 by Bill H. Ascue to honor 40 years of local baseball. The building is in Ascue's front yard.

Fans of unusual phenomena may remember that Cedar Bluff was the home of the celebrated little girl, Nannie Ruth Lowe, an extraordinary child who walked and talked at the age of nine months and predicted her own death at age seven. People came from miles around to hear her read the Bible at age three. The tot led revivals and excelled in Biblical knowledge, spelling and arithmetic.

To experience the area's history first hand, be sure to attend the Cedar Bluff Heritage Festival in September. Arts and crafts are center stage, along with a country store, antiques and vintage clothing. You can watch cider, apple butter and soap being made, while local historians and storytellers entertain. For more information on Cedar Bluff and the festival, call James K. McGlothlin at (703) 964-4889.

Visitors to the county will also want to see historic Pocahontas, the most interesting town in the county, designated a Virginia Historic Landmark. It has a colorful past as the early "capitol" of the famous and vast Pocahontas Coalfield and is the oldest mining town in the world. The first mine there was opened in 1882.

Proud citizens have since renovated many of its landmarks, including the Pocahontas Exhibition Mine, showing a spectacular 13-foot-high coal seam. The mine's "smokeless" coal made it the chosen fuel of the U.S. Navy during the mine's 73 years of operation. In that time, it produced more than 44 million tons of coal, enough to fill a train 6,000 miles long. The mine is open May through October. For tour information, call (703) 945-5959. Also nearby, in Boissevain, is the Coal Miner's Memorial.

Hungarian and Southern African-American miners brought their rich culture into the mountainous wilds of the emerging coal fields. Much of the beautiful, European-influenced architecture in Pocahontas dating from that period — the Opera House and the original Company Store — still stands today, a monument to a unique civilization. Built in 1895, the Opera House was the first theater in the area, staging many first-run Broadway shows. It was forced to close its doors during the Depression. Since, it has been restored as a dinner theater by Historic Pocahontas Inc.

In the midst of Pocahontas is the Silver Dollar Saloon, a testimony to a more boisterous and colorful era. On a more reverent note, another landmark to see is the ornate St. Elizabeth's Catholic Church, founded in 1898 and featuring 10 life-sized, hand-painted murals.

The town of Richlands boasts a 35-acre park adjacent to the town along the Clinch River. It includes a Junior Olympic pool, wading pool and multipurpose sports courts. Richlands is also known as the town of festivals, highlighted by the Tazewell County Fair in August and Richlands Festival, which is simply an excuse for five days of nonstop entertainment.

While visiting Tazewell, you'll find lots of good, old-fashioned family restaurants to visit. There's RC's on Main Street in Tazewell and Cuz' Uptown Barbeque, a restored barn in Pounding Mill that features a "Cow and Elvis" theme decor lounge. For the uninitiated, going to Cuz' will make a trip to Tazewell worthwhile. Some call the decor "Early Pee Wee Herman," while others have called it "the Jackalope from Hell." If you've never been to a restaurant where none of the menus look the same, you've got to try Cuz'. We recommend the ribs, which look like something Fred Flintstone might've ordered. Bet you can't finish them! Doggy-bags abound! Both the decor and the food pack people in nearly every night they're open. As unorthodox as this place is, the owners have hit upon a unique formula that truly entertains.

However, if you love refinement and fantastic, fussy and delicious food and tea, don't miss the Tea and Sympathy gift shop and tea room on Route 19 S. in Claypool Hill. Sisters D.R. Rife and Sandra Horn will pamper you and make you feel truly special in the midst of the mountains. It's worth the time just to sit a spell on their plump, over-stuffed chairs, smell the pot-pourri and have a sip of tea. A nice place to stay is the Comfort Inn in Bluefield, Virginia, (800) 228-5150.

For more information on places to eat and stay, call the Tazewell Area Chamber of Commerce & Visitors Center at (703) 988-5091, the Richlands Area Chamber of Commerce at (703) 963-3385, or Greater Bluefield Chamber of Commerce at (304) 327-7184.

Buchanan County

Located in the Appalachian Plateau of Southwestern Virginia, this is real Coal Country. The county of Buchanan, named for the former U.S. President James Buchanan, was explored about 1750 but sparsely settled until the 1930s, when coal mining made it big — so big, in fact, that Buchanan now produces nearly half of Virginia's coal, which translates to nearly 50 million tons.

With towns with such names as "Dismal," one may expect a high unemployment rate (nearly 8 percent) among the county's 34,200 people. When they can work, many make their living from coal mines and companies that make roof bolts and mining equipment. Coal Country's industrial giants are located here, including Island Creek, Consolidated, United and Jewell Coal and Coke.

Buchanan County's people, however, do know how to have a good time and are proud of the recreational opportunities they can offer visitors, including the county's newest recreational facility, the William P. Harris Park, which has a swimming pool, basketball and baseball fields, and Breaks Interstate Park, 4,200 acres nicknamed the "Grand Canyon of the South."

Breaks park, which is shared by Kentucky and the Dickenson County border, sports the largest canyon east of the Mississippi, carved by the Russell Fork River to a depth of 1,600 feet guarded by sheer vertical walls. In a succession of waterfalls and rapids, the river lunges over and around massive boulders. Whitewater rafting is available, water conditions permitting. Located 20 minutes from Grundy, the county seat, the park is open April through October. In the spring, it is famous for its blooming rhododendron, foliage and wild-

flowers. Rhododendron Lodge, located near the park, has a restaurant, gift shop featuring lovely mountain crafts and a lodge with rustic rooms. Cottages and a camping area are also available. Call (703) 865-4413 for park information or (703) 865-4414 for the lodge.

Once at the park, the visitor center is the main feature of the interpretive complex. It houses exhibits and displays of the natural and historic features of the area. Its coal exhibit probably is the most popular. An amphitheater in a shaded setting offers visitors an opportunity to view dramas and nature slide and film programs. It also is the location of the annual, three-day Autumn Gospel Sing Festival on Labor Day weekend.

Laurel Lake provides fishing opportunities and pedal boats for visitors who like the water. A pool is located near the lake and includes bath facilities and a children's pool. Breaks Interstate Park can be reached by U.S. Route 460 from Grundy to Harman Junction, then Route 609 to the Breaks. The state stocks trout in the stream at Dismal, which draws a large number of anglers when the season opens in the spring.

On Route 639, you'll find a public golf course, Mountain Top, with nine holes on 30 acres of previously strip-mined land in the Compton Mountain area. It features artificial greens and is the first course of its kind in the United States.

Another point of interest is Mountain Mission School, established in Grundy in 1921 for Christian education from ages one to 21. It has a world-famous choir.

When visiting Buchanan County, choose from five motels and numerous family-style restaurants along the Route 460 corridor. General and speciality shopping can be found in the same area, as well as on routes 80 and 83.

For more information, call the Buchanan County Chamber of Commerce at (703) 935-4147.

Russell County

Russell County, population 31,761, is famous for its coal mines, agriculture and incredible mountain scenery. Even the nomad, Daniel Boone, found Russell, "The Redbud Capital of the World," so beautiful that he put down roots here for a couple of years.

Teddy Roosevelt described the area's pioneers as "tough and supple as the hickory out of which they fashioned the handles of their axes." Long ago, however, the sturdy hickory made way for the coal industry.

In Russell County, you'll find the booming technology of the coal industry and headquarters of the nation's leading exporter of coal, Pittston, in Lebanon. Appalachian Power, which uses the Blue Ridge lakes of Smith Mountain and Claytor for its northern energy sources, here turns southwest Virginia coal into electrical power at its huge plant in Carbo. The manufacture of furniture, clothing, shoes and interiors for the auto industry also provides employment to locals.

Russell County was founded in 1786 and named for Gen. William Russell, who assisted in the drafting of the Declaration of Independence. More than 20 historic homes still stand, including the H.C. Stuart Mansion, built in 1913 at Elk Garden for Virginia's Governor Stuart; John Howard Mansion, five miles outside of Lebanon on Route 71; Dickenson Bundy Log House, a public building standing beside the Old Court House in Dickensonville; and the present courthouse in Lebanon, in use since 1874. If you're a history buff, photographer, artist or just enjoy old architecture, don't miss seeing these Russell County landmarks.

Another site you won't want to miss is Russell County's unusual House and Barn Mountain, a mountain named for these particular shapes.

For some of the best fishing east of the Mississippi, don't pass up the Clinch River. It's also known for its canoeing expeditions from Blackford to St. Paul. Camping facilities are offered next to the 300-acre Hidden Valley Lake. Big Cedar Creek, nicknamed "Big Bass Pond," is a fisherman's delight with camping, hiking and picnic facilities.

Lebanon's county park is home to a crystal clear waterfall. Camping is permitted, and locals say there's nothing visiting campers remark about more than the pleasure of waking up to the soothing sound of a waterfall. Afterward, a pleasant morning walk can be taken at J.S. Easterly Park, which also offers hiking trails and tennis courts.

Glade Hollow Park is another nice place to spend the day. Near Cleveland, Lake Bonaventure Country Club has golfing on a nine-hole course, swimming and fishing.

Russell Countians celebrate on many occasions. The most popular is the Honaker Redbud Festival, named for the delicate Virginia budding tree that dots the mountains each spring. The month-long festival starts in March and continues into April, with events as varied as an essay contest, canoe race, parade and homecoming dinner. The county's fair in Castlewood each September is another fun event, with a rodeo and drafthorse pulling contest taking top billing, along with the "Biggest Pumpkin" contest. The Southwest Virginia Music Festival in Belfast, held Labor Day weekend, is another popular affair.

While staying in Russell County, consider the Carriage House Motel, (703) 889-2884, in Lebanon and Town and Country Motor Lodge, (703) 889-2772, on Highway 19. Dine at restaurants such as Bonanza and Western Sizzlin' in Lebanon, all on Highway 19. For an interesting shopping excursion, visit the Russell County People's Market, between Lebanon Elementary and Middle School, each Saturday through September. It features farm produce and local handcrafts.

For more information about Russell County, call the Russell County Chamber of Commerce at (703) 889-8041.

Dickenson County

Located in the heart of Virginia's coal fields, where many are employed by Pittston Coal Company, Dickenson County is rich in history and mountain heritage. Kentucky is its northwest boundary along the crest of the Cumberland Mountains, to the point where the mountain breaks up, allowing the Russell Fork River to flow through Dickenson County and into the Breaks Canyon to the north.

The Russell Fork provides world-class whitewater rafting, Class 3 to 5+, and some of the most breathtaking scenery east of the Grand Canyon! Business owners are confident that whitewater rafting will soon blossom into a multimillion-dollar industry.

Hundreds of people each weekend brave the river, putting in at historic Yellow Poplar Splashdam, where Route 611 crosses the Russell Fork River. Many rafting enthusiasts say it's the most challenging river they've ever tackled! Outfitters such as Russell Fork Whitewater Adventures take trips nearly each weekend down the ravine. Call or write the Dickenson County Chamber at (703) 926-4328 for a rafting schedule.

The internationally renowned Breaks Interstate Park encompasses an area of 4,500 acres surrounding the Breaks Canyon, referred to as the "Grand Canyon of the South." The park features a 122-acre campground, motel, restaurant and visitors center. Call (703) 865-4413 for more information.

Twelve miles south is John W.

Flannagan Reservoir, a 1,143-acre lake noted for monstrous walleye fish and surrounded by 7,500 acres of woodlands teeming with wildlife. The dam was finished in 1964. It is 250 feet high and 916 feet long and forms a 1,145-acre lake proclaimed to be one of the cleanest in the world.

Visitors enjoy outstanding fishing, boating and water skiing. Campsites, picnic areas, tennis courts and a softball field are located near the lake, and horseback riding and hiking abound throughout the county. One of the most picturesque hikes is the 26-mile-long trek from Pound Gap to Potter's Flats, near Breaks Park, along the crest of the Cumberland Mountains that divide Virginia and Kentucky. For additional information, call the U.S. Army Corps of Engineers at (703) 835-9544.

Each fall, Pioneer Days and the county fair celebrate a rich Appalachian heritage. The Cumberland Museum and Art Gallery in the county seat of Clintwood is dedicated to the preservation of the area's vanishing art and artifacts, "Things of Toil and Love." You can see wood carvings, fossils, a miniature coal mine and hundreds of tools and survival items of early mountain settlers. It's been called "The Most Interesting Place in the Mountains." For more information, call (703) 926-6632.

Another notable site is the historic Fremont Train Station, which has been restored near its original site at the intersection of routes 63 and 83. Yet another landmark is the homeplace of Ralph and Carter Stanley, the legendary bluegrass music duo, "The Stanley Brothers." The old farm, located on Highway 643, is where Ralph holds his annual Bluegrass Festival.

If you're a railroad fan, don't miss Dennis Reedy's own railroad museum in Clinchco. He'll show you around by appointment; call (703) 835-9593.

While in Clintwood, get some family-style food from the White Star Cafe, across from the courthouse. Here, you can sample the atmosphere, pace and pricing of a bygone era. For information on other restaurants, lodging and shopping, call the Dickenson County Chamber at (703) 926-4326).

Wise County

Wise County, like others nearby, is a treasure trove of scenery, cul-

The temperature of the Southwestern Virginia mountains is usually 10 degrees cooler than other areas of the Blue Ridge — and snow can be a factor here when there is none in other areas of the Blue Ridge. Be prepared with sufficient clothing, whether you're planning to camp overnight or just touring.

Insiders' Tips

ture and attractions. However, it has more of them than most of its neighbors, with numerous recreational areas, a major outdoor drama and four museums.

Located in the heart of the Appalachian Mountains, Wise County was named for Gov. Henry Wise. Its 50,000 people reside mostly in the towns of Wise, Norton, Appalachian, Big Stone Gap, Coeburn, Pound and St. Paul. Wise also is in the heart of coal country and a center of health care and higher education, as well, with Clinch Valley College of the University of Virginia, a four-year, liberal arts college, and Mountain Empire Community College.

Recreational opportunities abound in the Jefferson National Forest. Norton offers Flag Rock Recreational Area and High Knob, where you can see several states from one viewpoint. Another scenic overlook is Powell Valley. There's fishing and camping in North Fork Reservoir in Point and Oxbow Lake in St. Paul. The North Fork of Pound Lake is another recreational area where you can boat, fish, camp and picnic. The U.S. Army Corps of Engineers can give you more information by calling (304) 529-2311.

If you've got the bug to go backpacking but hate the thought of buying expensive equipment, call Joseph's Backpacking in Big Stone Gap at (703) 679-3532. They'll supply you with equipment "to go boldly on a new adventure" on High Knob Mountain, so there's no reason why you can't explore the highlands with nothing but sheer determination. Do call for reservations, however.

Locals also have taken to mountain biking in a big way. Ride and Stride Shop, (703) 679-0118, can give you information. Holiday Inn of Norton, (703) 679-7000, offers special mountain bike motel rates.

Car racing is another popular sport in the region. Lonesome Pine International Raceway offers lots of fast cars in a continuing schedule of races featuring famous drivers such as Davey Allison, Mike Waltrip and Sterling Marlin. Call (703) 395-3338 for more information.

Wise County's towns are also worth exploring. You'll know Big Stone Gap is special when you see that its visitor's center is located in a restored railway car, Interstate Car #101, which has a long, illustrious history. Built in 1870 for the South Carolina & Georgia Railroad, the car was retired in 1959 from the tracks and transported to Wise to serve as a hunting camp. In 1988, the car was donated to Wise by Humphrey's Enterprises. A successful community fund-raising effort resulted in the car being moved to Big Stone Gap, where it was restored for use as the present visitor's center. It looks nearly exactly as it did in 1870! For more information, call (703) 523-2060.

After you've seen the #101, it's time to see the rest of Big Stone Gap. The town is noted for its outdoor drama, *Trail of the Lonesome Pine,* staged during July and August at June Tolliver Playhouse. The play, based on the John Fox, Jr., novel, is performed on the actual site of this historic event and has

Dickenson County, Virginia.
Rugged, Scenic, Different!

For Information, contact:
Dickenson County
Chamber of
Commerce
P. O. Box 1068
Clintwood, VA 24228
(703) 865-4443

been telling the story of a proud mountain folk since 1964. For more information, call (800) TRAIL-LP.

In addition to the drama, Lonesome Pine Arts & Crafts Inc. was organized in 1963 for the historical, cultural and economic benefit of Southwestern Virginia. For nearly 30 years, it has had an impact on the lives of hundreds of young people through its touring theater and marketing program for artisans and craftspeople. You can see their handiwork at the June Tolliver House and Craft Shop — weaving, painting, woodcraft and other unique mountain hand-made crafts. Call (703) 523-1235.

Also stop by to see John Fox, Jr., Museum, a national and Virginia Historical Landmark, which serves as both a museum and a memorial to the Fox family. John, who eventually wrote 500 short stories, grew up in the house. His *Trail of the Lonesome Pine* became the first American novel to sell a million copies; later, it became a popular movie. Call (703) 523-2747.

Big Stone Gap is also home to two other museums. They invite you to step across the threshold of the not-so-distant past to a time when "Gap Fever" brought a host of talented young men and women from all over the country who hoped to make their fortunes from the area's abundant natural resources. Among them was Virginia Attorney General Rufus Ayers, whose 1893 three-story, native cut stone home would eventually house the Southwest Virginia Museum. In it, you'll now see that Ayers spared no expense to build one of the finest

homes in Virginia. The museum is operated by the Department of Conservation and Recreation's Division of State Parks and is open July 16 through Labor Day Monday through Thursday from 10 AM to 4 PM, Friday 9 AM to 4 PM, Saturday 10 AM to 5 PM and Sunday 1 to 5 PM. From Labor Day through December 31, the park is closed on Mondays, Thanksgiving and Christmas. It is closed through January and February, and is closed on Mondays from March 1 through Memorial Day. For more information, call (703) 523-1322.

Another popular museum is the Harry Meador Coal Museum, E. Shawnee Street and Shawnee Avenue, which provides a fascinating history of this area's cornerstone industry. The museum contains artifacts painstakingly assembled from private homes and public buildings that illustrate the coal mining heritage of the area and its effect on the local life-style. Owned by Westmoreland Coal Company and operated by the Big Stone Gap Deptartment of Parks and Recreation, admission is free. The department also oversees Miners Park, a monument to coal field workers in downtown. The museum is dedicated to Harry W. Meador, Jr., former vice president of Westmoreland Coal and a tireless advocate of the coal mining industry. Call (703) 523-4950 for more information.

Each October, Mountain Empire College in Big Stone Gap celebrates a Home Crafts Day, with traditional Appalachian crafts, demonstrations, storytelling, ethnic foods, dancing and music.

The town of Norton is another focal point of home crafts and historical preservation. Country Cabin is co-sponsored by Clinch Valley College and Appalachian Traditions, a nonprofit organization dedicated to preservation, promotion and perpetuation of traditional Appalachian culture. It is used for everything from teaching clogging to a cultural exchange for tourists of other cultures. Here, you may hear the Sorghum Lickers Band or watch the Virginia Sugarcane Cloggers perform. The public is invited to visit the cabin each Saturday night for performances of traditional mountain music. Appalachian Traditions also sponsors the annual Dock Boggs Festival, a one-day celebration of traditional mountain music, on the second Saturday in September at the Wise County Fairground. Call (703) 328-0100 for more information.

One of the nicest places to stay in Wise County is the Norton Holiday Inn, "The Friendliest Hotel in Southwest Virginia," a favorite gathering place for those who enjoy fine dining, quality accommodations and excellent meeting facilities. Call them at (703) 679-7000. While you're staying in Wise County, you'll find great family restaurants to please all palates. Mosby's at Norton Shopping Plaza has a varied menu that includes such traditional fare as the New York strip or the more regional flavor of the General Lee Sandwich. Call for reservations at (703) 679-1046.

The town of Appalachia, named for the mountain range, focuses on coal. The village sprang up at a railroad junction during the coal and land boom in neighboring Big Stone Gap.

Also be sure to see Bee Rock Tunnel on U.S. Highway 23-Business. It's featured in *Ripley's Believe It or Not* as the "Shortest Railroad Tunnel in the World." Other attractions are the Bullitt Mine Complex, Westmoreland Coal dump train and the Rotary Dump, a machine that turns railroad cars upside down and empties their contents into a bin below. You also can see coal camps on Route 68 at Imboden, Lower Exeter, Exeter and Keokee, built by coal mining barons of the early 20th century for their employees.

For more sites to see, call the Wise County Chamber of Commerce at (703) 679-0961.

Scott County

Daniel Boone passed through this scenic wonderland on the Wilderness Road. Scott County still prides itself on being a land with gorgeous scenery "the way Mother Nature made it" — so beautiful, in fact, that it inspired the famous country ballad, "Wildwood Flower." It's also home to the "Eighth Wonder of the World," Natural Tunnel State Park.

Scott County, formed in 1814, was named after the War of 1812 hero Gen. Winfield Scott. The county's 24,700 citizens can choose from enjoying mountain streams or backpacking trails through an unspoiled natural setting. There are laurel-lined mountains in Hanging Rock Canyon in the Jefferson National Forest near Dungannon. Outside Nickelsville, the Kilgore Fort House, reconstructed from the frontier era, links the county to Boone's passage along the Wilderness Road. At Powell Mountain on Highway 58, you can see a view of three states.

The centuries-old Holston and Clinch rivers flow through this county, lending themselves freely to the leisurely activities of canoeing and fishing — great for family outings. Recreational areas are located at Scott County Park (with a golf course and tennis courts), Hanging Rock Picnic Area, Bark Camp Lake and Devils Fork Recreational Area, and its waterfalls are all overseen by the U.S. Forest Service.

The star attraction, however, is the Natural Tunnel Park in Duffield. Since 1880, when statesman William Jennings Bryan declared it the "Eighth Wonder of the World," Natural Tunnel has attracted sightseers from all parts of the country. Daniel Boone was one of the first to see it, and the area was well known to Native Americans. However, the tunnel got its start long before people were on the scene, as it is believed to be about 1 million years old. The walls of the limestone basin are nearly vertical, rising to heights of more than 400 feet.

While you're at the visitor center, drop by and see the video, "Stay Awhile," which highlights historical and recreational attractions nearby. For more information, call the state park at (703) 940-2674.

Another major attraction is the Carter Family Fold, "Where Music Began," the homeplace of Sara and Maybelle Carter. Maybelle's daughter, June, is the wife of singer Johnny Cash. It features a country music museum and live music every Saturday night and is located on A.P. Carter Highway in Hiltons. Call (703) 386-9480.

While you're staying in Scott County, consider the Ramada Inn in Duffield, offering package rates. Call (800) VA-BYWAY. The Ramada also features Winfield's Restaurant. There are fast food places and markets in the Gate City, Nickelsville and Duffield areas. For more information, call the Scott County Chamber of Commerce at (703) 386-6665

Lee County

Last but certainly not least, at the tip of Virginia, triangle-shaped Lee County, bordering Kentucky and Tennessee, offers beautiful rolling hills and valleys nestled in the Tennessee River Basin. It is home to 24,500 people and the Cumberland Gap, used by early settlers as the only means of passage during westward expansion. Cumberland Gap National Historical Park and the Jefferson National Park are also both located here.

People here frequently work either in the coal fields or on the farm. Tobacco is an important crop, but manufacturing, especially textiles, is gaining more importance. Tourism is also becoming a chief industry.

The northern part of Lee has nearly 12,000 acres of the Jefferson forest, which provide opportunities for hiking, hunting, camping, picnicking, backpacking and sightseeing. It contains Lake Keokee, a 92-acre waterway for fishing, boating and picnicking, and Cave Springs Recreation Area, a small lake for swimming and camping. Stone Mountain Trail, 11 miles long, is a difficult but popular hiking trail here, with one of the nicest natural settings in Southwestern Virginia. Call (703) 328-2931 for more information about the Jefferson National Forest.

The Cumberland Gap Park, commemorating Daniel Boone and other early settlers, is located in the extreme western portion of the county. Also located on the edge of the park is Cudjo's Caverns, three levels of natural caves used by Native Americans and Civil War soldiers. The camp features camping, hiking and the Hensley Settlement, a restored turn of the century mountain community that is a symbol of the determination and true grit of the early American pioneer. Shuttle bus service is provided, or you can go by horseback. Call (606) 248-2817.

The 26-acre Cumberland Bowl Park in Jonesville has swimming facilities, picnic tables and pavilions, a walking trail and children's playground. Plays are performed regularly in the amphitheater. Leeman Field, in Pennington Gap, has swimming, tennis courts and a horse ring and is the site of the annual Lee County Fair in August and Tobacco and Fall Festival in October.

Monte Vista Golf Course, a nine-hole course, also has a swimming pool and clubhouse. It is located off U.S. Highway 58 in Ewing.

Another interesting site is the African-American Historical Cultural Center in Pennington Gap, which contains a comprehensive collection of historical artifacts. A full-time curator presides. For more information, call (703) 546-5144.

A mile north of Pennington Gap on Old Harlan Road, Highway 421, look for Stone Face Rock, a fascinating rock formation that can be seen day or night and looks like an Indian head. Widely believed to be a natural phenomenon, some theorists claim it is an ancient Cherokee Indian head carved by the Cherokees to mark the entrance to their holy grounds.

Lee is located a few hours away from the Great Smokey Mountains and the Tennessee Valley Authority lakes.

If you decide to trek along the Daniel Boone Heritage Trail, which starts in Duffield and ends in Lee County, there are several nice places to stay. The Jonesville Motor Court, (703) 346-3210, is on Highway 58, as is Convenient Inn, (703) 546-5350, in Pennington Gap and Ritchie House Bed and Breakfast, (703) 445-4505, in Ewing.

Family restaurants and fast food strips are located mostly in Pennington Gap and Jonesville.

For more information, call the Lee County Chamber of Commerce at (703) 346-7766.

Index of Advertisers

200 South Street	337	Fox and Hounds Restaurant	Insert
309 First Street Restaurant	411	Frederick House	317
Afton House Antiques	Insert	Garment District	269
Afton Mountain Vineyards	Insert	George C. Marshall Museum	25
Ann Woods Ltd.	265	Go Pal Bicycle	267
Artists in Cahoots	25	Graves' Mountain Lodge	319
Ashby Inn	329	Greenberry's Coffee and Tea	285
AuPair Care	486	Greenskeeper Restaurant	269
Awful Arthur's Restaurant	387	Hearth 'n Holly Inn	323
Baja Bean Company	267	Heartwood Books	267
Barr-ee Station	269	Heritage House	319
Barracks Road		Holt's	Insert
Shopping Center	281, 283, 285	Honey Suckle Hill	Insert
Bent Mountain Lodge	71	Hot Cakes	283
Billy's Ritz	411	Hotel Strasburg	381
Birthplace Gift Shoppe	Insert	House of Laird	329
Blue Ridge Mountain Sports	283	Howard Johnson's-Charlottesville	391
Blue Ridge Restaurant, Inc.	69	Hummingbird Inn	323
Blue Ridge Terrace		Inn at Union Run	321
Mountain Crafts	Insert	Inn at Monticello	325
Boar's Head Inn	301	Inn At The Crossroads	319
Brasa Restaurant	427	Innovations	271
Brierley Hill	321	J Rugles Restaurant	Insert
Budget West Lawn Motel	Insert	Jefferson Vineyards	155
C & O Restaurant	429	Jolly Roger Haggle Shop	Insert
Captain Sam's Landing	Insert	Jordan Hollow Farm Inn	327
Carlos Restaurant	411	Joshua Wilton House	327
Center In The Square	Inside Front Cover	Kenwood Bed & Breakfast	Insert
Charlottesville Guide	47	Knights Inn	385
Chateau Morrisette Winery	505	La Maison Restaurant	413
Clifton Country Inn	345	Lambsgate Inn	Insert
Collector's Choice	Insert	les fabriques	281
College Inn	269	Lexington Historical Shop	25
Corned Beef and Company	411	Little John's	269
Cox Cable-Roanoke	27	Llewellyn Lodge	317
Crafters' Gallery	279	Looking Glass House	329
Depot Antiques	Insert	Lovingston Cafe	437
Derek's-U Spirit	271	Lynchburg College	489
Dickenson County	531	Macado's	267
Doe Run Lodge	504	Magic Tricks	Insert
Dusty's Antique Market	Insert	Mallard Point	465
Edelweiss German Restaurant	Insert	Mediterranean Italian	
Fantasies	25	& Continental Cuisine	411
Fort Lewis Lodge	327	Memory & Company	425
Fountain Hall	317	Memory Lane	Insert

Mincers	267	Silver Thatch Inn	341
Mountain Lake Resort	303	Sleepy Hollow Farm	325
Museum of American		South River Restaurant	Insert
Frontier Culture	Insert, 211	St Anne's Belfield Middle School	491
Nelson County Division of Tourism	Insert	Staunton Mall	Insert
New Mountain Merchantile	71	Staunton Visitor's Bureau	49
Oakencroft Vineyards	157	Stonewall Jackson House	25
Oktoberfestival	Insert	Subway	271
Old World Carpets	21	Talbots	285
Olde Mill Golf Course	504	Tastings Restaurant	435
Once Upon A Time	Insert	The Beverley Restaurant	Insert
Opera Roanoke	207	The Christmas Store	Insert
Oregano Joe's	431	The Colony of Virginia, Ltd.	21
P. Buckley Moss Museum	Insert, 203	The Count Pulaski	21
Palmer Country Manor	333	The Depot Grille	Insert
Pampered Palate Cafe	Insert	The Iris Inn	Insert
Pappagallo	25	The Keep Bed & Breakfast	321
Pat's Antique Mall	Insert	The Olde Prospector	Insert
Peaks of Otter	393	The Park-Oak Grove	
Plow and Hearth	283	Retirement Community	477
Primland Hunting Reserve	505	The Phoenix	271
Prince Michel De Virginia	153	The Pullman Restaurant	Insert
Prospect Hill Inn	339	The Purple Foot	Insert
Pulaski Antique Center	21	The Renaissance	21
Pulaski Main Street, Inc.	21	The Sampson Eagon Inn	Insert
Radford University	493	The Three-Legged Cow	71
Ramada Group	378	The Virginia Shop	285
Redwood Lodge	323	Tivoli	325
Reflections	Insert	Tuckahoe Antique Mall	Insert
Richmond Homes	Inside Back Cover	Upstairs Downstairs Boutique	21
Rising Sun Bakery	271	Valley Framing Studio & Gallery	Insert
Roanoke Marriott	395	Valley Green Arts and Crafts	Insert
Roanoke United Methodist Home	475	Vanucci's Restaurant	411
Roanoke Valley Convention and		Virginia Apparel Outlet	Insert
Visitors Bureau	29	Virginia Born and Bred	25
Rocky's Gold and		Virginia Central Railroad	Insert
Silver Antique Mall	Insert	Virginia Horse Center	25
Rococo's	433	Virginia Metalcrafters	Insert, 163
Rodes Farm Inn	Insert	Virginia Military Institute Museum	89
Rowe's Restaurant	Insert	Virginia Parkway Hosts Association	504
Scarpa	281	Walnut Hills Campground	Insert
Schoolhouse Fabrics	69	Waynesboro Village Factory Outlets	Insert
Scotto's Italian Restaurant	Insert	Weasies Kitchen	Insert
Second Story	25	Wharf Gallery	Insert
Shenandoah Acres	Insert	Whimsies	281
Shenandoah Valley Travel Association	15	Whitehouse Antiques	Insert
Shenanigan's	281	Willie's Hair Design	267
Signet Bank	31	Willson Walker House	25
Silver Linings	Insert	Wintergreen Farm Sheepskin Shoppe	69
		Wonderful World of Miniature Horses	133

Index

Symbols

1740 House Antiques   278
200 South Street   357
309 First Street   456

A

Aberdeen Barn   424
Abingdon General Store   521
Abingdon Mercantile and Frame Gallery and
   Antiques   521
Abram's Delight Museum   202
Acorn Inn   357
African-American Historical Cultural Center   535
Afton House Antiques   279
Afton Mountain Vineyards   158
Aileen Stores Inc.   262
Airports   479
Alexander's   410
Alleghany Highlands Arts & Crafts Center   242, 255
Alley Antiques   278
Always Roxie's   296
Amerind Gallery   273
Amherst County Historical Museum   54
Anchy's   442
Andre Viette Farm and Nursery   20
Andrew Johnston Museum &
   Research Center   227, 253
Ann Woods Ltd.   278
Annual Kite Day   180
Annual Sun and Sand Beach Weekend   184
Annual Zoo Boo   194
Antique Barn   268
Antique Car Show   179
Antique Collectors   278
Antique Mart, The   262
Antique Orchid Herbary   521
Antiques by Burt Long   262
Appalachia Coal and Railroad Days   189
Appalachian Arts and Crafts Festival   124
Appalachian Center for Poets and Writers   521
Appalachian Mountain Christmas   196, 302
Appalachian Trail   26, 32, 113, 185, 511
Apple Barn   273
Apple Butter Making Festival   193
Apple Core Village Gift Shop   381
Appomattox Court House National Historical Park   94
Arborgate Inn   397
Arnette's   282
Art Farm Galleries
Art Needlework Inc.   286
Arthurs   266
Artists in Cahoots   270
Arts Depot   521
Arts in the Park   124
Artworks   280
Asbury Center at Birdmont   513
Ash Lawn-Highland   46, 118, 234
Ashleys   297

Ashton Country House   322
Asian French Cafe   412
Augusta-Staunton-Waynesboro Visitors Bureau   22
Autumn Gospel Sing Festival   526
Autumn Hill Vineyards/Blue Ridge Winery   155
Awful Arthur's   424

B

Bacchanalian Feast   192
Bacova Guild Factory Outlet   297
Baja Bean Co.   425
Balcony, The   458
Barboursville Ruins   43
Barboursville Vineyards   41, 156
Barracks Road Shopping Center   284
Barree Station   282
Barr's Fiddle Shop   510
Barter Theatre   520
Bass Bonanza   181
Bateau Festival   52
Bateau Landing   438
Bath County Historical Society Museum   235, 256
Battle of Cedar Creek   87, 192, 203
Battle of Cloyd's Mountain   86
Battle of Front Royal   91
Battle of New Market   84
Bavarian Chef   423
Bay Pottery, The   263
Beale Treasure   59
Bedford City/County Museum   96, 244
Bedrooms of America Museum   16, 204
Bee Rock Tunnel   533
Belle Boyd Cottage   91
Belle Grae Inn   265, 324, 454
Belle Grove Plantation   12, 88, 203
Beltrone & Company   279
Bent Mountain Lodge   372
Bernard's Landing Resort   55, 306, 441
Bertines North   423
Best Western,   389, 383, 396, 445
Bestseller, The   272
Beth Gallery and Press   229
Beverley, The   406
Big Meadows   103, 107, 113
Big Meadows Lodge   103
Big Stone Gap Country Fair   183
Big Walker Lookout   515
Bikecentennial Trail   31
Biking   179, 186, 300, 302, 312, 511, 531
Billy's Ritz   412
Biltmore Grill   425, 457
Birthday Celebration for Stonewall Jackson   176
Birthday Convocationfor Robert E. Lee   176
Bisset Park   73
Bits, Bytes & Books   260
Black Dog Jazz Concert Series   160
Blacksburg   64
Blacksburg Marriott   394
Blackwater Creek Natural Area   53

Bland County Fair and Horse Show   516
Bleak-Thrift House   277
Blessing of the Hounds   304
Bleu Rock Inn   342, 421
Blue Bend   121
Blue Bird Cafe   426
Blue Ridge Balloons   56
Blue Ridge Brewing Company   426, 457
Blue Ridge Folklife Festival   194, 247
Blue Ridge Heritage Festival   188
Blue Ridge Institute   60, 247
Blue Ridge Mountain Sports   286
Blue Ridge Music Festival   184, 242
Blue Ridge Parkway   99
Blue Ridge Pottery   41, 278
Blue Ridge Restaurant   70, 446
Blue Ridge Summer Dinner Theatre   61
Blue Ridge Terrace Gifts Inc.   280
Blue Stone Inn   403
Blue Wheel Bicycles   282
Bluefield Area Arts and Crafts Center   523
Bluefield Chamber of Commerce Coal Show   524
Bluefield College   522
Bluegrass Festival   529
Bluemont Concert Series   183
Bluewater Cruise Company   56
Boar's Head Inn & Sports Club   172, 303, 389, 426
Boating   57, 120, 124
Bob Beard Antiques   274
Bogen's   443
Book Gallery, The   284
Booker T. Washington National Monument   56, 60, 247
Books, Strings & Things   275
Boone's Country Store   42, 62, 289
Boones Mill Apple Festival   61
Botetourt Museum Building   28
Bottle and Pottery Show and Sale   189
Boxwood Inn Bed & Breakfast   514
Braford Antiques   270
Brasa Restaurant and Tapas Bar   426
Breaks Interstate Park   526, 528
Bridge Street Antiques   289
Bridgewater Air Park   483
Bridgewater College   17, 489
Bridgewater Marina   57
Bridgewater Para-Sail   288
Bridgewater Plaza   55
Brierley Hill   330
Brookfield Christmas Tree Plantation   70, 292
Brookneal-Campbell County Airport Authority   484
Brush Mountain Inn   368
Bryce Resort   141
Buchanan County   525
Buck Mountain Grille   413
Buckhorn Art and Antiques   510
Buddy's   458
Buffalo Springs Herb Farm   272
Burke's Garden   521, 522
Burnley Vineyards   41, 43, 156
Byrd's Walden Pond Products   70

C

C and O Restaurant   427
C&S Galleries   295
Cabin on the River   520
Cabins   104

Cafe Albert   450
Cafe France   438
Cafe Sofia   401
Cambria Emporium   68, 291
Cambria Whistlestop Arts Festival   185
Camping   106, 107, 124,
          125, 131, 132, 511, 514, 518, 520
Candy Shop, The   268
Canoeing   118
Capt'n Sam's Landing   404
Carlos Brasilian International Cuisine   412
Carol Lee Doughnuts   458
Carol M. Newman Library   199, 250
Carolina Hosiery   287
Carriage Court   375
Carter Family Fold   534
Cascades Club Restaurant   451
Cascades Recreation Area   116
Cascades Waterfall   72
Casey's Country Store   291
Casino, The   451
Cass Scenic Railroad   78
Castle Rock Recreation Area   72
Cat & Owl Steak and Seafood House   449
Cave House Craft Shop   521
Cedar Battlefield   13
Cedar Bluff Heritage Festival   524
Cedar Creek Battlefield Foundation Re-enactment   88
Cedar Springs Sportsman's Lodge   514
Center in the Square   34, 226
Chalot's Antiques   262
Champions Italian Eatery and Cafe   458
Charades   456
Charleys   439
Charlottesville Transit Service   485
Charlottesville-Albemarle Airport   479
Chateau Morrisette Winery Inc.   160, 292, 446
Chautauqua Festival in the Park   185, 513
Cheers   456
Cheese Shop, The   20, 268
Chermont Winery Inc.   158
Chessie Nature Trail   26
Chestnut Creek Golf Course   56
Children's Corner, The   275
Chilhowie Apple Festival   192, 518
Chili Cook-Off & Independence Day Celebration   188
Christendom College   488
Christiansburg Depot Museum   68
Christmas at the Manse   196
Christmas Gallery, The   262
Christmas Store   268, 270
Church Mouse, The   276
Civil War   83
Civil War Battle Re-enactments   13, 87, 36, 87, 180, 185
Claiborne House Bed and Breakfast   366
Clarkcrest Bed and Breakfast   518
Classic Collections   288
Clayborne's   454
Clayton's   439
Claytor Lake   75, 120, 124, 129
Clifton—The Country Inn   351
Clinch Valley College   531
Clinch Valley Mountain Wildlife Area   518
Clothes Line   264
Coal Miner's Memorial   524
Cockram Mill   508

Cockram's General Store   70, 251, 291, 459
Cocoa Mill Chocolates   272
Coffee Exchange   428
Collector's Choice   266
Collector's Corner   294
College Inn   429
Colonial Art and Craft Shop   260
Colony House Motor Lodge   385
Colony of Virginia Ltd.   295
Comfort Inn   383, 384, 391, 394, 396, 397
Confederate Breastworks   81
Confederate Museum   13
Consolidated Shoe Store   287
Contra Corners 230
Coopers Corner   441
Cooper's Vantage   302
Copper Kettle Lounge   142
Copper Mine, The   302
Corned Beef & Co.   414
Corner Downtown Cafe   519
Count Pulaski Bed & Breakfast and Gardens   295, 372
Country Cabin   533
Country Fare   316
Country Garden Antiques   277
Country Inn, The   428
Country Manor   276
Country Records   293
Country Store Antique Mall   277
County Christmas House   293
Coupe de Ville's   429, 457
Court Square   46
Court Square Tavern   429
Courtyard by Marriott   389
Covered Bridges   161, 509
Cox Cable of Roanoke   28
Crabtree Falls   44
Craddock-Terry Shoe Factory Outlet   287
Crafter's Gallery   280
Craig Creek Recreation Area   33
Cudjo's Caverns   535
Cumberland Bowl Park   535
Cumberland Gap Park   535
Cumberland Museum and Art Gallery   529
Curiosity Shop   263
Cuz' Uptown Barbeque   525

D

Daedalus Bookshop   279
Damascus Appalachian Trail Days Festival   521
Daniel Boone Heritage Trail   535
Daniel HarrisonHouse (Fort Harrison)   207
Days Inn   391
Dayton Farmer's Market   263, 264
Dedmon Center   74
Deer Meadow Vineyard   150
Depot Antiques   265
Depot Grille   19, 406
Derek's U-Spirit   280
Design Accessories   275
Dickenson County   528
Dinner At Dusk   184
Dixie Caverns   169
Dixie Pottery   521
Dock Boggs Memorial Festival   192, 533
Doe Run Lodge Resort and
     Conference Center   108, 314, 397

Dogwood Festival   39, 178
Dolley Madison's Birthday   181
Donkenny Fashion Outlet   291
Donovan's Framery   206
Dooley's   457
Douthat Park Restaurant   449
Douthat State Park   77, 117, 120
Downriver Canoe Company   119
Downtown Charlottesville Art and Antique
     Center   278
Draper Mercantile   295
Draper Valley Golf Club   516
Dudley Mart & Restaurant   441
Dulwich Manor   360
Dun Roaming Stables   138
Durty Nelly's Pub   430
Dusty's Antique Market   265
Dux & Company Lounge   396

E

E.A. Clore Sons Inc.   277
Eagle Rock   30
Eagles Nest   483
Eagle's Nest Restaurant   78, 449
Early Time Antiques and Fine Art   278
East Coast Raw Bar   458
Eastern Mennonite College and Seminary   17, 488
Eastern Regional Coal Archives   523
Edelweiss German Restaurant   407
Edgewood Farm Bed & Breakfast   347
Edgewood Farm Nursery   278
Edinburg Mill   91
El Charro   403
El Dorado   401
El Rodeo Mexican Restaurant   414
Elder's Antique and Classic Autos   266
Elephant Walk   456
Eljo's   282
Elks National Home   244
Elkwallow Wayside   107
Elmer's Antiques   276
Emerson Creek Pottery Outlet   275
Emil's   439
Emory & Henry College   497, 519
Endless Caverns   16, 167
Endless Caverns Campgrounds   167
Exchange Hotel   43
Executive Motel   396
Explore Park   223

F

Fairview Bed & Breakfast   361
Fairystone State Park   508
Fall Foliage Festival   193
Fall Food Festival   190
Falwell Aviation Inc   484
Family Craft Weekend   207
Fantasies   272
Fantasyland   164
Farfelu Vineyards   41, 153
Farm Basket, The   287, 439
Farmer's Market   18
Farmhouse, The   444
Fassifern   335
Fellini's   457

Ferrum College   42, 60, 61, 496
Festival by the James   184
Festival in the Park   35, 182
Fincastle Festival   191
Fine Arts Center   293
Firmstone Manor Bed & Breakfast   373
First Night Roanoke   197
First Night Virginia   196
First Night Winchester   195
Fishing   57, 62, 124, 125,
     300, 304, 308, 310, 312,
     514, 518, 527, 528, 535
Flag Rock Recreational Area   531
Flea Market, The   262
Fletcher Collins Theater   241
Flossie Martin Gallery   253
Floyd County   68
Fly Fisher's Symposiums   126
For the Birds   275
Fort Harrison   17, 93
Fort Lewis Lodge   376
Fort Loudoun   12
Fort Young   77
Fountain Hall Bed & Breakfast   345
Four & Twenty Blackbirds   422
Four County Players   41, 233
Fox and Hounds Pub & Restaurant   405
Foxfield Race Course   172, 178
Framer's Daughter Gallery   510
Frederick County Fair   186
Frederick House   326
Free Fishing Days   127
Freeman-Victorious Framing   282
Fremont Train Station   529
Friendship Inn   385
From the Heart   290
Front Royal Canoe Co.   118

G

Galax Mountain Music Jamboree   509
Gallery 109   510
Gallery Cafe   445
Garden Terrace   302
Garment District, The   282
Garth Newel Music Center   79, 256
Gatewood Reservoir Park   75
Gen. Stonewall Jackson's Headquarters   88
General Store, The   26, 270
George C. Marshall Museum   24
George Washington National Forest   16, 18, 124
George Washington's Birthday Celebration   176
Germanna Archeological Site   43
Gift and Thrift Shop   263
Gifts Ahoy   288
Giles Little Theatre   73
Gilmore, Hamm and Snyder Inc.   286
Ginseng Mountain Farm   297
Glade Hollow Park   528
Glass Slipper   296
"Go Pal" Bicycle Shop   282
Golden Tub Bath Shop   266
Golf   56, 130, 299, 300, 301,
     304, 306, 309, 311, 381,
     511, 516, 526, 528
Goodwill Tinker Mountain Industries   30
Grady's Antiques   290

Graham Recreational Park   523
Grand Caverns   16, 168
Grandin Movie Theatre   225
Grandma's Bait Clothing Store   266
Grandma's Memories   294
Graves Mountain Lodge   388
Grayson County   511
Grayson County Old Time Fiddler's Convention   185
Grayson Highlands State Park   511, 512
Great American Duck Race   188
Great Wagon Road   12
Greater Lynchburg Transit Company   485
Green Hill Equestrian Park   36
Green Tree, The   421
Greenberry's Coffee and Tea   430
Greenbrier, The   310
Greene House Shops   277
Greenskeeper Restaurant   430
Greenwood Antique Center   279
Grille, The   451
Gristmill, The   302
Guilford Ridge Vineyard   16, 151
Gunstock Creek Cooperative   58
Gypsy Hill Park   19, 122

H

Hale Fishing Lake   514
Hall of Valor Museum   15, 92
Hamiltons   289
Hampton Inn   384
Handcraft House   277
Handworks Gallery   260
Happy Goose, The   260
Harbortown Golf   288
Harbs' Bistro   215, 408, 455
Hardware Company Restaurant   521
Hardware Store Restaurant   430
Harmon's Museum   510
Harrison Museum of African-American Culture   220
Harry Meador Coal Museum   532
Harvest Festival on the Market   194
Haunted Caverns   194
Hearth N' Holly Inn   322
Heartwood Bookshop   279
Heirloom Originals   290
Henry County   509
Hensley Settlement   535
Heritage House Antiques   516
High Country Restaurant at
     Doe Run Lodge   109, 314, 397
High Knob   531
High Meadows   367
High Valley Antiques and Collectibles   296
Highland County Arts Council   219, 255
Highland County Crafts   297
Highland County Maple Festival   80, 176
Highland Inn   398, 452
Highlands Arts & Crafts Center   296
Hiking   112, 113, 300, 302, 310,
     312, 511, 515, 518, 519, 529, 535
Hillsville Gun Show and Flea Market   511
Hilton — Lynchburg   392
Historic Car & Carriage Caravan   167
Historic Crab Orchard Museum and Pioneer Park   523
Historic Garden Week   177
Hofauger Farmhouse   36

Holiday Inn   382, 383, 386, 389, 390, 392, 395, 398, 443, 450
Holladay House   348
Hollins College   36, 491
Holt's China   266
Holy Land USA   59, 245
Homeplace, The   414
Homestead Club, The   459
Homestead Dining Room   451
Homestead, The   79, 137, 146, 308
Honaker Redbud Festival   179, 528
Horse Center   24
Horseback Riding   124, 126, 133, 300, 302, 304, 310, 312, 337, 511, 518, 529
Hospitals   38, 53, 513
Hot Air Ballooning   303
Hot Cakes   431
Hotel Strasburg   14, 380, 402
Hottest Fun in the Sun Beach Day   188
House and Barn Mountain   527
House of Hunan   518
Howard Johnson Lodge   384, 390, 393
Howe House   124
Huckleberry, The   444
Hull's Drive-In Theatre   217
Hummingbird Inn   336
Humpback Bridge   161, 162
Hungry Mother Arts and Crafts Festival   518
Hungry Mother State Park   120, 138, 517
Hunters Restaurant   396
Hunting   138
Hupp's Hill Battlefield Park & Study Center   89
Huyard's Country Kitchen   264, 403

I

Ice Cream Cottage   288
Ikenberry Orchard   273
Imagine That!   516
Imperial Wok   450
Ingalls Field   484
Inn at Burwell Place   340
Inn at Gristmill Square   79
Inn at Little Washington   343, 422
Inn at Meander Plantation   345
Inn at Monticello   353
Inn at Narrow Passage   318
Inn at Orchard Gap   510
Inn at the Crossroads   353
Inn at Union Run   333, 408
Innkeeper Lynchburg   393
Innkeeper Motel   386
Innovations   280
Iris Inn, The   338
Iroquois Club   456
Ivy Creek Natural Area   118

J

J Rugles Restaurant   406
J.S. Easterly Park   527
Jack Tale Players   61
Jackson, Gen. Thomas J. "Stonewall"   10, 22, 84
Jackson Statue   94
Jacob's Lantern   443
James Burke House Eatery   450

James Madison Museum, The   43, 231
James Madison University   17, 488
James Madison University Dinner Theater   207
James McHone Antique Jewelry   263
James River Basin Canoe Livery Ltd.   120
James River Reeling and Rafting   120
James River Runners Inc.   119
Jasbo's at Ramada Inn   409
Jazz on the Lawn   160, 194
Jeff Matthews Memorial Museum   510
Jefferson Lodge   386
Jefferson National Forest   58
Jeff's Antiques   263
Jeweler's Eye, The   284
JM's Pub and Deli   454
John Fox, Jr., Museum   532
John Sevier Gallery   204
John W. Flannagan Reservoir   528
Johnny Appleseed Restaurant   381
Johnny Bull's Restaurant   392
Joker's   454
Jolly Roger Haggle Shop   265
Jones Memorial Library   51, 243
Jordan Hollow Farm Inn   135, 318
Joseph's Backpacking   531
Joshua Wilton House   320, 403
June Tolliver House and Craft Shop   532

K

K.M.H. Hightower   284
Kafkafe   431, 458
Kaleidoscope   52, 190
Katie's Country Club   457
Keep, The   332
Keller & George   286
Kenwood   326
Keswick   48
Keswick Hall   304
Kids Kastoffs   289
Kilgore Fort House   534
Kimberly's Antiques and Linens   260
King William Regional Arts Center   521
Kinsinger's Kountry Kitchen   20, 268
Knights Inn   390
Krissia   286
Kurtz Cultural Center   12, 202

L

La Maison Du Gourmet   415
La Varenne   311
Lake Bonaventure Country Club   528
Lake Keokee   535
Lake Moomaw   77, 128
Lambsgate   330
Landing, The   308
Landmark Steakhouse and Lounge   440
Langhorne Manor   362
L'Arche   369
Latimer-Shaeffer Theatre   207
L'Auberge Provençale   401
Lavender Hill Farm   337
Layman Orchard   273
Le Chien Noir Restaurant   70
Lee Chapel   23
Lee, Gen. Robert E.   10, 22, 84

Lee Hi Truck Stop Restaurant   410
Lee Statue   94
Lenfest Center for the Performing Arts   216
Les Fabriques   284
Levy's   286
Lewis Glaser Inc.   280
Lewis Mountain Cabins   104
Lexington Historical Shop   270
Liberty Lake Park   58
Liberty University   52, 495
Library, The   415
Lily's   416
Lime Kiln Theatre   10, 24
Limeton Pottery   260
Linden Vineyards   41, 152
Link's Farm Bridge   162
L'Italia Restaurant and Lounge   404
Little Gallery   288
Little John's   432
Little Sorrel   23
Live Arts   234
Llewellyn Lodge at Lexington   334
Log Cabin Antiques   263
Log House Restaurant   514
Lonesome Pine International Raceway   531
Longdale Recreation Area   76
Looking Glass House   358
Lord Browne Antiques   278
Lovingston Cafe   408
Lowell's Restaurant and Lounge   456
Luigi's   416
Luray Caverns   16, 166
Luray Caverns Airport   482
Luray Caverns Car and Carriage Caravan   206
Luray Reptile Center and Dinosaur Park   17
Luray Singing Tower   167
Lynchburg College   52, 494
Lynchburg General Hospital   53
Lynchburg Mansion Inn Bed and Breakfast   363
Lynchburg Museum at Old Court House   95, 241
Lynchburg Red Sox   173
Lynchburg Regional Airport   480

M

Mabry Mill Blue Ridge Parkway Visitors Center   70
Mabry Mill Coffee Shop   109
Macado's Restaurant and Delicatessen   445
Madison Antiques Center   277
Madison House Bed & Breakfast   363
Magic City Station   274
Magic Tricks   282
Maharaja   432
Maier Museum   52, 241
Main Street Grill   432
Mama's Treasures   261
Manor at Taylor's Store   367
Maple Hall   410
Maple Museum   81, 256
Marion's Cafe   450
Mark Addy, The   359
Market Station   276
Marriott Ranch   134
Marshall, Gen. George C.   22
Martha Washington Inn   520
Martha's Cafe   433
Martinsville Speedway   509

Mary Baldwin College   19, 489
Mary Bladon House   339
Massanutten Mountain Cloggers   202
Massanutten Resort   18, 143, 382
Maury River Mercantile   26
Mayberry Trading Post   508
McCormick's Pub and Restaurant   454
McDowell Battlefield   82
McDowell Presbyterian Church   96
McGuffey Art Center   46, 229
Meadow Lane Lodge   126, 377
Meadows of Dan   508
Meander Inn at Penny Lane Farm   360
Mediterranean Italian & Continental Cuisine   416
Meems Bottom Bridge   161
Memorial Day Horse Fair and Auction   180
Memory & Company   433
Meredyth Vineyards   152
Merrie Olde England Christmas Festival   304
Michie Tavern   235, 434
Mid-Atlantic Chamber Orchestra
Middleburg Antiques Center   276
Miki Liszt Dance Company   230
Mill Mountain Star   33
Mill Mountain Zoo   163, 226
Mill Street Grill   454
Miller School of Albemarle   498
Miller's   457
Milmont Greenhouses   20
Milton Hall Bed & Breakfast Inn   374
Mincer's   282
Miners Park   532
Miniature Gift Shop   312
Miniature Graceland   35, 227
Mish Mish   275, 290
Misty Mountain Vineyards Inc.   41, 155
Monongahela National Forest   125
Montdomaine Cellars   157
Monte Vista Golf Course   535
Montfair Stables   136
Montgomery County Historical Festival   184
Montgomery County Park   68
Monticello   45, 235
Monticello Wine and Food Festival   193
Montpelier   41, 43, 237
Montpelier Hunt Races   195
Montpelier Wine Festival   180
Mosby's   533
Mount Rogers National Recreation
  Area   115, 141, 511
Mount Rogers Naturalist Rally   182
Mount Rogers Ramp Festival   182
Mountain Cove Vineyards   159
Mountain Empire Community College   531
Mountain Farm Trail   114
Mountain Lake   446
Mountain Lake Hotel and Resort   72, 312
Mountain Lake Symposium & Gallery   216, 251
Mountain Mission School   526
Mountain Springs Stables   134
Mountain Store   277
Mountaintop Ranch   135
Movie Theaters   26, 46
Murray's Fly Shop   126
Museum of American Frontier Culture   18
Music for Americans   187

N

Naked Creek Pottery   266
Naked Mountain Vineyard   152
National Blue Ridge Folk Life Institute   42
Natural Bridge Caverns   168
Natural Bridge Hotel   169
Natural Bridge of Virginia   10, 26, 302, 384
Natural Bridge Village Restaurants   410
Natural Bridge Wax Museum   26, 303
Natural Bridge Zoo   162
Natural Chimneys Jousting Tournament   18, 183
Natural Chimneys Regional Park   18
Natural Tunnel Park   534
Nature by Design   286
Needlecrafter   288
Nelson County Community Development Office   45
New Castle Mercantile   274
New London Airport   484
New Market Airport   483
New Market Battlefield Days Inn   380
New Market Battlefield Historical Park   15, 91
New Market Battlefield Museum and
    Hall of Valor   23, 92
New Market Heritage Days   180
New Mountain Mercantile   70, 250, 292
New River Canoe Livery   72, 118, 120
New River Community College   75
New River Cruise Company   447
New River Fine Arts Gallery   295
New River Trail State Park   511, 512
New River Valley Airport   483
New River Valley Horse Show   188
New River Valley Mall   290
New River Valley Speedway   174
Norfields Farm Bed & Breakfast   347
North Mountain Vineyard & Winery   150
North-South Skirmish Association Fall Nationals   192
Norwood Art Gallery and Encore Gift Shop   294

O

Oak Manor Farms   136
Oak Ridge   41, 44, 238
Oakencroft Vineyard and Winery   157
Oaks, The   371
Oasis Vineyard   14, 41, 152
Of Things Past   265
Oktoberfest   193
Old Country Store and Deli   288
Old Fiddler's Convention   189
Old Hardware Store   284
Old Newbern   74
Old Post Office Restaurant & Lounge   401
Old Rock House   513
Old Salem Days   38
Old South Antiques Ltd.   270
Old Town Hoe Down   188
Old White Club   459
Old World Carpets   294
Olde Mill Golf Resort   130, 511
Olde Prospector, The   268
Olde Salem Days   191
Olde Virginia Barbecue   442
Oliver's   402
Omni Charlottesville Hotel   390
Once Upon a Time Clock Shop   266

Orchard Gap Deli   109
Oregano Joe's   434
Orkney Springs Hotel   15
Orvis Factory Outlet   275
Oscar's Restaurant   388
Other Times LTD   290
Otter Creek Restaurant   109
Outdoor Art Show   181
Outlet Shopping   274, 287, 289,
    290, 291, 293, 297, 509, 513
Outpost, The   444
Overnight Wilderness Camping   134

P

P. Buckley Moss Museum   20
P.J.'s Christmas Carousel   513
Paddle Wheel Cruises   441
Paint Bank State Trout Hatchery   77
Paint Lick Mountain   523
Palais Royal   284
Palmer Country Manor   354
Palms, The   455
Pampered Palate, The   266, 407
Panorama Restaurant   107
Paper Treasures   16, 262
Pappagallo   272
Parkhurst Restaurant   402
Patrick Henry Hotel   386
Peaks of Otter Lodge   107, 109, 394
Peddler's Shop   280
Peebles Department Store   290
Peking Palace Restaurant   443
Pendleton House Inn   518
Perspective Art Gallery   248
Pest House Medical Museum and
    Confederate Cemetery   95, 241
Pewter Corner   284
Philpott Reservoir   509
Phoenix, The   282
Pig 'N Steak   437
Pine Knoll Gift Shop   261
Pine Tavern   447, 459
Pioneer Days   529
PJ Brown & Company   521
PJ's Carousel Collection Christmas   295
Plains Promenaders Square Dance Group   202
Plantation Days Festival   186
Plow & Hearth   286
Plum Alley Eatery   521
Pocahontas Exhibition Mine   524
Point of Honor   51, 242
Poor Farmers Market   292
Poplar Forest   42, 59
Poultry Festival   17
President's Cottage Museum   312
Primland Hunting Preserve   509
Prince Michel Restaurant   423
Prince Michel de Virginia Vineyards   41, 154
Prism Coffeehouse   232, 457
Private Campgrounds   106
Prospect Hill   437
Prospect Hill Cemetery   91
Prospect Hill Inn   355
Pulaski Antique Center   294
Pulaski County Speedway   75
Pulaski Fine Arts Center   75

Pullman Restaurant 407
Purcell Oriental Rug Co. Ltd. 284

Q

Quality Inn 380, 381, 388
Quarter Creek 262
Quilts Unlimited 296

R

R.P. Collectibles 294
Radford University 63, 73, 497
Radford's Gallery Underground 458
Ragged Mountain Running Shop 282
Railroad Festival 94
Rails 266
Ralph Stanley Blue Grass Festival 183
Ramada Inn 384
Randolph-Macon Woman's College 495
Ray's 459
RC's 525
Real Estate 461
Rebec Vineyards 159
Red Fox Tavern 421
Red Hill Shrine 51, 243
Red Lobster Restaurant 440
Redcoat Antiques 286
Remington's 417
Reminisce 264
Renaissance Gifts 280
Renaissance, The 448
Reuel B. Pritchett Museum 206
Reynolds Homestead 508
Rhododendron Lodge 526
Richard's Antiques 262
Richlands Festival 525
Ride and Stride Shop 531
Ridgeview Park 121
Rising Sun Bakery 434
River Farm 16
River Rental & Campstore 119
River Ridge Ranch 136
River Run and Bicycle Ride 179
Riverfest 188
Riverside Park 95
Riverview B&B 510
Rivianna Reservoir 128
Roanoke Airport Marriott 387
Roanoke College 38, 492
Roanoke Comedy Club 455
Roanoke Express, The 173
Roanoke Railway Festival 194
Roanoke Regional Airport 481
Roanoke Valley Historical Society and Museum
    Center 221
Roanoke Valley Horse Show 184, 227
Roanoke Weiner Stand 417
Roanoker Restaurant 417
Roaring Run Furnace 30
Roaring Run Recreation Area 76
Rockbridge Vineyard 151
Rocky Knob Cabins 108
Rocky Knob Recreation Area 115
Rocky's Antique Mart 265
Rococo's 435
Rodes Farm Inn 45, 302, 438

Rodes Farm Stables 136
Rooftop of Virginia Cap Crafts 510
Rose River Vineyards and Trout Farm 41, 153
Rose Street Interiors 264
Rotunda/The University of Virginia 238
Rural Retreat Lake and Campground 514
Ruritans Bass Fishing Tournament 124
Rush River Company 275
Ruskin Freer Preserve 53
Russell County People's Market 528
Russell Fork Whitewater Adventures 528
Russell's Yesteryear 274
Ryan's Fruit Market 264

S

Sackett's 458
Saigon Cafe 435
Salem Buccaneers 173
Salem Fair and Exposition 37, 188
Sal's Pizza Restaurants 442
Salt-Making Week 517
Saltville Museum 517
Sam Snead's Tavern in the Village 310, 451
Sampson Eagon Inn 328
Sam's On the Market 275
Sand Trap Tavern 382
Sani-Mode Barber Shop 294
Sawhill Gallery 206
School House Fabrics 293
Schooners Restaurant 442
Scooch's 456
Scott County Park 534
Scotto's Italian Restaurant and Pizzeria 405
Scrooge's 514
Scruple's 454
Second Street Gallery, The 46
Second Story 272
Seminole Square 286
Seven Bends Gallery 262
Seven Hills Inn 334
Shadows Bed and Breakfast Inn 350
Sharks 455
Shenandoah Acres Resort 22, 121, 125
Shenandoah Apple Blossom Festival 12, 179
Shenandoah Caverns 16, 166
Shenandoah National Park 13, 16, 18, 113, 134
Shenandoah River Outfitters Inc. 119
Shenandoah Summer Music Theatre 201
Shenandoah University 488
Shenandoah Valley Art Center 20
Shenandoah Valley Bicycle Festival 186
Shenandoah Valley Crafts and Gifts 262
Shenandoah Valley Farm Craft Days 183, 203
Shenandoah Valley Heritage Museum 17, 206
Shenandoah Valley Music Festival 15, 186, 205
Shenandoah Valley Regional Airport 483
Shenandoah Vineyards 150
Shenanigans 284
Shenvalee Golf Resort 381
Sherando Lake State Park 22
Sheraton Hotel 454
Sheraton Inns 383, 387, 390, 394
Sheridan, Gen. Philip 9
Sherwood Anderson Short Story Competition 517
Shot Tower Historical Park 515
Showalter's Orchard and Greenhouse 264

Signet Bank   28
Silver Dollar Saloon   525
Silver Linings   266
Silver Thatch Inn   356, 435
Silversmith Inn   520
Sinking Creek Covered Bridge   162
Skiing   300, 301, 310, 312
Sky Bryce Airport   482
Sky Meadows State Park   116
Skyland Lodge   102, 107, 382
Skyline Caverns   14, 166
Skyline Drive   14, 16, 99
Sleepy Hollow Farm   349
Smith Mountain Flowers   288
Smith Mountain Lake   42, 54, 124, 128
Smith Mountain Lake Airport   484
Smith Mountain Tour of Homes   56
Smith Mountain Visitors Center & Dam 244
Smith Mountain Yacht Club   57
Smokehouse, The   435
Smyth County   516
Snooper's Antique and Craft Mall   513
Snowshoe Ski Resort   78
Sorghum Molasses Festival   193
South Holston Lake   519
South Main Cafe   458
South River, An American Grill   405
South Street Antiques   278
Southern Culture   436
Southern Inn   409
Southern Kitchen   403
Southern Lamp & Shade Showroom   290
Southern Soldier Statue   95
Southwest Virginia Community College   522
Southwest Virginia Museum   532
Southwest Virginia Music Festival   528
Sperryville Emporium   276
Sports   169
Spring Balloon Festival   178
Spring Fly-In   179
Spring Garden Show   178
Spring Hill Cemetery   95
Spring Hill Farm Antiques   277
Spring House, The   402
Spring Wildflower Symposium   180, 302
Springhouse Antiques   276
Spurs   456
St. Anne's-Belfield Middle School   498
St. Maarten's Cafe   436
Star Hill Café   436
Starkey's Bistro   386
Starving Artist Cafe   521
Statler Brothers Museum   19
Staunton Military Academy   19
Stepping Out   189
Stone Face Rock   535
Stone's Cafeteria   444
Stonewall Brigade Band   211
Stonewall Jackson Cemetery   23, 93
Stonewall Jackson House   23, 93
Stonewall Jackson's Headquarters   204
Stonewall Vineyards   159
Stony Mountain Fibers   280
Strasburg Emporium   14, 260
Strasburg Museum   89, 204
Stuart Hall School   19
Studios on the Square   274

Sugar Tour   81
Sugar Tree Country Store and Sugar House   296
Sun Bow Trading Company   279
Sunnybrook Inn Restaurant   418
Sunrise House Chinese Restaurant   443
Super 8 Motel   396
Suter's   263
Swannanoa   44
Swedenburg Winery   151
Sweeney's Curious Goods   286
Sweet Briar College   52, 54, 494
Sweet Chalybeate Pools   77
Swimming   121
Sycamore Tree, The   369

T

T.G.I.F.   272
T.S. Eways   284
Talbott's   284
Tastings   436
Tazewell County Fair   525
Tea and Sympathy   525
Tea Room Cafe at the 1817   437
Tennis   123, 300, 302, 303, 304, 309, 312
Texas Steak House   440
Texas Tavern   418
TGIF Outlets   290
The Emporium   266
The Nicholas & Alexandra Gallery   279
The Peddlar Antiques   289
The Personal Touch   297
Theater at Lime Kiln   181
Theatre at Washington   228
Theda's Studio   294
Third Street Coffeehouse   456
Thomas Jefferson Visitors Center   45, 236
Thomas Jefferson's Tomato Fair   189
Thornrose House   328
Three Legged Cow Cafe   447
Three O Nine First Street   419
Tingler's Mill   32
Tivoli   348
Top Rail, The   456
Totier Creek Vineyard   158
Touch the Earth   264
Trading Post   276
Traditional Frontier Festival   190
Trail of the Lonesome Pine Outdoor Drama   531
Traveller   24
Travelodge — Roanoke North   385
Trax Max   457
Trebark Outfitters   274
Troutville Antique Mart   30, 273
Trudy's Antiques   274
Tuckahoe Antique Mall   279
Tuesday Evening Concert Series   231
Tully's Restaurant & Pub   454
Tultex Mill Outlet   287
Turtle Lane   266
Tuttle & Spice General Store Museum   205
Twin Porches   370

U

Uncle Bill's Treasures   294
University of Science and Philosophy   214

University of Virginia 45, 492
Upstairs, Downstairs 295

V

Valley Country 456
Valley Crafters 261
Valley Framing Studio & Gallery 208, 268
Valley Green 280
Valley MetroGreater Roanoke Transit Company 485
Valley Pike Inn 74, 448
Vanucci's Italian Cuisine 419
Verona Flea Market 265
Victoria and Albert Inn 520
Victorian Highland Inn 81
Village Accents 288
Village Inn 404
Village Square 288
Villager Antiques 263
Vinegar Hill Theater 46
Vinton Dogwood Festival 182
Virginia Apparel Outlet 290
Virginia Baptist Hospital 53
Virginia Born & Bred 259, 272
Virginia Center for the Creative Arts 54, 240
Virginia Chili Cook-off 182
Virginia Division of Tourism 11
Virginia Fall Foliage Festival 193
Virginia Festival of American Film 48, 193, 239
Virginia Garlic Festival 194
Virginia Handcrafts Inc. 286
Virginia Highland Llamas 516
Virginia Highlands Community College 519
Virginia Highlands Festival 189, 521
Virginia Horse Center 172
Virginia Horse Festival 178
Virginia Institute for the Deaf and the Blind 19
Virginia Made Shop 265
Virginia Metalcrafters Factory Showroom 268
Virginia Military Institute 10, 22, 94, 490
Virginia Mountain Outfitters 26, 126, 137
Virginia Museum of Natural History 509
Virginia Parkway Hosts 100
Virginia Polo Center 171
Virginia School of the Arts 53, 243
Virginia Shop 286
Virginia Special Olympics 176
Virginia Tech 63, 496
Virginia Tech Airport 483
Virginia Trout Company 81
Virginian, The 437
VMI Museum 10

W

Waccamaw Pottery 275
Walnut Hills Campground 106
Walnuthill 340
Walton House, The 459
Walton's Mountain Museum 44, 231
Ward's Rock Cafe 420, 456
Warm Springs Spa 96
Warren County 13
Warren Rifles Confederate Museum 91

Warren-Sipe Museum 93
Warwickton Mansion B&B 78
Washington and Lee University 23, 93, 490
Washington County Fair and Burley Tobacco
     Festival 521
Washington's Office Museum 203
Waterwheel Restaurant 452
Waynesboro Village Factory Outlets 268
Wayside Inn and Restaurant 401
Wayside Theatre 13, 202
Weasies Kitchen 406
Wharf Gallery 266
Whetstone Ridge 108
Whimsies 284
White Horse Antiques 293
White Star Cafe 529
Whitehouse Antiques 279
White's Mill 519
Whitetop Mountain Maple Festival 177
Whitewater Rafting 528
Whitey Taylor's Franklin County Speedway 63
Widow Kip's Bed and Breakfast and Antique Shop 261
Wilderness Battlefields, The 43
Wilderness Road Museum 74, 96
Wildflour Cafe and Catering 420
Wildflower Weekend 180
William P. Harris Park 526
Williams Corner Bookstore 284, 458
Willie's Hair Design 282
Willow Bend Farm B&B 516
Willow Grove Inn 349, 424
Willowcroft Farm Vineyards 151
Willson-Walker House 409
Wilson Warehouse 30
Winchester Regional Airport 482
Windsor House 421
Windsurfing 300
Wine and Cheese Festival 182
Winridge Bed & Breakfast 364
Wintergreen 301, 391
Wintergreen Farm Sheepskin Shoppe 292
Wintergreen Resort 41, 44
Wintergreen Vineyard & Winery 159
Winton Country Club 54
Wolf Creek Golf Club 516
Wonderful World of Miniature Horses Theme
     Park 164
Woodberry Forest 499
Woodland 293
Woodlane Craft Shop 296
Woodrow Wilson Museum 18
Woodstock Museum 15, 205
Woodstone Meadows Stable 135
Words and Music Irish Cafe 514
Wythe County Community Hospital 513
Wythe Raceway 515
Wytheville Community College 513
Wytheville State Fish Hatchery 514

Z

Zib's Country Connection 261
Zoos 162

ORDER FORM
Fast and Simple!

Mail to:
Insiders Guides®, Inc.
P.O. Drawer 2057
Manteo, NC 27954

Or:
for VISA or
Mastercard orders call
1-800-765-BOOK

Name _____

Address _____

City/State/Zip _____

Qty.	Title/Price	Shipping	Amount
	Insiders' Guide to Richmond/$12.95	$2.50	
	Insiders' Guide to Williamsburg/$12.95	$2.50	
	Insiders' Guide to Virginia's Blue Ridge/$12.95	$2.50	
	Insiders' Guide to Virginia's Chesapeake Bay/$12.95	$2.50	
	Insiders' Guide to Washington, DC/$12.95	$2.50	
	Insiders' Guide to Charlotte/$14.95	$2.50	
	Insiders' Guide to North Carolina's Triangle/$14.95	$2.50	
	Insiders' Guide to North Carolina's Outer Banks/$12.95	$2.50	
	Insiders' Guide to Wilmington, NC/$12.95	$2.50	
	Insiders' Guide to North Carolina's Crystal Coast/$12.95	$2.50	
	Insiders' Guide to Charleston, SC/$12.95	$2.50	
	Insiders' Guide to Myrtle Beach/$12.95	$2.50	
	Insiders' Guide to Mississippi/$12.95 (8/94)	$2.50	
	Insiders' Guide to Orlando/$12.95	$2.50	
	Insiders' Guide to Sarasota/Bradenton/$12.95 (8/94)	$2.50	
	Insiders' Guide to Northwest Florida/$12.95 (7/94)	$2.50	
	Insiders' Guide to Lexington, KY/$12.95	$2.50	
	Insiders' Guide to Louisville/$12.95 (12/94)	$2.50	
	Insiders' Guide to the Twin Cities/$12.95 (12/94)	$2.50	
	Insiders' Guide to Boulder/$12.95 (11/94)	$2.50	
	Insiders' Guide to Denver/$12.95 (11/94)	$2.50	
	Insiders' Guide to The Civil War (Eastern Theater)/$12.95	$2.50	
	Insiders' Guide to Western North Carolina/$12.95 (2/95)	$2.50	
	Insiders' Guide to Atlanta/$12.95 (2/95)	$2.50	

Payment in full(check or money order)
must accompany this order form.
Please allow 2 weeks for delivery.

N.C. residents add 6% sales tax _____

Total _____

To Virginia's Blue Ridge

Offer subject to modification by supplier without notice.
Unless otherwise stated expires: 4/31/96

To Virginia's Blue Ridge

Offer subject to modification by supplier without notice.
Unless otherwise stated expires: 4/31/96

To Virginia's Blue Ridge

Offer subject to modification by supplier without notice.
Unless otherwise stated expires: 4/31/96

Who you are and what you think is important to us.

Fill out the coupon and we'll give you an Insiders' Guide® for half price ($6.48 off)

Which book(s) did you buy? _____

Where do you live?_____

In what city did you buy your book? _____

Where did you buy your book?   ( ) catalog   ( ) bookstore   ( ) newspaper ad
( ) retail shop   ( ) other

How often do you travel?   ( ) yearly   ( ) bi-annually   ( ) quarterly
( ) more than quarterly

Did you buy your book because you were   ( ) moving   ( ) vacationing
( ) wanted to know more about your home town   ( ) other

Will the book be used by a   ( ) family   ( ) couple   ( ) individual   ( ) group

What is your annual income?   ( ) under $25,000   ( ) $25,000 to $35,000
( ) $35,000 to $50,000   ( ) $50,000 to $75,000   ( ) over $75,000

How old are you?   ( ) under 25   ( ) 25-35   ( ) 36-50   ( ) 51-65   ( ) over 65

How often has your family moved?   ( ) never   ( ) once   ( ) twice
( ) three times   ( ) more than three times

Did you use the book before you left for your destination?   ( ) yes   ( ) no

Did you use the book while at your destination?   ( ) yes   ( ) no

Is there anything you would like to tell us about Insiders' Guides?_____

_____

_____

Name_____ Address_____

City _____State_____Zip_____

We'll send you a voucher for $6.48 off any Insiders' Guide® and a list of available titles as soon as we get this card from you. Thanks for being an Insider!

BUSINESS REPLY MAIL

FIRST CLASS   PERMIT NO. 20   MANTEO, NC

POSTAGE WILL BE PAID BY ADDRESSEE

The Insiders' Guides®, Inc.
PO Box 2057
Manteo, NC 27954